A Guide to
Critical Reviews:

Part I:
American Drama, 1909-1969

Second edition

by
JAMES M. SALEM

The Scarecrow Press, Inc.
Metuchen, N.J.   1973

Library of Congress Cataloging in Publication Data

Salem, James M
   A guide to critical reviews.

   CONTENTS: pt. 1. American drama, 1909-1969.
   1. Theater--Reviews--Indexes. 2. Moving-
pictures--Reviews--Indexes. I. Title.
Z5782.S342   016.809'2   73-3120
ISBN 0-8108-0608-8

To Tim

FOREWORD

The purpose of Part I (Second Edition) of A Guide to
Critical Reviews is to provide a bibliography of critical reviews of American plays on the New York stage from 1909
to 1969. The productions listed are, for the most part,
Broadway productions, though Off-Broadway presentations
have been included when accurate statistical data could be
obtained. In the case of plays premiering in university or
regional theaters (indicated by an asterisk in this bibliography), I have listed reviews without production information.

Some 290 dramatists are included in this volume, and
over 1, 700 plays. To the original 52 playwrights in the first
edition I have added eighteenth, nineteenth, and twentieth
century dramatists whose works appeared in New York during
the past sixty years. I have entered American dramatists
who are important in American dramatic history (Royall
Tyler); who have written a play judged to be a critical success (David Rayfiel for P. S. 193); who have written a long
running play (Anne Nichols for Abie's Irish Rose, 2, 327
performances); who have written popular, commercial drama
(Samuel Shipman's 23 plays); who have attempted to bring
poetry to the theater (Robinson Jeffers); and promising new
American playwrights (Leonard Melfi).

Playwrights included in this bibliography are presented
alphabetically, with plays listed alphabetically under each
dramatist. Opening dates and performance totals are pro-
vided for most plays. No conscious effort has been made to
include foreign language or amateur productions.

The reviews cited in this volume are those which appeared in American or Canadian periodicals and in the New
York Times. With the exception of some now defunct dramatic periodicals like the Dramatic Mirror and the New York
Clipper, most of the reviews should be available in college
and public libraries. Reviews in other New York newspapers
have not been indexed, but New York Theatre Critics' Reviews which has reprinted reviews from the New York Jour-
nal-American, Daily News, Post, Mirror, World Telegram

v

and Sun, Herald Tribune, and Times since 1940, has been cited for plays produced after that date.

As no attempt has been made to include critical articles from the scholarly journals, the student of American drama should supplement this bibliography with annual bibliographies in American Literature, American Quarterly, Educational Theatre Journal, Modern Drama, and PMLA. In addition, Bulletin of Bibliography is important for bibliographies of many modern American dramatists. Especially helpful is "A Selected Bibliography of Bibliographies, " compiled by Marvin Carlson in Modern Drama, VII (May 1965), 112-118; especially convenient is the Goldentree bibliography of American drama compiled by E. Hudson Long (New York: The Meredith Corp., 1970).

In preparing this edition, I owe a debt of thanks to Donna Snow, Debbie Driver, and Chuck Herrin. I am also indebted to the reference and circulation librarians at the University of Alabama Library who again made exceptions for my work habits. And as usual, my wife Donna helped out near the end of the project.

James M. Salem

University, Alabama
August, 1972

TABLE OF CONTENTS

xii

ABBOTT, GEORGE

Broadway   (See entry under Dunning, Philip)

Coquette   (with Ann Preston Bridgers)
    Productions:
        Opened November 8, 1927 for 366 performances.
    Reviews:
        American Mercury 13:120-21, Jan 1928
        Dial 84:80, Jan 1928
        Drama 18: 241-2, May 1928
        Dramatist 19:1360-61, Jan 1927
        Independent 119:606, Dec 17, 1927
        Life (NY) 90:21, Dec 8, 1927
        New York Times IX, p. 2, Oct 16, 1927
                       p. 23, Nov 9, 1927
                       IX, p. 1, Nov 13, 1927
                       p. 27, Apr 25, 1928
                       p. 26, Apr 26, 1928
        Outlook 147:369, Nov 23, 1927
        Theatre Arts 12:17-18, Jan 1928
        Theatre Magazine 47:24-6+, Feb 1928
        Vogue 71:64-5+, Jan 1, 1928

The Fall Guy   (See entry under Gleason, James)

Four Walls   (with Dana Burnet)
    Productions:
        Opened September 19, 1927 for 144 performances.
    Reviews:
        Dramatist 18:354-5, Oct 1927
        Nation 125:343-4, Oct 5, 1927
        New York Times p. 33, Sep 20, 1927
                       VIII, p. 1, Oct 2, 1927
                       VIII, p. 2, Oct 2, 1927
        Vogue 70:166, Nov 15, 1927

Heat Lightning   (with Leon Abrams)
    Productions:
        Opened September 15, 1933 for 44 performances.
    Reviews:
        Catholic World 138:219, Nov 1933
        Literary Digest 116:18, Oct 14, 1933

1

ABBOTT, GEORGE (cont.)
  Heat Lightning (cont.)
        Nation 137:390-1, Oct 4, 1933
        New York Times p. 9, Sep 16, 1933

  A Holy Terror (See entry under Smith, Winchell)

  Ladies' Money (Based on a play by Lawrence Hazard and
        Richard Flournoy)
      Productions:
        Opened November 1, 1934 for 36 performances.
      Reviews:
        Catholic World 140:343, Dec 1934
        New York Times p. 26, Nov 2, 1934
        Newsweek 4:27, Nov 10, 1934
        Theatre Arts 18:904, Dec 1934

  Lilly Turner (See entry under Dunning, Philip)

  Love 'Em and Leave 'Em (with John V. A. Weaver)
      Productions:
        Opened February 3, 1926 for 152 performances.
      Reviews:
        Bookman 63:217, Apr 1926
        Life (NY) 87:21, Mar 4, 1926
        New York Times p. 20, Feb 4, 1926
                        VIII, p. 1, Feb 14, 1926
                        VIII, p. 1, Mar 28, 1926
        Theatre Magazine 43:26-8+, May 1926
                          44:22+, Nov 1926
        Vogue 67:94-5, Apr 1, 1926

  Ringside (with Edward E. Paramore and Hyatt Daab)
      Productions:
        Opened August 29, 1928 for 37 performances.
      Reviews:
        Life (NY) 92:11, Sep 21, 1928
        New York Times p. 13, Aug 30, 1928
                        IX, p. 1, Sep 9, 1928
        Theatre Magazine 48:30+, Oct 1928
                          48:47-8, Nov 1928
        Vogue 72:110, Oct 27, 1928

  Sweet River (Adapted from Harriet Beecher Stowe's
        Uncle Tom's Cabin)
      Productions:
        Opened October 28, 1936 for 5 performances.

Reviews:
    New Republic 89:78, Nov 18, 1936
    New York Times X, p. 2, Oct 18, 1936
                 p. 30, Oct 29, 1936
    Theatre Arts 20:935, Dec 1936

Those We Love (with S. K. Lauren)
    Productions:
    Opened February 19, 1930 for 77 performances.
    Reviews:
    New York Times p. 22, Feb 20, 1930
    Outlook 154:390, Mar 5, 1930
    Theatre Magazine 51:47-8, Apr 1930

Three Men on a Horse (with John Cecil Holm)
    Productions:
    Opened January 30, 1935 for 835 performances.
    Opened October 9, 1942 for 28 performances.
    Reviews:
    Catholic World 140:723-4, Mar 1935
    Commonweal 21:458, Feb 15, 1935
    Literary Digest 119:20, Feb 9, 1935
    New York Theatre Critics' Reviews 1942:209
    New York Times p. 22, Jan 22, 1935
                 p. 22, Jan 31, 1935
                 p. 16, Feb 19, 1936
                 p. 22, Mar 11, 1936
                 X, p. 2, Mar 15, 1936
                 p. 26, Mar 24, 1936
                 IX, p. 1, Jun 2, 1936
                 p. 10, Oct 10, 1942
    Vanity Fair 44:41, Apr 1935

ADE, GEORGE

The County Chairman
    Productions:
    Opened May 25, 1936 for 8 performances.
    Reviews:
    Commonweal 24:190, June 12, 1936
    Literary Digest 121:20, Jan 6, 1936
    New York Times IX, p. 2, May 24, 1936
                 p. 26, May 26, 1936
                 X, p. 1, May 31, 1936

3

ADE, GEORGE (cont.)
Mrs. Peckham's Carouse
Productions:
Opened April 21, 1913 for 24 performances.
Reviews:
Dramatic Mirror 69:6, Apr 23, 1913

Nettie
Productions:
Opened October 17, 1914 in repertory (The Princess Players).
Reviews:
Bookman 40:550, Jan 1915
Dramatic Mirror 72:8, Dec 2, 1914
Green Book 13:383-4, Feb 1915
New York Times p. 11, Mar 25, 1919

AKINS, ZOE

The Crown Prince (Adapted from the Hungarian of Ernest Vajda)
Productions:
Opened March 23, 1927 for 45 performances.
Reviews:
Bookman 65:448, Jun 1927
Life (NY) 89:18, Apr 14, 1927
New York Times VII, p. 4, Feb 27, 1927
p. 23, Mar 24, 1927

Daddy's Gone A-Hunting
Productions:
Opened August 31, 1921 for 129 performances.
Reviews:
Bookman 54:230, Nov 1921
Dial 76:94, Jan 1924
Dramatic Mirror 84:376, Sep 10, 1921
Everybody's 45:93-100, Dec 1921
Life (NY) 78:18, Sep 22, 1921
Nation 113:324-5, Sep 21, 1921
New York Clipper 69:20, Sep 7, 1921
New York Times p. 18, Sep 1, 1921
VI, p. 1, Sep 4, 1921
VI, p. 1, Sep 25, 1921
VII, p. 1, Oct 2, 1921
Theatre Magazine 34:315, Nov 1921
Weekly Review 5:234, Sep 10, 1921

Déclassée
Productions:
    Opened October 6, 1919 for 257 performances.
Reviews:
    Current Opinion 68:187-93, Feb 1920
    Dial 76:94, Jan 1924
    Dramatic Mirror 80:1612, Oct 16, 1919
    Dramatist 11:999-1000, Apr 1920
    Hearst 37:46-7+, Jan 1920
    Nation 109:548, Oct 25, 1919
    New Republic 22:95, Mar 17, 1920
    New York Times p. 22, Oct 7, 1919
                   p. 20, Aug 6, 1935
    Theatre Magazine 30:440, Dec 1919

*Did It Really Happen?
    Reviews:
    New York Times p. 9, Nov 27, 1916

First Love (Adapted from Louis Verneuil's Pile ou Face)
Productions:
    Opened November 8, 1926 for 50 performances.
Reviews:
    Life (NY) 88:23, Nov 25, 1926
    New York Times p. 31, Nov 9, 1926
    Theatre Magazine 45:16+, Feb 1927

Footloose (Adapted from For-get-me-not by Herman
        Merivale and F. C. Grove)
Productions:
    Opened May 10, 1920 for 32 performances.
Reviews:
    Dramatic Mirror 82:994, May 15, 1920
    Dramatist 17:1294, Jan 1926
    Forum 64:98, Jul 1920
    Life (NY) 75:992, May 27, 1920
    New York Clipper 68:16, May 19, 1920
    New York Times p. 12, May 11, 1920
                   VI, p. 1, May 16, 1920
    Theatre Magazine 31:526, Jan 1920

The Furies
    Productions:
    Opened March 7, 1928 for 45 performances.
Reviews:
    Dial 84:438-9, May 1928
    Nation 126:356, Mar 28, 1928

5

AKINS, ZOE (cont.)
New Republic 54:155-6, Mar 21, 1928
New York Times p. 23, Mar 8, 1928
Outlook 148:545, Apr 4, 1928
Theatre Arts 12:317+, May 1928
Vogue 71:136+, May 1, 1928

The Greeks Had A Word For It
Productions:
Opened September 25, 1930 for 253 performances.
Reviews:
Bookman 73:70, Mar 1931
Life (NY) 96:18, Oct 17, 1930
National Magazine 59:138, Dec 1930
New York Times p. 16, Sep 26, 1930
                p. 22, Nov 23, 1934
Vanity Fair 35:92, Dec 1930
Vogue 76:126+, Nov 24, 1930

The Happy Days (Adapted from Claude-André Puget's Les
    Jours Heureux)
Productions:
Opened May 13, 1941 for 23 performances.
Reviews:
Commonweal 34:135, May 30, 1941
Nation 152:648, May 31, 1941
New York Theatre Critics' Reviews 1941:324
New York Times p. 24, May 14, 1941
Time 37:44, May 26, 1941

*I Am Different
Reviews:
New York Times IX, p. 2, Aug 28, 1938

The Love Duel   (Adapted from the play by Lili Hatvany)
Productions:
Opened April 15, 1929 for 88 performances.
Reviews:
Catholic World 129:332-3, June 1929
Life (NY) 93:24, May 10, 1929
New York Time p. 32, Apr 16, 1929
Outlook 152:72, May 8, 1929
Theatre Magazine 49:44, Jun 1929

The Magical City (with Pierre Patelin)
Productions:
Season of 1915-16 in repertory (Washington Square
Players).

6

Reviews:
   Current Opinion 60:331, May 1916
   Dramatic Mirror 75:8, Apr 1, 1916
   Forum 55:507-50, May 1916
   New York Times p. 9, Mar 21, 1916
                  II, p. 8, Mar 26, 1916
                  p. 9, Sep 19, 1916

Mrs. January and Mr. Ex
Productions:
   Opened March 31, 1944 for 43 performances.
Reviews:
   Catholic World 159:170, May 1944
   Commonweal 40:14-5, Apr 21, 1944
   Nation 158:456, Apr 15, 1944
   New Republic 110:532, Apr 15, 1944
   New York Theatre Critics' Reviews 1944:235
   New York Times p. 10, Apr 1, 1944
   New Yorker 20:44, Apr 8, 1944
   Newsweek 23:92, Apr 10, 1944
   Theatre Arts 28:328+, Jun 1944
   Time 43:44, Apr 10, 1944

The Moon-Flower (Adapted from the Hungarian of Lajos Biro)
Productions:
   Opened February 25, 1924 for 48 performances.
Reviews:
   American Mercury 1:497-8, Apr 1924
   Independent 112:231-2, Apr 26, 1924
   Life (NY) 83:20, Mar 13, 1924
   New York Times VII, p. 2, Jan 27, 1924
                  p. 15, Feb 26, 1924
                  VIII, p. 1, Mar 2, 1924
   Theatre Magazine 39:19, May 1924

O Evening Star
Productions:
   Opened January 8, 1936 for 5 performances.
Reviews:
   Commonweal 23:356, Jan 24, 1936
   Literary Digest 121:19, Jan 18, 1936
   New York Times p. 20, Dec 26, 1935
                  p. 24, Jan 9, 1936
                  IX, p. 1, Jan 19, 1936
   Pictorial Review 37:50, Apr 1936

AKINS, ZOE (cont.)

The Old Maid (Based on a novel by Edith Wharton)
    Productions:
      Opened January 7, 1935 for 305 performances.
    Reviews:
      Catholic World 140:602, Feb 1935
      Commonweal 21:375, Jan 25, 1935
      New Republic 82:162, Mar 20, 1935
      New York Times p. 26, Jan 8, 1935
                 IX, p. 1, Jan 13, 1935
                 p. 21, May 7, 1935
                 p. 17, May 8, 1935
                 p. 21, May 8, 1935
                 XI, p. 1, May 26, 1935
                 p. 19, Feb 24, 1937
                 p. 20, Jan 27, 1949
      Newsweek 5:25, May 18, 1935
      Player's Magazine 11:11, Mar-Apr 1935
      Theatre Arts 19:168+, Mar 1935
      Time 25:25, Jan 21, 1935

Papa
    Productions:
      Opened April 10, 1919 for 12 performances.
    Reviews:
      New York Times p. 9, Apr 11, 1919
                 IV, p. 2, Apr 20, 1919
      Theatre Magazine 29:344, Jun 1919

Plans for Tomorrow (see Mrs. January and Mr. Ex)

A Royal Fandango
    Productions:
      Opened November 12, 1923 for 24 performances.
    Reviews:
      American Mercury 1:118-19, Jan 1924
      Independent 111:257, Nov 24, 1923
      Nation 117:615, Nov 28, 1923
      New York Times VIII, p. 2, Nov 11, 1923
                 p. 25, Nov 13, 1923
                 VIII, p. 1, Nov 18, 1923

The Texas Nightingale
    Productions:
      Opened November 20, 1922 for 32 performances.
    Reviews:

Bookman 56:746-7, Feb 1923
New York Clipper 70:20, Nov 29, 1922
New York Times p. 15, Nov 21, 1922
                    VIII, p. 1, Dec 3, 1922
Theatre Magazine 37:19, Jan 1923

*Thou Desperate Pilot
    Reviews:
    Life (NY) 89:21, Mar 24, 1927
    New York Times p. 23, Mar 8, 1927

*Two Mothers
    Reviews:
    New York Times p. 19, Feb 24, 1937

The Varying Shore
    Productions:
    Opened December 5, 1921 for 66 performances.
    Reviews:
    Dramatic Mirror 84:845, Dec 10, 1921
    Nation 113:763, Dec 28, 1921
    New York Clipper 69:20, Dec 14, 1921
    New York Times p. 24, Dec 6, 1921
                    VI, p. 1, Dec 11, 1921
    Theatre Magazine 35:75+, Feb 1922

ALBEE, EDWARD

The American Dream
    Productions:
        (Off Broadway) Opened January 24, 1961 for 370
            performances.
        (Off Broadway) Opened February 11, 1962 for 55
            performances.
        (Off Broadway) Opened September 4, 1962 for 30
            performances.
        (Off Broadway) Opened May 28, 1963 for 143 per-
            formances.
        (Off Broadway) Opened April 21, 1964 for 48 per-
            formances.
        Opened October 2, 1968 in repertory for 12 per-
            formances.
    Reviews:
    America 108:891-2, Jun 22, 1963
    Catholic World 193:335-6, Aug 1961
    Christian Century 78:275, Mar 1, 1961

9

ALBEE, EDWARD (cont.)
  The American Dream (cont.)
          Horizon 3:117, Jul 1961
          Nation 192:125-6, Feb 11, 1961
          New Republic 144:30, Mar 27, 1961
          New York Times p. 28, Jan 25, 1961
                        p. 33, Oct 25, 1961
                        p. 27, Feb 12, 1962
                        VI, p. 30, Feb 25, 1962
                        p. 39, May 29, 1963
                        p. 72, Oct 20, 1963
                        p. 10, Feb 13, 1965
                        p. 55, Oct 3, 1968
          New Yorker 36:62+, Feb 4, 1961
          Saturday Review 44:54, Feb 11, 1961
          Theatre Arts 45:68, Mar 1961
          Time 77:53+, Feb 3, 1961

  The Ballad of the Sad Cafe (Adapted from the story by
          Carson McCullers)
      Productions:
      Opened October 30, 1963 for 123 performances.
      Reviews:
          America 110:26, Jan 4, 1964
          Catholic World 198:264, Jan 1964
          Commonweal 79:256, Nov 22, 1963
          Nation 197:353-4, Nov 23, 1963
          National Review 16:34-5, Jan 14, 1964
          New Republic 149:28-9, Nov 16, 1963
          New York Theatre Critics' Reviews 1963:212
          New York Times II, p. 1, Oct 27, 1963
                        p. 27, Oct 31, 1963
                        II, p. 1, Nov 10, 1963
          New Yorker 39:95, Nov 9, 1963
          Newsweek 62:76, Nov 11, 1963
          Saturday Review 46:54, Nov 16, 1963
          Time 82:67, Nov 8, 1963
          Vogue 143:20, Jan 1, 1964

  Box
      Productions:
      Opened September 30, 1968 in repertory for 12 per-
          formances.
      Reviews:
          Commonweal 89:120+, Oct 25, 1968
          Nation 206:420, Mar 25, 1968
          New York Theatre Critics' Reviews 1968:213
                                          1968:228

New York Times p. 48, Mar 8, 1968
          II, p. 1, Mar 17, 1968
          p. 39, Oct 1, 1968
          II, p. 5, Oct 13, 1968
New Yorker 44:103-4+, Oct 12, 1968
Newsweek 71:109, Mar 18, 1968
Saturday Review 51:34, Mar 23, 1968
Time 92:73, Oct 11, 1968
Vogue 152:92, Nov 15, 1968

Box-Mao-Box (see entries under Box and Quotations from
     Chairman Mao-Tse-Tung.)

The Death of Bessie Smith
     Productions:
          (Off Broadway) Opened March 1, 1961 for 328 per-
          formances.
          Opened October 2, 1968 in repertory for 12 per-
          formances.
     Reviews:
          Catholic World 193:335, Aug 1961
          Horizon 3:116, Jul 1961
          Nation 192:242, Mar 18, 1961
          New Republic 144:29-30, Mar 27, 1961
          New York Times p. 33, Oct 25, 1961
                        p. 19, Mar 2, 1961
                        p. 29, Jun 11, 1963
                        p. 55, Oct 3, 1968
          New Yorker 37:114, Mar 11, 1961
          Theatre Arts 45:56, May 1961

A Delicate Balance
     Productions:
          Opened September 22, 1966 for 132 performances.
     Reviews:
          America 115:432-3, Oct 8, 1966
          Christian Century 83:55-6, Oct 14, 1966
          Life 61:119, Oct 28, 1966
          Nation 203:361-3, Oct 10, 1966
          National Review 19:99, Jan 24, 1967
          New Republic 155:35-6, Oct 8, 1966
          New York Theatre Critics' Reviews 1966:294
          New York Times p. 35, Aug 16, 1966
                        p. 44, Sep 23, 1966
                        II, p. 1, Oct 2, 1966
                        p. 35, Oct 28, 1967
          New Yorker 42:121, Oct 1, 1966

11

ALBEE, EDWARD (cont.)
A Delicate Balance (cont.)
      Newsweek 68:98, Oct 3, 1966
      Reporter 35:52-3, Oct 20, 1966
      Saturday Review 49:90, Oct 8, 1966
      Time 88:88, Sep 20, 1966
      Vogue, 148:150, Nov 1, 1966

Everything in the Garden (Based on the play by Giles
      Cooper)
Productions:
      Opened November 29, 1967 for 84 performances.
Reviews:
      America 118:19, Jan 6, 1968
      Commonweal 87:444+, Jan 12, 1968
      Life 64:16, Feb 2, 1968
      Nation 205:669, Dec 18, 1967
      New Republic 157:25-7, Dec 16, 1967
      New York Theatre Critics' Reviews 1967:204
                                         1967:211
      New York Times p. 50, Oct 24, 1967
                  II, p. 1, Nov 26, 1967
                  p. 60, Nov 30, 1967
                  II, p. 5, Dec 10, 1967
      Newsweek 70:96, Dec 11, 1967
      Reporter 37:38-9, Dec 28, 1967
      Saturday Review 50:24, Dec 16, 1967
      Time 90:96, Dec 8, 1967
      Vogue 151:28, Jan 15, 1968

Fam and Yam
Productions:
      (Off Broadway) Season of 1960-1961.
Reviews:
      New York Times p. 44, Oct 26, 1960

Malcolm (Based on James Purdy's novel)
Productions:
      Opened January 11, 1966 for 7 performances.
Reviews:
      Commonweal 83:584-5, Feb 18, 1966
      New Republic 154:34+, Jan 29, 1966
      New York Theatre Critics' Reviews 1966:392
      New York Times II, p. 1, Jan 7, 1966
                     p. 29, Jan 12, 1966
      New Yorker 41:74, Jan 22, 1966
      Newsweek 67:82, Jan 24, 1966

Time 87:50, Jan 21, 1966
Vogue 147:56, Feb 15, 1966

Quotations from Chairman Mao-Tse-Tung
Productions:
Opened September 30, 1968 in repertory for 12 per-
formances.
Reviews:
Commonweal 89:120+, Oct 25, 1968
Nation 206:420, Mar 25, 1968
New York Theatre Critics' Reviews 1968:213
1968:228
New York Times p. 48, Mar 8, 1968
II, p. 1, Mar 17, 1968
p. 39, Oct 1, 1968
II, p. 5, Oct 13, 1968
New Yorker 44:103-4+, Oct 12, 1968
Newsweek 71:109, Mar 18, 1968
Saturday Review 51:34, Mar 23, 1968
Time 92:73, Oct 11, 1968
Vogue 152:92, Nov 15, 1968

The Sandbox
Productions:
(Off Broadway) Season of 1959-1960.
(Off Broadway) Opened February 11, 1968 for 55
performances.
Reviews:
New York Times p. 42, May 17, 1960
p. 27, Feb 12, 1962
VI, p. 30, Feb 25, 1962

Tiny Alice
Productions:
Opened December 29, 1964 for 167 performances.
Reviews:
America 112:336-7, Mar 6, 1965
Catholic World 200:384, Mar 1965
Commonweal 81:543, Jan 22, 1965
84:583-5, Sep 16, 1966
Esquire 63:58+, Apr 1965
Life 58:14, Jan 29, 1965
Nation 200:65, Jan 18, 1965
New Republic 152:33-4+, Jan 23, 1965
New York Theatre Critics' Reviews 1964:95
New York Times p. 38, Dec 18, 1964
II, p. 1, Dec 27, 1964

ALBEE, EDWARD (cont.)
  Tiny Alice (cont.)

p. 14, Dec 30, 1964
p. 14, Dec 31, 1964
II, p. 1, Jan 10, 1965
p. 22, Jan 21, 1965
p. 33, Mar 23, 1965
II, p. 1, Apr 11, 1965

New Yorker 40:84, Jan 9, 1965
Newsweek 65:75, Jan 11, 1965
Reporter 32:53-4, Jan 28, 1965
Saturday Review 48:40, Jan 16, 1965
               48:38-9+, Jan 30, 1965
               48:21, Feb 20, 1965
Time 85:32, Jan 8, 1965
     85:68+, Jan 15, 1965
Vogue 145:50, Feb 15, 1965

Who's Afraid of Virginia Woolf?
  Productions:
  Opened October 13, 1962 for 664 performances.
  Reviews:
  America 107:1105-6, Nov 17, 1962
  Atlantic 213:122+, Apr 1964
  Catholic World 196:263-4, Jan 1963
  Commentary 35:296-301, Apr 1963
             36:272+, Oct 1963
  Commonweal 77:175-6, Nov 9, 1962
  Esquire 60:69+, Dec 1963
  Life 53:107-8, Dec 14, 1962
  Nation 195:273-4, Oct 27, 1962
  National Review 14:35-6, Jan 15, 1963
  New Republic 147:29-30, Nov 3, 1962
  New York Theatre Critics' Reviews 1962:251
  New York Times II, p. 1, Oct 7, 1962

p. 33, Oct 15, 1962
p. 79, Oct 16, 1962
II, p. 1, Oct 28, 1962
p. 15, Aug 16, 1963
p. 68, Oct 6, 1963
p. 15, Nov 9, 1963
p. 15, Feb 8, 1964
p. 52, Nov 26, 1964

New Yorker 38:85, Oct 20, 1962
Newsweek 60:52, Oct 29, 1962
Reporter 28:48, Apr 25, 1963
Saturday Review 45:29, Oct 27, 1962

Theatre Arts 46:10, Nov 1962
Time 80:84+, Oct 26, 1962

The Zoo Story
    Productions:
        (Off Broadway) Opened January 14, 1960 for 582
            performances.
        (Off Broadway) Opened September 12, 1961 for 32
            performances.
        (Off Broadway) Opened February 11, 1962 for 55
            performances.
        (Off Broadway) Opened September 4, 1962 for 30
            performances.
        (Off Broadway) Opened May 28, 1963 for 143 per-
            formances.
        (Off Broadway) Opened June 8, 1965 for 168 per-
            formances.
        Opened October 9, 1968 in repertory for 5 perform-
            ances.
    Reviews:
        America 108:891-2, Jun 22, 1963
        Commonweal 82:501-2, Jul 9, 1965
        Esquire 55:48-50, Apr 1961
        Nation 190:153, Feb 13, 1960
        New Republic 142:21, Feb 22, 1960
        New York Times p. 45, Sep 29, 1959
                       p. 37, Jan 15, 1960
                       II, p. 1, Jan 31, 1960
                       p. 23, Feb 15, 1960
                       p. 13, Aug 26, 1960
                       p. 39, May 29, 1963
                       p. 29, Jun 11, 1963
                       p. 10, Feb 13, 1965
                       p. 42, Jun 9, 1965
                       p. 41, Oct 11, 1968
        New Yorker 35:75-6, Jan 23, 1960
        Saturday Review 43:32, Feb 6, 1960

ALFRED, WILLIAM

    *Agamemnon
        Reviews:
        New York Times p. 29, Jan 12, 1966

    Hogan's Goat
        Productions:

15

ALFRED, WILLIAM (cont.)
  Hogan's Goat (cont.)
          (Off Broadway) Opened November 11, 1965 for 607
          performances.
  Reviews:
          Catholic World 202:318-20, Feb, 1966
          Commonweal 83:441, Jan 14, 1966
          Life 60:17, Feb 4, 1966
          Nation 201:427-8, Nov 29, 1965
          New Republic 153:46, Nov 27, 1965
          New York Times p. 56, Nov 12, 1965
                        p. 14, Nov 13, 1965
                        II, p. 1, Nov 21, 1965
                        II, p. 5, Nov. 21, 1965
          New Yorker 41:150-2, Nov 20, 1965
          Newsweek 66:92, Dec 6, 1965
          Reporter 34:47-8, Feb 24, 1966
          Time 87:65, Feb 18, 1966

ALLEN, JAY

  Forty Carats (Adapted from a play by Pierre Barillet and
          Jean-Pierre Gredy)
  Productions:
          Opened December 26, 1968 for 780 performances.
  Reviews:
          America 120:148, Feb 1, 1969
          Life 66:10, Feb 14, 1969
          Nation 208:125, Jan 27, 1969
          New York Theatre Critics' Reviews 1968:119
          New York Times p. 45, Dec 27, 1968
                        II, p. 1, Jan 5, 1969
                        II, p. 5, Feb 9, 1969
                        p. 48, Jan 6, 1970
          New Yorker 44:59, Jan 4, 1969
          Newsweek 73:57, Jan 6, 1969
          Time 93:64+, Jan 3, 1969
          Vogue 153:54, Feb 15, 1969

  The Prime of Miss Jean Brodie
  Productions:
          Opened January 16, 1968 for 378 performances.
  Reviews:
          America 118:330, Mar 9, 1968
          Christian Century 86:92-3, Jan 15, 1969
          Commonweal 87:592-3, Feb 16, 1968
          Life 64:14, Apr 5, 1968

Nation 206:186, Feb 5, 1968
New York Theatre Critics' Reviews 1968:376
1968:381
New York Times p. 39, Jan 17, 1968
II, p. 1, Jan 28, 1968
New Yorker 42:85, Jul 9, 1966
43:84, Jan 27, 1968
Newsweek 71:76, Jan 29, 1968
Reporter 38:43-4, Mar 7, 1968
Saturday Review 51:45, Feb 3, 1968
Time 91:45, Jan 26, 1968
Vogue 151:104, Mar 1, 1968

ALLEN, WOODY

Don't Drink the Water
    Productions:
    Opened November 17, 1966 for 598 performances.
    Reviews:
    America 116:26, Jan 7, 1967
    Commonweal 85:348, Dec 23, 1966
    Nation 203:652, Dec 12, 1966
    New York Theatre Critics' Reviews 1966:246
    New York Times p. 37, Nov 18, 1966
                    II, p. 1, Dec 25, 1966
    New Yorker 42:155, Dec 3, 1966
    Saturday Review 49:69, Dec 3, 1966
    Time 88:8, Nov 25, 1966

Play It Again, Sam
    Productions:
    Opened February 12, 1969 for 453 performances.
    Reviews:
    America 120:434, Apr 5, 1969
    Commonweal 90:438, Jul 11, 1969
    Nation 208:282-3, Mar 3, 1969
    New York Theatre Critics' Reviews 1969:360
    New York Times II, p. 1, Feb 9, 1969
                    p. 52, Feb 13, 1969
                    p. 26, Feb 14, 1969
                    II, p. 1, Feb 23, 1969
                    p. 25, Feb 7, 1970
    New Yorker 45:89, Feb 22, 1969
    Saturday Review 52:45, Mar 1, 1969
    Time 93:42, Feb 21, 1969
    Vogue 153:150, Apr 1, 1969

ANDERSON, MAXWELL

Anne of the Thousand Days
    Productions:
        Opened December 8, 1948 for 286 performances.
    Reviews:
        Catholic World 168:321-2, Jan 1949
        Commonweal 49:281 Dec 24, 1948
        Forum 111:92-3, Feb 1949
        Life 26:74-6, Jan 17, 1949
        Nation 168:24-5, Jan 1, 1949
        New Republic 119:29, Dec 27, 1948
        New York Theatre Critics' Reviews 1948:128
        New York Times, p. 49, Dec 9, 1948
                      II, p. 3, Dec 19, 1948
                      II, p. 1, Sep 18, 1949
        New York Times Magazine, p. 40-1, Nov 28, 1948
        New Yorker 24:48+, Dec 18, 1948
        Newsweek 32:72, Dec 20, 1948
        Saturday Review 31:24-26, Dec 25, 1948
        Theatre Arts 32:11-12, Oct 1948
                      33:52+, Mar 1949
        Time 52:60, Dec 20, 1948
        Vogue 113:113, Jan 1949

Bad Seed (Adapted from William March's novel)
    Productions:
        Opened December 8, 1954 for 332 performances.
    Reviews:
        America 92:346, Dec 25 1954
        Catholic World 180:387-8, Feb 1955
        Commonweal 61:358-9, Dec 31, 1954
        Life 38:53-4+, Jan 10, 1955
        Nation 179:556-7, Dec 25, 1954
        New Republic 131:21, Dec 27, 1954
        New York Theatre Critics' Reviews 1954:223
        New York Times p. 41, Dec 9, 1954
                      II, p. 3, Dec 19, 1954
                      VI, p. 22, Jan 16, 1955
                      II, p. 3, May 1, 1955
        New Yorker 30:61, Dec 18, 1954
        Newsweek 44:57 Dec 20, 1954
        Saturday Review 37:22, Dec 25, 1954
                      38:26, Apr 30, 1955
        Theatre Arts 39:18-20, Feb 1955
                      39:26, Apr 1955
                      39:33-4, Dec 1955
        Time 64:59, Dec 20, 1954

Barefoot in Athens
    Productions:
        Opened October 31, 1951 for 30 performances.
    Reviews:
        Catholic World 174:226-7, Dec 1951
        Commonweal 55:142-3, Nov 16, 1951
        Nation 173:430-1, Nov 17, 1951
        New York Theatre Critics' Reviews 1951:183
        New York Times II, p. 1, Oct 28, 1951
                        p. 35, Nov 1, 1951
                        II, p. 1, Nov 11, 1951
        New Yorker 27:66+, Nov 10, 1951
        Newsweek 38:92, Nov 12, 1951
        Saturday Review 35:28, Feb 23, 1952
                        34:26-8, Nov 24, 1951
        Theatre Arts 35:3 Dec 1951
                        36:81 Jan 1952
        Time 58:60+, Nov 12, 1951

Both Your Houses
    Productions:
        Opened March 6, 1933 for 120 performances.
    Reviews:
        Catholic World 173:80-1, Apr 1933
        Commonweal 17:582, Mar 22, 1933
        Literary Digest 115:15, Mar 25, 1933
        Nation 136:355, Mar 29, 1933
        New Outlook 161:46, Apr 1933
        New Republic 74:188, Mar 29, 1933
        New York Times p. 20, Mar 7, 1933
                        IX, p. 1, Mar 12, 1933
                        p. 22, May 23, 1933
        Newsweek 1:29, Mar 18, 1933
        Stage 10:6+, Apr 1933
        Theatre Arts 17:338-40, May 1933
        Time 21:40, Mar 13, 1930
        Vanity Fair 40:31-2+, May 1933
        Vogue 81:84, May 1, 1933

The Buccaneer (with Laurence Stallings)
    Productions:
        Opened October 2, 1925 for 20 performances.
    Reviews
        Nation 121:469, Oct 21, 1925
        New York Times p. 10, Oct 3, 1925
        Theatre Magazine 42:16, Dec 1925

ANDERSON, MAXWELL (cont.)
    Candle in the Wind
        Productions:
            Opened October 22, 1941 for 95 performances.
        Reviews:
            Catholic World 154:334-5, Dec 1941
            Commonweal 35:71, Nov 7, 1941
            Current History ns 1:379-80, Dec 1941
            Nation 153:462, Nov 8, 1941
            New Republic 105:621 Nov 10, 1941
            New York Theatre Critics' Reviews 1941:258
            New York Times p. 19, Sep 16, 1941
                          p. 26, Oct 23, 1941
                          IX, p. 1, Nov 2, 1941
            New Yorker 17:40+, Nov 1, 1941
            Newsweek 18:58, Nov 3, 1941
            Player's Magazine 18:11, Jan 1942
            Theatre Arts 25:861-2+, Dec 1941
                         26:80, Feb 1942

City Forgotten (See Night Over Taos)

The Day the Money Stopped (with Brendan Gill.   Based on
        Brendan Gill's novel)
Productions:
        Opened February 20, 1958 for 4 performances.
    Reviews:
        New York Theatre Critics' Reviews 1958:349
        New York Times, p. 19, Feb 21, 1958
        New Yorker 34:56+, Mar 1, 1958
        Time 71:74, Mar 3, 1958

Elizabeth and Essex (See Elizabeth the Queen)

Elizabeth the Queen
    Productions:
        Opened November 3, 1930 for 147 performances.
        (Off Broadway) Opened November 9, 1962 for 9 per-
            formances (Equity Library Theatre).
        Opened November 3, 1966 for 14 performances (City
            Center Drama Company).
    Reviews:
        Bookman 72:628, Feb 1931
        Catholic World 132:335, Dec 1930
        Collier's 87:10, Feb 7, 1931
        Commonweal 13:76, Nov 19, 1930
        Drama Magazine 21:11-12, Dec 1930

20

Literary Digest 107:17-18, Nov 22, 1930
Life (NY) 96:14, Nov 21, 1930
Nation 131:562, Nov 1930
National Review 19:99, Jan 24, 1967
New Republic 65:17-19, Nov 19, 1930
New York Times IX, p. 4, Oct 5, 1930
                  p. 37, Nov 4, 1930
               IX, p. 1, Nov 9, 1930
                  p. 18, Nov 9, 1935
                  p. 23, Jul 28, 1936
                  p. 25, Oct 30, 1936
                  p. 24, Aug 25, 1937
                  p. 30, Nov 4, 1966
Outlook 156:472, Nov 19, 1930
Theatre Arts 15:10-12, Jan 1931
Theatre Magazine 53:66, Jan 1931
Vanity Fair 35:30, Jan 1931
Woman's Journal ns 15:15, Dec 1930

The Eve of St. Mark
Productions:
    Opened October 7, 1942 for 307 performances.
Reviews:
    Catholic World 156:214-15, Nov 1942
    Commonweal 37:15, Oct 23, 1942
    Current History ns 3:264-5, Nov 1942
    Independent Woman 21:368, Dec 1942
    Life 13:51-2+, Oct 19, 1942
    Nation 155:425, Oct 24, 1942
    New Republic 107:546, Oct 26, 1942
    New York Theatre Critics' Reviews 1942:211
    New York Times VIII, p. 1, Oct 4, 1942
                       p. 30, Oct 8, 1942
                    VIII, p. 1, Oct 18, 1942
                       p. 8, Jan 25, 1943
    New Yorker 18:36 Oct 17, 1942
    Newsweek 20:76-8, Oct 19, 1942
    Player's Magazine 19:12, Dec 1942
    Scholastic 41:20, Nov 9, 1942
    Theatre Arts 26:735-7+, Dec 1942
                 33:54, May 1949
    Time 40:60+, Oct 19, 1942

First Flight (with Laurence Stallings)
Productions:
    Opened September 17, 1925 for 12 performances.
Reviews:

ANDERSON, MAXWELL (cont.)
  First Flight (cont.)
        American Mercury 6:376-7, Nov 1925
        Nation 121:390-1, Oct 7, 1925
        New York Times p. 26, Sep 18, 1925
                 VII, p. 1, Sep 27, 1925

Gods of the Lightning (with Harold Hickerson)
  Productions:
    Opened October 24, 1928 for 29 performances.
    (Off Broadway) Opened November 4, 1961 for 10 per-
      formances (Equity Library Theatre).
  Reviews:
    Catholic World 128:338-9, Dec 1928
    Dial 86:80-2, Jan 1929
    Life (NY) 92:14, Nov 9, 1928
    Nation 127:528, Nov 14, 1928
          127:593, Dec 5, 1928
    New Republic 56:326-7, Nov 7, 1928
    New York Times p. 27, Oct 25, 1928
               p. 17, Nov 27, 1935
    Theatre Arts 13:11-13, Jan 1929
    Theatre Magazine 49:47, Jan 1929
    Vogue 72:99, Dec 8, 1928

The Golden Six
  Productions:
    (Off Broadway) Season of 1958-59.
  Reviews:
    Commonweal 69:175-6, Nov 14, 1958
    New York Times p. 31, May 2, 1958
               p. 31, Oct 27, 1958
    New Yorker 34:91-3, Nov 8, 1958
    Theatre Arts 43:66, Jan 1959
    Time 72:50, Nov 3, 1958

Gypsy
  Productions:
    Opened January 14, 1929 for 64 performances.
  Reviews:
    Catholic World 128:724-5, Mar 1929
    Commonweal 9:406, Feb 6, 1929
    Life (NY) 93:23, Feb 1, 1929
    Nation 128:168, Feb 6, 1929
    New York Times p. 22, Jan 15, 1929
                IX, p. 1, Jan 27, 1929
                IX, p. 2, Oct 13, 1929
    Outlook 151:171, Jan 30, 1929

High Tor
    Productions:
        Opened January 9, 1937 for 171 performances.
    Reviews:
        Catholic World 144:728-9, Mar 1937
        Commonweal 25:388 Jan 29, 1937
                            26:132, May 28, 1937
        Forum 97:353, Jun 1937
        Literary Digest 123:21, Jan 23, 1937
        Nation 144:136, Jan 30, 1937
        New Republic 89:411-12, Feb 3, 1937
                            90:295, Apr 14, 1937
        New York Times X, p. 3, Dec 27, 1936
                            p. 20, Dec 31, 1936
                            p. 15, Jan 11, 1937
                            X, p. 1, Jan 17, 1937
                            X, p. 2, Feb 14, 1937
                            X, p. 1, Feb 21, 1937
                            X, p. 1, Apr 4, 1937
        Newsweek 9:32, Jan 16, 1937
        Scribner's Magazine 101:65-6, Jun 1937
        Stage 14:40-42, Jan 1937
              14:73-6, Feb 1937
              14:41-4, Mar 1937
        Theatre Arts 21:175-9, Mar 1937
        Time 29:47, Jan 18, 1937

Joan of Lorraine
    Productions:
        Opened November 18, 1946 for 199 performances.
    Reviews:
        Catholic World 164:357-8, Jan 1947
        Commonweal 45:200, Dec 6, 1946
        Life 21:51-2+, Dec 2, 1946
        Nation 163:671 Dec 7, 1946
        New Republic 115:726, Dec 2, 1946
        New York Theatre Critics' Reviews 1946:255
        New York Times p. 29, Oct 30, 1946
                            VI, p. 22, Nov 10, 1946
                            p. 40, Nov 19, 1946
                            II, p. 1, Nov 24, 1946
                            II, p. 3, Dec 1, 1946
                            p. 29, Nov 14, 1947
                            p. 12, Mar 26, 1955
        New York Times Magazine p. 22-3, Nov 30, 1946
        New Yorker 22:58, Nov 30, 1946
        Newsweek 28:94+, Dec 2, 1946

ANDERSON, MAXWELL (cont.)
    Joan of Lorraine (cont.)
                29:84, Jan 27, 1947
        Saturday Review 29:24-5, Dec 21, 1946
        Theatre Arts 31:12-13+, Jan 1947
        Time 48:54, Dec 2, 1946

Journey to Jerusalem
    Productions:
        Opened October 5, 1940 for 17 performances.
    Reviews:
        American Mercury 51:481-3, Dec 1940
        Arts and Decoration 52:40, Nov 1940
        Catholic World 152:216-17, Nov 1940
        Commonweal 32:530, Oct 18, 1940
        Nation 151:373, Oct 19, 1940
        New Republic 103:557, Oct 21, 1940
        New York Theatre Critics' Reviews 1940:262
        New York Times IX, p. 1, Sep 29, 1940
                        p. 21, Oct 7, 1940
        New Yorker 16:46, Oct 12, 1940
        Newsweek 16:74, Oct 14, 1940
        Theatre Arts 24:850+, Dec 1940
        Time 36:62, Oct 14, 1940

Key Largo
    Productions
        Opened November 27, 1939 for 105 performances.
    Reviews:
        Catholic World 150:467-8, Jan 1940
        Commonweal 31:163, Dec 8, 1939
        Forum 103:32, Jan 1940
        Nation 149:656+, Dec 9, 1939
        New Republic 101:230, Dec 13, 1939
        New York Theatre Critics' Reviews 1940:451
        New York Times p. 26, Oct 31, 1939
                        X, p. 3, Nov 19, 1939
                        p. 30, Nov 28, 1939
                        IX, p. 5, Dec 3, 1939
                        X, p. 3, Dec 10, 1939
                        VIII, p. 1, Jun 21, 1942
        Newsweek 14:34, Dec 11, 1939
        One Act Play Magazine 3:179-80, Feb 1940
        Theatre Arts 24:81-3+, Feb 1940
        Time 34:49, Dec 11, 1939

Mary of Scotland
    Productions:

Opened November 27, 1933 for 248 performances.
Reviews:
    Canadian Forum 15:275, Apr 1935
    Catholic World 138:473-5, Jan 1934
    Commonweal 19:189-90, Dec 15, 1933
    Nation 137:688+, Dec 13, 1933
    New Outlook 163:42, Jan 1934
    New Republic 77:130-1, Dec 13, 1933
    New York Times p. 28, Nov 28, 1933
                    IX, p. 5, Dec 3, 1933
                      IX, p. 2, Apr 14, 1935
    Newsweek 2:32, Dec 9, 1933
    Player's Magazine 10:32, May-Jun 1934
    Review of Reviews 89:39, Feb 1934
    Saturday Review 10:496, Feb 17, 1934
    Stage 11:10-11, Dec 1933
        11:8+, Jan 1934
    Theatre Arts 18:14-18, Jan 1934
    Time 22:48-9, Dec 4, 1933
    Vanity Fair 41:41, Feb 1934

The Masque of Kings
    Productions:
    Opened February 8, 1937 for 89 performances.
Reviews:
    Catholic World 144:731-2, Mar 1937
    Commonweal 25:502, Feb 26, 1937
                 26:216, Jun 18, 1937
    Literary Digest 123:24, Feb 20, 1937
    Nation 144:221-2, Feb 20, 1937
    New Republic 90:111-12, Mar 3, 1937
    New York Times p. 28, Jan 19. 1937
                  XI, p. 2, Jan 31, 1937
                  X, p. 2, Feb 7, 1937
                  p. 19, Feb 9, 1937
                  X, p. 1, Feb 21, 1937
                  X, p. 1, May 8, 1938
    Newsweek 9:24, Feb 20, 1937
    Saturday Review 15:23, Mar 13, 1937
    Theatre Arts 21:260-1, Apr 1937
    Time 29:39, Feb 15, 1937

Night Over Taos
    Productions:
    Opened March 9, 1932 for 13 performances.
Reviews:
    Arts and Decoration 37:56, May 1932

ANDERSON, MAXWELL (cont.)
  Night Over Taos (cont.)
          Catholic World 135:76, Apr 1932
          Nation 134:378, Mar 30, 1932
          New Republic 70:181-2, Mar 30, 1932
          New York Times p. 24, Feb 24, 1932
                        p. 25, Mar 10, 1932
          Stage 9:32-5, May 1932
          Theatre Arts 16:60-2, May 1932
          Theatre Guild Magazine 9:3, Apr 1932
          Vogue 79:100+, May 15, 1932

  Outside Looking In
    Productions:
          Opened September 7, 1925 for 113 performances.
    Reviews:
          Independent 115:393, Oct 3, 1925
          Life (NY) 86:20, Sep 24, 1925
          Nation 121:338, Sep 23, 1925
          New Republic 44:123-4, Sep 23, 1925
          New York Times, p. 28, Sep 8, 1925
                        VIII, p. 1, Sep 13, 1925
                        IX, p. 2, Oct 4, 1925
                        VIII, p. 2, Oct 11, 1925
                        VIII, p. 2, Oct 25, 1925
                        VIII, p. 2, Nov 15, 1935
                        VIII, p. 2, Jun 23, 1929
          Survey 55:46-7, Oct 1, 1925
          Theatre Arts 9:710-11, Nov 1925
          Theatre Magazine 42:16, Nov 1925

  Saturday's Children
    Productions:
          Opened January 26, 1927 for 310 performances.
          Opened April 9, 1928 for 16 performances.
    Reviews:
          American Mercury 10:503-4, Apr 1927
          Bookman 65:207, Apr 1927
          Life (NY) 89:19, Feb 17, 1927
          Nation 124:194, Feb 16, 1927
          New Republic 49:357, Jan 27, 1927
          New York Times p. 13, Jan 27, 1927
                        VII, p. 1, Feb 6, 1927
                        p. 32, Apr 10, 1928
                        p. 17, Jul 30, 1935
                        p. 22, Jul 7, 1936
                        IX, p. 3, May 12, 1940
          Theatre Magazine 45:22, May 1927

Theatre Magazine 46:24-5+, Jul 1927
Vogue 69:132, Apr 1, 1927

The Star Wagon
Productions:
Opened September 29, 1937 for 223 performances.
Reviews:
Catholic World 146:215-16, Nov 1937
Commonweal 26:580, Oct 15, 1937
Independent Woman 16:351+, Nov 1937
Nation 145:411, Oct 16, 1937
New Republic 92:302, Oct 20, 1937
New York Times p. 28, Sep 17, 1937
                p. 18, Sep 30, 1937
                XI, p. 1, Oct 10, 1937
Newsweek 10:27, Oct 11, 1937
One Act Play Magazine 1:857, Jan 1938
Scribner's Magazine 102:53-4, Dec 1937
Stage 15:69, Nov 1937
Theatre Arts 21:838+, Nov 1937
Time 30:52-3, Oct 11, 1937
Vogue 90:90, Nov 1, 1937

Storm Operation
Productions:
Opened January 11, 1944 for 23 performances.
Reviews:
Catholic World 158:489-90, Feb 1944
Commonweal 39:398-9, Feb 4, 1944
Nation 158:105-7, Jan 22, 1944
New Republic 110:148, Jan 31, 1944
New York Theatre Critics' Reviews 1944:289
New York Times II, p. 1, Sep 19, 1943
                  p. 28, Jan 12, 1944
New York Times Magazine pp. 10-11, Dec 26, 1943
New Yorker 19:34, Jan 22, 1944
Theatre Arts 28:133-6, Mar 1944
Time 43:40, Jan 24, 1944

Truckline Cafe
Productions:
Opened February 27, 1946 for 13 performances
Reviews:
Commonweal 43:533-4, Mar 15, 1946
Forum 105:753-5, Apr 1946
Nation 162:324, Mar 16, 1946
New Republic 114:349, Mar 11, 1946

ANDERSON, MAXWELL (cont.)
  Truckline Cafe (cont.)
        New York Theatre Critics' Reviews 1946:441
        New York Times II, p. 1, Feb 24, 1946
                        p. 19, Feb 28, 1946
        New Yorker 22:43-4, Mar 9, 1946
        Newsweek 27:82, Mar 11, 1946
        Theatre Arts 30:260+, May 1946
        Time 47:86, Mar 11, 1946

  Valley Forge
    Productions:
      Opened December 10, 1934 for 58 performances.
    Reviews:
      Catholic World 140:596-7, Feb 1935
      Commonweal 21:264, Dec 28, 1934
      Literary Digest 118:22, Dec 22, 1934
      Nation 139:750, Dec 26, 1934
      New Republic 81:196, Dec 26, 1934
      New York Times p. 26, Nov 27, 1934
                     p. 28, Dec 11, 1934
                     IX, p. 1, Dec 23, 1934
      Newsweek 4:24, Dec 22, 1934
      Stage 12:24-7, Jan 1935
      Theatre Arts 19:94-6, Feb 1935
      Time 24:46-8, Dec 10, 1934
      Vanity Fair 43:37-8, Feb 1935

  What Price Glory? (with Laurence Stallings)
    Productions:
      Opened September 3, 1924 for 299 performances.
    Reviews:
      American Mercury 3:372-3, Nov 1924
      Bookman 60:328, Nov 1924
      Canadian Magazine 64:74, Apr 1925
      Classic 20:46, Dec 1924
      Current Opinion 77:612+, Nov 1924
      Dial 77:440, Nov 1924
      Drama Magazine 15:4, Oct 1924
      Independent 113:403, Nov 15, 1924
      Life (NY) 84:18, Sep 24, 1924
      Literary Digest 83:30-1, Oct 4, 1924
                      84:30-1, Jan 10, 1925
                      92:24-5, Mar 5, 1927
                      117:21, Jun 30, 1934
      Living Age 324:68, Jan 3, 1925
      Nation 119:316-7, Sep 24, 1924

New Republic 40:98, Sep 24, 1924
         40:160-61, Oct 15, 1924
New York Times p. 14, Sep 6, 1924
              VIII, p. 1, Sep 14, 1924
              VII, p. 1, Sep 21, 1924
              p. 14, Sep 27, 1924
              VII, p. 1, Sep 27, 1924
              p. 14, Sep 29, 1924
              p. 22, Oct 2, 1924
              IV, p. 7, Oct 12, 1924
              VIII, p. 1, Jun 28, 1925
              IX, p. 2, Apr 28, 1929
              p. 25, Oct 30, 1936
              IX, p. 1, Sep 24, 1939
              p. 33, Mar 3, 1949
Outlook 138:439-41, Nov 19, 1924
Saturday Review 28:18, Dec 8, 1945
Theatre Arts 11:659, Sep 1927
            25:578, Aug 1941
Theatre Magazine 39:14-15, Nov 1924
              40:15, Nov 1924
              40:28, Dec 1924
              41:19, Jan 1925
              44:7, Jul 1926
Vogue 101:80, Feb 1, 1943
Woman Citizen 9:11, Oct 18, 1924

White Desert
    Productions:
    Opened October 18, 1923 for 12 performances.
    Reviews:
    New York Times p. 17, Oct 19, 1923

The Wingless Victory
    Productions:
    Opened December 23, 1936 for 110 performances.
    Reviews:
    Catholic World 144:598-9, Feb 1937
    Commonweal 25:304, Jan 8, 1937
    Forum 97:354, Jun 1937
    Nation 144:53-4, Jan 9, 1937
    New Republic 89:411, Feb 3, 1937
    New York Times p. 17, Nov 25, 1936
                   p. 20, Dec 24, 1936
                   X, p. 1, Jan 3, 1937
                   X, p. 1, Feb 21, 1937

29

ANDERSON, MAXWELL (cont.)
  The Wingless Victory (cont.)
      Newsweek 9:22, Jan 2, 1937
      Scholastic 30:19, Feb 13, 1937
      Scribner's Magazine 101:69-70, Mar 1937
      Stage 14:38-9+, Jan 1937
      Theatre Arts 21:89-95, Feb 1937
                29:309, May 1945
      Time 29:29, Jan 4, 1937
      Vogue 89:64, Feb 1, 1937

Winterset
  Productions:
      Opened September 25, 1935 for 195 performances.
      (Off Broadway) Opened February 9, 1966 for 30 per-
      formances.
  Reviews:
      Catholic World 142:211-12, Nov 1935
      Commonweal 22:585, Oct 11, 1935
                24:218, Jun 19, 1936
      Forum 95:345-6, Jun 1936
      Literary Digest 120:20, Oct 5, 1935
      Nation 141:420, Oct 9, 1935
            141:638, Dec 4, 1935
            142:484-5, Apr 15, 1936
      New Republic 84:274, Oct 16, 1935
                84:365, Nov 6, 1935
                85:257, Jan 8, 1936
      New York Times p. 19, Sep 26, 1935
                XI, p. 1, Oct 6, 1935
                IX, p. 1, Feb 16, 1936
                p. 35, Jun 2, 1936
                p. 32, Feb 10, 1966
                p. 28, Jul 23, 1968
      Newsweek 6:32-3, Oct 5, 1935
              7:32, Apr 4, 1936
              8:20, Dec 5, 1936
      Player's Magazine 12:2+, Jan-Feb, 1936
      Saturday Review 12:16, Oct 12, 1935
      Stage 13:56-8, Nov 1935
      Theatre Arts 19:815-20, Nov 1935
                20:465, Jun 1936
                31:30, Nov 1947
      Time 26:38+, Oct 7, 1935
      Vanity Fair 45:39, Dec 1935

All Summer Long (Adapted from Donald Wetzel's novel)
    Productions:
        Opened September 23, 1954 for 60 performances.
    Reviews:
        America 92:110, Oct 23, 1954
        Catholic World 180:144-5, Nov 1954
        Commonweal 61:60, Oct 22, 1954
        Nation 179:314, Oct 9, 1954
        New Republic 131:22, Oct 4, 1954
        New York Theatre Critics' Reviews 1954:304
        New York Times p. 23, Jan 29, 1953
                    II, p. 3, Sep 19, 1954
                    p. 26, Sep 24, 1954
                    II, p. 1, Oct 3, 1954
        New Yorker 30:63, Oct 2, 1954
        Newsweek 44:83, Oct 4, 1954
        Saturday Review 37:26, Oct 9, 1954
        Theatre Arts 38:20, 90, Dec 1954
        Time 64:56, Oct 4, 1954

Come Marching Home
    Productions:
        Opened May 18, 1946 for 19 performances.
    Reviews:
        Commonweal 44:166, May 31, 1946
        New York Times p. 18, May 20, 1946

*The Days Between
    Reviews:
        Life 59:20, Nov 19, 1965
        New York Times p. 28, Feb 19, 1965
                    p. 39, Jun 4, 1965
                    II, p. 1, Jun 27, 1965

The Footsteps of Doves (see You Know I Can't Hear You
    When the Water's Running)

I Never Sang for My Father
    Productions:
        Opened January 25, 1968 for 124 performances.
    Reviews:
        America 118:356, Mar 16, 1968
        Christian Century 85:405-6, Mar 27, 1968
        Life 64:10, Mar 1, 1968
        Nation 206:221, Feb 12, 1968
        New York Theatre Critics' Reviews 1968:367
                                        1968:373

ANDERSON, ROBERT (cont.)
    I Never Sang for My Father (cont.)
        New York Times p. 30, Jan 26, 1968
                        II, p. 1, Feb 4, 1968
        New Yorker 43:77, Feb 3, 1968
        Newsweek 71:81, Feb 5, 1968
        Saturday Review 51:39, Feb 10, 1968
        Time 91:47, Feb 2, 1968
        Vogue 151:44, Mar 15, 1968

    I'll Be Home for Christmas (see You Know I Can't Hear
      You When the Water's Running)

    I'm Herbert (see You Know I Can't Hear You When the
      Water's Running)

    The Shock of Recognition (see You Know I Can't Hear You
      When the Water's Running)

    Silent Night, Lonely Night
      Productions:
        Opened December 3, 1959 for 124 performances.
        (Off Broadway) Season of 1967-68.
      Reviews:
        America 102:428, Jan 9, 1960
        Christian Century 77:16, Jan 6, 1960
        Commonweal 71:395, Jan 1, 1960
        Nation 189:476, Dec 19, 1959
        New York Theatre Critics' Reviews 1959:204
        New York Times p. 12, Nov 14, 1959
                   p. 36, Dec 4, 1959
                   II, p. 3, Dec 13, 1959
        New Yorker 35:102-3, Dec 12, 1959
        Saturday Review 42:24, Dec 19, 1959
        Time 74:77, Dec 14, 1959

    Tea and Sympathy
      Productions:
        Opened September 30, 1953 for 712 performances.
      Reviews:
        America 90:107+, Oct 24, 1953
        Catholic World 178:148-9, Nov 1953
        Commonweal 59:90, Oct 30, 1953
        Life 35:121-3, Oct 19, 1953
        Nation 177:317-18, Oct 17, 1953
        New Republic 129:20-1, Oct 19, 1953
        New York Theatre Critics' Reviews 1953:266

New York Times II, p. 3, Sep 27, 1953
           p. 35, Oct 1, 1953
           II, p. 1, Oct 11, 1953
           VI, p. 14, Oct 11, 1953
           II, p. 3, Nov 8, 1953
           II, p. 1, Aug 15, 1954
           p. 50, Dec 4, 1956
           p. 22, Apr 26, 1957
New Yorker 29:71, Oct 10, 1953
Newsweek 42:84, Oct 12, 1953
           42:60, Dec 21, 1953
Saturday Review 36:35, Oct 17, 1953
           36:45, Dec 12, 1953
Theatre Arts 37:62-7, Nov 1953
           37:18-19, Dec 1953
Time 62:49, Oct 12, 1953

You Know I Can't Hear You When the Water's Running
    ("The Shock of Recognition, " "The Footsteps of Doves, "
    "I'll be Home for Christmas, " "I'm Herbert").
Productions:
    Opened March 13, 1967 for 755 performances.
Reviews:
    America 116:793, May 27, 1967
    Christian Century 84:1048-9, Aug 16, 1967
    Commonweal 86:175-6, Apr 28, 1967
    Life 62:23, Apr 28, 1967
    Nation 204:444, Apr 3, 1967
    New York Theatre Critics' Reviews 1967:343
    New York Times p. 54, Mar 14, 1967
               p. 54, Mar 15, 1967
               II, p. 1, Mar 26, 1967
               p. 33, Mar 29, 1968
    New Yorker 43:119, Mar 25, 1967
    Newsweek 69:110, Mar 27, 1967
    Reporter 36:43. 4, Apr 20, 1967
    Saturday Review 50:42, Apr 1, 1967
    Time 89:69, Mar 24, 1967

ANSPACHER, LOUIS K.

    Dagmar (Adapted from a play by Ferencz Herczeg)
    Productions:
        Opened January 22, 1923 for 56 performances.
    Reviews:
        Life (NY) 81:18, Feb 8, 1923
        New York Clipper 70:14, Jan 31, 1923

ANSPACHER, LOUIS K. (cont.)
Dagmar (cont.)
New York Times p. 18, Jan 23, 1923

Our Children
Productions:
Opened September 10, 1915 for 18 performances.
Reviews:
Dramatic Mirror 74:8, Sep 15, 1915
Life (NY) 66:566, Sep 23, 1915
Nation 101:364-5, Sep 16, 1915
New York Drama News 61:19, Sep 18, 1915
Theatre Magazine 22:167-8, Oct 1915

The Rhapsody
Productions:
Opened September 15, 1930 for 16 performances.
Reviews:
Commonweal 12:555, Oct 1, 1930
Nation 131:355, Oct 1, 1930
New York Times p. 30, Sep 16, 1930

That Day
Productions:
Opened October 3, 1922 for 15 performances.
Reviews:
Dramatic Mirror 77:34, Aug 11, 1917
Dramatist 13:1131-2, Oct 1922
New York Times p. 11, Jul 4, 1922
                 p. 27, Oct 4, 1922

The Unchastened Woman
Productions:
Opened October 9, 1915 for 193 performances.
Opened February 15, 1926 for 31 performances.
Reviews:
Book News 34:181-2, Dec 1915
Bookman 42:380+, Dec 1915
Current Opinion 59:400-4, Dec 1915
Drama 22:285-93, May 1916
Dramatic Mirror 74:9, Oct 16, 1915
Dramatist 7:638-9, Jan 1916
Green Book 15:18-19, Jan 1916
Hearst 29:106-8+, Feb 1916
Nation 101:476-7, Oct 14, 1915
New York Drama News 61:17, Oct 16, 1915
New York Times p. 12, Feb 17, 1926

VII, p. 1, Feb 21, 1926
Smart Set 47:147, Dec 1915

A Woman of Impulse
    Productions:
        Opened March 1, 1909 for 16 performances.
    Reviews:
        Forum 41:337-9, Apr 1909
        Theatre Magazine 9:105+, Apr 1909

ARCHIBALD, WILLIAM

The Cantilevered Terrace
    Productions:
        (Off Broadway) Opened January 17, 1962 for 39 per-
            formances.
    Reviews:
        America 106:632, Feb 10, 1962
        New York Times p. 24, Jan 18, 1962
                    II, p. 1, Jan 28, 1962
        New Yorker 37:73-4+, Jan 27, 1962
        Saturday Review 45:38, Feb 17, 1962
        Time 79:56, Jan 26, 1962

The Innocents (Based on Henry James' The Turn of the
    Screw)
    Productions:
        Opened February 1, 1950 for 141 performances.
        (Off Broadway) Season of 1958-1959.
    Reviews:
        Catholic World 170:469, Mar 1950
                       189:321, Jul 1959
        Commonweal 51:509, Feb 17, 1950
        Life 28:91-2+, Apr 3, 1950
        Nation 170:141, Feb 11, 1950
        New Republic 122:20, Feb 27, 1950
        New York Theatre Critics' Reviews 1950:359
        New York Times p. 30, Feb 2, 1950
                       II, p. 1, Feb 12, 1950
                       II, p. 3, Mar 26, 1950
                       II, p. 2, Apr 23, 1950
                       p. 9, Jul 4, 1952
                       p. 41, Apr 21, 1959
        New Yorker 25:44, Feb 11, 1950
                   35:97-9, May 2, 1959
        Newsweek 35:80, Feb 13, 1950
        Saturday Review 33:32+, Feb 25, 1950

ARCHIBALD, WILLIAM (cont.)
  The Innocents (cont.)
                    School and Society 71:214-15, Apr 8, 1950
                    Theatre Arts 34:16, Apr 1950
                                       34:22-3+, Jun 1950
                    Time 55:52-3, Feb 13, 1950

  Portrait of A Lady (Based on Henry James' novel)
         Productions:
                    Opened December 21, 1954 for 7 performances.
         Reviews:
                    America 92:407, Jan 15, 1955
                    Commonweal 61:429, Jan 21, 1955
                    Nation 180:36, Jan 8, 1955
                    New York Theatre Critics' Reviews 1954:211
                    New York Times II, p. 3, Dec 19, 1954
                                       p. 30, Dec 21, 1954
                                       p. 27, Dec 22, 1954
                    New Yorker 30:42+, Jan 1, 1955
                    Newsweek 45:43, Jan 3, 1955
                    Saturday Review 38:25, Jan 8, 1955
                    Time 65:35, Jan 3, 1955

ARDREY, ROBERT

  Casey Jones
         Productions:
                    Opened February 19, 1938 for 25 performances.
         Reviews:
                    Commonweal 27:554, Mar 11, 1938
                    Nation 146:281, Mar 5, 1938
                    New York Times p. 14, Feb 21, 1938
                    One Act Play Magazine 1:1021-2, Mar 1938
                    Theatre Arts 22:248-50, Apr 1938

  How to Get Tough About It
         Productions:
                    Opened February 8, 1938 for 23 performances.
         Reviews:
                    Catholic World 146:730, Mar 1938
                    Commonweal 27:496, Feb 25, 1938
                    New York Times p. 16, Feb 9, 1938
                    One Act Play Magazine 1:943-4, Feb 1938
                    Theatre Arts 22:250-1, Apr 1938
                    Time 31:42, Feb 21, 1938

Jeb
   Productions:
      Opened February 21, 1946 for 9 performances.
   Reviews:
      Forum 105:753, Apr 1946
      New Republic 114:349, Mar 11, 1946
      New York Theatre Critics' Reviews 1946:446
      New York Times II, p. 1, Feb 17, 1946
                      p. 20, Feb 22, 1946
                      II, p. 1, Mar 3, 1946
      New Yorker 22:41-3, Mar 2, 1946
      Newsweek 27:79, Mar 4, 1946
      Theatre Arts 30:203-5, Apr 1946

Shadow of Heroes (Stone and Star)
   Productions:
      (Off Broadway) Opened December 5, 1961 for 20
         performances.
   Reviews:
      Commonweal 75:389, Jan 5, 1962
      New York Times p. 59, Dec 6, 1961
      New Yorker 37:98+, Dec 16, 1961
      Reporter 26:38, Jan 4, 1962
      Saturday Review 45:25, Jan 6, 1962
      Theatre Arts (p. 15) 46:74-5, Feb 1962

Sing Me No Lullaby
   Productions:
      Opened October 14, 1954 for 30 performances.
   Reviews:
      America 92:221, Nov 20, 1954
      Commentary 18:522-5, Dec 1954
      Commonweal 61:189, Nov 19, 1954
      Nation 179:390, Oct 30, 1954
      New Republic 131:23, Nov 1, 1954
      New York Theatre Critics' Reviews 1954:279
      New York Times p. 17, Oct 15, 1954
                      II, p. 1, Oct 24, 1954
      New Yorker 30:79, Oct 23, 1954
      Newsweek 44:93, Oct 25, 1954
      Saturday Review 37:27, Oct 30, 1954
      Theatre Arts 38:81, 92, Dec 1954
      Time 64:42, Oct 25, 1954

Star Spangled
   Productions:
      Opened March 10, 1936 for 23 performances.

ARDREY, ROBERT (cont.)
  Star Spangled (cont.)
    Reviews:
      Catholic World 143:89, Apr 1936
      Literary Digest 121:19, Mar 21, 1936
      New York Times p. 25, Mar 6, 1936
                     p. 23, Mar 11, 1936

  Stone and Star (see Shadow of Heroes)

  Thunder Rock
    Productions:
      Opened November 14, 1939 for 23 performances.
    Reviews:
      Commonweal 31:137, Dec 1, 1939
      Nation 149:586, Nov 25, 1939
      New York Times p. 18, Nov 15, 1939
                     X, p. 3, Nov 19, 1939
                     p. 10, Jul 29, 1940
                     IV, p. 2, Aug 4, 1940
                     IX, p. 2, Aug 11, 1940
                     p. 18, Feb 27, 1956
      Newsweek 14:23, Nov 27, 1939
      Theatre Arts 24:16-17+, Jan 1940
      Time 36:52, Aug 12, 1940

ATLAS, LEOPOLD

  But for the Grace of God
    Productions:
      Opened January 12, 1937 for 42 performances.
    Reviews:
      Commonweal 25:418, Feb 5, 1937
      Nation 144:108, Jan 23, 1937
      New York Times X, p. 3, Jan 10, 1937
                     p. 21, Jan 13, 1937
      Theatre Arts 21:182-3, Mar 1937

  Wednesday's Child
    Productions:
      Opened January 16, 1934 for 56 performances.
    Reviews:
      Catholic World 138:732, Mar 1934
      Literary Digest 117:23, Feb 24, 1934
      New Outlook 163:33, Mar 1934
      New York Times p. 23, Jan 17, 1934
                     X, p. 2, Jan 21, 1934
                     IX, p. 1, Jan 28, 1934

Newsweek 3:33, Jan 27, 1934
Review of Reviews 89:47, Mar 1934
Stage 11:10-11, Mar 1934
Theatre Arts 18:170-1, Mar 1934
Time 23:34, Jan 29, 1934

AURTHUR, ROBERT ALAN

Carry Me Back to Morningside Heights
Productions:
Opened February 27, 1968 for 7 performances.
Reviews:
New York Theatre Critics' Reviews 1968:343
New York Times p. 41, Feb 28, 1968

A Very Special Baby
Productions:
Opened November 14, 1956 for 5 performances.
Reviews:
Nation 183:485, Dec 1, 1956
New York Theatre Critics' Reviews 1956:206
New York Times p. 43, Nov 15, 1956
New Yorker 32:123, Nov 24, 1956
Saturday Review 39:50, Dec 1, 1956
Theatre Arts 41:27, Jan 1957
Time 68:58, Nov 26, 1956

AXELROD, GEORGE

Goodbye, Charlie
Productions:
Opened December 16, 1959 for 109 performances.
Reviews:
Commonweal 71:630-1, Mar 4, 1960
New York Theatre Critics' Reviews 1959:186
New York Times p. 50, Dec 17, 1959
New Yorker 35:48+, Dec 26, 1959
Newsweek 54:43, Dec 28, 1959
Saturday Review 43:30, Jan 2, 1960

The Seven Year Itch
Productions:
Opened November 20, 1952 for 1, 141 performances
Reviews:
Catholic World 176:307, Jan 1953
Commonweal 57:259, Dec 12, 1952
Life 33:145-8, Dec 1952

AXELROD, GEORGE (cont.)
   The Seven Year Itch (cont.)
          Nation 175:563, Dec 13, 1952
          New York Theatre Critics' Reviews 1952:186
          New York Times p. 21, Nov 21, 1952
                    II, p. 1, Nov 30, 1952
                    II, p. 3, Mar 1, 1953
                    p. 26, May 18, 1953
          New Yorker 28:67, Dec 6, 1952
          Newsweek 40:79, Dec 1, 1952
          Saturday Review 35:25, Dec 13, 1952
          Theatre Arts 37:27-8, Feb 1953
          Time 60:78+, Dec 1, 1952

Will Success Spoil Rock Hunter?
   Productions:
   Opened October 13, 1955 for 444 performances.
   Reviews:
      America 94:138, Oct 29, 1955
      Catholic World 182:226, Dec 1955
      Commonweal 63:141, Nov 11, 1955
      Nation 181:405, Nov 5, 1955
      New Republic 134:20, Jan 2, 1956
      New York Theatre Critics' Reviews 1955:246
      New York Times p. 22, Oct 14, 1955
      New Yorker 31:88, Oct 22, 1955
      Newsweek 46:54, Oct 24, 1955
      Saturday Review 38:20, Oct 29, 1955
      Theatre Arts 39:26, Dec 1955
      Time 66:86, Oct 24, 1955

BALDERSTON, JOHN

   Berkeley Square (Suggested by Henry James' "A Sense of
        the Past.")
   Productions:
   Opened November 4, 1929 for 229 performances.
   Reviews:
      American Mercury 19:116-17, Jan 1930
      Catholic World 130:464-6, Jan 1930
      Commonweal 11:85, Nov 20, 1929
      Life (NY) 94:24, Nov 22, 1929
             95:18, Jun 6, 1930
      Literary Digest 103:19, Nov 30, 1929
      Nation 129:604-5, Nov 20, 1929
      New Republic 60:374-5, Nov 20, 1929
      New York Times p. 19, Oct 7, 1926

VIII, p. 2, Oct 24, 1926
p. 32, Nov 5, 1929
X, p. 1, Nov 9, 1929
X, p. 1, Dec 1, 1929
p. 25, Aug 20, 1935

Outlook 153:470, Nov 20, 1929
Sketch Book 7:29, Jan 1930
Theatre Arts 14:11-12, Jan 1930
Theatre Magazine 50:76, Dec 1929
51:32-5+, Jan 1930

Dracula (with Hamilton Deane. Based on Bram Stoker's novel)
  Productions:
    Opened October 5, 1927 for 261 performances.
    Opened April 13, 1931 for 8 performances.
  Reviews:
    New York Times p. 29, Oct 6, 1927
                VIII, p. 3, Dec 25, 1927
                p. 33, Apr 14, 1931
    Theatre Magazine 46:84, Dec 1927
    Vogue 70:172, Dec 1, 1927

Red Planet (with J. E. Hoare)
  Productions:
    Opened December 17, 1932 for 7 performances.
  Reviews:
    Commonweal 17:271, Jan 4, 1933
    Nation 136:27-8, Jan 4, 1933
    New York Times p. 19, Dec 19, 1932
    Stage 10:8-9, Feb 1933
    Theatre Arts 17:105-6, Feb 1933

BALDWIN, JAMES

The Amen Corner
  Productions:
    Opened April 15, 1965 for 84 performances.
  Reviews:
    America 112:690, May 8, 1965
    Catholic World 201:215-6, Jun 1965
    Commonweal 82:221-2, May 7, 1965
    Life 58:16, May 14, 1965
    Nation 200:514-5, May 10, 1965
    New York Theatre Critics' Reviews 1965:349
    New York Times p. 37, Mar 5, 1965
                II, p. 1, Apr 11, 1965

BALDWIN, JAMES (cont.)
The Amen Corner (cont.)
                        p. 35, Apr 16, 1965
                        II, p. 1, Apr 25, 1965
                        p. 82, Jun 13, 1965
                        p. 19, Aug 9, 1965
New Yorker 41:85, Apr 25, 1965
Newsweek 65:90, Apr 26, 1965
Saturday Review 48:49, May 1, 1965
Time 85:59, Apr 23, 1965
Vogue 145:68, Jun 1965

Blues for Mr. Charlie
Productions:
Opened April 23, 1964 for 148 performances.
Reviews:
America 110:776-7, May 30, 1964
Catholic World 199:263-4, Jul 1964
Commonweal 80:299-300, May 29, 1964
Ebony 19:188, Jun 1964
Nation 198:495-6, May 11, 1964
National Review 16:780-1, Sep 8, 1964
New Republic 150:35-7, May 16, 1964
New York Theatre Critics' Reviews 1964:276
New York Times, II, p. 1, Apr 19, 1964
                        p. 24, Apr 24, 1964
                        II, p. 1, May 3, 1964
                        p. 18, Jun 29, 1964
                        p. 52, May 5, 1965
New Yorker 40:143, May 9, 1964
Newsweek 63:46, May 4, 1964
Saturday Review 47:27-8, May 2, 1964
                        47:36, May 9, 1964
Time 83:50, May 1, 1964
          83:96, Jun 5, 1964
Vogue 144:32, Jul 1964

BARKER, JAMES NELSON
No Productions.

BARRY, PHILIP
The Animal Kingdom
Productions:
Opened January 12, 1932 for 183 performances.
Reviews:

Arts and Decoration 36:63-4, Mar 1932
Bookman 74:562-3, Jan 1932
Catholic World 134:714-15, Mar 1932
Commonweal 15:441-2, Feb 17, 1932
Nation 134:141 Feb 3, 1932
New Republic 69:293-4, Jan 27, 1932
New York Times p. 26, Jan 13, 1932
                 VIII, p. 1, Jan 24, 1932
                 p. 14, Jul 27, 1938
North American Review 234:173, Aug 1932
Outlook 160:118, Jan 27, 1932
Theatre Arts 16:187-8, Mar 1932
Theatre Guild Magazine 9:15-17, Mar 1932
Vogue 79:100, Mar 1, 1932

Bright Star
   Productions:
      Opened October 15, 1935 for 7 performances.
   Reviews:
      Commonweal 23:19, Nov 1, 1935
      Nation 141:520, Oct 30, 1935
      New York Times IX, p. 1, Oct 13, 1935
                  p. 26, Oct 16, 1935
      Theatre Arts 19:899-900, Dec 1935
      Time 26:39, Oct 28, 1935

Cock Robin (with Elmer Rice)
   Productions:
      Opened January 12, 1928 for 100 performances.
   Reviews:
      American Mercury 13:376-7, Mar 1928
      Life (NY) 91:21, Feb 2, 1928
      Nation 126:130, Feb 1, 1928
      New York Times p. 26, Jan 13, 1928
                  VIII, p. 2, Jan 15, 1928
      Outlook 148:423, Mar 14, 1928
      Theatre Arts 12:172, Mar 1928
      Theatre Magazine 47:40, Mar 1928
      Vogue 71:83+, Mar 1, 1928

Foolish Notion
   Productions
      Opened March 13, 1945 for 104 performances.
   Reviews:
      Catholic World 161:70, Apr 1945
      Commonweal 41:589, Mar 30, 1945
      Nation 160:340-1, Mar 24, 1945

BARRY, PHILIP (cont.)
   Foolish Notion (cont.)
         New Republic 112:421, Mar 26, 1945
         New York Theatre Critics' Reviews 1945:254
         New York Times VI, p. 24, Feb 25, 1945
                   p. 23, Mar 14, 1945
                  II, p. 1, Mar 18, 1945
         New York Times Magazine p. 24-5, Feb 25, 1945
         New Yorker 21:48 Mar 24, 1945
         Newsweek 25:88 Mar 26, 1945
         Saturday Review 28:18-19, Mar 24, 1945
         Theatre Arts 29:199, Apr 1945
                   29:269-70, May 1945
         Time 45:70+, Mar 26, 1945

Here Come the Clowns
   Productions:
      Opened December 7, 1938 for 88 performances.
      (Off Broadway) Season of 1960-61.
      (Off Broadway) Opened May 13, 1966 for 9 perform-
      ances (Equity Theatre).
   Reviews:
      America 104:100, Oct 15, 1960
      Catholic World 148:473-4, Jan 1939
                  179:308, Jul 1954
      Commonweal 29:244, Dec 23, 1938
               29:552, Mar 10, 1939
      Forum 101:72, Feb 1939
      Nation 147:700, Dec 24, 1938
      New Republic 97:230, Dec 28, 1938
      New York Times p. 36, Dec 8, 1938
                 p. 30, Dec 20, 1938
                 IX, p. 3, Jan 8, 1939
                 p. 36, May 5, 1954
                 p. 48, Sep 20, 1960
      New Yorker 36:131-2, Oct 1, 1960
      Newsweek 12:25, Dec 19, 1938
      North American Review 247, no. 1:156-7, Mar 1939
      One Act Play Magazine 2:671-3, Jan 1939
      Theatre Arts 23:89-91+, Feb 1939
      Time 32:43-4, Dec 19, 1938

Holiday
   Productions:
      Opened November 26, 1928 for 229 performances.
   Reviews:
      American Mercury 16:245, Feb 1929

Bookman 68:684-5, Feb 1929
Commonweal 9:405, Feb 6, 1929
Drama 19:103, 128, Jan 1929
New Republic 57:96-7, Dec 12, 1928
New York Times p. 36, Nov 27, 1928
             p. 26, Nov 28, 1928
             X, p. 1, Dec 9, 1928
             p. 21, Feb 6, 1930
             p. 15, Jul 23, 1941
Outlook 151:11 Jan 2, 1929
Review of Reviews 79:160, Feb 1929
Theatre Magazine 49:78, Feb 1929
             49:18, Apr 1929
             50:15, Jul 1929
             52:47, Aug 1930

Hotel Universe
    Productions:
        Opened April 14, 1930 for 81 performances.
    Reviews:
        Catholic World 131:327-8, Jun 1930
        Commonweal 11:741, Apr 30, 1930
        Life (NY) 95:18, May 2, 1930
        Nation 130:525-6, Apr 30, 1930
        New Republic 62:326-8, May 7, 1930
        New York Times p. 29, Apr 15, 1930
                      VIII, p. 1, Apr 20, 1930
        Outlook 154:711, Apr 30, 1930
        Review of Reviews 81:130, Jun 1930
        Sketch Book 7:29, Jul 1930
        Theatre Arts 14:462-3, Jun 1930
        Theatre Magazine 51:43-4+, Jun 1930
        Vogue 75:122, Jun 7, 1930

In A Garden
    Productions:
        Opened November 16, 1925 for 73 performances.
    Reviews:
        Bookman 62:705, Feb 1926
        Dial 80:73, Jan 1926
        Independent 116:48, Jan 9, 1926
        Life (NY) 86:18, Dec 10, 1925
        New York Times p. 29, Nov 17, 1925
                      VIII, p. 1, Nov 22, 1925
        Theatre Magazine 43:15, Jan 1926
        Vogue 67:87, Jan 15, 1926

BARRY, PHILIP (cont.)
  John
    Productions:
      Opened November 2, 1927 for 11 performances.
    Reviews:
      Dial 84:81, Jan 1928
      Life (NY) 90:23, Nov 24, 1927
      Nation 125:582-3, Nov 23, 1927
      New York Times p. 16, Nov 5, 1927
      Theatre Arts 12:4, Jan 1928
                   12:19, Jan 1928

  The Joyous Season
    Productions:
      Opened January 29, 1934 for 16 performances.
    Reviews:
      Catholic World 138:729-30, Mar 1934
      Commonweal 19:413, Feb 9, 1934
                 19:469, Feb 23, 1934
      Literary Digest 117:23, Feb 24, 1934
      Nation 138:200-2, Feb 14, 1934
      New Republic 78:21, Feb 14, 1934
      New York Times p. 16, Jan 30, 1934
                   II, p. 9, Nov 24, 1935
      Newsweek 3:39, Feb 10, 1934
      Review of Reviews 89:47, Mar 1934
      Stage 11:17, Mar 1934
      Theatre Arts 18:244, Apr 1934
      Time 23:34, Feb 5, 1934
      Vanity Fair 42:45-6, Apr 1934

  Liberty Jones
    Productions:
      Opened February 5, 1941 for 22 performances.
    Reviews:
      Catholic World 152:725-6, Mar 1941
      Commonweal 33:447, Feb 21, 1941
      Nation 152:192, Feb 15, 1941
      New Republic 104:276, Feb 24, 1941
      New York Theatre Critics' Reviews 1941:391
      New York Times p. 24, Feb 6, 1941
      New Yorker 17:30, Feb 15, 1941
      Newsweek 17:67, Feb 17, 1941
      Theatre Arts 25:261, Apr 1941
      Time 37:85, Feb 17, 1941

  My Name Is Aquilon (Adapted from the play by Jean
        Pierre Aumont)

Productions:
    Opened February 9, 1949 for 31 performances.
Reviews:
    Nation 168:256, Feb 26, 1949
    New York Theatre Critics' Reviews 1949:362
    New York Times p. 38, Feb 10, 1949
    New Yorker 24:60, Feb 19, 1949
    Newsweek 33:79, Feb 21, 1949
    Theatre Arts 33:24-5, May 1949
    Time 53:76, Feb 21, 1949

Paris Bound
    Productions:
    Opened December 27, 1927 for 234 performances.
Reviews:
    American Mercury 13:376-7, Mar 1928
    Bookman 67:288-90, May 1928
    Drama Magazine 18:139, Feb 1928
    Life (NY) 91:21, Jan 19, 1928
    Nation 126:75-6, Jan 18, 1928
    New Republic 53:273, Jan 25, 1928
    New York Times p. 26, Dec 28, 1927
                 VIII, p. 1, Jan 1, 1928
                 VIII, p. 1, Jan 15, 1928
                 X, p. 1, Dec 2, 1928
                 p. 28, May 1, 1929
                 IX, p. 1, May 19, 1929
    Outlook 148:147, Jan 25, 1928
    Saturday Review 4:515-6, Jan 14, 1928
    Theatre Arts 12:166, 169, Mar 1928
    Theatre Magazine 47:40, Mar 1928
    Vogue 71:86-7, Feb 15, 1928

The Philadelphia Story
    Productions:
    Opened March 28, 1939 for 417 performances.
Reviews:
    Catholic World 149:216-17, May 1939
    Commonweal 29:692, Apr 14, 1939
    Life 6:39-40+, Apr 24, 1939
    Nation 148:410-11, Apr 8, 1939
    New York Theatre Critics' Reviews 1950:487
    New York Times p. 14, Feb 17, 1939
                 XI, p. 2, Mar 19, 1929
                 p. 21, Mar 29, 1939
                 X, p. 1, Apr 2, 1939
                 p. 8, Jun 4, 1949

BARRY, PHILIP (cont.)
The Philadelphia Story (cont.)
                            p. 32, Jun 28, 1949
                            p. 3, Sep 27, 1949
                            p. 46, Jun 22, 1967
        Newsweek 13:28-9, Apr 10, 1939
        North American Review 247:366, Summer 1939
        Stage 16:16-18, Apr 1, 1939
        Theatre Arts 23:324-25, May 1939
        Time 33:56, Apr 10, 1939
        Vogue 93:90, May 1, 1939

Second Threshold (with revisions by Robert E. Sherwood)
    Productions:
        Opened January 2, 1951 for 126 performances.
    Reviews:
        Catholic World 172:385, Feb 1951
        Christian Science Monitor Magazine p. 6, Jan 6, 1951
        Commonweal 53:398, Jan 26, 1951
        Life 30:53-4, Jan 29, 1951
        Nation 172:44, Jan 13, 1951
        New Republic 124:22, Feb 5, 1951
        New York Theatre Critics' Reviews 1951:398
        New York Times II, p. 1, Dec 31, 1950
                            p. 23, Jan 3, 1951
                            II, p. 1, Jan 14, 1951
                            VI, p. 32, Jan 14, 1951
                            p. 38, Sep 25, 1952
                            II, p. 3, Oct 12, 1952
        New Yorker 26:42+, Jan 13, 1951
        Newsweek 37:78, Jan 15, 1951
        Saturday Review 34:25-7, Jan 27, 1951
        School and Society 73:183, Mar 24, 1951
        Theatre Arts 35:16, Mar 1951
                    35:17, Sep 1951
        Time 57:39, Jan 15, 1951

Spring Dance
    Productions:
        Opened August 25, 1936 for 24 performances.
    Reviews:
        Commonweal 24:487, Sep 18, 1936
        Literary Digest 122:19, Jul 25, 1936
                        122:24, Sep 5, 1936
        Nation 143:284, Sep 5, 1936
        New Republic 88:160, Sep 16, 1936
        New York Times p. 22, Jul 7, 1936

p. 17, Aug 26, 1936
Newsweek 8:27, Sep 5, 1936
Time 28:53, Sep 7, 1936

Tomorrow and Tomorrow
    Productions:
        Opened January 13, 1931 for 206 performances.
    Reviews:
        Arts and Decoration 34:84, Mar 1931
        Bookman 73:72-3, Mar 1931
        Catholic World 132:717-18, Mar 1931
        Commonweal 13:357-8, Jan 28, 1931
        Drama Magazine 21:10-11, Mar 1931
        Dramatist 22:1431, Jan 1931
        Life (NY) 97:18, Jan 30, 1931
        Nation 132:108, Jan 28, 1931
        New Republic 65:322-3, Feb 4, 1931
        New York Times p. 26, Jan 14, 1931
                       VIII, p. 2, Feb 1, 1931
                       p. 17, Jun 24, 1941
        Outlook 157:152, Jan 28, 1931
        Theatre Arts 15:185-6, Mar 1931
        Theatre Magazine 53:24, Mar 1931
        Theatre Magazine 53:33-5+, May 1931
        Vogue 77:59, Mar 1, 1931

White Wings
    Productions:
        Opened October 15, 1926 for 27 performances.
    Reviews:
        Dial 82:77, Jan 1927
        Life (NY) 88:23, Nov 11, 1926
        New York Times p. 15, Oct 16, 1926
                       VIII, p. 1, Oct 24, 1926
        Theatre Magazine 44:72, Dec 1926
        Vogue 68:77+, Dec 15, 1926

Without Love
    Productions:
        Opened November 10, 1942 for 113 performances.
    Reviews:
        Catholic World 156:336-7, Dec 1942
        Commonweal 37:144, Nov 27, 1942
        Current History ns 3:456, Jan 1943
        Life 12:78+, May 11, 1942
        Nation 155:553-4, Nov 21, 1942
        New Republic 107:679-80, Nov 23, 1942

49

BARRY, PHILIP (cont.)
  Without Love (cont.)
        New York Theatre Critics' Reviews, 1942:182
        New York Times p. 20, Mar 5, 1942
                    p. 17, Apr 28, 1942
                    IV, p. 2, May 3, 1942
                    VII, p. 12, Nov 8, 1942
                    p. 28, Nov 11, 1942
                    VIII, p. 1, Nov 29, 1942
        New Yorker 18:36+, Nov 21, 1942
        Newsweek 20:73, Nov 23, 1942
        Theatre Arts 27:15, Jan 1943
        Time 39:61, Apr 27, 1942
             40:53, Nov 23, 1942

  You and I
    Productions:
        Opened February 19, 1923 for 136+ performances.
    Reviews:
        Bookman 57:318-9, May 1923
               58:58-9, Sep 1923
        Current Opinion 74:702-7, Jun 1923
        Dial 75:100-101, Jun 1923
        Dramatist 14:1153-4, Apr 1923
        Hearst 44:85-7+, Oct 1923
        Independent 110:207, Mar 17, 1923
        Life (NY) 81:18, Mar 15, 1923
        Nation 116:346, Mar 21, 1923
        New York Clipper 71:14, Feb 28, 1923
        New York Times p. 12, Feb 20, 1923
                      VII, p. 1, Feb 25, 1923
                      p. 29, Oct 20, 1925
        Scribner's Magazine 74:69, Jul 1923
        Theatre Magazine 37:16, Apr 1923
        Theatre Magazine 38:28+, Jul 1923

  The Youngest
    Productions:
        Opened December 22, 1924 for 104 performances.
    Reviews:
        American Mercury 4:247-8, Feb 1925
        Current Opinion 78:436-44, Apr 1925
        Life (NY) 85:18, Jan 8, 1925
        New York Times p. 17, Dec 23, 1924
        Theatre Arts 9:151, Mar 1925
        Theatre Magazine 41:19, Mar 1925

*Ann Vroome
  Reviews:
    New York Times VIII, p. 2, Jul 27, 1930

Brothers
  Productions:
    (Off Broadway) Season of 1919-20.
  Reviews:
    New York Times p. 14, Dec 6, 1919

The Clod
  Productions:
    Season of 1915-16 in repertory (Washington Square
      Players).
  Reviews:
    Bookman 43:23, Mar 1916
    Dramatic Mirror 75:8, Jan 22, 1916
    New York Times p. 11, Jan 11, 1916
                   p. 11, Jun 6, 1916

The Goose Hangs High
  Productions:
    Opened January 29, 1924 for 159+ performances.
  Reviews:
    Bookman 59:203, Apr 1924
    Drama 16:66, Nov 1925
    Dramatist 15:1210-11, Apr 1924
    Life (NY) 83:18, Feb 14, 1924
    New York Times p. 16, Jan 30, 1924
                   VII, p. 1, Feb 3, 1924
    Theatre Magazine 39:15-16, Apr 1924

Merry Andrew
  Productions:
    Opened January 21, 1929 for 24 performances.
  Reviews:
    Commonweal 4:431, Feb 13, 1929
    Life (NY) 93:25, Feb 15, 1929
    Nation 128:168, Feb 6, 1929
    New York Times VIII, p. 2, Jan 13, 1929
                        p. 22, Jan 22, 1929
    Vogue 73:150, Mar 16, 1929

A Square Peg
  Productions:
    Opened January 27, 1923 for 41 performances.

BEACH, LEWIS (cont.)
  A Square Peg (cont.)
    Reviews:
        Bookman 57:194-5, Apr 1923
        Life (NY) 81:18, Feb 15, 1923
        Nation 116:224, Feb 21, 1923
        New York Clipper 71:14, Feb 7, 1923
        New York Times p. 10, Jan 29, 1923
                        VII, p. 1, Feb 11, 1923

BEHRMAN, S. N.

  Amphitryon 38 (Adapted from the original by Jean Girau-
        doux)
    Productions:
    Opened November 1, 1937 for 153 performances.
    Reviews:
        Catholic World 146:338-9, Dec 1937
        Commonweal 27:78, Nov 12, 1937
        Life 3:70, Jul 1937
        Literary Digest 1:35, Nov 20, 1935
        Nation 145:539, Nov 13, 1937
        New Republic 93:44, Nov 17, 1937
                      94:132, Mar 9, 1938
        New York Times p. 30, Jun 24, 1937
                      p. 32, Nov 2, 1937
                      XI, p. 1, Nov 7, 1937
        Newsweek 10:20-1, Jul 3, 1937
                 10:22, Nov 8, 1937
        Scribner's Magazine 102:66+, Dec 1937
        Stage 15:46-9, Oct 1937
              15:94, Nov 1937
              15:44-5, Jan 1938
        Theatre Arts 21:924, Dec 1937
        Time 30:25, Nov 8, 1937

  Biography
    Productions:
    Opened December 12, 1932 for 267 performances.
    Opened February, 1934 for 283 performances.
    Reviews:
        Arts and Decoration 38:56, Feb 1933
        Catholic World 136:590, Feb 1933
        Commonweal 17:245, Dec 28, 1932
        Nation 135:654, Dec 28, 1932
               136:327-8, Mar 22, 1933
        New Outlook 161:46, Jan 1933

New Republic 73:188-9, Dec 28, 1932
New York Times p. 25, Dec 13, 1932
              IX, p. 1, Jan 22, 1933
              p. 24, Feb 6, 1934
              IX, p. 2, May 20, 1934
              II, p. 12, Apr 11, 1937
              p. 14, Aug 3, 1938
Player's Magazine 9:11, Mar-Apr 1933
Saturday Review 9:438, Feb 18, 1933
Stage 10:1+, Feb 1933
Theatre Arts 17:103-5, Feb 1933
              18:495-6, Jul 1934
Vanity Fair 39:60, Feb 1933
Vogue 81:56+, Feb 1, 1933

Brief Moment
  Productions:
    Opened November 9, 1931 for 129 performances.
  Reviews:
    Arts and Decoration 36:78, Jan 1932
    Catholic World 134:469-70, Jan 1932
    Commonweal 15:134, Dec 2, 1931
    Nation 133:621-2, Dec 2, 1931
    New Republic 69:70, Dec 2, 1931
                  69:136, Dec 16, 1931
    New York Times p. 16, Feb 25, 1932
                  VIII, p. 1, Feb 28, 1932
                  VIII, p. 2, Oct 25, 1931
                  p. 28, Nov 10, 1931
    Outlook 159:407, Nov 25, 1931
    Theatre Arts 16:20, Jan 1932
    Theatre Guild Magazine 9:4-6, Dec 1931

But for Whom Charlie
  Productions:
    Opened March 12, 1964 for 34 performances (Reper-
      tory Theatre of Lincoln Center).
  Reviews:
    America 110:657, May 9, 1964
    Commonweal 80:90, Apr 10, 1964
    Nation 198:335-6, Mar 30, 1964
    New York Theatre Critics' Reviews 1964:322
    New York Times II, p. 5, Mar 8, 1964
                  p. 42, Mar 13, 1964
    New Yorker 40:64, Mar 21, 1964
    Newsweek 63:70, Mar 23, 1964
    Saturday Review 47:21, Mar 28, 1964

BEHRMAN, S. N. (cont.)
   But for Whom Charlie (cont.)
            Time 83:55, Mar 20, 1964
            Vogue 143:62, May 1964

The Cold Wind and the Warm
   Productions:
      Opened December 8, 1958 for 120 performances.
   Reviews:
      America 100:438, Jan 10, 1959
      Catholic World 188:421, Feb 1959
      Commentary 27:256-60, Mar 1959
      Commonweal 69:496-7, Feb 6, 1959
      New York Theatre Critics' Reviews 1958:175
      New York Times II, p. 8, Dec 7, 1958
                     p. 55, Dec 9, 1958
                     II, p. 1, Jan 18, 1959
      New Yorker 34:69, Dec 20, 1958
      Newsweek 52:46, Dec 22, 1958
      Theatre Arts 43:201, Feb 1959
      Time 72:54, Dec 22, 1958

Dunnigan's Daughter
   Productions:
      Opened December 26, 1945 for 38 performances.
   Reviews:
      Catholic World 162:456, Feb 1946
      Nation 162:81, Jan 19, 1946
      New York Theatre Critics' Reviews 1945:54
      New York Times p. 16, Dec 27, 1945
                     II, p. 1, Jan 6, 1946
      New Yorker 21:43-4, Jan 5, 1946
      Theatre Arts 30:138, Mar 1946
      Time 47:86+, Jan 7, 1946

End of Summer
   Productions:
      Opened February 17, 1936 for 153 performances.
   Reviews:
      Catholic World 143:86-7, Apr 1936
      Commonweal 23:497, Feb 28, 1936
      Literary Digest 121:19, Feb 29, 1936
      Nation 142:291-2, Mar 4, 1936
      New Republic 86:113, Mar 4, 1936
                   86:141, Mar 11, 1936
      New York Times p. 17, Jan 31, 1936
                     X, p. 2, Feb 9, 1936

p. 26, Feb 18, 1936
IX, p. 1, Mar 1, 1936
Newsweek 7:31-2, Feb 29, 1936
Stage 13:28-9, Mar 1936
Theatre Arts 20:258-60, Apr 1936
Time 27:59, Mar 2, 1936

I Know My Love (Adapted from Marcel Achard's Auprès
    de Ma Blonde)
    Productions:
    Opened November 2, 1949 for 246 performances.
    Reviews:
    Catholic World 170:229, Dec 1949
    Forum 112:337-8, Dec 1949
    Nation 169:498, Nov 19, 1949
    New Republic 121:19, Nov 21, 1949
    New York Theatre Critics' Reviews 1949:233
    New York Times p. 29, Feb 24, 1949
                   p. 36, Nov 3, 1949
                   VI, p. 24, Nov 13, 1949
                   II, p. 1, Nov 20, 1949
    New Yorker 25:54+, Nov 12, 1949
    Newsweek 34:84, Nov 14, 1949
    Saturday Review 32:54-5, Dec 3, 1949
    Theatre Arts 34:13, Jan 1950
    Time 53:58, Mar 7, 1949
         54:49, Nov 14, 1949

Jacobowsky and the Colonel (Based on the play by Franz
    Werfel)
    Productions:
    Opened March 14, 1944 for 417 performances.
    Reviews:
    Catholic World 159:169-70, May 1944
                   159:457-8, Aug 1944
    Commonweal 39:589-90, Mar 31, 1944
    Life 16:49-50+, Apr 10, 1944
    Nation 158:373, Mar 25, 1944
           158:429-30, Apr 8, 1944
    New Republic 110:407, Mar 27, 1944
    New York Theatre Critics' Reviews 1944:243
    New York Times II, p. 3, Jan 9, 1944
                   VI, p. 24, Mar 5, 1944
                   II, p. 1, Mar 12, 1944
                   p. 17, Mar 15, 1944
                   II, p. 1, Mar 19, 1944
                   VI, p. 16, Apr 9. 1944

BEHRMAN, S. N. (cont.)
Jacobowsky and the Colonel (cont.)
                        II, p. 1, May 21, 1944
                        II, p. 1, Jun 24, 1945
    New Yorker 20:52, Mar 25, 1944
    Newsweek 23:105-6, Mar 27, 1944
    Theatre Arts 28:143-50, Mar 1944
                  28:204, Apr 1944
                  28:261-2+, May 1944
    Time 43:60+, Mar 27, 1944

Jane (Suggested by a story of W. Somerset Maugham's)
    Productions:
    Opened February 1, 1952 for 100 performances.
    Reviews:
    Catholic World 174:465, Mar 1952
    Commonweal 55:496, Feb 22, 1952
    Nation 174:162, Feb 16, 1952
    New Republic 126:23, Feb 18, 1952
    New York Theatre Critics' Reviews 1952:376
    New York Times p. 10, Feb 2, 1952
                    II, p. 1, Feb 10, 1952
    New Yorker 27:56-7, Feb 9, 1952
    Newsweek 39:82, Feb 11, 1952
    Saturday Review 35:34, Feb 16, 1952
    School and Society 75:325, May 24, 1952
    Theatre Arts 31:59, Apr 1947
                  36:71, Apr 1952
    Time 59:79, Feb 11, 1952

Lord Pengo (Based on Behrman's The Days of Duveen)
    Productions:
    Opened November 19, 1962 for 175 performances.
    Reviews:
    America 108:52, Jan 12, 1963
    Life 54:51-2, Feb 22, 1963
    Nation 196:214, Mar 9, 1963
    New York Theatre Critics' Reviews 1962:192
    New York Times II, p. 1, Nov 18, 1962
                    p. 41, Nov 20, 1962
    New Yorker 38:118, Dec 1, 1962
    Newsweek 60:63, Dec 3, 1962
    Theatre Arts 47:11, Jan 1963
    Time 80:53, Nov 30, 1962

Love Is Like That (with Kenyon Nicholson)
    Productions:

Opened April 18, 1927 for 24 performances.
Reviews:
    Life (NY) 89:25, May 5, 1927
    New York Times p. 24, Apr 19, 1927
    Theatre Magazine 45:25, Jun 1927

The Mechanical Heart (See The Talley Method)

Meteor
  Productions:
    Opened December 23, 1929 for 92 performances.
  Reviews:
    Catholic World 130:724-5, Mar 1930
    Commonweal 11:310, Jan 15, 1930
    Life (NY) 95:20, Jan 10, 1930
    Nation 130:78-9, Jan 15, 1930
    New Republic 61:250, Jan 22, 1930
    New York Times X, p. 2, Dec 8, 1929
               p. 15, Dec 24, 1929
               p. 24, Jan 20, 1930
    Outlook 154:73, Jan 8, 1930
    Sketch Book 7:21, Mar 1930
    Theatre Magazine 51:45-6, Mar 1930
               51:8, Apr 1930
    Vogue 75:118, Feb 15, 1930

No Time for Comedy
  Productions:
    Opened April 17, 1939 for 185 performances.
  Reviews:
    Catholic World 149:344-5, Jun 1939
    Commonweal 30:48, May 5, 1939
    Nation 148:509-10, Apr 29, 1939
    New Republic 98:378, May 3, 1939
    New York Times p. 18, Mar 31, 1939
               p. 26, Apr 18, 1939
               XI, p. 1, Apr 30, 1939
               X, p. 2, May 7, 1939
               p. 47, Mar 31, 1940
    Newsweek 13:45, May 1, 1939
    North American Review 247 no 2:367-8, Jun 1939
    Stage 16:22, Apr 1, 1939
        16:18-21, Apr 15, 1939
    Theatre Arts 23:395-6, Jun 1939
    Time 33:61, May 1, 1939

BEHRMAN, S. N. (cont.)
The Pirate (Suggested by a play by Ludwig Fulda)
Productions:
Opened November 25, 1942 for 177 performances.
Reviews:
Catholic World 156:475-6, Jan 1943
Commonweal 37:206, Dec 11, 1942
Current History ns 3:455, Jan 1943
Independent Woman 21:367, Dec 1942
Life 13:89-92, Oct 5, 1942
Nation 155:659, Dec 12, 1942
New Republic 107:792-3, Dec 14, 1942
New York Theatre Critics' Reviews 1942:162
New York Times p. 18, Sep 15, 1942
p. 39, Nov 26, 1942
VIII, p. 1, Dec 6, 1942
p. 18, May 26, 1943
New York Times Magazine pp. 16-17, Oct 4, 1942
Newsweek 20:74, Dec 7, 1942
Poet Lore 49:286, Autumn 1943
Theatre Arts 26:605, Oct 1942
27:12+, Jan 1943
Time 40:54-5, Dec 7, 1942

Rain from Heaven
Productions:
Opened December 24, 1934 for 99 performances.
Reviews:
Canadian Forum 15:194-5, Feb 1935
Catholic World 140:599, Feb 1935
Commonweal 21:318, Jan 11, 1935
Nation 140:55-6, Jan 9, 1935
New Republic 81:308, Jan 23, 1935
New York Times p. 26, Dec 11, 1934
XI, p. 2, Dec 16, 1934
p. 28, Dec 25, 1934
IX, p. 3, Dec 30, 1934
IX, p. 1, Jan 6, 1935
Stage 12:2-3, Feb 1935
Theatre Arts 19:96, Feb 1935
Time 25:40, Jan 7, 1935
Vanity Fair 44:47, Mar 1935

The Second Man
Productions:
Opened April 11, 1927 for 178 performances.
Reviews:

American Mercury 11:249-50, Jun 1927
Dial 82:535-6, Jun 1927
Dramatist 18:1343, Jun 1927
Life (NY) 89:19, Apr 28, 1927
Nation 124:484, Apr 27, 1927
New Republic 50:274, Apr 27, 1927
New York Times p. 24, Apr 12, 1927
                  VII, p. 1, Apr 24, 1927
                  VIII, p. 2, Feb 12, 1928
                  IX, p. 2, May 25, 1930
Theatre Magazine 46:18, Jul 1927
Vogue 69:75+, Jun 1, 1927
      70:118, Oct 1, 1927

Serena Blandish
Productions:
    Opened January 23, 1929 for 93 performances.
Reviews:
    Catholic World 128:722-3, Mar 1929
    Commonweal 9:430-1, Feb 13, 1929
    Life (NY) 93:25, Feb 15, 1929
    Nation 128:212-14, Feb 13, 1929
    New Republic 57:346-7, Feb 13, 1929
    New York Times VIII, p. 2, Jan 13, 1929
                p. 30, Jan 24, 1929
                IX, p. 2, Jan 27, 1929
                VIII, p. 1, Feb 3, 1929
    Outlook 151:262, Feb 13, 1929
    Theatre Magazine 49:45, Apr 1929
            50:14, Jul 1929
    Vogue 73:104, Mar 16, 1929

The Talley Method
Productions:
    Opened February 24, 1941 for 56 performances.
Reviews:
    American Mercury 52:355-6, Mar 1941
    Catholic World 153:85-6, Apr 1941
    Commonweal 33:519, Mar 14, 1941
    Nation 152:277, Mar 8, 1941
    New Republic 104:340, Mar 10, 1941
    New York Theatre Critics' Reviews 1941:373
    New York Times p. 26, Feb 23, 1941
                p. 26, Feb 25, 1941
                IX, p. 1, Mar 2, 1941
                IX, p. 4, Mar 23, 1941
                IX, p. 3, Mar 30, 1941

BEHRMAN, S. N. (cont.)
    The Talley Method (cont.)
            New Yorker 17:34+, Mar 8, 1941
            Newsweek 17:66, Mar 10, 1941
            Theatre Arts 25:256+, Apr 1941
            Time 37:44, Mar 10, 1941

    Wine of Choice
        Productions:
            Opened February 21, 1938 for 43 performances.
        Reviews:
            Catholic World 147:85, Apr 1938
            Commonweal 27:554, Mar 11, 1938
            Nation 146:280-1, Mar 5, 1938
            New Republic 94:132, Mar 9, 1938
            New York Times p. 32, Dec 14, 1937
                          p. 18, Feb 22, 1938
                          X, p. 1, Feb 27, 1938
            One Act Play Magazine 1:953-4, Feb 1938
                                  1:1023-4, Mar 1938
            Theatre Arts 22:253-4, Apr 1938
            Time 31:52, Mar 7, 1938

BELASCO, DAVID

    The Comedian (Adapted from a play by Sacha Guitry)
        Productions:
            Opened March 13, 1923 for 87 performances.
        Reviews:
            Dial 74:635-6, Jun 1923
            Hearst 44:85-7+, Jul 1923
            Life (NY) 81:20, Apr 5, 1923
            New York Clipper 71:14, Mar 21, 1923
            New York Times p. 14, Mar 14, 1923
                          VIII, p. 1, Mar 25, 1923
            Theatre Magazine 37:14+, May 1923

    Fanny (with Willard Mack)
        Productions:
            Opened September 21, 1926 for 63 performances.
        Reviews:
            Bookman 64:481, Dec 1926
            New York Times p. 30, Sep 22, 1926
            Theatre Magazine 44:15, Nov 1926
            Vogue 68:106, Nov 15, 1926

Girl of the Golden West
   Productions:
      (Off Broadway) Season of 1957-58.
   Reviews:
      New York Times p. 44, Nov 6, 1957
      Theatre Arts 42:25, Jan 1958

Kiki (Adapted from the French of Andre Picard.)
   Productions:
      Opened November 29, 1921 for 600 performances.
   Reviews:
      Bookman 54:573, Feb 1922
      Current Opinion 72:342-51, Mar 1922
      Dramatic Mirror 84:809, Dec 3, 1921
      Dramatist 13:1102-3, Apr 1922
      Hearst 42:85-7+, Jul 1922
      Life (NY) 78:18, Dec 15, 1921
      Nation 113:736, Dec 21, 1921
      New York Clipper 69:20, Dec 7, 1921
      New York Times p. 13, Nov 30, 1921
                      VII, p. 1, Dec 4, 1921
      Theatre Magazine 35:97-8+, Feb 1922

Laugh, Clown, Laugh! (with Tom Cushing) (Adapted from
   Faurto Martini's Ridi Pagliaccio.)
   Productions:
      Opened November 28, 1923, for 133 performances.
   Reviews:
      Life (NY) 82:18, Dec 20, 1923
      New Republic 37:94-5, Dec 19, 1923
      New York Times VIII, p. 2, Oct 28, 1923
                      p. 30, Nov 29, 1923
                      IX, p. 1, Dec 9, 1923
      Theatre Magazine 39:15-16, Feb 1924

The Lily (Adapted from the French of Pierre Wolff and
   Gaston Leroux)
   Productions:
      Opened December 23, 1909 for 164 performances.
   Reviews:
      Burr McIntosh Monthly 22:222-3, Mar 1910
      Current Literature 48:204, Feb 1910
      Dramatic Mirror 63:5, Jan 1, 1910
      Dramatist 1:45-8, Apr 1913
      Forum 43:190, Feb 1910
      Green Book 3:516-19, Mar 1910
      Hampton 24:407-8, Mar 1910

BELASCO, DAVID (cont.)
    The Lily (cont.)
                Life (NY) 55:37, Jan 6, 1910
                Metropolitan Magazine 31:818-9, Mar 1910
                Nation 89:659, Dec 30. 1909
                Pearson 23:368-72, Mar 1910
                Theatre Magazine 11:42-4, Feb 1910
                Twentieth Century Magazine 2:507-10, Sep 1910

    Mima (Adapted from Ferenc Molnar's The Red Mill)
        Productions:
            Opened December 12, 1928 for 180 performances.
        Reviews:
            American Mercury 16:249, Feb 1929
            Bookman 68:686, Feb 1929
            Catholic World 128:593-4, Feb 1929
            Life (NY) 93:23, Jan 18, 1929
            New York Times p. 24, Dec 13, 1928
                            VIII, p. 1, Dec 23, 1928
            Scientific American 140:244-5, Mar 1929
            Theatre Magazine 49:49, Feb 1929
            Vogue 73:118, Feb 2, 1929

    The Return of Peter Grimm
        Productions:
            Opened October 17, 1911 for 231 performances.
            Opened September 21, 1921 for 78 performances.
        Reviews:
            American Magazine 73:490, Feb 1912
            American Playwright 1:26-7, Jan 1912
                            1:89-96, Mar 1912
            Blue Book 13:9-11, May 1911
            Book News 31:194, Nov 1912
            Bookman 35:362-7, Dec 1911
            Current Literature 52:447-54, Apr 1912
            Dramatic Mirror 66:7, Oct 25, 1911
                            84:484, Oct 1, 1921
            Dramatist 3:210-12, Jan 1912
            Everybody's 26:91-5, Jan 1912
            Independent 72:503, Mar 7, 1912
            Life (NY) 58:762, Nov 2, 1911
            Munsey 46:427-8, Dec 1911
            New York Clipper 69:17, Sep 28, 1921
            New York Times p. 12, Sep 22, 1921
                            VI, p. 1, Sep 25, 1921
            Pearson 26:764-9, Dec 1911
            Red Book 18:561+, Jan 1912

Theatre Magazine 14:xi-xii, Nov 1911
                34:388+, Dec 1921
World Today 21:1501-16, Dec 1911

The Son-Daughter (with George Scarborough)
    Productions:
        Opened November 19, 1919 for 223 performances.
    Reviews:
        Dramatic Mirror 80:1861, Dec 4, 1919
        Dramatist 11:991-2, Apr 1920
        Life (NY) 74:898, Nov 27, 1919
        New York Times p. 11, Nov 20, 1919
        Theatre Magazine 31:17, Jan 1920

*Van der Decker
    Reviews:
        New York Times p. 8, Dec 8, 1915

BELLOW, SAUL

The Last Analysis
    Productions:
        Opened October 1, 1964 for 28 performances.
    Reviews:
        Life 57:17, Oct 30, 1964
        Nation 199:256-7, Oct 19, 1964
        New Republic 151:25-6, Oct 24, 1964
        New York Theatre Critics' Reviews 1964:206
        New York Times II, p. 1, Sep 27, 1964
                        p. 30, Oct 2, 1964
                        II, p. 1, Oct 11, 1964
        Newsweek 64:105, Oct 12, 1964
        Saturday Review 47:29, Oct 17, 1964
        Time 84:92, Oct 9, 1964
        Vogue 144:64, Nov 15, 1964

Orange Souffle (See Under the Weather)

Out From Under (See Under the Weather)

Under the Weather (Out From Under, Orange Souffle, and
    The Wen)
    Productions:
        Opened October 27, 1966 for 12 performances.
    Reviews:
        Commonweal 85:199-201, Nov 18, 1966
        Nation 203:5234, Nov 14, 1966

BELLOW, SAUL (cont.)
  Under the Weather (cont.)
        New York Theatre Critics' Reviews 1966:254
        New York Times p. 42, Jun 8, 1966
                    p. 14, Jul 16, 1966
                    p. 35, Oct 28, 1966
                    II, p. 1, Dec 25, 1966
        New Yorker 42:127, Nov 5, 1966
        Newsweek 68:96, Nov 7, 1966
        Saturday Review 49:34, Nov 12, 1966
        Time 88:85, Nov 4, 1966

  The Wen (See Under the Weather)

BENET, STEVEN VINCENT

  John Brown's Body (Adapted by Charles Laughton)
        Productions:
        Opened February 14, 1953 for 65 performances.
        (Off Broadway) Season of 1960-61.
        (Off Broadway) Opened March 3, 1969 for 3 perform-
           ances.
        Reviews:
        Colliers 130:24-7, Dec 6, 1952
        New York Theatre Critics' Reviews 1953:358
        New York Times p. 25, Nov 3, 1952
                    p. 43, Dec 16, 1952
                    p. 17, Feb 16, 1953
                    II, p. 1, Feb 22, 1953
                    II, p. 3, Mar 8, 1953
                    p. 31, Jun 22, 1960
                    II, p. 1, Aug 21, 1960
                    p. 33, Jun 29, 1964
                    p. 49, Feb 13, 1968
        Newsweek 40:88, Nov 24, 1952

  Nerves (with John Farrar)
        Productions:
        Opened September 1, 1924 for 16 performances.
        Reviews:
        New York Times p. 22, Sep 2, 1924
                    VI, p. 1, Sep 7, 1924
                    VII, p. 2, Sep 7, 1924

  That Awful Mrs. Eaton (with John Farrar)
        Productions:
        Opened September 29, 1924 for 16 performances.

Reviews:
New York Times VII, p. 1, Jul 20, 1924
p. 27, Sep 30, 1924
Theatre Magazine 39:19, Dec 1924

BENTHAM, JOSEPHINE

Janie (with Herschel Williams)
Productions:
Opened September 10, 1942 for 642 performances
Reviews:
Catholic World 156:90-1, Oct 1942
Commonweal 36:543, Sep 25, 1942
Independent Woman 21:378, Dec 1942
Life 13:119-22+, Sep 28, 1942
Nation 155:278, Sep 26, 1942
New York Theatre Critics' Reviews 1942:244
New York Times p. 24, Sep 11, 1942
II, p. 2, Dec 17, 1944
New Yorker 18:34, Sep 19, 1942
Newsweek 20;78, Sep 21, 1942
Theatre Arts 26:674+, Nov 1942
Time 40:42, Sep 21, 1942

BERG, GERTRUDE

Dear Me, the Sky Is Falling (See entry under Spigelgass,
Leonard)
Me and Molly
Productions:
Opened February 26, 1948 for 156 performances.
Reviews:
Catholic World 167:71, Apr 1948
Commonweal 47:546, Mar 12, 1948
New York Theatre Critics' Reviews 1948:322
New York Times p. 27, Feb 27, 1948
II, p. 1, Mar 7, 1948
New Yorker 24:52, Mar 6, 1948
Newsweek 31:75, Mar 8, 1948
Theatre Arts 32:31, Apr 1948
Time 51:50, Mar 8, 1948
Vogue 111:151, Apr 1, 1948

BIRD, ROBERT MONTGOMERY
No Productions.

BOKER, GEORGE HENRY
No Productions

BOLTON, GUY

Adam and Eva (with George Middleton)
    Productions:
    Opened September 13, 1919 for 312 performances.
    Reviews:
        Current Opinion 68:782-8, Jun 1920
        Dramatic Mirror 80:1503, Sep 25, 1919
        Dramatist 10:969-70, Oct 1919
        Hearst 38:41-3+, Jul 1920
        Life (NY) 74:548-9, Sep 25, 1919
        New York Times p. 15, Sep 16, 1919
                        IV, p. 2, Sep 21, 1919

Anastasia (Adapted from a play by Marcelle Maurette)
    Productions:
    Opened December 29, 1954 for 272 performances.
    Reviews:
        America 92:461, Jan 29, 1955
        Catholic World 180:386, Feb 1955
        Commonweal 61:582-3, Mar 4, 1955
        Life 38:32-3, Feb 14, 1955
        Nation 180:24, Jan 22, 1955
        New Republic 132:22, Feb 7, 1955
        New York Theatre Critics' Reviews 1954:192
        New York Times II, p. 3, Dec 26, 1954
                        p. 13, Dec 30. 1954
                        II, p. 1, Jan 16, 1955
        New Yorker 30:66, Jan 8, 1955
        Newsweek 45:62, Jan 10, 1955
        Saturday Review 38:31, Jan 15, 1955
        Theatre Arts 39:19+, Mar 1955
                    39:28+, Jun 1955
                    40:34-61, May 1956
        Time 65:35, Jan 10, 1955

The Cave Girl (with George Middleton)
    Productions:
    Opened August 18, 1920 for 37 performances.
    Reviews:
        Dramatic Mirror p. 9, Jul 3, 1920
                        p. 371, Aug 28, 1920
        Independent 103:261, Sep 4, 1920
        New York Clipper 68:19, Aug 25, 1920

New York Times p. 12, Aug 19, 1920
Theatre 32:242, Oct 1920

Chicken Feed (Wages for Wives)
    Productions:
    Opened September 24, 1923 for 144 performances.
    Reviews:
        Nation 117:412, Oct 10, 1923
        New York Times p. 10, Sep 25, 1923
        Theatre Magazine 38:56+, Nov 1923

Child of Fortune (Adapted from Wings of the Dove by
        Henry James)
    Productions:
    Opened November 13, 1956 for 23 performances.
    Reviews:
        Commonweal 65:383, Jan 11, 1957
        New York Theatre Critics' Reviews 1956:209
        New York Times p. 41, Nov 14, 1956
        New Yorker 32:124, Nov 24, 1956
        Saturday Review 39:50, Dec 1, 1956
        Theatre Arts 41:27, Jan 1957
        Time 68:58, Nov 26, 1956

Children (with Tom Carlton)
    Productions:
    Opened October 4, 1915 in repertory (Washington
        Square Players)
    Reviews:
        Dramatic Mirror 75:8, Apr 1, 1916
        New York Times p. 9, Mar 21, 1916

The Fallen Idol
    Productions:
    Opened January 23, 1915 for nine performances.
    Reviews:
        Current Opinion 58:177-8, Mar 1915
        Dramatic Mirror 73:24, Jan 27, 1915
        Green Book 13:765-6, Apr 1915
        Life (NY) 65:196, Feb 4, 1915
        New York Dramatic News 60:17, Jan 30, 1915
        New York Times p. 9, Jan 25, 1915
        Theatre Magazine 21:149, Mar 1915

The Five Million (with Frank Mandel)
    Productions:
    Opened July 8, 1919 for 91 performances.

67

BOLTON, GUY (cont.)
   The Five Million (cont.)
      Reviews:
         Current Opinion 67:160-4, Sep 1919
         Forum 62:243-4, Aug 1919
         Hearst 36:42-3+, Oct 1919
         New York Times p. 14, Jul 9, 1919
         Theatre Magazine 30:149, Sep 1919

   Golden Wings (R.A.F.) (with William Jay)
      Productions:
         Opened December 8, 1941 for six performances.
      Reviews:
         New York Theatre Critics' Reviews 1941:178
         New York Times p. 33, Nov 25, 1941
                       p. 46, Dec 9, 1941
         Newsweek 18:61, Dec 22, 1941
         Theatre Arts 26:79, Feb 1942

   Grounds for Divorce (Adapted from the Hungarian of
         Ernest Vajda)
      Productions:
         Opened September 23, 1924 for 127 performances.
      Reviews:
         Nation 119:394-5, Oct 8, 1924
         New York Times VIII, p. 2, Mar 2, 1924
                        p. 20, Sep 24, 1924

   Hit-the-Trail-Holiday (See entry under Cohan, George M.)

   *Larger Than Life
      Reviews:
         New York Times p. 33, Feb 8, 1950
                        II, p. 3, Mar 12, 1950

   The Light of the World (with George Middleton)
      Productions:
         Opened January 6, 1920 for 31 performances.
      Reviews:
         Dramatic Mirror 82:51, Jan 15, 1920
         Life (NY) 75:148, Jan 22, 1920
         New York Clipper 67:25, Jan 14, 1920
         New York Times p. 17, Jan 7, 1920
         Theatre Magazine 31:142, Feb 1920

   The Nightcap (with Max Marcin)
      Productions:

Opened August 15, 1921 for 96 performances.
Reviews:
Dramatic Mirror 84:285, Aug 20, 1921
New York Clipper 69:24, Aug 14, 1921
New York Times p. 18, Aug 16, 1921
Theatre Magazine 34:236, Oct 1921
Weekly Review 5:215, Sep 3, 1921

Nobody Home (with Paul Rubens)
Productions:
Opened April 20, 1915 for 135 performances.
Reviews:
Dramatic Mirror 73:8, Apr 28, 1915
Green Book 14:59-60, Jul 1915
14:191-2, Jul 1915
Life (NY) 65:808, May 16, 1915
Theatre Magazine 21:280+, Jun 1915

Nobody's Business (with Frank Mandel)
Productions:
Opened October 22, 1923 for 40 performances.
Reviews:
New York Times p. 17, Oct 23, 1923
VIII, p. 1, Oct 28, 1923

Polly Preferred
Productions:
Opened January 11, 1923 for 184 performances.
Reviews:
New York Clipper 70:14, Jan 17, 1923
New York Times p. 13, Jan 12, 1923

Polly With A Past (with George Middleton)
Productions:
Opened September 8, 1917 for 315 performances.
Reviews:
Bookman 46:284-5, Nov 1917
Dramatic Mirror 77:5+, Sep 15, 1917
Green Book 18:774-8, Nov 1917
Life (NY) 70:466, Sep 20, 1917
New York Dramatic News 64:6, Sep 15, 1917
New York Times p. 7, Sep 7, 1917
II, p. 5, Sep 16, 1917
p. 13, Mar 3, 1921
Theatre Magazine 26:197+, Oct 1917

R.A.F. (see Golden Wings)

BOLTON, GUY (cont.)
   The Rule of Three
      Productions:
         Opened February 16, 1914 for 80 performances.
      Reviews:
         Bookman 39:145, Apr 1914
         Dramatic Mirror 71:6, Feb 18, 1914
         Green Book 11:776, May 1914
                 11:972-4, Jun 1914
                 11:1058-68, Jun 1914
         Hearst 25:685-700, May 1914
         Life (NY) 63:409, Mar 5, 1914
         Munsey 51:585, Apr 1914
         New York Dramatic News 59:20, Feb 21, 1914
         New York Times p. 11, Feb 17, 1914
         Theatre Magazine 19:170+, Apr 1914

   Theatre (with Somerset Maugham)
      Productions:
         Opened November 12, 1941 for 69 performances.
      Reviews:
         Catholic World 154:473, Jan 1942
         Commonweal 35:144, Nov 28, 1941
         New Republic 105:762, Dec 8, 1941
         New York Theatre Critics' Reviews 1941:226
         New York Times IX, p. 2, Oct 26, 1941
                 p. 34, Nov 13, 1941
         Theatre Arts 26:15, Jan 1942

   Wages for Wives (See Chicken Feed)

BOOTHE, CLARE

   Abide with Me
      Productions:
         Opened November 21, 1935 for 36 performances.
      Reviews:
         Commonweal 23:162, Dec 6, 1935
         New York Times p. 19, Nov 22, 1935
         Theatre Arts 20:20, Jan 1936
         Time 26:68, Dec 2, 1935

   Child of the Morning
      Productions:
         (Off Broadway) Season of 1957-58.
      Reviews:
         America 99:151, Apr 26, 1958

Catholic World 187:311, Jul 1958
Commonweal 68:153-4, May 9, 1958
New York Times p. 40, Apr 22, 1958
            p. 37, Feb 18, 1959

Kiss the Boys Good-bye
  Productions:
    Opened September 28, 1938 for 286 performances.
  Reviews:
    Catholic World 148:212-13, Nov 1938
    Commonweal 28:644, Oct 14, 1938
    Independent Woman 17:348+, Nov 1938
    Life 5:66-9, Oct 17, 1938
    Nation 147:362, Oct 8, 1938
    New Republic 96:331, Oct 26, 1938
    New York Times, p. 30, Sep 29, 1938
    Theatre Arts 22:778+, Nov 1938
    Time 32:48, Oct 10, 1938
    Vogue 92:75, Nov 1, 1935

Margin for Error
  Productions:
    Opened November 3, 1939 for 264 performances.
  Reviews:
    Catholic World 150:339, Dec 1939
    Commonweal 31:118, Nov 24, 1939
    Forum 103:33, Jan 1940
    Life 7:60-61, Nov 20, 1939
    New York Theatre Critics' Reviews 1940:460
    New York Times p. 48, Oct 15, 1939
                 p. 11, Nov 4, 1939
                 IX, p. 1, Nov 12, 1939
                 IX, p. 2, Aug 11, 1940
    Newsweek 14:36, Nov 20, 1939
    Spectator 156:146, Aug 9, 1940
    Theatre Arts 24:18-19, Jan 1940
    Time 34:58, Nov 13, 1939

The Women
  Productions:
    Opened December 26, 1936 for 657 performances.
  Reviews:
    Catholic World 144:599-600, Feb 1937
    Commonweal 25:332, Jan 15, 1937
    Life 2:38+, Jan 25, 1937
         13:4-6, Dec 21, 1942
    Literary Digest 123:24-5, Jan 9, 1937

71

BOOTHE, CLARE (cont.)
  The Women (cont.)
        New Republic 90:263, Apr 7, 1937
        New York Times p. 30, Dec 8, 1936
                     p. 13, Dec 28, 1936
                     X, p. 3, Oct 31, 1937
                     II, p. 2, May 22, 1938
                     p. 14, Nov 5, 1938
                     X, p. 3, Mar 5, 1939
                     p. 21, Apr 21, 1939
                     X, p. 2, May 7, 1939
                     p. 14, Jun 10, 1939
        Newsweek 9:22, Jan 2, 1937
        Stage 14:50, Jan 1937
              14:48-9, Feb 1937
              14:41-4, Mar 1937
        Theatre Arts 21:101-2, Feb 1937
        Time 29:30, Jan 4, 1937
        Vogue 89:78-9, Jan 15, 1937
              101:44-5, Jan 1, 1943

BOUCICAULT, DION

  *After Dark
     Reviews:
        Life (NY) 93:21, Feb 22, 1929
        Literary Digest 101:24-6, Apr 6, 1929
        Nation 128:54, Jan 9, 1929
        New York Times p. 35, Dec 11, 1928
        Theatre Magazine 49:51+, Feb 1929

  Life in Louisiana (See The Octoroon)

  London Assurance
     Productions:
        Opened February 18, 1937 for 5 performances.
     Reviews:
        New York Times p. 14, Feb 19, 1937

  The Octoroon (or Life in Louisiana)
     Productions:
        Opened March 12, 1929
        Opened January 27, 1961 for 45 performances.
     Reviews:
        America 104:714, Feb 25, 1961
        Commonweal 73:636, Mar 17, 1961
        Life 50:39-40+, Feb 24, 1961

Nation 128:380, Mar 27, 1929
       192:126, Feb 11, 1961
New York Theatre Critics' Reviews 1961:382
New York Times p. 28, Mar 13, 1929
              p. 24, Sep 1, 1936
              II, p. 3, Jan 22, 1961
              p. 13, Jan 28, 1961
New Yorker 36:75-6+, Feb 11, 1961
Saturday Review 44:41, Feb 25, 1961

*The Shaughraun
    Reviews:
        New York Times p. 54, May 22, 1968

The Streets of New York, or Poverty Is No Crime
    Productions:
        Opened October 6, 1931 for 87 performances.
    Reviews:
        Bookman 74:564, Jan-Feb 1932
        Catholic World 134:210, Nov 1931
        Commonweal 19:608, Oct 21, 1931
        Literary Digest 111:19, Nov 14, 1931
        Nation 133:467-8, Oct 28, 1931
        New Republic 68:301, Oct 28, 1931
        New York Times p. 29, Apr 26, 1929
                       VIII, p. 4, Oct 4, 1931
                       p. 29, Oct 7, 1931
                       p. 14, Jul 21, 1934
        Outlook 159:248, Oct 21, 1931
        Stage 9:10, Jul 1932
        Theatre Arts 15:984, Dec 1931
        Vogue 78:60-61, Dec 1, 1931

BOWLES, JANE

In the Summer House
    Productions:
        Opened December 29, 1953 for 55 performances.
        (Off Broadway) Opened March 25, 1964 for 15 per-
        formances.
    Reviews:
        America 90:406, Jan 16, 1954
        Catholic World 178:386, Feb 1954
        Commonweal 59:449-50, Feb 5, 1954
        Nation 178:58, Jan 16, 1954
        New Republic 130:20-21, Jan 11, 1954
        New York Theatre Critics' Reviews 1953:168

BOWLES, JANE (cont.)
    In the Summer House (cont.)
            New York Times II, p. 5, Dec 27, 1953
                          p. 17, Dec 30, 1953
                          II, p. 1, Jan 10, 1954
                          p. 43, Mar 26, 1964
            New Yorker 29:61-2, Jan 9, 1954
            Saturday Review 37:31, Jan 16, 1954
                          37:61-2, Jan 23, 1954
            Theatre Arts 38:19, Mar 1954
            Time 63:67, Jan 11, 1954

BREIT, HARVEY

    The Disenchanted (See entry under Schulberg, Budd)

    The Guide (with Patricia Rinehart) (Based on the novel by
        R. K. Naryan.)
        Opened March 6, 1968 for 5 performances.
        Reviews:
            New York Theatre Critics' Reviews 1968:329
            New York Times p. 50, Mar 7, 1968
            New Yorker 44:130, Mar 16, 1968

BRIDGERS, ANN

    Coquette (See entry under Abbott, George)

BROKAW, CLARE (See Booth, Clare)

BROWNE, PORTER EMERSON

    The Bad Man
        Productions:
        Opened August 30, 1920 for 342 performances.
        Reviews:
            Bookman 53:407+, Jul 1921
            Current Opinion 69:812-22, Dec 1920
            Dramatic Mirror p. 415, Sep 4, 1920
            Dramatist 12:1054, Apr 1921
            Hearst 39:41-3+, Jan 1921
            Life (NY) 76:500, Sep 16, 1920

New York Clipper 68:29, Sep 8, 1920
New York Times p. 7, Aug 31, 1920
Outlook 126:183, Sep 29, 1920
Theatre Magazine 32:278-9, Nov 1920

Chains (Adapted from the play by Elizabeth Baker.)
Productions:
Opened December 16, 1912 for one matinee.
Reviews:
American Playwright 2:7-9, Jan 1913
Bookman 36:640-1, Feb 1913
Dramatic Mirror 68:6, Dec 18, 1912
Munsey 48:845, Feb 1913
New York Drama News 57:26, Dec 21, 1912
Theatre Magazine 17:xv+, Feb 1913

A Fool There Was
Productions:
Opened March 24, 1909 for 93 performances.
Reviews:
Collier's 43:20, May 22, 1909
Dramatist 7:621-2, Oct 1915
Forum 41:449-50, May 1909
Green Book 2:257-83, Aug 1909
Hampton 23:109-111, Jul 1909
Theatre Magazine 9:135-6+, May 1909

The Spendthrift
Productions:
Opened April 11, 1910 for 88 performances.
Reviews:
Collier's 45:34, May 7, 1910
Dramatic Mirror 63:7-8, Apr 23, 1910
Dramatist 2:105-6, Oct 1910
Green Book 4:98-9, Jul 1910
4:929-50, Nov 1910
Hampton 24:824-5, Jun 1910
Leslies' Weekly 110:437, May 5, 1910
Metropolitan Magazine 32:538-9, Jul 1910
World Today 19:1099-105, Oct 1910

BUCK, PEARL S.

A Desert Incident
Productions:
Opened March 24, 1959 for 7 performances.

BUCK, PEARL S. (cont.)
  A Desert Incident (cont.)
    Reviews:
        New York Theatre Critics' Reviews 1959:332
        New York Times p. 40, Mar 25, 1959
        New Yorker 35:112+, Apr 4, 1959
        Saturday Review 42:35, Apr 11, 1959
        Theatre Arts 43:11, Jun 1959

  The First Wife
    Productions:
        (Off Broadway) December 1945 (Chinese Theatre).
    No Reviews.

  *Flight Into China
    Reviews:
        New York Times p. 28, Sep 12, 1939

  The Good Earth (See entry under Davis, Owen)

BURROWS, ABE

  Cactus Flower (Based on a play by Pierre Barillet and
        Jean Pierre Gredy)
    Productions:
        Opened December 8, 1965 for 1,234 performances.
    Reviews:
        America 114:54, Jan 8, 1966
        Commonweal 83:410, Jan 7, 1966
        Life 60:35-6, Feb 11, 1966
        National Review 18:739-40, Jul 26, 1966
        New York Theatre Critics' Reviews 1965:229
        New York Times p. 60, Dec 9, 1965
                      p. 58, Dec 10, 1965
                      II, p. 2, Jul 31, 1966
                      p. 48, Dec 16, 1967
        New Yorker 41:152, Dec 18, 1965
        Newsweek 66:72, Dec 20, 1965
        Saturday Review 48:41, Dec 25, 1965
        Time 86:40, Dec 17, 1965
        Vogue 147:99, Feb 1, 1966

BUTLER, RACHEL BARTON

  Mama's Affair

Productions:
Opened January 19, 1920 for 98 performances.
Reviews:
Dramatic Mirror 82:132, Jan 29, 1920
Life (NY) 75:184, Jan 29, 1920
Nation 110:211, Feb 14, 1920
New York Clipper 67:25, Jan 28, 1920
New York Times p. 10, Jan 20, 1920
VIII, p. 2, Jan 25, 1920
Theatre Magazine 31:181+, Mar 1920

CALDWELL, ERSKINE

Journeyman (See entry under Hayes, Alfred)

Tobacco Road (See entry under Kirkland, Jack)

*Trouble in July
Reviews:
New York Times p. 36, Dec 2, 1949

CAPOTE, TRUMAN

The Grass Harp (Based on his novel)
Productions:
Opened March 27, 1952 for 36 performances.
Reviews:
Catholic World 175:147-8, May 1952
177:228, Jun 1953
Commonweal 56:68-9, Apr 25, 1952
58:179, May 22, 1953
Life 32:142+, Apr 14, 1952
Nation 174:353, Apr 12, 1952
176:421, May 16, 1953
New Republic 126:22-3, Apr 14, 1952
New York Theatre Critics' Reviews 1952:328
New York Times II, p. 1, Mar 23, 1952
p. 26, Mar 28, 1952
II, p. 1, Apr 6, 1952
p. 32, Apr 28, 1953
II, p. 1, May 24, 1953
New Yorker 28:70, Apr 5, 1952
Newsweek 39:94, Apr 7, 1952
Saturday Review 35:43-4, Apr 19, 1952
36:30, May 16, 1953

CAPOTE, TRUMAN (cont.)
  The Grass Harp (cont.)
            School and Society 75:323-4, May 24, 1952
            Theatre Arts 36:17-18, Jun 1952
                        37:16, Jul 1953
            Time 59:77, Apr 7, 1952

CAROLE, JOSEPH

  Separate Rooms (with Alan Dinehart)
    Productions:
      Opened March 23, 1940 for 613 performances.
    Reviews:
      New York Theatre Critics' Reviews 1940:359
                                        1941:487
      New York Times p. 10, Mar 25, 1940
                  IX, p. 2, Aug 18, 1940
      Stage 1:17, Nov 1940
            1:18, Dec 1940

  Thanks for My Wife (See Separate Rooms)

CHAPMAN, ROBERT

  Billy Budd (See entry under Coxe, Louis O.)

  Uniform of Flesh (See entry under Coxe, Louis O.)

CHASE, MARY COYLE

  Bernadine
    Productions:
      Opened October 16, 1952 for 157 performances.
    Reviews:
      Catholic World 176:227-8, Dec 1952
      Commonweal 57:119, Nov 7, 1952
      Life 33:83-4+, Nov 24, 1952
      Nation 175:414, Nov 1, 1952
      New York Theatre Critics' Reviews 1952:231
      New York Times p. 33, Oct 17, 1952
                  II, p. 1, Nov 9, 1952
                  II, p. 1, Nov 23, 1952
      New Yorker 28:74, Oct 25, 1952
      Newsweek 40:78, Oct 27, 1952

Saturday Review 35:26, Nov 1, 1952
School and Society 76:403, Dec 20, 1952
Theatre Arts 36:26-8, Dec 1952
Time 60:75, Oct 27, 1952

Harvey
  Productions:
  Opened November 1, 1944 for 1,775 performances.
  Reviews:
    Catholic World 160:260, Dec 1944
    Commonweal 41:124, Nov 17, 1944
    Cosmopolitan 119:34-5+, Jul 1945
    Life 17:96-8+, Nov 27, 1944
        18:55-8+, Jan 8, 1945
    Nation 59:624, Nov 18, 1944
    New Republic 111:661, Nov 20, 1944
    New York Theatre Critics' Reviews 1944:95
    New York Times p. 23, Nov 2, 1944
                    II, p. 1, Nov 12, 1944
                    VI, p. 28, Jan 7, 1945
                    p. 16, May 8, 1945
                    II, p. 1, May 13, 1945
                    p. 36, Mar 11, 1947
                    II, p. 3, Mar 16, 1947
                    p. 27, Jul 15, 1947
                    II, p. 1, Sep 7, 1947
                    II, p. 1, Oct 26, 1947
                    p. 31, Nov 24, 1947
                    p. 30, Apr 7, 1948
                    p. 29, Oct 19, 1948
                    p. 29, Jan 6, 1949
                    II, p. 1, Jan 16, 1949
                    II, p. 3, Feb 13, 1949
                    p. 34, Mar 24, 1949
                    p. 14, Feb 13, 1950
                    p. 10, Oct 21, 1950
                    II, p. 5, Nov 26, 1950
                    II, p. 3, Dec 31, 1950
                    II, p. 2, Jun 3, 1951
    New Yorker 20:44, Nov 11, 1944
              23:40+, Jul 26, 1947
    Newsweek 24:82-3, Nov 13, 1944
            30:78-9, Jul 28, 1947
    Player's Magazine 22:5, Sep-Oct 1945
    Saturday Review 27:10-11, Dec 30, 1944
    Theatre Arts 29:2, 5-6+, Jan 1945
                29:85, Feb 1945

CHASE, MARY COYLE (cont.)
Harvey (cont.)
                    32:20, Fall 1948
         Time 44:60, Nov 13, 1944
               49:74, Jun 16, 1947
               53:31, Apr 25, 1949

Midgie Purvis
    Productions:
        Opened February 1, 1961 for 21 performances.
    Reviews:
        Nation 192:155-6, Feb 18, 1961
        New York Theatre Critics' Reviews 1961:375
        New York Times p. 25, Feb 2, 1961
                        II, p. 1, Feb 12, 1961
        New Yorker 36:75, Feb 11, 1961
        Saturday Review 44:41, Feb 25, 1961
        Time 77:68, Feb 10, 1961

Mrs. McThing
    Productions:
        Opened February 20, 1952 for 350 performances.
    Reviews:
        Catholic World 175:68, Apr 1952
        Commonweal 55:567, Mar 14, 1952
        Life 32:149-50+, Mar 10, 1952
        Nation 174:258, Mar 15, 1952
        New Republic 126:22, Mar 17, 1952
        New York Theatre Critics' Reviews 1952:359
        New York Times II, p. 1, Feb 17, 1952
                          p. 22, Feb 21, 1952
                          II, p. 1, Mar 2, 1952
                          II, p. 3, Mar 30, 1952
        New Yorker 28:58, Mar 1, 1952
        Newsweek 39:61, Mar 3, 1952
        Saturday Review 35:28, Mar 15, 1952
        School and Society 75:182-3, Mar 22, 1952
        Theatre Arts 36:28-9, 38-41, May 1952
        Time 59:63, Mar 3, 1952

The Next Half Hour
    Productions:
        Opened October 29, 1945 for 8 performances.
    Reviews:
        New Republic 113:639, Nov 12, 1945
        New York Theatre Critics' Reviews 1945:130
        New York Times II, p. 1, Nov 4, 1945

New Yorker 21:44+, Nov 10, 1945
Theatre Arts 30:12, Jan 1946

Now You've Done It
    Productions:
    Opened March 5, 1937 for 43 performances.
    Reviews:
    New York Times p. 10, Mar 6, 1937

CHAYEFSKY, PADDY

Gideon
    Productions:
    Opened November 9, 1961 for 236 performances.
    Reviews:
    America 106:453-4, Jan 6, 1962
    Catholic World 194:216-21, Jan 1962
    Christian Century 78:1500-1, Dec 13, 1961
    Commonweal 75:257-9, Dec 1, 1961
    Life 51:118-19, Dec 15, 1961
    Nation 193:437-8, Nov 25, 1961
    New Republic 145:21-3, Nov 27, 1961
    New York Theatre Critics' Reviews 1961:174
    New York Times II, p. 1, Nov 5, 1961
                    p. 38, Nov 10, 1961
                    II, p. 1, Nov 19, 1961
    New Yorker 37:96, Nov 18, 1961
    Newsweek 58:69, Nov 20, 1961
    Reporter 25:62, Dec 7, 1961
    Saturday Review 44:27, Dec 9, 1961
                    45:30, May 19, 1962
    Theatre Arts 46:10-11, Jan 1962
    Time 78:71, Nov 17, 1961

*The Latent Heterosexual
    Reviews:
    Life 64:16, Apr 20, 1968
    New York Times p. 52, Mar 22, 1968
                    II, p. 3, Mar 31, 1968
    Newsweek 71:87, Apr 1, 1968
    Saturday Review 51:20, Apr 6, 1968
    Time 91:91, Mar 29, 1968

Middle of the Night
    Productions:
    Opened February 8, 1956 for 477 performances.
    Reviews:

CHAYEFSKY, PADDY (cont.)
  Middle of the Night (cont.)
          America 94:619, Mar 3, 1956
          Catholic World 183:66, Apr 1956
          Commonweal 63:663, Mar 30, 1956
          Life 40:99-100+, Feb 27, 1956
          Nation 182:166, Feb 25, 1956
          New Republic 134:21, Feb 27, 1956
          New York Theatre Critics' Reviews 1956:370
          New York Times p. 39, Feb 9, 1956
                         II, p. 1, Feb 19, 1956
                         II, p. 1, Jul 15, 1956
          New York Times Magazine p. 78, Jan 29, 1956
          New Yorker 31:60+, Feb 18, 1956
          Newsweek 47:93, Feb 20, 1956
          Saturday Review 39:26, Feb 25, 1956
          Theatre Arts 40:20, Apr 1956
          Time 67:90, Feb 20, 1956

  The Passion of Josef D.
    Productions:
      Opened February 11, 1964 for 15 performances.
    Reviews:
      Commonweal 79:693, Mar 6, 1964
      New York Theatre Critics' Reviews 1964:354
      New York Times II, p. 1, Feb 9, 1964
                     p. 29, Feb 12, 1964
                     p. 25, Feb 17, 1964
                     II, p. 1, Feb 23, 1964
      New Yorker 40:92, Feb 22, 1964
      Newsweek 63:61, Feb 24, 1964
      Saturday Review 47:26, Feb 29, 1964
      Time 83:62, Feb 21, 1964

  The Tenth Man
    Productions:
      Opened November 5, 1959 for 623 performances.
      Opened November 8, 1967 for 23 performances.
    Reviews:
      America 102:362, Dec 12, 1959
      Christian Century 76:1528-9, Dec 30, 1959
      Commentary 28:523-7, Dec 1959
      Life 47:127-8+, Dec 7, 1959
      Nation 189:388, Nov 21, 1959
      New Republic 141:21-2, Nov 23, 1959
      New York Theatre Critics' Reviews 1959:232
      New York Times p. 24, Nov 6, 1959

II, p. 1, Nov 15, 1959
                     VI, p. 106, Nov 15, 1959
                     p. 68, Feb 7, 1960
                     p. 23, Apr 14, 1961
                     p. 46, Oct 3, 1962
                     p. 54, Nov 9, 1967
          New Yorker 35:118+, Nov 14, 1959
          Newsweek 54:109, Nov 16, 1959
          Reporter 21:39, Dec 10, 1959
          Saturday Review 42:31+, Nov 21, 1959
                     50:70, Nov 25, 1967
          Time 74:57, Nov 16, 1959

CHODOROV, EDWARD

   Common Ground
      Productions:
         Opened April 25, 1945 for 69 performances.
      Reviews:
         Catholic World 161:261, Jun 1945
         Commonweal 42:93, May 11, 1945
         New York Theatre Critics' Reviews 1945:221
         New York Times p. 19, Apr 12, 1945
                        p. 27, Apr 26, 1945
                        p. 16, May 1, 1945
                        II, p. 1, May 6, 1945
         New Yorker 21:42, May 5, 1945
         Newsweek 25:81, May 7, 1945
         Theatre Arts 29:389, Jul 1945
         Time 45:74, May 7, 1945

   Cue for Passion (with H. S. Kraft)
      Productions:
         Opened December 19, 1940 for 12 performances.
      Reviews:
         New York Theatre Critics' Reviews 1940:185
         New York Times p. 33, Dec 20, 1940
         New Yorker 16:29, Dec 28, 1940
         Theatre Arts 25:98, Feb 1941

   Decision
      Productions:
         Opened February 2, 1944 for 160 performances.
      Reviews:
         Catholic World 158:585-6, Mar 1944
         Commonweal 39:447, Feb 18, 1944

                        83

CHODOROV, EDWARD (cont.)
    Decision (cont.)
                Life 16:47-8+, May 27, 1944
                Nation 158:235, Feb 19, 1944
                New Republic 110:242, Feb 21, 1944
                New York Theater Critics' Reviews 1944:265
                New York Times p. 23, Feb 3, 1944
                                II, p. 1, Feb 13, 1944
                                II, p. 1, May 21, 1944
                Newsweek 23:72, Feb 14, 1944
                Theater Arts 28:197-99+, Apr 1944
                Time 43:62, Feb 14, 1944

    Kind Lady (Adapted from a story by Hugh Walpole)
        Productions:
            Opened April 23, 1935 for 102 performances.
            Opened September 9, 1935 for 20 performances.
            Opened September 3, 1940 for 107 performances.
        Reviews:
            Catholic World 141:340-1, Jun 1935
                            152:88, Oct 1940
            Commonweal 22:47, May 10, 1935
                        32:449, Sep 20, 1940
            Literary Digest 119:16, May 4, 1935
            Nation 140:554, May 8, 1935
            New Republic 82:370, May 8, 1935
            New York Theatre Critics' Reviews 1940:286
            New York Times p. 24, Apr 24, 1935
                            X, p. 1, Apr 28, 1935
                            p. 24, Jul 23, 1935
                            p. 27, Nov 19, 1935
                            p. 19, Jun 12, 1936
                            p. 22, Jul 14, 1936
                            p. 23, Jul 6, 1937
                            p. 19, Jul 21, 1937
                            p. 14, Jul 11, 1938
                            p. 28, Sep 4, 1940
            Newsweek 5:24, May 4, 1935
            Stage 1:14, Nov 1940
            Theater Arts 24:775+, Nov 1940
                        (p. 775) 24:779, Nov 1940
            Time 25:40, May 6, 1935

    Oh, Men! Oh Women!
        Productions:
            Opened December 17, 1953 for 382 performances.
        Reviews:

America 90:386, Jan 9, 1954
Catholic World 178:389, Feb 1954
Commonweal 59:403, Jan 22, 1954
Life 36:49-50+, Jan 11, 1954
Nation 178:57, Jan 16, 1954
New Republic 130:21, Jan 4, 1954
          130:21, May 31, 1954
New York Theatre Critics' Reviews 1953:184
New York Times p. 37, Dec 18, 1953
New Yorker 29:38-9, Jan 2, 1954
Newsweek 42:47, Dec 28, 1953
Saturday Review 37:30, Jan 9, 1954
Theater Arts 38:17, Mar 1954
Time 62:34, Dec 28, 1953

Last Judgment (See Cue for Passion)

Those Endearing Young Charms
    Productions:
    Opened June 16, 1943 for 61 performances.
    Reviews:
    Catholic World 157:523, Aug 1943
    Commonweal 38:234-5, Jul 2, 1943
    New York Theatre Critics' Reviews 1943:318
    New York Times p. 16, Jun 17, 1943
    New Yorker 19:33, Jun 26, 1943

Wonder Boy (with Arthur Barton)
    Productions:
    Opened October 22, 1931 for 44 performances.
    Reviews:
    Commonweal 15:102, Nov 25, 1931
    Nation 133:525-6, Nov 11, 1931
    New York Times p. 20, Oct 24, 1931
    Vogue 78:57, Dec 15, 1931

CHODOROV, JEROME

Anniversary Waltz (with Joseph A. Fields)
    Productions:
    Opened April 7, 1954 for 615 performances.
    Reviews:
    America 91:116, Apr 24, 1954
    Catholic World 179:226, Jun 1954
    Commonweal 60:143, May 14, 1954
    Nation 178:370, Apr 24, 1954

CHODOROV, JEROME (cont.)
  Anniversary Waltz (cont.)
        New York Theatre Critics' Reviews 1954:339
        New York Times p. 34, Apr 8, 1954
                        II, p. 1, Apr 25, 1954
                        p. 18, Apr 8, 1955
                        p. 31, Dec 2, 1955
                        II, p. 7, Dec 11, 1955
        New Yorker 30:66-8, Apr 17, 1954
        Newsweek 43:66, Apr 19, 1954
        Saturday Review 37:24, Apr 24, 1954
        Theater Arts 38:20, Jun 1954
        Time 63:88, Apr 19, 1954

  The French Touch (See entry under Fields, Joseph A.)

  Junior Miss (with Joseph A. Fields)
     Productions:
        Opened November 18, 1941 for 710 performances.
     Reviews:
        Catholic World 154:471-2, Jan 1942
        Commonweal 35:178, Dec 5, 1941
        Life 11:103, Dec 15, 1941
            15:82, Aug 2, 1943
        Nation 153:548, Nov 29, 1941
        New Republic 113:161, Aug 1, 1945
        New York Theatre Critics' Reviews 1941:211
        New York Times p. 28, Nov 19, 1941
                        IV, p. 2, Nov 23, 1941
                        IX, p. 1, Nov 30, 1941
                        p. 23, Jan 7, 1942
                        II, p. 1, Apr 18, 1943
        New Yorker 17:39, Nov 29, 1941
        Newsweek 18:71, Dec 1, 1941
        Theater Arts 26:9+, Jan 1942
        Time 38:67, Dec 1, 1941

  My Sister Eileen (See entry under Fields, Joseph A.)

  The Ponder Heart (See entry under Fields, Joseph A.)

  Schoolhouse on the Lot (See entry under Fields, Joseph A.)

  3 Bags Full (Based on a play by Claude Magnier)
     Productions:
        Opened March 6, 1966 for 33 performances.
     Reviews:

America 114:453, Apr 2, 1966
New York Theater Critics' Reviews 1966:339
New York Times p. 22, Mar 7, 1966
New Yorker 42:160, May 19, 1966
Newsweek 67:97, Mar 21, 1966
Time 87:80, Mar 18, 1966
Vogue 147:145, May 1966

CLEMENTS, COLIN

Glamour Preferred (See entry under Ryerson, Florence)

Harriet (See entry under Ryerson, Florence)

Morality Clause (See Glamour Preferred)

Strange Bedfellows (See entry under Ryerson, Florence)

COFFEE, LEONORE (MRS. W. J. COWEN)

Family Portrait (with William Joyce Cowen)
    Productions:
        Opened March 8, 1939 for 111 performances.
        (Off Broadway) Season of 1958-59.
    Reviews:
        Catholic World 149:89-90, Apr 1939
        Commonweal 29:609, Mar 24, 1939
        New York Times p. 18, Mar 9, 1939
                        XI, p. 1, Mar 19, 1939
                        IX, p. 2, Jun 30, 1940
                        p. 48, May 6, 1959
        New Yorker 35:87-8, May 16, 1959
        Newsweek 13:33, Mar 20, 1939
        North American Review 247:No 2:370-1, Jun 1939
        Player's Magazine 17:11-12, Jan 1941
        Stage 16:24-5, Mar 15, 1939
        Theatre Arts 23:318-19+, May 1939
        Time 33:60-61, Mar 20, 1939

COHAN, GEORGE M.

American Born
    Productions:
        Opened October 5, 1925 for 88 performances.

COHAN, GEORGE M. (cont.)
  American Born (cont.)
    Reviews:
      Life (NY) 86:18, Oct 29, 1925
      New York Times p. 31, Oct 6, 1925

Baby Cyclone
  Productions:
    Opened September 12, 1927 for 184 performances.
  Reviews:
    Life (NY) 90:21, Oct 6, 1927
    New York Times VII, p. 2, Aug 14, 1927
                    p. 37, Sep 13, 1927
    Theatre Magazine 46:23, Nov 1927

Broadway Jones
  Productions:
    Opened September 23, 1912 for 176 performances.
  Reviews:
    Blue Book 16:229-34, Dec 1912
    Bookman 36:281, Nov 1912
    Dramatic Mirror 68:6-7, Sep 25, 1912
    Dramatist 4:377-9, Jul 1913
    Everybody's 27:817-18, Dec 1912
    Green Book 8:924-6+, Dec 1912
               9:534-52, Mar 1913
    Hearst 23:315-26, Feb 1913
    Leslies' Weekly 115:490, Nov 14, 1912
    Life (NY) 60:1912, Oct 3, 1912
    Munsey 48:354, Nov 1912
    New York Times p. 3, Feb 4, 1914
    Red Book 20:374-7+, Dec 1912
    Theatre Magazine 16:134, Nov 1912

*Confidential Service
  Reviews:
    New York Times VIII, p. 2, Apr 3, 1932

Dear Old Darling
  Productions:
    Opened March 2, 1936 for 16 performances.
  Reviews:
    Commonweal 23:580, Mar 20, 1936
    Literary Digest 121:19, Mar 14, 1936
    Nation 142:359-60, Mar 18, 1936
    New Republic 86:169, Mar 18, 1936
    New York Times p. 10, Dec 31, 1935

IX, p. 1, Feb 2, 1936
p. 25, Mar 3, 1936
Newsweek 7:39-40, Mar 14, 1936
Stage 13:29-30, Jan 1936
Theatre Arts 20:260-1, Apr 1936
Time 27:42, Mar 9, 1936

Friendship
    Productions:
        Opened August 31, 1931 for 24 performances.
    Reviews:
        Arts and Decoration 36:73, Nov 1931
        Commonweal 14:470, Sep 16, 1931
        Life (NY) 98:18, Sep 18, 1931
        New York Times VIII, p. 2, May 10, 1931
                          p. 30, Sep 1, 1931
                     IX, p. 1, Sep 13, 1931
        Outlook 159:86, Sep 16, 1931
        Theatre Arts 15:887-8, Nov 1931
        Vogue 78:106, Nov 1, 1931

Fulton of Oak Falls (Based on a story by Parker Fennelly)
    Productions:
        Opened February 10, 1937 for 37 performances.
    Reviews:
        New York Times p. 15, Jan 2, 1937
                       p. 18, Feb 11, 1937
        Newsweek 9:21-4, Feb 20, 1937
        Stage 14:65, Feb 1937
        Time 29:46, Feb 22, 1937

Gambling
    Productions:
        Opened August 26, 1929 for 152 performances.
    Reviews:
        Catholic World 130:209-10, Nov 1929
        Commonweal 10:645, Oct 23, 1929
        Life (NY) 94:20, Sep 20, 1929
        New York Times IX, p. 2, May 19, 1929
                          p. 31, Aug 27, 1929
        Outlook 153:72, Sep 11, 1929
        Theatre Magazine 50:42, Oct 1929

Get-Rich-Quick Wallingford (Adapted from the novel by
        George Randolph Chester)
    Productions:
        Opened September 19, 1910 for 424 performances.

COHAN, GEORGE M. (cont.)
   Get-Rich-Quick Wallingford (cont.)
      Opened May 7, 1917 for 16 performances.
    Reviews:
      Blue Book 12:638-9, Jan 1911
      Collier's 46:17, Dec 24, 1910
      Current Literature 51:185-91, Aug 1911
      Dramatist 2:118-19, Jan 1911
      Green Book 4:1222-23, Dec 1910
               5:239+, Feb 1911
      Hampton 25:828-9, Dec 1910
      Literary Digest 44:1356, Jun 29, 1912
      Metropolitan Magazine 33:404-5, Dec 1910
      Munsey 44:410, Dec 1910
      New York Times p. 9, May 9, 1917
               VIII, p. 7, May 13, 1917
      Pearson 24:806-7, Dec 1910
      Red Book 16:566-71, Jan 1911
      Theatre Magazine 12:141+, Nov 1910
      Worlds' Work 21:14112-21, Mar 1911
              22:14322-8, May 1911
              22:14274-9, Jun 1911

Hit-the-Trail-Holiday (Suggested by George Middleton and
   Guy Bolton)
   Productions:
      Opened September 13, 1915 for 336 performances.
    Reviews:
      Bookman 42:267-8, Nov 1915
      Dramatic Mirror 74:8, Sep 15, 1915
               75:2+, Jan 8, 1916
      Everybody's 34:502, Apr 1916
      Green Book 14:973-5, Dec 1915
               14:981-2, Dec 1915
      Life (NY) 66:566, Sep 23, 1915
      National Magazine 43:379-80, Nov 1915
      New Republic 4:211-, Sep 25, 1915
      New York Drama News 61:19, Sep 18, 1915
      New York Times p. 11, Sep 14, 1915

The Home Towners
   Productions:
      Opened August 23, 1926 for 64 performances.
    Reviews:
      Bookman 64:341-2, Nov 1926
      Dial 81:520, Dec 1926
      Independent 117:421, Oct 9, 1926

Life (NY) 88:20, Sep 16, 1926
New York Times VIII, p. 2, May 16, 1926
                  p. 19, Aug 24, 1926
                  VII, p. 1, Aug 29, 1926
                  VII, p. 1, Sep 5, 1926
Theatre Magazine 44:66+, Oct 1926
Vogue 68:80+, Oct 15, 1926

The Little Millionaire
Productions:
Opened September 25, 1911 for 192 performances.
Reviews:
Blue Book 14:463-5, Jan 1912
Dramatic Mirror 66:11, Sep 27, 1911
Green Book 6:1195-6, Dec 1911
Leslies' Weekly 113:409, Oct 12, 1911
Life (NY) 58:618, Oct 12, 1911
Munsey 46:426, Dec 1911

Madeleine and the Movies
Productions:
Opened March 6, 1922 for 80 performances.
Reviews:
Bookman 55:283, May 1922
Life (NY) 79:18, Mar 23, 1922
New York Clipper 70:22, Mar 15, 1922
New York Times p. 11, Mar 7, 1922
               p. 17, Mar 9, 1922
Theatre Magazine 35:336, May 1922

The Miracle Man (Based on Frank L. Packard's story)
Productions:
Opened September 21, 1914 for 97 performances.
Reviews:
American Magazine 79:87-8, Feb 1915
Book News 33:230-1, Jan 1915
Bookman 40:256-8, Nov 1914
Dramatic Mirror 72:8, Sep 30, 1914
Dramatist 6:530-1, Jan 1915
Everybody's 31:702, Nov 1914
Green Book 12:1140, Dec 1914
Life (NY) 64:584, Oct 1, 1914
Munsey 53:360, Nov 1914
Nation 99:415, Oct 1, 1914
New Republic 1:23, Nov 14, 1914
New York Drama News 59:18, Sep 26, 1914
New York Times VIII, p. 6, Jul 19, 1914

COHAN, GEORGE M. (cont.)
The Miracle Man (cont.)
p. 11, Sep 22, 1914
VII, p. 8, Nov 15, 1914
Theatre Magazine 20:205+, Nov 1914

Pigeons and People
Productions:
Opened January 16, 1933 for 70 performances.
Reviews:
Arts and Decoration 38:42, Mar 1933
Catholic World 136:716-17, Mar 1933
Commonweal 17:385, Feb 1, 1933
Nation 136:160, Feb 8, 1933
New Outlook 161:49, Mar 1933
New York Times IX, p. 2, Jan 1, 1933
p. 22, Jan 17, 1933
Stage 10:11, Feb 1933
Theatre Arts 17:180+, Mar 1933
19:325, May 1935
Time 21:22, Jan 30, 1933
Vogue 81:51+, Mar 15, 1933

A Prince There Was (Based on a story by Dorrough
Aldrich)
Productions:
Opened December 24, 1918 for 159 performances.
Reviews:
Dramatic Mirror 80:47-8, Jan 11, 1919
Nation 108:104, Jan 18, 1919
New Republic 18:279, Mar 29, 1919
New York Times p. 13, Dec 25, 1918

The Return of the Vagabond
Productions:
Opened May 17, 1940 for 7 performances.
Reviews:
Commonweal 32:129, May 31, 1940
Life 8:72-4, May 27, 1940
New York Theatre Critics' Reviews 1940:307
New York Times p. 19, Apr 12, 1940
p. 20, Apr 13, 1940
IX, p. 1, Apr 21, 1940
p. 27, May 14, 1940
Newsweek 15:48, May 27, 1940

<u>Seven Keys to Baldpate</u> (Based on the novel by Earl Derr
    Biggers)
  Productions:
    Opened September 22, 1913 for 320 performances.
    Opened May 27, 1935 for 8 performances.
  Reviews:
    American Magazine 2:303-5, Oct 1913
                      5:447-9, Apr 1914
    Blue Book 18:836-7, Mar 1914
    Bookman 38:262-3, Nov 1913
    Commonweal 22:190, Jun 14, 1935
    Current Opinion 55:408-12, Dec 1913
    Dramatic Mirror 70:10, Sep 24, 1913
    Green Book 10:960-3, Dec 1913
               10:1058-60, Dec 1913
    Life (NY) 62:567, Oct 2, 1913
    Literary Digest 119:23, Jun 1, 1935
    Munsey 50:299, Nov 1913
    New York Drama News 58:19-20, Sep 27, 1913
    New York Times p. 11, Sep 23, 1913
                   p. 11, Jun 2, 1914
                   p. 3, Apr 2, 1919
                   p. 25, Jan 8, 1930
                   IX, p. 1, May 19, 1935
                   p. 30, May 28, 1935
    Newsweek 5:22-3, Jun 8, 1935
    Stage 12:6-9, May 1935
          12:32-5, Jul 1935
    Theatre Magazine 18:161+, Nov 1913

<u>The Song and Dance Man</u>
  Productions:
    Opened December 31, 1923 for 96 performances.
    Opened June 16, 1930 for 16 performances.
  Reviews:
    Metropolitan Magazine 59:38+, Apr 1924
    New York Times p. 21, Jan 1, 1924
                   VIII, p. 1, Jun 15, 1930
                   p. 25, Jun 17, 1930
    Theatre Magazine 39:16, Mar 1924

<u>The Tavern</u>
  Productions:
    Opened May 23, 1921 for 27 performances.
    Opened May 19, 1930 for 32 performances.
    (Off Broadway) Opened April 3, 1962 for 11 per-
      formances (APA Repertory).

COHAN, GEORGE M. (cont.)
  The Tavern (cont.)
      (Off Broadway) Opened March 5, 1964 for 12 per-
    formances (Association of Producing Artists).
  Reviews:
    Commonweal 12:134-5, Jun 4, 1930
    Dramatic Mirror p. 591, Oct 2, 1920
                    83:929, May 28, 1921
    Life (NY) 76:680, Oct 14, 1920
              77:840, Jun 9, 1921
              95:18, Jun 6, 1930
    New Republic 146:38, May 14, 1962
    New York Clipper 68:29, Oct 6, 1920
                     69:23, Jun 1, 1921
    New York Times VI, p. 1, Oct 10, 1920
                       p. 20, May 18, 1921
                       p. 20, May 24, 1921
                       VIII, p. 1, May 18, 1930
                       p. 32, May 20, 1930
                       VIII, p. 4, Nov 16, 1930
                       p. 29, Apr 5, 1962
                       p. 39, Mar 6, 1964
    New Yorker 38:108, Apr 14, 1962
    Outlook 155:193, Jun 4, 1930
    Saturday Review 45:38, Apr 28, 1962
    Theatre Magazine 32:370+, Dec 1930
                     52:40-41, Jul 1930

  The Voice of McConnell
    Productions:
      Opened December 25, 1918 for 30 performances.
    Reviews:
      Dramatic Mirror 80:48, Jan 11, 1919
      Forum 61:246, Feb 1919
      Life (NY) 73:56, Jan 9, 1919
      New York Times p. 9, Dec 26, 1918
      Theatre Magazine 29:79+, Feb 1919

  Whispering Friends
    Productions:
      Opened February 20, 1928 for 112 performances.
    Reviews:
      Life (NY) 91:19, Mar 22, 1928
      New York Times p. 18, Feb 21, 1928

CONKLE, E. P.

Afternoon Storm
    Productions:
        Opened April 11, 1948 for 8 performances.
    Reviews:
        New York Times p. 24, Apr 12, 1948

Minnie Field
    Productions:
        (Off Broadway) Season of 1940-41.
    No Reviews

Prologue to Glory
    Productions:
        Opened March 17, 1938 for 70 performances.
        Reopened September 19, 1938 for 99 performances.
    Reviews:
        Catholic World 147:213-14, May 1938
        Commonweal 27:636, Apr 1, 1938
        Life 4:41-2+, Apr 11, 1938
        Nation 146:395, Apr 2, 1938
        New York Times p. 22, Mar 18, 1938
                       X, p. 1, Mar 27, 1938
        One Act Play Magazine 1:1122-3, Apr 1938
        Theatre Arts 22:329-30, May 1938
        Time 31:24, Mar 28, 1938

200 Were Chosen
    Productions:
        Opened November 20, 1936 for 35 performances.
    Reviews:
        Catholic World 144:472, Jan 1937
        Commonweal 25:162, Dec 4, 1936
        Literary Digest 122:19-20, Dec 5, 1936
        Nation 143:677, Dec 5, 1936
        New York Times XI, p. 3, Nov 15, 1936
                          p. 21, Nov 21, 1936
                       XII, p. 1, Nov 29, 1936
        Newsweek 8:20, Nov 28, 1936
        Survey 26:41, Jan 1937
        Theatre Arts 21:17-18, Jan 1937
        Time 28:54, Nov 30, 1936

What D'You Call It
    Productions:
        Opened March 19, 1940 for 38 performances.

CONKLE, E. P. (cont.)
  What D'You Call It (cont.)
    Reviews:
      New York Times p. 36, Mar 20, 1940

CONNELLY, MARC

  Beggar On Horseback (See entry under Kaufman, George
    S.)

  The Deep Tangled Wildwood (See entry under Kaufman
    George S.)

  Dudley (See entry under Kaufman, George S.)

  Everywhere I Roam (with Arnold Sundguard)
    Productions:
      Opened December 29, 1918 for 13 performances.
    Reviews:
      Catholic World 148:597, Feb 1939
      Commonweal 29:330, Jan 13, 1939
      Nation 148:73-4, Jan 14, 1939
      New York Times p. 15, Apr 22, 1938
                    p. 10, Dec 30, 1938
                    IX, p. 1, Jan 8, 1939
                    IX, p. 2, Jan 15, 1939
                    IX, p. 8, Jan 22, 1939
      Stage 16:39, Jan 1939
      Theatre Arts 23:164, Mar 1939
      Time 33:25, Jan 9, 1939

  The Farmer Takes A Wife (with Frank B. Elser) (Based
    on Walter D. Edmonds' Rome Haul)
    Productions:
      Opened October 30, 1934 for 104 performances.
    Reviews:
      Catholic World 140:340, Dec 1934
      Commonweal 21:122, Nov 23, 1934
      Literary Digest 118:20, Nov 17, 1934
      Nation 139:573, Nov 14, 1934
      New Republic 81:21, Nov 14, 1934
      New York Times p. 17, Oct 9, 1934
                    IX, p. 3, Oct 28, 1934
                    p. 17, Oct 31, 1934
                    IX, p. 1, Nov 11, 1934
                    IX, p. 1, Jan 6, 1935

Newsweek 4:27, Nov 10, 1934
Stage 12:12, Nov 1934
    12:28-9, Dec 1934
Theatre Arts 18:902-3, Dec 1934
Time 24:36+, Nov 12, 1934

The Flowers of Virtue
Productions:
    Opened February 5, 1942 for 4 performances.
Reviews:
    Catholic World 154:732, Mar 1942
    Commonweal 35:437, Feb 20, 1942
    New York Theatre Critics' Reviews 1942:354
    New York Times p. 22, Feb 6, 1942
    New Yorker 17:28, Feb 14, 1942
    Theatre Arts 26:225, Apr 1942

Green Pastures (Based on Roark Bradford's Ol' Man Adam an' His Chillun'.)
Productions:
    Opened February 26, 1930 for 640 performances.
    Opened February 26, 1935 for 73 performances.
    Opened March 15, 1951 for 44 performances.
Reviews:
    Arts and Decoration 33:105, May, 1930
    Bookman 71:340, Jun 1930
        73:294-5, May 1931
    Catholic World 131:210-11, May 1930
        133:596-8, Aug 1931
        173:145, May 1951
    Christian Century 47:1278-81, Oct 22, 1930
        49:1316, Oct 26, 1932
        52:399-401, Mar 27, 1935
    Collier's 85:23+, May 10, 1930
    Commonweal 11:561, Mar 19, 1930
        17:481, Mar 1, 1933
        53:646, Apr 6, 1951
    Dramatist 22:1435-6, Jan 1931
    Ladies Home Journal 52:8-9+, Sep 1935
    Life (NY) 95:18+, Mar 21, 1930
        95:16, May 23, 1930
    Life 30:67-9, Apr 16, 1951
    Literary Digest 104:20-1, Mar 22, 1930
        105:22-3, Jun 21, 1930
        105:18, Jun 28, 1930
        107:19-20, Dec 20, 1930
        119:25, Mar 9, 1935

CONNELLY, MARC (cont.)
Green Pastures (cont.)
           Living Age 338:501, Jun 15, 1930
           Nation 130:376, Mar 26, 1930
                  130:415, Apr 9, 1930
                  130:600, May 21, 1930
                  130:376, 415, Mar 26, 1930
                  172:305, Mar 31, 1951
           National Magazine 59:172, Jan 1931
           New Republic 62:128-9, Mar 18, 1930
                  63:128, Jun 18, 1930
                  63:150-1, Jun 25, 1930
                  124:30, Apr 16, 1951
           New York Theatre Critics' Reviews 1951:312
           New York Times p. 26, Feb 27, 1930
                  IX, p. 1, Mar 9, 1930
                  p. 26, Mar 19, 1930
                  VIII, p. 1, May 18, 1930
                  IX, p. 1, Jun 8, 1930
                  VIII, p. 5, Jun 29, 1930
                  VIII, p. 1, Mar 1, 1931
                  p. 14, Aug 31, 1931
                  p. 17, Aug 3, 1932
                  p. 24, Sep 1, 1932
                  p. 26, Oct 11, 1932
                  p. 17, Oct 17, 1932
                  X, p. 2, Sep 10, 1933
                  p. 24, Oct 5, 1933
                  IX, p. 1, Oct 22, 1933
                  X, p. 3, Jan 7, 1934
                  IX, p. 3, Feb 25, 1934
                  p. 26, Mar 22, 1934
                  X, p. 3, Sep 23, 1934
                  p. 19, Oct 4, 1934
                  VIII, p. 2, Feb 3, 1935
                  p. 16, Feb 27, 1935
                  VIII, p. 2, Mar 3, 1935
                  p. 35, Mar 16, 1951
                  II, p. 1, Apr 1, 1951
           New Yorker 27:56+, Mar 24, 1951
           Newsweek 5:28-9, Mar 9, 1935
                  37:90, Mar 26, 1951
           Outlook 154:429, Mar 12, 1930
           Review of Reviews 81:145, Apr 1930
           Saturday Review 34:28-30, Apr 7, 1951
           School and Society 73:246-7, Apr 21, 1951
           Sketch Book 7:37, May 1930

Survey 64:156, May 1, 1930
Theatre Arts 14:369-70, May 1930
35:22, May 1951
42:64-6+, Nov 1958
Theatre Magazine 51:46, Mar 1930
51:15-16, Apr 1930
51:46, Mar 1930
51:23+, Jun 1930
53:14, Mar 1931
Time 25:35-7, Mar 4, 1935
35:68, Jan 29, 1940
57:67, Mar 26, 1951
Vogue 75:82-3+, May 10, 1930
110:181, Sep 1, 1947

*Hunger's Moon
Reviews:
New York Times II, p. 3, Mar 16, 1958

Merton of the Movies (See entry under Kaufman, George S.)

A Story for Strangers
Productions:
Opened September 21, 1948 for 15 performances.
Reviews:
Commonweal 48:618, Oct 8, 1948
Nation 167:381, Oct 2, 1948
New York Theatre Critics' Review 1948:231
New York Times p. 39, Sep 22, 1948
New Yorker 24:51, Oct 2, 1948
Time 52:59, Oct 4, 1948

To the Ladies (See entry under Kaufman, George S.)

The Wild Man of Borneo (with Herman J. Mankiewicz)
Productions:
Opened September 13, 1927 for 15 performances.
Reviews:
New Republic 52:148-9, Sep 28, 1927
New York Times p. 29, Sep 14, 1927
VIII, p. 1, Sep 25, 1927

The Wisdom Tooth
Productions:
Opened February 15, 1926 for 160 performances.
Reviews:
Bookman 63:341, May 1926

CONNELLY, MARC (cont.)
   The Wisdom Tooth (cont.)
            Dramatist 17:1300-1, Apr 1926
            Independent 116:332, Mar 20, 1926
            Life (NY) 87:22, Mar 18, 1926
            Nation 122:238, Mar 3, 1926
            New Republic 46:45, Mar 3, 1926
            New York Times p. 22, Feb 16, 1926
                        VIII, p. 1, Feb 28, 1926
                        VIII, p. 1, Mar 14, 1926
            Theatre Magazine 43:16, May 1926
                        43:30, May 1926
                        43:26+, Jun 1926
            Vogue 67:117+, Apr 15, 1926

CORMACK, BARTLETT

   *Hey Diddle Diddle
      Reviews:
      New York Times p. 24, Jan 22, 1937

   The Racket
      Productions:
      Opened November 22, 1927 for 119 performances.
      Reviews:
      Life (NY) 90:21, Dec 8, 1927
      New York Times p. 28, Nov 23, 1927
                  IX, p. 1, Dec 18, 1927

COWEN, WILLIAM JOYCE

   Family Portrait (See Coffee, Leonore)

COXE, LOUIS O.

   Billy Budd (with Robert Chapman) (Based on the novel by
      Herman Melville)
      Productions:
      Opened February 10, 1951 for 105 performances.
      (Off Broadway) Season of 1954-55.
      (Off Broadway) Season of 1958-59 (Equity Library
         Theatre)
      Reviews:
      Commonweal 53:518, Mar 2, 1951

Nation 172:189, Feb 24, 1951
New York Theatre Critics' Reviews 1951:353
New York Times p. 18, Feb 12, 1951
           II, p. 1, Feb 18, 1951
           II, p. 1, Apr 15, 1951
           II, p. 1, May 6, 1951
           II, p. 3, Oct 21, 1951
           p. 35, May 4, 1955
           p. 13, Feb 28, 1959
New Yorker 27:70, Feb 17, 1951
Newsweek 37:82-3, Feb 19, 1951
Time 57:68+, Feb 19, 1951

Uniform of Flesh (with R. H. Chapman) (Based on Herman
    Melville's Billy Budd
    Productions:
        (Off Broadway) Season of 1948-49 (Experimental
          Theatre).
    Reviews:
        New York Times p. 15, Jan 31, 1949

The Witchfinders
    Productions:
        (Off Broadway) Season of 1955-56.
    Reviews:
        New York Times p. 22, May 11, 1956

CRAVEN, FRANK

The First Year
    Productions:
        Opened October 20, 1920 for 760 performances.
    Reviews:
        Bookman 53:408-10, Jul 1921
        Current Opinion 70:343-51, Mar 1921
        Dramatic Mirror p. 795, Oct 30, 1920
        Dramatist 12:1055-6, Apr 1921
        Everybody's 44:54-5, Feb 1921
        Hearst 39:21-3+, Mar 1921
        Independent 104:177, Nov 6, 1920
        Life (NY) 76:872, Nov 11, 1920
        New York Clipper 68:28, Oct 27, 1920
        New York Times p. 11, Oct 21, 1920
                VI, p. 1, Oct 31, 1920
                VII, p. 6, Dec 19, 1926
      Theatre Magazine 33:27+, Jan 1921
                33:402+, Jun 1921

CRAVEN, FRANK (cont.)
Money from Home
Productions:
Opened February 28, 1927 for 32 performances.
Reviews:
Life (NY) 89:21, Mar 24, 1927
New York Times p. 30, Mar 1, 1927
Vogue 69:138, May 1, 1927

New Brooms
Productions:
Opened November 17, 1924 for 88 performances.
Reviews:
American Mercury 4:120, Jan 1925
Current Opinion 78:60-65, Jan 1925
New York Times p. 23, Nov 18, 1924
Overland 86:51, Feb 1928
Theatre Magazine 40:16, Feb 1925

The 19th Hole
Productions:
Opened October 11, 1927 for 119 performances.
Reviews:
Life (NY) 90:23, Nov 10, 1927
New York Times VIII, p. 4, Oct 2, 1927
                p. 30, Oct 12, 1927
Outlook 148:23, Jan 4, 1928
Theatre Magazine 46:42-3, Dec 1927
Vogue 70:172, Dec 1, 1927

Spite Corner
Productions:
Opened September 25, 1922 for 121 performances.
Reviews:
Dramatic Mirror 84:85, Jul 16, 1921
Hearst 43:93-5+, Jan 1923
New York Clipper 70:21, Oct 4, 1922
New York Times p. 18, Sep 26, 1922

That's Gratitude
Productions:
Opened September 11, 1930 for 197 performances.
Opened June 16, 1932 for 8 performances.
Reviews:
Arts and Decoration 34:67, Nov 1930
Catholic World 135:595-6, Aug 1932
Drama 21:15-16, Nov 1930

Life (NY) 96:18, Oct 3, 1930
Nation 131:355, Oct 1, 1930
National Magazine 59:138, Dec 1930
New York Times p. 28, Sep 12, 1930
               IX, p. 1, Sep 21, 1930
               p. 23, Feb 2, 1931
               p. 24, Jun 17, 1932
Sketch Book 8:29, Nov 1930
Theatre Magazine 52:24-5, Nov 1930
Vogue 76:116, Nov 10, 1930

This Way Out
   Productions:
      Opened August 30, 1917 for 28 performances.
   Reviews:
      Dramatic Mirror 77:8, Sep 8, 1917
      New York Times p. 8, Aug 31, 1917
      Theatre Magazine 26:206, Oct 1917

Too Many Cooks
   Productions:
      Opened February 24, 1914 for 223 performances.
   Reviews:
      American Magazine 77:105-6, Jun 1914
      American Playwright 3:129-30, Apr 1914
      Book News 32:404, Apr 1914
      Bookman 39:143-5, Apr 1914
      Dramatic Mirror 71:6, Mar 4, 1914
      Dramatist 5:478-9, Jul 1914
      Green Book 11:712-13, May 1914
               11:773-5, May 1914
      Munsey 51:588, Apr 1914
      New York Drama News 59:19, Mar 7, 1914
      New York Times p. 9, Jan 27, 1914
               p. 9, Feb 26, 1914
      Theatre Magazine 19:170-1+, Apr 1914

CROTHERS, RACHEL

As Husbands Go
   Productions:
      Opened March 5, 1931 for 148 performances.
      Opened January 19, 1933 for 148 performances.
   Reviews:
      Arts and Decoration 35:88, May 1931
      Bookman 73:296, May 1931

CROTHERS, RACHEL (cont.)
  As Husbands Go (cont.)
          Catholic World 133:205, May 1931
          Commonweal 13:552-3, Mar 18, 1931
          Drama 21:11, Apr 1931
          Life (NY) 97:25, Mar 27, 1931
          Nation 132:338, Mar 25, 1931
          New York Times p. 26, Mar 6, 1931
                          IX, p. 1, Mar 15, 1931
                          p. 20, Jan 20, 1933
                          p. 24, Jul 2, 1935
          Theatre Arts 15:370-1, May 1931
          Vogue 77:59+, May 1, 1931

  *Bon Voyage
     Reviews:
     New York Times VIII, p. 4, Dec 29, 1929

  Caught Wet
     Productions:
     Opened November 4, 1931 for 13 performances.
     Reviews:
     Catholic World 134:334, Dec 1931
     New York Times p. 29, Nov 5, 1931

  Everyday
     Productions:
     Opened November 16, 1921 for 30 performances.
     Reviews:
     Dramatic Mirror 84:773, Nov 26, 1921
     New York Clipper 69:20, Nov 23, 1921
     New York Times p. 15, Nov 17, 1921

  Expressing Willie
     Productions:
     Opened April 16, 1924 for 69+ performances.
     Reviews:
     American Mercury 2:246, Jun 1924
     Arts and Decoration 21:38, Jul 1924
     Bookman 59:452, Jun 1924
     Classic 19:46+, Aug 1924
     Current Opinion 76:799-807, Jun 1924
     Dramatist XV:1239, Oct 1924
     New York Times p. 22, Apr 17, 1924
                     VIII, p. 1, Apr 27, 1924
                     VIII, p. 1, May 4, 1924
     Theatre Magazine 39:15-16, Jun 1924

39:14, Jul 1924
39:26+, Aug 1924
Woman Citizen ns 8:13, May 17, 1924

He and She
    Productions:
    Opened February 12, 1920 for 28 performances.
    Reviews:
    Dramatic Mirror 82:310, Feb 21, 1920
    Dramatist 11:994-5, Apr 1920
    New York Clipper 68:21, Feb 18, 1920
    New York Times p. 16, Feb 13, 1920
                III, p. 5, Feb 22, 1920
                III, p. 6, Feb 22, 1920
    Review 2:262+, Mar 13, 1920
    Theatre Magazine 31:269-70, Apr 1920

*The Heart of Paddy Whack
    Reviews:
    New York Times p. 13, Nov 24, 1914

A Lady's Virtue
    Productions:
    Opened November 23, 1925 for 136 performances.
    Reviews:
    New York Times p. 28, Nov 24, 1925
                VIII, p. 5, Dec 6, 1925
                VII, p. 2, Feb 21, 1926

Let Us Be Gay
    Productions:
    Opened February 19, 1929 for 132 performances.
    Reviews:
    American Mercury 17:118-9, May 1929
    Arts and Decoration 31:64, May 1929
    Catholic World 129:82-3, Apr 1929
    Commonweal 9:750, May 1, 1929
    Life (NY) 93:20, Mar 22, 1929
    New York Times p. 19, Feb 22, 1929
                X, p. 4, Mar 10, 1929
                p. 18, Jun 29, 1937
    Outlook 151:423, Mar 13, 1929
    Theatre Arts 13:330-3, May 1929
    Theatre Magazine 49:28-9+, Jun 1929

A Little Journey
    Productions:

CROTHERS, RACHEL (cont.)
A Little Journey (cont.)
Opened December 26, 1918 for 252 performances.
Reviews:
Dramatic Mirror 80:47, Jan 11, 1919
Dramatist 11:1001-2, Apr 1920
Hearst 36:42-3+, Aug 1919
Life (NY) 73:57, Jan 9, 1919
73:615, Apr 10, 1919
New York Times p. 9, Dec 27, 1918
Theatre Magazine 29:77+, Feb 1919

A Man's World
Productions:
Opened February 8, 1910 for 71 performances.
Reviews:
Bookman 31:139-42, Apr 1910
Burr McIntosh Monthly 22:394-5, May 1910
Dial 59:326, Oct 14, 1915
Dramatic Mirror 63:6, Feb 19, 1910
Everybody's 22:703+, May 1910
Green Book 3:697, Apr 1910
3:1006-8, May 1910
Hampton 24:579, Apr 1910
Harper's Weekly 54:24, Mar 26, 1910
Life (NY) 55:324, Feb 24, 1910
Metropolitan Magazine 32:266-7, May 1910
Nation 90:146, Feb 10, 1910
Pearson 23:552, Apr 1910
Theatre Magazine 11:68-9, Mar 1910

Mary the Third
Productions:
Opened February 5, 1923 for 152+ performances.
Reviews:
Nation 116:278, Mar 7, 1923
New York Clipper 71:14, Feb 14, 1923
New York Times p. 14, Feb 6, 1923
Scribner's Magazine 74:269, Jul 1923
Theatre Magazine 37:20, Apr 1923

Mother Carey's Chickens (with Kate Douglas Wiggin)
(Based on Miss Wiggin's novel)
Productions:
Opened September 25, 1917 for 39 performances.
Reviews:
Dramatic Mirror 77:7, Oct 16, 1917

Dramatist 9:873-4, Jan 1918
New York Drama News 64:10, Sep 29, 1917
New York Times p. 11, Sep 26, 1917
                III, p. 8, Sep 30, 1917
Theatre Magazine 26:279+, Nov 1917

Nice People
    Productions:
        Opened March 2, 1921 for 120+ performances.
    Reviews:
        Bookman 53:275, May 1921
        Dramatist 15:1201-2, Jan 1924
        Everybody's 45:87-94, Nov 1921
        Hearst 40:25-7+, Jul 1921
        Independent 105:281, Mar 19, 1921
        Life (NY) 77:428, Mar 24, 1921
        New York Clipper 69:23, Mar 9, 1921
        New York Times p. 11, Mar 3, 1921
        Scribner's Magazine 72:105, Jul 1922
        Theatre Magazine 33:339, May 1921
                        34:16+, Jul 1921
        Weekly Review 4:345-6, Apr 13, 1921

Old Lady 31 (Suggested by Louise Forsslund's novel)
    Productions:
        Opened October 30, 1916 for 160 performances.
    Reviews:
        Book News 36:304-5, Apr 1918
        Bookman 44:396-8, Dec 1916
        Collier's 58:8+, Jan 27, 1917
        Current Opinion 61:389-92, Dec 1916
        Dramatic Mirror 76:10, Sep 16, 1916
                        76:7, Nov 11, 1916
        Everybody's 36:65-6, Jan 1917
        Green Book 17:4-5+, Jan 1917
        Life (NY) 68:858-9, Nov 16, 1916
        Nation 103:470, Nov 16, 1916
        New Republic 9:217-18, Dec 23, 1916
        New York Drama News 63:14, Nov 4, 1916
        New York Times p. 11, Oct 31, 1916
                        II, p. 6, Nov 5, 1916
        Theatre Magazine 24:357, Dec 1916
        Woman's Home Companion 44:45, Apr 1917

Once Upon A Time
    Productions:
        Opened April 15, 1918 for 24 performances.

CROTHERS, RACHEL (cont.)
Once Upon A Time (cont.)
Reviews:
Dramatic Mirror 78:584-5, Apr 27, 1918
Green Book 20:14-17, Jul 1918
New York Times p. 11, Apr 16, 1918

Ourselves
Productions:
Opened November 12, 1913 for 29 performances.
Reviews:
Bookman 38:496-9, Jan 1914
Dramatic Mirror 70:6-7, Nov 19, 1913
Dramatist 5:421-2, Jan 1914
Everybody's 30:264, Feb 1914
Green Book 11:346-7, Feb 1914
Harper's Weekly 58:12-17, Dec 6, 1913
                58:26, Jan 10, 1914
Life (NY) 62:922-3, Nov 27, 1913
Munsey 51:124, Feb 1914
New York Drama News 58:20, Nov 22, 1913
New York Times p. 13, Nov 11, 1913
                p. 11, Nov 14, 1913
Theatre Magazine 18:xviii+, Dec 1913

*Rector
Reviews:
New York Times p. 7, Apr 26, 1926

Revenge, or the Pride of Lilian LeMar
Productions:
Opened February 25, 1913 for one matinee.
No reviews.

Susan and God
Productions:
Opened October 7, 1937 for 288 performances.
Opened December 13, 1944 for 8 performances.
Reviews:
Catholic World 146:219-20, Nov 1937
Commonweal 26:606, Oct 22, 1937
Independent Woman 16:351, Nov 1937
Life 4:31, Feb 21, 1938
Literary Digest 123:20+, May 15, 1937
                125:21, Jan 8, 1939
Nation 145:455-6, Oct 23, 1937
New Republic 92:342, Oct 27, 1937

New York Times II, p. 12, Apr 11, 1937
　　　　　　　　X, p. 2, Apr 25, 1937
　　　　　　　　p. 26, Oct 8, 1937
　　　　　　　　XI, p. 1, Oct 17, 1937
　　　　　　　　XI, p. 3, Nov 7, 1937
　　　　　　　　p. 29, Jun 8, 1938
　　　　　　　　X, p. 10, Jun 12, 1938
　　　　　　　　p. 17, Nov 24, 1943
　　　　　　　　II, p. 3, Dec 12, 1943
　　　　　　　　p. 30, Dec 14, 1943
Newsweek 10:25, Oct 25, 1937
Stage 15:7-8, Mar 1938
Theatre Arts 21:918-19, Dec 1937
Time 30:36, Oct 18, 1937

*Talent

Reviews:
New York Times p. 18, Aug 4, 1933
　　　　　　　　IX, p. 3, Dec 31, 1933

39 East

Productions:
Opened March 31, 1919 for 160 performances.
Reviews:
Dramatist 11:987, Jan 1920
Forum 61:629, May 1919
Independent 102:309, Jun 5, 1920
New York Times p. 9, Apr 1, 1919
Review 1:131-2, Jun 21, 1919
Theatre Magazine 29:275+, May 1919

Venus

Productions:
Opened December 26, 1927 for 8 performances.
Reviews:
New York Times p. 26, Dec 26, 1927

When It Strikes Home (See Ourselves)

When Ladies Meet

Productions:
Opened October 6, 1932 for 173 performances.
Opened Spring, 1933 for 18 performances.
Reviews:
Catholic World 136:208-9, Nov 1932
Commonweal 16:621, Oct 26, 1932
Nation 135:408, Oct 26, 1932

CROTHERS, RACHEL (cont.)
    When Ladies Meet (cont.)
            New Outlook 161:46, Nov 1932
            New York Times IX, p. 1, Aug 14, 1932
                            p. 19, Oct 7, 1932
                            IX, p. 1, Oct 16, 1932
                            p. 15, Apr 27, 1933
            Player's Magazine 9:20, Nov-Dec, 1932
            Stage 10:11, Nov 1932
                    10:8-9, Dec 1932
            Theatre Arts 16:958, Dec 1932
            Town and Country 87:22-3, Nov 1, 1932
            Vogue 80:61, Dec 1, 1932

    Young Wisdom
        Productions:
            Opened January 5, 1914 for 56 performances.
        Reviews:
            American Playwright 3:6-7, Jan 1914
            Book News 32:403-4, Apr 1914
            Bookman 39:66, Mar 1914
            Collier's 52:24, Feb 21, 1914
            Dramatic Mirror 71:10, Jan 7, 1914
            Green Book 11:408-10, Mar 1914
                        11:525-6, Mar 1914
            Harper's Weekly 58:5, Jan 31, 1914
            Life (NY) 63:150-1, Jan 22, 1914
            Munsey 51:341, Mar 1914
            New York Drama News 58:13, Jan 10, 1914
            New York Times p. 6, Jan 6, 1914
            Theatre Magazine 19:60-1+, Feb 1914

CROUSE, RUSSEL

    The Great Sebastians (See entry under Lindsay, Howard)

    I'd Rather Be Right (See State of the Union)

    Life With Father (See entry under Lindsay, Howard)

    Life With Mother (See entry under Lindsay, Howard)

    The Prescott Proposals (See entry under Lindsay, Howard)

    Remains to be Seen (See entry under Lindsay, Howard)

State of Union (See entry under Lindsay, Howard)

Strip for Action (See entry under Lindsay, Howard)

Tall Story (See entry under Lindsay, Howard)

CROWLEY, MART

The Boys in the Band
    Productions:
        (Off Broadway) Opened April 15, 1968 for 1,002
            performances
    Reviews:
        America 118:652, May 11, 1968
        Commonweal 88:335, May 31, 1968
        Life 64:18, May 24, 1968
        Nation 206:580, Apr 29, 1968
        New York Times p. 48, Apr 15, 1968
                        II, p. 1, Apr 28, 1968
                        II, p. 3, Sep 29, 1968
                        p. 52, Feb 13, 1969
                        p. 36, Feb 18, 1969
                        II, p. 23, Jun 1, 1969
                        p. 21, Sep 20, 1969
                        p. 34, Apr 18, 1970
        New Yorker 44:84+, Apr 27, 1968
        Newsweek 71:93-4, Apr 29, 1968
        Saturday Review 51:26, May 11, 1968
        Time 91:97, Apr 26, 1968
        Vogue 152:64, Aug 1, 1968

CUMMINGS, E. E.

Him
    Productions:
        Opened April 18, 1928 for 27 performances.
    Reviews:
        Dial 85:77-81, Jul 1928
        New Republic 54:325-6, May 2, 1928
                     54:383, May 16, 1928
                     119:26, Aug 9, 1948
        New York Times IX, p. 4, Apr 15, 1928
                        p. 23, Apr 19, 1928
                        IX, p. 1, Apr 22, 1928
                        IX, p. 2, Apr 27, 1928

CUMMINGS, E. E. (cont.)
  Him (cont.)
        Theatre Arts 12:392-3, Jun 1928
        Vogue 71:98, Jun 15, 1928

  Santa Claus
      Productions:
        (Off Broadway) Season of 1956-57 (ANTA).
        (Off Broadway) Season of 1960-61.
      Reviews:
        New York Times p. 42, Dec 18, 1957
                       p. 13, Jul 22, 1960

DALY, AUGUSTIN

  Under the Gaslight
      Productions:
        Opened April 2, 1929 for 23 performances.
        (Off Broadway) Opened December 8, 1967 for 9 per-
          formances (Equity Theatre).
      Reviews:
        Life (NY) 93:20, Apr 26, 1929
        New York Times p. 27, Apr 3, 1929

DAVIS, J. FRANK

  The Ladder
      Productions:
        Opened October 22, 1926 for 789 performances.
      Reviews:
        Collier's 81:17+, Feb 18, 1928
        New York Times p. 15, Oct 23, 1926
                       p. 28, Dec 20, 1926
                       p. 30, Dec 26, 1926
                       p. 30, Jan 9, 1927
                       p. 30, Apr 5, 1927
                       VII, p. 2, Aug 28, 1927
                       p. 24, Oct 7, 1927
                       p. 28, Nov 23, 1927
                       p. 22, Nov 24, 1927
                       p. 24, Nov 25, 1927
                       p. 29, Dec 9, 1927
                       p. 19, Feb 22, 1928
                       p. 8, Feb 26, 1928
                       p. 25, Jul 12, 1928

VIII, p. 1, Jul 15, 1928
p. 24, Aug 22, 1928
p. 20. Aug 23, 1928
p. 21, Nov 10, 1928
p. 30, Nov 11, 1928
p. 26, Nov 14, 1928
Outlook 149:63, May 9, 1928
Theatre Arts 48:15-16+, Nov 1928

DAVIS, OSSIE

Purlie Victorious
    Productions:
        Opened September 28, 1961 for 261 performances.
        (Off Broadway) Opened March 7, 1969 for 9 per-
            formances (Equity Library Theater).
    Reviews:
        America 106:376, Dec 9, 1961
        Ebony 17:55-6+, Mar 1962
        Nation 193:254-5, Oct 14, 1961
        New Republic 145:22, Nov 6, 1961
        New York Theatre Critics' Reviews 1961:256
        New York Times II, p. 1, Sep 24, 1961
                        p. 29, Sep 29, 1961
                    II, p. 1, Oct 8, 1961
        New Yorker 37:130, Oct 7, 1961
        Reporter 25:52, Oct 26, 1961
        Saturday Review 44:78, Oct 14, 1961
        Theatre Arts 45:12, Dec 1961
        Time 78:88, Oct 6, 1961

DAVIS, OWEN

Any House
    Productions:
        Opened February 14, 1916 for 16 performances.
    Reviews:
        Dramatic Mirror 75:8, Feb 19, 1916
                        75:4, Feb 26, 1916
                        75:2, Mar 4, 1916
        New York Dramatic News 62:17-18, Feb 9, 1916
        New York Times p. 9, Feb 15, 1916
                    II, p. 7, Feb 20, 1916

DAVIS, OWEN (cont.)
  At 9:45
    Productions:
      Opened June 28, 1919 for 139 performances.
    Reviews:
      Dramatist 10:967-8, Oct 1919
      Forum 62:243, Aug 1919
      Independent 99:169, Aug 9, 1919
      New York Times p. 16, Jun 30, 1919
      Theatre Magazine 30:81+, Aug 1919

  Beware of Widows
    Productions:
      Opened December 1, 1925 for 55 performances.
    Reviews:
      Life (NY) 86:18, Dec 24, 1925
      New York Times p. 22, Dec 2, 1925
      Vogue 67:108+, Feb 1, 1926

  *The Big Deal
    Reviews:
      New York Times p. 13, Mar 7, 1953

  Big Jim Garrity
    Productions:
      Opened October 16, 1914 for 27 performances.
    Reviews:
      American Playwright 3:371-3, Nov 1914
      Dramatic Mirror 72:8, Oct 28, 1914
      Green Book 12:1095-1107, Dec 1914
      Munsey 53:557, Dec 1914
      New York Dramatic News 60:16-17, Oct 24, 1914
      New York Times p. 11, Oct 17, 1914

  The Bronx Express (Adapted from the Russian of Ossip
      Dymow)
    Productions:
      Opened April 26, 1922 for 58+ performances.
    Reviews:
      Life (NY) 79:18, May 18, 1922
      New York Clipper 70:20, May 3, 1922
      New York Times p. 12, Apr 27, 1922
      Theatre Magazine 36:7+, Jul 1922

  Carry On
    Productions:
      Opened January 23, 1928 for 8 performances.

114

Reviews:
    New York Times p. 26, Jan 24, 1928
    Vogue 71:158, Mar 15, 1928

*Coming Spring
    Reviews:
    New York Times X, p. 2, Sep 23, 1934

The Detour
    Productions:
    Opened August 23, 1921 for 48 performances.
    Reviews:
    Bookman 54:147-8, Oct 1921
    Current Opinion 71:603-12, Nov 1921
    Dramatic Mirror 84:85, Jul 16, 1921
                     84:305, Aug 21, 1921
    Dramatist 13:1119, Jul 1922
    Independent 106:113, Sep 17, 1921
    Life (NY) 78:18, Sep 15, 1921
    Nation 113:299, Sep 14, 1921
    New York Clipper 69:17, Aug 31, 1921
    New York Times p. 12, Aug 24, 1921
                   VI, p. 1, Sep 24, 1921
    Theatre Magazine 34:313, Nov 1921

The Donovan Affair
    Productions:
    Opened August 30, 1926 for 128 performances.
    Reviews:
    Independent 117:421, Oct 9, 1926
    Life 88:21, Sep 23, 1926
    New York Times p. 15, Aug 31, 1926
    Theatre Magazine 44:16+, Nov 1926
    Vogue 68:90-91, Nov 1, 1926

*Dread
    Reviews:
    New York Times IX, p. 2, Oct 27, 1929

Dreams for Sale
    Productions:
    Opened September 13, 1922 for 13 performances.
    Reviews:
    New York Clipper 70:22, Sep 20, 1922
    New York Times p. 24, Sep 14, 1922

115

DAVIS, OWEN (cont.)
  Easy Come, Easy Go
      Productions:
        Opened October 26, 1925 for 180 performances.
      Reviews:
        Life (NY) 68:20, Nov 19, 1925
        New York Times p. 20, Oct 27, 1925

  Ethan Frome (with Donald Davis) (Based on Edith Wharton's
        novel)
      Productions:
        Opened January 21, 1936 for 120 performances.
        (Off Broadway) Opened July 7, 1947 (On Stage).
      Reviews:
        Catholic World 142:723-4, Mar 1936
        Commonweal 23:414, Feb 7, 1936
        Literary Digest 121:19, Feb 1, 1936
        Nation 142:167-8, Feb 5, 1936
        New Republic 86:78, Feb 26, 1936
        New York Times p. 24, Jan 7, 1936
                       p. 15, Jan 22, 1936
                       IX, p. 1, Feb 2, 1936
                       X, p. 3, Feb 9, 1936
        Newsweek 7:33, Feb 1, 1936
        Player's Magazine 14:28, Dec 1937
        Stage 13:20-25, Feb 1936
              13:37, Mar 1936
        Theatre Arts 20:181-2, Mar 1936
        Time 27:25, Feb 3, 1936
        Vogue 37:50, Feb 15, 1936

  The Family Cupboard
      Productions:
        Opened August 21, 1913 for 140 performances
      Reviews:
        American Playwright 2:281-3, Sep 1913
        Blue Book 18:10-12+, Nov 1913
        Bookman 38:134, Oct 1913
        Current Opinion 55:325-8, Nov 1913
        Dramatic Mirror 70:6, Aug 27, 1913
                        70:5, Nov 12, 1913
        Dramatist 5:415, Oct 1913
        Everybody's 29:684, Nov 1913
        Green Book 10:722-3, Nov 1913
                   10:866-7, Nov 1913
                   10:1043-57, Dec 1913
        Munsey 50:297, Nov 1913

New York Times p. 9, Aug 22, 1913
Theatre Magazine 18:x-xi, Oct 1913

Forever After
  Productions:
  Opened September 9, 1918 for 312 performances.
  Reviews:
  Dramatic Mirror 79:301, Aug 31, 1918
                  79:434-5, Sep 21, 1918
  Life (NY) 72:417, Sep 19, 1918
  New York Times p. 11, Sep 10, 1918
                  IV, p. 2, Sep 22, 1918

Gentle Grafters
  Productions:
  Opened October 27, 1926 for 13 performances.
  Reviews:
  New York Times p. 23, Oct 28, 1926

The Good Earth (with Donald Davis and Pearl Buck)
  Productions:
  Opened October 17, 1932 for 56 performances.
  Reviews:
  Arts and Decoration 38:57, Dec 1932
  Catholic World 136:338-9, Dec 1932
  Commonweal 17:23-4, Nov 2, 1932
  Literary Digest 114:17, Nov 5, 1932
  Nation 135:438, Nov 2, 1932
  New Outlook 161:47, Dec 1932
  New Republic 72:330-1, Nov 2, 1932
               73:19-20, Nov 16, 1932
  New York Times IX, p. 1, Sep 25, 1932
                 p. 23, Oct 18, 1932
                 IX, p. 1, Oct 23, 1932
  Stage 10:13-16, Nov 1932
  Theatre Arts 17:16-17, Jan 1933
  Town and Country 87:22, Nov 15, 1932
  Vogue 80:61+, Dec 1, 1932

The Great Gatsby (Adapted from the novel by F. Scott
      Fitzgerald)
  Productions:
  Opened February 2, 1926 for 112 performances.
  Reviews:
  Bookman 63:216, Apr 1926
  Life (NY) 87:21, Mar 4, 1926
            88:24, Dec 16, 1926

DAVIS, OWEN (cont.)
The Great Gatsby (cont.)
Nation 122:211-12, Feb 24, 1926
New Republic 46:145, Mar 24, 1926
New York Times p. 22, Feb 3, 1926
VII, p. 1, Feb 7, 1926
Theatre Magazine 43:19+, Apr 1926
Vogue 67:126, Apr 1, 1926

*Harbor Light
Reviews:
New York Times IX, p. 2, Aug 7, 1932

The Haunted House
Productions:
Opened September 2, 1924 for 103 performances.
Reviews:
New York Times p. 12, Sep 3, 1924
Theatre Magazine 39:19+, Nov 1924

Home Fires
Productions:
Opened August 20, 1923 for 48 performances.
Reviews:
Bookman 58:181-2, Oct 1923
Life (NY) 82:20, Sep 6, 1923
New York Times VI, p. 1, Sep 2, 1923
Theatre Magazine 38:16+, Oct 1923

Icebound
Productions:
Opened February 10, 1923 for 145+ performances.
Reviews:
Bookman 57:317-18, May 1923
58:59:60, Sep 1923
Current Opinion 74:574-9, May 1923
Hearst 44:85-7+, Sep 1923
Life (NY) 81:18, Mar 1, 1923
New York Clipper 71:14, Feb 21, 1923
New York Times p. 16, Feb 12, 1923
Theatre Magazine 37:20, Apr 1923
37:28+, May 1923

The Insect Comedy (See The World We Live In)

Jezebel
Productions:

Opened December 19, 1933 for 32 performances.
Reviews:
Catholic World 138:604-5, Feb 1934
Commonweal 19:273, Jan 5, 1934
Nation 138:28, Jan 3, 1934
New Republic 77:226, Jan 3, 1934
New York Times p. 26, Dec 20, 1933
Newsweek 2:30, Dec 30, 1933
Stage 11:19-21, Feb 1934
Theatre Arts 18:95-7, Feb 1934
Time 23:23, Jan 1, 1934

Just to Remind You
Productions:
Opened September 7, 1931 for 16 performances.
Reviews:
Arts and Decoration 36:73, Nov 1931
Literary Digest 110:15, Sep 26, 1931
Nation 133:316, Sep 23, 1931
New York Times p. 39, Sep 8, 1931
Outlook 159:119, Sep 23, 1931
Theatre Arts 15:891-2, Nov 1931
Vogue 78:68+, Nov 1, 1931

Lazybones
Productions:
Opened September 22, 1924 for 79 performances.
Reviews:
New York Times p. 23, Sep 23, 1924

Making Good
Productions:
Opened February 5, 1912 for 8 performances.
Reviews:
American Playwright 1:71-5, Mar 1912
Dramatic Mirror 67:7, Feb 7, 1912
Theatre Magazine 15:xiv-xv, Mar 1912

Marry the Poor Girl
Productions:
Opened September 25, 1920 for 18 performances.
Reviews:
Dramatic Mirror p. 591, Oct 2, 1920
New York Clipper 68:19, Sep 29, 1920
New York Times p. 18, Sep 27, 1920

DAVIS, OWEN (cont.)

Mile-a-Minute Kendall
Productions:
Opened November 28, 1916 for 47 performances.
Reviews:
Dramatic Mirror 76:7+, Dec 9, 1916
Dramatist 8:763-4, Jan 1917
Green Book 17:204-7, Feb 1917
New York Times p. 9, Nov 29, 1916
Theatre Magazine 25:23, Jan 1917

Mr. and Mrs. North (Based on the stories by Frances
and Richard Lockridge)
Productions:
Opened January 12, 1941 for 163 performances.
Reviews:
Catholic World 152:727-8, Mar 1941
Commonweal 33:375, Jan 31, 1941
Nation 152:109, Jan 25, 1941
New Republic 104:116, Jan 27, 1941
New York Theatre Critics' Reviews 1941:413
New York Times p. 11, Jan 13, 1941
                IX, p. 1, Feb 23, 1941
Stage 1:25, Feb 1941
Theatre Arts 25:189, Mar 1941

The Nervous Wreck (Based on a story by E. J. Rath)
Productions:
Opened October 9, 1923 for 279 performances.
Reviews:
Bookman 58:439-40, Dec 1923
Classic 19:46, Mar 1924
Dramatist 15:1206-7, Apr 1924
Life (NY) 82:20, Nov 1, 1923
New York Times p. 16, Oct 10, 1923
                VIII, p. 1, Oct 21, 1923
                VIII, p. 2, Oct 19, 1924
                p. 28, Dec 16, 1924
                X, p. 4, Dec 9, 1928
Theatre Magazine 38:68+, Dec 1923

The 9th Guest
Productions:
Opened August 25, 1930 for 72 performances.
Reviews:
Life (NY) 96:16, Sep 12, 1930
National Magazine 59:137, Dec 1930

120

New York Times p. 24, Aug 26, 1930
Outlook 156:71, Sep 10, 1930
Vogue 76:116, Oct 13, 1930

No Way Out
Productions:
Opened October 30, 1944 for 8 performances.
Reviews:
New York Theatre Critics' Reviews 1944:100
New York Times p. 23, Oct 31, 1944

Opportunity
Productions:
Opened July 30, 1920 for 138 performances.
Reviews:
Dramatic Mirror p. 229, Aug 7, 1920
New York Clipper 68:23, Aug 4, 1920
New York Times p. 5, Jul 31, 1920
Theatre Magazine 32:188, Oct 1920

*Peacocks
Reviews:
New York Times VIII, p. 2, Mar 2, 1924

*Robin Hood and his Merry Men
Reviews:
New York Times IV, p. 7, Apr 26, 1914

Sandalwood (with Fulton Oursler)
Productions:
Opened September 22, 1926 for 39 performances.
Reviews:
Bookman 64:480-1, Dec 1926
Life (NY) 88:23, Oct 14, 1926
Nation 123:384-5, Oct 13, 1926
New York Times p. 23, Sep 23, 1926
                 VIII, p. 1, Oct 3, 1926
Theatre Magazine 44:15, Nov 1926
Vogue 68:79+, Nov 15, 1926

A Saturday Night
Productions:
Opened February 28, 1933 for 40 performances.
Reviews:
Arts and Decoration 38:49+, Apr 1933
Catholic World 137:78-9, Apr 1933
Commonweal 17:553, Mar 15, 1933

DAVIS, OWEN (cont.)
A Saturday Night (cont.)
Nation 136:300, Mar 15, 1933
New Outlook 161:47, Apr 1933
New York Times p. 13, Mar 1, 1933
IX, p. 1, Mar 19, 1933
Theatre Arts 17:343, May 1933
Vanity Fair 40:32+, May 1933
Vogue 81:84, May 1, 1933

The Scrap of Paper (with Arthur Somers Roche)
Productions:
Opened September 17, 1917 for 40 performances.
Reviews:
Dramatic Mirror 77:4+, Sep 29, 1917
Life (NY) 70:549, Oct 4, 1917
New York Times p. 7, Sep 18, 1917
Theatre Magazine 26:278, Nov 1917

Sinners
Productions:
Opened January 7, 1915 for 220 performances.
Reviews:
American Playwright 4:41-4, Feb 1915
Bookman 40:641-2, Feb 1915
Current Opinion 58:177, Mar 1915
Dramatic Mirror 73:8, Jan 13, 1915
Dramatist 7:648-9, Jan 1916
Green Book 13:477-8, Mar 1915
13:619-33, Apr 1915
Hearst 27:440-3, May 1915
Life (NY) 65:112-13, Jan 21, 1915
Munsey 54:338-9, Mar 1915
Nation 100:61, Jan 14, 1915
New York Drama News 60:14-15, Jan 16, 1915
New York Times p. 11, Jan 8, 1915
Smart Set 45:285-6, Mar 1915
Theatre Magazine 21:101, Feb 1915

The Snark Was A Boojum (Based on Richard Shattuck's
novel)
Productions:
Opened September 1, 1943 for 5 performances.
Reviews:
New York Theatre Critics' Reviews 1943:288
New York Times p. 14, Sep 2, 1943
New Yorker 19:44, Sep 11, 1943

Spring Freshet
    Productions:
        Opened October 4, 1934 for 12 performances.
    Reviews:
        New York Times p. 19, Oct 2, 1934
                        p. 28, Oct 5, 1934
        Vanity Fair 43:46, Dec 1934

*Ten Minute Alibi
    Reviews:
        New York Times p. 24, Jun 11, 1935
                        p. 19, Jul 20, 1937

Those Who Walk In Darkness
    Productions:
        Opened August 14, 1919 for 28 performances.
    Reviews:
        New York Times p. 12, Aug 15, 1919
                        VI, p. 2, Aug 24, 1919
        Theatre Magazine 30:224-5, Oct 1919

Tonight at 12
    Productions:
        Opened November 13, 1928 for 60 performances.
    Reviews:
        New York Times p. 28, Nov 16, 1928
        Theatre Magazine 49:45, Jan 1929
        Vogue 73:67+, Jan 5, 1929

Too Many Boats (Based on a novel by Charles L. Clifford)
    Productions:
        Opened September 11, 1934 for 7 performances.
    Reviews:
        New York Times p. 26, Sep 12, 1934
        Vogue 84:74, Oct 15, 1934

The Triumphant Bachelor
    Productions:
        Opened September 15, 1927 for 12 performances.
    Reviews:
        New York Times p. 21, Sep 16, 1927

*Two Time Mary
    Reviews:
        New York Times p. 20, Aug 3, 1937

DAVIS, OWEN (cont.)
Up the Ladder
Productions:
Opened March 6, 1922 for 117+ performances.
Reviews:
Dramatist 13:1106-7, Apr 1922
New York Clipper 70:20, Mar 29, 1922
New York Times p. 11, Mar 7, 1922

What Happened to Mary
Productions:
Opened March 24, 1913 for 56 performances.
Reviews:
American Playwright 2:115-16, Apr 1913
Blue Book 17:448-50, Jul 1913
Dramatic Mirror 69:6, Mar 26, 1913
Dramatist 4:343, Apr 1913
Green Book 9:932-4+, Jun 1913
9:1079-80, Jun 1913
Life (NY) 61:734, Apr 10, 1913
New York Drama News 57:20-21, Mar 29, 1913
New York Times p. 8, Mar 25, 1913
Red Book 21:315-17, Jun 1913
Theatre Magazine 17:130, May 1913

*Wife's Away
Reviews:
New York Times IX, p. 3, Nov 23, 1930

The World We Live In (The Insect Comedy) (Adapted from
the play by Josef and Karel Capek)
Productions:
Opened October 31, 1922 for 111 performances.
Opened June 3, 1948 for 14 performances.
Reviews:
Bookman 56:610-11, Jan 1923
Catholic World 116:501-3, Jan 1923
Commonweal 43:235, Jun 18, 1948
Drama 13:130-1, Jun 1923
Forum 110:20-2, Jul 1948
Independent 109:320-1, Nov 25, 1922
Living Age 313:617-20, Jun 3, 1922
Nation 115:556, Nov 22, 1922
New Republic 118:28-9, Jun 21, 1948
New York Clipper 70:20, Nov 8, 1922
New York Times p. 16, Nov 1, 1922
p. 26, Jun 4, 1948
School and Society 67:478, Jun 26, 1948

DAYTON, KATHERINE

First Lady (with George S. Kaufman)
    Productions:
        Opened November 26, 1935 for 246 performances.
        Opened May 28, 1952 for 16 performances.
    Reviews:
        Catholic World 142:468-9, Jan 1936
                     175:309, Jul 1952
        Commonweal 23:188, Dec 13, 1935
                 56:269, Jun 20, 1952
        Literary Digest 120:20, Dec 7, 1935
        Nation 141:694+, Dec 11, 1935
        New Republic 85:175, Dec 18, 1935
        New York Theatre Critics' Reviews 1952:273
        New York Times p. 21, Nov 11, 1935
                    p. 17, Nov 17, 1935
                    X, p. 3, Dec 8, 1935
                    p. 17, Oct 9, 1937
                    p. 16, May 23, 1952
                    II, p. 3, May 25, 1952
                    p. 18, May 29, 1952
        Newsweek 6:41, Dec 7, 1935
        Stage 13:22+, Jan 1936
        Theatre Arts 20:16+, Jan 1936
                 20:379-83, May 1936
                 36:72, Aug 1952
        Time 26:52, Dec 9, 1935

Save Me the Waltz
    Productions:
        Opened February 28, 1938 for 8 performances.
    Reviews:
        Commonweal 27:608, Mar 25, 1938
        Nation 146:310, Mar 12, 1938
        New York Times p. 19, Mar 1, 1938
        Newsweek 11:22, Mar 14, 1938
        Stage 15:26, Mar 1938

DELL, FLOYD

Cloudy With Showers (with Thomas Mitchell)
    Productions:
        Opened September 1, 1931 for 71 performances.
    Reviews:
        Arts & Decorations 36:51, Nov 1931

DELL, FLOYD (cont.)
Cloudy With Showers (cont.)
    Life (NY) 98:18, Sep 18, 1931
    New York Times VIII, p. 2, Aug 23, 1931
                     p. 17, Sep 2, 1931
                 VIII, p. 3, Oct 4, 1931
    Outlook 159:86, Sep 16, 1931
    Sketch Book 8:21, Oct 1931

Little Accident (with Thomas Mitchell)
    Productions:
    Opened October 9, 1928 for 303 performances.
    Reviews:
    Commonweal 9:431, Feb 13, 1929
    Life (NY) 92:21, Nov 2, 1928
    New York Times p. 32, Oct 10, 1928
    Outlook 150:1031, Oct 24, 1928
    Theatre Magazine 48:46-7, Dec 1928
    Vogue 72:76-7, Nov 24, 1928

*Sweet and Twenty
    Reviews:
    New York Times p. 28, Nov 8, 1921

DENKER, HENRY

A Case of Libel (Based on Louis Nizer's My Life in
    Court)

    Productions:
    Opened October 10, 1963 for 242 performances.
    Reviews:
    America 109:751, Dec 7, 1963
    Commonweal 79:194, Nov 8, 1963
    Nation 197:306+, Nov 9, 1963
    New York Theatre Critics' Reviews 1963:244
    New York Times p. 43, Oct 11, 1963
                     II, p. 1, Oct 27, 1963
                     p. 79, Feb 12, 1968
    New Yorker 39:99, Oct 19, 1963
    Newsweek 62:104, Oct 21, 1963
    Saturday Review 46:18, Nov 2, 1963
    Theatre Arts 48:66, Jan 1964
    Time 82:78, Oct 18, 1963

A Far Country
    Productions:

Opened April 4, 1961 for 271 performances.
Reviews:
America 105-408+, Jun 3, 1961
Nation 192:359, Apr 22, 1961
New Republic 144:20-2, Apr 17, 1961
New York Theatre Critics' Reviews 1961:310
New York Times II, p. 3, Mar 26, 1961
            p. 32, Apr 5, 1961
            II, p. 1, Apr 16, 1961
New Yorker 37:76, Apr 15, 1961
Newsweek 57:69, Apr 17, 1961
Saturday Review 44:31, Apr 22, 1961
Theatre Arts 45:28-9, Jun 1961
Time 77:106, Apr 14, 1961
Vogue 138:22, Sep 1, 1961

Time Limit! (With Ralph Berkey)
Productions:
Opened January 24, 1956 for 127 performances.
Reviews:
America 94:599, Feb 25, 1956
Commonweal 63:542-3, Feb 24, 1956
Life 40:65-6+, Feb 6, 1956
Nation 182:125-6, Feb 11, 1956
New York Theatre Critics' Reviews 1956:381
New York Times II, p. 1, Jan 22, 1956
            p. 27, Jan 25, 1956
            II, p. 1, Feb 5, 1956
New Yorker 31:60, Feb 4, 1956
Newsweek 47:42, Feb 6, 1956
Saturday Review 39:22, Feb 11, 1956
Theatre Arts 40:17, Apr 1956
Time 67:67, Feb 6, 1956

Venus At Large
Productions:
Opened April 12, 1962 for 4 performances.
Reviews:
New York Theatre Critics' Reviews 1962:296
New York Times p. 30, Apr 13, 1962
New Yorker 38:85, Apr 21, 1962
Saturday Review 45:38, Apr 28, 1962

What Did We Do Wrong?
Productions:
Opened October 22, 1967 for 48 performances.
Reviews:

DENKER, HENRY (cont.)
What Did We Do Wrong? (cont.)
America 117:623, Nov 18, 1967
New York Theatre Critics' Reviews 1967:231
1967:247
New York Times p. 56, Oct 23, 1967
II, p. 5, Nov 12, 1967
New Yorker 43:162, Nov 4, 1967

DODD, LEE WILSON

The Changelings
Productions:
Opened September 17, 1923 for 128 performances.
Reviews:
Bookman 58:307-8, Nov 1923
Life (NY) 82:22, Oct 4, 1923
Nation 117:359-60, Oct 3, 1923
New York Times p. 16, Sep 18, 1923
II, p. 1, Sep 30, 1923
Theatre Magazine 38:16, Nov 1923
38:26+, Dec 1923

His Majesty Bunker Bean (Adapted from Harry Leon Wil-
son's novel)
Productions:
Opened October 2, 1916 for 72 performances.
Reviews:
Dramatic Mirror 76:7, Oct 7, 1916
Green Book 16:970-2, Dec 1916
Nation 103:358, Oct 12, 1916
New York Drama News 63:10-11, Oct 7, 1916
New York Times p. 9, Oct 3, 1916
Theatre Magazine 23:152, Mar 1916
24:284, Nov 1916

Pals First (Based on Francis Perry Elliott's novel)
Productions:
Opened February 26, 1917 for 152 performances.
Reviews:
Dramatic Mirror 77:7+, Mar 3, 1917
Green Book 17:779+, May 1917
Life (NY) 69:444, Mar 15, 1917
New York Drama News 64:2, Mar 3, 1917
New York Times p. 9, Feb 27, 1917
Theatre Magazine 25:215+, Apr 1917

The Return of Eve
    Productions:
        Opened March 17, 1909 for 29 performances
    Reviews:
        Collier's 43:20, May 22, 1909
        Dramatist 1:27-9, Jan 1910
        Forum 41:341-2, Apr 1909
        Theatre Magazine 9:134-5, May 1909

Speed
    Productions:
        Opened September 9, 1911 for 33 performances.
    Reviews:
        American Playwright 1:26, Jan 1912
        Blue Book 14:475-7, Jan 1912
        Collier's 48:17, Sep 30, 1911
        Dramatic Mirror 66:9, Sep 13, 1911
        Dramatist 3:191-2, Oct 1911
        Green Book 6:996, Nov 1911
                    6:1199-1200, Dec 1911
        Life (NY) 58:478, Sep 21, 1911
        Munsey 46:279, Nov 1911
        Red Book 14:186-9, Nov 1911
        Theatre Magazine 14:114+, Oct 1911

A Strong Man's House
    Productions:
        Opened September 16, 1929 for 24 performances.
    Reviews:
        Commonweal 10:592, Oct 9, 1929
        Life (NY) 94:24, Oct 11, 1929
        New York Times VIII, p. 1, Jun 30, 1929
                          p. 34, Sep 17, 1929
        Theatre Magazine 50:47, Nov 1929

DOS PASSOS, JOHN

    *Airways, Inc.
        Reviews:
            Dial 86:442, May 1929
            New York Times p. 30, Feb 21, 1929

    The Garbage Man (See The Moon Is A Gong)

    The Moon Is A Gong
        Productions:

DOS PASSOS, JOHN (cont.)
  The Moon Is A Gong (cont.)
    Opened March 12, 1926 for 18 performances.
    Reviews:
      New Republic 46:174, Mar 31, 1926
      New York Times p. 21, Mar 13, 1926
                     VIII, p. 2, Mar 21, 1926
      Theatre Magazine 43:16+, Jun 1926

  U.S.A. (with Paul Shyre) (Based on Dos Passos' novel)
    Productions:
      (Off Broadway) Opened October 28, 1959 for 256
        performances
    Reviews:
      Nation 189:367, Nov 14, 1959
      New York Times II, p. 5, Oct 25, 1959
                       p. 38, Oct 29, 1959
                       II, p. 1, Nov 8, 1959
      New Yorker 35:88, Nov 7, 1959
      Theatre Arts 44:24-50, Jun 1960

DREISER, THEODORE

  The Girl in the Coffin
    Productions:
      Opened October 31, 1917 in repertory (Washington
        Square Players).
    Reviews:
      New York Times p. 11, Dec 4, 1917
      Theatre Magazine 27:15+, Jan 1918

  The Hand of the Potter
    Productions:
      Opened December 5, 1921 for 21 performances.
    Reviews:
      Nation 109:340, Sep 6, 1919
             113:762-3, Dec 28, 1921

DUBERMAN, MARTIN

  In White America
    Productions:
      (Off Broadway) Opened October 31, 1963 for 493
        performances.
      (Off Broadway) Opened May 18, 1965 for 32 per-

formances.
Reviews:
America 109:754, Dec 7, 1963
Commonweal 79:693, Mar 6, 1964
Nation 199:254-6, Oct 19, 1964
New Republic 149:28-9, Nov 16, 1963
New York Times p. 26, Nov 1, 1963
             p. 55, Aug 2, 1964
             p. 42, Feb 9, 1965
New Yorker 39:98-9, Nov 9, 1963

Metaphors
Productions:
(Off Broadway) Opened May 8, 1968 for 80 perform-
ances.
Reviews:
Harper's Bazaar 237:113-15, Oct 1968
Nation 206:772+, Jun 10, 1968
New York Times p. 55, May 9, 1968
             II, p. 1, May 19, 1968
New Yorker 44:74, May 18, 1968

DUNLAP, WILLIAM
No Productions.

DUNNING, PHILIP

Broadway (with George Abbott)
Productions:
Opened September 16, 1926 for 603 performances.
Reviews:
American Mercury 9:504, Dec 1926
Dial 82:77, Jan 1927
Dramatist 17:1317-18, Oct 1926
Independent 118:21, Jan 1, 1927
Life (NY) 88:23, Oct 14, 1926
Nation 123:330, Oct 6, 1926
New Republic 50:45, Mar 2, 1927
New York Times p. 19, Sep 17, 1926
             VIII, p. 1, Sep 26, 1926
             p. 23, Dec 23, 1926
             VII, p. 2, Jan 9, 1927
             VIII, p. 2, Oct 23, 1927
             VIII, p. 2, Feb 12, 1928
             p. 5, Mar 11, 1928

DUNNING, PHILIP (cont.)
  Broadway (cont.)
                              IX, p. 4, Apr 15, 1928
                                  p. 34, Oct 12, 1928
                                  p. 34, Dec 6, 1928
            Theatre Magazine 44:66, Nov 1926
                              45:26+, Jan 1927
            Vogue 68:78-9, Nov 15, 1926

  Dawn Glory (See Night Hostess)

  East of Broadway (See Night Hostess)

  Get Me in the Movies (with Charlton Andrews)
      Productions:
        Opened May 21, 1928 for 32 performances.
      Reviews:
        Life (NY) 91:26, Jun 7, 1928
        New York Times p. 18, May 22, 1928
                            VIII, p. 1, May 27, 1928
        Vogue 17:98, Jul 15, 1928

  Kill That Story (with Harry Madden)
      Productions:
        Opened August 29, 1934 for 117 performances.
      Reviews:
        New York Times p. 22, Aug 30, 1934

  Lilly Tuner (with George Abbott)
      Productions:
        Opened September 19, 1932 for 24 performances.
      Reviews:
        New York Times p. 26, Sep 20, 1932
        Theatre Arts 16:868+, Nov 1932
        Vogue 80:89, Nov 1, 1932

  Night Hostess
      Productions:
        Opened September 12, 1928 for 117 performances.
      Reviews:
        Drama 19:44, Nov 1928
        Life (NY) 92:15, Oct 5, 1928
        Nation 127:327-8, Oct 3, 1928
        New York Times VII, p. 2, Jul 29, 1928
                            p. 31, Sep 13, 1928
        Vogue 72:150, Nov 10, 1928

Page Miss Glory (with Joseph Schrank)
    Productions:
    Opened November 27, 1934 for 63 performances.
    Reviews:
    Catholic World 140:469, Jan 1935
    Golden Book 21:28a+
    New York Times p. 24, Nov 28, 1934
                 X, p. 2, Dec 9, 1934
    Newsweek 4:26, Dec 8, 1934
    Time 24:51, Dec 10, 1934

Remember The Day (with Philo Higley)
    Productions:
    Opened September 25, 1935 for 122 performances.
    Reviews:
    Catholic World 142:213-14, Nov 1935
    Commonweal 22:585, Oct 11, 1935
    New York Times p. 24, Jul 9, 1935
                 p. 19, Sep 26, 1935
                 XI, p. 2, Oct 6, 1935
                 IX, p. 1, Oct 13, 1935
                 X, p. 2, Nov 3, 1935
    Stage 13:72, Dec 1935
    Theatre Arts 19:825, Nov 1935
    Time 26:38, Oct 7, 1935

Sweet Land of Liberty
    Productions:
    Opened September 23, 1929 for 8 performances.
    Reviews:
    New York Times p. 29, Sep 24, 1929
    Theatre Magazine 50:72, Nov 1929

D'USSEAU, ARNAUD

Deep Are the Roots (with James Gow)
    Productions:
    Opened September 26, 1945 for 477 performances.
    (Off Broadway) Season of 1959-60.
    Reviews:
    Catholic World 162:164, Nov 1945
    Commonweal 42:624, Oct 12, 1945
    Life 19:51-2+, Oct 15, 1945
    Nation 161:384, Oct 13, 1945
    New Republic 113:499, Oct 15, 1945
                 114:446, Apr 1, 1946

D'USSEAU, ARNAUD (cont.)
  Deep Are the Roots (cont.)
    New York Theatre Critics' Reviews 1945:160
    New York Times p. 24, Sep 27, 1945
                II, p. 1, Oct 7, 1945
                II, p. 1, Oct 14, 1945
                p. 26, Apr 28, 1947
                p. 17, Jul 10, 1947
                II, p. 2, Aug 24, 1947
                p. 47, Oct 4, 1960
    New Yorker 21:46+, Oct 6, 1945
    Newsweek 26:94-5, Oct 8, 1945
    Saturday Review 28:38+, Oct 13, 1945
    Theatre Arts 29:622-4, Nov 1945
              29:678, Dec 1945
              31:37, Oct 1947
    Time 46:77, Oct 8, 1945

  The Ladies of the Corridor (See entry under Parker,
    Dorothy)

  Legend of Sarah (See entry under Gow, James)

  Tomorrow the World (See entry under Gow, James)

ELIOT, T. S.

  The Cocktail Party
    Productions:
      Opened January 21, 1950 for 409 performances.
      Opened October 7, 1968 for 44 performances (A. P. A.
        Phoenix).
    Reviews:
      America 119:445-7, Nov 9, 1968
      American Mercury 70:557-8, May 1950
      Catholic World 170:466, Mar 1950
                 171:469-70, Sep 1950
      Christian Science Monitor Magazine, p. 6, May 27,
        1950
      Commonweal 51:463, Feb 3, 1950
              51:507-8, Feb 17, 1950
      Fortnightly 174 (ns 168):391-8, Dec 1950
      Life 27:16+, Sep 26, 1949
      Nation 170:94-5, Jan 28, 1950
      New Republic 122:30, Feb 13, 1950
      New York Theatre Critics' Reviews 1950:376

New York Times p. 28, Aug 23, 1949
                II, p. 2, Sep 11, 1949
                p. 17, Jan 23, 1950
                II, p. 1, Jan 29, 1950
                VI, p. 14, Jan 29, 1950
                II, p. 1, Apr 16, 1950
                p. 33, May 4, 1950
                II, p. 2, May 7, 1950
                II, p. 3, May 21, 1950
                II, p. 3, Dec 17, 1950
                p. 42, Oct 8, 1968
                II, p. 1, Oct 20, 1968
New Yorker 25:47, Jan 28, 1950
           26:26-9, Apr 1, 1950
           44:159, Oct 19, 1968
Newsweek 35:66, Jan 30, 1950
Saturday Review 33:28-30, Feb 4, 1950
                33:48, Feb 11, 1950
School and Society 72:180-2, Sep 16, 1950
Theatre Arts 34:8, May 1950
             34:10, Apr 1950
Time 54:58, Sep 5, 1949
     55:37, Jan 30, 1950
     92:72+, Oct 18, 1968

The Confidential Clerk
  Productions:
    Opened February 11, 1954 to 117 performances.
  Reviews:
    America 90:608+, Mar 6, 1954
    Catholic World 179:68-9, Apr 1954
    Commentary 17:367-72, Apr 1954
    Commonweal 59:475-6, Feb 12, 1954
               59:599, Mar 19, 1954
    Life 36:56-8+, Feb 1, 1954
    Nation 178:184+, Feb 27, 1954
    New Republic 129:17-18, Sep 21, 1953
                 130:22, Feb 22, 1954
                 131:124-5, Nov 22, 1954
    New York Theatre Critics' Reviews 1954:370
    New York Times p. 20, Dec 22, 1952
                   p. 22, Aug 26, 1953
                   p. 21, Aug 27, 1953
                   II, p. 2, Aug 30, 1953
                   II, p. 3, Oct 11, 1953
                   II, p. 1, Feb 7, 1954

T. S. ELIOT (cont.)
    The Confidential Clerk (cont.)
                        p. 22, Feb 12, 1954
                        II, p. 1, Feb 21, 1954
            New York Times Magazine pp. 36-7, Sep 6, 1953
                        p. 16, Feb 21, 1954
            New Yorker 29:110-11, Oct 10, 1953
                        30:62+, Feb 20, 1954
            Newsweek 43:94, Feb 22, 1954
            Saturday Review 36:26-8, Aug 29, 1953
                        36:44-6, Sep 12, 1953
                        37:26-8, Feb 27, 1954
            Theatre Arts 37:81-2, Nov 1953
                        38:22-3, Apr 1954
                        38:22-5, May 1954
            Time 63:80+, Feb 22, 1954
            Vogue 123:130-1, Mar 1, 1954

    *The Elder Statesman
        Reviews:
            Life 45:108, Nov 24, 1958
            New York Times p. 21, Aug 20, 1958
                        p. 35, Aug 26, 1958
                        II, p. 3, Aug 31, 1958
            New Yorker 34:168, Nov 1, 1958
            Saturday Review 41:30-1, Sep 13, 1958
            Time 72:43+, Sep 8, 1958

    The Family Reunion
        Productions:
            (Off Broadway) Opened December, 1947 (On Stage).
            Opened October 20, 1958 for 20 performances.
            (Off Broadway) Opened November 20, 1967 for 3 per-
                formances (Equity Theatre).
        Reviews:
            America 100:174, Nov 8, 1958
            Catholic World 188:331, Jan 1959
            Christian Century 75:1380-2, Nov 26, 1958
            Commonweal 69:232-4, Nov 28, 1958
            Nation 148:676, Jun 10, 1939
                    187:347, Nov 8, 1958
            New Republic 98:384-5, May 3, 1939
            New York Theatre Critics' Reviews 1958:255
            New York Times X, p. 1, Apr 9, 1939
                        p. 9, Nov 29, 1947
                        p. 13, Jun 9, 1956
                        p. 39, Oct 21, 1958

```
                    II, p. 1, Oct 26, 1958
                        p. 26, Dec 10, 1960
New Yorker 34:99-101, Nov 1, 1958
One Act Play Magazine 3:82, Jan 1940
Reporter 19:35, Nov 27, 1958
Saturday Review 19:12, Apr 1, 1939
                        41:25, Nov 8, 1958
Theatre Arts 41:23-4, May 1957
                        42:64, Dec 1958
Time 72:48, Nov 3, 1958
Yale Review 28:836-8, Summer, 1939
```

Murder in the Cathedral
  Productions:
```
    Opened March 20, 1936 for 38 performances.
    Opened February 16, 1938 for 21 performances.
```
  Reviews:
```
    Catholic World 143:209-11, May 1936
    Christian Century 52:1636, Dec 18, 1935
    Commonweal 23:636, Apr 3, 1936
                27:524, Mar 4, 1938
    Forum 95:346-7, Jun 1936
    Life 19:123-7, Oct 1, 1945
    Nation 141:417, Oct 9, 1935
           142:459-60, Apr 8, 1936
    New Republic 85:290, Jan 15, 1936
                 86:253, Apr 8, 1936
                 94:101, Mar 2, 1938
    New York Times p. 12, Nov 2, 1935
                   IX, p. 1, Feb 16, 1936
                   p. 13, Mar 21, 1936
                   IX, p. 1, Mar 29, 1936
                   p. 16, Feb 17, 1938
                   XI, p. 1, Feb 20, 1938
                   II, p. 1, Apr 26, 1953
                   p. 12, Mar 22, 1958
                   p. 38, Jun 21, 1966
    New Yorker 29:87, May 2, 1953
    Newsweek 7:26, Mar 28, 1936
    Saturday Review 12:10-11, Oct 12, 1935
                    49:41, Jul 9, 1966
    Stage 13:97, Nov 1935
    Theatre Arts 20:25-6, Jan 1936
                 20:341-3, May 1936
                 22:254-5, Apr 1938
    Time 31:34, Feb 28, 1938
    Yale Review 25:427-9, Winter 1936
```

EMERY, GILBERT

Episode
  Productions:
    Opened February 4, 1925 for 21 performances.
  Reviews:
    American Mercury 4:502-3, Apr 1925
    Nation 120:221-2, Feb 25, 1925
    New York Times p. 23, Feb 5, 1925
                VII, p. 1, Feb 8, 1925
                VII, p. 1, Feb 15, 1925
    Theatre Magazine 41:18, Apr 1925

Far-Away Horses (with Michael Birmingham)
  Productions:
    Opened March 21, 1933 for 4 performances.
  Reviews:
    Nation 136:382, Apr 5, 1933
    New York Times p. 21, Mar 22, 1933

The Hero
  Productions:
    Opened March 14, 1921 for 5 matinees.
    Opened September 5, 1921 for 80 performances.
  Reviews:
    Bookman 53:276, May 1921
            54:229-30, Nov 1921
    Current Opinion 71:751-60, Dec 1921
    Dramatist 83:488, Mar 19, 1921
           84:376, Sep 10, 1921
    Everybody's 46:123-30, Mar 1922
    Life (NY) 77:464-5, Mar 31, 1921
    Nation 113:381, Oct 5, 1921
    New York Drama News 69:19, Mar 16, 1921
               69:23, Sep 14, 1921
    New York Times p. 14, Mar 15, 1921
           VI, p. 1, Mar 20, 1921
           p. 13, Sep 6, 1921
           VI, p. 1, Sep 11, 1921
    Review 4:301-3, Mar 30, 1921
    Theatre Magazine 35:16+, Jan 1922
    Weekly Review 4:302-3, Mar 30, 1921
            5:255-6, Sep 17, 1921

Housewarming
  Productions:
    Opened April 7, 1932 for 4 performances.

Reviews:
New York Times p. 25, Apr 8, 1932

Love In A Mist (with Amelie Rives)
Productions:
Opened April 12, 1926 for 118 performances.
Reviews:
Life (NY) 87:21, Apr 29, 1926
Nation 122:484, Apr 28, 1926
New York Times p. 28, Apr 13, 1926

Tarnish
Productions:
Opened October 1, 1923 for 248 performances.
Reviews:
Bookman 58:440, Dec 1923
Current Opinion 76:186-94, Feb 1924
Dramatist 15:1190-91, Jan 1924
Life (NY) 82:18, Oct 25, 1923
Nation 117:444, Oct 17, 1923
New York Times p. 10, Oct 2, 1923
Theatre Magazine 38:18+, Dec 1923
39:26+, Feb 1924

FAULKNER, WILLIAM

Requiem for a Nun (With Ruth Ford) (Adapted from
Faulkner's novel)
Productions:
Opened January 30, 1959 for 43 performances.
Reviews:
America 100:614, Feb 21, 1959
Catholic World 189:61, Apr 1959
Nation 188:193-4, Feb 28, 1959
New Republic 140:22, Mar 9, 1959
New York Theatre Critics' Reviews 1959:390
New York Times II, p. 1, Jan 25, 1959
p. 32, Jan 30, 1959
p. 13, Jan 31, 1959
II, p. 1, Feb 8, 1959
New Yorker 34:82+, Feb 7, 1959
Newsweek 53:56+, Feb 9, 1959
Saturday Review 42:32, Feb 14, 1959
Theatre Arts 43:23+, Apr 1959
Time 73:70, Feb 9, 1959

FERBER, EDNA

Bravo! (with George S. Kaufman)
    Productions:
        Opened November 11, 1948 for 44 performances.
    Reviews:
        Commonweal 49:195, Dec 3, 1948
        New Republic 119:28-9, Nov 29, 1948
        New York Theatre Critics' Reviews 1948:165
        New York Times p. 31, Nov 12, 1948
        New Yorker 24:58+, Nov 20, 1948
        Newsweek 32:80, Nov 22, 1948
        School and Society 68:454-5, Dec 25, 1948
        Time 52:85, Nov 22, 1948

Dinner at Eight (See entry under Kaufman, George S.)

The Land Is Bright (See entry under Kaufman, George S.)

Minick (See entry under Kaufman, George S.)

Old Man Minick (See Minick)

Our Mrs. McChesney (with George V. Hobert) (Adapted
        from the Ferber stories)
    Productions:
        Opened October 19, 1915 for 151 performances.
    Reviews:
        American Magazine 80:40-42+, Nov 1915
        Book News 34:179-80, Dec 1915
        Bookman 42:384+, Dec 1915
        Dramatic Mirror 74:8, Oct 30, 1915
        Dramatist 7:635-6, Jan 1916
        Harper's Weekly 61:440, Nov 6, 1915
        Nation 101:527-8, Oct 28, 1915
        National Magazine 43:244-7, Nov 1915
        New York Drama News 61:18, Oct 23, 1915
        New York Times p. 11, Oct 20, 1915
                        VI, p. 6, Oct 24, 1915

The Royal Family (See entry under Kaufman, George S.)

Stage Door (See entry under Kaufman, George S.)

Theatre Royal (See The Royal Family)

FERRIS, WALTER

Death Takes A Holiday (Adapted from the Italian of Alberto
    Casella)
    Productions:
    Opened December 26, 1929 for 180 performances.
    Opened February 16, 1931 for 32 performances.
    Reviews:
    Catholic World 130:725-6, Mar 1930
    Commonweal 11:369, Jan 29, 1930
    Life (NY) 95:20, Jan 17, 1930
    Literary Dibest 104:18, Jan 18, 1930
    Nation 138:342, Mar 21, 1934
    New Republic 61:675-6, Jan 29, 1930
    New York Times X p. 4, Nov 24, 1929
                    p. 26, Dec 27, 1929
                    VIII, p. 2, Jan 5, 1930
                    p. 22, Jan 29, 1930
                    p. 29, Feb 17, 1931
    Theatre Arts 14:191-2, Mar 1930
    Vogue 75:122, Feb 15, 1930

The First Stone (Based on a story by Mary Heaton Vorse)
    Productions:
    Opened January 16, 1928 for 3 performances.
    Reviews:
    Drama 18:201, Apr 1928
    New York Times p. 12, Jan 14, 1928

Judas (with Basil Rathbone)
    Productions:
    Opened January 24, 1929 for 12 performances.
    Reviews:
    Life (NY) 93:25, Feb 15, 1929
    New York Times p. 20, Jan 25, 1929

FIELD, SALISBURY

The Rented Earl
    Productions:
    Opened February 8, 1915 for 16 performances.
    Reviews:
    Current Opinion 58:249-50, Apr 1915
    Dramatic Mirror 72:7, Sep 16, 1914
                    73:8, Feb 17, 1915
    Green Book 13:958, May 1915

FIELD, SALISBURY (cont.)
The Rented Earl (cont.)
New York Times p. 9, Feb 9, 1915

Twin Beds (With Margaret Mayo)
Productions:
Opened August 14, 1914 for 411 performances.
Reviews:
Bookman 40:186, Oct 1914
Dramatic Mirror 72:8, Aug 19, 1914
Dramatist 6:533-4, Jan 1915
Green Book 12:90+, Jul 1914
12:697-9, Oct 1914
12:940-7, Nov 1914
Munsey 53:358-9, Nov 1914
New York Drama News 59:11, Aug 22, 1914
New York Times p. 9, Aug 15, 1914
Theatre Magazine 20:154+, Oct 1914

Wedding Bells
Productions:
Opened November 10, 1919 for 168 performances.
Reviews:
Dramatic Mirror 80:1825, Nov 27, 1919
Dramatist 11:998-9, Apr 1920
New York Times p. 11, Nov 13, 1919
IX, p. 2, Dec 7, 1919
Theatre Magazine 30:367, Dec 1919

Zander the Great
Productions:
Opened April 9, 1923 for 80+ performances.
Reviews:
Bookman 57:438-9, Jun 1923
Current Opinion 75:189-94+, Aug 1923
Hearst 44:85-7+, Aug 1923
Independent 110:302, Apr 28, 1923
Life (NY) 81:18, Apr 26, 1923
New York Clipper 71:14, Apr 18, 1923
New York Times p. 24, Apr 10, 1923
VII, p. 1, Apr 15, 1923
Theatre Magazine 37:14+, Jun 1923

FIELDS, JOSEPH

Anniversary Waltz (See entry under Chodorov, Jerome)

The Doughgirls
    Productions:
        Opened December 30, 1942 for 671 performances.
    Reviews:
        Catholic World 156:599-600, Feb 1943
        Commonweal 37:350, Jan 22, 1943
        Independent Woman 22:144, May 1943
        Life 14:68-9, Feb 1, 1943
        Nation 156:103, Jan 16, 1943
        New York Theatre Critics' Reviews 1942:124
        New York Times p. 19, Dec 31, 1942
                        VIII, p. 1, Jan 10, 1943
                        II, p. 2, Jan 9, 1944
        Theatre Arts 27:139-40, Mar 1943
        Time 41:64, Jan 11, 1943

The French Touch (with Jerome Chodorov)
    Productions:
        Opened December 8, 1945 for 33 performances.
    Reviews:
        Commonweal 43:287, Dec 28, 1945
        Harper's Bazaar 79:128, Dec 1945
        New York Theatre Critics' Reviews 1945:77
        New York Times p. 18, Dec 10, 1945
        New Yorker 21:60, Dec 15, 1945
        Theatre Arts 30:79, Feb 1946
        Time 46:72, Dec 17, 1945

I Gotta Get Out (with Ben Sher)
    Productions:
        Opened September 25, 1947 for 4 performances.
    Reviews:
        New York Theatre Critics' Reviews 1947:343
        New York Times II, p. 1, Sep 21, 1947
                        p. 27, Sep 26, 1947
        New Yorker 23:50, Oct 4, 1947

Junior Miss (See entry under Chodorov, Jerome)

My Sister Eileen (with Jerome Chodorov) (Based on the
        stories of Ruth McKenney)
    Productions:
        Opened December 26, 1940 for 865 performances.
        (Off Broadway) Opened April 26, 1948
    Reviews:
        Life 10:49, Feb 17, 1941
        Nation 152:53, Jan 11, 1941

FIELDS, JOSEPH (cont.)
My Sister Eileen (cont.)
New Republic 104:84, Jan 20, 1941
New York Theatre Critics' Reviews 1940:175
1941:445
New York Times p. 23, Dec 27, 1940
IX, p. 1, Jan 5, 1941
IX, p. 2, May 18, 1941
Newsweek 17:52, Jan 6, 1941
Stage 1:20-21, Feb 1941
Theatre Arts 25:94, Feb 1941
Time 37:41, Jan 6, 1941

The Ponder Heart (with Jerome Chodorov)
Productions:
Opened February 16, 1956 for 149 performances.
Reviews:
America 94:703, Mar 24, 1956
Catholic World 183:64-5, Apr 1956
Commonweal 64:22, Apr 6, 1956
Life 40:111-12+, Mar 5, 1956
Nation 182:204, Mar 10, 1956
New Republic 134:29, Mar 12, 1956
New York Theatre Critics' Reviews 1956:358
New York Times VI, p. 44, Jan 22, 1956
p. 26, Feb 1, 1956
p. 14, Feb 17, 1956
II, p. 1, Feb 26, 1956
New Yorker 32:90, Feb 25, 1956
Newsweek 47:61, Mar 5, 1956
Saturday Review 39:22, Mar 3, 1956
Theatre Arts 40:22-3, Apr 1956
Time 67:61, Feb 27, 1956

Schoolhouse On the Lot (with Jerome Chodorov)
Productions:
Opened March 22, 1938 for 55 performances.
Reviews:
Catholic World 147:217, May 1938
New York Times p. 18, Mar 23, 1938
Newsweek 11:22, Mar 14, 1938
11:25, Apr 4, 1938
One Act Play Magazine 2:69-70, May 1938
Time 31:22, Apr 4, 1938

The Tunnel of Love (with Peter DeVries) (Based on De-
Vries' novel)

Productions:
  Opened February 13, 1957 for 417 performances.
Reviews:
  America 96:629, Mar 2, 1957
  Catholic World 185:69, Apr 1957
  Commonweal 65:662, Mar 29, 1957
  New York Theatre Critics' Reviews 1957:347
  New York Times VI, p. 62, Feb 3, 1957
                 p. 31, Feb 14, 1957
                 p. 47, Dec 5, 1957
  New York Times Magazine p. 62, Feb 3, 1957
  New Yorker 33:69, Feb 23, 1957
  Newsweek 49:75, Feb 25, 1957
  Saturday Review 40:26, Mar 2, 1957
  Theatre Arts 41:18, Apr 1957
  Time 69:52, Feb 25, 1957

FISHER, ROBERT (BOB)

Happiness Is Just a Little Thing Called a Rolls Royce
    (with Arthur Alsberg)
  Productions:
  Opened May 11, 1968 for 1 performance.
Reviews:
  New York Theatre Critics' Reviews 1968:277
  New York Times p. 54, May 13, 1968
                 p. 39, May 14, 1968
  New Yorker 44:73, May 18, 1968

The Impossible Years (with Arthur Marx)
  Productions:
  Opened October 13, 1965 for 670 performances.
Reviews:
  Commonweal 83:243, Nov 26, 1965
  Life 59:72B, Nov 5, 1965
  New York Theatre Critics' Reviews 1965:311
  New York Times II, p. 10, Apr 22, 1965
                  p. 55, Oct 14, 1965
  Newsweek 66:102, Oct 25, 1965
  Time 86:103A, Oct 22, 1965

FITCH, CLYDE

The Bachelor
  Productions:

FITCH, CLYDE (cont.)
The Bachelor (cont.)
Opened March 15, 1909 for 56 performances.
Reviews:
Forum 41:340-1, Apr 1909

Beau Brummell
Productions:
Opened April 24, 1916 for 24 performances.
Reviews:
Dramatic Mirror 75:8, Apr 29, 1916
Green Book 16:79+, Jul 1916
Munsey 58:521, Aug 1916
Nation 102:483, May 4, 1916
New York Times p. 11, Apr 26, 1916
VII, p. 7, Apr 30, 1916
Stage 14:93, Aug 1937
Theatre Magazine 23:334-5, Jun 1916

Captain Jinks of the Horse Marines
Productions:
Opened January 25, 1938 for 2 performances (WPA
Federal Theatre Project).
Reviews:
New York Times p. 16, Jan 28, 1938

The City
Productions:
Opened December 21, 1909 for 190 performances.
Reviews:
Bookman 31:63-6, Mar 1910
Burr McIntosh Monthly 22:226, Mar 1910
Colliers 44:7, Jan 15, 1910
Current Literature 48:201-2, Feb 1910
Dramatic Mirror 63:5-6, Jan 1, 1910
Dramatist 1:39-41, Apr 1910
Forum 43:190-1, Feb 1910
Green Book 3:513-16, Mar 1910
Hampton 24:401-4, Mar 1910
Harper's Weekly 54:24, Jan 15, 1910
54:24, Apr 16, 1910
Life (NY) 55:36, Jan 6, 1910
Metropolitan Magazine 32:114-15, Apr 1910
Pearson 23:373-6, Mar 1910
Theatre Magazine 11:34+, Feb 1910

146

Girls
Productions:
Opened March 23, 1908 for 64 performances.
Opened February 8, 1909 for one week.
Reviews:
New York Times p. 3, Sep 11, 1913
Theatre Magazine 8:vii+, May 1908

The Happy Marriage
Productions:
Opened April 12, 1909 for 24 performances.
Reviews:
Dramatic Mirror 61:3, Apr 24, 1909
Forum 41:455-7, May 1909
Independent 66:90, Apr 29, 1909
Nation 88:392, Apr 15, 1909

*Nathan Hale
Reviews:
New York Times p. 11, May 1, 1926

The Truth
Productions:
Opened April 14, 1914 for 55 performances.
Reviews:
Book News 32:456-7, May 1914
Current Opinion 57:24-7, Jul 1914
Dramatic Mirror 71:12, Apr 15, 1914
Green Book 11:1015-17, Jun 1914
12:462-71, Sep 1914
Harper's Weekly 58:21, May 2, 1914
Life (NY) 63:740-1, Apr 23, 1914
Nation 98:418+, Apr 16, 1914
New York Times VIII, p. 6, Apr 12, 1914
p. 11, Apr 13, 1914
Theatre Magazine 7:301+, Feb 1907
19:265, May 1914

FITZGERALD, F. SCOTT

The Great Gatsby (See entry under Davis, Owen)

The Vegetable
Productions:
Opened April 10, 1929 for 13 performances.
(Off Broadway) Opened October 26, 1963 for 8 per-

FITZGERALD, F. SCOTT (cont.)
  The Vegetable (cont.)
        formances. (Equity Library Theatre)
    Reviews:
        Bookman 56:57-8, Sep 1923
        Dramatist 14:1183-4, Oct 1923
        Life (NY) 93:24, May 3, 1929
        New York Times p. 32, Apr 11, 1929

FLAVIN, MARTIN

  Achilles Had a Heel
    Productions:
        Opened October 13, 1935 for 8 performances.
    Reviews:
        Commonweal 23:19, Nov 1, 1935
        New York Times X, p. 1, Apr 28, 1935
                        p. 20, Oct 14, 1935
        Time 26:51, Oct 21, 1935

  Around the Corner
    Productions:
        Opened December 28, 1936 for 16 performances.
    Reviews;
        New York Times p. 17, Dec 29, 1936
        Theatre Arts 21:102, Feb 1937

  Broken Dishes
    Productions:
        Opened November 5, 1929 for 178 performances.
    Reviews:
        Catholic World 130:466-7, Jan 1930
        Commonweal 11:115-16, Nov 27, 1929
        Life (NY) 94:48, Dec 6, 1929
        New York Times p. 28, Nov 6, 1929
        Theatre Magazine 51:45-6+, Jan 1930
        Vogue 75:118, Feb 15, 1930

  Children of the Moon
    Productions:
        Opened August 17, 1923 for 117 performances.
    Reviews:
        Bookman 58:180-1, Oct 1923
        Dramatist 14:1184-5, Oct 1923
        Life (NY) 82:18, Sep 13, 1923
        Metropolitan Magazine 58:38+, Jan 1924

Nation 117:273, Sep 12, 1923
New York Times p. 10, Aug 18, 1923
VI, p. 2, Sep 2, 1923
VIII, p. 1, Nov 7, 1926
XI, p. 3, May 4, 1930
Theatre Magazine 38:14-15, Oct 1923
38:26+, Nov 1923

The Criminal Code
    Productions:
        Opened October 2, 1929 for 173 performances.
    Reviews:
        Catholic World 180:331-2, Dec 1929
        Commonweal 11:115, Nov 27, 1929
        Drama 21:26-7, Mar 1931
        Life (NY) 94:22, Oct 25, 1929
        Literary Digest 103:19-20, Nov 2, 1929
        New York Times p. 28, Oct 2, 1929
                      IX, p. 1, Oct 13, 1929
                      IX, p. 4, Oct 20, 1929
                      p. 30, Dec 19, 1929
        Outlook 153:314, Oct 23, 1929
        Review of Reviews 80:156, Dec 1929
        Theatre Arts 13:875-6, Dec 1929
        Theatre Magazine 50:41-2+, Dec 1929
        Vogue 74:116, Nov 23, 1929

Cross Roads
    Productions:
        Opened November 11, 1929 for 28 performances.
    Reviews:
        Commonweal 11:116, Nov 27, 1929
        Life (NY) 94:48, Dec 26, 1929
        Nation 129:640-2, Nov 27, 1929
        New York Times p. 34, Nov 12, 1929
        Theatre Magazine 51:46, Jan 1930

Grist of the Mill (See Cross Roads)

Lady of the Rose
    Productions:
        Opened May 19, 1925 for 8 performances.
    Reviews:
        New York Times p. 26, May 20, 1925

Service for Two
    Productions:

FLAVIN, MARTIN (cont.)
Service for Two (cont.)
Opened August 30, 1926 for 24 performances.
Reviews:
New York Times p. 15, Aug 31, 1926
VII, p. 1, Sep 5, 1926
Theatre Magazine 44:18, Nov 1926

Tapestry in Gray
Productions:
Opened December 27, 1935 for 24 performances.
Reviews:
Catholic World 142:602, Feb 1936
Commonweal 23:330, Jan 17, 1936
Literary Digest 121:20, Jan 11, 1936
New York Times p. 10, Dec 28, 1935

FORBES, JAMES

The Commuters
Productions:
Opened August 15, 1910 for 160 performances.
Reviews:
Blue Book 12:661-3, Feb 1911
Bookman 32:349-, Dec 1910
Dramatic Mirror 64:7-8, Aug 27, 1910
Dramatist 2:102-5, Oct 1910
Green Book 5:307-8, Feb 1911
Hampton 25:524, Oct 1910
Life (NY) 56:434, Sep 15, 1910
Metropolitan Magazine 33:122-3, Oct 1910
Munsey 44:125, Oct 1910
Theatre Magazine 12:xv, Sep 1910

The Endless Chain
Productions:
Opened September 4, 1922 for 40 performances.
Reviews:
Life (NY) 80:18, Sep 21, 1922
New York Clipper 70:20, Sep 13, 1922
New York Times p. 21, Sep 5, 1922

The Famous Mrs. Fair
Productions:
Opened December 22, 1919 for 183 performances.
Reviews:

Current Opinion 69:192-9, Aug 1920
Dramatic Mirror 81:2023, Jan 1, 1920
Dramatist 12:1039-40, Jan 1921
Forum 63:246, Feb 1920
Life (NY) 75:72, Jan 8, 1920
Nation 110:210-11, Feb 14, 1920
New York Times p. 12, Dec 23, 1919
            p. 20, Apr 24, 1920
Theatre Magazine 21:83+, Feb 1920

*Final Fling
Reviews:
New York Times IX, p. 2, Oct 7, 1928

Matrimony PFD (With Grace George) (Adapted from the
    play by Louis Verneuil)
Productions:
Opened November 12, 1936 for 61 performances.
Reviews:
Catholic World 144:473, Jan 1937
Nation 143:642, Nov 28, 1936
New York Times p. 28, Nov 6, 1936
            p. 26, Nov 13, 1936
Theatre Arts 21:22, Jan 1937
Time 28:36, Nov 23, 1936

Precious
Productions:
Opened January 14, 1929 for 24 performances.
Reviews:
New York Times p. 22, Jan 15, 1929

A Rich Man's Son
Productions:
Opened November 4, 1912 for 32 performances.
Reviews:
Blue Book 16:692-5, Feb 1913
Bookman 36:377, Dec 1912
Dramatic Mirror 68:5, Nov 13, 1912
Everybody's 28:257-8, Feb 1913
New York Drama News 56:19-20, Nov 16, 1912

The Show Shop
Productions:
Opened December 31, 1914 for 156 performances.
Reviews:
American Magazine 79:85-6, May 1915

FORBES, JAMES (cont.)
  The Show Shop (cont.)
          Bookman 40:641, Feb 1915
          Current Opinion 58:328-31, May 1915
          Dramatic Mirror 73:8-9, Jan 6, 1915
          Dramatist 6:558-60, Apr 1915
          Green Book 13:474-6, Mar 1915
                        13:763-4, Apr 1915
          Life (NY) 65:68, Jan 14, 1915
          Nation 100:31, Jan 7, 1915
          New Republic 2:131, Mar 6, 1915
          New York Drama News 60:18, Jan 9, 1915
          New York Times p. 17, Jan 1, 1915
                        VII, p. 6, Jan 24, 1915
          Smart Set 45:285, Mar 1915
          Theatre Magazine 21:57-8, Feb 1915

  Young Blood
    Productions:
      Opened November 24, 1925 for 73 performances.
    Reviews:
      New York Times p. 15, Nov 25, 1925
                      VIII, p. 1, Nov 29, 1925
      Theatre Magazine 43:18, Feb 1926

FORD, RUTH

  Requiem for a Nun (See entry under Faulkner, William)

FOSTER, PAUL

  Balls
    Productions:
      (Off Broadway) Opened February 10, 1965 for 23
        performances (Theatre 1965 New Playwrights
        Series).
    Reviews:
      New York Times II, p. 1, Feb 7, 1965
                       p. 45, Feb 11, 1965
      Newsweek 65:93, Feb 22, 1965

  The Recluse
    Productions:
      (Off Broadway) Opened April 12, 1966 for 16 per-
        formances.

Reviews:
Nation 202:405-6, Apr 4, 1966
New York Times II, p. 15, Apr 10, 1966
p. 36, Apr 13, 1966

Tom Paine
Productions:
(Off Broadway) Opened March 25, 1968 for 295 performances.
Reviews:
America 118:652, May 11, 1968
Nation 206:516, Apr 15, 1968
New York Times p. 38, Mar 26, 1968
II, p. 1, May 12, 1968
p. 71, Mar 30, 1969
New Yorker 44:110-11, Apr 6, 1968
Newsweek 71:131, Apr 8, 1968
Saturday Review 51:40, May 4, 1968

FRANKEN, ROSE

Another Language
Productions:
Opened April 25, 1932 for 344 performances.
Opened May 8, 1933 for 89 performances.
Reviews:
Arts and Decoration 37:58, Sep 1932
Bookman 75:176-7, May 1932
Catholic World 135:338, Jun 1932
Commonweal 16:76-7, May 18, 1932
Literary Digest 113:17, May 28, 1932
Nation 134:580, May 18, 1932
New Republic 70:351-2, May 11, 1932
New York Times p. 25, Apr 26, 1932
VIII, p. 1, May 15, 1932
IX, p. 1, Dec 25, 1932
IX, p. 1, Jan 8, 1933
p. 20, May 9, 1933
North American Review 234:172-3, Aug 1932
Player's Magazine 9:13, Sep-Oct, 1932
Stage 9:14-17, Jun 1932
Town and Country 87:24, Jun 1, 1932
Vogue 79:41+, Jun 15, 1932

Claudia
Productions:
Opened February 12, 1941 for 722 performances.

FRANKEN, ROSE (cont.)
  Claudia (cont.)
        Reopened May 24, 1942 for 24 performances.
    Reviews:
        Commonweal 33:475, Feb 28, 1941
        Life 10:120-23, Mar 31, 1941
              11:118-22+, Nov 17, 1941
        Nation 152:221, Feb 22, 1941
        New York Theatre Critics' Reviews 1941:378
        New York Times p. 24, Feb 13, 1941
                          IX, p. 1, Mar 9, 1941
                          IX, p. 3, Apr 20, 1941
                          IX, p. 1, Jul 27, 1941
                          IX, p. 1, Aug 10, 1941
                          p. 28, Jul 28, 1942
                          VIII, p. 2, Sep 27, 1942
                          VIII, p. 2, Oct 4, 1942
        Newsweek 17:60, Feb 24, 1941
        Player's Magazine 17:11, May 1941
        Theatre Arts 25:258+, Apr 1941
                     (p. 258) 25:262, Apr 1941
        Time 37:58, Feb 24, 1941

  Doctors Disagree
    Productions:
        Opened December 28, 1943 for 23 performances.
    Reviews:
        Commonweal 39:328, Jan 14, 1944
        New York Theater Critics' Reviews 1943:186
        New York Times p. 15, Dec 29, 1943
        New Yorker 19:38, Jan 8, 1944
        Newsweek 23:89, Jan 10, 1944
        Theatre Arts 28:141, Mar, 1944
        Time 43:72, Jan 10, 1944

  The Hallams
    Productions:
        Opened March 4, 1948 for 12 performances.
    Reviews:
        Commonweal 47:566, Mar 19, 1948
        New Republic 118:34, Mar 22, 1948
        New York Theatre Critics' Reviews 1948:313
        New York Times p. 18, Mar 5, 1948
        New Yorker 24:48, Mar 13, 1948
        Newsweek 31:79, Mar 15, 1948
        Time 51:65, Mar 15, 1948
        Vogue 111:151, Apr 1, 1948

Outrageous Fortune
    Productions:
        Opened November 3, 1943 for 77 performances.
    Reviews:
        Catholic World 159:298, Dec 1943
        Commonweal 39:116, Nov 19, 1943
        New Republic 109:686, Nov 15, 1943
        New York Theatre Critics' Review 1943:237
        New York Times p. 28, Nov 4, 1943
                        II, p. 1, Nov 21, 1943
        Newsweek 22:96, Nov 15, 1943
        Player's Magazine 20:13, Jan 1944
        Theatre Arts 28:8-11, Jan 1944

Soldier's Wife
    Productions:
        Opened October 4, 1944 for 253 performances.
    Reviews:
        Catholic World 160:169-70, Nov 1944
        Nation 159:482-3, Oct 21, 1944
        New Republic 111:521, Oct 23, 1944
        New York Theatre Critics' Reviews 1944:121
        New York Times p. 18, Oct 5, 1944
                        II, p. 1, Oct 15, 1944
                        p. 13, Sep 2, 1946
        New Yorker 20:42, Oct 14, 1944
        Newsweek 24:85, Oct 16, 1944
        Theatre Arts 28:696+, Dec 1944
        Time 44:52, Oct 16, 1944

FRIEDMAN, BRUCE JAY

Scuba Duba
    Productions:
        (Off Broadway) Opened October 10, 1967 for 692
            performances.
    Reviews:
        America 117:486-7, Oct 28, 1967
        Commentary 44:84, Dec 1967
        Commonweal 87:624, Feb 23, 1968
        Life 63:119-20+, Nov 17, 1967
        Nation 205:438-9+, Oct 30, 1967
        New Republic 157:31-3, Oct 28, 1967
        New York Times p. 36, Oct 11, 1967
                        II, p. 3, Oct 22, 1967
                        VI, p. 13, Jan 14, 1968

155

FRIEDMAN, BRUCE JAY (cont.)
  Scuba Duba (cont.)
                              p. 51, Apr 7, 1969
              New York Times Magazine p. 30-2+, Jan 14, 1968
              New Yorker 43:82+, Oct 21, 1967
              Newsweek 70:113+, Oct 23, 1967
              Reporter 38:43, Jan 25, 1968
              Time 90:82+, Oct 20, 1967

FRINGS, KETTI

  Look Homeward, Angel (Based on Thomas Wolfe's novel)
      Productions:
      Opened November 28, 1957 for 564 performances.
    Reviews:
      America 98:551, Feb 8, 1957
      Catholic World 186:385-6, Feb 1958
      Christian Century 75:469, Apr 16, 1958
      Commonweal 68:16-18, Apr 4, 1958
      Life 43:79-82, Dec 16, 1957
      Nation 185:463-4, Dec 14, 1957
      New York Theatre Critics' Reviews 1957:166
      New York Times II, p. 1, Nov 24, 1957
                       p. 33, Nov 29, 1957
                       II, p. 5, Dec 8, 1957
                       VI, p. 18, Dec 15, 1957
                       II, p. 1, Aug 31, 1958
      New York Times Magazine p. 18+, Dec 15, 1957
      New Yorker 33:95-6, Dec 7, 1957
      Newsweek 50:70-1, Dec 9, 1957
      Reporter 17:33, Dec 26, 1957
      Saturday Review 40:27-8, Nov 23, 1957
                      40:22, Dec 14, 1957
      Theatre Arts 42:18-19, Feb 1958
      Time 70:72, Dec 9, 1957

  The Long Dream (Based on Richard Wright's novel)
      Productions:
      Opened February 17, 1960 for 5 performances
    Reviews:
      New York Theatre Critics' Reviews 1960:362
      New York Times p. 36, Feb 18, 1960
      New Yorker 36:120, Mar 5, 1960
      Reporter 22:38-9, Mar 17, 1960

<u>Mr. Sycamore</u> (Based on a story by Robert Ayre)
    Productions:
       Opened November 13, 1942 for 19 performances.
    Reviews:
       Commonweal 37:144, Nov 27, 1942
       Current History 3:456, Jan 1943
       Independent Woman 21:378, Dec 1942
       Nation 155:598, Nov 28, 1942
       New Republic 107:714, Nov 30, 1942
       New York Theatre Critics' Reviews 1942:179
       New York Times p. 13, Nov 14, 1942
                  VIII, p. 1, Nov 29, 1942
       Newsweek 20:73, Nov 23, 1942
       Theatre Arts 27:20, Jan 1943
       Time 40:53, Nov 23, 1942

FROST, ROBERT

<u>Masque of Reason</u>
    Productions:
       (Off Broadway) Season of 1959-60 (ANTA).
    Reviews:
       New York Times p. 19, Nov 25, 1959

FUNT, JULIAN

<u>The Dancer</u> (with Milton Lewis)
    Productions:
       Opened June 5, 1946 for 5 performances.
    Reviews:
       New York Theatre Critics' Reviews 1946:368
       New York Times p. 16, Jun 6, 1946
       New Yorker 22:40, Jun 15, 1946

<u>The Magic and the Loss</u>
    Productions:
       Opened April 9, 1954 for 27 performances.
    Reviews:
       America 91:145, May 1, 1954
       Commonweal 60:175, May 21, 1954
       Nation 178:390, May 1, 1954
       New Republic 130:21, May 3, 1954
       New York Theatre Critics' Reviews 1954:332
       New York Times p. 10, Apr 10, 1954
       New Yorker 30:63, Apr 17, 1954
       Newsweek 43:66, Apr 19, 1954

FUNT, JULIAN (cont.)
  The Magic and the Loss (cont.)
        Saturday Review 37:24, Apr 24, 1954
        Theatre Arts 38:21, Jun 1954
        Time 63:86+, Apr 19, 1954

GALE, ZONA

  Miss Lulu Bett
    Productions:
        Opened December 27, 1920 for 198+ performances.
    Reviews:
        Bookman 52:567-8, Feb 1921
        Colliers 67:13, Jan 29, 1921
        Current Opinion 70:487-95, Apr 1921
        Dramatic Mirror 83:40, Jan 1, 1921
        Hearst 40:25-7+, Sep 1921
        Independent 105:57, Jan 15, 1921
        Life (NY) 77:64-5, Jan 13, 1921
                  80:18, Jul 13, 1922
        Literary Digest 68:26-7, Feb 12, 1921
        Nation 112:189, Feb 2, 1921
        New Republic 25:204-5, Jan 19, 1921
        New York Clipper 68:19, Jan 5, 1921
        New York Times p. 11, Dec 27, 1920
                       p. 9, Dec 28, 1920
                       VI, p. 1, Jan 9, 1921
                       VI, p. 1, Jan 23, 1921
                       VI, p. 1, Feb 6, 1921
        Outlook 127:579-80, Apr 13, 1921
        Theatre Magazine 33:180-81+, Mar 1921
        Weekly Review 4:90, Jan 26, 1921

  Mr. Pitt
    Productions:
        Opened January 22, 1924 for 87 performances.
    Reviews:
        American Mercury 1:374-5, Mar 1924
        Freeman 8:520-1, Feb 6, 1924
        Life (NY) 83:20, Feb 7, 1924
        New York Times VII, p. 1, Jan 6, 1924
                       p. 15, Jan 23, 1924
        Theatre Magazine 39:17, Apr 1924

  Neighbors
    Productions:

Opened October 31, 1917 in repertory (Washington
Square Players).
Reviews:
Dial 50:112-13, Aug 15, 1915
Dramatic Mirror 75:8, Apr 1, 1916
New York Times p. 13, Oct 22, 1917
p. 11, Dec 4, 1917

GARDNER, DOROTHY

Eastward in Eden
Productions:
Opened November 18, 1947 in 15 performances.
(Off Broadway) Season of 1955-56.
Reviews:
Commonweal 47:196, Dec 5, 1947
Nation 165:628-9, Dec 6, 1947
New Republic 117:31, Dec 1, 1947
New York Theatre Critics' Reviews 1947:261
New York Times p. 33, Nov 19, 1947
p. 25, Apr 18, 1956
New Yorker 23:58+, Nov 29, 1947
Newsweek 30:80, Dec 1, 1947
Theatre Arts 32:12, 14, Jan 1948
Time 50:66, Dec 1, 1947

GARDNER, HERB

The Goodbye People
Productions:
Opened December 3, 1968 for 7 performances.
Reviews:
New York Theatre Critics' Reviews 1968:157
New York Times p. 52, Dec 4, 1968
p. 59, Dec 9, 1968
II, p. 5, Dec 15, 1968
New Yorker 44:180, Dec 14, 1968
Newsweek 72:114, Dec 16, 1968

A Thousand Clowns
Productions:
Opened April 5, 1962 for 428 performances.
Reviews:
Commonweal 76:116-17, Apr 27, 1962
Life 52:57-8, Jun 15, 1962

GARDNER, HERB (cont.)
A Thousand Clowns (cont.)
Nation 194:408, May 5, 1962
New York Theatre Critics' Reviews 1962:302
New York Times p. 31, Apr 6, 1962
II, p. 1, Apr 13, 1962
New Yorker 38:106+, Apr 14, 1962
Newsweek 59:100, Apr 16, 1962
Saturday Review 45:46, Apr 21, 1962
Theatre Arts 46:57-8, Jun 1962
Time 79:82, Apr 13, 1962

GAZZO, MICHAEL V.

A Hatful of Rain
Productions:
Opened November 9, 1955 for 398 performances.
Reviews:
America 94:286, Dec 3, 1955
Catholic World 182:309-10, Jan 1956
Commonweal 63:331, Dec 30, 1955
Life 39:85-6+, Dec 19, 1955
Nation 181:465, Nov 26, 1955
New Republic 134:20, Jan 2, 1956
New York Theatre Critics' Reviews 1955:213
New York Times VI, p. 76, Oct 30, 1955
p. 44, Nov 10, 1955
II, p. 1, Dec 4, 1955
New Yorker 31:121-3, Nov 19, 1955
Newsweek 46:66+, Nov 21, 1955
Saturday Review 38:26, Nov 26, 1955
Theatre Arts 40:22, Jan 1956
Time 66:110, Nov 21, 1955

The Night Circus
Productions:
Opened December 2, 1958 for 7 performances.
Reviews:
New York Theatre Critics' Review 1958:183
New York Times II, p. 3, Sep 14, 1958
p. 44, Dec 3, 1958
New Yorker 34:106-7, Dec 13, 1958
Saturday Review 41:32, Dec 20, 1958
Time 72:44, Dec 15, 1958

GELBER, JACK

The Apple
   Productions:
      (Off Broadway) Opened December 7, 1961 for 64
        performances.
   Reviews:
      Christian Century 79:233-4, Feb 21, 1962
      Commentary 33:331-4, Apr 1962
      Commonweal 75:364-5, Dec 29, 1961
      National Review 12:68, Jan 30, 1962
      New Republic 145:20+, Dec 25, 1961
      New York Times II, p. 3, Nov 26, 1961
                       p. 44, Dec 8, 1961
                       p. 22, Apr 20, 1962
                       p. 33, Apr 23, 1962
      New Yorker 37:97-8, Dec 16, 1961
      Newsweek 58:72, Dec 18, 1961
      Theatre Arts 46:13-14, Feb 1962

The Connection
   Productions:
      (Off Broadway) Opened July 15, 1959 for 722 per-
        formances
      (Off Broadway) Opened September 12, 1961 for 120
        performances.
   Reviews:
      Esquire 55:45-7, Apr 1961
      Harper's Bazaar 220:26-8, Apr 1960
      Nation 189:80, Aug 15, 1959
      New Republic 141:29-30, Sep 28, 1959
      New York Times p. 30, Jul 16, 1959
                    II, p. 1, Feb 7, 1960
                     p. 23, Feb 15, 1960
                     p. 30, Feb 23, 1961
                     p. 17, Mar 4, 1961
                     p. 29, Jun 16, 1961
      New Yorker 35:126-9, Oct 10, 1959
      Saturday Review 42:27, Sep 26, 1959
      Time 75:61, Jan 25, 1960

The Cuban Thing
   Productions:
      Opened September 24, 1968 for 1 performance.
   Reviews:
      New Republic 159:36, Oct 19, 1968
      New York Theatre Critics' Reviews 1968:245

GELBER, JACK (cont.)
    The Cuban Thing (cont.)
        New York Times p. 39, Sep 13, 1968
                      II, p. 1, Sep 15, 1968
                      p. 36, Sep 25, 1968
        New Yorker 44:95-6, Oct 5, 1968

    Square in the Eye
        Productions:
        (Off Broadway) Opened May 19, 1965 for 31 per-
            formances.
        Reviews:
        Commonweal 82:474, Jul 2, 1965
        New Republic 152:30, Jun 26, 1965
        New York Times p. 54, May 20, 1965
                      p. 18, May 22, 1965
                      II, p. 1, Jun 6, 1965
                      p. 44, Jun 15, 1965
        New Yorker 41:56+, May 29, 1965
        Newsweek 65:76, May 31, 1965
        Reporter 33:42, Jul 1, 1965
        Time 85:83, May 28, 1965
        Vogue 146:38, Jul 1965

GIBBS, WOLCOTT

    Season in the Sun
        Productions:
        Opened September 28, 1950 for 367 performances.
        Reviews:
        Catholic World 172:149-50, Nov 1950
        Christian Science Monitor Magazine p. 11, Oct 7,
            1950
        Commonweal 53:42, Oct 20, 1950
        Life 29:111-14, Oct 9, 1950
        Nation 171:320-1, Oct 7, 1950
        New Republic 123:22, Oct 16, 1950
        New York Theatre Critics' Reviews 1950:258
        New York Times p. 31, Sep 29, 1950
                      II, p. 1, Oct 8, 1950
                      II, p. 3, Oct 13, 1950
                      II, p. 3, Nov 26, 1950
        New Yorker 26:54+, Oct 7, 1950
        Newsweek 36:84, Oct 9, 1950
        Saturday Review 33:26-7+, Oct 21, 1950
        School and Society 73:184, Mar 24, 1951

Theatre Arts 34:15, Nov 1950
35:82, Sep 1951
Time 56:85, Oct 9, 1950

GIBSON, WILLIAM

A Cry of Players
Productions:
Opened November 14, 1968 for 72 performances.
Reviews:
America 119:634, Dec 14, 1968
Nation 207:604-5, Dec 2, 1968
New York Theatre Critics' Reviews 1968:179
New York Times p. 40, Nov 15, 1968
II, p. 9, Nov 24, 1968
II, p. 1, Dec 1, 1968
New Yorker 44:122+, Nov 23, 1968
Newsweek 72:126, Nov 25, 1968
Saturday Review 51:60, Nov 30, 1968
Vogue 152:170, Dec 1968

Dinny and the Witches
Productions:
(Off Broadway) Opened December 9, 1959 for 29
performances.
Reviews:
America 102:482, Jan 16, 1960
New York Times p. 53, Dec 10, 1959
New Yorker 35:82+, Dec 19, 1959
Saturday Review 42:24-5, Dec 26, 1959

The Miracle Worker (Based on the life of Helen Keller)
Productions:
Opened October 19, 1959 for 700 performances.
Reviews:
America 102:217, Nov 14, 1959
Christian Century 76:1470, Dec 16, 1959
Commonweal 71:289, Dec 4, 1959
Life 47:127-8, Sep 28, 1959
Nation 189:366, Nov 14, 1959
New Republic 141:28-9, Nov 9, 1959
New York Theatre Critics' Reviews 1959:254
New York Times VI, p. 67, Sep 27, 1959
II, p. 1, Oct 18, 1959
p. 44, Oct 20, 1959
II, p. 1, Nov 1, 1959

GIBSON, WILLIAM (cont.)
  The Miracle Worker (cont.)
                        II, p. 5, Dec 20, 1959
                        II, p. 1, Mar 5, 1961
                        p. 19, Mar 10, 1961
                        p. 22, Mar 20, 1961
                        p. 40, Mar 28, 1961
                        p. 11, Apr 1, 1961
                        p. 31, Apr 5, 1961
                        p. 43, Apr 11, 1961
                        p. 29, Apr 21, 1961
                        p. 35, May 1, 1961
                        p. 22, May 19, 1961
                        p. 28, May 31, 1961
                        p. 20, Aug 21, 1961
    New Yorker 35:132-4, Oct 31, 1959
    Newsweek 54:97, Nov 2, 1959
    Saturday Review 42:28, Nov 7, 1959
    Theatre Arts 43:14, Dec 1959
                44:26-9+, Jan 1960
    Time 74:51, Oct 5, 1959
        74:30, Nov 2, 1959
        74:46-8+, Dec 21, 1959
    Vogue 135:112-13+, Jan 1, 1959

Two for the Seesaw
  Productions:
    Opened January 16, 1958 for 750 performances.
  Reviews:
    America 98:552, Feb 8, 1959
    Catholic World 187:67-8, Apr 1958
    Commonweal 67:540-1, Feb 21, 1958
    Life 44:95-6, Feb 17, 1958
    Nation 186:107, Feb 1, 1958
    New York Theatre Critics' Reviews 1958:394
    New York Times II, p. 1, Jan 12, 1958
                    p. 15, Jan 17, 1958
                    II, p. 1, Jan 26, 1958
                    VII, p. 5, Mar 15, 1959
                    II, p. 1, Apr 12, 1959
                    p. 34, Sep 4, 1963
    New Yorker 33:56+, Jan 25, 1958
    Newsweek 51:63, Jan 27, 1958
    Reporter 18:36, Mar 6, 1958
    Saturday Review 41:25, Feb 1, 1958
    Theatre Arts 42:9, Mar 1958
    Time 71:86+, Jan 27, 1958

GILLETTE, WILLIAM

All The Comforts of Home (Adapted from a play by Carl
    Laufs)
    Productions:
    Opened May 25, 1942 for 8 performances.
    Reviews:
    New York Theatre Critics' Reviews 1942:280
    New York Times p. 24, May 26, 1942

The Dream Maker
    Productions:
    Opened November 21, 1921 for 82 performances.
    Reviews:
    Bookman 54:573-4, Feb 1922
    Dramatic Mirror 84:773, Nov 26, 1921
    New York Clipper 69:20, Nov 30, 1921
    New York Times p. 17, Nov 22, 1921

Electricity
    Productions:
    Opened October 31, 1910 for 16 performances.
    Reviews:
    Blue Book 12:863, Feb 1911
    Bookman 32:352, Dec 1910
    Dramatic Mirror 64:7, Nov 2, 1910
    Dramatist 2:118-20, Jan 1911
    Leslies' Weekly 111:515, Nov 17, 1910
    Life (NY) 56:864, Nov 17, 1910
    Metropolitan Magazine 33:666-7, Feb 1911
    Munsey 44:561, Jan 1911
    Theatre Magazine 12:165+, Dec 1910

Held by the Enemy
    Productions:
    Opened December 5, 1910 in repertory.
    Reviews:
    Dramatic Mirror 65:7, Mar 29, 1911
    Leslies' Weekly 112:617, Jan 1, 1911

The Private Secretary
    Productions:
    Opened December 5, 1910 in repertory.
    Reviews:
    Dramatic Mirror 64:8, Dec 14, 1910

GILLETTE, WILLIAM (cont.)
    Secret Service
        Productions:
            Opened December 5, 1910 in repertory.
            Opened November 8, 1915 for two weeks.
        Reviews:
            Dramatic Mirror 74:8, Nov 13, 1915
            Dramatist 7:649-50, Jan 1916
            Munsey 45:286, May 1911
            New York Times p. 9, Nov 9, 1915
                            VI, p. 8, Nov 14, 1915
            Theatre Arts 27:471, Aug 1943

    Sherlock Holmes (Based on the novels of Arthur Conan
            Doyle)
        Productions:
            Opened December 5, 1910 in repertory.
            Opened October 11, 1915 for four weeks.
            Opened February 20, 1928 for 16 performances.
            Opened November 25, 1929 for 45 performances.
        Reviews:
            Commonweal 11:198, Dec 18, 1929
            Current Literature 50:73-81, Jan 1911
            Dramatic Mirror 74:9, Oct 16, 1915
            New York Times p. 11, Oct 12, 1915
                            VI, p. 8, Oct 17, 1915
                            p. 18, Feb 21, 1928
                            V, p. 14, Nov 10, 1929
                            p. 28, Nov 26, 1929
            Saturday Review 13:18, Jan 4, 1936
            Stage 13:76, Oct 1935
                  14:90-91, Aug 1937
            Theatre Arts 14:105+, Feb 1930
            Theatre Magazine 51:68, Feb 1930

    Too Much Johnson
        Productions:
            Opened December 5, 1910 in repertory.
            (Off Broadway) Opened January 15, 1964 for 23
                performances.
        Reviews:
            New York Times p. 29, Jan 26, 1964
            New Yorker 39:74+, Jan 25, 1964

GILROY, FRANK D.

The Only Game in Town
    Productions:
        Opened May 20, 1968 for 16 performances.
    Reviews:
        Commonweal 88:382+, Jun 14, 1968
        New York Theatre Critics' Reviews 1968:274
        New York Times p. 42, May 21, 1968
        New Yorker 44:102, Jun 1, 1968
        Newsweek 71:102, Jun 3, 1968

The Subject Was Roses
    Productions:
        Opened May 25, 1964 for 832 performances.
    Reviews:
        America 110:853, Jun 20, 1964
        Life 56:17, Jun 19, 1964
            57:71-3, Sep 4, 1964
        Nation 198:611, Jun 15, 1964
        New York Theatre Critics' Reviews 1964:252
        New York Times p. 45, May 26, 1964
                II, p. 1, Jun 7, 1964
                p. 25, Jul 2, 1964
        New Yorker 40:86, Jun 6, 1964
        Newsweek 63:69, Jun 8, 1964
        Saturday Review 47:44, Jun 13, 1964
        Time 83:75, Jun 5, 1964
        Vogue 144:30, Aug 1, 1964

That Summer--That Fall
    Productions:
        Opened March 16, 1967 for 12 performances.
    Reviews:
        Commonweal 86:153-4, Apr 21, 1967
        New York Theatre Critics' Reviews 1967:340
        New York Times p. 33, Mar 17, 1967
                II, p. 3, Apr 2, 1967
        Newsweek 69:110, Mar 27, 1967
        Saturday Review 50:42, Apr 1, 1967
        Time 89:69, Mar 24, 1967

Who'll Save the Plowboy?
    Productions:
        (Off Broadway) Opened January 9, 1962 for 56 per-
           formances.
    Reviews:

GILROY, FRANK D. (cont.)
Who'll Save the Plowboy? (cont.)
America 106:605, Feb 3, 1962
Nation 194:127, Feb 10, 1962
New Republic 146:29-30, Feb 5, 1962
New York Times p. 24, Jan 10, 1962
II, p. 1, Jan 28, 1962
New Yorker 37:69, Jan 20, 1962
Reporter 26:48, Mar 1, 1962
Theatre Arts 46:61-2, Mar 1962
Time 79:56, Jan 26, 1962

GLASPELL, SUSAN

Alison's House
Productions:
Opened December 1, 1930 for 41 performances.
Reviews:
Bookman 72:514, Jan 1931
Catholic World 132:591-2, Feb 1931
Commonweal 13:127, Dec 13, 1930
Drama Magazine 21:13, Jan 1931
Life (NY) 97:18, Jan 2, 1931
Nation 132:590-1, May 27, 1931
New York Times p. 31, Dec 2, 1930
VIII, p. 1, May 10, 1931
IX, p. 3, Nov 13, 1932
Outlook 156:711, Dec 31, 1930
Sketch Book 8:23, Feb 1931
Theatre Arts 15:99+, Feb 1931
Theatre Magazine 53:25, Feb 1931
Vogue 77:84, Feb 1, 1931

*Bernice
Reviews:
New York Times IV, p. 2, Mar 30, 1919

Chains of Dew
Productions:
Opened April 27, 1922 for 16 performances.
Reviews:
Nation 114:627, May 24, 1922
New York Times p. 20, Apr 28, 1922

*Close the Book
Reviews:

New York Times p. 11, May 14, 1918

The Comic Artist (with Norman Matson)
    Productions:
        Opened April 19, 1933 for 21 performances.
    Reviews:
        Commonweal 18:49-50, May 12, 1933
        Nation 136:539-40, May 10, 1933
        New Republic 74:365-6, May 10, 1933
        New York Times VIII, p. 1, Jul 22, 1928
                            p. 20, Apr 20, 1933
        Newsweek 1:26, Apr 29, 1933
        Player's Magazine 9:15, May-Jun 1933
        Stage 10:11, Jun 1933
        Theatre Arts 17:418, Jun 1933
        Time 21:43, May 1, 1933

Inheritors
    Productions:
        Season of 1920-21.
        Opened March 15, 1927 for 17 performances.
    Reviews:
        Bookman 53:526-8, Aug 1921
        Independent 105:329, Apr 2, 1921
        Nation 112:515, Apr 6, 1921
               116:393, Apr 4, 1923
        New York Times VII, p. 1, Mar 27, 1921
                            p. 24, Sep 28, 1925
                            p. 23, Mar 8, 1927
                        VIII, p. 1, Mar 20, 1927
        Review 4:344-6, Apr 13, 1921
        Vogue 69:138, May 1, 1927

Suppressed Desires (with George Cram Cook)
    Productions:
        Opened October 31, 1917 in repertory (Washington
        Square Players).
    Reviews:
        New York Times p. 7, Jan 24, 1918

*Tickless Time (with George Cram Cook)
    Reviews:
        New York Times p. 13, Dec 21, 1918

Trifles
    Productions:
        Opened August 30, 1916 in repertory. (Washing-

GLASPELL, SUSAN (cont.)
Trifles (cont.)
‾‾‾‾‾‾ton Square Players)
Reviews:
Dramatic Mirror 76:7, Nov 25, 1916
New York Times p. 8, Nov 14, 1916
Theatre Magazine 25:21+, Jan 1917

The Verge
Productions:
Opened November 14, 1921 for 38 performances.
Reviews:
Nation 113:708-9, Dec 14, 1921
New Republic 29:47, Dec 7, 1921
New York Clipper 69:20, Nov 23, 1921
New York Times p. 23, Nov 15, 1921
VI, p. 1, Nov 20, 1921

A Woman's Honor
Productions:
Opened April 18, 1918 in repertory. (Greenwich Village Players)
Reviews:
Dramatic Mirror 78:766, Jun 1, 1918
New York Times p. 13, May 21, 1918

GLEASON, JAMES

The Fall Guy (with George Abbott)
Productions:
Opened March 10, 1925 for 95 performances.
Reviews:
American Mercury 5:119, May 1925
Nation 120:362-3, Apr 1, 1925
New York Times VII, p. 1, Jul 20, 1924
p. 19, Mar 11, 1925
Theatre Magazine 42:26+, Sep 1925

Is Zat So? (with Richard Taber)
Productions:
Opened January 5, 1925 for 618 performances.
Reviews:
American Mercury 5:119, May 1925
Bookman 61:338, May 1925
Life (NY) 85:18, Jan 29, 1925
Literary Digest 85:26-7, May 16, 1925

New Republic 42:160-, Apr 1, 1925
New York Times p. 23, Jan 6, 1925
                VII, p. 1, Feb 1, 1925
                p. 12, Feb 17, 1926
                p. 25, Jun 25, 1926
Theatre Magazine 41:17-18, Apr 1925

*Puffy
    Reviews:
    New York Times VII, p. 2, Jul 29, 1928

Shannons of Broadway
    Productions:
    Opened September 26, 1927 for 288 performances.
    Reviews:
    Life (NY) 90:25, Oct 20, 1927
    New York Times p. 30, Sep 27, 1927
                    VIII p. 1, Oct 9, 1927
    Outlook 147:213-14, Oct 19, 1927
    Theatre Magazine 46:74, Nov 1927

GODFREY, THOMAS
No productions.

GOETZ, RUTH and AUGUSTUS

The Heiress (Suggested by Henry James' Washington
        Square)
    Productions:
    Opened September 29, 1947 for 410 performances.
    Opened February 8, 1950 for 16 performances.
    Reviews:
    Catholic World 166:168, Nov 1947
    Commonweal 47:16, Oct 17, 1947
    Forum 108:370-1, Dec 1947
    Life 23:149-50+, Nov 3, 1947
    Nation 165:425-6, Oct 18, 1947
    New Republic 117:36, Oct 13, 1947
    New York Theatre Critics' Reviews 1947:335
    New York Times p. 22, Sep 30, 1947
                    II, p. 1, Oct 5, 1947
                    II, p. 3, Nov 16, 1947
                    p. 34, Feb 9, 1950
    New Yorker 23:50, Oct 11, 1947
    Newsweek 30:80, Oct 13, 1947

171

GOETZ, RUTH and AUGUSTUS (cont.)
  The Heiress (cont.)
          Publisher's Weekly 153:1130, Feb 28, 1948
          School and Society 67:167, Feb 28, 1948
          Theatre Arts 31:12-13, Dec 1947
                     32:32, Apr 1948
                     32:21, Oct 1948
                     34:18, Apr 1950
          Time 50:70+, Oct 13, 1947
          Vogue 110:190, Nov 15, 1947

  The Hidden River (Based on Storm Jameson's novel)
      Productions:
          Opened January 23, 1957 for 61 performances.
      Reviews:
          Catholic World 185:69, Apr 1957
          Commonweal 65:569, Mar 1, 1957
          Nation 184:146, Feb 16, 1957
          New York Theatre Critics' Reviews 1957:378
          New York Times II, p. 1, Jan 20, 1957
                          p. 32, Jan 24, 1957
                          p. 41, Apr 14, 1959
          New Yorker 32:70+, Feb 2, 1957
          Newsweek 49:78, Feb 4, 1957
          Reporter 16:40, Mar 7, 1957
          Saturday Review 40:25, Feb 9, 1957
          Theatre Arts 41:14, Apr 1957
          Time 69:56, Feb 4, 1957

  The Immoralist (Based on Andre Gide's novel)
      Productions:
          Opened February 8, 1954 for 96 performances.
          (Off Broadway) Opened November 7, 1963 for 210
            performances.
      Reviews:
          America 90:581, Feb 27, 1954
          Catholic World 179:70, Apr 1954
          Commonweal 79:283-4, Nov 29, 1963
          Nation 178:156, Feb 20, 1954
          New Republic 130:21, Mar 22, 1954
          New York Theatre Critics' Reviews 1954:373
          New York Times II, p. 1, Jan 31, 1954
                          p. 22, Feb 9, 1954
                          II, p. 1, Feb 14, 1954
                          p. 36, Nov 8, 1963
          New Yorker 29:61, Feb 13, 1954
          Newsweek 43:94, Feb 22, 1954

Saturday Review 37:28, Feb 27, 1954
Theatre Arts 38:17, Apr 1954
Time 63:80, Feb 22, 1954

One-Man Show
  Productions:
    Opened February 8, 1945 for 36 performances.
  Reviews:
    Catholic World 160:551, Mar 1945
    Commonweal 41:475, Feb 23, 1945
    Nation 160:229, Feb 24, 1945
    New Republic 112:295, Feb 26, 1945
    New York Theatre Critics' Reviews 1945:269
    New York Times p. 21, Feb 9, 1945
                 II, p. 1, Feb 18, 1945
    Newsweek 25:84, Feb 19, 1945
    Theatre Arts 29:204, Apr 1945
    Time 45:69, Feb 19, 1945

GOLDMAN, JAMES

Blood, Sweat, and Stanley Poole (with William Goldman)
  Productions:
    Opened October 5, 1961 for 84 performances.
  Reviews:
    America 106:134, Oct 28, 1961
    New York Theatre Critics' Reviews 1961:244
    New York Times p. 31, Oct 6, 1961
    New Yorker 37:165, Oct 14, 1961
    Newsweek 58:102, Oct 16, 1961
    Theatre Arts 45:13+, Dec 1961
    Time 78:58, Oct 13, 1961

The Lion in Winter
  Productions:
    Opened March 3, 1966 for 92 performances.
  Reviews:
    America 114:452, Apr 2, 1966
    Commonweal 84:114, Apr 15, 1966
    Nation 202:374, Mar 28, 1966
    New Republic 154:37, Aug 26, 1966
    New York Times Critics' Reviews 1966:344
    New York Times p. 23, Mar 4, 1966
                 II, p. 1, Mar 13, 1966
    New Yorker 42:110, May 12, 1966
    Newsweek 62:94, Mar 14, 1966

GOLDMAN, JAMES (cont.)
The Lion in Winter (cont.)
Saturday Review 49:55, Mar 19, 1966
Time 87:52, Mar 11, 1966
Vogue 147:145, May 1966

GOLDSMITH, CLIFFORD

What A Life
Productions:
Opened April 13, 1938 for 538 performances.
Reviews:
Catholic World 147:347, Jun 1938
Commonweal 28:21, Apr 29, 1938
Life 4:48-51, Jun 6, 1938
New York Times p. 26, Apr 14, 1938
IX, p. 3, Feb 26, 1939
p. 17, Aug 2, 1939
One Act Play Magazine 2:77-8, May 1938
Stage 15:28, May 1938
Theatre Arts 22:396+, Jun 1938
Time 31:39-40, Apr 25, 1938

GOODHART, WILLIAM

Generation
Productions:
Opened October 6, 1965 for 299 performances.
Reviews:
Commonweal 83:125-6, Oct 28, 1965
Life 59:72A-72B, Nov 5, 1965
New York Theatre Critics' Reviews 1965:262
New York Times p, 5, Oct 8, 1965
New Yorker 41:195-6, Oct 16, 1965
Newsweek 66:114, Oct 18, 1965
Saturday Review 48:74, Oct 23, 1965
Time 86:75, Oct 15, 1965
Vogue 146:68, Nov 15, 1965

GOODMAN, RUTH (see Goetz, Ruth)

GOODRICH, FRANCES

Bridal Wise (See entry under Hackett, Albert)

The Diary of Anne Frank (with Albert Hackett) (Based on
    Anne Frank: The Diary of a Young Girl)
Productions:
    Opened October 5, 1955 for 717 performances.
Reviews:
    America 94:110+, Oct 22, 1955
    Catholic World 182:223, Dec 1955
    Commentary 20:464-7, Nov 1955
    Commonweal 63:91-2, Oct 28, 1955
                65:87, Oct 26, 1956
    Life 39:162-3, Oct 17, 1955
    Nation 181:370, Oct 29, 1955
    New Republic 134:20, Jan 2, 1956
    New York Theatre Critics' Reviews 1955:257
    New York Times VI, p. 47, Sep 25, 1955
                    II, p. 1, Oct 2, 1955
                    p. 24, Oct 6, 1955
                    II, p. 1, Oct 16, 1955
                    II, p. 3, Oct 23, 1955
                    II, p. 1, Sep 30, 1956
                    p. 39, Oct 2, 1956
                    p. 30, Oct 3, 1956
                    p. 18, Oct 6, 1956
                    VI, p. 2, Oct 7, 1956
                    II, p. 1, Oct 14, 1956
                    p. 43, Nov 29, 1956
                    II, p. 7, Dec 9, 1956
    New Yorker 31:75-6, Oct 15, 1955
    Newsweek 46:103, Oct 17, 1955
                48:112, Oct 15, 1956
    Reporter 13:31, Dec 29, 1955
    Saturday Review 38:27, Oct 22, 1955
    Theatre Arts 39:24, Dec 1955
                41:29-30, May 1957
    Time 66:51, Oct 17, 1955
        68:50+, Oct 15, 1956

The Great Big Doorstep (with Albert Hackett) (Based on
    E. P. O'Donell's novel)
Productions:
    Opened November 26, 1942 for 28 performances.
Reviews:
    Catholic World 156:474, Jan 1943

GOODRICH, FRANCES (cont.)
  The Great Big Doorstep (cont.)
          Commonweal 37:206, Dec 11, 1942
          Current History 3:457, Jan 1943
          New York Theatre Critics' Reviews 1942:160
          New York Times p. 26, Nov 27, 1942
                        p. 8, Mar 18, 1950
          Newsweek 20:76, Dec 7, 1942
          Theatre Arts 27:17, Jan 1943
          Time 40:54, Dec 7, 1942

  Up Pops the Devil (See entry under Hackett, Albert)

  *Western Union (with Albert Hackett)
    Reviews:
        New York Times p. 22, Jul 13, 1937

GORDON, RUTH

  The Leading Lady
    Productions:
        Opened October 18, 1948 for 8 performances.
    Reviews:
        Commonweal 49:94, Nov 5, 1948
        New Republic 119:25-6, Nov 8, 1948
        New York Theatre Critics' Reviews 1948:190
        New York Times p. 38, Sep 15, 1948
                      p. 30, Oct 18, 1948
                      p. 33, Oct 19, 1948
        New Yorker 24:42+, Oct 30, 1948
        Newsweek 32:74, Nov 1, 1948
        Time 52:52, Nov 1, 1948

  Miss Jones (See Years Ago)

  Over 21
    Productions:
        Opened January 3, 1944 for 221 performances.
    Reviews:
        Catholic World 158:488, Feb 1944
        Commonweal 359:351-2, Jan 21, 1944
        Life 16:107-8+, Feb 14, 1944
        Nation 158:107, Jan 22, 1944
        New York Theatre Critics' Reviews 1944:297
        New York Times p. 20, Jan 4, 1944
                      II, p. 1, Jan 9, 1944

New Yorker 19:36, Jan 15, 1944
Newsweek 23:70, Jan 17, 1944
Theatre Arts 28:137-8, Mar 1944
Time 43:90, Jan 17, 1944

A Very Rich Woman (Based on a play by Phillippe Heriat)
Productions:
Opened September 30, 1965 for 28 performances.
Reviews:
Commonweal 83:98, Oct 22, 1965
New York Theatre Critics' Reviews 1965:268
New York Times p. 5, Oct 5, 1965
New Yorker 41:184, Oct 9, 1965
Newsweek 66:93, Oct 11, 1965
Saturday Review 48:75, Oct 16, 1965
Time 86:68, Oct 8, 1965
Vogue 146:71, Nov 15, 1965

Years Ago
Productions:
Opened December 3, 1946 for 206 performances.
Reviews:
Catholic World 164:359, Jan 1947
Commonweal 45:254, Dec 20, 1946
Life 22:58-60, Jan 6, 1947
Nation 163:738, Dec 21, 1946
New Republic 115:878, Dec 23, 1946
New York Theatre Critics' Reviews 1946:229
New York Times VI, p. 38, Dec 1, 1946
                     p. 44, Dec 4, 1946
                     II, p. 3, Dec 15, 1946
                     II, p. 1, Jan 12, 1947
                     II, p. 3, May 11, 1947
New Yorker 22:60+, Dec 14, 1946
Newsweek 28:94, Dec 16, 1946
Saturday Review 30:30-2, Mar 22, 1947
Scholastic 50:20, Feb 3, 1947
Theatre Arts 31:16+, Feb 1947
Time 48:70, Dec 16, 1946

GORDONE, CHARLES

No Place To Be Somebody
Productions:
(Off Broadway) Season of 1968-69 (The Other Stage).
(Off Broadway) Opened May 4, 1969 for 250 per-

GORDONE, CHARLES (cont.)
  No Place To Be Somebody (cont.)
        formances.
    Reviews:
        America 121:145, Sep 6, 1969
        Nation 208:644, May 19, 1969
        New York Times p. 53, May 5, 1969
                        II, p. 1, May 18, 1969
                        II, p. 22, May 18, 1969
                        II, p. 1, Jun 8, 1969
                        p. 17, Dec 31, 1969
                        II, p. 1, Jan 25, 1970
                        II, p. 1, May 17, 1970
        New Yorker 45:112+, May 17, 1969
                    45:64, Jan 10, 1970
        Newsweek 73:101, Jun 2, 1969
        Saturday Review 52:18, May 31, 1969
        Time 93:85-6, May 16, 1969

GOW, JAMES

    Deep are The Roots (See entry under d'Usseau, Arnaud)

    Legend of Sarah (with Arnaud d'Usseau)
        Productions:
        Opened October 11, 1950 for 29 performances.
    Reviews:
        Christian Science Monitor Magazine p. 6, Oct 21,
            1950
        Commonweal 53:95, Nov 3, 1950
        Nation 171:370, Oct 21, 1950
        New York Theatre Critics' Reviews 1950:247
        New York Times p. 42, Oct 12, 1950
        New Yorker 26:55-7, Oct 21, 1950
        Newsweek 36:85, Oct 23, 1950
        Theatre Arts 34:14, Dec 1950
        Time 56:58, Oct 23, 1950

    Tomorrow the World (with Arnaud d'Usseau)
        Productions:
        Opened April 14, 1943 for 500 performances.
    Reviews:
        Catholic World 157:298-9, Jun 1943
        Commonweal 38:40, Apr 30, 1943
        Life 14:63-4+, May 31, 1943
        Nation 156:642, May 1, 1943

New Republic 108:637, May 10, 1943
New York Theatre Critics' Reviews 1943:334
New York Times p. 22, Apr 15, 1943
             II, p. 1, Apr 25, 1943
             II, p. 1, May 2, 1943
             p. 24, Apr 26, 1944
New Yorker 19:28, Apr 24, 1943
Newsweek 21:86, Apr 26, 1943
Theatre Arts 27:331-2+, Jun 1943
Time 41:66, Apr 26, 1943

GREEN, PAUL

*Common Glory
  Reviews:
  New York Times p. 11, Jul 19, 1947
               II, p. 1, Jul 27, 1947
               II, p. 13, Jun 26, 1949

*The Confederacy
  Reviews:
  New York Times p. 20, Jul 3, 1958
               II, p. 1, Jul 13, 1958
               IV, p. 8, Jul 20, 1958

*The Cross and the Sword
  Reviews:
  New York Times p. 32, Jun 28, 1965

*Enchanted Maze
  Reviews:
  New York Times p. 10, Dec 14, 1935
               XI, p. 5, Dec 15, 1935

*Faith of Our Fathers
  Reviews:
  New York Times II, p. 1, Jul 1, 1950
               p. 72, Aug 6, 1950
               II, p. 1, Aug 13, 1950
               p. 5, May 26, 1951

*The Founders
  Reviews:
  New York Times p. 14, Aug 24, 1956
               II, p. 3, May 12, 1957
               p. 39, May 14, 1957

GREEN, PAUL (cont.)
The Field God
Productions:
Opened April 21, 1927 for 45 performances.
Reviews:
Life (NY) 89:24, Jun 2, 1927
Nation 125:510-11, May 4, 1927
New York Times p. 18, Apr 22, 1927
VIII, p. 1, May 1, 1927
Theatre Magazine 46:19, Jul 1927

*Highland Call
Reviews:
New York Times p. 19, Nov 21, 1939
North Carolina Historical Review 19:305-7, Jul 1942

The House of Connelly
Productions:
Opened September 28, 1931 for 91 performances.
Reviews:
Arts and Decoration 36:68, Dec 1931
Bookman 74:298-9, Nov 1931
75:290, Jun-Jul, 1932
Catholic World 134:207-8, Nov 1931
Commonweal 14:583-4, Oct 14, 1931
Literary Digest 111:17, Oct 24, 1931
Nation 133:408, Oct 14, 1931
New Republic 68:234-6, Oct 14, 1931
New York Times p. 22, Sep 29, 1931
VIII, p. 1, Oct 4, 1931
Outlook 159:215, Oct 14, 1931
Saturday Review 8:199+, Oct 17, 1931
Theatre Arts 15:75-7, Dec 1931
16:92+, Feb 1932
Vogue 78:100, Dec 1, 1931

Hymn to the Rising Sun
Productions:
Opened May 6, 1937 for 10 performances (Federal
Theatre Project).
Season of 1937-38 in repertory for 22 performances
(Federal Theatre Project).
Reviews:
New York Times p. 14, Jul 13, 1936
p. 28, May 7, 1937
Newsweek 9:29, May 22, 1937

In Abraham's Bosom
  Productions:
    Opened December 30, 1926 for 200 performances.
    Opened September 6, 1927 for 88 performances.
  Reviews:
    Bookman 65:706-7, Aug 1927
    Drama 17:136, Feb 1927
    Dramatist 18:1347, Jul 1927
    Life (NY) 89:24, Jun 2, 1927
    Literary Digest 93:27-8, May 28, 1927
    Nation 124:73, Jan 19, 1927
          124:510-11, May 4, 1927
    New Republic 50:46-7, Mar 2, 1927
    New York Times p. 10, Dec 31, 1926
                VII, p. 1, Feb 20, 1927
                VII, p. 1, May 8, 1927
                p. 26, May 9, 1927
                p. 35, Sep 7, 1927
                X, p. 1, Dec 2, 1928
    Survey 57:591, Feb 1, 1927
    Theatre Magazine 46:18, Jul 1927
                46:24-6+, Aug 1927

Johnny Johnson (with Kurt Weill)
  Productions:
    Opened November 19, 1936 for 68 performances.
    (Off Broadway) Opened May 2, 1941 (Theatre
      Associates).
    (Off Broadway) Season of 1956-57.
  Reviews:
    Catholic World 144:468-9, Jan 1937
    Commonweal 25:162, Dec 4, 1936
    Forum 97:354, Jun 1937
    Literary Digest 123:23, Jan 2, 1937
    Nation 143:674+, Dec 5, 1936
          183:439, Nov 17, 1956
    New Republic 89:179, Dec 9, 1936
    New York Times p. 26, Nov 20, 1936
                XI, p. 2, Nov 22, 1936
                XII, p. 1, Nov 29, 1936
                p. 20, May 3, 1941
                p. 24, Oct 22, 1956
    Newsweek 8:19, Nov 28, 1936
    Scribner's Magazine 101:66-7, Jun 1937
    Theatre Arts 21:15-17, Jan 1937
                21:426-7, Jun 1937
    Time 28:54, Nov 30, 1936

GREEN, PAUL (cont.)
*Last of the Lowries
   Reviews:
     New York Times p. 15, May 7, 1927

*Lost Colony
   Reviews:
     Holiday 1:74-6, Jun 1946
     Life 7:58-9, Jul 31, 1939
     Magazine of Art 31:690-3+, Dec 1938
     New York Times X, p. 2, Jul 11, 1937
                X, p. 1, Aug 15, 1937
                p. 14, Jun 30, 1952
     Player's Magazine 16:10+, Apr 1940
     Reader's Digest 37:30, Jul 1940
     Saturday Review 39:31, Aug 4, 1956
     Theatre Arts 23:518-22, Jul 1939
                36:72-3, Jul 1952
                40:69-70+, Jul 1956
     Time 34:48, Jul 10, 1939

Native Son (with Richard Wright) (Based on Richard
     Wright's novel)
   Productions:
     Opened March 24, 1941 for 114 performances.
     Opened October 23, 1942 for 84 performances.
   Reviews:
     Catholic World 153:217, May 1941
     Commonweal 33:622, Apr 11, 1941
     Independent Woman 21:378, Dec 1942
     Life 10:94-6, Apr 7, 1941
     Nation 152:417, Apr 5, 1941
     New Republic 104:468-9, Apr 7, 1941
     New York Theatre Critics' Reviews 1941:349
     New York Times p. 26, Mar 25, 1941
                  IX, p. 1, Mar 30, 1941
                  IX, p. 1, Apr 6, 1941
                  p. 10, Oct 24, 1942
                  VIII, p. 1, Nov 1, 1942
     Theatre Arts 25:329-32, May 1941
                25:467-70, Jun 1941
                26:744, Dec 1942
     Time 37:76, Apr 7, 1941

Peer Gynt (Adapted from Henrik Ibsen's play)
   Productions:
     Opened January 28, 1951 for 32 performances.

Reviews:
Catholic World 172:464, Mar 1951
Commonweal 53:468-9, Feb 16, 1951
Nation 172:139-40, Feb 10, 1951
New Republic 124:22-3, Mar 5, 1951
New York Theatre Critics' Reviews 1951:373
New York Times II, p. 3, Jan 21, 1951
      p. 15, Jan 29, 1951
      II, p. 1, Feb 4, 1951
New Yorker 26:61, Feb 10, 1951
School and Society 73:184, Mar 24, 1951
Theatre Arts 35:14, Apr 1951

The Potter's Field (See Roll, Sweet Chariot)

Roll, Sweet Chariot
Productions:
Opened October 2, 1934 for 7 performances.
Reviews:
New York Times IX, p. 1, Sep 30, 1934
      p. 24, Oct 3, 1934
      X, p. 1, Oct 14, 1934
Stage 12:5, Nov 1934
Theatre Arts 18:813-14, Nov 1934
Vanity Fair 43:46, Dec 1934

*Salvation on a String
Reviews:
America 91:425, Jul 24, 1954
New York Times p. 23, Jul 7, 1954

Saturday Night
Productions:
(Off Broadway) Season of 1940-41.
No Reviews.

*Shroud My Body Down
Reviews:
New York Times II, p. 1, Dec 9, 1934
Theatre Arts 19:311, Apr 1935
      19:961-2, Dec 1935

*Tread the Green Grass
Reviews:
New York Times IX, p. 1, Jul 24, 1932
      p. 19, Apr 21, 1950
Player's Magazine 9:10, Sep-Oct 1932

GREEN, PAUL (cont.)
Tread the Green Grass (cont.)
Theatre Arts 16:1003, Dec 1932

Unto Such Glory
Productions:
Opened May 6, 1937 for 10 performances (Federal
Theatre Project).
Season of 1937-38 in repertory for 22 performances
(Federal Theatre Project).
Reviews:
New York Times p. 14, Jan 13, 1936
                p. 28, May 7, 1937
Newsweek 9:29, May 22, 1937

*Wilderness Road
Reviews:
New York Times p. 43, Jun 19, 1955
                p. 17, Jun 30, 1955
                p. 20, Jun 30, 1955
Saturday Review 39:30, Aug 4, 1956

HACKETT, ALBERT

Bridal Wise (with Frances Goodrich)
Productions:
Opened May 30, 1932 for 128 performances.
Reviews:
Catholic World 135:464-5, Jul 1932
Commonweal 16:188, Jun 15, 1932
New York Times p. 15, May 31, 1932
Stage 9:2-3, Jul 1932

The Diary of Anne Frank (See entry under Goodrich,
Frances)

The Great Big Doorstep (See entry under Goodrich,
Frances)

Up Pops the Devil (with Frances Goodrich)
Productions:
Opened September 1, 1930 for 148 performances.
Reviews:
Arts and Decoration 34:96, Nov 1930
Catholic World 132:205, Nov 1930
Drama 21:15, Nov 1930

Life (NY) 96:16, Sep 19, 1930
National Magazine 59:107, Nov 1930
New York Times p. 19, Sep 2, 1930
                  VIII, p. 1, Sep 14, 1930
Outlook 156:113, Sep 17, 1930
Theatre Magazine 52:25-6, Nov 1930
Vogue 76:100, Oct 27, 1930

Western Union (See entry under Goodrich, Frances)

HAGAN, JAMES

Guns
   Productions:
     Opened August 6, 1928 for 48 performances.
   Reviews:
     New York Times p. 25, Aug 7, 1928

Mid-West
   Productions:
     Opened January 7, 1936 for 22 performances.
   Reviews:
     Commonweal 23:356, Jan 24, 1936
     Literary Digest 121:19, Jan 18, 1936
     Nation 142:112, Jan 22, 1936
     New York Times p. 21, Jan 2, 1936
                  IX, p. 3, Jan 5, 1936
                  p. 22, Jan 8, 1936
     Theatre Arts 20:175-6, Mar 1936

One Sunday Afternoon
   Productions:
     Opened February 15, 1933 for 322 performances.
   Reviews:
     Arts and Decoration 38:58, Apr 1933
     Catholic World 137-38, Apr 1933
     Commonweal 17:610, Mar 29, 1933
     Nation 136:272, Mar 8, 1933
     New Outlook 161:47, Apr 1933
     New York Times p. 23, Feb 16, 1933
                  IX, p. 2, Mar 26, 1933
                  X, p. 2, Sep 17, 1933
     Player's Magazine 9:25, May-Jun 1933
     Stage 10:28-9, Apr 1933
     Theatre Arts 17:262-4, Apr 1933
     Vanity Fair 40:60, May 1933

HAGAN, JAMES (cont.)
  One Sunday Afternoon (cont.)
       Vogue 81:86, Apr 15, 1933

HAINES, WILLIAM WISTER

  Command Decision
     Productions:
     Opened October 1, 1947 for 408 performances.
     Reviews:
       Catholic World 166:170, Nov 1947
       Commonweal 47:16, Oct 17, 1947
       Forum 108:368-70, Dec 1947
       Life 23:107-8+, Oct 20, 1947
       Nation 165:480-1, Nov 1, 1947
       New Republic 117:36, Oct 13, 1947
       New York Theatre Critics' Reviews 1947:328
       New York Times p. 59, Sep 21, 1947
                      VI, p. 30, Sep 28, 1947
                      p. 30, Oct 2, 1947
                      II, p. 1, Oct 12, 1947
                      II, p. 3, Nov 23, 1947
       New Yorker 23:50+, Oct 11, 1947
       Newsweek 30:80, Oct 13, 1947
       Saturday Review 30:30-3, Oct 25, 1947
       School and Society 66:326-7, Oct 25, 1947
       Theatre Arts 31:13-14, 60, Dec 1947
                    32:30, Apr 1948
       Time 50:70, Oct 13, 1947
       Vogue 110:112, Nov 15, 1947

HANLEY, WILLIAM

  Mrs. Dally
     Productions:
     Opened September 22, 1965 for 53 performances.
     Reviews:
       America 113:508, Oct 30, 1965
       Commonweal 83:61-2, Oct 15, 1965
       New York Theatre Critics' Review 1965:270
       New York Times p. 5, Sep 25, 1965
       New Yorker 41:176, Oct 2, 1965
       Newsweek 66:94, Oct 4, 1965
       Saturday Review 48:34, Oct 9, 1965
       Time 86:67, Oct 1, 1965

Mrs. Dally Has A Lover
    Productions:
        (Off Broadway) Opened October 1, 1962 for 48 per-
            formances.
    Reviews:
        Commonweal 77:123, October 26, 1962
        New York Times p. 47, Oct 2, 1962
        New Yorker 38:183, Oct 13, 1962

Slow Dance On The Killing Ground
    Productions:
        Opened November 30, 1964 for 88 performances.
    Reviews:
        America 113:508, Oct 30, 1965
        Commonweal 81:485-6, Jan 8, 1965
                    83:61-2, Oct 15, 1965
        Life (NY) 58:10, Jan 15, 1965
        Nation 199:523-4, Dec 28, 1964
        New Republic 152:32, Jan 23, 1965
        New York Theatre Critics' Review 1964:127
        New York Times p. 50, Dec 1, 1964
                       p. 56, Dec 2, 1964
                       II, p. 5, Dec 13, 1964
        New Yorker 41:176, Oct 2, 1965
        Newsweek 64:84+, Dec 14, 1964
                 66:94, Oct 4, 1965
        Saturday Review 47:24-5, Dec 19, 1964
                        48:34, Oct 9, 1965
        Time 84:73, Dec 11, 1964
             86:67, Oct 1, 1965
        Vogue 145:27, Jan 15, 1965

Whisper Into My Good Ear
    Productions:
        (Off Broadway) Opened October 1, 1962 for 48 per-
            formances.
    Reviews:
        Commonweal 77:123, Oct 26, 1962
        New York Times p. 47, Oct 2, 1962
        New Yorker 38:182, Oct 13, 1962

HANSBERRY, LORRAINE

A Raisin in the Sun
    Productions:
        Opened March 11, 1959 for 530 performances.

HANSBERRY, LORRAINE (cont.)
  A Raisin in the Sun (cont.)
      Reviews:
          America 101:286-7, May 2, 1959
          Catholic World 189:159, May 1959
                          190:31-5, Oct 1959
          Commentary 27:527-30, Jun 1959
          Commonweal 70:81, Apr 17, 1959
          Life 46:137-8, Apr 27, 1959
          Nation 188:301-2, Apr 4, 1959
          New Republic 140:21, Apr 13, 1959
          New York Theatre Critics' Reviews 1959:344
          New York Times II, p. 3, Mar 8, 1959
                          p. 27, Mar 12, 1959
                          p. 25, Mar 13, 1959
                          II, p. 1, Mar 29, 1959
                          p. 32, Aug 5, 1959
                          p. 19, Jul 27, 1965
          New Yorker 35:100-2, Mar 21, 1959
          Newsweek 53:76, Mar 23, 1959
          Reporter 20:34-5, Apr 16, 1959
          Saturday Review 42:28, Apr 4, 1959
          Theatre Arts 43:22-3, May 1959
                       43:58-61, Jul 1959
          Time 73:58+, Mar 23, 1959

The Sign in Sidney Brustein's Window
  Productions:
      Opened October 15, 1964 for 101 performances.
  Reviews:
      America 111:758, Dec 5, 1964
      Commonweal 81:197, Nov 6, 1964
      Nation 199:340, Nov 9, 1964
      National Review 17:250, Mar 23, 1965
      New York Theatre Critics' Reviews 1964:190
      New York Times II, p. 1, Oct 11, 1964
                      p. 32, Oct 16, 1964
                      II, p. 1, Nov 1, 1964
      New Yorker 40:93, Oct 24, 1964
      Newsweek 64:101, Oct 26, 1964
      Saturday Review 47:31-, Oct 31, 1964
      Time 84:67, Oct 23, 1964

To Be Young, Gifted and Black (Adapted by Richard
        Nemiroff)
  Productions:
      (Off Broadway) Opened January 2, 1969 for 380

performances.
Reviews:
Commonweal 90:542-3, Sep 5, 1969
Nation 208:548, Apr 28, 1969
New York Times p. 15, Jan 3, 1969
    II, p. 1, May 25, 1969
    p. 36, Sep 22, 1969

The World of Lorraine Hansberry (See To Be Young,
 Gifted and Black)

HARRIGAN, EDWARD
No Productions.

HART, MOSS

The American Way (See entry under Kaufman, George S.)

Christopher Blake
 Productions:
 Opened November 30, 1946 for 114 performances.
 Reviews:
  Catholic World 164:357-8, Jan 1947
  Commonweal 45:255, Dec 20, 1946
  Life (NY) 22:95-6+, Jan 13, 1947
  Nation 163:738, Dec 21, 1946
  New Republic 115:824, Dec 16, 1946
  New York Theatre Critics' Reviews 1946:233
  New York Times p. 33, Dec 2, 1946
       II, p. 5, Dec 8, 1946
  New Yorker 22:67-9, Dec 7, 1946
  Newsweek 28:92, Dec 9, 1946
  Theatre Arts 31:12-13+, Feb 1947
  Time 48:83, Dec 9, 1946

The Climate of Eden (Based on Edgar Mittelholzer's novel
 Shadows Move Among Them)
 Productions:
 Opened November 14, 1952 for 20 performances.
 Reviews:
  Commonweal 57:223, Dec 5, 1952
  Nation 175:473, Nov 22, 1952
  New York Theatre Critics' Reviews 1952:204
  New York Times II, p. 1, Nov 2, 1952
      p. 20, Nov 7, 1952

HART, MOSS (cont.)
The Climate of Eden (cont.)
II, p. 1, Nov 16, 1952
p. 11, Nov 21, 1953
New Yorker 28:69, Nov 15, 1952
Newsweek 40:74, Nov 17, 1952
Saturday Review 35:37-8, Nov 22, 1952
Theatre Arts 37:23-4, Jan 1953
Time 60:102+, Nov 17, 1952

The Fabulous Invalid (with George S. Kaufman)
Productions:
Opened October 8, 1938 for 65 performances.
Reviews:
Catholic World 148:210-11, Nov 1938
Commonweal 28:677, Oct 21, 1938
Independent Woman 17:347, Nov 1938
Nation 147:432, Oct 22, 1938
New Republic 96:334, Oct 26, 1938
New York Times p. 15, Oct 10, 1938
IX, p. 1, Oct 16, 1938
IX, p. 3, Oct 1930
p. 23, Jan 26, 1950
Newsweek 12:34, Oct 24, 1938
Publishers' Weekly 134:1581, Oct 29, 1938
Stage 16:7+, Nov 1938
16:34, Nov 1938
Theatre Arts 22:862-4, Dec 1938
Time 32:50, Oct 17, 1938

George Washington Slept Here (See entry under Kaufman,
George S.)

Light Up the Sky
Productions:
Opened November 18, 1948 for 216 performances.
Reviews:
Catholic World 168:324, Jan 1949
Commonweal 49:196, Dec 3, 1948
Forum 111:92, Feb 1949
Life 25:115-16+, Dec 6, 1948
Nation 167:674, Dec 11, 1948
New Republic 119:37-8, Dec 6, 1948
New York Theatre Critics' Reviews 1948:148
New York Times p. 34, Nov 19, 1948
II, p. 5, Dec 5, 1948
II, p. 1, Jan 2, 1949

New Yorker 24:55, Nov 27, 1948
Newsweek 32:82, Nov 29, 1948
Saturday Review 31:24-5, Dec 11, 1948
School and Society 69:154, Feb 26, 1949
Time 52:78, Nov 29, 1948
    54:59, Aug 8, 1949
Vogue 113:116, Jan 1949

The Man Who Came To Dinner (with George S. Kaufman)

Productions:
    Opened October 16, 1939 for 739 performances.
Reviews:
    Catholic World 150:339-40, Dec 1939
    Commonweal 31:47, Nov 3, 1939
    Life 7:88-9, Oct 30, 1939
    Nation 149:474-5, Oct 28, 1939
    New Republic 100:368, Nov 1, 1939
    New York Theatre Critics' Reviews 1940:472
                         1941:492
    New York Times p. 21, Sep 26, 1939
           IX, p. 2, Oct 1, 1939
           p. 31, Oct 17, 1939
           IX, p. 1, Oct 22, 1939
           IX, p. 1, Oct 29, 1939
           p. 19, Feb 10, 1940
           IX, p. 3, Feb 18, 1940
           p. 17, Feb 26, 1941
           IV, p. 2, Mar 2, 1941
           IX, p. 1, Mar 23, 1941
           p. 13, Jul 29, 1941
           IX, p. 4, Dec 14, 1941
    Newsweek 14:38, Oct 30, 1939
    Stage 1:18, Nov 1940
        1:19, Dec 1940
        1:13, Jan 1941
    Theatre Arts 23:770, 788-98, Nov 1939
              23:851-2+, Dec 1939
              24:407, Jun 1940
    Time 34:42, Oct 30, 1939
        35:50, Jan 22, 1940
        38:31, Aug 11, 1941
    Vogue 94:63-4, Nov 15, 1939

Merrily We Roll Along (See entry under Kaufman, George S.)

Once in A Lifetime (See entry under Kaufman, George S.)

HART, MOSS (cont.)
  Winged Victory
    Productions:
      Opened November 20, 1943 for 212 performances.
    Reviews:
      American Magazine 137:28-9, Jun 1944
      Catholic World 158:392, Jan 1944
      Commonweal 39:204-5, Dec 10, 1943
      Life 15:58-64, Nov 29, 1943
      Nation 157:675, Dec 4, 1943
      New Republic 109:808, Dec 4, 1943
      New York Theatre Critics' Reviews 1943:216
      New York Times p. 22, Nov 3, 1943
                     VI, p. 8, Nov 7, 1943
                     p. 56, Nov 21, 1943
                     p. 24, Nov 22, 1943
                     II, p. 1, Nov 28, 1943
      New Yorker 19:51-2, Dec 4, 1943
      Newsweek 22:86, Nov 29, 1943
      Theatre Arts 27:723, Dec 1943
                   28:6-8, Jan 1944
                   28:88+, Feb 1944
      Time 42:43-4, Nov 29, 1943
           45:84, Apr 16, 1945

You Can't Take It With You (with George S. Kaufman)
    Productions:
      Opened December 14, 1936 for 837 performances.
      Opened March 26, 1945 for 17 performances.
      Opened November 23, 1965 for 255 performances.
      Opened February 10, 1967 for 16 performances
        (APA Repertory Co.).
    Reviews:
      America 113:762-3, Dec 11, 1965
      Catholic World 144:597-8, Feb 1937
      Commonweal 25:249, Dec 25, 1936
      Life 2:54-5, Jun 28, 1937
          56:16, Dec 17, 1965
      Literary Digest 122:22, Dec 26, 1936
      Nation 143:770, Dec 26, 1936
             201:484, Dec 13, 1965
      New Republic 89:273, Dec 30, 1936
                   153:28, Dec 8, 1965
      New York Theatre Critics' Reviews 1965:248
      New York Times p. 30, Dec 1, 1936
                     XII, p. 6, Dec 6, 1936
                     p. 31, Dec 15, 1936

XI, p. 3, Dec 20, 1936
X, p. 1, Aug 29, 1937
X, p. 3, Oct 31, 1937
X, p. 1, Jan 9, 1938
X, p. 1, Jan 16, 1938
p. 23, Mar 27, 1945
p. 8, Apr 7, 1951
II, p. 1, Nov 21, 1965
p. 32, Nov 24, 1965
p. 66, Nov 25, 1965
II, p. 5, Dec 5, 1965
Newsweek 8:38, Dec 26, 1936
25:87, Apr 9, 1945
Saturday Review 15:3-4, May 8, 1937
Stage 14:52-3, Jan 1937
14:41-4, May 1937
Theatre Arts 21:96-7, Feb 1937
Time 28:33, Dec 28, 1936
Vogue 89:69, Jan 15, 1937

HAWTHORNE, RUTH

Mrs. Partridge Presents (See entry under Kennedy, Mary)

Queen Bee (with Louise Fox Connell)
Productions:
Opened November 12, 1929 for 21 performances.
Reviews:
New York Times p. 25, Nov 13, 1929

HAYDEN, JOHN

Lost Horizons (Based on a play by Harry Segall)
Productions:
Opened October 15, 1934 for 56 performances.
Reviews:
Catholic World 140:338, Dec 1934
Commonweal 20:618, Oct 26, 1934
Literary Digest 118:24, Oct 27, 1934
Nation 139:517, Oct 31, 1934
New Republic 80:341, Oct 31, 1934
New York Times p. 31, Oct 16, 1934
IX, p. 1, Oct 21, 1934
Theatre Arts 18:903-4, Dec 1934

HAYDEN, JOHN (cont.)
  Lost Horizons (cont.)
      Time 24:44, Oct 29, 1934

HAYES, ALFRED

  The Girl on the Via Flaminia
      Productions:
      Opened February 9, 1954 for 111 performances.
      Reviews:
        America 90:581, Feb 27, 1954
        Catholic World 179:69, Apr 1954
        Life 36:57-8+, Mar 15, 1954
        Nation 178:184+, Feb 27, 1954
        New Republic 130:21, May 3, 1954
        New York Theatre Critics' Reviews 1954:349
        New York Times p. 37, Feb 10, 1954
                    II, p. 3, May 16, 1954
                    p. 26, Oct 13, 1954
        New Yorker 30:65, Feb 20, 1954
        Saturday Review 37:25, Mar 6, 1954
        Theatre Arts 38:22, Jun 1954
        Time 63:74, Apr 12, 1954

  Journeyman (with Leon Alexander) (Based on Erskine
      Caldwell's novel)
      Productions:
      Opened January 29, 1938 for 41 performances.
      Reviews:
        Nation 146:190, Feb 12, 1938
        New York Times p. 14, Jan 31, 1938
        One Act Play Magazine 1:945, Feb 1938

HAYES, JOSEPH

  Calculated Risk (Based on a play by George Ross and
      Campbell Singer)
      Productions:
      Opened October 31, 1962 for 221 performances.
      Reviews:
        Commonweal 77:280, Dec 7, 1962
        New York Theatre Critics' Reviews 1962:214
        New York Times p. 33, Oct 17, 1962
                    p. 35, Nov 1, 1962
        New Yorker 38:146, Nov 10, 1962

Newsweek 60:62, Nov 12, 1962
Theatre Arts 46:12-13, Dec 1962
Time 80:64, Nov 9, 1962

The Desperate Hours (Based on his novel)
    Productions:
        Opened February 10, 1955 for 212 performances.
    Reviews:
        America 92:685-6, Mar 26, 1955
        Catholic World 181:65-6, Apr 1955
        Life 38:75-6+, Feb 28, 1955
        Nation 180:186, Feb 26, 1955
        New Republic 132:19-20, Mar 7, 1955
        New York Theatre Critics' Reviews 1955:370
        New York Times II, p. 1, Jan 30, 1955
                        p. 20, Feb 11, 1955
                      II, p. 1, Feb 20, 1955
                      II, p. 3, May 1, 1955
                      II, p. 3, Jun 2, 1955
        New Yorker 31:76-7, Feb 19, 1955
        Newsweek 45:90, Feb 21, 1955
        Saturday Review 38:22, Feb 26, 1955
        Theatre Arts 39:20-1, 24-5, Apr 1955
        Time 65:54, Feb 21, 1955

Leaf and Bough
    Productions:
        Opened January 21, 1949 for 3 performances.
    Reviews:
        New York Theatre Critics' Reviews 1949:381
        New York Times p. 10, Jan 22, 1949
        New Yorker 24:42+, Jan 29, 1949
        Newsweek 33:71, Jan 31, 1949
        Saturday Review 31:24, Apr 3, 1948
        Time 53:44, Jan 31, 1949

*Midnight Sun
    Reviews:
        New York Times p. 26, Nov 6, 1959

HECHT, BEN

The Egotist
    Productions:
        Opened December 25, 1922 for 48 performances.
    Reviews:

HECHT, BEN (cont.)
The Egotist (cont.)
New York Clipper 70:20, Jan 10, 1923
New York Times p. 12, Dec 27, 1922
Theatre Magazine 37:19, Mar 1923

A Flag Is Born
Productions:
Opened September 5, 1946 for 120 performances
Reviews:
Catholic World 164:71, Oct 1946
Life 21:87-8, Sep 30, 1946
New Republic 115:351, Sep 23, 1946
New York Theatre Critics' Reviews 1946:348
New York Times p. 10, Sep 7, 1946
　　　　　　　　II, p. 21, Sep 15, 1946
　　　　　　　　p. 19, Oct 16, 1946
New Yorker 22:48+, Sep 14, 1946
Newsweek 28:92, Sep 16, 1946
　　　　　　30:74, Nov 10, 1947
Time 48:85, Sep 16, 1946

The Front Page (with Charles MacArthur)
Productions:
Opened August 14, 1928 for 276 performances.
Opened September 4, 1946 for 79 performances.
Opened May 10, 1969 for 64 performances.
Reviews:
America 120:673-4, Jun 7, 1969
　　　　　121:434, Nov 8, 1969
American Mercury 15:251, Oct 1928
Catholic World 128:211-12, Nov 1928
　　　　　　　　164:72, Oct 1946
Commonweal 90:437-8, Jul 11, 1969
Dial 86:82-3, Jan 1929
Life (NY) 92:12, Aug 30, 1928
Life 21:78-80, Sep 23, 1946
Literary Digest 98:29, Sep 29, 1928
Nation 127:207, Aug 29, 1928
　　　　　208:676, May 26, 1969
New Republic 56:73-4, Sep 5, 1928
　　　　　　　115:351, Sep 23, 1946
New York Theatre Critics' Reviews 1946:355
　　　　　　　　　　　　　　　1969:287
New York Times p. 19, Aug 15, 1928
　　　　　　　　VII, p. 1, Aug 26, 1928
　　　　　　　　VIII, p. 4, Jan 6, 1929

p. 27, Nov 12, 1937
p. 22, Sep 5, 1946
II, p. 21, Sep 15, 1946
p. 85, Oct 20, 1968
p. 52, May 12, 1969
p. 54, May 12, 1969
II, p. 1, May 25, 1969
p. 86, Nov 2, 1969
p. 67, Feb 2, 1970
New Yorker 22:46, Sep 14, 1946
45:112, May 17, 1969
44:160, Oct 19, 1968
Newsweek 28:92, Sep 16, 1946
73:133, May 26, 1969
Outlook 149:705, Aug 29, 1928
Saturday Review 5:706, Feb 23, 1929
29:24-6, Oct 26, 1946
Theatre Arts 12:701-6, Oct 1928
Theatre Magazine 48:24-6+, Aug 1928
48:40, Oct 1928
Time 48:85, Sep 16, 1946
93:75, May 23, 1969
Vogue 72:94-5+, Oct 13, 1928

The Great Magoo (with Gene Fowler)
Productions:
Opened December 2, 1932 for 11 performances.
Reviews:
Nation 135:625-6, Dec 21, 1932
New York Times IX, p. 2, Nov 27, 1932
p. 20, Dec 3, 1932
Theatre Arts 17:112, Feb 1933
Vanity Fair 39:41, Feb 1933

The Hero of Santa Maria (with Kenneth Goodman)
Productions:
Opened August 30, 1916 in repertory (Washington
Square Players).
Reviews:
Dramatic Mirror 77:7, Feb 24, 1917
New York Times p. 7, Feb 14, 1917
Theatre Magazine 25:213+, Apr 1917

Ladies and Gentlemen (See entry under MacArthur,
Charles)

HECHT, BEN (cont.)
Lily of the Valley
Productions:
Opened January 26, 1942 for 8 performances.
Reviews:
Catholic World 154:732, Mar 1942
Commonweal 35:418, Feb 13, 1942
New Republic 106:204, Feb 9, 1942
New York Theatre Critics' Reviews 1942:365
New York Times p. 25, Jan 27, 1942
                  IX, p. 1, Feb 1, 1942
Theatre Arts 26:225, Apr 1942

*Man Eating Tiger
Reviews:
New York Times VIII, p. 4, Sep 25, 1927

The Stork (Adapted from the play by Laszlo Fodor)
Productions:
Opened January 26, 1925 for 8 performances.
Reviews:
New York Times p. 14, Jan 27, 1925

Swan Song (with Charles MacArthur) (Based on a story
     by Ramon Romero and Harriet Hinsdale)
Productions:
Opened May 15, 1946 for 158 performances.
Reviews:
Catholic World 163:360, Jul 1946
New York Theatre Critics' Reviews 1946:386
New York Times p. 29, May 16, 1946
New Yorker 22:46-7, May 25, 1946
Time 47:66, May 27, 1946

To Quito and Back
Productions:
Opened October 6, 1937 for 46 performances.
Reviews:
Catholic World 146:218-19, Nov 1937
Commonweal 26:606, Oct 22, 1937
Independent Woman 16:368, Nov 1937
Life 3:120-22+, Oct 11, 1937
Nation 145:412, Oct 16, 1937
New Republic 92:342, Oct 27, 1937
New York Times XI, p. 2, Sep 19, 1937
               p. 29, Sep 21, 1937
               XI, p. 3, Sep 26, 1937

p. 30, Oct 7, 1937
Newsweek 10:25, Oct 18, 1937
Theatre Arts 21:919, 20, Dec 1937
Time 30:32+, Oct 18, 1937

20th Century (with Charles MacArthur)
    Productions:
    Opened December 29, 1932 for 152 performances.
    Reviews:
    Arts and Decoration 38:63, Mar 1933
    Catholic World 136:589, Feb 1933
                 172:387-8, Feb 1951
    Commonweal 17:329, Jan 18, 1933
                 53:349, Jan 12, 1951
    Christian Science Monitor Magazine p. 9, Dec 30,
        1950
    Life 30:117-18+, Feb 19, 1951
    Nation 136:75, Jan 18, 1933
           172:18, Jan 6, 1951
    New Outlook 161:48, Feb 1933
    New Republic 124:22, Jan 8, 1951
    New York Theatre Critics' Reviews 1950:163
    New York Times p. 15, Dec 30, 1932
                   IX, p. 3, Jan 1, 1933
                   IX, p. 3, Jan 29, 1933
                   IX, p. 1, Feb 12, 1933
                   II, p. 4, Dec 24, 1950
                   p. 23, Dec 25, 1950
    New Yorker 26:54+, Jan 6, 1951
    Newsweek 37:80, Jan 22, 1951
    Saturday Review 34:25-7, Mar 24, 1951
    Stage 10:32-3, Feb 1933
    Theatre Arts 17:178, Mar 1933
                 35:12, 22-3, Mar 1951
    Time 21:40, Jan 9, 1933
         57:30, Jan 8, 1951

Winkelberg
    Productions:
    (Off Broadway) Season of 1957-58.
    Reviews:
    New Republic 138:21, Feb 3, 1958
    New York Times II, p. 3, Jan 12, 1958
                   p. 26, Jan 15, 1958
    Saturday Review 41:25, Feb 1, 1958

HEGGEN, THOMAS

Mister Roberts (See entry under Logan, Joshua)

HELLER, JOSEPH

We Bombed in New Haven
    Productions:
        Opened Oct 16, 1968 for 85 performances.
    Reviews:
        America 119:447, Nov 9, 1968
        Life 64:14, Jan 12, 1968
        Nation 206:26-7, Jan 1, 1968
                207:477-8, Nov 4, 1968
        New York Theatre Critics' Reviews 1968:206
        New York Times II, p. 1, Dec 3, 1967
                        p. 58, Dec 7, 1967
                        II, p. 3, Dec 17, 1967
                        p. 49, Sep 10, 1968
                        p. 51, Oct 17, 1968
                        II, p. 1, Oct 27, 1968
        New Yorker 44:139, Oct 26, 1968
        Newsweek 70:96, Dec 18, 1967
                72:135, Oct 28, 1968
        Reporter 38:44, Jan 25, 1968
        Saturday Review 51:53, Nov 2, 1968
        Time 90:87, Dec 15, 1967
            92:69, Oct 25, 1968

HELLMAN, LILLIAN

Another Part of the Forest
    Productions:
        Opened November 20, 1946 for 182 performances.
    Reviews:
        Catholic World 164:360, Jan 1947
        Commonweal 45:201, Dec 6, 1946
        Life 21:71-2+, Dec 9, 1946
        Nation 163:671, Dec 7, 1946
        New Republic 115:822, Dec 16, 1946
        New York Theatre Critics' Reviews 1946:247
        New York Times II, p. 1, Nov 17, 1946
                        VI, p. 68, Nov 17, 1946
                        p. 42, Nov 21, 1946
                        II, p. 1, Dec 1, 1946

II, p. 3, Feb 16, 1947
             p. 19, Oct 17, 1949
             p. 34, Oct 18, 1949
             p. 83, Nov 13, 1949
New Yorker 22:58+, Nov 30, 1946
Newsweek 28:94, Dec 14, 1946
Saturday Review 29:20-3, Dec 14, 1946
School and Society 65:251, Apr 5, 1947
Theatre Arts 31:14, 17, Jan 1947
Time 48:56, Dec 2, 1946

The Autumn Garden
    Productions:
        Opened March 7, 1951 for 101 performances.
    Reviews:
        Catholic World 173:67, Apr 1951
        Commonweal 53:645, Apr 6, 1951
        Nation 172:257, Mar 17, 1951
        New Republic 124:21-2, Mar 26, 1951
        New York Theatre Critics' Reviews 1951:325
        New York Times II, p. 1, Feb 25, 1951
                        p. 36, Mar 8, 1951
                      II, p. 1, Mar 18, 1951
        New Yorker 27:52+, Mar 17, 1951
        Newsweek 37:84, Mar 19, 1951
        Theatre Arts 35:18, May 1951
                     35:17+, Sep 1951
        Time 57:51, Mar 19, 1951

The Children's Hour
    Productions:
        Opened November 20, 1934 for 691 performances.
        Opened December 18, 1952 for 189 performances.
    Reviews:
        Catholic World 140:466-7, Jan 1935
                       176:388, Feb 1953
        Commonweal 57:377, Jan 16, 1953
        Golden Book 21:28A, Feb, 1935
        Life 34:51+, Jan 19, 1953
        Literary Digest 118:20, Dec 1, 1934
                        120:20, Dec 28, 1935
        Nation 139:656-7, Dec 5, 1934
               140:610, May 22, 1935
               176:18, Jan 3, 1953
        New Republic 81:169, Dec 19, 1934
                     128:30-1, Jan 5, 1953
        New York Theatre Critics' Reviews 1952:151

201

HELLMAN, LILLIAN (cont.)
The Children's Hour (cont.)
New York Times p. 23, Nov 21, 1934
X, p. 1, Dec 2, 1934
IX, p. 3, Nov 17, 1935
VI, p. 11, Dec 22, 1935
IX, p. 1, Jun 7, 1936
p. 27, Nov 13, 1936
XII, p. 2, Nov 29, 1936
II, p. 3, Dec 14, 1952
p. 35, Dec 19, 1952
II, p. 1, Dec 28, 1952
p. 39, Nov 10, 1953
New Yorker 28:30, Jan 3, 1953
Newsweek 40:40, Dec 29, 1952
Saturday Review 11:523, Mar 2, 1935
11:528, Mar 16, 1935
36:30, Jan 10, 1953
School and Society 77:117-18, Feb 21, 1953
Stage 12:28-9, Jan 1935
Theatre Arts 19:13-15, Jan 1935
Time 24:24, Dec 3, 1934
60:55, Dec 29, 1952
Vanity Fair 43:37, Feb 1935

Days to Come
Productions:
Opened December 15, 1936 for 7 performances.
Reviews:
Commonweal 25:276, Jan 1, 1937
Literary Digest 122:22, Dec 26, 1936
Nation 143:769-70, Dec 26, 1936
New Republic 89:274, Dec 30, 1936
New York Times XI, p. 4, Dec 13, 1936
p. 35, Dec 16, 1936

Ladies and Gentlemen (See Another Part of the Forest)

The Lark (Adapted from the play by Jean Anouilh)
Productions:
Opened November 17, 1955 for 229 performances.
Reviews:
America 90:420-1, Jan 23, 1954
94:363, Dec 24, 1955
95:109-10, Apr 28, 1956
Catholic World 182:308-9, Jan 1952
Commonweal 63:304, Dec 23, 1955

Holiday 19:77+, Mar 1956
Life 39:113-114+, Dec 12, 1955
Nation 181:485-6, Dec 3, 1955
New Republic 133:21, Dec 5, 1955
New York Theatre Critics' Reviews 1955:206
New York Times II, p. 1, Nov 13, 1955
            II, p. 1, Nov 27, 1955
New Yorker 31:112+, Dec 3, 1955
Newsweek 46:110, Nov 28, 1955
Reporter 13:31, Dec 29, 1955
Saturday Review 38:24, Feb 19, 1955
Theatre Arts 39:23, Apr 1955
           40:63-4+, Mar 1956
           40:8-10, May 1956
Time 66:76+, Nov 28, 1955

The Little Foxes
  Productions:
    Opened February 15, 1939 for 410 performances.
    Opened October 26, 1967 for 100 performances
     (Repertory Theatre of Lincoln Center).
  Reviews:
    America 117:723, Dec 9, 1967
    Catholic World 149:87-8, Apr 1939
    Christian Century 85:332, Mar 13, 1968
    Commonweal 29:525, Mar 3, 1939
              87:304-5, Dec 1, 1967
    Harper's Bazaar 80:220, Dec 1946
    Life 6:70-73, Mar 6, 1939
    Nation 148:244, Feb 25, 1939
    New Republic 98:279, Apr 12, 1939
    New York Theatre Critics' Reviews 1940:490
                               1967:237
    New York Times p. 16, Feb 16, 1939
                 IX, p. 1, Feb 26, 1939
                 VIII, p. 2, Nov 1, 1942
                 II, p. 1, Oct 22, 1967
                 p. 53, Oct 27, 1967
                 II, p. 1, Nov 5, 1967
                 p. 24, Jan 6, 1968
    New Yorker 43:162, Nov 4, 1967
    Newsweek 13:26, Feb 27, 1939
           70:86, Nov 6, 1967
    One Act Play Magazine 2:748-9, Feb 1939
    Reporter 38:36, Jan 11, 1968
    Saturday Review 50:26, Nov 11, 1967
    Stage 16:36-7+, Apr 1, 1939

HELLMAN, LILLIAN (cont.)
   The Little Foxes (cont.)
            Theatre Arts 23:244+, Apr 1939
            Time 33:38+, Feb 27, 1939
                 90:64+, Nov 3, 1967

Montserrat (Adapted from the French of Emmanuel Robles)
   Productions:
      Opened October 29, 1949 for 65 performances.
      (Off Broadway) Season of 1960-61.
   Reviews:
      America 104:577, Jan 28, 1961
      Catholic World 170:227-8, Dec 1949
      Commonweal 51:179-80, Nov 1949
      Forum 112:338-9, Dec 1949
      Nation 169:478, Nov 12, 1949
      New Republic 121:21-2, Dec 5, 1949
      New York Theatre Critics' Reviews 1949:244
      New York Times p. 21, Oct 31, 1949
                     II, p. 3, May 11, 1952
                     p. 34, May 26, 1954
                     p. 30, Jan 9, 1961
      New Yorker 36:68-70, Jan 21, 1961
                 25:62+, Nov 5, 1949
      Newsweek 34:80-1, Nov 7, 1949
      Saturday Review 32:53-4, Nov 19, 1949
      School and Society 71:25-6, Jan 14, 1950
      Theatre Arts 34:10, Jan 1950
      Time 54:79, Nov 7, 1949

My Mother, My Father and Me (Based on Burt Blechman's
      How Much?)
   Productions:
      Opened March 23, 1963 for 17 performances.
   Reviews:
      Nation 196:334, Apr 20, 1963
      New York Theatre Critics' Reviews 1963:302
      New York Times p. 5, Mar 25, 1963
      New Yorker 39:108, Mar 30, 1963
      Newsweek 61:85, Apr 8, 1963
      Reporter 28:48, Apr 25, 1963
      Saturday Review 46:27, Apr 27, 1963
      Theatre Arts 47:69-70, May 1963
      Time 81:56, Apr 5, 1963

The Searching Wind
   Productions:

Opened April 12, 1944 for 318 performances.
Reviews:
    Catholic World 159:170-1, May 1944
    Commonweal 40:40, Apr 28, 1944
    Life 16:43-4+, May 1, 1944
    Nation 158:494, Apr 22, 1944
    New Republic 110:604, May 1, 1944
    New York Theatre Critics' Reviews 1944:217
    New York Times II, p. 1, Apr 9, 1944
                    p. 25, Apr 13, 1944
                    II, p. 1, Apr 23, 1944
    New York Times Magazine p. 19, Apr 23, 1944
    New Yorker 20:42+, Apr 22, 1944
    Newsweek 23:86+, Apr 24, 1944
    Quarterly Journal of Speech 31:22-8, Feb 1945
    Theatre Arts 28:331-3, Jun 1944
    Time 43:72, Apr 24, 1944

Toys in the Attic
    Productions:
    Opened February 25, 1960 for 556 performances.
Reviews:
    America 103:323, May 28, 1960
    Christian Century 77:511, Apr 27, 1960
    Life 48:53-4+, Apr 4, 1960
    Nation 190:261, Mar 19, 1960
    New Republic 142:22, Mar 14, 1960
    New York Theatre Critics' Reviews 1960:345
    New York Times II, p. 3, Feb 21, 1960
                    p. 23, Feb 26, 1960
                    II, p. 1, Mar 6, 1960
    New Yorker 36:124-5, Mar 5, 1960
    Newsweek 55:89, Mar 7, 1960
    Reporter 22:43, Mar 31, 1960
    Saturday Review 43:71-2, Mar 12, 1960
    Time 75:50, Mar 7, 1960

Watch on the Rhine
    Productions:
    Opened April 1, 1941 for 378 performances.
Reviews:
    Catholic World 153:215-16, May 1941
    Commonweal 34:15-16, Apr 25, 1941
    Life 10:81-2+, Apr 14, 1941
    Nation 152:453, Apr 12, 1941
    New Republic 104:498-9, Apr 14, 1941
    New York Theatre Critics' Reviews 1941:341

HELLMAN, LILLIAN (cont.)
Watch on the Rhine (cont.)
New York Times p. 26, Mar 25, 1941
              p. 26, Apr 2, 1941
              IV, p. 8, Apr 6, 1941
              IX, p. 1, Apr 13, 1941
              IX, p. 1, Apr 20, 1941
              p. 20, Apr 24, 1941
              VI, p. 2, Apr 27, 1941
              IX, p. 1, Aug 24, 1941
              VIII, p. 1, May 3, 1942
              p. 10, Feb 26, 1945
New Yorker 17:32, Apr 12, 1941
Newsweek 17:70, Apr 14, 1941
Theatre Arts 25:409-11, Jun 1941
           25:791, Nov 1941
Time 37:64, Apr 14, 1941
     38:56, Nov 3, 1941

HEMINGWAY, ERNEST

A Farewell to Arms (See entry under Stallings,
        Laurence)

The Fifth Column (Adapted by Benjamin Glazer from
        Hemingway's published play)
Productions:
    Opened March 6, 1940 for 87 performances.
Reviews:
    Catholic World 151:97-8, Apr 1940
    Commonweal 31:475, Mar 22, 1940
    Forum 103:272, May 1940
    Life 8:100-1, Mar 25, 1940
    Nation 150:371-2, Mar 16, 1940
    New Republic 102:408, Mar 25, 1940
    New York Theatre Critics' Reviews 1940:370
    New York Times p. 9, Jan 27, 1940
                   IX, p. 1, Feb 4, 1940
                   p. 18, Mar 7, 1940
                   X, p. 1, Mar 17, 1940
    New Yorker 16:44, Mar 16, 1940
    Newsweek 15:52, Mar 18, 1940
    Theatre Arts 24:310-11+, May 1940
    Time 35:65-7, Mar 18, 1940

HERBERT, F. HUGH

The Best House in Naples (Adapted from the play by
    Eduardo de Felippo)
  Productions:
    Opened October 26, 1956 for 3 performances.
  Reviews:
    New York Theatre Critics' Reviews 1956:243
    New York Times p. 16, Oct 27, 1956
    New Yorker 32:73, Nov 3, 1956
    Theatre Arts 41:20, Jan 1957

A Girl Can Tell
  Productions:
    Opened October 29, 1953 for 60 performances.
  Reviews:
    America 90:215, Nov 21, 1953
    Catholic World 178:231, Dec 1953
    Commonweal 59:164, Nov 20, 1953
    Nation 177:434, Nov 21, 1953
    New York Theatre Critics' Reviews 1953:237
    New York Times II, p. 3, Oct 25, 1953
                   p. 28, Oct 30, 1953
    New Yorker 29:76+, Nov 7, 1953
    Newsweek 42:60, Nov 9, 1953
    Saturday Review 36:38, Nov 14, 1953
    Theatre Arts 38:17, Jan 1954
    Time 62:72, Nov 9, 1953

For Keeps
  Productions:
    Opened June 14, 1944 for 29 performances.
  Reviews:
    Catholic World 159:459, Aug 1944
    Commonweal 40:255, Jun 30, 1944
    New York Theatre Critics' Reviews 1944:169
    New York Times p. 17, Jun 15, 1944
    New Yorker 20:47, Jun 1944

For Love or Money
  Productions:
    Opened November 4, 1947 for 265 performances.
  Reviews:
    Catholic World 166:267, Dec 1947
    New Republic 117:32, Nov 17, 1947
    New York Theatre Critics' Reviews 1947:271
    New York Times II, p. 1, Nov 2, 1947

HERBERT, F. HUGH (cont.)
  For Love or Money (cont.)
                    p. 36, Nov 5, 1947
          New Yorker 23:54+, Nov 15, 1947
          Newsweek 30:84, Nov 17, 1947
          School and Society 66:421-2, Nov 29, 1947
          Time 50:87, Nov 17, 1947

  Kiss and Tell
     Productions:
          Opened March 17, 1943 for 956 performances.
     Reviews:
          Catholic World 157:18, May 6, 1943
          Commonweal 37:590, Apr 2, 1943
          Independent Woman 22:155, May 1943
          Life 14:41-2, Apr 12, 1943
          Nation 156:534, Apr 10, 1943
          New York Theatre Critics' Reviews 1943:356
          New York Times p. 22, Mar 8, 1943
                         II, p. 1, Mar 28, 1943
                         II, p. 1, Apr 4, 1943
          Newsweek 21:58, May 29, 1943
          Theatre Arts 27:276, May 1943
          Time 41:55, Mar 29, 1943

  The Moon Is Blue
     Productions:
          Opened March 8, 1951 for 924 performances.
          (Off Broadway) Opened June 7, 1961 in repertory.
     Reviews:
          Catholic World 173:147, May 1951
          Commonweal 53:618, Mar 30, 1951
          Life 30:87-8, Apr 2, 1951
          New Republic 124:21, Apr 9, 1951
          New York Theatre Critics' Reviews 1951:322
          New York Times p. 29, Mar 9, 1951
                         II, p. 3, Mar 25, 1951
                         p. 24, Jul 8, 1953
                         II, p. 1, Aug 9, 1953
                         p. 29, Aug 9, 1961
          New Yorker 27:56, Mar 17, 1951
          Newsweek 37:84, Mar 19, 1951
          Theatre Arts 35:19, May 1951
          Time 57:52, May 19, 1951

  Quiet Please (with Hanz Kraly) (Based on a story by
          Ferdinand Reyher)

Productions:
Opened November 8, 1940 for 16 performances.
Reviews:
Commonweal 33:127, Nov 22, 1940
New York Theatre Critics' Reviews 1940:224
New York Times IX, p. 2, Oct 20, 1940
p. 20, Nov 9, 1940
Newsweek 16:60, Nov 18, 1940

HERNE, JAMES A.

*Drifting Apart, or the Fisherman's Child
Reviews:
New York Times p. 16, Aug 20, 1941

HEYWARD, DOROTHY AND DUBOSE

Brass Ankle (Dubose Heyward)
Productions:
Opened April 23, 1931 for 44 performances.
Reviews:
Arts and Decoration 35:82, Jul 1931
Catholic World 133:335-7, Jun 1931
Commonweal 14:16, May 6, 1931
Drama Magazine 21:10-11, May 1931
Life (NY) Vol. 97, May 8, 1931
Nation 132:538-9, May 13, 1931
New Republic 66:357, May 13, 1931
New York Times p. 26, Apr 24, 1931
Outlook 158:26, May 6, 1931
Vogue 77:100, Jun 15, 1931

Cinderalative (Dorothy Heyward with Dorothy De Jagers)
Productions:
Opened September 18, 1930 for 4 performances.
Reviews:
New York Times p. 18, Sep 19, 1930

The Dud (See Nancy Ann)

Mamba's Daughters (From Dubose Heyward's novel)
Productions:
Opened January 3, 1939 for 162 performances.
Opened March 23, 1940 for 17 performances.
Reviews:

  Mamba's Daughters (cont.)
        Catholic World 148:597-8, Feb 1939
        Commonweal 29:358, Jan 20, 1939
        Life 6:49-51, Jan 23, 1939
        Nation 148:74, Jan 14, 1939
        New Republic 97:315, Jan 18, 1939
        New York Times IX, p. 3, Jan 1, 1939
                        p. 24, Jan 4, 1939
                        IX, p. 1, Jan 15, 1939
                        p. 10, Mar 25, 1940
                        p. 12, Mar 21, 1953
        North American Review 247 no. 2:366-7, Jun 1939
        Newsweek 13:26, Jan 16, 1939
        Theatre Arts 23:169, Mar 1939
        Time 33:41, Jan 16, 1939

Nancy Ann (Dorothy Heyward)
    Productions:
        Opened March 31, 1924 for 40 performances.
    Reviews:
        Dramatist 15:1205-6, Apr 1924
        Life (NY) 83:20, Apr 17, 1924
        New York Times VIII, p. 2, Mar 9, 1924
                        p. 18, Apr 1, 1924
                        VIII, p. 1, Apr 6, 1924
        Theatre Magazine 39:19, Jun 1924

Porgy
    Productions:
        Opened October 10, 1927 for 367 performances.
        Opened September 13, 1929 for 34 performances.
    Reviews:
        Dial 83:529-30, Dec 1927
        Independent 119:606, Dec 17, 1927
        Literary Digest 95:27-8, Nov 5, 1927
        Nation 125:457-8, Oct 26, 1927
        New Republic 52:261-2, Oct 26, 1927
        New York Times p. 26, Oct 11, 1927
                        IX, p. 1, Oct 16, 1927
                        IX, p. 2, Apr 29, 1928
                        p. 17, May 29, 1928
                        VIII, p. 1, Jul 1, 1928
                        X, p. 1, Dec 2, 1928
                        p. 32, Apr 11, 1929
                        IX, p. 1, Apr 28, 1929
                        p. 28, May 9, 1929

p. 17, Sep 14, 1929
Outlook 147:402-3, Nov 30, 1927
Saturday Review 4:251, Oct 29, 1927
Survey 57:465-6, Jan 1, 1928
Theatre Arts 11:901-4, Dec 1927
Theatre Magazine 46:82, Dec 1927
Vogue 70:87, Dec 1, 1927

Set My People Free (Dorothy Heyward)
 Productions:
  Opened November 3, 1948 for 36 performances.
  (Off Broadway) Season of 1948-49 (Neighborhod
    Playhouse).
 Reviews:
  Catholic World 168:241-2, Dec 1948
  Commonweal 49:142, Nov 19, 1948
  Forum 110:353-4, Dec 1948
  Nation 167:586, Nov 20, 1948
  New Republic 119:28-9, Nov 22, 1948
  New York Theatre Critics' Reviews 1948:171
  New York Times p. 38, Nov 4, 1948
             II, p. 1, Nov 14, 1948
  New Yorker 24:60+, Nov 13, 1948
  Newsweek 32:82, Nov 15, 1948
  School and Society 68:389, Dec 4, 1948
  Time 52:84, Nov 15, 1948
  Vogue 112:183, Dec 1948

South Pacific (Dorothy Heyward with Howard Rigsby)
 Productions:
  Opened December 29, 1943 for 5 performances.
 Reviews:
  Commonweal 29:328-9, Jan 14, 1944
  New York Theatre Critics' Reviews 1943:184
  New York Times p. 11, Dec 30, 1943
  New Yorker 19:38, Jan 8, 1944
  Newsweek 23:89, Jan 10, 1944
  Theatre Arts 28:136-7, Mar 1944
  Time 43:72, Jan 10, 1944

HOPKINS, ARTHUR

Burlesque (See entry under Watters, George Manker)

Conquest
 Productions:

HOPKINS, ARTHUR (cont.)
    Conquest (cont.)
        Opened February 18, 1933 for 10 performances.
        Reviews:
            Commonweal 17:526, Mar 8, 1933
            Nation 136:270, Mar 8, 1933
            New Republic 74:159, Mar 22, 1933
            New York Times p. 11, Feb 20, 1933
            Theatre Arts 17:343-4, May 1933
            Vogue 81:86, Apr 15, 1933

    The Fatted Calf
        Productions:
            Opened February 19, 1912 for 8 performances.
        Reviews:
            Dramatic Mirror 67:6, Feb 28, 1912
            Dramatist 3:247, Apr 1912
            Green Book 7:1068-9, May 1912

    *Moonshine
        Reviews:
            Dramatic Mirror 68:7, Sep 25, 1912
            New York Times III, p. 7, Jun 23, 1918
                        p. 11, Sep 17, 1918

HOROVITZ, ISRAEL

    The Honest-to-God Schnozzola
        Productions:
            (Off Broadway) Opened April 21, 1969 for 8 per-
                formances.
        Reviews:
            New York Times p. 40, Apr 22, 1969
            New Yorker 45:108-9, May 3, 1969
            Newsweek 73:118, May 5, 1969

    The Indian Wants the Bronx
        Productions:
            (Off Broadway) Opened January 17, 1968 for 204
                performances.
        Reviews:
            Nation 206:221, Feb 12, 1968
            New York Times p. 47, Jan 18, 1968
            New Yorker 43:86-7, Jan 27, 1968
            Reporter 38:35, May 2, 1968
            Vogue 151:166, May 1968

It's Called the Sugar Plum
    Productions:
        (Off Broadway) Opened January 17, 1968 for 204
            performances.
    Reviews:
        New York Times p. 47, Jan 18, 1968
        New Yorker 43:87, Jan 27, 1968

Leader
    Productions:
        (Off Broadway) Opened April 21, 1969 for 8 per-
            formances.
    Reviews:
        New York Times p. 40, Apr 22, 1969
        New Yorker 45:108-9, May 3, 1969
        Newsweek 73:118, May 5, 1969

Line
    Productions:
        (Off Broadway) Season of 1967-1968 (La Mama Ex-
            perimental Theatre Club).
    No Reviews.

Morning
    Productions:
        Opened November 28, 1968 for 52 performances.
    Reviews:
        Commonweal 89:471-2, Jan 10, 1969
        Nation 207:665-6, Dec 16, 1968
        New York Theatre Critics' Reviews 1968:168
        New York Times p. 52, Nov 29, 1968
                       II, p. 7, Dec 8, 1968
                       p. 54, Dec 10, 1968
        New Yorker 44:139-40, Dec 7, 1968
        Time 92:71-2, Dec 6, 1968

Rats
    Productions:
        (Off Broadway) Opened May 8, 1968 for 80 per-
            formances.
    Reviews:
        Harper's Bazaar 237:113-15, Oct 1968
        Nation 206:772+, Jun 10, 1968
        New York Times p. 55, May 9, 1968
                       II, p. 1, May 19, 1968
        New Yorker 44:74, May 18, 1968

HOWARD, GEORGE BRONSON

The Henrietta (See The New Henrietta under Smith, Winchell)

The Only Law (with Wilson Mizner)
   Productions:
   Opened August 2, 1909 for 48 performances.
   Reviews:
      Dramatic Mirror 62:5, Aug 14, 1909
      Forum 42:360-1, Oct 1909
      Green Book 2:777-9, Oct 1909
      Hampton 23:542, Oct 1909
      Metropolitan Magazine 31:126-7, Oct 1909
      Munsey 42:248-53, Nov 1909
      Pearson 22:506, Oct 1909
      Theatre Magazine 10:73-4, Sep 1909
      World To-Day 17:912, Sep 1909

HOWARD, SIDNEY

Alien Corn
   Productions:
   Opened February 20, 1933 for 98 performances.
   Reviews:
      Arts and Decoration 38:48-9, Apr 1933
      Catholic World 137:77, Apr 1933
      Commonweal 17:553, Mar 15, 1933
      Literary Digest 115:20, Mar 11, 1933
      Nation 136:299-300, Mar 15, 1933
      New Outlook 161:46, Apr 1933
      New Republic 74:101-2, Mar 8, 1933
      New York Times p. 19, Feb 14, 1933
                     p. 17, Feb 21, 1933
                     IX, p. 1, Feb 26, 1933
                     X, p. 3, Jan 20, 1935
                     p. 26, Jul 6, 1939
                     IX, p. 2, Jul 23, 1939
      Newsweek 1:26, Feb 25, 1933
      Stage 10:7-9, Mar 1933
            10:12-13, Mar 1933
      Theatre Arts 17:342, May 1933
      Time 21:18, Feb 27, 1933
      Vanity Fair 40:31-2, May 1933
      Vogue 81:61+, Apr 15, 1933

Bewitched (See entry under Sheldon, Edward)

214

Casanova (Adapted from the play by Lorenzo de Azertis)
    Productions:
    Opened September 26, 1923 for 77 performances.
    Reviews:
        Nation 117:412, Oct 10, 1923
        New Republic 36:180-1, Oct 10, 1923
        New York Times p. 10, Sep 27, 1923
        Theatre Magazine 38:13+, Nov 1923

Dodsworth (Based on the novel by Sinclair Lewis)
    Productions:
    Opened February 24, 1934 for 147 performances.
    Opened August 20, 1934 for 168 performances.
    Reviews:
        Catholic World 139:86-7, Apr 1934
        Collier's 95:16+, Jan 12, 1935
        Commonweal 19:554, Mar 16, 1934
        Golden Book Magazine 20:376, Oct 1934
        Literary Digest 117:22, Mar 17, 1934
        Nation 138:311-12+, Mar 14, 1934
        New Outlook 163:44, Apr 1934
        New Republic 78:134, Mar 14, 1934
        New York Times p. 20, Feb 26, 1934
                      p. 12, Aug 21, 1934
                      IX, p. 2, Apr 5, 1936
                      p. 26, Feb 23, 1938
                      XI, p. 3, Mar 13, 1938
        Newsweek 3:34, Mar 3, 1934
        Review of Reviews 89:48, Apr 1934
        Saturday Review 10:569-70, Mar 24, 1934
        Stage 11:6+, Mar 1934
              12:9-10, Oct 1934
        Theatre Arts 18:325-6, May 1934
        Time 23:40, Mar 5, 1934

*Gather Ye Rosebuds (with R. Littell)
    Reviews:
        New York Times p. 33, Nov 29, 1934
                      X, p. 1, Dec 2, 1934

The Ghost of Yankee Doodle
    Productions:
    Opened November 22, 1937 for 48 performances.
    Reviews:
        Catholic World 146:467, Jan 1938
        Commonweal 27:191, Dec 10, 1937
        Nation 145:664, Dec 11, 1937

HOWARD, SIDNEY (cont.)
    The Ghost of Yankee Doodle (cont.)
            New York Times p. 28, Oct 28, 1937
                        XI, p. 2, Nov 7, 1937
                        XI, p. 2, Nov 21, 1937
                        p. 26, Nov 23, 1937
            Newsweek 10:32, Dec 6, 1937
            Theatre Arts 22:20-1, Jan 1938
            Time 30:41, Dec 6, 1937

Half Gods
    Productions:
        Opened December 21, 1929 for 17 performances.
    Reviews:
        Drama Magazine 20:138, Feb 1930
        Life (NY) 95:20, Jan 10, 1930
        Nation 130:52, Jan 8, 1930
        New York Times p. 18, Dec 23, 1929
        Theatre Arts 14:109, Feb 1930
        Theatre Magazine 51:66, Feb 1930
        Vogue 75:118, Feb 15, 1930

The Late Christopher Bean (Adapted from the French of
        Rene Fauchois)
    Productions:
        Opened October 31, 1932 for 224 performances.
    Reviews:
        Arts and Decoration 38:50, Jan 1933
        Catholic World 136:335-6, Dec 1932
        Commonweal 17:75, Nov 16, 1932
        Nation 135:484-5, Nov 16, 1932
        New Outlook 161:46, Dec 1932
        New York Times p. 24, Nov 1, 1932
                    p. 15, May 17, 1933
                    p. 13, Aug 28, 1935
        Player's Magazine 9:13, Nov-Dec 1932
        Stage 10:35, Dec 1932
        Theatre Arts 17:18+, Jan 1933
        Town and Country 87:26+, Dec 1, 1932
        Vogue 80:48, Dec 15, 1932

Lucky Sam McCarver
    Productions:
        Opened October 21, 1925 for 29 performances.
    Reviews:
        Life (NY) 86:20, Nov 12, 1925
        New York Times p. 22, Oct 22, 1925

VIII, p. 1, Nov 1, 1925
VII, p. 1, Feb 21, 1926
p. 10, Apr 15, 1950
Theatre Arts 10:15-16, Jan 1926

Madam Will You Walk
Productions:
Opened December 1, 1953 for 42 performances.
Reviews:
America 90:346, Dec 26, 1953
Catholic World 178:307, Jan 1954
Commonweal 59:330, Jan 1, 1954
Nation 177:554, Dec 19, 1953
New York Theatre Critics' Reviews 1953:201
New York Times p. 20, Nov 14, 1939
p. 2, Dec 2, 1953
New Yorker 29:87-8, Dec 12, 1953
Newsweek 42:61, Dec 14, 1953
Saturday Review 36:28, Dec 19, 1953
Time 62:94, Dec 14, 1953

Marseilles (Adapted from the French of Marcel Pagnol)
Productions:
Opened November 17, 1930 for 16 performances.
Reviews:
Commonweal 13:160, Dec 10, 1930
New York Times IX, p. 3, Nov 9, 1930
p. 28, Nov 18, 1930
Theatre Arts 15:18-19, Jan 1931

Muse of All Work (See The Late Christopher Bean)

Ned McCobb's Daughter
Productions:
Opened November 29, 1926 for 156 performances.
Reviews:
Bookman 64:731, Feb 1927
Dramatist 18:1331-2, Jan 1927
Independent 118:270, Mar 5, 1927
Life (NY) 88:19, Dec 23, 1926
Nation 123:697, Dec 29, 1926
New Republic 49:108-9, Dec 15, 1926
New York Times p. 26, Nov 30, 1926
VIII, p. 2, Dec 5, 1926
VII, p. 2, Feb 6, 1927
VIII, p. 2, Mar 20, 1927
p. 29, Jan 7, 1948

217

HOWARD, SIDNEY (cont.)
  Ned McCobb's Daughter (cont.)
        Theatre Magazine 45:15, Feb 1927
        Vogue 16:120, Feb 1, 1927
        Yale Review 17:175, Oct 1927

  Ode to Liberty (Adapted from the French of Michel
        Duran)
        Productions:
        Opened December 21, 1934 for 67 performances.
        Reviews:
        Catholic World 140:598-9, Feb 1935
        New York Times p. 28, Dec 11, 1934
                     p. 20, Dec 22, 1934
                     p. 24, Jul 9, 1935
                     p. 20, Aug 6, 1935
        Time 24:24, Dec 31, 1934

  Paths of Glory (Adapted from Humphrey Cobb's novel)
        Productions:
        Opened September 26, 1935 for 23 performances.
        Reviews:
        Catholic World 142:212-13, Nov 1935
        Commonweal 22:585, Oct 11, 1935
        Literary Digest 121:19, Jan 4, 1936
        New Republic 84:302, Oct 23, 1935
        New York Times p. 29, Sep 19, 1935
                     p. 24, Sep 27, 1935
                     IX, p. 1, Oct 13, 1935
                     p. 16, Oct 14, 1935
                     p. 23, Mar 19, 1936
        Newsweek 6:33, Oct 5, 1935
        Theatre Arts 19:813-15, Nov 1935
                     20:74-6, Jan 1936
        Time 26:38, Oct 7, 1935

  Salvation (with Charles MacArthur)
        Productions:
        Opened January 31, 1928 for 31 performances.
        Reviews:
        Dial 84:351-2, Apr 1928
        Life (NY) 91:19, Feb 23, 1928
        Nation 126:220, Feb 22, 1928
        New Republic 54:18-19, Feb 22, 1928
        New York Times p. 31, Feb 1, 1928
                     VIII, p. 1, Feb 12, 1928
        Vogue 71:142, Apr 1, 1928

The Silver Cord
    Productions:
        Opened December 20, 1926 for 112 performances.
    Reviews:
        Bookman 65:70-71, Mar 1927
        Dial 82:259-60, Mar 1927
        Drama Magazine 17:171, Mar 1927
        Dramatist 18:1337-8, Apr 1927
        Independent 118:270, Mar 5, 1927
        Life (NY) 89:21, Jan 6, 1927
        Nation 124:20-1, Jan 5, 1927
        New Republic 49:328, Feb 9, 1927
        New York Times p. 21, Dec 21, 1926
                        p. 29, Sep 14, 1927
                        VIII, p. 1, Oct 2, 1927
                        IX, p. 2, Oct 16, 1927
                        IX, p. 2, Apr 29, 1928
        Theatre Magazine 45:58, Feb 1927
                         45:19, Mar 1927
                         45:50, Mar 1927
        Vogue 69:80-81+, Feb 15, 1927

Swords
    Productions:
        Opened September 1, 1921 for 36 performances.
    Reviews:
        Bookman 54:228-9, Nov 1921
        Dramatic Mirror 84:376, Sep 10, 1921
        Independent 106:137, Sep 24, 1921
        Life (NY) 78:18, Sep 22, 1921
        Nation 113:325, Sep 21, 1921
        New Republic 28:77, Sep 14, 1921
        New York Clipper 69:22, Sep 7, 1921
        New York Times p. 9, Sep 2, 1921
                        VI, p. 1, Nov 20, 1921
        Theatre Magazine 34:16, Nov 1921
        Weekly Review 5:255, Sep 17, 1921

They Knew What They Wanted
    Productions:
        Opened November 24, 1924 for 192 performances.
        Opened October 2, 1939 for 24 performances.
        Opened February 16, 1949 for 61 performances.
    Reviews:
        Bookman 60:741, Feb 1925
        Catholic World 150:217, Nov 1939
                       169:64, Apr 1949

HOWARD, SIDNEY (cont.)
  They Knew What They Wanted (cont.)
            Commonweal 30:587, Oct 20, 1939
                        49:591, Mar 25, 1949
        Current Opinion 78:188-95, Feb 1925
        Dial 78:82, Jan 1925
        Forum 111:287-8, May 1949
        Independent 114:51, Jan 10, 1925
        Motion Picture Classic 21:46+, Mar 1925
        Nation 119:662-3, Dec 10, 1924
                168:312, Mar 12, 1949
        New York Theatre Critics' Reviews 1949:354
        New York Times VIII, p. 1, Nov 20, 1924
                        p. 27, Nov 25, 1924
                        p. 19, Apr 27, 1925
                        p. 14, Jun 4, 1925
                        p. 17, Jul 7, 1936
                        p. 14, Jul 8, 1936
                        p. 10, Jul 30, 1938
                        p. 19, Oct 3, 1939
                        II, p. 1, Feb 13, 1949
                        p. 28, Feb 17, 1949
        New Yorker 25:50-1, Feb 26, 1949
        Newsweek 14:44, Oct 16, 1939
                33:73, Feb 28, 1949
        School and Society 69:233, Mar 26, 1949
        Theatre Arts 9:77, Feb 1925
                23:862, Dec 1939
                33:24, 26, May 1949
        Theatre Magazine 41:19, Feb 1925
                        41:19, Mar 1925
                        42:7, Jul 1925
                        42:26+, Aug 1925
        Time 34:56, Oct 16, 1939
            53:57, Feb 28, 1949

  Yellow Jack (with Paul de Kruif)
    Productions:
        Opened March 6, 1934 for 79 performances.
        Opened February 27, 1947 for 21 performances.
        (Off Broadway) Opened December 11, 1964 for 9
            performances (Equity Library Theatre).
    Reviews:
        Catholic World 139:89-90, Apr 1934
                165:71, Apr 1947
        Commonweal 19:580, Mar 23, 1934
                45:566, Mar 21, 1947

Literary Digest 117:32, Mar 31, 1934
Nation 138:340-1, Mar 21, 1934
        164:312-3, Mar 15, 1947
New Outlook 163:44, Apr 1934
New Republic 116:41, Mar 17, 1947
New York Theatre Critics' Reviews 1947:443
New York Times p. 22, Mar 7, 1934
                X, p. 1, Mar 11, 1934
                IX, p. 1, Mar 18, 1934
                p. 26, Feb 28, 1947
New Yorker 23:56, Mar 8, 1947
Newsweek 3:38, Mar 17, 1934
        29:82, Mar 10, 1947
Review of Reviews 89:49, May 1934
Saturday Review 10:569-70, Mar 24, 1934
School and Society 65:252, Apr 5, 1947
Stage 11:8-10, Apr 1934
Survey Graphic 23:241, May 1934
Theatre Arts 18:326-8, May 1934
Time 23:35-6, Mar 19, 1934
        49:46, Mar 10, 1947

HOWELLS, WILLIAM DEAN
    No Productions.

HOYT, CHARLES HALE

    *Temperance Town
    Reviews:
        New York Times VIII, p. 2, Aug 11, 1929

    Texas Steer
    Productions:
        (Off Broadway) Season of 1968-69 (American
            Theatre Club).
    Reviews:
        New York Times p. 39, Nov 13, 1968

HUGHES, HATCHER

    Hell-Bent For Heaven
    Productions:
        Opened January 4, 1924 for 122 performances.
    Reviews:

HUGHES, HATCHER (cont.)
Hell-Bent For Heaven (cont.)
Arts and Decoration 20:24, Apr 1924
Life (NY) 83:20, Feb 7, 1924
Nation 118:68-9, Jan 16, 1924
New York Times p. 9, Dec 31, 1923
p. 10, Jan 5, 1924
p. 21, Feb 5, 1924
VII, p. 1, Feb 10, 1924
Theatre Magazine 39:19, Apr 1924
39:26+, Jul 1924

*Honeymooning on High
Reviews:
New York Times VII, p. 4, Feb 27, 1927

It's A Grand Life (with Alan Williams)
Productions:
Opened February 10, 1930 for 25 performances.
Reviews:
Commonweal 11:480, Feb 26, 1930
Nation 130:254, Feb 26, 1930
New Republic 62:47, Feb 26, 1930
New York Times VIII, p. 2, Feb 2, 1930
p. 30, Feb 11, 1930

The Lord Blesses the Bishop
Productions:
Opened November 27, 1934 for 7 performances.
Reviews:
New York Times p. 24, Nov 28, 1934

"Ruint"
Productions:
Opened April 7, 1925 for 30 performances.
Reviews:
American Mercury 5:247, Jun 1925
Nation 120:473-4, Apr 22, 1925
New York Times p. 24, Apr 8, 1925

Wake Up, Jonathan! (with Elmer Rice)
Productions:
Opened January 17, 1921 for 105 performances.
Reviews:
Dramatic Mirror 83:163, Jan 22, 1921
Life (NY) 77:172, Feb 3, 1921
Nation 112:189, Feb 2, 1921

New York Clipper 68:19, Jan 26, 1921
New York Times p. 14, Jan 18, 1921
VI, p. 1, Jan 23, 1921
Review 4:112-14, Feb 2, 1921
Theatre Magazine 33:261, Apr 1921
Weekly Review 4:112-14, Feb 2, 1921

HUGHES, LANGSTON

Black Nativity
Productions:
(Off Broadway) Opened December 11, 1961 for 57
performances.
(Off Broadway) Season of 1968-69 in repertory
(Afro-American Studio).
Reviews:
New York Times p. 54, Dec 12, 1961
p. 37, Aug 15, 1962

Don't You Want To Be Free
Productions:
(Off Broadway) Opened June 10, 1938 in repertory
(New Theatre League).
No Reviews.

Jerico-Jim Crow
Productions:
(Off Broadway) Opened January 12, 1964 for 31
performances.
(Off Broadway) Season of 1967-68.
Reviews:
New York Times p. 25, Jan 13, 1964
p. 22, Mar 23, 1968

Mulatto
Productions:
Opened October 24, 1935 for 373 performances.
(Off Broadway) Season of 1967-68.
Reviews:
New York Times p. 13, Aug 8, 1935
p. 25, Oct 25, 1935
p. 61, Nov 16, 1967
Theatre Arts 19:902, Dec 1935
Time 26:58+, Nov 4, 1935

HUGHES, LANGSTON (cont.)
   The Prodigal Son
      Productions:
         (Off Broadway) Opened May 20, 1965 for 141 per-
            formances.
      Reviews:
         America 113:62, Jul 10, 1965
         New York Times p. 19, May 21, 1965

   Shakespeare in Harlem
      Productions:
         (Off Broadway) Season of 1959-60.
      Reviews:
         America 102:747, Mar 19, 1960
         New York Times p. 43, Feb 10, 1960
                        II, p. 1, Feb 21, 1960

HURLBUT, WILLIAM J.

   Are You a Crook? (with Frances Whitehouse)
      Productions:
         Opened May 1, 1913 for 12 performances.
      Reviews:
         Blue Book 17:652-5, Aug 1913
         Dramatic Mirror 69:6, May 7, 1913
         Dramatist 4:376-7, Jul 1913
         Green Book 10:10-12+, Jul 1913
         Life (NY) 61:980-1, May 15, 1913
         New York Drama News 57:18, May 10, 1913
         New York Times p. 11, May 2, 1913
         Red Book 21:507-11, Jul 1913
         Theatre Magazine 17:181, Jun 1913

   The Bride
      Productions:
         Opened September 27, 1913 in repertory (The
            Princess Players).
      No Reviews.

   Bride of the Lamb
      Productions:
         Opened March 30, 1926 for 109 performances.
      Reviews:
         Dramatic Mirror 70:6, Oct 15, 1913
         Dramatist 17:1306-7, Jul 1926
         Green Book 10:1064, Dec 1913

Life (NY) 87:21, Apr 22, 1926
Nation 121:426-7, Apr 14, 1926
New Republic 46:301-2, Apr 28, 1926
New York Times p. 20, Mar 31, 1926
                p. 26, Mar 29, 1934
Theatre Magazine 18:143, Nov 1913
                 43:5+, Jun 1926
                 44:26-8+, Aug 1926
Vogue 67:80+, Jun 1, 1926

Chivalry
    Productions:
    Opened December 15, 1925 for 23 performances.
    Reviews:
    New York Times p. 22, Dec 16, 1925
    Theatre Magazine 43:16, Mar 1926

The Cup
    Productions:
    Opened November 12, 1923 for 16 performances.
    Reviews:
    New York Times p. 25, Nov 13, 1923

Hail and Farewell
    Productions:
    Opened February 19, 1923 for 40 performances.
    Reviews:
    New York Clipper 71:14, Feb 28, 1923
    New York Times p. 12, Feb 20, 1923

Hidden
    Productions:
    Opened October 4, 1927 for 79 performances.
    Reviews:
    Dramatist 18:1353-4, Oct 1927
    Life (NY) 90:25, Oct 20, 1927
    New York Times VIII, p. 4, Sep 25, 1927
                   p. 30, Oct 5, 1927
    Theatre Magazine 46:43-4, Dec 1927

Lilies of the Field
    Productions:
    Opened October 4, 1921 for 169 performances.
    Reviews:
    Dramatic Mirror 84:520, Oct 8, 1921
    New York Clipper 69:20, Oct 12, 1921
    New York Times p. 20, Oct 5, 1921

HURLBUT, WILLIAM J. (cont.)
  Lilies of the Field (cont.)
        Theatre Magazine 34:363+, Dec 1921

  New York
    Productions:
        Opened October 17, 1910 for 16 performances.
    Reviews:
        Blue Book 12:431-3, Jan 1911
        Dramatic Mirror 64:7, Oct 19, 1910
        Life (NY) 56:704, Oct 27, 1910

  On the Stairs
    Productions:
        Opened September 25, 1922 for 80 performances.
    Reviews:
        New York Clipper 70:21, Oct 4, 1922
        New York Times p. 18, Sep 26, 1922

  Paradise
    Productions:
        Opened December 26, 1927 for 8 performances.
    Reviews:
        New York Times p. 26, Dec 26, 1927

  A Primer for Lovers
    Productions:
        Opened November 18, 1929 for 24 performances.
    Reviews:
        Nation 129:669, Dec 4, 1929
        New York Times p. 26, Nov 19, 1929

  Romance and Arabella
    Productions:
        Opened October 17, 1917 for 29 performances.
    Reviews:
        Dramatic Mirror 77:7, Oct 27, 1917
        Life (NY) 70:714-15, Nov 1, 1917
        New York Drama News 64:6, Oct 27, 1917
        New York Times p. 13, Oct 18, 1917

  Saturday to Monday
    Productions:
        Opened October 1, 1917 for 16 performances.
    Reviews:
        Dramatic Mirror 77:15, Jun 2, 1917
                        77:8, Oct 13, 1917

Life (NY) 70:591, Oct 11, 1917
New York Times p. 11, Oct 2, 1917
Theatre Magazine 26:265+, Nov 1917

*Story to be Whispered
   Reviews:
      New York Times p. 21, Aug 20, 1937

The Strange Woman
   Productions:
      Opened November 17, 1913 for 88 performances.
   Reviews:
      Blue Book 18:631-3, Feb 1914
      Book News 32:257-8, Jan 1913
      Bookman 38:495, Jan 1914
      Collier's 52:30, Jan 10, 1914
      Dramatic Mirror 70:10, Nov 16, 1913
      Green Book 11:238-9, Feb 1914
              11:350-1, Feb 1914
      Hearst 25:275-86, Feb 1914
      Munsey 50:728, Jan 1914
      New York Times p. 11, Nov 18, 1913
      Theatre Magazine 19:6-8, Jan 1914

Trimmed in Scarlet
   Productions:
      Opened February 2, 1920 for 14 performances.
   Reviews:
      Dramatic Mirror 82:206, Feb 7, 1920
      Life (NY) pp. 322-3, Feb 19, 1920
      New York Times p. 18, Feb 3, 1920
      Theatre Magazine 31:185+, Mar 1920

The Writing On the Wall
   Productions:
      Opened April 26, 1909 for 32 performances.
   Reviews:
      Forum 41:548-9, Jun 1909
      Hampton 23:111, Jul 1909
      Nation 88:447, Apr 29, 1909
      New York Times p. 25, Jul 3, 1923
      Theatre Magazine 9:169-70+, Jun 1909

HUSTON, JOHN

In Time to Come (See entry under Koch, Howard)

INGE, WILLIAM

Bus Stop
    Productions:
    Opened March 2, 1955 for 478 performances.
    Reviews:
        America 93:54, Apr 9, 1955
        Catholic World 181:147, May 1955
        Commonweal 62:14, Apr 8, 1955
        Life 38:77-80, Mar 28, 1955
        Nation 180:245, Mar 19, 1955
        New Republic 132:22, May 2, 1955
        New York Theatre Critics' Reviews 1955:346
        New York Times II, p. 3, Feb 27, 1955
                        p. 23, Mar 3, 1955
                     II, p. 1, Mar 13, 1955
                     II, p. 1, Apr 3, 1955
        New York Times Magazine p. 59, Mar 20, 1955
        New Yorker 31:62+, Mar 12, 1955
        Newsweek 45:99, Mar 14, 1955
        Saturday Review 38:24, Mar 19, 1955
        Theatre Arts 39:16, 22, May 1955
        Time 65:58, Mar 14, 1955

Come Back Little Sheba
    Productions:
    Opened February 15, 1950 for 123 performances.
    Reviews:
        Catholic World 171:67, Apr 1950
        Christian Science Monitor Magazine p. 4, Feb 25,
            1950
        Commonweal 51:558, Mar 3, 1950
        Life 28:93+, Apr 17, 1950
        New Republic 122:22-3, Mar 13, 1950
        New York Theatre Critics' Reviews 1950:348
        New York Times p. 28, Feb 16, 1950
                     II, p. 1, Feb 26, 1950
                     II, p. 3, Apr 2, 1950
                     II, p. 1, Jul 23, 1950
        New Yorker 26:68+, Feb 25, 1950
        Newsweek 35:74, Feb 27, 1950
        School and Society 71:345, Jan 3, 1950
        Theatre Arts 34:20, Apr 1950
                     34:22-3, May, 1950
        Time 55:81, Feb 27, 1950

The Dark at the Top of the Stairs
  Productions:
    Opened December 5, 1957 for 468 performances.
  Reviews:
    America 98:436, Jan 11, 1958
    Catholic World 186:385, Feb 1958
    Christian Century 75:17-18, Jan 1, 1958
    Commonweal 67:615-16, Mar 14, 1958
    Life 44:74-7, Jan 6, 1958
    Nation 185:483, Dec 21, 1957
    New Republic 137:21, Dec 30, 1957
    New York Theatre Critics' Reviews 1957:158
    New York Times II, p. 1, Dec 1, 1957
                   p. 38, Dec 6, 1957
                   II, p. 3, Dec 15, 1957
                   II, p. 1, Mar 16, 1958
    New York Times Magazine pp. 80-1, Nov 24, 1957
    New Yorker 33:83, Dec 14, 1957
    Newsweek 50:81, Dec 16, 1957
    Reporter 17:34, Dec 26, 1957
    Saturday Review 40:27, Dec 21, 1957
    Theatre Arts 42:20-21, Feb 1958
                 42:62-4, Jul 1958
    Time 70:42+, Dec 16, 1957

*Farther Off from Heaven
  Reviews:
    New York Times p. 33, Jun 4, 1947

Glory in the Flower
  Productions:
    (Off Broadway) Season of 1958-1959 (ANTA).
  Reviews:
    New York Times p. 57, Dec 9, 1959

A Loss of Roses
  Productions:
    Opened November 28, 1959 for 25 performances.
  Reviews:
    America 102:402+, Jan 2, 1960
    Christian Century 77:15, Jan 6, 1960
    Commonweal 71:395, Jan 1, 1960
    Nation 189:475, Dec 19, 1959
    New Republic 141:23-4, Dec 21, 1959
    New York Theatre Critics' Reviews 1959:211
    New York Times II, p. 3, Nov 22, 1959
                   p. 27, Nov 30, 1959

INGE, WILLIAM (cont.)
A Loss of Roses (cont.)
                              II, p. 5, Dec 6, 1959
        New Yorker 35:99-100, Dec 12, 1959
        Newsweek 54:96, Dec 7, 1959
        Saturday Review 42:24, Dec 19, 1959
        Theatre Arts 44:10-13, Feb 1960
        Time 74:56, Dec 7, 1959

Natural Affection
    Productions:
        Opened January 31, 1963 for 36 performances.
    Reviews:
        Commonweal 77:598, Mar 1, 1963
        Nation 196:148, Feb 16, 1963
        New Republic 148:29, Feb 23, 1963
        New York Theatre Critics' Reviews 1963:383
        New York Times p. 5, Feb 2, 1963
        New Yorker 38:66+, Feb 9, 1963
        Newsweek 61:84, Feb 11, 1963
        Reporter 28:48-9, Apr 25, 1963
        Saturday Review 46:25, Feb 16, 1963
        Theatre Arts 47:58-9, Mar 1963
        Time 81:56, Feb 8, 1963

Picnic
    Productions:
        Opened February 19, 1953 for 477 performances.
    Reviews:
        America 88:632, Mar 7, 1953
                89:147, May 2, 1953
        Catholic World 177:69, Apr 1953
        Commonweal 57:603, Mar 20, 1953
        Life 34:136-7, Mar 16, 1953
        Nation 176:213, Mar 7, 1953
        New Republic 128:22-3, Mar 16, 1953
        New York Theatre Critics' Reviews 1953:348
        New York Times II, p. 3, Feb 15, 1953
                         p. 14, Feb 20, 1953
                         II, p. 1, Mar 1, 1953
                         II, p. 1, Aug 30, 1953
                         p. 32, Feb 21, 1957
        New Yorker 29:65, Feb 28, 1953
        Newsweek 41:84, Mar 2, 1953
        Saturday Review 36:33, Mar 7, 1953
        Theatre Arts 37:14-15, May 1953
                      37:28-9, Oct 1953

Time 61:72+, Mar 2, 1953

Where's Daddy?
Productions:
Opened March 2, 1966 for 22 performances.
Reviews:
Commonweal 84:83, Apr 8, 1966
New Republic 154:36, Mar 26, 1966
New York Theatre Critics' Reviews 1966:347
New York Times p. 27, Mar 3, 1966
New Yorker 42:110, Mar 12, 1966
Newsweek 67:94, Mar 14, 1966
Saturday Review 49:55, Mar 19, 1966
Time 87:52, Mar 11, 1966
Vogue 147:64, Apr 5, 1966

IRVING, WASHINGTON

No Productions.

JAMES, DANIEL L.

Winter Soldiers
Productions:
Opened November 29, 1942 for 25 performances.
Reviews:
American Mercury 56:237-8, Feb 1943
Current History 3:459, Jan 1943
New York Times p. 19, Nov 30, 1942
Theatre Arts 27:79+, Feb 1943

JAMES, HENRY

Disengaged
Productions:
Opened March 11, 1909 for 1 performance.
Reviews:
Forum 41:342-3, Apr 1909
Theatre Magazine 9:xii-xiii, Apr 1909

Portrait of A Lady (See entry under Archibald, William)

JAMES, HENRY (cont.)
Pyramus and Thisbe
Productions:
(Off Broadway) Season of 1968-69 (American
Theatre Club).
No Reviews

The Salon
Productions:
(Off Broadway) Season of 1968-69 in repertory
(American Theatre Club).
No Reviews

"A Sense of the Past" (See Berkeley Square under Balder-
sten, John)

The Turn of the Screw (See The Innocents under Archibald
William)

Washington Square (See The Heiress under Goetz, Ruth)

Wings of the Dove (See Child of Fortune under Bolton,
Guy)

JEFFERS, ROBINSON

Cretan Woman
Productions:
(Off Broadway) Season of 1954-1955.
Reviews:
Catholic World 179:469-71, Sep 1954
Commonweal 60:558, Sep 10, 1954
Life 37:142+, Sep 13, 1954
New York Times p. 17, May 21, 1954
                p. 18, Jul 8, 1954
                II, p. 1, Sep 5, 1954
Saturday Review 37:25, Jun 5, 1954

Dear Judas (Adapted by Michael Myerberg)
Productions:
Opened October 5, 1947 for 17 performances.
Reviews:
Commonweal 47:71, Oct 31, 1947
Forum 108:371, Dec 1947
New York Theatre Critics' Reviews 1947:315
New York Times II, p. 1 Aug 3, 1947

232

```
                p.  26,  Aug  5,  1947
                II,  p.  1,  Oct  5,  1947
                II,  p.  3,  Oct  5,  1947
                p.  26,  Oct  6,  1947
                II,  p.  6,  Oct  19,  1947
New  Yorker  23:59-61,  Oct  18,  1947
Newsweek  30:91,  Oct  20,  1947
Time  50:59,  Aug  25,  1947
        50:73,  Oct  20,  1947
```

The Double Axe
    Productions:
        (Off Broadway) Season of 1968-69 (American
            Theatre Club).
    No Reviews

Medea (Adapted from the tragedy by Euripides)
    Productions:
        Opened October 20, 1947 for 214 performances.
        Opened May 2, 1949 for 16 performances.
        (Off Broadway) Season of 1960-61.
        (Off Broadway) Opened November 28, 1965 for 77
            performances.
    Reviews:
        Catholic World 166:263-4, Dec 1947
                       169:228-9, Jun 1949
        Commonweal 47:94, Nov 7, 1947
        Life 23:112-14, Nov 17, 1947
        Nation 165:509-10, Nov 8, 1947
        New Republic 117:36, Nov 3, 1947
        New York Theatre Critics' Reviews 1947:295
        New York Times VI, p. 56, Oct 12, 1947
                       II, p. 1, Oct 19, 1947
                       p. 27, Oct 21, 1947
                       II, p. 1, Oct 26, 1947
                       II, p. 1, Nov 9, 1947
                       II, p. 4, Dec 14, 1947
                       p. 9, Sep 4, 1948
                       p. 32, Sep 30, 1948
                       p. 31, May 3, 1949
                       p. 22, Sep 14, 1951
                       II, p. 9, Sep 16, 1951
                       p. 24, Oct 6, 1955
                       p. 25, Jul 26, 1960
                       p. 46, Nov 29, 1965
        New Yorker 23:44, Nov 1, 1947
        Newsweek 30:76, Nov 3, 1947

JEFFERS, ROBINSON (cont.)
Medea (cont.)
Saturday Review 30:24-7, Nov 22, 1947
School and Society 67:163-4, Feb 28, 1948
Survey 31:31-4, Nov 1937
Theatre Arts 31:10-12, 36, Dec 1947
Time 50:68, Nov 3, 1947
Vogue 110:168-9, Dec 1947

The Tower Beyond Tragedy (Based on the works of
Aeschylus)
Productions:
Opened November 26, 1950 for 32 performances.
Reviews:
Catholic World 172:308, Jan 1951
Christian Science Monitor Magazine p. 5, Dec 9,
1950
Commonweal 53:279, Dec 22, 1950
New Republic 124:22, Jan 8, 1951
New York Theatre Critics' Reviews 1950:180
New York Times II, p. 1, Nov 26, 1950
p. 29, Nov 27, 1950
II, p. 5, Dec 10, 1950
New Yorker 26:62+, Dec 9, 1950
School and Society 72:416-19, Dec 23, 1950
Theatre Arts 35:15, Feb 1951
Time 56:65, Dec 4, 1950

JONES, LEROI

The Baptism
Productions:
(Off Broadway) Opened May 1, 1964 for 3 per-
formances.
No Reviews.

Dante
Productions:
(Off Broadway) Opened October 29, 1961 for 16
performances.
No Reviews.

Dutchman
Productions:
(Off Broadway) Opened January 12, 1964 for 2 per-
formances (Theater 1964 Playwrights' Unit).

(Off Broadway) Opened March 23, 1964 for 80
performances.
Reviews:
New York Times p. 46, Mar 25, 1964
p. 34, Jun 28, 1965
p. 53, Nov 17, 1965
New Yorker 40:78-9, Apr 4, 1964
Newsweek 63:60, Apr 13, 1964
Vogue 144:32, Jul 1964

The Slave
Productions:
(Off Broadway) Opened December 16, 1964 for 151
performances.
Reviews:
Nation 200:16-17, Jan 4, 1965
National Review 17:249, Mar 23, 1965
New Republic 152:32-3, Jan 23, 1965
New York Times p. 51, Dec 17, 1964
p. 53, Nov 17, 1965
New Yorker 40:50+, Dec 26, 1964
Newsweek 64:56, Dec 28, 1964
Saturday Review 48:46, Jan 9, 1965
Time 84:62-3, Dec 25, 1964
Vogue 145:98, Feb 1, 1965

The Toilet
Productions:
(Off Broadway) Opened December 16, 1964 for 151
performances.
Reviews:
Nation 200:16, Jan 4, 1965
National Review 17:249, Mar 23, 1965
New Republican 152:32-3, Jan 23, 1965
New York Times p. 51, Dec 17, 1964
New Yorker 40:50+, Dec 26, 1964
Newsweek 64:56, Dec 28, 1964
Saturday Review 48:46, Jan 9, 1965
Time 84:62, Dec 25, 1964
Vogue 145:98, Feb 1, 1965

KANIN, FAY

Goodbye, My Fancy
Productions:
Opened November 17, 1948 for 446 performances.

KANIN, FAY (cont.)
　　Goodbye, My Fancy (cont.)
　　　　Reviews:
　　　　　　Catholic World 168:323, Jan 1949
　　　　　　Commonweal 49:196, Dec 3, 1948
　　　　　　Independent Woman 28:38-40, Feb 1949
　　　　　　Life 25:69-72, Dec 13, 1948
　　　　　　Nation 167:646-7, Dec 4, 1948
　　　　　　New Republic 119:30, Dec 13, 1948
　　　　　　New York Theatre Critics' Reviews 1948:152
　　　　　　New York Times p. 35, Nov 18, 1948
　　　　　　　　　　　　　　II, p. 1, Nov 28, 1948
　　　　　　　　　　　　　　II, p. 4, Dec 19, 1948
　　　　　　　　　　　　　　p. 19, Jul 1, 1952
　　　　　　New Yorker 24:56+, Nov 27, 1948
　　　　　　Newsweek 32:81, Nov 29, 1948
　　　　　　Saturday Review 32:30-2, Jan 8, 1949
　　　　　　Theatre Arts 33:13, Jan 1949
　　　　　　Time 52:76, Nov 29, 1948
　　　　　　Vogue 113:117, Jan 1949

　　His and Hers (with Michael Kanin)
　　　　Productions:
　　　　　　Opened January 7, 1954 for 76 performances.
　　　　Reviews:
　　　　　　America 90:463, Jan 30, 1954
　　　　　　Catholic World 178:467, Mar 1954
　　　　　　New York Theatre Critics' Reviews 1954:393
　　　　　　New York Times p. 18, Jan 8, 1954
　　　　　　New Yorker 29:54-6, Jan 16, 1954
　　　　　　Newsweek 43:59, Jan 18, 1954
　　　　　　Saturday Review 37:27, Jan 30, 1954
　　　　　　Theatre Arts 38:15, Mar 1954
　　　　　　Time 63:54, Jan 18, 1954

　　Rashomon (with Michael Kanin) (Based on the stories of
　　　　Ryunosuke Akutagawa)
　　　　Productions:
　　　　　　Opened January 27, 1959 for 159 performances.
　　　　Reviews:
　　　　　　America 100:670-1, Mar 7, 1959
　　　　　　Catholic World 189:59, Apr 1959
　　　　　　Commonweal 69:650, Mar 20, 1959
　　　　　　Nation 188:146, Feb 14, 1959
　　　　　　Coronet 46:12, May 1959
　　　　　　New York Theatre Critics' Reviews 1959:397
　　　　　　New York Times II, p. 1, Jan 18, 1959

                    p. 36, Jan 28, 1959
                    II, p. 1, Feb 8, 1959
New Yorker 34:81-2, Feb 7, 1959
Newsweek 53:56, Feb 9, 1959
Reporter 20:39, Mar 19, 1959
Saturday Review 42:32, Feb 14, 1959
Theatre Arts 43:12-13+, Feb 1959
                    43:9, Apr 1959
Time 73:70+, Feb 9, 1959
Vogue 133:112-13, Mar 1, 1959

KANIN, GARSON

Born Yesterday
    Productions:
        Opened February 4, 1946 for 1,642 performances.
        (Off Broadway) Season of 1957-58 (Equity Library
            Theatre).
    Reviews:
        Catholic World 162:552, Mar 1946
        Commonweal 43:479, Feb 22, 1946
        Life 20:81-2+, Feb 25, 1946
        Nation 162:205, Feb 16, 1946
        New Republic 114:254, Feb 18, 1946
                    114:280-2, Feb 25, 1946
        New York Theatre Critics' Reviews 1946:466
        New York Times p. 18, Feb 5, 1946
                    II, p. 1, Feb 10, 1946
                    II, p. 1, Apr 7, 1946
                    II, p. 1, May 5, 1946
                    II, p. 1, Jul 21, 1946
                    p. 32, Nov 5, 1946
                    II, p. 3, Feb 2, 1947
                    II, p. 3, Feb 9, 1947
                    II, p. 1, May 18, 1947
                    II, p. 1, Jul 27, 1947
                    II, p. 1, Oct 12, 1947
                    II, p. 3, Dec 28, 1947
                    VI, p. 16, Mar 4, 1951
                    p. 16, Jan 1, 1954
                    p. 12, Mar 22, 1958
        New Yorker 22:46+, Feb 16, 1946
        Newsweek 27:92, Feb 18, 1946
        Theatre Arts 30:200-1+, Apr 1946
                    31:58, Apr 1947
        Time 47:49, Feb 18, 1946

KANIN, GARSON (cont.)
    Come On Strong
        Productions:
        Opened October 4, 1962 for 36 performances.
        Reviews:
            New York Theatre Critics' Reviews 1962:256
            New York Times p. 29, Oct 5, 1962
                          p. 12, Oct 6, 1962
                          p. 19, Oct 8, 1962
            New Yorker 38:180+, Oct 13, 1962
            Newsweek 60:68, Oct 15, 1962
            Theatre Arts 46:12-13, Nov 1962

    A Gift of Time (Based on Lael Tucker Wertenbaker's
        Death of A Man.)
        Productions:
        Opened February 22, 1962 for 92 performances.
        Reviews:
            Catholic World 195:127-8, May 1962
            Commonweal 76:16, Mar 30, 1962
            Nation 194:221-2, Mar 10, 1962
            New York Theatre Critics' Reviews 1962:340
            New York Times p. 34, Feb 23, 1962
                          II, p. 1, Mar 4, 1962
            New Yorker 38:93, Mar 3, 1962
            Newsweek 59:73, Mar 5, 1962
            Saturday Review 45:32, Mar 10, 1962
            Theatre Arts 46:61, Apr 1962
            Time 79:42, Mar 2, 1962

    The Good Soup (Adapted from the play by Felicien Mar-
        ceau)
        Productions:
        Opened March 2, 1960 for 21 performances.
        Reviews:
            America 103:27, Apr 2, 1960
            Nation 190:263, Mar 19, 1960
            New York Theatre Critics' Reviews 1960:330
            New York Times VI, p. 79, Feb 21, 1960
                          II, p. 1, Feb 28, 1960
                          p. 26, Mar 3, 1960
            New Yorker 36:113-14, Mar 12, 1960
            Saturday Review 43:26-7, Mar 19, 1960
            Theatre Arts 43:14, Jul 1959
            Time 75:73, Mar 14, 1960

The Live Wire
    Productions:
        Opened August 17, 1950 for 28 performances.
    Reviews:
        Christian Science Monitor Magazine p. 8, Aug 26,
            1950
        Commonweal 52:510, Sep 1, 1950
        New Republic 123:23, Sep 4, 1950
        New York Theatre Critics' Reviews 1950:277
        New York Times p. 26, Jul 19, 1950
                      p. 16, Aug 18, 1950
                      II, p. 1, Aug 27, 1950
        New Yorker 26:50, Aug 26, 1950
        Newsweek 36:75, Aug 28, 1950
        Theatre Arts 34:11, Oct 1950
        Time 56:70, Aug 28, 1950

The Rat Race
    Productions:
        Opened December 22, 1949 for 84 performances.
    Reviews:
        Catholic World 170:386, Feb 1950
        Commonweal 51:390, Jan 13, 1950
        New Republic 122:31, Jan 16, 1950
        New York Theatre Critics' Reviews 1949:190
        New York Times p. 16, Dec 23, 1949
        New Yorker 25:40-1, Dec 31, 1949
        Newsweek 35:48, Jan 2, 1950
        Theatre Arts 34:9, Mar 1950
        Time 55:52, Jan 2, 1950

The Smile of the World
    Productions:
        Opened January 12, 1949 for 5 performances.
    Reviews:
        Forum 111:161, Mar 1949
        New Republic 120:30, Jan 31, 1949
        New York Theatre Critics' Reviews 1949:396
        New York Times p. 26, Jan 13, 1949
        New Yorker 24:44-6, Jan 22, 1949
        Newsweek 33:70, Jan 24, 1949
        Theatre Arts 33:17, Apr 1949
        Time 53:52, Jan 24, 1949

KAUFMAN, GEORGE S.

The American Way (with Moss Hart)
    Productions:
        Opened January 21, 1939 for 164 performances.
        Opened July 17, 1939 for 80 performances.
    Reviews:
        Catholic World 148:728-9, Mar 1939
        Commonweal 29:441, Feb 10, 1939
        Life 6:32, Feb 6, 1939
        Nation 148:157-8, Feb 4, 1939
        New Republic 98:14, Feb 8, 1939
        New York Times p. 9, Jan 23, 1939
                        IX, p. 1, Jan 29, 1939
        Newsweek 13:24, Feb 6, 1939
        North American Review 247, no. 1:153-5, Mar 1939
        One Act Play Magazine 2:746-7, Feb 1939
        Theatre Arts 23:162-4, Mar 1939
        Time 33:28, Jan 30, 1939

Beggar On Horseback (with Marc Connelly)
    Productions:
        Opened February 12, 1924 for 144+ performances.
        Opened March 23, 1925 for 16 performances.
    Reviews:
        American Mercury 1:499-500, Apr 1924
        Bookman 59:201, Apr 1924
        Classic 19:46+, Jul 1924
        Dial 76:384, Apr 1924
        Freeman 8:617-18, Mar 5, 1924
        Life (NY) 83:20, Mar 6, 1924
        Metropolitan Magazine 59:48, Jul 1924
        Nation 118:238-9, Feb 27, 1924
        New Republic 38:45-6, Mar 5, 1924
        New York Times p. 17, Feb 13, 1924
                        VII, p. 1, Feb 17, 1924
                        p. 22, May 8, 1925
                        p. 24, Nov 12, 1925
                        p. 18, Nov 12, 1925
        Theatre Magazine 39:19, 62, Apr 1924
                        53:49, Feb 1931

Bravo! (See entry under Ferber, Edna)

The Butter and Egg Man
    Productions:
        Opened September 23, 1925 for 243 performances.

(Off Broadway) Opened October 17, 1966 for 32
    performances.
Reviews:
    America 115:524, Oct 29, 1966
    Bookman 62:480, Dec 1925
    Independent 116:20, Jan 2, 1926
    Nation 203:493, Nov 7, 1966
    New Republic 44:202, Oct 14, 1925
    New York Times p. 28, Sep 24, 1925
                    p. 28, Aug 23, 1927
                    p. 19, Aug 31, 1927
                    p. 15, Sep 17, 1927
                    p. 49, Oct 18, 1966
                    p. 34, Nov 4, 1966
    New Yorker 42:98-9, Oct 29, 1966

The Channel Road (with Alexander Woolcott)
    Productions:
    Opened October 17, 1929 for 60 performances.
Reviews:
    Catholic World 130:333-4, Dec 1929
    Life (NY) 94:28, Nov 8, 1929
    Nation 129:530, Nov 6, 1929
    New York Times p. 24, Oct 18, 1929
                   IX, p. 1, Oct 27, 1929
    Outlook 153:389, Nov 6, 1929
    Theatre Arts 13:881-2, Dec 1929
    Theatre Magazine 50:24, Dec 1929

The Dark Tower (with Alexander Woolcott)
    Productions:
    Opened November 25, 1933 for 57 performances.
Reviews:
    Catholic World 138:475-6, Jan 1934
    Commonweal 19:160, Dec 8, 1933
    Nation 137:690, Dec 13, 1933
    New Outlook 163:42, Jan 1934
    New Republic 81:78, Nov 28, 1934
    New York Times p. 20, Nov 27, 1933
                   IX, p. 5, Dec 3, 1933
    Stage 11:18-19, Jan 1934
    Time 22:48, Dec 4, 1933
    Vanity Fair 41:42, Feb 1934

The Deep Tangled Wildwood (with Marc Connelly)
    Productions:
    Opened November 5, 1923 for 16 performances.

241

KAUFMAN, GEORGE S. (cont.)
The Deep Tangled Wildwood (cont.)
Reviews:
Life (NY) 82:18, Nov 22, 1923
New York Times p. 22, Nov 6, 1923

Dinner at Eight (with Edna Ferber)
Productions:
Opened October 22, 1932 for 232 performances.
Opened September 27, 1966 for 127 performances.
Reviews:
America 115:524, Oct 29, 1966
Arts and Decoration 38:51, Dec 1932
Christian Century 84:144, Feb 1, 1967
Commonweal 17:49, Nov 9, 1932
            85:78, Oct 21, 1966
Life 61:127-30, Nov 25, 1966
Nation 135:464-5, Nov 9, 1932
        203:397-8, Oct 17, 1966
National Review 19:99, Jan 24, 1967
New Outlook 161:46, Dec 1932
New Republic 72:355-7, Nov 9, 1932
New York Theatre Critics' Reviews 1966:289
New York Times p. 18, Oct 24, 1932
                IX, p. 3, Oct 30, 1932
                IX, p. 1, Nov 6, 1932
                p. 11, Jan 7, 1933
                IX, p. 1, Jan 29, 1933
                IX, p. 1, Apr 9, 1933
                p. 21, Oct 6, 1933
                p. 26, Oct 17, 1933
                II, p. 1, Sep 25, 1966
                p. 38, Sep 28, 1966
                II, p. 1, Oct 9, 1966
Newsweek 68:104, Oct 10, 1966
Saturday Review 49:63, Oct 15, 1966
Stage 10:13-16, Dec 1932
Theatre Arts 17:22, Jan 1933
Time 88:92, Oct 9, 1966
Town and Country 87:26, Dec 1, 1932
Vanity Fair 39:25, Nov 1932
Vogue 80:92, Dec 1, 1932

Dulcy (with Marc Connelly)
Productions:
Opened August 13, 1921 for 246 performances.
Reviews:
Bookman 54:144-6, Oct 1921

Dramatic Mirror 83:408, Mar 5, 1921
               84:265, Aug 20, 1921
Hearst 40:21-3+, Oct 1921
Life (NY) 78:18, Sep 1, 1921
Nation 113:299, Sep 14, 1921
New Republic 28:33, Aug 31, 1921
New York Clipper 69:24, Aug 17, 1921
New York Times p. 14, Aug 15, 1921
              VI, p. 1, Aug 21, 1921
              VI, p. 1, Nov 6, 1921
              II, p. 1, Jun 22, 1947
Theatre Magazine 34:234, Oct 1921
              34:237, Oct 1921
              34:372+, Dec 1921
Weekly Review 5:216, Sep 3, 1921

Eldorado (See entry under Stallings, Laurence)

The Fabulous Invalid (See entry under Hart, Moss)

Fancy Meeting You Again (with Leueen MacGrath)
    Productions:
        Opened January 14, 1952 for 8 performances.
    Reviews:
        Commonweal 55:423, Feb 1, 1952
        New York Theatre Critics' Reviews 1952:392
        New York Times p. 23, Jan 15, 1952
        New Yorker 27:54, Jan 26, 1952
        Saturday Review 35:30, Feb 2, 1952
        Theatre Arts 36:71, Mar 1952

First Lady (See entry under Dayton, Katherine)

George Washington Slept Here (with Moss Hart)
    Productions:
        Opened October 18, 1940 for 173 performances.
    Reviews:
        American Mercury 51:483-5, Dec 1940
        Catholic World 152:335, Dec 1940
        Commonweal 33:80, Nov 8, 1940
        Nation 151:430, Nov 2, 1940
        New Republic 103:629, Nov 4, 1940
        New York Theatre Critics' Reviews 1940:246
                           1941:466
        New York Times p. 27, Sep 24, 1940
                  p. 20, Oct 19, 1940
                  IX, p. 1, Oct 27, 1940
                  X, p. 5, Dec 15, 1940

KAUFMAN, GEORGE S. (cont.)
George Washington Slept Here (cont.)
                    p. 27, Jul 1, 1941
      New Yorker 16:36, Oct 26, 1940
      Newsweek 16:62, Nov 4, 1940
      Stage 1:10, Nov 1940
            1:10, Dec 1940
            1:39, Feb 1941
      Theatre Arts 24:849, Dec 1940
      Time 36:67, Oct 28, 1940

The Good Fellow (with Herman J. Mankiewicz)
   Productions:
      Opened October 5, 1926 for 7 performances.
   Reviews:
      New York Times p. 22, Oct 6, 1926
      Theatre Magazine 44:18, Dec 1926

June Moon (See entry under Lardner, Ring)

The Land Is Bright (with Edna Ferber)
   Productions:
      Opened October 28, 1941 for 79 performances.
   Reviews:
      Catholic World 154:337-8, Dec 1941
      Commonweal 35:93, Nov 14, 1941
      Current History 1:379-80, Dec 1941
      Life 11:53-6, Dec 1, 1941
      Nation 153:491, Nov 15, 1941
      New York Theatre Critics' Reviews 1941:253
      New York Times p. 28, Oct 21, 1941
                     p. 26, Oct 29, 1941
                     p. 22, Oct 30, 1941
                     IV, p. 2, Nov 2, 1941
                     IX, p. 1, Nov 2, 1941
                     IX, p. 1, Nov 9, 1941
      New Yorker 17:36+, Nov 8, 1941
      Newsweek 18:70, Nov 10, 1941
      Theatre Arts 26:10, Jan 1942
      Time 38:55, Nov 10, 1941

The Late George Apley (See entry under Marquand, John
      P.)

The Man Who Came to Dinner (See entry under Hart,
      Moss)

Merrily We Roll Along (with Moss Hart)
   Productions:
      Opened September 29, 1934 for 155 performances.
   Reviews:
      Catholic World 140:209, Nov 1934
      Commonweal 20:589, Oct 19, 1934
      Golden Book 20:636+, Dec 1934
      Literary Digest 118:18, Oct 13, 1934
      Nation 139:460, Oct 17, 1934
      New York Times p. 14, Oct 1, 1934
                    IX, p. 1, Oct 7, 1934
                    X, p. 3, Oct 14, 1934
                    II, p. 2, Jan 13, 1935
                    p. 15, Jun 30, 1936
      Scholastic 25:3, Oct 20, 1934
      Stage 12:2, 6, Nov 1934
         12:13-14, Dec 1934
         12:26, May 1935
      Theatre Arts 18:815-16, Nov 1934
      Time 24:46, Oct 8, 1934
      Vanity Fair 43:45, Dec 1934
      Vogue 84:51, Oct 15, 1934

Merton of the Movies (with Marc Connelly) (Adapted from
      Harry Leon Wilson's story)
   Productions:
      Opened November 13, 1922 for 248+ performances.
   Reviews:
      Life (NY) 80:18, Nov 30, 1922
      New York Clipper 70:20, Nov 22, 1922
      New York Times p. 16, Nov 14, 1922
                    VII, p. 1, Nov 19, 1922
                    p. 20, Apr 13, 1923
                    p. 20, Apr 27, 1923
                    p. 62, Sep 26, 1968
      Theatre Magazine 37:25, Jan 1923

Minick (with Edna Ferber)
   Productions:
      Opened September 24, 1924 for 141 performances.
   Reviews:
      American Mercury 3:376-7, Nov 1924
      Current Opinion 77:732-9, Dec 1924
      Independent 113:551, Dec 20, 1924
      Life (NY) 84:18, Oct 16, 1924
      Motion Picture Classic 28:48+, Jan 1925
      Nation 119:423-4, Oct 15, 1924

KAUFMAN, GEORGE S. (cont.)
   Minick (cont.)
         New York Times VII, p. 1, Aug 24, 1924
                            p. 20, Sep 25, 1924
         Overland 86:19, Jan 1928
         Survey 53:162-4, Nov 1, 1924
         Theatre Arts 8:804+, Dec 1924
         Theatre Magazine 40:16, Dec 1924
                            40:18, Dec 1924

Old Man Minick (See Minick)

Once in A Lifetime (with Moss Hart)
   Productions:
      Opened September 24, 1930 for 406 performances.
      (Off Broadway) Opened January 28, 1964 for 1
         performance.
   Reviews:
      Bookman 74:72, Sep 1931
      Catholic World 132:204-5, Nov 1930
      Commonweal 12:584, Oct 8, 1930
      Drama 21:15-16, Nov 1930
      Life (NY) 96:18, Oct 17, 1930
      Nation 131:386, Oct 8, 1930
             132:392, Apr 8, 1931
      New York Times IX, p. 2, Sep 7, 1930
                         p. 22, Sep 25, 1930
                         IX, p. 1, Dec 7, 1930
                         VIII, p. 1, Feb 1, 1931
                         p. 13, Feb 24, 1933
                         p. 30, Oct 30, 1962
                         p. 20, Jan 29, 1964
      Outlook 156:233, Oct 8, 1930
      Sketch Book 8:31, Dec 1930
      Theatre Magazine 52:26, Dec 1930
                        52:35-7+, Dec 1930
      Vanity Fair 35:46+, Dec 1930
      Vogue 76:69+, Nov 24, 1930

The Royal Family (with Edna Ferber)
   Productions:
      Opened December 28, 1927 for 345 performances.
      Opened January 10, 1951 for 15 performances.
   Reviews:
      American Mercury 13:378, Mar 1928
      Commonweal 32:390, Aug 30, 1940
      Dramatist 19:1366-7, Apr 1928

Life (NY) 91:21, Jan 19, 1928
Life 9:46-8, Sep 23, 1940
Literary Digest 96:26-7, Jan 21, 1928
New York Theatre Critics' Reviews 1951:392
New York Times p. 26, Dec 29, 1927
                VIII, p. 1, Jan 8, 1928
                IX, p. 1, Apr 12, 1931
                p. 24, Oct 24, 1934
                IX, p. 1, Nov 11, 1934
                p. 15, Jul 16, 1936
                p. 15, Aug 12, 1936
                p. 15, Aug 13, 1940
                IV, p. 2, Aug 18, 1940
                p. 28, Jan 11, 1951
Outlook 148:67, Jan 11, 1928
Saturday Review 4:531-2, Jan 21, 1928
School and Society 73:102-103, Feb 17, 1951
Theatre Arts 12:171-2, Mar 1928
          35:18, Mar 1951
Theatre Magazine 47:28-30+, Mar 1928
Vogue 71:124, Feb 15, 1928

The Small Hours (with Leueen MacGrath)
   Productions:
     Opened February 15, 1951 for 20 performances.
   Reviews:
     Commonweal 53:542, Mar 9, 1951
     New York Theatre Critics' Reviews 1951:344
     New York Times II, p. 1, Feb 11, 1951
                p. 22, Feb 16, 1951
     New Yorker 27:66+, Feb 24, 1951
     Newsweek 37:49, Feb 26, 1951
     Theatre Arts 35:20, Apr 1951
     Time 57:50, Feb 26, 1951

Some One in the House (with Larry Evans and Walter
   Percival)
   Productions:
     Opened September 9, 1918 for 32 performances.
   Reviews:
     Dramatic Mirror 79:435, Sep 21, 1918
     Independent 95:370, Sep 21, 1918
     New York Times p. 11, Sep 10, 1918
                VIII, p. 1, Sep 15, 1918
     Theatre Magazine 28:274+, Nov 1918

KAUFMAN, GEORGE S. (cont.)
  The Solid Gold Cadillac (with Howard Teichmann)
    Productions:
      Opened November 5, 1953 for 526 performances.
    Reviews:
      America 90:278, Dec 5, 1953
      Business Week p. 128+, Nov 14, 1953
      Catholic World 178:306-7, Jan 1954
      Commonweal 59:306, Dec 25, 1953
      Fortune 48:100, Dec 1953
      Harpers 208:93-4, Jan 1954
      Life 35:65-6+, Nov 23, 1953
      Nation 177:433, Nov 21, 1953
      New York Theatre Critics' Reviews 1953:222
      New York Times II, p. 3, Nov 1, 1953
                     p. 24, Nov 6, 1953
                     II, p. 1, Nov 15, 1953
      New Yorker 29:70+, Nov 14, 1953
      Newsweek 42:60, Nov 16, 1953
               42:60, Dec 21, 1953
      Saturday Review 36:50, Nov 21, 1953
                      35:46, Dec 12, 1953
      Theatre Arts 38:19, Jan 1954
      Time 62:90, Nov 16, 1953

  Stage Door (with Edna Ferber)
    Productions:
      Opened October 22, 1936 for 169 performances.
    Reviews:
      Catholic World 144:471, Jan 1937
      Commonweal 25:51, Nov 6, 1936
      Nation 143:557, Nov 7, 1936
      New Republic 89:50, Nov 11, 1936
      New York Times p. 35, Sep 29, 1936
                     IX, p. 2, Oct 4, 1936
                     p. 26, Oct 23, 1936
                     X, p. 3, Oct 25, 1936
                     X, p. 1, Nov 1, 1936
                     p. 19, Mar 15, 1939
      Newsweek 8:24, Oct 31, 1936
      Stage 14:48-9, Nov 1936
      Theatre Arts 20:923-4, Dec 1936
      Time 28:46, Nov 2, 1936

  Theatre Royal (See The Royal Family)

To the Ladies (with Marc Connelly)
    Productions:
        Opened February 20, 1922 for 128 performances.
    Reviews:
        Life (NY) 79:18, Mar 9, 1922
        Nation 114:294, Mar 8, 1922
        New York Clipper 70:22, Mar 8, 1922
        New York Times p. 20, Feb 21, 1922
                        VI, p. 1, Mar 5, 1922
                        VI, p. 1, Mar 12, 1922
        Theatre Magazine 35:307-8, May 1922

You Can't Take It With You (See entry under Hart,
    Moss)

KELLY, GEORGE

Behold the Bridegroom
    Productions:
        Opened December 26, 1927 for 88 performances.
    Reviews:
        American Mercury 13:375-6, Mar 1928
        Dramatist 19:1359-60, Jan 1928
        Life (NY) 91:21, Jan 12, 1928
        Nation 126:51, Jan 11, 1928
        New Republic 53:246-7, Jan 18, 1928
        New York Times p. 24, Dec 27, 1927
                       VIII, p. 1, Jan 1, 1928
                       IX, p. 4, Apr 1, 1928
        Outlook 148:105, Jan 18, 1928
        Saturday Review 4:547-8, Jan 28, 1928
        Theatre Arts 12:169-71, Mar 1928
        Theatre Magazine 47:38, Mar 1928
                       47:28-30+, Apr 1928
        Vogue 71:87, Feb 15, 1928

Craig's Wife
    Productions:
        Opened October 12, 1925 for 360 performances.
        (Off Broadway) Opened February 1946 (Playhouse
           des Artistes).
        Opened February 12, 1947 for 69 performances.
    Reviews:
        American Mercury 6:504-5, Dec 1925
        Bookman 62:596, Jan 1926
        Catholic World 165:72, Apr 1947

KELLY, GEORGE (cont.)
    Craig's Wife (cont.)
        Commonweal 45:492, Feb 28, 1947
        Dramatist 17:1305-6, Jul 1926
        Independent 115:586, Nov 21, 1925
        Mentor 14:36-7, Jun 1926
        Nation 121:521-2, Nov 4, 1925
               164:256, Mar 1, 1947
        New Republic 44:281-2, Nov 4, 1925
                   116:40, Feb 24, 1947
        New York Theatre Critics' Reviews 1947:457
        New York Times p. 21, Oct 13, 1925
                     IX, p. 1, Oct 18, 1925
                     II, p. 1, Feb 9, 1947
                     p. 35, Feb 13, 1947
                     II, p. 1, Mar 30, 1947
        New Yorker 23:53, Feb 22, 1947
        Newsweek 29:92, Feb 24, 1947
        Outlook 142:49-50, Jan 13, 1926
        Saturday Review 30:32-4, Mar 8, 1947
        Theatre Arts 31:19, Apr 1947
        Theatre Magazine 42:15, Dec 1925
                     43:29, Jan 1926
                     43:26+, Apr 1926
                     44:9+, Oct 1926
        Time 49:58, Feb 24, 1947

Daisy Mayme
    Productions:
    Opened October 25, 1926 for 112 performances.
    Reviews:
        Bookman 64:618-20, Jan 1927
        Independent 118:21, Jan 1, 1927
        Life (NY) 88:23, Nov 11, 1926
        Nation 123:488, Nov 10, 1926
        New Republic 48:375-6, Nov 17, 1926
        New York Times p. 24, Oct 26, 1926
                    VIII, p. 1, Oct 31, 1926
        Theatre Arts 11:11-12, Jan 1927
        Theatre Magazine 45:16, Jan 1927
        Vogue 68:76-7, Dec 15, 1926

The Deep Mrs. Sykes
    Productions:
    Opened March 19, 1945 for 72 performances.
    Reviews:
        Commonweal 41:625, Apr 6, 1945

Nation 160:395, Apr 7, 1945
New Republic 112:447, Apr 2, 1945
New York Theatre Critics' Reviews 1945:246
New York Times p. 22, Mar 20, 1945
               II, p. 1, Mar 25, 1945
New Yorker 21:40+, Mar 31, 1945
Newsweek 25:84, Apr 2, 1945
Theatre Arts 29:271, May 1945
Time 45:58+, Apr 2, 1945

Fatal Weakness
Productions:
    Opened November 19, 1946 for 119 performances.
Reviews:
    Catholic World 164:359, Jan 1947
    Commonweal 45:201, Dec 6, 1946
    Nation 164:81, Jan 18, 1947
    New Republic 115:764, Dec 9, 1946
    New York Theatre Critics' Reviews 1946:251
    New York Times p. 43, Nov 20, 1946
                 II, p. 3, Feb 9, 1947
    New Yorker 22:60, Nov 30, 1946
    Newsweek 28:94, Dec 2, 1946
    Saturday Review 29:23, Dec 21, 1946
    Theatre Arts 31:21, 30, Jan 1947
    Time 48:54, Dec 2, 1946

Maggie the Magnificent
Productions:
    Opened October 21, 1929 for 32 performances.
Reviews:
    Commonweal 11:21, Nov 6, 1929
    Life (NY) 94:28, Nov 8, 1929
    New Republic 60:323-5, Nov 6, 1929
    New York Times p. 26, Oct 22, 1929
                IX, p. 1, Nov 3, 1929
    Review of Reviews 80:158-9, Dec 1929
    Theatre Arts 14:17-18, Jan 1930
    Theatre Magazine 50:68, Dec 1929

Philip Goes Forth
Productions:
    Opened January 12, 1931 for 97 performances.
Reviews:
    Bookman 73:70-1, Mar 1931
    Catholic World 132:722, Mar 1931
    Commonweal 13:241, Dec 31, 1930

KELLY, GEORGE (cont.)
  Philip Goes Forth (cont.)
        Drama 21:13, Feb 1931
        Nation 132:107, Jan 28, 1931
        New Republic 65:301-2, Jan 28, 1931
        New York Times VIII, p. 2, Jan 4, 1931
                        p. 35, Jan 13, 1931
                        VIII, p. 1, Jan 18, 1931
                        VIII, p. 3, Feb 8, 1931
        Outlook 157:152, Jan 28, 1931
        Sketch Book 8:25, Mar 1931
        Theatre Arts 15:183-5, Mar 1931
        Theatre Magazine 53:24-5, Mar 1931
        Vogue 77:59, Mar 1, 1931

  Reflected Glory
    Productions:
        Opened September 21, 1936 for 127 performances.
    Reviews:
        Catholic World 144:217-18, Nov 1936
        Commonweal 24:560, Oct 9, 1936
        Literary Digest 122:18-19, Aug 8, 1936
                        122:19, Oct 3, 1936
        Nation 143:401-2, Oct 3, 1936
        New Republic 88:257, Oct 7, 1936
        New York Times p. 23, Jul 22, 1936
                        p. 19, Sep 18, 1936
                        p. 30, Sep 22, 1936
                        X, p. 1, Sep 27, 1936
                        p. 14, Apr 17, 1937
                        II, p. 10, May 2, 1937
        Newsweek 8:22, Aug 1, 1936
        Player's Magazine 13:8, Nov-Dec, 1936
        Theatre Arts 20:849-50, Nov 1936
        Time 28:42, Oct 5, 1936

  The Show-Off
    Productions:
        Opened February 5, 1924 for 571 performances.
        Opened December 12, 1932 for 119 performances.
        Opened May 31, 1950 for 6 performances.
        Opened December 5, 1967 for 81 performances.
        Opened September 13, 1968 for 19 performances.
    Reviews:
        America 118:131, Jan 27, 1968
        American Mercury 1:500-501, Apr 1924
        Bookman 59:204-5, Apr 1924

Canadian Forum 10:347, Jun 1930
Canadian Magazine 64:104-5+, May 1925
Catholic World 171:309, July 1950
Christian Science Monitor Magazine p. 9, Jun 17, 1950
Classic 19:46+, Jun 1924
Commonweal 17:187, Dec 14, 1932
          17:245, Dec 28, 1932
          87:471, Jan 19, 1968
Current Opinion 76:673-6+, May 1924
Freeman 8:592-3, Feb 27, 1924
Life (NY) 83:18, Feb 21, 1924
Metropolitan Magazine 59:46, Aug 1924
Nation 118:351-2, Mar 26, 1924
     135:654, Dec 28, 1932
     170:603, Jun 17, 1950
     206:27, Jan 1, 1968
New Republic 122:21, Jun 19, 1950
          158:41-2, Jan 6, 1968
New York Theatre Critics' Reviews 1950:292
                       1967:201
New York Times VII, p. 2, Jan 20, 1924
             p. 16, Feb 6, 1924
             VII, p. 1, Feb 17, 1924
             VII, p. 1, Feb 15, 1925
             p. 25, Dec 13, 1932
             p. 24, Jun 1, 1950
             II, p. 1, Jun 11, 1950
             p. 40, Dec 6, 1967
             p. 61, Dec 7, 1967
             II, p. 3, Dec 17, 1967
Newsweek 35:83, Jun 12, 1950
        70:94, Dec 18, 1967
Reporter 38:37, Jan 11, 1968
Saturday Review 51:26, Jan 6, 1968
Theatre Magazine 39:16, 19, Apr 1924
              39:26+, Sep 1924
Time 55:57, Jun 12, 1950
    90:87, Dec 15, 1967

The Torch Bearers

Productions:
    Opened August 29, 1922 for 135 performances.
Reviews:
    Bookman 57:324-5, Nov 1922
            58:56-7, Sep 1923
    Dramatist 14:1175, Jul 1923

KELLY, GEORGE (cont.)
  The Torch Bearers (cont.)
          Independent 109:397-8, Dec 23, 1922
          Life (NY) 80:18, Sep 21, 1922
          Nation 115:286, Sep 20, 1922
          New Republic 32:100-101, Sep 20, 1922
          New York Clipper 70:20, Sep 27, 1922
          New York Times p. 10, Aug 30, 1922
                        VI, p. 1, Sep 3, 1922
                        p. 30, Mar 22, 1929
          Playground 16:357-60, Nov 1922
          Theatre Magazine 36:298, Nov 1922
                        38:42, Jul 1923

KENNEDY, ADRIANNE

  A Beast's Story (See Cities in Bezique)

  Cities in Bezique (The Owl Answers and A Beast's
        Story)
      Productions:
        (Off Broadway) Opened January 4, 1969 for 67 per-
          formances (New York Shakespeare Festival Public
          Theatre).
      Reviews:
        New York Times p. 26, Jan 13, 1969
                      II, p. 3, Jan 19, 1969
        New Yorker 44:77, Jan 25, 1969

  Funnyhouse of a Negro
      Productions:
        (Off Broadway) Opened January 14, 1964 for 46
          performances.
      Reviews:
        New York Times p. 25, Jan 15, 1964
        New Yorker 39:76+, Jan 25, 1964

  *In His Own Write (With John Lennon and Victor Spinetti)
      Reviews:
        New York Times p. 50, Jun 20, 1968
                      p. 30, Jul 9, 1968
                      II, p. 4, Jul 14, 1968

  The Owl Answers (See Cities in Bezique)

KENNEDY, CHARLES RANN

The Admiral
    Productions:
        Opened April 17, 1924 for 4 performances.
    Reviews:
        Living Age 322:664, Sep 27, 1924
        New York Times p. 20, Apr 25, 1924
                        VIII, p. 1, May 4, 1924

The Army with Banners
    Productions:
        Opened April 9, 1918 for 17 performances.
    Reviews:
        Dramatic Mirror 78:584+, Apr 27, 1918
        New Republic 14:360, Apr 20, 1928
        New York Times IV, p. 6, Apr 14, 1918
        Theatre Magazine 27:285-6, May 1918

The Chastening
    Productions:
        Opened March 12, 1923 for 18 performances.
    Reviews:
        Literary Digest 77:36-7, Apr 7, 1923
        New York Clipper 71:14, Feb 21, 1923
        New York Times p. 9, Feb 17, 1923

The Flower of the Palace of Han (with Louis Laloy)
        (Adapted from the Chinese)
    Productions:
        Opened March 19, 1912 for 39 performances.
    Reviews:
        Blue Book 15:252-4, Jun 1912
        Bookman 35:246, May 1912
        Dramatic Mirror 67:6, Mar 27, 1912
        Green Book 7:1094-5+, Jun 1912
                    8:352-68, Aug 1912
        Life (NY) 59:700, Apr 4, 1912
        New York Drama News 55:26, Mar 30, 1912
        Red Book 19:568-70, Jul 1912
        Theatre Magazine 15:139-40+, May 1912

The Servant in the House
    Productions:
        Opened April 24, 1918 for 21 performances.
        Opened May 2, 1921 for 3 performances.
        Opened April 7, 1925 for 8 performances.

KENNEDY, CHARLES RANN (cont.)
  The Servant in the House (cont.)
     Opened May 3, 1926 for 12 performances.
   Reviews:
     Arena 41:57-73, Jan 1909
     Book News 27:611-2, Apr 1909
     Bookman 63:590, Jul 1926
     Dramatic Mirror 78:656, May 11, 1918
     Dramatist 3:234-5, Apr 1912
     Everybody's 22:122-7, Jan 1910
     New York Clipper 69:19, May 11, 1921
     New York Times p. 10, Apr 25, 1918
               IV, p. 9, Apr 28, 1918
               p. 20, May 3, 1921
               p. 24, Apr 8, 1925
               p. 30, May 4, 1926
     Poet Lore 20:438-43, Nov-Dec 1909
     Theatre Magazine 8:90, Apr 1908
                8:116-7+, May 1908
                14:24-6, Jul 1911
                27:349, Jun 1918
     Weekly Review 4:496, May 21, 1921

The Seventh Trumpet
   Productions:
     Opened November 21, 1941 for 11 performances.
   Reviews:
     Commonweal 35:178, Dec 5, 1941
     New York Theatre Critics' Reviews 1941:204
     New York Times p. 10, Nov 22, 1941

The Terrible Meek
   Productions:
     Opened March 19, 1912 for 39 performances.
   Reviews:
     Blue Book 15:680-1, Aug 1912
     Book News 31:60-1, Sep 1912
     Bookman 35:246-7, May 1912
     Collier's 49:21, Apr 6, 1912
     Dramatic Mirror 67:6, Mar 27, 1912
     Dramatist 3:235-6, Apr 1912
     Green Book 7:1185-7, Jun 1912
             7:1204, Jun 1912
     Life (NY) 59:700, Apr 4, 1912
     Literary Digest 44:644-5, Mar 30, 1912
               44:758, Apr 13, 1912
     Nation 94:294-5, Mar 21, 1912

New York Drama News 55:26, Mar 30, 1912
New York Times XI, p. 3, May 4, 1930
Red Book 19:566+, Jul 1912
Theatre Magazine 15:139-40, May 1912

KENNEDY, MARY

Mrs. Partridge Presents (with Ruth Hawthorne)
    Productions:
        Opened January 5, 1925 for 144 performances.
    Reviews:
        Life (NY) 85:18, Jan 29, 1925
        New York Times p. 23, Jan 6, 1925
                        VII, p. 1, Jan 11, 1925
                        p. 10, Feb 29, 1936
        Theatre Magazine 40:16+, Mar 1925
        Woman Citizen 9:9, Feb 7, 1925

KERR, JEAN

Jenny Kissed Me
    Productions:
        Opened December 23, 1948 for 20 performances.
    Reviews:
        Catholic World 168:403, Feb 1949
        New York Theatre Critics' Reviews 1948:112
        New York Times p. 12, Dec 24, 1948
        New Yorker 24:36, Jan 1, 1949
        Newsweek 33:54, Jan 3, 1949
        Time 53:49, Jan 3, 1949

King of Hearts (with Eleanor Brooke)
    Productions:
        Opened April 1, 1954 for 279 performances.
    Reviews:
        America 91:114+, Apr 24, 1954
        Catholic World 179:149, May 1954
        Commonweal 60:143, May 14, 1954
        Life 36:97-8+, Apr 26, 1954
        Nation 178:342, Apr 17, 1954
        New Republic 130:21, May 31, 1954
        New York Theatre Critics' Reviews 1954:342
        New York Times II, p. 1, Mar 28, 1954
                        p. 23, Apr 2, 1954
                        II, p. 1, Apr 11, 1954

KERR, JEAN (cont.)
King of Hearts (cont.)
                              p. 16, Aug 4, 1955
        New Yorker 30:60+, Apr 10, 1954
        Newsweek 43:92, Apr 12, 1954
        Saturday Review 37:22, Apr 17, 1954
        Theatre Arts 38:17, Jun 1954
                           38:17, Jul 1954
        Time 63:74, Apr 12, 1954

Mary, Mary
     Productions:
        Opened March 8, 1961 for 1,572 performances.
     Reviews:
        America 105:27, Apr 1, 1961
        Commonweal 74:79-80, Apr 14, 1961
        Coronet 50:16, Jun 1961
        Nation 192:311, Apr 8, 1961
        New York Theatre Critics' Reviews 1961:335
        New York Times p. 24, Mar 9, 1961
                       p. 16, Jul 29, 1963
                       p. 14, Mar 7, 1964
                       p. 55, Dec 8, 1964
        New Yorker 37:124, Mar 18, 1961
        Newsweek 57:88, Mar 20, 1961
        Reporter 24:46, Apr 13, 1961
        Saturday Review 44:35, Mar 25, 1961
                        44:27, Mar 18, 1961
        Theatre Arts 45:58, May 1961
        Time 77:42, Mar 17, 1961

Poor Richard
     Productions:
        Opened December 2, 1964 for 118 performances.
     Reviews:
        Look 29:67-70, Mar 9, 1965
        New York Theatre Critics' Reviews 1964:120
        New York Times p. 59, Dec 3, 1964
                       p. 37, Mar 5, 1965
        New Yorker 40:152+, Dec 12, 1964
        Newsweek 64:84, Dec 14, 1964
        Saturday Review 47:25, Dec 19, 1964
        Time 84:73, Dec 11, 1964
        Vogue 145:27, Jan 15, 1965

The Song of Bernadette (with Walter Kerr) (Adapted from
        Franz Werfel's novel)

Productions:
  Opened March 26, 1946 for 3 performances.
Reviews:
  America 99:179, May 3, 1958
  New York Theatre Critics' Reviews 1946:418
  New York Times p. 22, Mar 27, 1946

KESSELRING, JOSEPH O.

Arsenic and Old Lace
  Productions:
    Opened January 10, 1941 for 1,444 performances.
  Reviews:
    Catholic World 152:599, Feb 1941
    Commonweal 33:351, Jan 24, 1941
    Life 16:57-8+, Apr 3, 1944
    Nation 152:108-9, Jan 25, 1941
    New Republic 104:116, Jan 27, 1941
    New York Theatre Critics' Reviews 1941:417
    New York Times p. 13, Jan 11, 1941
                   IX, p. 1, Jan 12, 1941
                   IX, p. 3, Jan 19, 1941
                   IX, p. 3, Feb 9, 1941
                   IX, p. 1, Feb 23, 1941
                   IX, p. 1, Jun 22, 1941
                   IX, p. 2, Sep 7, 1941
                   IX, p. 3, Feb 1, 1942
                   p. 25, Mar 24, 1942
                   p. 26, Jan 1, 1943
                   VIII, p. 1, Jan 10, 1943
                   p. 16, Feb 26, 1943
                   II, p. 1, May 30, 1943
                   p. 7, Jul 3, 1944
    New Yorker 16:34, Jan 18, 1941
    Newsweek 17:63, Jan 20, 1941
             19:56, May 18, 1942
    Stage 1:24-5, Feb 1941
    Theatre Arts 25:185-6+, Mar 1941
    Time 37:40, Jan 20, 1941
         46:64, Jul 9, 1945
    Vogue 97:77, Mar 1, 1941

Cross-Town
  Productions:
    Opened March 17, 1937 for 5 performances.
  Reviews:

KESSELRING, JOSEPH O. (cont.)
    Cross-Town (cont.)
        New York Times p. 21, Mar 18, 1937

    Four Twelves Are 48
        Productions:
            Opened January 17, 1951 for 2 performances.
        Reviews:
            Commonweal 53:447, Feb 9, 1951
            New York Theatre Critics' Reviews 1951:384
            New York Times p. 30, Jan 18, 1951
            New Yorker 26:54, Jan 27, 1951
            Newsweek 37:83, Jan 29, 1951
            Theatre Arts 35:20, Mar 1951
            Time 57:49, Jan 29, 1951

    There's Wisdom in Women
        Productions:
            Opened October 30, 1935 for 46 performances.
        Reviews:
            Catholic World 142:343, Dec 1935
            Commonweal 23:76, Nov 15, 1935
            New York Times p. 24, Jul 16, 1935
                          p. 17, Oct 31, 1935
            Vanity Fair 45:46, Jan 1936

KINGSLEY, SIDNEY

    Darkness At Noon (Based on the novel by Arthur
        Koestler)
        Productions:
            Opened January 13, 1951 for 186 performances.
            (Off Broadway) Opened March 29, 1963 for 9 per-
                formances (Equity Library Theatre).
        Reviews:
            Catholic World 172:465, Mar 1951
            Commonweal 53:425, Feb 2, 1951
            Life 30:77-8+, Feb 5, 1951
            Nation 172:92-3, Jan 27, 1951
            New Republic 124:22-3, Feb 5, 1951
            New York Theatre Critics' Reviews 1951:388
            New York Times II, p. 1, Jan 7, 1951
                          p. 13, Jan 15, 1951
                          II, p. 1, Jan 21, 1951
                          II, p. 3, Feb 4, 1951
                          II, p. 1, Mar 18, 1951

                    p. 34, Apr 4, 1951
    New Yorker 26:54, Jan 20, 1951
    Newsweek 37:80, Jan 22, 1951
    Saturday Review 34:22-4, Feb 3, 1951
    School and Society 73:105-6, Feb 17, 1951
    Theatre Arts 35:19, 42, Mar 1951
                    35:41+, 373, Sep 1951
    Time 57:38, Jan 22, 1951

Dead End
    Productions:
        Opened October 28, 1935 for 687 performances.
    Reviews:
        Catholic World 142:339-40, Dec 1935
        Commonweal 23:48, Nov 8, 1935
                    23:76, Nov 15, 1935
        Literary Digest 120:17, Nov 9, 1935
        Nation 141:575-6, Nov 13, 1935
        New Republic 85:21, Nov 13, 1935
                    85:49, Nov 20, 1935
        New York Times p. 17, Oct 29, 1935
                    X, p. 1, Nov 3, 1935
                    IX, p. 1, Nov 10, 1935
                    XI, p. 5, Dec 15, 1935
                    X, p. 3, Nov 1, 1936
                    p. 17, Jan 15, 1937
                    p. 18, Jun 29, 1937
                    p. 23, Aug 17, 1937
        Newsweek 6:26, Nov 9, 1935
        Player's Magazine 12:13+, Jan-Feb, 1936
        Stage 13:26-8, Dec 1935
                13:66, Jan 1936
        Survey Graphic 25:52, Jan 1936
        Theatre Arts 19:888-93, Dec 1935
                    20:462-3, Jun 1936
        Time 26:40, Nov 11, 1935
        Vanity Fair 45:45+, Jan 1936

Detective Story
    Productions:
        Opened March 23, 1949 for 581 performances.
        (Off Broadway) Season of 1953-54 (Equity Library
            Theatre).
    Reviews:
        Catholic World 169:144, May 1949
        Christian Science Monitor Magazine p. 7, Apr 15,
            1950

KINGSLEY, SIDNEY (cont.)
  Detective Story (cont.)
          Commonweal 49:638, Apr 8, 1949
          Life 26:131-2+, May 2, 1949
          Nation 168:424-5, Apr 9, 1949
          New Republic 120:25, Apr 11, 1949
          New York Theatre Critics' Reviews 1949:330
          New York Times II, p. 1, Mar 20, 1949
                          p. 34, Mar 24, 1949
                          II, p. 1, Apr 3, 1949
                          p. 18, Mar 27, 1950
                          II, p. 2, Jun 3, 1951
                          p. 11, Feb 13, 1954
                          p. 37, May 11, 1968
          New Yorker 25:50, Apr 2, 1949
          Newsweek 33:78, Apr 4, 1949
          Saturday Review 32:50-2, Apr 16, 1949
          School and Society 70:362-3, Dec 3, 1949
          Theatre Arts 33:11, Jan 1949
          Time 53:75-6, Apr 4, 1949
          Vogue 113:116-17, May 1, 1949

  Lunatics and Lovers
    Productions:
      Opened December 13, 1954 for 336 performances.
    Reviews:
      America 92:366, Jan 1, 1955
      Catholic World 180:388, Feb 1955
      Commonweal 61:406, Jan 14, 1955
      Life 38:57-8+, Jan 17, 1955
      Nation 180:18, Jan 1, 1955
      New Republic 132:20, Mar 7, 1955
      New York Theatre Critics' Reviews 1954:219
      New York Times II, p. 3, Dec 12, 1954
                      p. 44, Dec 14, 1954
                      p. 31, Dec 21, 1954
      New Yorker 30:44-6, Dec 25, 1954
      Newsweek 45:43, Jan 3, 1955
      Saturday Review 38:62, Jan 1, 1955
      Theatre Arts 39:17, 90, Feb 1955
      Time 64:32, Dec 27, 1954

  Men In White
    Productions:
      Opened September 26, 1933 for 351 performances.
    Reviews:
      Catholic World 138:215-17, Nov 1933

Commonweal 18:563-4, Oct 13, 1933
Hygeia 12:358-60, Apr 1934
Literary Digest 116:19, Nov 4, 1933
Nation 137:419-20, Oct 11, 1933
New Outlook 162:43, Nov 1933
New Republic 76:241-2, Oct 11, 1933
New York Times p. 24, Sep 27, 1933
                IX, p. 1, Oct 1, 1933
                IX, p. 2, Oct 15, 1933
                p. 16, Jun 29, 1934
                p. 13, Feb 26, 1955
Newsweek 2:29, Oct 7, 1933
Review of Reviews 89:39, Feb 1934
Stage 11:27-9, Nov 1933
Theatre Arts 17:915-16, Dec 1933

Night Life
    Productions:
    Opened December 15, 1962 for 63 performances.
    Reviews:
    Catholic World 196:199, Dec 1962
    Commonweal 77:232, Nov 23, 1962
    New York Theatre Critics' Reviews 1962:234
    New York Times p. 27, May 26, 1962
                    p. 45, Oct 2, 1962
                    II, p. 3, Oct 21, 1962
                    p. 44, Oct 24, 1962
    New Yorker 38:111, Nov 3, 1962
    Newsweek 60:75, Nov 5, 1962
    Saturday Review 45:28, Nov 10, 1962
    Theatre Arts 46:12-13, Dec 1962
    Time 80:82, Nov 2, 1962

The Patriots
    Productions:
    Opened January 29, 1943 for 173 performances.
    Opened December 20, 1943 for 8 performances.
    Reviews:
    American Mercury 56:486-7, Apr 1943
    Catholic World 156:726-7, Mar 1943
    Commonweal 37:422, Feb 12, 1943
    Current History ns 4:88-91, Mar 1943
    Independent Woman 22:143, May 1943
    Life 14:57-8+, Mar 8, 1943
    Nation 156:248, Feb 13, 1943
    New Republic 108:211, Feb 15, 1943
    New York Theatre Critics' Reviews 1943:385

KINGSLEY, SIDNEY (cont.)
    The Patriots (cont.)
        New York Times p. 11, Jan 30, 1943
                          V, p. 16, Jan 31, 1943
                          II, p. 1, Feb 7, 1943
                          p. 22, Dec 21, 1943
        New York Times Magazine p. 16-17, Jan 31, 1943
        New Yorker 18:31, Feb 6, 1943
        Newsweek 21:82+, Feb 8, 1943
        Saturday Review 26:26+, Apr 17, 1943
        Scholastic 42:20, Mar 15, 1943
        Theatre Arts 27:201-4, Apr 1943
        Time 41:36, Feb 8, 1943

Ten Million Ghosts
    Productions:
        Opened October 23, 1936 for 11 performances.
    Reviews:
        Nation 143:558, Nov 7, 1936
        New York Times p. 23, Oct 24, 1936
        Stage 14:50, Nov 1936
        Theatre Arts 20:932, Dec 1936
        Time 28:49, Nov 2, 1936

The World We Make (Based on Millen Brand's The Out-
        ward Room)
    Productions:
        Opened Nov. 20, 1939 for 80 performances.
    Reviews:
        Catholic World 150:470, Jan 1940
        Forum 103:32-3, Jan 1940
        Life 8:27-9, Jan 1, 1940
        Nation 149:627-9, Dec 2, 1939
        New York Theatre Critics' Reviews 1940:454
        New York Times p. 19, Nov 21, 1939
                          IX, p. 1, Nov 26, 1939
                          IX, p. 5, Dec 3, 1939
                          IX, p. 3, Dec 17, 1939
        Newsweek 14:39, Dec 4, 1939
        North American Review 248 No. 2:402-3 (Dec) 1939
        Theatre Arts 24:15, Jan 1940
        Time 34:38+, Dec 4, 1939

KIRKLAND, JACK

    Frankie and Johnnie
        Productions:

Opened September 25, 1930 for 61 performances.
Reviews:
Life (NY) 90:19, Oct 17, 1930
National Magazine 59:136, Dec 1920
New York Times p. 16, Sep 26, 1930
Theatre Arts 16:456-8, Jun 1932

I Must Love Someone (with Leyla Georgie)
Productions:
Opened February 7, 1939 for 191 performances.
Reviews:
New York Times p. 18, Feb 8, 1939
Time 33:55, Feb 20, 1939

The Man With The Golden Arm
Productions:
(Off Broadway) Season of 1955-56.
Reviews:
New York Times p. 28, May 22, 1956
Saturday Review 39:32, Jun 16, 1956

Mandingo (Based on Kyle Onstott's novel)
Productions:
Opened May 22, 1961 for 8 performances.
Reviews:
New York Times p. 43, May 23, 1961
New Yorker 37:90, Jun 3, 1961
Theatre Arts 45:10, Jul 1961
Time 77:85-6, Jun 2, 1961

Mr. Adam (Based on Pat Frank's novel)
Productions:
Opened May 25, 1949 for 5 performances.
Reviews:
New York Theatre Critics' Reviews 1949:292
New York Times p. 34, May 26, 1949
New Yorker 25:46+, Jun 4, 1949
Theatre Arts 33:5, Aug 1949
Time 53:70, Jun 6, 1949

Suds in Your Eye (Based on a novel by Mary Lasswell)
Productions:
Opened January 12, 1944 for 37 performances.
Reviews:
Catholic World 150:490, Feb 1944
New York Theatre Critics' Reviews 1944:287
New York Times p. 15, Jan 13, 1944

KIRKLAND, JACK (cont.)
 Suds in Your Eye (cont.)
          Theatre Arts 28:141, Mar 1944
          Time 43:40, Jan 24, 1944

 Tobacco Road (Based on Erskine Caldwell's novel)
     Productions:
          Opened December 4, 1933 for 3, 182 performances.
          Opened September 5, 1942 for 34 performances.
          Opened September 4, 1943 for 66 performances.
          Opened March 6, 1950 for 7 performances.
          (Off Broadway) Season of 1959-60.
     Reviews:
          Catholic World 138:603-4, Feb 1934
          Commonweal 34:185, Jun 13, 1941
                        39:140-1, Nov 26, 1943
          Golden Book Magazine 20:246+, Sep 1934
          Life 2:36-7, Jan 11, 1937
               9:30, Dec 16, 1940
          Literary Digest 118:18+, Dec 15, 1934
          Nation 137:718, Dec 20, 1933
          New Outlook 163:43, Jan 1934
          New Republic 77:168-9, Dec 20, 1933
          New York Theatre Critics' Reviews 1940:498
                                              1941:498
                                              1950:333
          New York Times p. 31, Dec 5, 1933
                          IX, p. 3, Jan 28, 1934
                          p. 24, Jun 20, 1934
                          X, p. 1, Jul 1, 1934
                          X, p. 2, Dec 2, 1934
                          p. 17, Oct 30, 1935
                          p. 17, Nov 27, 1935
                          XI, p. 7, Dec 1, 1935
                          II, p. 1, Jan 19, 1936
                          p. 25, Jan 23, 1936
                          XI, p. 1, Mar 22, 1936
                          p. 31, Apr 7, 1936
                          XII, p. 1, Nov 29, 1936
                          XI, p. 2, Mar 21, 1937
                          p. 16, May 20, 1937
                          p. 27, Nov 23, 1937
                          XI, p. 2, Nov 21, 1937
                          IX, p. 3, Nov 27, 1937
                          IX, p. 3, Nov 27, 1938
                          p. 17, Nov 4, 1939
                          VII, p. 6, Nov 12, 1939

IX, p. 3, Nov 12, 1939
VII, p. 12, Dec 24, 1939
XI, p. 1, Mar 10, 1940
X, p. 3, Dec 1, 1940
p. 32, Dec 5, 1940
p. 18, May 24, 1941
p. 20, Jun 3, 1941
IX, p. 3, Nov 30, 1941
p. 34, Sep 7, 1942
p. 21, Sep 6, 1943
p. 26, Aug 26, 1947
p. 27, Aug 11, 1949
p. 23, Mar 7, 1950
p. 44, May 11, 1960
Newsweek 7:32, Apr 4, 1936
8:22, Dec 5, 1936
14:32-3, Nov 27, 1939
17:58, Jun 9, 1941
Photoplay 18:50-51, Apr 1941
Review of Reviews 89:47, Mar 1934
Stage 11:29, Jan 1934
1:20, Nov 1940
1:19, Dec 1940
Theatre Arts 18:93-5, Feb 1934
31:67-9, Apr 1947
34:16, May 1950
Time 22:31, Dec 18, 1933
24:32, Jul 2, 1934
24:50-51, Dec 17, 1934
30:57, Dec 13, 1937
37:53, Jun 9, 1941
55:61, Mar 20, 1950

Tortilla Flat (Based on John Steinbeck's novel)
Productions:
Opened January 12, 1938 for 5 performances.
Reviews:
New York Times p. 16, Jan 13, 1938
Time 31:47, Jan 24, 1938

KOBER, ARTHUR

Having Wonderful Time
Productions:
Opened February 20, 1937 for 372 performances.
Reviews:

KOBER, ARTHUR (cont.)
  Having Wonderful Time (cont.)
          Catholic World 145:85, Apr 1937
          Commonweal 25:528, Mar 5, 1937
          Literary Digest 123:25, Mar 6, 1937
          Nation 144:276-7, Mar 6, 1937
          New York Times X, p. 1, Feb 14, 1937
                            p. 12, Feb 22, 1937
                            XI, p. 1, Feb 28, 1937
                            XI, p. 1, Mar 21, 1937
          Newsweek 9:22-4, Feb 27, 1937
          Stage 14:50-53, Mar 1937
                14:78, Apr 1937
          Theatre Arts 21:262, Apr 1937
          Time 29:47-8, Mar 1, 1937

  A Mighty Man Is He (with George Oppenheimer)
    Productions:
      Opened January 6, 1960 for 5 performances.
    Reviews:
      New York Theatre Critics' Reviews 1960:397
      New York Times p. 25, Jan 7, 1960
      New Yorker 35:86+, Jan 16, 1960

KOCH, HOWARD

  Give Us This Day
    Productions:
      Opened Octuber 27, 1933 for 3 performances.
    Reviews:
      New York Times p. 20, Oct 28, 1933

  In Time to Come (with John Huston)
    Productions:
      Opened December 28, 1941 for 40 performances.
    Reviews:
      Catholic World 154:599-600, Feb 1942
      Commonweal 35:344-5, Jan 23, 1942
      Current History 1:568, Feb 1942
      Life 12:33-4+, Feb 2, 1942
      Nation 154:74, Jan 17, 1942
      New Republic 106:147, Feb 2, 1942
      New York Theatre Critics' Reviews 1941:158
      New York Times p. 20, Dec 29, 1941
                    IX, p. 1, Jan 4, 1942
      Scholastic 39:24, Jan 19, 1942

Theatre Arts 26:149-50, Mar 1942
        28:606, Oct 1944
Time 39:42, Jan 12, 1942
Vogue 99:61, Feb 15, 1942

KOPIT, ARTHUR

The Day the Whores Came Out to Play Tennis
    Productions:
        (Off Broadway) Opened March 15, 1965 for 24 per-
            formances.
    Reviews:
        Nation 200:374, Apr 5, 1965
        New Republic 152:24, Apr 10, 1965
        New York Times p. 45, Mar 16, 1965
        New Yorker 41:146-7, May 27, 1965
        Newsweek 65:82, Mar 29, 1965
        Time 85:58, Mar 26, 1965
        Vogue 145:142, May 1965

*Indians
    Reviews:
        New York Times p. 30, Jul 9, 1968
                    II, p. 12, Jul 21, 1968
        Newsweek 72:97, Jul 29, 1968

Oh Dad, Poor Dad, Mamma's Hung You In the Closet
and I'm Feelin' So Sad
    Productions:
        (Off Broadway) Opened February 26, 1962 for 454
            performances.
        Opened August 27, 1963 for 47 performances.
    Reviews:
        Commonweal 76:41, Apr 6, 1962
        National Review 12:416-17, Jun 5, 1962
        New Republic 146:31, Mar 19, 1962
        New York Theatre Critics' Reviews 1963:294
        New York Times p. 19, Jul 6, 1961
                    p. 28, Feb 27, 1962
                    II, p. 1, Mar 11, 1962
                    p. 28, Aug 28, 1963
        New Yorker 38:84-5, Mar 10, 1962
        Saturday Review 45:35, Mar 17, 1962
        Theatre Arts (p. 63) 46:60-1, May 1962

KOPIT, ARTHUR (cont.)
Sing to Me Through Open Windows
    Productions:
        (Off Broadway) Opened March 15, 1965 for 24 per-
            formances.
    Reviews:
        Nation 200:373-4, Apr 5, 1965
        New Republic 152:24, Apr 10, 1965
        New York Times p. 45, Mar 16, 1965
        Newsweek 65:82, Mar 29, 1965

KRAMM, JOSEPH

    *Build With One Hand
        Reviews:
            New York Times p. 42, Nov 29, 1956

    Giants, Sons of Giants
        Productions:
            Opened January 6, 1962 for 9 performances.
        Reviews:
            New York Theatre Critics' Reviews 1962:388
            New York Times p. 26, Jan 8, 1962

    The Shrike
        Productions:
            Opened January 15, 1952 for 161 performances.
            Opened November 25, 1953 for 15 performances.
            (Off Broadway) Opened February 1, 1964 for 8 per-
                formances (Equity Library Theatre).
        Reviews:
            America 90:306, Dec 12, 1953
            Catholic World 174:465, Mar 1952
                         178:309, Jan 1954
            Commonweal 55:422, Feb 1, 1952
            New Republic 126:23, Feb 4, 1952
            New York Theatre Critics' Reviews 1952:389
            New York Times p. 20, Jan 16, 1952
                         II, p. 1, Jan 27, 1952
                         II, p. 1, Feb 24, 1952
                         p. 51, Nov 26, 1953
            New Yorker 27:53, Jan 26, 1952
            Newsweek 39:83, Jan 28, 1952
            Saturday Review 35:22-3, Feb 9, 1952
                         35:28, May 17, 1952
            School and Society 75:181-2, Mar 22, 1952

Theatre Arts 36:71, Mar 1952
                36:4, Jul 1952
                38:20, Feb 1954
        Time 59:43, Jan 28, 1952

KRASNA, NORMAN

Dear Ruth
    Productions:
        Opened December 13, 1944 for 683 performances.
    Reviews:
        Catholic World 160:454, Feb 1945
        Commonweal 41:275, Dec 29, 1944
        Life 18:57-8+, Jan 22, 1944
        Nation 159:810, Dec 30, 1944
        New York Theatre Critics' Reviews 1944:56
        New York Times p. 29, Dec 14, 1944
                        II, p. 1, Dec 31, 1944
                        II, p. 1, Jan 7, 1945
                        p. 14, Jan 27, 1945
                        p. 26, Oct 24, 1945
                        p. 17, Mar 1, 1946
        New Yorker 20:38, Dec 23, 1944
        Newsweek 24:69, Dec 25, 1944
        Saturday Review 28:24, Mar 17, 1945
        Theatre Arts 29:74-5, Feb 1945
                     29:334, Jun 1945
        Time 44:56, Dec 25, 1944

John Loves Mary
    Productions:
        Opened February 4, 1947 for 423 performances.
    Reviews:
        Catholic World 164:552, Mar 1947
        Commonweal 45:469, Feb 21, 1947
        Life 22:125-6+, Apr 14, 1947
        New Republic 116:40, Feb 17, 1947
        New York Theatre Critics' Reviews 1947:465
        New York Times II, p. 1, Feb 2, 1947
                        p. 29, Feb 5, 1947
                        II, p. 1, Apr 13, 1947
                        II, p. 1, Jul 13, 1947
        New Yorker 22:48+, Feb 15, 1947
        Newsweek 29:88, Feb 17, 1947
        School and Society 66:327-8, Oct 25, 1947
        Theatre Arts 31:18, Apr 1947

KRASNA, NORMAN (cont.)
John Loves Mary (cont.)
Time 49:53, Feb 17, 1947

Kind Sir
Productions:
Opened November 4, 1953 for 166 performances.
Reviews:
America 90:249+, Nov 28, 1953
Catholic World 178:310, Jan 1954
Commonweal 59:224-5, Dec 4, 1953
Life 35:160-4, Oct 12, 1953
Nation 177:434, Nov 21, 1953
New York Theatre Critics' Reviews 1953:225
New York Times VI, p. 19, Sep 20, 1953
            p. 21, Sep 28, 1953
            II, p. 3, Oct 18, 1953
            p. 41, Nov 5, 1953
New Yorker 29:69-70, Nov 14, 1953
Newsweek 42:60, Dec 21, 1953
        42:56+, Nov 9, 1953
Saturday Review 36:47, Nov 21, 1953
Theatre Arts 37:11, Aug 1953
            38:18, Jan 1954
Time 62:90, Nov 16, 1953

Louder, Please
Productions:
Opened November 12, 1931 for 68 performances.
Reviews:
New York Times p. 26, Nov 13, 1931
Theatre Guild Magazine 9:34-5, Jan 1932

Love in E-Flat
Productions:
Opened February 13, 1967 for 24 performances.
Reviews:
New York Theatre Critics' Reviews 1967:367
New York Times p. 38, Feb 14, 1967

The Man With Blond Hair
Productions:
Opened November 4, 1941 for 7 performances.
Reviews:
New York Theatre Critics' Reviews 1941:241
New York Times p. 30, Nov 5, 1941

272

Small Miracle
    Productions:
        Opened September 26, 1934 for 117 performances.
    Reviews:
        Catholic World 140:213-14, Nov 1934
        Golden Book 20:510, Nov 1934
        New York Times p. 24, Sep 27, 1934
        Stage 12:2+, Nov 1934
        Time 24:46, Oct 8, 1934

Sunday in New York
    Productions:
        Opened November 29, 1961 for 188 performances.
    Reviews:
        America 106:453, Jan 6, 1962
        New York Theatre Critics' Reviews 1961:158
        New York Times p. 40, Nov 30, 1961
        New Yorker 37:160, Dec 9, 1961
        Newsweek 58:65, Dec 11, 1961
        Reporter 26:38, Jan 4, 1962
        Theatre Arts 46:12-13, Feb 1962
        Time 78:75, Dec 8, 1961

Time for Elizabeth (with Groucho Marx)
    Productions:
        Opened September 27, 1948 for 8 performances.
    Reviews:
        Nation 167:410, Oct 9, 1948
        New Republic 119:27, Oct 18, 1948
        New York Theatre Critics' Review 1948:218
        New York Times p. 32, Sep 28, 1948
        New Yorker 24:62, Oct 9, 1948
        Time 52:78+, Oct 11, 1948

Who Was That Lady I Saw You With?
    Productions:
        Opened March 3, 1958 for 208 performances.
    Reviews:
        America 99:93+, Apr 12, 1958
        Catholic World 187:145-6, May 1958
        Commonweal 68:128, May 2, 1958
        Nation 186:261, Mar 22, 1958
        New York Theatre Critics' Reviews 1958:337
        New York Times p. 33, Mar 4, 1958
        New Yorker 34:89-90, Mar 15, 1958
        Newsweek 51:91, Mar 17, 1958
        Saturday Review 41:56, Mar 15, 1958

Who Was That Lady I Saw You With? (cont.)
Time 71:86, Mar 17, 1958

KUMMER, CLARE

Amourette
    Productions:
        Opened September 27, 1933 for 22 performances.
    Reviews:
        Catholic World 138:217, Nov 1933
        Commonweal 18:544, Oct 13, 1933
        Stage 11:5-6, Oct 1933

Banco (Adapted from the French of Alfred Savoir)
    Productions:
        Opened September 20, 1922 for 69 performances.
    Reviews:
        Life (NY) 80:10, Oct 12, 1922
        New York Clipper 70:39, Oct 4, 1922
        New York Times p. 18, Sep 21, 1922
        Theatre Magazine 36:297, Nov 1922

Be Calm, Camilla
    Productions:
        Opened October 31, 1918 for 84 performances.
    Reviews:
        Dramatic Mirror 79:723, Nov 16, 1918
        Independent 96:193, Nov 16, 1918
        Life (NY) 72:712, Nov 14, 1918
        New York Drama News 65:11, Nov 9, 1918
        New York Times p. 13, Nov 1, 1918
                        IV, p. 2, Nov 10, 1918
        Theatre Magazine 28:380, Dec 1918

Bridges
    Productions:
        Opened February 28, 1921 for 5 Matinees.
    Reviews:
        Dramatic Mirror 83:408+, Mar 5, 1921

Good Gracious Annabelle
    Productions:
        Opened October 31, 1916 for 111 performances.
    Reviews:
        Dramatic Mirror 76:7, Nov 11, 1916

Green Book 17:10+, Jan 1917
International 11:29, Jan 1917
Nation 103:470, Nov 16, 1916
National Magazine 45:576-7, Jan 1917
New Republic 9:331, Jan 20, 1917
New York Times p. 9, Nov 1, 1916
    II, p. 6, Nov 5, 1916
    II, p. 7, Nov 12, 1916
Theatre Magazine 24:358, Dec 1916

Her Master's Voice
Productions:
Opened October 23, 1933 for 224 performances.
(Off Broadway) Opened December 26, 1964 for 18
 performances.
Reviews:
Catholic World 138:341, Dec 1933
Commonweal 19:104, Nov 24, 1933
Nation 137:550, Nov 8, 1933
New Outlook 162:46, Dec 1933
New York Times p. 24, Oct 24, 1933
    IX, p. 7, Dec 3, 1933
    X, p. 1, Dec 10, 1933
    p. 33, Dec 28, 1964
New Yorker 40:84+, Jan 9, 1965
Newsweek 2:28, Nov 4, 1933
Stage 11:7, Dec 1933
Theatre Arts 17:920, Dec 1933
Vanity Fair 41:42, Jan 1934

Many Happy Returns
Productions:
Opened January 5, 1945 for 3 performances.
Reviews:
New York Theatre Critics' Reviews 1945:296
New York Times p. 15, Jan 6, 1945
New Yorker 20:40, Jan 13, 1945

The Mountain Man
Productions:
Opened December 12, 1921 for 163 performances.
Reviews:
Dramatic Mirror 84:881, Dec 17, 1921
Life (NY) 79:18, Jan 5, 1922
New Republic 29:309-10, Feb 8, 1922
New York Clipper 69:12, Dec 21, 1921
New York Times p. 24, Dec 13, 1921

KRASNA, NORMAN (cont.)
The Mountain Man (cont.)
Theatre Magazine 35:128, Feb 1922

Pomeroy's Past
Productions:
Opened April 19, 1926 for 94 performances.
Reviews:
Life (NY) 87:23, May 13, 1926
Nation 122:510, May 5, 1926
New York Times p. 24, Apr 20, 1926
VIII, p. 1, May 2, 1926
Theatre Magazine 44:16, Jul 1926
44:26, Oct 1926
Vogue 67:79+, Jun 15, 1926

The Rescuing Angel
Productions:
Opened October 8, 1917 for 32 performances.
Reviews:
Dramatic Mirror 77:7, Oct 20, 1917
Life (NY) 70:672, Oct 25, 1917
New York Drama News 64:7, Oct 13, 1917
New York Times p. 9, Oct 9, 1917
III, p. 6, Oct 14, 1917
Theatre Magazine 27:349+, Dec 1917

The Robbery
Productions:
Opened February 28, 1921 for 5 matinees.
Reviews:
Dramatic Mirror 83:408+, Mar 5, 1921
New York Times p. 18, Mar 1, 1921
VIII, p. 1, Mar 13, 1921

Rollo's Wild Oat
Productions:
Opened November 23, 1920 for 228 performances.
Reviews:
Collier's 66:11, Dec 25, 1920
Dramatic Mirror p. 1051, Dec 4, 1920
Hearst 39:21-3+, May 1921
Independent 104:385, Dec 18, 1920
New York Clipper 67:25, Feb 4, 1920
68:23, Dec 1, 1920
New York Times p. 14, Nov 24, 1920
VI, p. 1, Jan 23, 1921

Theatre Magazine 33:83+, Feb 1921

Spring Thaw
Productions:
Opened March 21, 1938 for 8 performances.
Reviews:
New York Times p. 18, Mar 22, 1938
Newsweek 11:25, Apr 4, 1938
One Act Play Magazine 2:69, May 1938
Stage 15:31, Apr 1938

A Successful Calamity
Productions:
Opened February 5, 1917 for 144 performances.
Opened February 12, 1934 in repertory.
Reviews:
American Magazine 85:30, Feb 1918
Book News 35:283, Mar 1917
Current Opinion 62:249-52, Apr 1917
Dramatic Mirror 77:7, Feb 10, 1917
Green Book 17:581+, Apr 1917
International 11:95, Mar 1917
Nation 104:198, Feb 15, 1917
New York Drama News 63:6, Feb 10, 1917
New York Times p. 10, Feb 6, 1917
II, p. 2, Feb 11, 1917
p. 11, Mar 19, 1921
Theatre Magazine 25:145+, Mar 1917

LARDNER, RING

Elmer the Great
Productions:
Opened September 24, 1928 for 40 performances.
Reviews:
Drama 19:43-4, Nov 1928
Life (NY) 92:17, Oct 12, 1928
New York Times p. 29, Sep 25, 1928
IX, p. 1, Sep 30, 1928
p. 32, Nov 1, 1940
Theatre Arts 12:775+, Nov 1928
Time 36:44, Aug 5, 1940

June Moon (with George S. Kaufman)
Productions:
Opened October 9, 1929 for 273 performances.

LARDNER, RING (cont.)
  June Moon (cont.)
        Opened May 15, 1933 for 49 performances.
    Reviews:
        American Mercury 18:502-3, Dec 1929
        Life (NY) 94:22, Nov 1, 1929
        New York Times VIII, p. 1, Aug 4, 1929
                         IX, p. 4, Oct 6, 1929
                         p. 34, Oct 10, 1929
        Outlook 153:431, Nov 13, 1929
        Theatre Arts 13:880-1, Dec 1929
        Theatre Magazine 50:47-8, Dec 1929
                         51:32-5+, Feb 1930
        Vogue 74:164, Dec 7, 1929

  The Love Nest (See entry under Sherwood, Robert E.)

LAURENTS, ARTHUR

  The Bird Cage
    Productions:
        Opened February 22, 1950 for 21 performances.
    Reviews:
        Commonweal 51:607, Mar 17, 1950
        Nation 170:236, Mar 11, 1950
        New Republic 122:23, Mar 13, 1950
        New York Theatre Critics' Reviews 1950:341
        New York Times p. 32, Feb 23, 1950
        New Yorker 26:58, Mar 4, 1950
        Newsweek 35:82, Mar 6, 1950
        Theatre Arts 34:14, May 1950
        Time 55:71, Mar 6, 1950

  A Clearing in the Woods
    Productions:
        Opened January 10, 1957 for 36 performances.
        (Off Broadway) Season of 1958-59.
    Reviews:
        America 96:510, Feb 2, 1957
        Catholic World 184:470, Mar 1957
        Christian Century 74:235, Feb 20, 1957
        Commonweal 65:489, Feb 8, 1957
        New York Theatre Critics' Reviews 1957:393
        New York Times p. 20, Jan 11, 1957
                       II, p. 1, Jan 20, 1957
                       p. 32, Feb 13, 1959
        New Yorker 32:57, Jan 19, 1957

Saturday Review 40:23, Jan 26, 1957
                42:25, Feb 28, 1959
Theatre Arts 41:20, Mar 1957
Time 69:72, Jan 21, 1957

Home of the Brave
Productions:
Opened December 27, 1945 for 69 performances.
(Off Broadway) Season of 1946-47 (Associated Play-
wright, Inc.).
Reviews:
Catholic World 162:457, Feb 1946
Forum 105:657-9, Mar 1946
New York Theatre Critics' Reviews 1945:51
New York Times p. 13, Dec 28, 1945
                II, p. 1, Jan 6, 1946
                II, p. 1, Jan 13, 1946
New Yorker 21:42-4, Jan 12, 1946
Newsweek 27:82, Jan 7, 1946
Theatre Arts 30:141, 145-6, Mar 1946
Time 47:88, Jan 7, 1946

Invitation to a March
Productions:
Opened October 29, 1960 for 113 performances.
(Off Broadway) Season of 1966-67 for 10 perform-
ances (Equity Theatre).
Reviews:
America 104:352, Dec 3, 1960
Christian Century 77:1382, Nov 23, 1960
Nation 191:420-1, Nov 26, 1960
New Republic 143:20-1, Nov 14, 1960
New York Theatre Critics' Reviews 1960:191
New York Times II, p. 1, Oct 23, 1960
                p. 27, Oct 31, 1960
New Yorker 36:116, Nov 5, 1960
Newsweek 56:61, Nov 14, 1960
Saturday Review 43:73, Nov 12, 1960
Theatre Arts 45:73, Jan 1961
Time 76:84, Nov 14, 1960

The Time of the Cuckoo
Productions:
Opened October 15, 1952 for 263 performances.
(Off Broadway) Season of 1958-59.
Reviews:
Catholic World, 176:229-30, Dec 1952

LAURENTS, ARTHUR (cont.)
  The Time of the Cuckoo (cont.)
          Commonweal 57:118, Nov 7, 1952
          Nation 175:413, Nov 1, 1952
          New York Theatre Critics' Reviews 1952:235
          New York Times II, p. 3, Oct 12, 1952
                          p. 37, Oct 16, 1952
                          II, p. 1, Nov 2, 1952
                          II, p. 1, Jan 4, 1953
                          p. 40, Oct 28, 1958
          New Yorker 28:77-8, Oct 25, 1952
          Newsweek 40:77, Oct 27, 1952
          Saturday Review 35:28, Oct 18, 1952
                          35:26, Nov 1, 1952
          School and Society 77:117, Feb 21, 1953
          Theatre Arts 36:26-7, Dec 1952
          Time 60:75, Oct 27, 1952

  *The Way Back
    Reviews:
    New York Times p. 9, Jan 29, 1949

LAVERY, EMMET

  *Dawn's Early Light
    Reviews:
    New York Times p. 76, Aug 9, 1959

  The First Legion
    Productions:
    Opened October 1, 1934 for 112 performances.
    Reviews:
    Catholic World 140:210, Nov 1934
    Commonweal 20:563, Oct 12, 1934
                21:654, Apr 3, 1935
                23:104, Nov 22, 1935
    New York Times p. 18, Oct 2, 1934
                   VIII, p. 2, Mar 10, 1935
                   p. 19, Mar 12, 1936
                   p. 30, Jun 8, 1937
                   X, p. 2, Aug 15, 1937
    Stage 12:13, Nov 1934
          12:63-4, Dec 1934
    Theatre Arts 20:89, Feb 1936

The Gentleman from Athens
    Productions:
        Opened December 9, 1947 for 7 performances.
    Reviews:
        New York Theatre Critics' Reviews 1947:241
        New York Times p. 78, Nov 30, 1947
                       II, p. 5, Dec 7, 1947
                          p. 42, Dec 10, 1947
        New Yorker 23:48+, Dec 20, 1947
        Newsweek 30:76, Dec 22, 1947
        Time 50:74, Dec 22, 1947

The Magnificent Yankee
    Productions:
        Opened January 22, 1946 for 160 performances.
    Reviews:
        Catholic World 162:550-1, Mar 1946
        Commonweal 43:429, Feb 8, 1946
                    43:456, Feb 15, 1946
        Forum 105:659, Mar 1946
        Life 20:56-8, Feb 11, 1946
        New Republic 114:189, Feb 11, 1946
        New York Theatre Critics' Reviews 1946:477
        New York Times p. 23, Jan 2, 1946
                       VI, p. 28, Jan 13, 1946
                          p. 21, Jan 23, 1946
                       II, p. 1, Feb 3, 1946
                       II, p. 1, Mar 31, 1946
        New Yorker 21:36-8, Feb 2, 1946
        Newsweek 27:80, Feb 4, 1946
        Saturday Review 29:28-30, Feb 23, 1946
        Theatre Arts 30:140, Mar 1946
        Time 47:62, Feb 4, 1946

LAWRENCE, JEROME

    Auntie Mame (with Robert E. Lee) (Based on Patrick
        Dennis's novel)
    Productions:
        Opened October 31, 1956 for 639 performances.
        Opened August 11, 1958 for 24 performances.
    Reviews:
        America 96:310, Dec 8, 1956
        Catholic World 184:305-6, Jan 1957
        Commonweal 65:382, Jan 11, 1957

LAWRENCE, JEROME (cont.)
Auntie Mame (cont.)
    Life 41:129-30+, Nov 12, 1956
    Nation 183:485, Dec 1, 1956
    New York Theatre Critics' Reviews 1956:229
    New York Times VI, p. 17, Oct 28, 1956
                p. 47, Nov 1, 1956
                II, p. 1, Nov 11, 1956
                II, p. 3, Nov 18, 1956
                II, p. 1, Jun 8, 1958
                p. 3, Aug 12, 1958
    New Yorker 32:110+, Nov 10, 1956
    Newsweek 48:54, Nov 12, 1956
    Saturday Review 39:28, Nov 17, 1956
    Theatre Arts 41:22-3, Jan 1957
              41:33+, Aug 1957
              42:25-6+, Nov 1958
  Time 68:71, Nov 12, 1956

A Call On Kuprin (with Robert E. Lee)
  Productions:
    Opened May 25, 1961 for 12 performances.
  Reviews:
    Nation 192:504+, Jun 10, 1961
    New York Theatre Critics' Reviews 1961:282
    New York Times II, p. 1, May 21, 1961
                p. 29, May 26, 1961
                II, p. 1, Jun 4, 1961
    New Yorker 37:94, Jun 10, 1961
    Newsweek 57:85, Jun 5, 1961
    Theatre Arts 45:9-11, Jul 1961
    Time 77:85, Jun 2, 1961

Diamond Orchid (with Robert E. Lee)
  Productions:
    Opened February 10, 1965 for 5 performances.
  Reviews:
    New York Theatre Critics' Reviews 1965:378
    New York Times p. 44, Feb 11, 1965

The Gangs All Here (with Robert E. Lee)
  Productions:
    Opened October 1, 1959 for 132 performances.
  Reviews:
    America 102:213-14, Nov 14, 1959
    Commonweal 71:186, Nov 6, 1959
    Nation 189:239, Oct 17, 1959

New York Theatre Critics' Reviews 1959:289
New York Times p. 23, Oct 2, 1959
                II, p. 1, Oct 11, 1959
New Yorker 35:125-6, Oct 10, 1959
Newsweek 54:70, Oct 12, 1959
Reporter 21:37, Nov 12, 1959
Saturday Review 42:65, Oct 17, 1959
Theatre Arts 43:15, Dec 1959
Time 74:70, Oct 12, 1959

Inherit the Wind (with Robert E. Lee)
    Productions:
        Opened April 21, 1955 for 806 performances.
    Reviews:
        America 93:250, May 28, 1955
        Catholic World 181:225-6, Jun 1955
        Commonweal 62:278, Jun 17, 1955
        Life 38:119-20+, May 9, 1955
        Nation 180:410, May 7, 1955
        New York Theatre Critics' Reviews 1955:322
        New York Times p. 24, Jan 12, 1955
                       p. 28, Apr 5, 1955
                       II, p. 1, Apr 17, 1955
                       p. 20, Apr 22, 1955
                       VI, p. 17, May 22, 1955
                       II, p. 1, Sep 25, 1955
                       p. 31, Jun 3, 1957
                       p. 36, Feb 18, 1960
                       p. 50, Jun 23, 1967
        New Yorker 31:67, Apr 30, 1955
        Newsweek 45:82, May 2, 1955
        Saturday Review 38:25, May 14, 1955
        Theatre Arts 39:18-19, 23, Jul 1955
                     41:34-62, Aug 1957
        Time 65:78, May 2, 1955

Only in America (with Robert E. Lee) (Based on Harry
    Golden's book)
    Productions:
        Opened November 19, 1959 for 28 performances.
    Reviews:
        Commonweal 71:321, Dec 11, 1959
        Nation 189:427, Dec 5, 1959
        New York Theatre Critics' Reviews 1959:224
        New York Times p. 46, Nov 18, 1959
                       p. 35, Nov 20, 1959
        New Yorker 35:97, Dec 5, 1959

LAWRENCE, JEROME (cont.)
Only in America (cont.)
Newsweek 54:100, Nov 30, 1959
Saturday Review 42:29, Dec 5, 1959
Time 74:64, Nov 30, 1959

LAWSON, JOHN HOWARD

Gentlewoman
Productions:
Opened March 22, 1934 for 12 performances.
Reviews:
Nation 138:424, Apr 11, 1934
New York Times p. 28, Mar 23, 1934
Stage 11:10, Apr 1934
Time 23:26, Apr 2, 1934

The International
Productions:
Opened January 12, 1928 for 27 performances.
Reviews:
Life (NY) 92:21, Feb 2, 1928
Nation 126:130, Feb 1, 1928
New York Times p. 24, Jan 16, 1928

Loud Speaker
Productions:
Opened March 7, 1927 for 42 performances.
Reviews:
Bookman 65:332, May 1927
Independent 118:445, Apr 23, 1927
Life (NY) 89:21, Mar 24, 1927
Nation 124:324, Mar 23, 1927
New York Times p. 27, Mar 3, 1927
VII, p. 1, Mar 20, 1927
Vogue 69:82-3, May 1, 1927

Marching Song
Productions:
Opened February 17, 1937 for 61 performances.
Reviews:
Catholic World 145:85-6, Apr 1937
Commonweal 25:258, Mar 5, 1937
Nation 144:248-9, Feb 27, 1937
New Republic 90:166-7, Mar 17, 1937
New York Times p. 18, Feb 18, 1937

XI, p. 2, Feb 28, 1937
Theatre Arts 21:265, Apr 1937
Time 29:47, Mar 1937

Nirvana
    Productions:
        Opened March 3, 1926 for 6 performances.
    Reviews:
        Nation 122:295, Mar 17, 1926
        New Republic 46:173, Mar 31, 1926
        New York Times p. 19, Mar 4, 1926
        Theatre Magazine 43:16, May 1926

Processional
    Productions:
        Opened January 12, 1925 for 96 performances.
        Opened October 13, 1937 for 81 performances
            (WPA Federal Theatre Project).
    Reviews:
        American Mercury 4:372-3, Mar 1925
        Bookman 61:74-5, Mar 1925
        Catholic World 146:341-2, Dec 1937
        Dial 78:341-4, Apr 1925
        Drama 15:129-30, Mar 7, 1925
        Independent 114:275, Mar 7, 1925
        Independent Woman 16:368, Nov 1937
        Life (NY) 85:18, Feb 5, 1925
        Nation 120:99-100, Jan 28, 1925
                145:456, Oct 23, 1937
        New Republic 41:261, Jan 28, 1925
        New York Times p. 17, Jan 13, 1925
                        VII, p. 1, Jan 18, 1925
                        VII, p. 1, Jan 25, 1925
                        IV, p. 18, Feb 1, 1925
                        VII, p. 2, Feb 1, 1925
                        VII, p. 2, Feb 8, 1925
                        XI, p. 2, Oct 10, 1937
                        p. 23, Oct 14, 1937
                        XI, p. 1, Oct 24, 1937
        Theatre Magazine 40:19, Mar 1925

The Pure in Heart
    Productions:
        Opened March 20, 1934 for 7 performances.
    Reviews:
        New York Times p. 9, May 21, 1932
                        IX, p. 3, Oct 9, 1932

285

LAWSON, JOHN HOWARD (cont.)
  The Pure in Heart (cont.)
                        p. 24, Mar 21, 1934
            Stage 11:10, Apr 1934

  Roger Bloomer
      Productions:
      Opened March 1, 1923 for 50 performances.
      Reviews:
        Bookman 57:319, May 1923
        Freeman 7:111-12, Apr 11, 1923
        Independent 110:206, Mar 17, 1923
        Nation 116:346, Mar 21, 1923
        New Republic 34:100-1, Mar 21, 1923
        New York Clipper 71:14, Mar 7, 1923
        New York Times p. 18, Mar 2, 1923
                        VIII, p. 1, Mar 11, 1923
        Theatre Magazine 37:15, Apr 1923

  Success Story
      Productions:
      Opened September 26, 1932 for 121 performances.
      Reviews:
        Catholic World 136:207-8, Nov 1932
        Commonweal 16:566, Oct 12, 1932
        Nation 135:336-7, Oct 12, 1932
        New Outlook 161:46, Jan 1933
        New Republic 72:233-5, Oct 12, 1932
        New York Times p. 24, Sep 27, 1932
                        IX, p. 1, Oct 2, 1932
                        p. 17, Jan 2, 1934
        Theatre Arts 16:955-6, Dec 1932
        Vogue 80:59+, Nov 15, 1932

LEE, ROBERT E.

  Auntie Mame (See entry under Lawrence, Jerome)

  A Call on Kuprin (See entry under Lawrence, Jerome)

  Diamond Orchid (See entry under Lawrence, Jerome)

  The Gang's All Here (See entry under Lawrence, Jerome)

  Inherit the Wind (See entry under Lawrence, Jerome)

Only in America (See entry under Lawrence, Jerome)

LEVIN, IRA M.

Critic's Choice
    Productions:
        Opened December 14, 1960 for 189 performances.
    Reviews:
        America 104:548, Jan 21, 1961
        Nation 191:531, Dec 31, 1960
        New York Theatre Critics' Reviews 1960:138
        New York Times p. 61, Dec 15, 1960
                        p. 53, Dec 7, 1961
        New Yorker 36:38+, Dec 24, 1960
        Newsweek 56:53, Dec 26, 1960
        Saturday Review 43:28, Dec 31, 1960
        Theatre Arts 45:11, Feb 1961

Dr. Cook's Garden
    Productions:
        Opened September 25, 1967 for 8 performances.
    Reviews:
        New York Theatre Critics' Reviews 1967:290
        New York Times p. 52, Sep 26, 1967
        New Yorker 43:131, Oct 7, 1967

General Seeger
    Productions:
        Opened February 28, 1962 for 2 performances.
    Reviews:
        New York Theatre Critics' Reviews 1962:334
        New York Times p. 26, Mar 1, 1962
        New Yorker 38:83, Mar 10, 1962

Interlock
    Productions:
        Opened February 6, 1958 for 4 performances.
    Reviews:
        New Republic 138:22, Mar 3, 1958
        New York Theatre Critics' Reviews 1958:363
        New York Times p. 18, Feb 7, 1958
        New Yorker 33:58+, Feb 15, 1958
        Theatre Arts 42:25, Apr 1958

No Time for Sergeants (Adapted from Mac Hyman's
        novel)

LEVIN, IRA M. (cont.)
  No Time for Sergeants (cont.)
      Productions:
      Opened October 20, 1955 for 796 performances.
      Reviews:
          America 94:167, Nov 5, 1955
          Catholic World 182:226, Dec 1955
          Colliers 137:6, Mar 2, 1956
          Commonweal 63:141-2, Nov 11, 1955
          Life 39:113+, Nov 7, 1955
          Nation 181:406, Nov 5, 1955
          New York Theatre Critics' Reviews 1955:238
          New York Times VI, p. 38, Oct 9, 1955
                          p. 32, Oct 21, 1955
                          II, p. 1, Nov 6, 1955
                          p. 15, Aug 24, 1956
          New Yorker 31:88+, Oct 29, 1955
          Newsweek 46:55, Oct 31, 1955
          Saturday Review 38:26, Nov 5, 1955
          Theatre Arts 39:28-9, Dec 1955
          Time 66:73+, Oct 31, 1955

LEVITT, SAUL

  The Andersonville Trial
      Productions:
      Opened December 29, 1959 for 179 performances.
      Reviews:
          America 102:482-3, Jan 16, 1960
          Christian Century 77:136-7, Feb 3, 1960
          Commonweal 71:469, Jan 22, 1960
          Life 48:125-6, Feb 8, 1960
          Nation 190:87-8, Jan 23, 1960
          New Republic 142:21-2, Jan 18, 1960
          New York Theatre Critics' Review 1959:181
          New York Times p. 15, Oct 31, 1959
                          p. 15, Dec 30, 1959
                          II, p. 1, Jan 10, 1960
                          p. 33, Nov 25, 1960
          New Yorker 35:69-70+, Jan 9, 1960
          Newsweek 55:60, Jan 11, 1960
          Saturday Review 43:54, Jan 16, 1960
          Theatre Arts 44:12, Mar 1960
          Time 75:46, Jan 11, 1960

LEWIS, SINCLAIR

*Angela Is Twenty-Two
  Reviews:
    New York Times p. 6, Dec 31, 1938

Dodsworth (See entry under Howard, Sidney)

Hobohemia
  Productions:
    Opened February 8, 1919 for 89 performances.
  Reviews:
    Dramatic Mirror 80:267, Feb 22, 1919
    Life (NY) 73:293, Feb 20, 1919
    New York Times p. 20, Feb 9, 1919
    Theatre Magazine 29:205-6+, Apr 1919

It Can't Happen Here (with John C. Moffitt) (Based on
    the novel by Sinclair Lewis)
  Productions:
    Opened October 26, 1936 for 95 performances.
  Reviews:
    Catholic World 144:338, Dec 1936
    Commonweal 25:76, Nov 13, 1936
    Nation 143:558, Nov 7, 1936
    New Republic 89:50, Nov 11, 1936
    New York Times p. 30, Oct 28, 1936
                   X, p. 1, Nov 8, 1936
                   p. 22, Jul 26, 1938
    Newsweek 8:40, Nov 7, 1936
    Stage 14:78, Dec 1936
    Theatre Arts 20:930-1, Dec 1936
    Time 28:21, Nov 9, 1936

Jayhawker (with Lloyd Lewis)
  Productions:
    Opened November 5, 1934 for 24 performances.
  Reviews:
    Catholic World 140:342, Dec 1934
    Nation 139:600-1, Nov 21, 1934
    New York Times IX, p. 3, Nov 4, 1934
                   p. 34, Nov 6, 1934
                   VIII, p. 3, Feb 17, 1935
    Stage 12:26-7, Dec 1934
    Theatre Arts 19:9-10, Jan 1935
    Time 24:36, Nov 12, 1934

The Great Sebastians (with Russel Crouse)
    Productions:
        Opened January 4, 1956 for 174 performances.
    Reviews:
        America 94:515, Feb 4, 1956
        Commonweal 63:428, Jan 27, 1956
        Life 40:107-8+, Jan 30, 1956
        Nation 182:58, Jan 21, 1956
        New York Theatre Critics' Reviews 1956:397
        New York Times p. 27, Jan 5, 1956
                        II, p. 1, Jan 11, 1956
                        II, p. 1, Jan 15, 1956
        New Yorker 31:60+, Jan 14, 1956
        Newsweek 47:50, Jan 16, 1956
        Saturday Review 39:40, Jan 21, 1956
        Theatre Arts 40:18, Feb 1956
                  40:16, Mar 1956
        Time 67:79, Jan 16, 1956

I'd Rather Be Left (See State of the Union)

Life With Father (with Russel Crouse) (Based on the
    book by Clarence Day).
    Productions:
        Opened November 8, 1939 for 3,224 performances.
        Opened October 19, 1967 for 22 performances (City
           Center Drama Co.).
    Reviews:
        Catholic World 150:336, Dec 1939
                    156:90, Oct 1942
                    161:508-9, Sep 1945
                    163:554, Sep 1946
        Collier's 115:18+, Apr 21, 1945
        Commonweal 31:118, Nov 24, 1939
                  40:399-400, Aug 11, 1944
        Cosmopolitan 123:8, Sep 1947
        Forum 103:33, Jan 1940
        Ladies Home Journal 58:20-21+, May 1941
        Life 7:39-40+, Nov 27, 1939
           9:110+, Dec 2, 1940
        Nation 149:560, Nov 18, 1939
        New Republic 101:169, Nov 29, 1939
        New York Theatre Critics' Reviews 1940:457
                                1941:489
        New York Times p. 14, Aug 15, 1939

                    IX, p. 1, Nov 5, 1939
                    p. 26, Nov 9, 1939
                    X, p. 1, Nov 19, 1939
                    X, p. 5, Dec 10, 1939
                    X, p. 2, Mar 3, 1940
                    p. 29, Jul 28, 1940
                    IX, p. 1, Aug 18, 1940
                    IX, p. 2, Jun 1, 1941
                    p. 20, Sep 30, 1941
                    IX, p. 3, Nov 16, 1941
                    p. 26, Mar 25, 1942
                    VIII, p. 1, Nov 1, 1942
                    p. 8, Jun 19, 1943
                    p. 34, Dec 16, 1943
                    II, p. 1, Nov 5, 1944
                    p. 15, Aug 1, 1945
                    VI, p. 34, Nov 3, 1946
                    II, p. 3, Nov 24, 1946
                    II, p. 3, Apr 20, 1947
                    p. 34, Apr 30, 1947
                    p. 27, Jun 6, 1947
                    II, p. 1, Jun 8, 1947
                    p. 26, Jun 10, 1947
                    p. 52, Jun 14, 1947
                    p. 58, Oct 16, 1967
                    p. 53, Oct 20, 1967
                    p. 32, Jan 19, 1968
New York Times Magazine pp. 34-5, Nov 3, 1946
New Yorker 21:16-17, Jun 16, 1945
Newsweek 14:36, Nov 20, 1939
          29:86, Jun 16, 1947
          30:77, Aug 18, 1947
North American Review 248:no. 2:401, Dec 1939
Saturday Review 21:8-9, Nov 18, 1939
Stage 1:14, Nov 1940
      1:14, Dec 1940
Theatre Arts 24:13-15, Jan 1940
             24:397+, Jun 1940
             26:26-30, Jan 1942
             30:672, Nov 1946
             31:69, Apr 1947
             31:58+, Jul 1947
Time 34:69, Nov 20, 1939
     40:40, Sep 14, 1942
     49:27+, Mar 24, 1947
     49:74, Jun 16, 1947
     50:43, Jul 21, 1947

LINDSAY, HOWARD (cont.)
  Life with Father (cont.)
        Vogue 95:38-9, Jan 1, 1940
        Yale Review 30:421, Winter 1941

  Life With Mother (with Russel Crouse) (Based on the
      book by Clarence Day).
  Productions:
  Opened October 20, 1948 for 265 performances.
  Reviews:
     Catholic World 168:241, Dec 1948
     Commonweal 49:118, Nov 12, 1948
     Life 25:53-4, Jul 5, 1948
          25:149-50, Nov 15, 1948
          26:41, Feb 7, 1949
     Nation 167:528, Nov 6, 1948
     New Republic 119:26, Nov 8, 1948
     New York Theatre Critics' Reviews 1948:182
     New York Times p. 36, Jun 9, 1948
                      VI, p. 16, Jun 27, 1948
                      II, p. 3, Oct 17, 1948
                      p. 32, Oct 21, 1948
                      II, p. 1, Oct 31, 1948
                      II, p. 1, Mar 27, 1949
     New York Times Magazine p. 16-17, Jun 27, 1948
     New Yorker 24:40+, Oct 30, 1948
     Newsweek 32:74, Nov 1, 1948
     Saturday Review 31:25-8, Nov 20, 1948
                     32:30, Dec 31, 1949
     School and Society 68:455-6, Dec 25, 1948
     Theatre Arts 32:10-14, Aug 1948
                  32:28-9, Oct 1948
     Time 52:51, Nov 1, 1948
     Vogue 112:183, Dec 1948

  Oh, Promise Me (with Bertrand Robinson)
  Productions:
  Opened November 24, 1930 for 145 performances.
  Reviews:
     Commonweal 13:218, Dec 24, 1930
     Drama 21:12-13, Jan 1931
     Life (NY) 96:18, Dec 26, 1930
     New York Times p. 31, Nov 25, 1930
     Vogue 77:98, Jan 15, 1931

  The Prescott Proposals (with Russel Crouse)
  Productions:

Opened December 16, 1953 for 125 performances.
Reviews:
America 90:385, Jan 9, 1954
Catholic World 178:386-7, Feb 1954
Commonweal 59:404, Jan 22, 1954
Life 36:75-7, Jan 18, 1954
Nation 178:57, Jan 16, 1954
New Republic 130:21, Jan 4, 1954
New York Theatre Critics' Reviews 1953:187
New York Times II, p. 7, Dec 13, 1953
                p. 53, Dec 17, 1953
              II, p. 3, Dec 27, 1953
New Yorker 42:47, Dec 28, 1953
Saturday Review 37:55-6, Jan 2, 1954
Theatre Arts 38:21, Mar 1954
Time 62:34, Dec 28, 1953

Remains to Be Seen (with Russel Crouse)
Productions:
Opened October 3, 1951 for 199 performances.
Reviews:
Catholic World 174:148, Nov 1951
Commonweal 55:37-8, Oct 19, 1951
Life 31:169-70+, Oct 15, 1951
Nation 173:334, Oct 20, 1951
New York Theatre Critics' Reviews 1951:223
New York Times II, p. 3, Sep 30, 1951
                p. 37, Oct 4, 1951
              II, p. 3, Jan 25, 1953
New Yorker 27:84, Oct 13, 1951
Newsweek 38:85, Oct 15, 1951
Saturday Review 34:25-6, Oct 20, 1951
School and Society 75:185, Mar 22, 1952
Theatre Arts 35:3, 78, Dec 1951
Time 58:74, Oct 15, 1951

She Loves Me Not (Adapted from Edward Hope's novel)
Productions:
Opened November 20, 1933 for 360 performances.
Reviews:
Catholic World 138:477, Jan 1934
Literary Digest 118:23, Jul 14, 1934
Nation 137:662, Dec 6, 1933
New Outlook 163:42, Jan 1934
New York Times IX, p. 3, Nov 19, 1933
                p. 22, Nov 21, 1933
              IX, p. 5, Dec 17, 1933

293

LINDSAY, HOWARD (cont.)
  She Loves Me Not (cont.)
                          IX, p. 3, Feb 18, 1934
                              p. 18, Mar 26, 1934
                              p. 25, May 2, 1934
                          X, p. 2, May 27, 1934
      Newsweek 2:32, Nov 25, 1933
      Review of Reviews 81:49, Jun 1934
      Stage 11:20-22, Jan 1934
      Theatre Arts 18:9-11+, Jan 1934
      Time 22:49, Dec 4, 1933

A Slight Case of Murder (with Damon Runyon)
      Productions:
      Opened September 11, 1935 for 69 performances.
      Reviews:
      Commonweal 22:528, Sep 27, 1935
      Literary Digest 120:22, Sep 28, 1935
      Nation 141:364, Sep 25, 1935
               122:24, Sep 5, 1936
      New York Times p. 28, Sep 12, 1935
                     X, p. 1, Sep 22, 1935
      Newsweek 8:27, Sep 5, 1936
      Theatre Arts 19:822, Nov 1935
      Time 26:54-5, Sep 23, 1935
      Vanity Fair 45:41, Nov 1935

State of the Union (with Russel Crouse)
      Productions:
      Opened November 14, 1945 for 765 performances.
      Reviews:
      Catholic World 162:357, Jan 1946
      Commonweal 43:169, Nov 30, 1945
      Forum 105:466-8, Jan 1946
      Harper's Bazaar 79:128, Dec 1945
      Life 19:84-5+, Dec 10, 1945
      Nation 161:604, Dec 1, 1945
      New Republic 113:711, Nov 26, 1945
      New York Theatre Critics' Reviews 1945:102
      New York Times VI, p. 24, Nov 4, 1945
                         p. 21, Nov 7, 1945
                         p. 25, Nov 15, 1945
                         II, p. 1, Nov 25, 1945
                         II, p. 1, Apr 7, 1946
                         II, p. 1, Aug 4, 1946
                         II, p. 1, Sep 8, 1946
                         II, p. 1, Nov 10, 1946

II, p. 1, Jan 26, 1947
II, p. 3, May 18, 1947
p. 26, Jul 15, 1947
II, p. 1, Jul 20, 1947
New York Times Magazine p. 24-5, Nov 4, 1945
New Yorker 21:48+, Nov 24, 1945
Newsweek 26:96, Nov 26, 1945
Player's Magazine 25:21, Oct 1948
Saturday Review 28:18-20, Nov 24, 1945
Theatre Arts 29:677, Dec 1945
            30:5-6, Jan 1946
Time 46:48, Nov 26, 1945
Vogue 106:61, Dec 15, 1945

Strip for Action (with Russel Crouse)
    Productions:
    Opened September 30, 1942 for 110 performances.
    Reviews:
    New Republic 107:545, Oct 26, 1942
    New York Theatre Critics' Reviews 1942:220
    New York Times p. 26, Oct 1, 1942
                    VIII, p. 1, Oct 11, 1942
                    p. 18, Dec 14, 1942
    Newsweek 20:82+, Oct 12, 1942
    Theatre Arts 26:741, Dec 1942

Tall Story (with Russel Crouse) (Suggested by Howard
    Nemerov's The Homecoming Game)
    Productions:
    Opened January 29, 1959 for 108 performances.
    Reviews:
    America 100:614, Feb 21, 1959
    Catholic World 189:60-1, Apr 1959
    Commonweal 69:600, Mar 6, 1959
    New York Theatre Critics' Reviews 1959:393
    New York Times p. 33, Jan 30, 1959
    New Yorker 34:87-8, Feb 7, 1959
    Newsweek 53:56, Feb 9, 1959
    Saturday Review 42:34, Feb 21, 1959
    Theatre Arts 43:21-2, Apr 1959
    Time 73:73, Feb 9, 1959

Tommy (with Bertrand Robinson)
    Productions:
    Opened January 10, 1927 for 232 performances.
    Opened August 7, 1933 for 24 performances.
    Reviews:

295

LINDSAY, HOWARD (cont.)
  Tommy (cont.)
            Life (NY) 89:19, Feb 17, 1927
            New York Times p. 36, Jan 11, 1927
                        VII, p. 1,' Mar 27, 1927
                        p. 22, Aug 8, 1933
            Theatre Magazine 45:24+, May 1927
            Vogue 69:110+, Mar 1, 1927

  Your Uncle Dudley (with Bertrand Robinson)
     Productions:
        Opened November 18, 1929 for 96 performances.
     Reviews:
        Commonweal 11:145, Dec 4, 1929
        New York Times p. 26, Nov 19, 1929
        Theatre Magazine 51:46-7, Jan 1930
        Vogue 75:106, Jan 18, 1930

LOGAN, JOSHUA

  Mister Roberts (with Thomas Heggen) (Based on
        Thomas Heggen's novel)
     Productions:
        Opened February 18, 1948 for 1,157 performances
        Opened December 5, 1956 for 15 performances.
        (Off Broadway) Opened September 28, 1962 for 9
            performances (Equity Library Theatre).
     Reviews:
        Catholic World 167:70, Apr 1948
        Christian Science Monitor Magazine p. 7, Aug 5,
            1950
        Commonweal 47:521, Mar 5, 1948
        Life 24:93-6+, Mar 1, 1948
        Nation 166:402-3, Apr 10, 1948
        New Republic 118:29, Mar 8, 1948
        New York Theatre Critics' Reviews 1948:388
                                          1956:169
        New York Times p. 27, Feb 19, 1948
                    II, p. 1, Feb 29, 1948
                    p. 8, Feb 18, 1950
                    II, p. 1, May 21, 1950
                    p. 22, Jul 20, 1950
                    II, p. 1, Jul 23, 1950
                    p. 20, Feb 9, 1951
                    p. 29, Apr 2, 1951
                    II, p. 3, Feb 10, 1952

                    p. 46, Dec 6, 1956
New York Times Magazine p. 12-13, Feb 8, 1948
New Yorker 24:46+, Feb 28, 1948
Newsweek 31:65-6, Mar 1, 1948
            31:56, Apr 19, 1948
Saturday Review 31:24-6, Mar 6, 1948
Theatre Arts 32:28-9, Apr 1948
Theatre Guild Magazine 32:32, Summer 1948
                        32:23, Fall 1948
                        33:12+, Nov 1949
Time 51:63, Mar 1, 1948
      51:52, Apr 19, 1948
Vogue 111:150, Apr 1, 1948
       112:144-5+, Aug 15, 1948

The Wisteria Trees (Based on Anton Chekhov's The
      Cherry Orchard)
   Productions:
      Opened March 29, 1950 for 165 performances.
      Opened February 2, 1955 for 15 performances.
   Reviews:
      Catholic World 171:147, May 1950
                     180:468, Mar 1955
      Christian Science Monitor Magazine p. 4, Apr 1,
      1950
      Commonweal 52:69-70, Apr 28, 1950
      Life 28:68-70, Apr 24, 1950
      Nation 170:354-5, Apr 15, 1950
      New Republic 122:22, Apr 10, 1958
      New York Theatre Critics' Reviews 1950:320
                                        1955:377
      New York Times p. 22, Feb 7, 1950
                     II, p. 1, Mar 26, 1950
                     p. 39, Mar 30, 1950
                     II, p. 1, Apr 9, 1950
                     p. 20, Feb 3, 1955
      New York Times Magazine pp. 32-3, Mar 5, 1950
      New Yorker 26:63+, Apr 8, 1950
                 30:60, Feb 12, 1955
      Newsweek 35:77, Apr 10, 1950
      Saturday Review 38:24, Feb 19, 1955
      Theatre Arts 34:15, Jun 1950
                   39:22+, Apr 1955
      Time 55:68, Apr 10, 1950

                        297

LONG, JOHN LUTHER

Kassa
Productions:
Opened January 23, 1909 for 65 performances.
Reviews:
Hampton 22:543+, Apr 1909
Theatre Magazine 9:72-3+, Mar 1909

LONG, SUMNER ARTHUR

Cradle and All (See Never Too Late)

Never Too Late
Productions:
Opened November 27, 1962 for 1,007 performances.
Reviews:
America 108:53, Jan 12, 1962
Nation 195:430, Dec 15, 1962
New York Theatre Critics' Reviews 1962:187
New York Times p. 42, Nov 28, 1962
              p. 5, Dec 19, 1962
              p. 48, Sep 25, 1963
New Yorker 38:148, Dec 8, 1962
Newsweek 60:58, Dec 10, 1962
Theatre Arts 47:12-13, Jan 1963
Time 80:72, Dec 7, 1962

LOOS, ANITA

Cheri (Based on Colette's Cheri and The Last of Cheri)
Productions:
Opened October 12, 1959 for 56 performances.
Reviews:
America 102:214+, Nov 14, 1959
Nation 189:339, Nov 7, 1959
New Republic 141:19-20, Oct 26, 1959
New York Theatre Critics' Reviews 1959:267
New York Times II, p. 1, Oct 11, 1959
                  p. 44, Oct 13, 1959
New Yorker 35:91-2+, Oct 24, 1959
Newsweek 54:116, Oct 26, 1959
Saturday Review 42:26, Oct 31, 1959
Theatre Arts 43:14-16, Nov 1959
              (p. 86), 43:84, Dec 1959
Time 74:102+, Oct 26, 1959

The Fall of Eve (with John Emerson)
    Productions:
        Opened August 31, 1925 for 48 performances.
    Reviews:
        Life (NY) 86:18, Sep 17, 1925
        New Republic 44:95-6, Sep 16, 1925
        New York Times p. 18, Sep 1, 1925
                        VIII, p. 1. Sep 6, 1925
                        p. 13, Oct 17, 1926

Gentlemen Prefer Blondes (with John Emerson)
    Productions:
        Opened September 28, 1926 for 199 performances.
    Reviews:
        Bookman 64:479-80, Dec 1926
        Harper's Bazaar 60:117+, Oct 1926
        Life (NY) 88:23, Oct 21, 1926
        New Republic 48:245-6, Oct 20, 1926
        New York Times VIII, p. 1, Sep 3, 1926
                        p. 23, Sep 29, 1926
                        VIII, p. 2, Oct 10, 1926
                        p. 32, Apr 3, 1928
        Theatre Magazine 44:13+, Dec 1926
        Vanity Fair 27:54+, Oct 1926

Gigi (Based on the novel by Colette)
    Productions:
        Opened November 24, 1951 for 219 performances.
    Reviews:
        Catholic World 174:309-10, Jan 1952
        Commonweal 55:254, Dec 14, 1951
        Nation 173:530, Dec 15, 1951
        New York Theatre Critics' Reviews 1951:159
        New York Times p. 20, Nov 26, 1951
                        p. 27, May 24, 1956
        New Yorker 27:87, Dec 1, 1951
        Newsweek 38:60, Dec 3, 1951
        Saturday Review 34:32-3, Dec 15, 1951
        School and Society 75:107-8, Feb 16, 1952
        Theatre Arts 36:31, Feb 1952
                        36:41-7+, Jul 1952
        Time 58:49, Dec 3, 1951

Happy Birthday
    Productions:
        Opened October 31, 1946 for 564 performances.
    Reviews:

LOOS, ANITA (cont.)
  Happy Birthday (cont.)
            Catholic World 164:261, Dec 1946
            Commonweal 45:116, Nov 15, 1946
            Life 21:79-82, Nov 18, 1946
            Nation 163:565, Nov 16, 1946
            New Republic 115:662, Nov 18, 1946
            New York Theatre Critics' Reviews 1946:280
            New York Times VI, p. 27, Sep 22, 1946
                         VI, p. 30, Oct 27, 1946
                         p. 31, Nov 1, 1946
                         II, p. 1, Nov 10, 1946
                         II, p. 1, Jan 26, 1947
                         II, p. 1, Apr 20, 1947
                         II, p. 1, Oct 26, 1947
            New Yorker 22:55, Nov 9, 1946
            Newsweek 28:92, Nov 11, 1946
            Saturday Review 29:23, Dec 21, 1946
            School and Society 66:327-8, Oct 25, 1947
            Theatre Arts 31:18-19+, Jan 1947
            Time 48:56, Nov 11, 1946

  *The King's Mare
      Reviews:
            New York Times p. 23, Jul 21, 1966

  The Social Register (with John Emerson)
      Productions:
            Opened November 9, 1931 for 97 performances.
      Reviews:
            New York Times VIII, p. 2, Oct 4, 1931
                           p. 28, Nov 10, 1931

  The Whole Town's Talking (with John Emerson)
      Productions:
            Opened August 29, 1923 for 173 performances.
      Reviews:
            Dramatist 14:1168-9, Jul 1923
            Metropolitan Magazine 58:38-9+, Dec 1923
            Nation 117:304, Sep 19, 1923
            New York Times p. 8, Aug 30, 1923
                           VII, p. 1, Sep 9, 1923
            Theatre Magazine 38:66, Oct 1923

LOWELL, ROBERT

Benito Cereno (See The Old Glory)

Endecott and the Red Cross
    Productions:
        (Off Broadway) Opened May 7, 1968 for 15 perform-
        ances (American Place Theater).
    Reviews:
        America 119:149, Aug 31, 1968
        Nation 206:710, May 27, 1968
        New York Times p. 50, May 7, 1968
        New Yorker 44:84-6+, May 11, 1968
        Newsweek 71:109-10, May 13, 1968
        Saturday Review 51:40, May 25, 1968
        Time 91:74, May 10, 1968

My Kinsman, Major Molineux (See The Old Glory)

The Old Glory (Adapted from Nathaniel Hawthorne's My
        Kinsman, Major Molineux and Herman Melville's
        Benito Cereno.)
    Productions:
        (Off Broadway) Opened March 1, 1964 for 1 perform-
        ance (American Place Theater).
        (Off Broadway) Opened November 1, 1964 for 36
        performances (American Place Theater).
    Reviews:
        Catholic World 200:323-4, Feb 1965
        Nation 199:390-1, November 23, 1964
        New Republic 151:28+, November 21, 1964
        New York Times p. 62, Nov 2, 1964
                        II, p. 1, Nov 15, 1964
                        II, p. 7, Dec 6, 1964
        New Yorker 40:143-4, Nov 14, 1964
        Newsweek 64:92, Nov 16, 1964
        Reporter 36:44-5, Jun 15, 1967
        Vogue 145:68, Jan 1, 1965

*Prometheus Bound
    Reviews:
        Nation 204:829-30, Jun 26, 1967
        New York Times p. 52, May 11, 1967
                        II, p. 1, May 21, 1967
                        II, p. 1, Jun 11, 1967
        Newsweek 69:109, May 22, 1967
        Reporter 36:44-6, Jun 15, 1967

LOWELL, ROBERT (cont.)
 *Prometheus Bound (cont.)
    Saturday Review 50:49, May 27, 1967

LUCE, CLARE BOOTHE

    (See Boothe, Clare)

MACARTHUR, CHARLES

   The Front Page (See entry under Hecht, Ben)

   Johnny On A Spot (Based on a story by Parke Levy and
        Alan Lipscott)
      Productions:
      Opened January 8, 1942 for 4 performances.
      Reviews:
        New York Theatre Critics' Reviews 1942:391
        New York Times p. 24, Jan 9, 1942

   Ladies and Gentlemen (with Ben Hecht) (Adapted from
        Twelve in a Box by L. Bush-Fekete)
      Productions:
      Opened October 17, 1939 for 105 performances.
      Reviews:
        Catholic World 150:337-8, Dec 1939
        Independent Woman 19:50, Feb 1940
        Life 7:30-32, Aug 21, 1939
        New York Theatre Critics' Reviews 1940:469
        New York Times IX, p. 2, Sep 24, 1939
                       p. 30, Oct 18, 1939
                    IX, p. 1, Oct 22, 1939
                    IX, p. 1, Oct 29, 1939
        Newsweek 14:31-2, Jul 17, 1939
                 14:38, Oct 30, 1939
        Theatre Arts 23:856, Dec 1939
        Time 34:50, Jul 24, 1939
             34:43, Oct 30, 1939

   Lulu Belle (See entry under Sheldon, Edward)

   Salvation (See entry under Howard, Sidney)

   Swan Song (See entry under Hecht, Ben)

   Twentieth Century (See entry under Hecht, Ben)

MC CULLERS, CARSON

Ballad of the Sad Cafe (See entry under Albee, Edward)

The Member of the Wedding (Adapted from her novel)
Productions:
Opened January 5, 1950 for 501 performances.
Reviews:
Catholic World 170:467, Mar 1950
Commonweal 51:437-8, Jan 27, 1950
Life 28:63-6, Jan 23, 1950
Nation 170:44, Jan 14, 1950
New Republic 122:28, Jan 30, 1950
New York Theatre Critics' Reviews 1950:397
New York Times II, p. 3, Jan 1, 1950
p. 26, Jan 6, 1950
II, p. 1, Jan 15, 1950
II, p. 1, Sep 17, 1950
p. 20, Feb 6, 1957
New Yorker 25:46+, Jan 14, 1950
Newsweek 35:74, Jan 16, 1950
Saturday Review 33:27-9, Jan 28, 1950
School and Society 71:213-14, Apr 8, 1950
Theatre Arts 34:13, Mar 1950
Time 55:45, Jan 16, 1950

The Square Root of Wonderful
Productions:
Opened October 30, 1957 for 45 performances.
(Off Broadway) Opened April 19, 1963 for 9 per-
formances (Equity Library Theatre).
Reviews:
America 98:299, Nov 30, 1957
Catholic World 186:306, Jan 1958
Christian Century 74:1425, Nov 27, 1957
Commonweal 67:288-9, Dec 13, 1957
New York Theatre Critics' Reviews 1957:199
New York Times p. 40, Oct 31, 1957
Nation 185:394, Nov 23, 1957
New Yorker 33:103-5, Nov 9, 1957
Theatre Arts 42:24, Jan 1958
Time 70:93-4, Nov 11, 1957

MCENROE, ROBERT E.

Oliver Erwenter (See The Silver Whistle)

MCENROE, ROBERT E. (cont.)
The Silver Whistle
    Productions:
        Opened November 24, 1948 for 219 performances.
    Reviews:
        Catholic World 168:324, Jan 1949
        Commonweal 49:258, Dec 17, 1948
        Life 25:51-2, Dec 20, 1948
        Nation 167:704, Dec 18, 1948
        New Republic 119:31, Dec 13, 1948
        New York Theatre Critics' Reviews 1948:139
        New York Times p. 49, Nov 25, 1948
                      II, p. 7, Dec 5, 1948
        New Yorker 24:55, Dec 4, 1948
        Newsweek 32:86-7, Dec 6, 1948
        School and Society 69:232, Mar 26, 1949
        Theatre Arts 33:16, Jan 1949
        Time 52:90, Dec 6, 1948

MCGUIRE, WILLIAM ANTHONY

*The Bad Penny
    Reviews:
        New York Times VIII, p. 2, Aug 23, 1931

A Good Bad Woman
    Productions:
        Opened April 8, 1919 for 31 performances.
    Reviews:
        Dramatist 16:1276, Jul 1925
        Forum 61:628-9, May 1919
        New York Times p. 9, Apr 9, 1919
        Theatre Magazine 29:344-50, Jun 1919

The Heights
    Productions:
        Opened January 31, 1910 for 16 performances.
    Reviews:
        Dramatic Mirror 63:8, Feb 12, 1910
        Green Book 3:770, Apr 1910
        Life (NY) 55:284, Feb 17, 1910
        Theatre Magazine 11:vii, Mar 1910

If I Was Rich
    Productions:
        Opened September 2, 1926 for 92 performances.

Reviews:
Life (NY) 88:19, Sep 30, 1926
New York Times p. 15, Sep 3, 1926
VIII, p. 1, Sep 12, 1926
Overland 85:118, Apr 1927
Theatre Magazine 44:18, Nov 1926

It's A Boy
Productions:
Opened September 19, 1922 for 63 performances.
Reviews:
Life (NY) 80:18, Oct 5, 1922
New York Clipper 70:39, Oct 4, 1922
New York Times p. 18, Sep 20, 1922

Six-Cylinder Love
Productions:
Opened August 25, 1921 for 344+ performances.
Reviews:
Dramatic Mirror 84:229, Aug 13, 1921
84:341, Sep 3, 1921
Hearst 40:17-19+, Nov 1921
Independent 106:113, Sep 1921
Life (NY) 78:18, Sep 15, 1921
Nation 113:299, Sep 14, 1921
New York Clipper 69:17, Aug 31, 1921
New York Times p. 8, Aug 26, 1921
Theatre Magazine 34:291+, Nov 1921
Weekly Review 5:234-5, Sep 10, 1921

Twelve Miles Out
Productions:
Opened November 16, 1925 for 188 performances.
Reviews:
New York Times p. 29, Nov 17, 1925
VII, p. 6, Feb 21, 1926
VII, p. 1, Feb 20, 1927
Theatre Magazine 43:72, Apr 1926

MACKAYE, PERCY

Anti-Matrimony
Productions:
Opened September 22, 1910 for 20 performances.
Reviews:
Dramatic Mirror 64:6, Sep 28, 1910

MACKAYE, PERCY (cont.)
   Anti-Matrimony (cont.)
         Dramatist 4:374-5, Jul 1913
         Everybody's 23:844+, Dec 1910
         Hampton 25:680, Nov 1910
         Leslies' Weekly 111:385, Oct 13, 1910
         Life (NY) 56:364, Oct 6, 1910
         Living Age 268:318, Feb 4, 1911
         Nation 91:298, Sep 29, 1910

   The Antick
      Productions:
         Opened October 4, 1915 in repertory (Washington
            Square Players).
      Reviews:
         Dramatic Mirror 74:9, Oct 16, 1915
                        74:2, Nov 6, 1915
         New York Times p. 11, Oct 5, 1915

   Caliban of the Yellow Sands
      Productions:
         Opened May 24, 1916 for 10 performances.
      Reviews:
         Book News 34:445-6, Jun 1916
         Collier's 36:343-50, Jul 1, 1916
         Current Opinion 60:408-10, Jun 1916
         Dial 61:22, Jun 22, 1916
         Dramatic Mirror 75:8, Jun 3, 1916
         Independent 86:59-60, Apr 10, 1916
                     86:333, May 29, 1916
         Literary Digest 52:1760-1, Jun 10, 1916
         Nation 102:586, Jun 1, 1916
         National Magazine 46:697-8, Aug 1917
         Outlook 113:308+, Jun 7, 1916
         Survey 36:343-50, Jul 1, 1916
         Theatre Magazine 24:8-9, Jul 1916

   George Washington
      Productions:
         Opened March 1, 1920 for 16 performances.
      Reviews:
         Dramatic Mirror 82:414, Mar 6, 1920
         New York Clipper 68:14, Mar 10, 1920
         New York Times p. 13, Feb 24, 1920
                        p. 9, Mar 2, 1920
         Review 2:288-9, Mar 20, 1920
         Theatre Magazine 31:247+, Apr 1920

*The Ghost of Elsinore
    Reviews:
        New York Times p. 10, Apr 16, 1949
                       II, p. 1, Apr 23, 1949

*Jeanne d'Arc
    Reviews:
        New York Times III, p. 13, Jun 7, 1914

*Sanctuary
    Reviews:
        New York Times p. 9, Feb 25, 1914

The Scarecrow
    Productions:
        Opened January 17, 1911 for 23 performances.
        (Off Broadway) Season of 1953-54.
    Reviews:
        Blue Book 12:1118-20, Apr 1911
        Book News 27:358, Jan 1909
        Bookman 23:28-9, Mar 1911
        Collier's 46:33, Feb 25, 1911
        Drama 4:216-22, Nov 1911
        Dramatic Mirror 65:7-8, Jan 25, 1911
        Everybody's 24:556-8, Jan 25, 1911
        Hampton 26:360+, Mar 1911
                26:640-3+, May 1911
        Independent 70:406-7, Feb 23, 1911
        Life (NY) 57:260-1, Feb 2, 1911
        Munsey 44:871, Mar 1911
        New Republic 128:23, Jun 29, 1953
        New York Times p. 31, Jun 17, 1953
        Pearson 25:387, Mar 1911
        Red Book 16:1142-3+, Apr 1911
        Theatre Magazine 9:xi-xii, Feb 1909
                         11:56, Feb 1910
                         13:71-2+, Mar 1911
        World Today 20:281, Mar 1911

This Fine-Pretty World
    Productions:
        Opened December 26, 1923 for 33 performances.
    Reviews:
        Dial 76:288, Mar 1924
        Literary Digest 80:29-30, Jan 26, 1924
        Nation 118:68-9, Jan 16, 1924

MACKAYE, PERCY (cont.)
This Fine-Pretty World (cont.)
New York Times VII, pp. 2-3, Dec 23, 1923
p. 11, Dec 27, 1923

A Thousand Years Ago
Productions:
Opened January 6, 1914 for 87 performances.
Reviews:
American Magazine 77:43-4, Jun 1914
Bookman 38:613-14, Feb 1914
Colonnade 7:175-9, Feb 1914
Current Opinion 56:188-92, Mar 1914
Dramatic Mirror 71:22, Jan 14, 1914
Dramatist 5:4845, Jul 1914
Green Book 11:411, Mar 1914
11:526-7, Mar 1914
Munsey 51:343-4, Mar 1914
Nation 98:67, Jan 15, 1914
New York Drama News 58:32, Jan 17, 1914
New York Times p. 11, Jan 7, 1914
Theatre Magazine 19:61+, Feb 1914

*Washington
Reviews:
New York Times p. 9, Feb 18, 1919

MAC KAYE, STEELE
No Productions.

MACLEISH, ARCHIBALD

*Herakles
Reviews:
Life 59:10, Dec 3, 1965
New Republic 157:25-6+, Jul 22, 1967

J.B.
Productions:
Opened December 11, 1958 for 364 performances.
(Off Broadway) Opened March 17, 1962 for 9 per-
formances (Equity Library Theatre).
Reviews:
America 100:33, Oct 4, 1958
100:502, Jan 24, 1959

Catholic World 188:505, Mar 1959
               190:81-5, Nov 1959
Christian Century 75:692-3, Jun 11, 1958
               75:926, Aug 13, 1958
               76:9-11, Jan 7, 1959
               76:21-2, Jan 7, 1959
               76:106-7, Jan 28, 1959
Commentary 26:183-4, Aug 1958
           27:153-8, Feb 1959
Commonweal 70:153-4+, May 8, 1959
Harper's Bazaar 218:77-8+, Apr 1959
Library Journal 83:821, Mar 15, 1958
              84:36-7, Jan 1, 1959
Life 45:171+, Dec 22, 1958
    46:124-5, May 18, 1959
Nation 186:425-6, May 10, 1958
       188:19, Jan 3, 1959
New York Theatre Critics' Reviews 1958:168
New York Times p. 27, Jan 6, 1958
              p. 37, Apr 24, 1958
              II, p. 1, May 4, 1958
              p. 41, Nov 15, 1958
              II, p. 5, Dec 7, 1958
              p. 2, Dec 12, 1958
              II, p. 1, May 10, 1959
              p. 38, Nov 11, 1964
New Yorker 34:70-2, Dec 20, 1958
Newsweek 52:45, Dec 22, 1958
Reporter 20:37, Jan 8, 1959
Saturday Review 41:11-12+, Mar 8, 1958
              41:22, May 10, 1958
              42:22-3, Jan 3, 1959
              43:39+, Jan 30, 1960
Theatre Arts 42:9-11, Aug 1958
           43:9, Feb 1959
           43:60-63, Apr 1959
           44:29-32, Feb 1960
Time 71:87-8, May 24, 1958
      72:53-4, Dec 22, 1958
      73:95, Apr 13, 1959

Panic
    Productions:
        Opened March 14, 1935 for 2 performances.
    Reviews:
        Nation 140:369-70, Mar 27, 1935
        New Republic 82:190-191, Mar 27, 1935

MACLEISH, ARCHIBALD (cont.)
Panic (cont.)
82:217, Apr 3, 1935
New York Times p. 18, Mar 16, 1935
IX, p. 1, May 25, 1935
p. 38, Nov 26, 1936
Newsweek 5:29, Mar 23, 1935
Saturday Review 11:545+, Mar 16, 1935
Theatre Arts 19:325-7, May 1935
21:103-5, Feb 1937
Time 25:77, Mar 18, 1935
Yale Review 24:839-41, Summer 1935

This Music Crept By Me on the Waters
Productions:
(Off Broadway) Season of 1959-60 (ANTA matinee).
Reviews:
New York Times p. 20, Oct 23, 1953
p. 19, Nov 25, 1959

*The Trojan Horse
Reviews:
New York Times p. 20, Oct 23, 1953

MCLELLAN, C. M. S.

The Fountain
Productions:
Opened September 27, 1913 in repertory (The Prin-
cess Players).
Reviews:
New York Times III, p. 5, Feb 1, 1914

Judith Zaraine
Productions:
Opened January 16, 1911 for 16 performances.
Reviews:
Collier's 46:24, Feb 4, 1911
Dramatic Mirror 65:10, Jan 18, 1911
Green Book 5:481-519, Mar 1911

Leah Kleschna
Productions:
Opened April 21, 1924 for 32 performances.
Reviews:
American Mercury 2:242-3, Jun 1924

Bookman 59:580, Jul 1924
Dramatist 2:134-5, Jan 1911
New York Times p. 19, Apr 22, 1924
                    VIII, p. 1, Apr 27, 1924
Theatre Magazine 39:16, Jul 1924

MC NALLY, TERRENCE

And Things That Go Bump in the Night
    Productions:
        Opened April 26, 1965 for 16 performances.
    Reviews:
        Commonweal 82:290, May 21, 1965
        New York Theatre Critics' Reviews 1965:341
        New York Times p. 27, Apr 27, 1965
                    II, p. 1, May 9, 1965
        Saturday Review 48:24, May 15, 1965
        Time 85:88-9, May 7, 1965

Cuba Sí
    Productions:
        (Off Broadway) Opened December 9, 1968 for 2 per-
        formances (ANTA Matinee).
    Reviews:
        New York Times p. 53, Dec 10, 1968

The Lady of the Camellias (Based on a play by Giles
        Cooper)
    Productions:
        Opened March 20, 1963 for 13 performances.
    Reviews:
        Nation 196:333, Apr 20, 1963
        New York Theatre Critics' Review 1963:305
        New York Times p. 7, Mar 22, 1963
        New Yorker 39:110, Mar 30, 1963
        Newsweek 61:78, Apr 1, 1963
        Theatre Arts (p. 15) 47:70-1, May 1963
        Time 81:46, Mar 29, 1963

Next
    Productions:
        (Off Broadway) Opened February 10, 1969 for 546
        performances. (Still running on June 1, 1970.)
    Reviews:
        Nation 208:282, Mar 3, 1969
        New York Times p. 27, Feb 11, 1969

311

MC NALLY, TERRENCE (cont.)
Next (cont.)
                          II, p. 5, Feb 23, 1969
                              p. 46, Mar 12, 1970
    New Yorker 45:90+, Feb 22, 1969
    Saturday Review 52:45, Mar 1, 1969
    Time 93:42, Feb 21, 1969
    Vogue 153:150, Apr 1, 1969

Noon
    Productions:
    Opened November 28, 1968 for 52 performances.
    Reviews:
    Commonweal 89:471-2, Jan 10, 1969
    Nation 207:665-6, Dec 16, 1968
    New York Theatre Critics' Reviews 1968:168
    New York Times p. 52, Nov 29, 1968
                          II, p. 7, Dec 8, 1968
                              p. 54, Dec 10, 1968
    New Yorker 44:139-40, Dec 7, 1968
    Time 92:71-2, Dec 6, 1968

Sweet Eros
    Productions:
    (Off Broadway) Opened November 21, 1968 for 78
        performances.
    Reviews:
    Nation 207:665, Dec 16, 1968
    New York Times p. 38, Nov 22, 1968
                          II, p. 34, Nov 24, 1968
    New Yorker 44:140+, Dec 7, 1968
    Newsweek 72:106, Dec 2, 1968
    Time 92:71, Nov 29, 1968

Tour
    Productions:
    (Off Broadway) Opened May 8, 1968 for 80 per-
        formances.
    Reviews:
    Harper's Bazaar 237:113-15, Oct 1968
    Nation 206:772+, Jun 10, 1968
    New York Times p. 55, May 9, 1968
                          II, p. 1, May 19, 1968
    New Yorker 44:74, May 18, 1968

Witness
    Productions:

(Off Broadway) Opened November 21, 1968 for 78
 performances.
Reviews:
 Nation 207:665, Dec 16, 1968
 New York Times p. 38, Nov 22, 1968
 New Yorker 44:140+, Dec 7, 1968
 Time 92:71+, Nov 29, 1968

MAILER, NORMAN

The Deer Park
 Productions:
 (Off Broadway) Opened February 1, 1967 for 128
  performances.
 Reviews:
  Commonweal 85:657-8, Mar 10, 1967
  Life 62:8, Feb 24, 1967
  Nation 204:252-3, Feb 20, 1967
  New York Times II, p. 1, Jan 22, 1967
         p. 27, Feb 1, 1967
         II, p. 1, Feb 12, 1967
  New Yorker 42:116, Feb 11, 1967
  Newsweek 69:109+, Feb 13, 1967
  Reporter 36:47-8, Apr 6, 1967
  Saturday Review 50:45, Mar 4, 1967
  Time 89:58, Feb 10, 1967
  Vogue 149:94, Apr 1, 1967

MALTZ, ALBERT

Black Pit
 Productions:
 Opened March 20, 1935 for 85 performances.
 Reviews:
  Catholic World 141:213-4, May 1935
  Commonweal 21:654, Apr 5, 1935
  Nation 140:399-400, Apr 3, 1935
  New Republic 82:289, Apr 17, 1935
  New York Times p. 26, Mar 21, 1935
  Newsweek 5:29, Mar 30, 1935
  Theatre Arts 19:331-2, May 1935

Merry-Go-Round (with George Sklar)
 Productions:
 Opened April 22, 1932 for 48 performances.

MALTZ, ALBERT (cont.)
  Merry-Go-Round (cont.)
    Reviews:
      Catholic World 135:339, Jun 1932
      Nation 134:552, May 11, 1932
      New Republic 71:70-72, Jun 1, 1932
      New York Times p. 11, Apr 23, 1932
                    p. 1, May 1, 1932
      North American Review 234:171-2, Aug 1932
      Stage 9:30-32, Jun 1932

Peace On Earth (See entry under Sklar, George)

Private Hicks
  Productions:
    (Off Broadway) Season of 1935-36.
  Reviews:
    New York Times p. 14, Jan 13, 1936

Rehearsal
  Productions:
    (Off Broadway) Opened January 15, 1939 (New
      School for Social Research).
    (Off Broadway) April and May, 1939 (Flatbush Arts
      League).
    (Off Broadway) Opened April, 1939 (New York
      Players).
    (Off Broadway) Opened Spring, 1939 (International
      Workers Order).
  No Reviews.

MARKS, JOSEPHINE PRESTON PEABODY
  No Productions.

MARQUAND, JOHN P.

  The Late George Apley (with George S. Kaufman) (Based
    on Marquand's novel)
  Productions:
    Opened November 23, 1944 for 385 performances.
  Reviews:
    Catholic World 160:355, Jan 1945
    Commonweal 41:230, Dec 15, 1944
    Life 17:41-4, Dec 4, 1944
    Nation 159:725, Dec 9, 1944

New Republic 111:798, Dec 11, 1944
New York Theatre Critics' Reviews 1944:77
New York Times p. 16, Oct 20, 1944
                    p. 25, Nov 7, 1944
                    VI, p. 28, Nov 19, 1944
                    p. 26, Nov 22, 1944
                    II, p. 1, Nov 26, 1944
                    II, p. 1, Dec 3, 1944
New York Times Magazine p. 28-9, Nov 19, 1944
New Yorker 20:44, Dec 2, 1944
Newsweek 24:110, Dec 4, 1944
Saturday Review 27:24+, Dec 9, 1944
Scholastic 46:18, Mar 5, 1945
Theatre Arts 29:7, 11, Jan 1945
              29:221-5, Apr 1945
Time 44:48, Dec 4, 1944

Point of No Return (See entry under Osborne, Paul)

MARQUIS, DON

The Dark Hours
    Productions:
    Opened November 14, 1932 for 8 performances.
    Reviews:
    Nation 135:542, Nov 30, 1932
    New York Times IX, p. 2, Nov 13, 1932
                    p. 24, Nov 15, 1932
    Vanity Fair 39:60, Feb 1933

Everything's Jake
    Productions:
    Opened January 16, 1930 for 76 performances.
    Reviews:
    Catholic World 130:79-80, Apr 1930
    New York Times p. 20, Jan 17, 1930
    Theatre Magazine 51:13+, Mar 1930
    Vogue 75:108, Mar 15, 1930

*Master of the Revels
    Reviews:
    New York Times p. 16, Aug 14, 1935

The Old Soak
    Productions:
    Opened August 22, 1922 for 423 performances.

315

MARQUIS, DON (cont.)
  The Old Soak (cont.)
    Reviews:
      Bookman 56:322-4, Nov 1922
      Collier's 70:26, Sep 30, 1922
      Dial 73:464, Oct 1922
      Dramatist 15:1199-1200, Jan 1924
      Life (NY) 80:20, Sep 14, 1922
      National Magazine 52:236, Oct 1923
      New York Clipper 70:20, Aug 30, 1922
      New York Times p. 14, Aug 23, 1922
                          VI, p. 1, Sep 3, 1922
      Outlook 132:138-9, Sep 27, 1922
      Theatre Magazine 36:296+, Nov 1922

  Out of the Sea
    Productions:
      Opened December 5, 1927 for 16 performances.
    Reviews:
      New York Times p. 26, Dec 6, 1927
      Saturday Review 4:468-9, Dec 24, 1927
      Vogue 71:100, Feb 1, 1928

MAY, ELAINE

  Adaptation
    Productions:
      (Off Broadway) Opened February 10, 1969 for 546
        performances. (Still running on June 1, 1970.)
    Reviews:
      Nation 208:281-2, Mar 3, 1969
      New York Times p. 27, Feb 11, 1969
                          II, p. 1, Feb 23, 1969
                          p. 46, Mar 12, 1970
      New Yorker 45:90+, Feb 22, 1969
      Saturday Review 52:45, Mar 1, 1969
      Time 93:42, Feb 21, 1969
      Vogue 153:50, Apr 1, 1969

  *A Matter of Position
    Reviews:
      New York Times II, p. 1, Sep 23, 1962
                          p. 59, Oct 10, 1962

  Not Enough Rope
    Productions:

(Off Broadway) Opened March 1, 1962 for 4 per-
formances.
Reviews:
New York Times p. 24, Mar 2, 1962
New Yorker 38:83-4, Mar 10, 1962

MAYER, EDWIN JUSTUS

Children of Darkness
Productions:
Opened January 7, 1930 for 79 performances.
(Off Broadway) Season of 1957-58.
Reviews:
Catholic World 130:722, Mar 1930
                187:145, May 1958
Commonweal 68:105, Apr 25, 1958
Life (NY) 95:20, Jan 31, 1930
Nation 130:134, Jan 29, 1930
New Republic 62:20, Feb 19, 1930
New York Times VIII, p. 1, Jan 19, 1930
                VIII, p. 4, Feb 9, 1930
                p. 11, Mar 1, 1958
Theatre Arts 14:191+, Mar 1930
Theatre Magazine 51:72, Feb 1930
                 51:32-5+, Apr 1930
Vogue 75:106, Mar 1, 1930

The Firebrand
Productions:
Opened October 15, 1924 for 261 performances.
(Off Broadway) Opened December 10, 1965 for 9
performances (Equity Library Theatre).
Reviews:
American Mercury 4:120-21, Jan 1925
Dramatist 16:1245-6, Jan 1925
Life (NY) 84:20, Nov 6, 1924
Nation 119:501-2, Nov 5, 1924
New York Times p. 33, Oct 16, 1924
              p. 16, Feb 10, 1926
Theatre Magazine 39:16, Dec 1924
                 41:26+, May 1925

*Sunrise in My Pocket
Reviews:
New York Times IX, p. 1, Sep 28, 1941

317

MELFI, LEONARD

Birdbath
    Productions:
        (Off Broadway) Opened April 11, 1966 for 16 per-
            formances.
    Reviews:
        Nation 202:404, Apr 4, 1966
        New York Times II, p. 15, Apr 10, 1966
                         p. 43, Apr 12, 1966
        New Yorker 42:126, Apr 23, 1966

Night
    Productions:
        Opened November 28, 1968 for 52 performances.
    Reviews:
        Commonweal 89:471-2, Jan 10, 1969
        Nation 207:665-6, Dec 16, 1968
        New York Theatre Critics' Review 1968:168
        New York Times p. 52, Nov 29, 1968
                         II, p. 7, Dec 8, 1968
                         p. 54, Dec 10, 1968
        New Yorker 44:139-40, Dec 7, 1968
        Time 92:71-2, Dec 6, 1968

Stars and Stripes
    Productions:
        (Off Broadway) Opened May 8, 1968 for 80 per-
            formances.
    Reviews:
        Harpers Bazaar 237:113-15, Oct, 1968
        Nation 206:772+, Jun 10, 1968
        New York Times p. 55, May 9, 1968
                         II, p. 1, May 19, 1968
        New Yorker 44:74, May 18, 1968

*Times Square
    Reviews:
        New York Times p. 16, Jan 27, 1968

MELONEY, ROSE (See Franken, Rose)

MICHAELS, SIDNEY

Dylan
    Productions:

Opened January 18, 1964 for 273 performances.
Reviews:
America 110:238-9, Feb 15, 1964
Catholic World 198:391-2, Mar 1964
Commonweal 79:572-3, Feb 7, 1964
Nation 198:176, Feb 17, 1964
New York Theatre Critics' Reviews 1964:380
New York Times II, p. 1, Jan 12, 1964
              p. 18, Jan 20, 1964
New Yorker 39:72, Jan 25, 1964
Newsweek 63:58, Jan 27, 1964
Saturday Review 47:22, Feb 8, 1964
Time 83:54, Jan 31, 1964

Tchin-Tchin (Based on the play by Francois Billetdoux)
Productions:
Opened October 25, 1962 for 222 performances.
Reviews:
Nation 195:333-4, Nov 17, 1962
New York Theatre Critics' Reviews 1962:227
New York Times p. 37, Oct 9, 1962
            p. 26, Oct 26, 1962
            II, p. 1, Nov 25, 1962
New Yorker 38:111, Nov 3, 1962
Newsweek 60:74, Nov 5, 1962
Saturday Review 45:28, Nov 10, 1962
Theatre Arts 46:11, Dec 1962
Time 80:82, Nov 2, 1962

MIDDLETON, GEORGE

Accused (Adapted from the play by Eugene Brieux)
Productions:
Opened September 29, 1925 for 95 performances.
Reviews:
Life (NY) 86:26, Oct 22, 1925
Nation 121:446-7, Oct 14, 1925
New York Times p. 20, Sep 30, 1925
Theatre Magazine 42:16, Dec 1925

Adam and Eva (See entry under Bolton, Guy)

The Big Pond (with A. E. Thomas)
Productions:
Opened August 21, 1928 for 47 performances.
Reviews:

MIDDLETON, GEORGE (cont.)
  The Big Pond (cont.)
          Life (NY) 92:13, Sep 14, 1928
          New York Times p. 25, Aug 22, 1928
          Outlook 150:743, Sep 5, 1928
          Review 48:41, Oct 1928
          Theatre Magazine 48:32-4+, Nov 1928
          Vogue 72:126, Oct 13, 1928

  Blood Money (Based on a story by H. H. Van Loan)
      Productions:
      Opened August 22, 1927 for 64 performances.
      Reviews:
          Life (NY) 90:19, Sep 8, 1927
          New York Times p. 29, Aug 23, 1927
          Theatre Magazine 46:26-8+, Oct 1927
          Vogue 70:118, Oct 15, 1927

  The Cave Girl (with Guy Bolton)
      Productions:
      Opened August 18, 1920 for 37 performances.
      Reviews:
          Dramatic Mirror 9:Jul 3, 1920
                          p. 371, Aug 28, 1920
          Independent 103:261, Sep 4, 1920
          New York Clipper 68:19, Aug 25, 1920
          New York Times p. 12, Aug 19, 1920
          Theatre Magazine 32:242, Oct 1920

  Hit-the-Trail-Holiday (See entry under Cohan, George M.)

  The Light of the World (See entry under Bolton, Guy)

  Madame Capet (Adapted from the French of Marcelle
        Maurette)
      Productions:
      Opened October 25, 1938 for 7 performances.
      Reviews:
          Commonweal 29:76, Nov 11, 1938

  The Other Rose (Adapted from the French of Edouard
        Bourdet)
      Productions:
      Opened December 20, 1923 for 84 performances.
      Reviews:
          American Mercury 1:247, Feb 1924
          New York Times I, p. 2, Dec 16, 1923

p. 15, Dec 21, 1923
VII, p. 1, Dec 30, 1923
Theatre Magazine 39:15, Feb 1924

Polly with a Past (See entry under Bolton, Guy)

The Road Together
    Productions:
        Opened January 17, 1924 for 1 performance.
    Reviews:
        New Republic 8:275-6, Oct 14, 1916
        New York Times p. 21, Jan 18, 1924

MILLAY, EDNA ST. VINCENT

Aria Da Capo
    Productions:
        (Off Broadway) Season of 1957-58 (ANTA).
    Reviews:
        Drama 21:34, Mar 1931
        New York Times p. 14, Dec 6, 1919
                        p. 36, May 25, 1950
                        p. 40, May 21, 1958
                        p. 18, Jun 27, 1958

Conversation at Midnight
    Productions:
        Opened November 12, 1964 for 4 performances.
    Reviews:
        New York Theatre Critics' Reviews 1964:155
        New York Times p. 27, Nov 13, 1964

Launzi (Based on the play by Ferenc Molnar)
    Productions:
        Opened October 10, 1923 for 13 performances.
    Reviews:
        Life (NY) 82:20, Nov 1, 1923
        Nation 117:470, Oct 24, 1923
        New Republic 36:230-1, Oct 23, 1923
        New York Times p. 16, Oct 11, 1923
        Theatre Magazine 38:16, Dec 1923

MILLER, ARTHUR

After the Fall
    Productions:

MILLER, ARTHUR (cont.)
  After the Fall (cont.)
            Opened January 23, 1964 for 59 performances (Rep-
              ertory Theatre of Lincoln Center).
    Reviews:
      America 110:322, Mar 7, 1964
      Commonweal 79:600-1, Feb 14, 1964
      Life 56:64A, Feb 7, 1964
      Nation 198:153-4, Feb 10, 1964
      National Review 16:289-90, Apr 7, 1964
      New Republic 150:26-8+, Feb 8, 1964
      New York Theatre Critics' Reviews 1964:374
      New York Times p. 39, Oct 25, 1963
                     II, p. 1, Jan 19, 1964
                     p. 18, Jan 24, 1964
                     p. 14, Jan 31, 1964
                     II, p. 1, Feb 2, 1964
                     p. 37, Aug 11, 1964
                     p. 21, Jan 25, 1965
                     p. 26, Feb 1, 1966
      New Yorker 39:59, Feb 1, 1964
      Newsweek 63:49-52, Feb 3, 1964
      Reporter 30:46+, Feb 27, 1964
      Saturday Review 47:35, Feb 15, 1964
      Theatre Arts 48:12-16+, Jan 1964
      Time 83:54, Jan 31, 1964
      Vogue 143:66, Mar 15, 1964

All My Sons
  Productions:
      Opened January 29, 1947 for 328 performances.
      (Off Broadway) Opened November 15, 1968 for 9
        performances (Equity Library Theatre).
  Reviews:
      Catholic World 164:552-3, Mar 1947
      Commonweal 45:445-6, Feb 14, 1947
      Forum 107:271-5, Mar 1947
      Life 22:71-2+, Mar 10, 1947
      Nation 164:191+, Feb 15, 1947
      New Republic 116:42, Feb 10, 1947
      New York Theatre Critics' Reviews 1947:475
      New York Times p. 21, Jan 30, 1947
                     II, p. 1, Feb 9, 1947
                     II, p. 1, Apr 27, 1947
                     II, p. 3, Jun 29, 1947
                     II, p. 1, Sep 7, 1947
                     II, p. 1, Sep 21, 1947

II, p. 3, Oct 19, 1947
p. 26, Oct 21, 1947
II, p. 2, Jan 18, 1948
p. 33, May 12, 1948
New Yorker 22:50, Feb 8, 1947
Newsweek 29:85, Feb 10, 1947
Player's Magazine 25:47, Nov 1948
Saturday Review 30:22-24, Mar 1, 1947
School and Society 65:250, Apr 5, 1947
Theatre Arts 31:19, 50, Apr 1947
Time 49:68, Feb 10, 1947

The Crucible
Productions:
Opened January 22, 1953 for 197 performances.
(Off Broadway) Season of 1957-58 for 571 per-
formances.
Opened April 6, 1964 for 16 performances (National
Repertory Theatre).
Reviews:
American Record Guide 29:508-9+, Mar 1963
Catholic World 176:465-6, Mar 1953
193:394-5, Sep 1961
Commentary 15:265-71, Mar 1953
16:83-4, Jul 1953
Commonweal 57:498, Feb 20, 1953
Life 34:87-8+, Feb 9, 1953
Nation 176:131, Feb 7, 1953
New Republic 128:22-3, Feb 16, 1953
New York Theatre Critics' Reviews 1953:383
1964:295
New York Times II, p. 1, Jan 18, 1953
p. 15, Jan 23, 1953
II, p. 1, Feb 1, 1953
II, p. 3, Feb 8, 1953
VI, p. 20, Feb 15, 1953
p. 20, Jul 2, 1953
p. 8, Jul 29, 1955
p. 28, Apr 11, 1956
II, p. 3, Mar 9, 1958
p. 36, Mar 12, 1958
p. 21, Mar 17, 1958
II, p. 1, Jun 1, 1958
II, p. 1, May 17, 1959
p. 30, Apr 7, 1964
p. 35, Jan 20, 1965
p. 82, Jan 24, 1965

MILLER, ARTHUR (cont.)
  The Crucible (cont.)
            New Yorker 28:47, Jan 31, 1953
            Newsweek 41:68, Feb 2, 1953
            Saturday Review 36:24-6, Jan 31, 1953
                          36:41-2, Feb 14, 1953
            School and Society 77:185-6, Mar 21, 1953
            Theatre Arts 37:24-6, 65-9, Apr 1953
                         37:33-4, Oct 1953
                         40:80, Feb 1956
                         41:27, May 1957
            Time 61:48, Feb 2, 1953

Death of A Salesman
  Productions:
      Opened February 10, 1949 for 742 performances.
  Reviews:
      American Mercury 68:679-80, Jun 1949
      Canadian Forum 29:86-7, Jul 1949
      Catholic World 169:62-3, Apr 1949
                     171:110-16, May 1950
      Commonweal 49:520-1, Mar 4, 1949
                 81:670, Feb 19, 1965
      Fortune 39:79-80, May 1949
      Forum 111:219-21, Apr 1949
      Harper's Bazaar 83:161, Mar 1949
      House and Garden 95:218, May 1949
      Life 26:115+, Feb 21, 1949
      Nation 168:283-4, Mar 5, 1949
      New Republic 120:26-8, Feb 28, 1949
      New York Theatre Critics' Reviews 1949:358
      New York Times II, p. 1, Feb 6, 1949
                      p. 27, Feb 11, 1949
                      II, p. 1, Feb 20, 1949
                      VII, p. 12, May 29, 1949
                      p. 12, Jul 29, 1949
                      II, p. 1, Aug 7, 1949
                      VI, p. 11+, Aug 28, 1949
                      VI, p. 6, Sep 11, 1949
                      II, p. 1, Feb 5, 1950
                      p. 10, Mar 4, 1950
                      II, p. 1, Mar 12, 1950
                      p. 41, Mar 16, 1950
                      p. 25, Apr 28, 1950
                      p. 20, Sep 21, 1950
                      p. 42, Dec 10, 1954
                      p. 11, Jul 20, 1963

New Yorker 24:58+, Feb 19, 1949
Newsweek 33:78, Feb 21, 1949
Saturday Review 32:30-2, Feb 26, 1949
               46:34, Aug 24, 1963
School and Society 70:363-4, Dec 3, 1949
Theatre Arts 33:14-16, Apr 1949
           33:18-21, Oct 1949
           33:12-14, Nov 1949
Time 53:74-6, Feb 21, 1949
     54:59, Aug 8, 1949
Vogue 113:157, Mar 1, 1949

An Enemy of the People (Adapted from Henrik Ibsen's
   play)
  Productions:
    Opened December 28, 1950 for 36 performances.
    (Off Broadway) Season of 1958-59.
    (Off Broadway) Opened February 9, 1968 for 9 per-
    formances (Equity Library Theatre).
  Reviews:
    Catholic World 172:387, Feb 1951
    Christian Science Monitor Magazine p. 6, Jan, 1951
    Commonweal 53:374, Jan 19, 1951
    Nation 172:18, Jan 6, 1951
    New Republic 124:22, Jan 22, 1951
    New York Theatre Critics' Reviews 1950:154
    New York Times II, p. 3. Dec 24, 1950
                p. 14, Dec 29, 1950
                 II, p. 1, Jan 7, 1951
                 p. 24, Feb 5, 1959
    New Yorker 26:44, Jan 13, 1951
            34:68+, Feb 14, 1959
    Newsweek 37:67, Jan 8, 1951
    Saturday Review 42:34, Feb 21, 1959
    School and Society 73:105, Feb 17, 1951
    Theatre Arts 35:15, Mar 1951
    Time 57:31, Jan 8, 1951

Incident at Vichy
  Productions:
    Opened December 3, 1964 for 99 performances
    (Repertory Theatre of Lincoln Center).
  Reviews:
    America 112:147-9, Jan 23, 1965
    Life 58:39-40+, Jan 22, 1965
    Nation 199:504, Dec 21, 1964
    New Republic 151:26-7, Dec 26, 1964

MILLER, ARTHUR (cont.)
  Incident at Vichy (cont.)
          New York Theatre Critics' Reviews 1964:116
          New York Times II, p. 1, Nov 29, 1964
                         p. 44, Dec 4, 1964
                         p. 45, Dec 7, 1964
                         II, p. 3, Dec 20, 1964
                         VI, p. 10, Jan 30, 1965
                         p. 28, Jan 27, 1966
          New Yorker 40:152, Dec 12, 1964
          Newsweek 64:86, Dec 14, 1964
          Saturday Review 47:24, Dec 19, 1964
          Time 84:73, Dec 11, 1964
          Vogue 145:27, Jan 15, 1965

  The Man Who Had All the Luck
      Productions:
          Opened November 23, 1944 for 4 performances.
      Reviews:
          New York Theatre Critics' Reviews 1944:73
          New York Times p. 18, Nov 24, 1944

  A Memory of Two Mondays
      Productions:
          Opened September 29, 1955 for 149 performances.
          (Off Broadway) Opened October 30, 1964 for 9 per-
            formances (Equity Library Theatre).
      Reviews:
          America 94:223, Nov 19, 1955
          Catholic World 182:144-5, Nov 1955
          Commonweal 63:117, Nov 4, 1955
          Life 39:166-7, Oct 17, 1955
          Nation 181:348-9, Oct 22, 1955
          New York Theatre Critics' Reviews 1955:272
          New York Times p. 16, Aug 31, 1955
                         VI, p. 78, Sep 18, 1955
                         II, p. 1, Sep 25, 1955
                         p. 21, Sep 30, 1955
                         II, p. 1, Oct 9, 1955
                         p. 35, Oct 12, 1955
                         p. 34, Nov 9, 1956
          New Yorker 31:92+, Oct 8, 1955
          Saturday Review 38:25-6, Oct 15, 1955
          Theatre Arts 39:18-19, Dec 1955
                       40:31-2, Sep 1956
          Time 66:53, Oct 10, 1955

The Price
    Productions:
        Opened February 7, 1968 for 429 performances.
    Reviews:
        America 118:422-3, Mar 30, 1968
        Atlantic 221:120-2, Jun 1968
        Catholic World 207:74-5, May 1968
        Christian Century 85:405-6, Mar 27, 1968
        Commentary 45:74-6, Apr 1968
        Commonweal 87:655, Mar 1, 1968
        Life 64:18, Mar 8, 1968
        Nation 206:281-3, Feb 26, 1968
        National Review 20:511-12, May 21, 1968
        New Republic 158:39-41, Feb 24, 1968
        New York Theatre Critics' Reviews 1968:334
                         1968:352
        New York Times II, p. 1, Jan 28, 1968
                   p. 37, Feb 8, 1968
                   II, p. 1, Feb 18, 1968
                   p. 32, Mar 5, 1968
                   II, p. 1, Apr 21, 1968
                   p. 39, Oct 30, 1968
                   p. 36, Mar 6, 1969
        New Yorker 43:99, Feb 17, 1968
        Newsweek 71:104, Feb 19, 1968
        Reporter 38:42+, Mar 21, 1968
        Saturday Review 51:38, Feb 24, 1968
        Time 91:76-7, Feb 16, 1968

A View from the Bridge
    Productions:
        Opened September 29, 1955 for 149 performances.
        (Off Broadway) Opened January 28, 1965 for 780
          performances.
    Reviews:
        America 94:223, Nov 19, 1955
        Catholic World 182:144-5, Nov 1955
        Commonweal 63:117, Nov 4, 1955
                 81:670, Feb 19, 1965
        Life 39:166-7, Oct 17, 1955
        Nation 181:348-9, Oct 22, 1955
        New Republic 133:21-2, Dec 19, 1955
        New York Theatre Critics' Reviews 1955:272
        New York Times p. 16, Aug 31, 1955
                   VI, p. 78, Sep 18, 1955
                   II, p. 1, Sep 25, 1955
                   p. 21, Sep 30, 1955

MILLER, ARTHUR (cont.)
  A View from the Bridge (cont.)
                    II, p. 1, Oct 9, 1955
                    p. 35, Oct 12, 1955
                    p. 34, Nov 9, 1956
                    p. 24, Jan 29, 1965
                    II, p. 1, Aug 15, 1965
                    p. 45, Dec 3, 1966
          New Yorker 31:92+, Oct 8, 1955
                    40:94, Feb 6, 1965
          Newsweek 65:93, Mar 15, 1965
          Saturday Review 38:25-6, Oct 15, 1955
          Theatre Arts 39:18-19, Dec 1955
                    40:31-2, Sep 1956
          Time 66:53, Oct 10, 1955
          Vogue 145:56, Apr 15, 1965

MITCHELL, LANGDON

  Becky Sharp (Based on Thackeray's Vanity Fair)
      Productions:
      Opened March 20, 1911 for 16 performances.
      Opened June 3, 1929 for 8 performances.
      Reviews:
      Commonweal 10:189, Jun 19, 1929
      Dramatic Mirror 65:7, Mar 22, 1911
      Leslies' Weekly 112:423, Apr 13, 1911
      Life (NY) 93:22, Jun 28, 1929
      Literary Digest 101:23-4, Jun 29, 1929
      New York Times VIII, p. 2, Jun 2, 1929
                    p. 29, Jun 4, 1929
                    p. 24, Jun 10, 1929
      Outlook 152:313, Jun 19, 1929

  The Kreutzer Sonata (Adapted from the play by Jacob
      Gordin)
      Productions:
      Opened May 14, 1924 for 38 performances.
      Reviews:
      American Mercury 2:373-4, Jul 1924
      New York Times p. 22, May 15, 1924
      Theatre Magazine 6:xv, Sep 1906
                    39:15, Jul 1924

  Major Pendennis (Based on Thackeray's Vanity Fair)
      Productions:

Opened October 26, 1916 for 76 performances.
Reviews:
    Current Opinion 62:24-8, Jan 1917
    Dramatic Mirror 76:7, Nov 4, 1916
    Green Book 17:7+, Jan 1917
    Life (NY) 60:812, Nov 9, 1916
    Literary Digest 53:1328-9, Nov 18, 1916
                53:1409, Nov 25, 1916
    Nation 103:426-7, Nov 2, 1916
    New Republic 9:21, Nov 4, 1916
    New York Dramatic News 63:10-11, Nov 4, 1916
    New York Times p. 7, Oct 27, 1916
                II, p. 6, Oct 29, 1916
                II, p. 7, Nov 5, 1916
                II, p. 6, Nov 26, 1916
    Theatre Magazine 24:354+, Dec 1916

The New York Idea
    Productions:
        Opened September 28, 1915 in repertory (New York
        Playhouse Co.).
        Opened March 22, 1933 for 3 performances.
    Reviews:
        Book News 34:123, Nov 1915
        Bookman 42:263+, Nov 1915
        Dramatic Mirror 74:8, Oct 6, 1915
        Life (NY) 66:708, Oct 14, 1915
        Nation 101:443, Oct 7, 1915
        New Republic 4:263, Oct 9, 1915
                    119:31, Aug 30, 1948
        New York Times p. 13, Sep 29, 1915
                    p. 29, Aug 18, 1948
                    p. 12, Jul 13, 1963
        Smart Set 47:144-5, Dec 1915
        Theatre Magazine 7:2-3, Jan 1907
                    22:224, Nov 1915

MITCHELL, THOMAS

Cloudy With Showers (See entry under Dell, Floyd)

Glory Hallelujah (with Bertram Bloch)
    Productions:
        Opened April 6, 1926 for 15 performances.
    Reviews:
        Bookman 63:468-9, Jun 1926

329

MITCHELL, THOMAS (cont.)
  Glory Hallelujah (cont.)
        Life (NY) 87:21, Apr 29, 1926
        New York Times p. 26, Apr 7, 1926
                        VIII, p. 1, Apr 11, 1926

  Little Accident (See entry under Dell, Floyd)

MONKS, JOHN JR.

  Brother Rat (with Fred F. Finklehoffe)
    Productions:
        Opened December 16, 1936 for 577 performances.
    Reviews:
        Catholic World 144:599, Feb 1937
        Commonweal 25:276, Jan 1, 1937
        Literary Digest 123:22-3, Jan 2, 1937
        New York Times XII, p. 6, Dec 6, 1936
                        p. 30, Dec 8, 1936
                        XI, p. 5, Dec 13, 1936
                        p. 34, Dec 17, 1936
                        X, p. 3, Oct 31, 1937
                        p. 26, Nov 6, 1941
        Newsweek 8:38, Dec 26, 1936
        Stage 14:64, Feb 1937
        Theatre Arts 21:97, Feb 1937
        Time 28:33, Dec 28, 1936

MOODY, WILLIAM VAUGHN

  The Faith Healer
    Productions:
        Opened January 19, 1910 for 6 performances.
    Reviews:
        Book News 27:61, Apr 1909
        Collier's 44:33, Feb 12, 1910
        Current Literature 48:311-7, Mar 1910
        Dramatic Mirror 69:7-8, Jan 29, 1909
        Dramatist 1:33-4, Jan 1910
        Hampton 24:561-5, Apr 1910
        Independent 68:989-90, May 5, 1910
        Life (NY) 55:205, Feb 3, 1910
        Nation 88:175-6, Feb 18, 1909
        Theatre Magazine 9:xii, Mar 1909

The Great Divide
    Productions:
        Opened February 7, 1917 for 53 performances.
    Reviews:
        Book News 28:469, Feb 1910
        Dramatic Mirror 77:10, Feb 17, 1917
        Dramatist 4:354-6, Apr 1913
        Forum 43:90-92, Jan 1910
        Independent 67:932, Oct 21, 1909
        Nation 89:387, Oct 21, 1909
                104:197, Feb 15, 1917
        New Republic 10:137, Mar 3, 1917
        New York Times p. 11, Feb 8, 1917
                    II, p. 2, Feb 11, 1917
        Theatre Magazine 6:282-3+, Nov 1906
                    25:137+, Mar 1917

MOSEL, TAD

All the Way Home (Based on James Agee's novel A
        Death in the Family)
    Productions:
        Opened November 30, 1960 for 333 performances.
    Reviews:
        America 104:480, Jan 14, 1961
        Catholic World 193:206-8, Jun 1961
        Commonweal 73:588, Mar 3, 1961
        Life 50:93-4, Jan 27, 1961
        Nation 191:491, Dec 17, 1960
        New Republic 143:20-1, Dec 26, 1960
        New York Theatre Critics' Reviews 1960:163
        New York Times II, p. 1, Nov 27, 1960
                        p. 42, Dec 1, 1960
                        p. 46, Dec 9, 1960
                        II, p. 3, Dec 18, 1960
                        p. 26, Dec 27, 1960
        New Yorker 36:96+, Dec 10, 1960
        Saturday Review 43:29, Dec 17, 1960
        Theatre Arts 45:64-5+, Jun 1961
                    45:10-11, Feb 1961
        Time 76:76, Dec 12, 1960
        Vogue 137:166-7, Feb 1, 1961

331

MOWATT, ANNA CORA

Fashion, or Life in New York
    Productions:
        Opened February 3, 1924 for 152 performances.
        (Off Broadway) Season of 1958-59.
    Reviews:
        America 100:613, Feb 21, 1959
        Bookman 59:202, Apr 1924
        Catholic World 189:60, Apr 1959
        Dial 76:383-4, Apr 1924
        Drama 15:124, Mar 1925
                15:154, Apr 1925
        Freeman 8:567-8, Feb 20, 1924
        Literary Digest 81:28-9, Apr 19, 1924
        Nation 118:213, Feb 20, 1924
        New Republic 37:313, Feb 13, 1924
        New York Times p. 21, Feb 5, 1924
                        VII, p. 1, Feb 10, 1924
                        VIII, p. 2, Mar 16, 1924
                        VII, p. 1, Jul 20, 1924
                        VII, p. 14, Aug 10, 1924
                        p. 19, Jul 15, 1939
                        p. 27, Jan 21, 1959
        New Yorker 34:64+, Jan 31, 1959
        Theatre Magazine 25:143, Mar 1917
                        39:16+, Apr 1924
        Time 73:66, Feb 16, 1959

MURRAY, JOHN

Room Service (with Alan Boretz)
    Productions:
        Opened May 19, 1937 for 500 performances.
        Opened April 6, 1953 for 16 performances.
        (Off Broadway) Opened May 10, 1963 for 9 per-
            formances. (Equity Library Theatre)
    Reviews:
        America 89:116-17, Apr 25, 1953
        Catholic World 145:472-3, Jul 1937
        Commonweal 26:188, Jun 11, 1937
                    58:72, Apr 24, 1953
        Life 2:56, Jun 28, 1937
        Nation 144:628, May 29, 1937
        New York Theatre Critics' Reviews 1953:322
        New York Times p. 16, May 20, 1937

                    X, p. 1, May 30, 1937
                    X, p. 2, Jul 25, 1937
                    p. 35, Dec 16, 1937
                    X, p. 1, Jan 16, 1938
                    p. 34, Apr 7, 1953
          New Yorker 29:68+, Apr 18, 1953
          Newsweek 9:23, May 29, 1937
                    12:21, Sep 26, 1938
          Saturday Review 36:28, Apr 25, 1953
          Theatre Arts 21:500, Jul 1937
                    37:89, Jun 1953
          Time 29:34, May 31, 1937
                    32:36, Oct 3, 1938
                    61:72, Apr 20, 1953

NASH, N. RICHARD

  Girls of Summer
    Productions:
      Opened November 19, 1956 for 56 performances.
    Reviews:
      Catholic World 184:305, Jan 1957
      Commonweal 65:382, Jan 11, 1957
      Nation 183:506, Dec 8, 1956
      New York Theatre Critics' Reviews 1956:197
      New York Times p. 45, Nov 20, 1956
      New Yorker 32:117-18, Dec 1956
      Newsweek 48:50, Dec 3, 1956
      Saturday Review 39:29, Dec 8, 1956
      Theatre Arts 41:30, Jan 1957
      Time 68:82, Dec 3, 1956

  Handful of Fire
    Productions:
      Opened October 1, 1958 for 5 performances.
    Reviews:
      America 100:116+, Oct 25, 1958
      Commonweal 69:127-8, Oct 31, 1958
      New Republic 139:23, Oct 20, 1958
      New York Theatre Critics' Reviews 1958:285
      New York Times p. 45, Oct 2, 1958
      New Yorker 34:87-9, Oct 11, 1958
      Newsweek 52:112, Oct 13, 1958
      Theatre Arts 42:14+, Dec 1958

  Second Best Bed
    Productions:

                         333

NASH, N. RICHARD (cont.)
  Second Best Bed (cont.)
        Opened June 3, 1946 for 8 performances.
     Reviews:
        New York Theatre Critics' Reviews 1946:371
        New York Times p. 20, Jun 4, 1946
        New Yorker 22:40+, Jun 15, 1946

  The Rainmaker
     Productions:
        Opened October 28, 1954 for 125 performances.
     Reviews:
        America 92:284, Dec 4, 1954
        Catholic World 180:227, Dec 1954
        Commonweal 61:251+, Dec 3, 1954
        Life 37:143-4+, Nov 15, 1954
        Nation 179:429, Nov 13, 1954
        New York Theatre Critics' Reviews 1954:264
        New York Times p. 28, Oct 29, 1954
                        II, p. 1, Nov 7, 1954
                        II, p. 1, Nov 21, 1954
                           p. 26, Jun 1, 1956
                        II, p. 9, Dec 9, 1956
        New Yorker 30:82+, Nov 6, 1954
        Newsweek 44:60, Nov 8, 1954
        Saturday Review 37:26, Nov 13, 1954
        Theatre Arts 39:15, 20, Jan 1955
        Time 64:59, Nov 8, 1954

  See The Jaguar
     Productions:
        Opened December 3, 1952 for 5 performances.
     Reviews:
        Commonweal 57:333, Jan 2, 1953
        New York Theatre Critics' Reviews 1952:164
        New York Times p. 46, Dec 4, 1952
        New Yorker 28:86+, Dec 13, 1952
        Newsweek 40:63, Dec 15, 1952
        Saturday Review 35:26, Dec 20, 1952
        Theatre Arts 37:29, Feb 1953
        Time 60:73, Dec 15, 1952

  The Young and the Fair
     Productions:
        Opened November 22, 1948 for 48 performances.
     Reviews:
        Catholic World 168:323, Jan 1949

Commonweal 49:231, Dec 10, 1948
New Republic 119:38, Dec 6, 1948
New York Theatre Critics' Reviews 1948:143
New York Times p. 35, Nov 23, 1948
              p. 14, Jul 1, 1949
New Yorker 24:55-7, Dec 4, 1948
Newsweek 32:86, Dec 6, 1948
School and Society 68:455, Dec 25, 1948
Theatre Arts 33:16, Jan 1949
Time 52:91, Dec 6, 1948

NICHOLS, ANNE

Abie's Irish Rose
  Productions:
    Opened May 23, 1922 for 2,327 performances.
    Opened May 12, 1937 for 46 performances.
    Opened November 18, 1954 for 20 performances.
  Reviews:
    Catholic World 180:309, Jan 1955
    Classic 20:46, Oct 1924
    Collier's 74:5+, Jul 26, 1924
    Commonweal 26:160, Jun 4, 1937
    Current Opinion 77:192, Aug 1924
    Dial 78:432, May 1925
    Dramatist 15:1214-15, Apr 1924
    Ladies Home Journal 41:32+, Sep 1924
    Life (NY) 85:20, May 21, 1925
             85:18, Jun 25, 1925
             85:19, Feb 3, 1927
    Literary Digest 92:30, Feb 19, 1927
                    93:27, May 14, 1927
    Nation 125:467-8, Nov 2, 1927
    National Magazine 55:12+, Sep 1926
    New Republic 42:98-9, Mar 18, 1925
                 51:18-19, May 25, 1927
    New York Clipper 70:20, May 31, 1922
    New York Theatre Critics' Reviews 1954:248
    New York Times p. 22, May 24, 1922
                   VIII, p. 1, May 13, 1923
                   p. 6, Dec 18, 1925
                   p. 14, May 22, 1926
                   VII, p. 1, Aug 29, 1926
                   p. 12, Nov 6, 1926
                   p. 16, Jan 12, 1927
                   p. 23, Mar 29, 1927

NICHOLS, ANNE (cont.)
    Abie's Irish Rose (cont.)
                            p. 24, Apr 12, 1927
                            VII, p. 1, May 8, 1927
                            p. 23, May 24, 1927
                            p. 10, Jul 16, 1927
                            VII, p. 1, Jul 31, 1927
                            p. 27, Aug 9, 1927
                            II, p. 3, Sep 4, 1927
                            p. 29, Sep 30, 1927
                            VIII, p. 1, Oct 23, 1927
                            VIII, p. 2, Oct 23, 1927
                            p. 20, Oct 24, 1927
                            VIII, p. 2, Jun 10, 1928
                            X, p. 2, Aug 2, 1936
                            XI, p. 2, May 2, 1937
                            p. 30, May 13, 1937
                            p. 19, Nov 19, 1954
                            VI, p. 2, Dec 5, 1954
                            II, p. 1, May 13, 1962
                            p. 40, May 21, 1962
                            p. 44, May 23, 1962
        Newsweek 9:26+, May 22, 1937
        Theatre Arts 31:66-7, Apr 1947
                     39:13+, Feb 1955
        Theatre Magazine 36:95, Aug 1922
                         39:19+, Jul 1924
                         46:7-8, Jul 1927
        Time 64:50, Nov 29, 1954
        Vanity Fair 26:52+, May 1926

*Her Week-End
    Reviews:
        New York Times p. 28, Mar 20, 1936

Just Married (with Adelaide Matthews)
    Productions:
        Opened April 26, 1921.
    Reviews:
        Dramatic Mirror 83:733, Apr 30, 1921
        Life (NY) 77:688, May 12, 1921
        New York Clipper 69:23, May 4, 1921
        Theatre Magazine 34:9+, Jul 1921

*Nearly Married (with Adelaide Matthews)
    Reviews:
        New York Times IX, p. 4, Sep 22, 1929

Pre-Honeymoon (with Alford VanRonkel)
Productions:
Opened April 30, 1936 for 255 performances.
Reviews:
New York Times p. 19, May 1, 1936
Time 27:28, May 11, 1936

NICHOLSON, KENYON

Apple of his Eye (with Charles Robinson)
Productions:
Opened February 5, 1946 for 118 performances.
Reviews:
Catholic World 162:553, Mar 1946
Life 20:107-10, Apr 8, 1946
New Republic 114:254, Feb 18, 1946
New York Theatre Critics' Reviews 1946:463
New York Times p. 18, Feb 6, 1946
New Yorker 22:50, Feb 16, 1946
Theatre Arts 30:135, Mar 1946
              30:205, Apr 1946
Time 47:50, Feb 18, 1946

The Barker
Productions:
Opened January 18, 1927 for 172 performances.
Reviews:
Bookman 65:208, Apr 1927
Life (NY) 89:23, Feb 10, 1927
Nation 124:125, Feb 2, 1927
New York Times p. 20, Jan 19, 1927
              VII, p. 1, Jan 23, 1927
Theatre Magazine 45:24+, Apr 1927
Vogue 69:138, Mar 15, 1927

Before You're 25
Productions:
Opened April 16, 1929 for 23 performances.
Reviews:
Life (NY) 93:24, May 10, 1929
New York Times p. 30, Apr 17, 1929
Outlook 152:32, May 1, 1929

Dance Night
Productions:
Opened October 14, 1938 for 3 performances.

NICHOLSON, KENYON (cont.)
    Dance Night (cont.)
        Reviews:
            New York Times p. 20, Oct 15, 1938

    Eva the Fifth (with John Golden)
        Productions:
            Opened August 28, 1928 for 63 performances.
        Reviews:
            Life (NY) 92:13, Sep 14, 1928
            New York Times VII, p. 1, Jul 22, 1928
                            p. 19, Aug 29, 1928
            Outlook 150:785, Sep 12, 1928
            Theatre Magazine 48:48, Nov 1928

    The Flying Gerardos (with Charles Robinson)
        Productions:
            Opened December 29, 1940 for 24 performances.
        Reviews:
            New York Theatre Critics' Reviews 1940:165
                                            1941:437
            New York Times p. 21, Dec 30, 1940
            Time 37:57, Jan 13, 1941

    Love Is Like That (See entry under Behrman, S. N.)

    Out West of Eighth
        Productions:
            Opened September 20, 1951 for 4 performances.
        Reviews:
            Commonweal 54:620, Oct 5, 1951
            New York Theatre Critics' Reviews 1951:232
            New York Times p. 20, Sep 21, 1951
            New Yorker 27:66, Sep 29, 1951
            Theatre Arts 35:8, Nov 12, 1951

    Sailor, Beware! (with Charles Robinson)
        Productions:
            Opened September 28, 1933 for 500 performances.
            Opened May 3, 1935 for 16 performances.
        Reviews:
            New Outlook 162:42, Nov 1933
            New Republic 76:279, Oct 18, 1933
            New York Times p. 24, Sep 29, 1933
                            IX, p. 3, Jan 7, 1934
                            IX, p. 2, Feb 4, 1934
                            p. 22, Feb 7, 1935

p. 28, May 7, 1935
Review of Reviews 89:47, Mar 1934
Stage 11:9-10+, Nov 1933
    11:10-11, Feb 1934
    11:29, Mar 1934
Theatre Arts 17:918-19, Dec 1933

Stepdaughters of War (Adapted from the novel by Helen
    Zenna Smith)
Productions:
    Opened October 6, 1930 for 24 performances.
Reviews:
    Bookman 72:297, Nov 1930
    Commonweal 12:643-4, Oct 22, 1930
    Life (NY) 96:18, Oct 24, 1930
    Nation 131:451-2, Oct 22, 1930
    New York Times p. 27, Oct 7, 1930
    Outlook 156:314, Oct 22, 1930
    Theatre Magazine 52:28+, Dec 1930

Swing Your Lady (with Charles Robinson)
Productions:
    Opened October 18, 1936 for 105 performances.
Reviews:
    New Republic 89:50, Nov 11, 1936
    New York Times p. 22, Oct 19, 1936
    Stage 14:49, Dec 1936
    Theatre Arts 20:926+, Dec 1936
    Time 28:47, Nov 2, 1936

Torch Song
Productions:
    Opened August 27, 1930 for 87 performances.
Reviews:
    Arts and Decoration 34:67, Nov 1930
    Catholic World 132:206, Nov 1930
    Life (NY) 96:16, Sep 19, 1930
    Nation 131:303-4, Sep 17, 1930
    National Magazine 59:136-7, Dec 1930
    New Republic 64:152-3, Sep 24, 1930
    New York Times VIII, p. 3, Aug 3, 1930
                 p. 23, Aug 28, 1930
                 IX, p. 1, Sep 7, 1930
                 VIII, p. 4, Oct 4, 1930
    Sketch Book 7:33, Oct 1930
    Theatre Arts 14:909+, Nov 1930
    Theatre Magazine 52:24, Nov 1930

339

NICHOLSON, KENYON (cont.)
  Torch Song (cont.)
                    52:34-6+, Nov 1930
        Vanity Fair 35:86+, Nov 1930
        Vogue 76:83+, Oct 13, 1930

NUGENT, ELLIOTT and J. C.

  The Breaks
    Productions:
      Opened April 16, 1928 for 8 performances.
    Reviews:
      New York Times p. 26, Apr 17, 1928

  By Request
    Productions:
      Opened September 27, 1928 for 28 performances.
    Reviews:
      Life (NY) 92:19, Oct 19, 1928
      New York Times p. 30, Sep 28, 1928

  Dream Child (J. C. Nugent alone)
    Productions:
      Opened September 27, 1934 for 24 performances.
    Reviews:
      New York Times p. 26, Sep 28, 1934

  Dumb-Bell
    Productions:
      Opened November 26, 1923 for 2 performances.
    Reviews:
      New York Times p. 23, Nov 27, 1923
                    VIII, p. 1, Dec 2, 1923

  Fast Service
    Productions:
      Opened November 17, 1931 for 7 performances.
    Reviews:
      New York Times p. 26, Nov 18, 1931

  Human Nature
    Productions:
      Opened September 24, 1925 for 4 performances. •
    Reviews:
      New York Times p. 24, Sep 25, 1925

Kempy
    Productions:
        Opened May 15, 1922 for 38+ performances.
        Opened May 11, 1927 for 46 performances.
    Reviews:
        Current Opinion 73:213-20, Aug 1922
        Everybody's 47:83-8, Nov 1922
        Life (NY) 79:18, Jun 1, 1922
        New York Clipper 70:20, May 24, 1922
        New York Times p. 14, May 16, 1922
                        VI, p. 1, Jun 11, 1922
                        p. 25, May 12, 1927
                        VIII, p. 1, May 22, 1927
        Theatre Magazine 36:30-31, Jul 1922
                        36:230+, Oct 1922

The Male Animal (See entry under Thurber, James)

*Mr. Shaddy (J. C. Nugent alone)
    Reviews:
        New York Times p. 14, Jul 15, 1936

Nightstick (with John Wray, and Elaine Sterne Carring-
        ton)
    Productions:
        Opened November 10, 1927 for 52 performances.
        Reopened for 32 performances.
    Reviews:
        Life (NY) 90:21, Dec 8, 1927
        New York Times p. 20, Nov 11, 1927
                        IX, p. 4, Nov 20, 1927
        Vogue 71:100, Jan 1, 1928

A Place of Our Own (Elliott Nugent alone)
    Productions:
        Opened April 2, 1945 for 8 performances.
    Reviews:
        New York Theatre Critics' Reviews 1945:232
        New York Times p. 23, Apr 3, 1945

The Poor Nut
    Productions:
        Opened April 27, 1925 for 32 performances.
    Reviews:
        Nation 120:556-7, May 13, 1925
        New York Times p. 18, Apr 28, 1925
        Theatre Magazine 42:15, Jul 1925
                        42:26+, Oct 1925

NUGENT, ELLIOTT and J. C.
    The Rising Son
        Productions:
            Opened October 27, 1924 for 16 performances.
        Reviews:
            Life (NY) 84:18, Nov 13, 1924
            New York Times p. 27, Oct 28, 1924
            Theatre Magazine 40:20, Jan 1925

    That Old Devil (J. C. Nugent alone)
        Productions:
            Opened June 5, 1944 for 16 performances.
        Reviews:
            Commonweal 40:231, June 23, 1944
            New York Theatre Critics' Reviews 1944:177
            New York Times p. 14, Jun 6, 1944
            New Yorker 20:44, Jun 17, 1944

    The Trouper
        Productions:
            Opened March 8, 1926 for 24 performances.
        Reviews:
            New York Times p. 21, Mar 9, 1926
                          VIII, p. 1, Mar 14, 1926
            Theatre Magazine 43:18, May 1926

    *World's My Opinion
        Reviews:
            New York Times X, p. 1, Jun 16, 1935

ODETS, CLIFFORD

    Awake and Sing
        Productions:
            Opened February 19, 1935 for 209 performances.
            Opened September 9, 1935 for 24 performances.
            Opened March 7, 1939 for 45 performances.
        Reviews:
            Catholic World 141:91, Apr 1935
                           149:217-18, May 1939
            Commonweal 21:570, Mar 15, 1935
                       29:639, Mar 31, 1939
            Literary Digest 119:18, Apr 6, 1935
            Nation 140:314+, Mar 13, 1935
                   140:610, May 22, 1935
            New Republic 82:134, Mar 13, 1935

New York Times p. 23, Feb 20, 1935
                VIII, p. 1, Mar 10, 1935
                p. 15, Feb 21, 1938
                p. 16, Dec 23, 1938
                p. 18, Mar 8, 1939
                X, p. 1, Mar 26, 1939
                VIII, p. 2, May 31, 1941
                VIII, p. 2, May 31, 1942
Newsweek 5:31, Mar 2, 1935
Stage 12:23, Apr 1935
Theatre Arts 19:254-6, Apr 1935
             23:323, May 1939
Time 25:39, Mar 4, 1935
     33:60, Mar 20, 1939
Vanity Fair 44:24, Jun 1935

The Big Knife
    Productions:
        Opened February 24, 1949 for 108 performances.
        (Off Broadway) Season of 1959-60.
    Reviews:
        Catholic World 169:63, Apr 1949
        Commonweal 49:590-1, Mar 25, 1949
        Forum 111:286-7, May 1949
        Nation 168:340, Mar 19, 1949
        New Republic 120:28-9, Mar 14, 1949
        New York Theatre Critics' Reviews 1949:349
        New York Times p. 27, Feb 25, 1949
                        II, p. 1, Mar 6, 1949
                        p. 64, Jan 3, 1954
                        II, p. 4, Jan 17, 1954
                        p. 25, Nov 13, 1959
        New Yorker 25:56+, Mar 5, 1949
        Newsweek 33:84, Mar 7, 1949
        Saturday Review 32:34-5, Mar 19, 1949
        School and Society 69:340-1, May 7, 1949
        Theatre Arts 33:23-5, May 1949
        Time 53:58, Mar 7, 1949
        Vogue 113:206+, Apr 1, 1949

Clash By Night
    Productions:
        Opened December 27, 1941 for 49 performances.
    Reviews:
        Catholic World 154:601, Feb 1942
        Commonweal 35:319-20, Jan 16, 1942
        Current History ns 1:566-8, Feb 1942

343

ODETS, CLIFFORD (cont.)
  Clash By Night (cont.)
        Life 11:53-4, Nov 24, 1941
        Nation 154:45-6, Jan 10, 1942
        New York Theatre Critics' Reviews 1941:161
        New York Times IX, p. 1, Jan 11, 1942
                       IX, p. 1, Jan 18, 1942
                       IX, p. 3, Feb 1, 1942
        New Yorker 17:28+, Jan 3, 1942
        Newsweek 19:46, Jan 12, 1942
        Player's Magazine 18:13, Feb 1942
        Theatre Arts 26:150-2, Mar 1942

  The Country Girl
    Productions:
        Opened November 10, 1950 for 235 performances.
        (Off Broadway) Opened March 12, 1968 for 15 per-
        formances. (Billed as Winter Journey).
        Opened September 29, 1966 for 22 performances
        (City Center Drama Company).
    Reviews:
        American Mercury 72:350-1, Mar 1951
        Catholic World 172:310, Jan 1951
        Christian Science Monitor Magazine p. 4, Nov. 18,
        1950
        Commonweal 53:196, Dec 1, 1950
        Life 29:77-80, Dec 4, 1950
        Nation 171:493, Nov 25, 1950
               203:398, Oct 17, 1966
        National Review 19:99, Jan 24, 1967
        New Republic 123:29-30, Dec 11, 1950
        New York Theatre Critics' Reviews 1950:210
        New York Times II, p. 3, Nov 5, 1950
                         p. 10, Nov 11, 1950
                      II, p. 1, Nov 19, 1950
                      II, p. 3, Nov 26, 1950
                         p. 31, Apr 3, 1951
                         p. 21, Apr 4, 1952
                      II, p. 3, Apr 13, 1952
                         p. 55, Sep 30, 1966
                         p. 39, Mar 13, 1968
        New Yorker 26:77-9, Nov 18, 1950
        Newsweek 36:90, Nov 20, 1950
        Saturday Review 33:26-7, Dec 9, 1950
        School and Society 73:249-50, Apr 21, 1951
        Theatre Arts 35:14, Jan 1951
        Time 56:64, Nov 20, 1950

The Flowering Peach
    Productions:
        Opened December 28, 1954 for 135 performances.
    Reviews:
        America 92:434, Jan 22, 1955
        Catholic World 180:387, Feb 1955
        Commentary 20:74-6, Jul 1955
        Commonweal 61:502, Feb 11, 1955
        Nation 180:57-9, Jan 15, 1955
        New Republic 132:21, Jan 10, 1955
        New York Theatre Critics' Reviews 1954:196
        New York Times II, p. 1, Dec 26, 1954
                       p. 19, Dec 29, 1954
                       II, p. 1, Jan 9, 1955
                       II, p. 3, Mar 20, 1955
        New Yorker 30:62+, Jan 8, 1955
        Newsweek 45:62, Jan 10, 1955
        Saturday Review 38:30, Jan 15, 1955
        Theatre Arts 38:24-5, Oct 1954
                     39:18, 23+, Mar 1955
        Time 65:34, Jan 10, 1955

Golden Boy
    Productions:
        Opened November 4, 1937 for 250 performances.
        Opened March 12, 1952 for 55 performances.
    Reviews:
        Catholic World 146:342, Dec 1937
                       175:148, May 1952
        Commonweal 27:106, Nov 19, 1937
                   55:614-15, Mar 28, 1952
        Current History 48:54, Apr 1938
        Life 4:24-7, Jan 17, 1938
        Literary Digest 124:35, Nov 27, 1937
        Nation 145:540, Nov 13, 1937
               174:285, Mar 22, 1952
        New Republic 93:45, Nov 17, 1937
        New York Theatre Critics' Reviews 1952:344
        New York Times p. 18, Nov 5, 1937
                       XI, p. 1, Nov 21, 1937
                       p. 27, Jun 22, 1938
                       IX, p. 1, Jul 10, 1938
                       IX, p. 3, Oct 23, 1938
                       X, p. 3, Mar 5, 1939
                       II, p. 3, Mar 9, 1952
                       p. 24, Mar 13, 1952
                       II, p. 1, Mar 23, 1952

ODETS, CLIFFORD (cont.)
   Golden Boy (cont.)
      New Yorker 28:60, Mar 22, 1952
      Newsweek 39:100, Mar 24, 1952
      Saturday Review 35:26, Mar 29, 1952
      School and Society 75:326-7, May 24, 1952
      Scribner's Magazine 103:66, May 1938
      Theatre Arts 22:11-13, Jan 1938
      Time 30:25-6, Nov 15, 1937
           59:56, Mar 24, 1952

I Can't Sleep
   Productions:
      (Off Broadway) Season of 1967-68 in repertory
        (The Dove Company).
   No Reviews.

Night Music
   Productions:
      Opened February 22, 1940 for 20 performances.
      Opened April 8, 1951 for 8 performances.
   Reviews:
      Commonweal 31:435, Mar 8, 1940
           54:58, Apr 27, 1951
      Nation 150:316-7, Mar 2, 1940
      New Republic 102:377, Mar 18, 1940
           124:22, Apr 30, 1951
      New York Theatre Critics' Reviews 1940:385
               1951:300
      New York Times p. 18, Feb 23, 1940
           X, p. 1, Mar 3, 1940
           p. 29, Apr 9, 1951
      New Yorker 27:62+, Apr 21, 1951
      Newsweek 15:42, Mar 4, 1940
      Theatre Arts 24:230-1+, Apr 1940
      Time 35:34, Mar 4, 1940
      Yale Review 30:422, Winter 1941

Paradise Lost
   Productions:
      Opened December 9, 1935 for 73 performances.
   Reviews:
      Catholic World 142:600, Feb 1936
      Commonweal 23:244, Dec 27, 1935
      Forum 95:347, Jun 1936
      Literary Digest 120:20, Dec 21, 1936
      Nation 141:752, Dec 25, 1935

142:27-8, Jan 1, 1936
142:72-3, Jan 15, 1936
New Republic 85:202, Dec 25, 1935
86:283, Apr 15, 1936
New York Times p. 31, Dec 10, 1935
XI, p. 3, Dec 15, 1935
IX, p. 1, Dec 29, 1935
IX, p. 1, Jan 8, 1939
Newsweek 6:39, Dec 21, 1935
Stage 13:2+, Jan 1936
Theatre Arts 20:94-7, Feb 1936
20:465-6, Jun 1936
Time 26:31-2, Dec 23, 1935

Rocket to the Moon
    Productions:
    Opened November 24, 1938 for 131 performances.
    Reviews:
    Catholic World 148:476, Jan 1939
    Commonweal 29:190, Dec 9, 1938
    Forum 101:72, Feb 1939
    Nation 147:600-1, Dec 3, 1938
    New Republic 97:173, Dec 14, 1938
    New York Times p. 18, Nov 25, 1938
                    X, p. 5, Dec 4, 1938
                    p. 30, Mar 23, 1948
                    II, p. 3, Apr 11, 1948
    Newsweek 12:24, Dec 5, 1938
    North American Review 247 no. 1:157-8, Mar 1939
    One Act Play Magazine 2:599-602, Dec 1938
    Theatre Arts 23:11-13, Jan 1939
    Time 32:44, Dec 5, 1938

The Russian People (Adapted from the play by Konstantin
    Simonov)
    Productions:
    Opened December 29, 1942 for 39 performances.
    Reviews:
    Catholic World 156:599, Feb 1943
    Commonweal 37:349, Jan 22, 1943
    Current History ns3:549, Feb 1943
    Nation 156:103, Jan 16, 1943
    New York Theatre Critics' Reviews 1942:127
    New York Times p. 8, Jul 18, 1942
                    p. 17, Dec 30, 1942
    Newsweek 21:66, Jan 11, 1943
    Theatre Arts 27:70-1, Feb 1943
                  27:141-2+, Mar 1943

ODETS, CLIFFORD (cont.)
The Russians (See The Russian People)

Till the Day I Die
Productions:
Opened March 26, 1935 for 136 performances.
Reviews:
Catholic World 141:328+, May 1935
Commonweal 21:682, Apr 12, 1935
Nation 140:428, Apr 10, 1935
New Republic 82:247, Apr 10, 1935
New York Times p. 24, Mar 27, 1935
X, p. 3, Sep 27, 1936
X, p. 10, Jan 10, 1937
Theatre Arts 19:328+, May 1935

Waiting for Lefty
Productions:
Opened March 26, 1935 for 168 performances.
Opened September 9, 1935 for 24 performances.
(Off Broadway) Opened July 19, 1938 for 1 perform-
ance (Furrier's Worker's Union).
(Off Broadway) Season of 1967-68 in repertory
(Roundabout Theatre).
Reviews:
Catholic World 141:215, May 1935
Commonweal 21:682, Apr 12, 1935
Literary Digest 119:18, Apr 6, 1935
Nation 140:427-8, Apr 10, 1935
New Republic 82:247, Apr 10, 1935
New York Times p. 14, Feb 11, 1935
p. 24, Mar 27, 1935
p. 58, Dec 19, 1967
Theatre Arts 19:327-8, May 1935
Time 25:38, Jun 1935

Winter Journey (See The Country Girl)

O'NEILL, EUGENE

Abortion (See The Lost Works of Eugene O'Neill)

Ah, Wilderness
Productions:
Opened October 2, 1933 for 289 performances.
Opened October 2, 1941 for 29 performances.

(Off Broadway) Season of 1952-53 (Equity Library
  Theatre).
Reviews:
  Canadian Forum 14:188, Feb 1934
  Catholic World 138:214-5, Nov 1933
                154:212-213, Nov 1941
  Commonweal 18:620, Oct 27, 1933
                34:613, Oct 17, 1941
  Life 11:59-61, Nov 3, 1941
  Literary Digest 116:24, Oct 28, 1933
                120:22, Dec 28, 1935
  Nation 137:458-9, Oct 18, 1933
        153:381, Oct 18, 1941
  New Outlook 162:42, Nov 1933
  New Republic 76:280, Oct 18, 1933
                85:198, Dec 25, 1935
  New York Theatre Critics' Reviews 1941:282
  New York Times X, p. 1, Sep 10, 1933
                p. 26, Sep 26, 1933
                p. 28, Oct 3, 1933
                X, p. 1, Oct 8, 1933
                p. 26, Mar 20, 1934
                X, p. 2, Mar 25, 1934
                p. 26, Apr 10, 1934
                p. 26, May 1, 1934
                p. 23, Oct 30, 1934
                p. 18, Oct 31, 1934
                IX, p. 3, Jan 13, 1935
                VIII, p. 3, Jan 27, 1935
                p. 25, Aug 20, 1935
                p. 26, May 5, 1936
                IX, p. 2, Jun 7, 1936
                IX, p. 1, Jun 28, 1936
                p. 23, Aug 20, 1940
                p. 26, Oct 3, 1941
                p. 10, Feb 7, 1953
                II, p. 1, Feb 15, 1953
                p. 20, Aug 21, 1954
                II, p. 7, Mar 19, 1967
  Newsweek 2:29, Oct 7, 1933
            3:23, May 12, 1934
            6:38, Dec 14, 1935
  Review of Reviews 89:39, Feb 1934
  Saturday Review 10:217, Oct 28, 1933
  Stage 11:7-9, Nov 1933
  Theatre Arts 17:980-10, Dec 1933
                20:142-3, Feb 1936

O'NEILL, EUGENE (cont.)
Ah, Wilderness (cont.)
                    25:867-8, Dec 1941
          Time 22:26-7, Oct 9, 1933
                    26:44, Dec 9, 1935
          Vanity Fair 41:43+, Nov 1933

All God's Chillun Got Wings
     Productions:
     Opened May 15, 1924 (Provincetown Players).
     Reviews:
     American Mercury 1:129-48, Feb 1924
                      2:113-4, May 1924
     Bookman 59:582, Jul 1924
     Life (NY) 83:18, Mar 27, 1924
     Nation 118:664, Jun 4, 1924
     New Republic 39:22, May 28, 1924
     New York Times p. 22, Mar 3, 1924
                    p. 19, Mar 19, 1924
                    p. 21, Mar 20, 1924
                    IX, p. 5, May 11, 1924
                    p. 15, May 12, 1924
                    p. 22, May 16, 1924
                    VII, p. 1, May 18, 1924
                    p. 9, Aug 19, 1924
                    VII, p. 1, Aug 24, 1924
                    p. 19, Mar 14, 1933
     Theatre Arts 8:497-8, Jul 1924
                  17:423-4, Jun 1933
     Theatre Magazine 40:15, Jul 1924

The Ancient Mariner
     Productions:
     Opened April 6, 1924 for 33 performances.
     Reviews:
     American Mercury 2:243-4, Jun 1924
     Independent 112:259, May 10, 1924
     New York Times p. 15, Apr 7, 1924
                    VIII, p. 1, Apr 13, 1924
     Theatre Arts 8:357-8, Jun 1924
     Theatre Magazine 39:19, Jun 1924

Anna Christie
     Productions:
     Opened November 2, 1921 for 177 performances.
     Opened January 9, 1952 for 29 performances.
     Reviews:

Catholic World 174:462-3, Mar 1952
Commonweal 55:399, Jan 25, 1952
Current Opinion 72:57-66, Jan 1922
Dial 71:724-5, Dec 1921
Dramatic Mirror 84:701, Nov 12, 1921
Hearst 41:45-7+, Mar 1922
Independent 107:326, Dec 3, 1921
Life (NY) 78:18, Nov 24, 1921
Life 32:82-4+, Feb 4, 1952
Literary Digest 77:28-9, May 26, 1923
Metropolitan Magazine 55:36-7, Jun 1922
Nation 113:626, Nov 30, 1921
      120:242, Mar 4, 1925
      174:92, Jan 26, 1952
New Republic 29:20, Nov 30, 1921
New York Theatre Critics' Reviews 1952:395
New York Times p. 22, Nov 3, 1921
      VI, p. 1, Nov 13, 1921
      VI, p. 1, Dec 25, 1921
      III, p. 3, Jan 15, 1922
      p. 16, Apr 11, 1923
      VII, p. 2, Apr 15, 1923
      p. 18, Jun 24, 1924
      p. 33, Jun 11, 1930
      p. 30, Jun 12, 1930
      IX, p. 1, Aug 10, 1941
      p. 33, Jan 10, 1952
      II, p. 1, Jan 20, 1952
      p. 41, Nov 22, 1955
New Yorker 27:48, Feb 2, 1952
Saturday Review 35:32-4, Feb 16, 1952
School and Society 75:107, Feb 16, 1952
Theatre Arts 36:70, Mar 1952
Theatre Magazine 35:29, Jan 1922
      35:220+, Apr 1922
      41:20, Apr 1925
Time 59:73, Jan 21, 1952
(Also see Chris and Chris Christophersen)

Before Breakfast
  Productions:
    Opened March 5, 1929 for 27 performances.
    (Off Broadway) Season of 1957-58 (ANTA).
  Reviews:
    Arts and Decoration 81:104, May 1929
    Drama Magazine 19:200, Apr 29, 1929
    New York Times p. 33, Mar 6, 1929

O'NEILL, EUGENE (cont.)
Before Breakfast (cont.)
                  p. 36, Mar 12, 1958
      Theatre Arts 13:334, May 1924

Beyond the Horizon
    Productions:
        Opened February 2, 1920 for 111 performances.
        Opened November 30, 1926 for 79 performances.
    Reviews:
        Current Opinion 68:339-45, Mar 1920
        Drama 17:136, Feb 1927
        Dramatic Mirror 82:258, Feb 14, 1920
        Independent 101:382, Mar 13, 1920
        Life (NY) 75:322, Feb 19, 1920
        Literary Digest 64:33, Feb 28, 1920
        Nation 110:241-2, Feb 21, 1920
              123:646-7, Dec 15, 1926
        New Republic 25:173-4, Jan 5, 1921
        New York Clipper 68:21, Feb 11, 1920
        New York Times p. 12, Feb 4, 1920
                      VIII, p. 2, Feb 8, 1920
                      p. 9, Mar 10, 1920
                      VI, p. 2, Apr 11, 1920
                      p. 28, May 23, 1926
                      p. 27, Nov 23, 1926
                      p. 24, Dec 1, 1926
                      XI, p. 3, Mar 20, 1938
                      p. 27, Oct 26, 1962
      Player's Magazine 26:46, Nov 1949
      Review 2:185-6, Feb 21, 1920
      Theatre Arts 4:286-9, Oct 1920
              11:86, Feb 1927
      Theatre Magazine 31:185, Mar 1920
                43:185, Feb 1926

Bound East for Cardiff (See S. S. Glencairn for other
    productions.)
    Productions:
        (Off Broadway) Summer of 1916 (Provincetown
        Players).
        (Off Broadway) Opened November 3, 1916 (Province-
        town Players).
    Reviews:
        Commonweal 9:349, Jan 23, 1929
               48:185, Jun 4, 1948
        Current Opinion 61:323, Nov 1916

New Republic 118:27-9, Jun 7, 1948
New York Times p. 31, Nov 4, 1924
                VII, p. 1, Dec 28, 1924
                p. 24, Jan 10, 1929
                IX, p. 1, Jan 27, 1929
                p. 23, Oct 30, 1937
                p. 21, May 21, 1948
                II, p. 1, May 30, 1948
New Yorker 24:43, May 29, 1948
School and Society 67:478, Jun 26, 1948
Theatre Arts 13:172, Mar 1929
           27:400, Jul 1943
Theatre Guild Magazine 9:12, Nov 1931
Theatre Magazine 40:22, Jan 1925
Time 4:14, Nov 17, 1924

*Chris (an early version of Anna Christie).
   Reviews:
       Dramatic Mirror 82:577, Mar 27, 1920

*Chris Christophersen (An early version of Anna
       Christie)
   Reviews:
       New York Times IV, p. 2, Jun 1, 1919

Days Without End
   Productions:
       Opened January 8, 1934 for 57 performances.
   Reviews:
       American Review 2:491-5, Feb 1934
       Catholic World 138:513-17+, Feb 1934
       Christian Century 51:191-2, Feb 7, 1934
                         51:258, Feb 21, 1934
                         73:950, Aug 15, 1956
       Commonweal 19:327-9, Jan 19, 1934
                  19:357, Jan 26, 1934
                  19:469, Feb 23, 1934
                  19:496-7, Mar 2, 1934
                  19:608, Mar 30, 1934
                  20:46, May 11, 1934
       Literary Digest 117:17, Feb 10, 1934
       Living Age 347:554-6, Feb 1935
       Nation 138:110-11, Jan 24, 1934
       New Outlook 163:48, Feb 1934
       New Republic 77:312, Jan 24, 1934
       New York Times p. 19, Jan 9, 1934
                      IX, p. 1, Jan 14, 1934

O'NEILL, EUGENE (cont.)
   Days Without End (cont.)
                              p. 26, Apr 24, 1934
                              p. 23, Feb 5, 1935
                              VIII, p. 1, Mar 3, 1935
            Newsweek 3:34, Jan 20, 1934
            Saturday Review 10:419, Jan 20, 1934
            Stage 11:16-18, Feb 1934
            Theatre Arts 18:167-9+, Mar 1934
            Vanity Fair 42:42, Mar 1934

   Desire Under the Elms
      Productions:
            Opened November 11, 1924 for 208 performances.
            Opened January 16, 1952 for 46 performances.
            (Off Broadway) Opened January 8, 1963 for 380 per-
               formances.
      Reviews:
            America 108:275, Feb 23, 1963
            American Mercury 4:119, Jan 1925
            Bookman 60:621, Jan 1925
            Canadian Magazine 64:74, Apr 1925
            Catholic World 120:519-21, Jan 1925
                           174:464, Mar 1952
            Commonweal 55:423, Feb 1, 1952
                        77:543, Feb 15, 1963
            Dial 78:82, Jan 1925
            Independent 114:51, Jan 10, 1925
            Life (NY) 84:18, Dec 11, 1924
            Life 32:82-4, Feb 4, 1952
            Literary Digest 86:23-4, Aug 8, 1925
            Nation 119:578-80, Nov 26, 1924
                   120:346, Apr 1, 1925
                   122:548-9, May 19, 1926
                   196:106-7, Feb 2, 1963
            New Republic 41:44, Dec 3, 1924
                         148:26, Feb 2, 1963
            New York Theatre Critics' Reviews 1952:386
            New York Times p. 20, Nov 12, 1924
                           VIII, p. 5, Dec 7, 1924
                           p. 19, Feb 20, 1926
                           p. 15, Apr 10, 1926
                           p. 25, Apr 15, 1926
                           p. 8, Apr 16, 1926
                           p. 23, Aug 3, 1930
                           IX, p. 1, Nov 12, 1933
                           IX, p. 2, Feb 4, 1940
                           p. 45, Nov 22, 1951

p. 23, Jan 17, 1952
p. 17, May 23, 1952
II, p. 5, Mar 2, 1958
p. 5, Jan 11, 1963
New Yorker 27:53, Jan 26, 1952
38:62+, Jan 19, 1963
Newsweek 39:83, Jan 28, 1952
61:57, Jan 21, 1963
Saturday Review 35:32-4, Feb 16, 1952
46:32, Jan 26, 1963
School and Society 75:106-7, Feb 16, 1952
Survey 53:421-2, Jan 1, 1925
Theatre Arts 9:3-15, Jan 1925
36:70, Mar 1952
36:31-3, Apr 1952
47:10-11, Feb 1963
Theatre Guild Magazine 9:14, Nov 1931
9:12, Jan 1932
Theatre Magazine 41:22, Jan 1925
41:26+, Jun 1925
Time 59:44, Jan 28, 1952
81:42, Jan 18, 1963

Diff'rent
Productions:
(Off Broadway) Opened December 27, 1920 (Province-
town Players).
Opened February 4, 1921 for 100 performances.
(Off Broadway) Season of 1924-25.
Opened January 25, 1938 for 4 performances (WPA
Federal Theatre Project).
(Off Broadway) Opened October 17, 1961 for 88 per-
formances.
Reviews:
Bookman 52:565, Feb 1921
Commonweal 1:466, Mar 4, 1925
Independent 105:153, Feb 12, 1921
Nation 193:459-60, Dec 2, 1961
New Republic 42:45, Mar 4, 1925
New York Clipper 68:19, Jan 5, 1921
New York Times p. 8, Dec 29, 1920
p. 19, Feb 11, 1925
VII, p. 1, Mar 1, 1925
p. 23, Oct 30, 1937
II, p. 10, Nov 21, 1937
p. 26, Jan 26, 1938
p. 52, Oct 18, 1961

O'NEILL, EUGENE (cont.)
    Diff'rent (cont.)
        New Yorker 37:137, Oct 28, 1961
        Review 4:207-9, Mar 2, 1921
        Theatre Arts 45:70-1, Dec 1961
        Theatre Magazine 33:261, Apr 1921
        Time 5:13, Feb 23, 1925
        Vanity Fair 16:33, Apr 1921
        Weekly Review 4:207-9, Mar 2, 1921

The Dreamy Kid
    Productions:
        (Off Broadway) Opened October 31, 1919 (Province-
        town Players).
        Opened February 11, 1925 for 28 performances.
    Reviews:
        New York Times VIII, p. 2, Nov 9, 1919

Dynamo
    Productions:
        Opened February 11, 1929 for 50 performances.
    Reviews:
        American Mercury 16:119-20, Jan 1929
                       16:373-8, Mar 1929
        Arts and Decoration 30:72, Apr 1929
        Bookman 69:179-80, Apr 1929
        Catholic World 129:80-2, Apr 1929
        Commonweal 9:489-90, Feb 27, 1929
        Dial 86:349-50, Apr 1929
        Drama 19:201+, Apr 1929
        Life (NY) 93:24+, Mar 8, 1929
        Literary Digest 100:21-2, Mar 2, 1929
        Nation 128:264-6, Feb 27, 1929
        New Republic 58:43-4, Feb 27, 1929
        New York Times p. 22, Feb 12, 1929
                      VIII, p. 4, Mar 3, 1929
        Outlook 151:331, Feb 27, 1929
        Review of Reviews 79:158-60, Apr 1929
        Theatre Arts 13:245-7, Apr 1929
        Theatre Magazine 49:45, May 1929
        Vanity Fair 31:62+, Feb 1929
        Vogue 73:61+, Mar 30, 1929

The Emperor Jones
    Productions:
        Opened November 1, 1920 for 204 performances.
        Opened February 11, 1925 for 28 performances.

Opened February 16, 1926 for 35 performances.
Opened November 10, 1926 for 61 performances.
(Off Broadway) Opened January 16, 1945 in reper-
tory
Reviews:
Bookman 52:565, Feb 1921
Current Opinion 70:55-64, Jan 1921
Drama 14:132, Jan 1924
Dramatist 14:1176-7, Jul 1928
Everybody's 54:134-48, Apr 1926
Independent 105:158-9, Feb 12, 1921
Literary Digest 79:24-5, Dec 29, 1923
Nation 112:189, Feb 2, 1921
New York Clipper 68:19, Nov 24, 1920
New York Times VII, p. 1, Nov 7, 1920
                  p. 24, Nov 1, 1923
                  p. 18, Jan 10, 1924
                  p. 18, May 7, 1924
                  p. 16, Feb 12, 1925
                  p. 20, Sep 11, 1925
                  p. 11, Feb 17, 1926
                  p. 28, May 18, 1926
                  p. 23, Nov 11, 1926
                VII, p. 4, Feb 13, 1927
                  p. 10, Apr 1, 1930
                  p. 24, Aug 11, 1936
                  p. 25, Jun 20, 1939
                  p. 18, Jan 17, 1945
                II, p. 1, Jan 28, 1945
                  p. 20, Aug 6, 1964
                II, p. 5, Aug 16, 1964
Outlook 126:710-11, Dec 22, 1920
Review of Reviews 3:567-8, Dec 8, 1920
Theatre Arts 5:5-7, Jan 1921
                17:172+, Mar 1933
Theatre Magazine 33:8, Jan 1921
Weekly Review 3:567-8, Dec 8, 1920

Exorcism
   Productions:
      (Off Broadway) Opened March 26, 1920 (Province-
town Players).
   Reviews:
      New York Times VI, p. 6, Apr 4, 1920

The First Man
   Productions:

O'NEILL, EUGENE (cont.)
  The First Man (cont.)
        Opened March 4, 1922 for 27 performances.
     Reviews:
        Bookman 52:284, May 1922
        Freeman 5:184-5, May 3, 1922
        New York Clipper 70:22, Mar 15, 1922
        New York Times p. 9, Mar 6, 1922
        Theatre Arts 6:182, Jul 1922
        Theatre Magazine 35:308, May 1922

  The Fountain
     Productions:
        Opened December 10, 1925 for 28 performances.
     Reviews:
        American Mercury 7:247-9, Feb 1926
        Arts and Decoration 24:84-6, Feb 1926
        Bookman 62:704-5, Feb 1926
        Commonweal 3:189, Dec 23, 1925
        Dial 80:168-9, Feb 1926
        Drama 16:175-6, Feb 1926
        Life (NY) 86:18, Dec 31, 1925
        New Republic 45:160-1, Dec 30, 1925
        New York Times p. 26, Dec 11, 1925
        New Yorker 1:17, Dec 19, 1925
        Theatre Arts 10:77, Feb 1926
        Theatre Magazine 43:15, Feb 1926
        Vanity Fair 25:118, Feb 1926
        Vogue 67:60-61, Feb 1, 1926

  Gold
     Productions:
        Opened June 1, 1921 for 13 performances.
     Reviews:
        Bookman 53:528-30, Aug 1921
        Dramatic Mirror 83:1001, Jun 11, 1921
        Dramatist 13:1095-7, Jan 1922
        Independent 105:633, Jun 18, 1921
        Life (NY) 77:876, Jun 16, 1921
        Nation 112:902, Jun 22, 1921
        New York Clipper 69:19, Jun 8, 1921
        New York Times p. 14, Jun 2, 1921
        Review 4:584-5, Jun 18, 1921
        Theatre Magazine 34:97, Aug 1921

  Great God Brown
     Productions:

Opened January 23, 1926 for 271 performances.
Opened October 6, 1959 for 32 performances.
Reviews:
America 102:139-40, Oct 31, 1959
American Mercury 7:503-4, Apr 1926
Arts and Decoration 24:62, Mar 1926
Catholic World 122:805-7, Mar 1926
Commonweal 3:384, Feb 10, 1926
Drama 16:206, Mar 1926
Dramatist 17:1307-9, Jul 1926
Independent 116:275, Mar 6, 1926
Life (NY) 87:20, Feb 11, 1926
Nation 122:164-5, Feb 10, 1926
            189:259-60, Oct 24, 1959
New Republic 45:329-30, Feb 10, 1926
                   141:29, Oct 19, 1959
New York Theatre Critics' Reviews 1959:282
New York Times p. 26, Jan 25, 1926
                   VII, p. 1, Jan 31, 1926
                   VIII, p. 2, Feb 14, 1926
                   p. 25, Apr 20, 1926
                   VII, p. 1, Jul 24, 1927
                   IX, p. 1, Jun 28, 1936
                   II, p. 1, Oct 4, 1959
                   p. 48, Oct 7, 1959
                   II, p. 1, Oct 18, 1959
New Yorker 1:26, Feb 6, 1926
               35:131-3, Oct 17, 1959
Newsweek 54:80, Oct 19, 1959
Survey 56:43, Apr 1, 1926
Theatre Arts 10:145-6, Mar 1926
                43:88, Dec 1959
Theatre Magazine 43:18, Apr 1926
                      44:26+, Nov 1926
Time 74:56, Oct 19, 1959
Vanity Fair 26:78, Apr 1926
Vogue 67:106+, Mar 15, 1926

The Hairy Ape
   Productions:
      Opened March 9, 1922 for 108+ performances.
   Reviews:
      Bookman 55:284, May 1922
      Catholic World 116:714, Feb 1923
      Century 104:748-9+, Sep 1922
      Current Opinion 72:768-76, Jun 1922
      Dial 72:548-9, May 1922

O'NEILL, EUGENE (cont.)
The Hairy Ape (cont.)
Dramatist 13:1117-8, Jul 1922
Freeman 5:449, Jul 19, 1922
Independent 110:282-4, Apr 28, 1923
Life (NY) 79:18, Mar 30, 1922
Literary Digest 77:35, Apr 7, 1923
Living Age 337:417-18, Dec 1, 1929
Nation 114:349-50, Mar 22, 1922
New Republic 30:112-13, Mar 22, 1922
New York Clipper 70:22, Mar 22, 1922
New York Times p. 18, Mar 10, 1922
VI, p. 1, Apr 16, 1922
VI, p. 1, Apr 23, 1922
VIII, p. 4, Feb 19, 1928
p. 27, Sep 23, 1929
p. 29, May 12, 1931
Theatre Arts 6:182, Jul 1922
18:598, Aug 1934
Theatre Magazine 35:305, May 1922
35:370, Jun 1922
36:80+, Aug 1922

Hughie
Productions:
Opened December 22, 1964 for 51 performances.
Reviews:
Commonweal 70:187-8, May 15, 1959
81:518, Jan 15, 1965
Nation 200:65, Jan 18, 1965
New York Theatre Critics' Reviews 1964:99
New York Times p. 36, Sep 18, 1958
p. 24, Sep 19, 1953
VII, p. 5, Apr 19, 1959
p. 48, Oct 15, 1959
p. 29, Jun 11, 1963
p. 21, Dec 23, 1964
New Yorker 40:58, Jan 2, 1965
Newsweek 65:52, Jan 4, 1965
Saturday Review 41:27, Oct 4, 1958
48:40, Jan 16, 1965
Theatre Arts 43:14-15, Aug 1959
Time 85:53, Jan 1, 1965

The Iceman Cometh
Productions:
Opened October 9, 1946 for 136 performances.

(Off Broadway) Season of 1955-56.
Reviews:
America 95:251, Jun 2, 1956
Arizona Quarterly 3:293-300, Winter 1947
Atlantic 178:64-6, Nov 1946
Catholic World 164:168-9, Nov 1946
                183:310, Jul 1956
Commonweal 45:44-6, Oct 25, 1946
             64:515, Aug 24, 1956
Life 21:109-11, Oct 28, 1946
Nation 163:481, Oct 26, 1946
      182:458, May 26, 1956
New Republic 115:517-8, Oct 21, 1946
New York Theatre Critics' Reviews 1946:315
New York Times VI, p. 27, Sep 22, 1946
                p. 31, Oct 10, 1946
                II, p. 1, Oct 13, 1946
                VI, p. 22, Oct 13, 1946
                II, p. 1, Oct 20, 1946
                II, p. 1, Oct 27, 1946
                II, p. 1, Nov 10, 1946
                p. 35, Jun 9, 1948
                p. 38, May 9, 1956
                II, p. 1, May 20, 1956
                VI, p. 31, Nov 11, 1956
                p. 18, Jan 30, 1958
                II, p. 1, Oct 8, 1959
                p. 58, Apr 1, 1968
New York Times Magazine p. 22-3, Oct 13, 1946
New Yorker 22:53-7, Oct 19, 1946
          32:72+, May 26, 1956
Newsweek 28:92, Oct 21, 1946
Reporter 14:35-6, Jun 28, 1956
Saturday Review 29:26-8+, Oct 19, 1946
               39:24, May 26, 1956
Theatre Arts 30:635-6, Nov 1946
           30:684+, Dec 1946
           31:31, Jun 1947
           40:72-3, Oct 1956
Time 48:71-2+, Oct 21, 1946

'Ile
Productions:
Opened April 18, 1918 in repertory (Greenwich
Village Players).
Reviews:
Dramatist 10:960, Jul 1919

O'NEILL, EUGENE (cont.)
  'Ile (cont.)
      New York Times p. 13, Apr 19, 1918
                    IV, p. 2, May 11, 1919
      Theatre Magazine 27:356, Jun 1918
                    35:270, Apr 1922

In the Zone (See S. S. Glencairn for other productions)
    Productions:
      Opened October 31, 1917 in repertory (Washington
        Square Players).
    Reviews:
      Commonweal 9:349, Jan 23, 1929
                  48:185, Jun 4, 1948
      Current Opinion 65:159-62, Sep 1918
      New Republic 118:27-9, Jun 7, 1948
      New York Times p. 13, Nov 1, 1917
                    p. 31, Nov 4, 1924
                    VII, p. 1, Dec 28, 1924
                    p. 24, Jan 10, 1929
                    IX, p. 1, Jan 27, 1929
                    p. 23, Oct 30, 1937
                    p. 21, May 21, 1948
                    II, p. 1, May 30, 1948
      New Yorker 24:43, May 29, 1948
      School and Society 67:478, Jun 26, 1948
      Theatre Arts 13:172, Mar 1929
                   27:400, Jul 1943
      Theatre Guild Magazine 9:12, Nov 1931
      Theatre Magazine 26:352, Dec 1917
                       40:22, Jan 1925
      Time 4:14, Nov 17, 1924

*Lazarus Laughed
      (Opened April 9, 1928 in Pasadena, California for
        28 performances.)
    Reviews:
      Arts and Decoration 27:68-9, Sep 1927
      Catholic World 167:264, Jun 1948
      Commonweal 48:674, Apr 30, 1948
      Drama 18:244-6, May 1928
      Nation 126:19, Jan 4, 1928
      New York Times VIII, p. 1, Sep 11, 1927
                    p. 33, Apr 10, 1928
                    IX, p. 2, Apr 22, 1928
                    p. 19, Nov 19, 1928
      Review of Reviews 78:439-40, Oct 1928

362

Theatre Arts 12:447-8, Jun 1928
Theatre Magazine 48:42-4, Jul 1928

Long Day's Journey Into Night
  Productions:
    Opened November 7, 1956 for 390 performances.
    Opened May 15, 1962 for 2 performances (Royal
      Dramatic Theatre of Sweden).
  Reviews:
    America 95:141, May 5, 1956
    Christian Century 74:235, Feb 20, 1957
    Catholic World 184:306, Jan 1957
    Commonweal 63:614-5, Mar 16, 1956
              64:515, Aug 24, 1956
              65:467-8, Feb 1, 1957
    Harpers 212:96, Mar 1956
    Life 40:93-4+, Mar 12, 1956
        41:123-4+, Nov 19, 1956
    Madamoiselle 44:186, Feb 1957
    Nation 183:466, Nov 24, 1956
    New Republic 134:20, Mar 5, 1956
    New York Theatre Critics' Reviews 1956:217
                                       1962:285
    New York Times p. 26, Jan 5, 1956
                   p. 12, Feb 11, 1956
                   II, p. 1, Feb 19, 1956
                   VI, p. 56, Feb 19, 1956
                   VI, p. 28, Sep 16, 1956
                   p. 40, Oct 17, 1956
                   II, p. 1, Nov 4, 1956
                   p. 47, Nov 8, 1956
                   II, p. 1, Nov 18, 1956
                   II, p. 3, Nov 25, 1956
                   II, p. 1, Mar 1957
                   p. 14, Jul 3, 1957
                   p. 9, Jul 6, 1957
                   II, p. 1, Aug 11, 1957
                   p. 40, Sep 9, 1958
                   p. 21, Sep 26, 1958
                   p. 42, Mar 10, 1959
                   p. 30, Apr 29, 1959
                   p. 35, May 16, 1962
                   p. 85, Sep 30, 1962
                   p. 25, Jun 27, 1963
    New York Times Magazine p. 56, Feb 19, 1956
                            p. 74, Oct 21, 1956
    New Yorker 32:120+, Nov 24, 1956

O'NEILL, EUGENE (cont.)
Long Day's Journey Into Night (cont.)
Newsweek 47:92, Feb 20, 1956
48:117, Nov 19, 1956
Reporter 15:38-9, Dec 13, 1956
Saturday Review 39:15-16, Feb 25, 1956
39:58, Oct 20, 1956
39:30-1, Nov 24, 1956
Theatre Arts 40:25+, Apr 1956
40:65, May 1956
41:25-6, Jan 1957
Time 67:89, Feb 20, 1956
68:57, Nov 19, 1956
Vogue 128:105, Nov 15, 1956

Long Voyage Home (See S.S. Glencairn for other pro-
ductions)
Productions:
(Off Broadway) Opened November 2, 1917 (Province-
town Players).
(Off Broadway) Opened December 4, 1961 for 32 per
formances.
Reviews:
Commonweal 9:349, Jan 23, 1929
48:185, Jun 4, 1948
New Republic 118:27-9, Jun 7, 1948
New York Times p. 31, Nov 4, 1924
VII, p. 1, Dec 28, 1924
p. 24, Jan 10, 1929
IX, p. 1, Jan 27, 1929
p. 23, Oct 30, 1937
p. 21, May 21, 1948
II, p. 1, May 30, 1948
p. 49, Dec 5, 1961
New Yorker 24:43, May 29, 1948
School and Society 67:478, Jun 26, 1948
Theatre Arts 13:172, Mar 1929
27:400, Jul 1943
Theatre Guild Magazine 9:12, Nov 1931
Theatre Magazine 40:22, Jan 1925
Time 4:14, Nov 17, 1924

The Lost Works of Eugene O'Neill ("Abortion," "Movie
Man," "Sniper")
Productions:
(Off Broadway) Season of 1959-60.
Reviews:
New York Times p. 40, Oct 28, 1959

Marco Millions
  Productions:
    Opened January 9, 1928 for 92 performances.
    Opened March 3, 1930 for 8 performances.
    (Off Broadway) Season of 1938-39 (Marionette Pro-
      duction).
    Opened February 20, 1964 for 38 performances
      (Repertory Theatre of Lincoln Center).
  Reviews:
    America 110:656, May 9, 1964
    American Mercury 8:499-505, Aug 1926
    Arts and Decoration 28:62, Mar 1928
    Commonweal 80:89, Apr 10, 1964
    Drama 18:170, Mar 1928
    Dramatist 18:1341-2, Jul 1927
    Life (NY) 91:19, Jan 26, 1928
    Literary Digest 96:26-7, Feb 4, 1928
    Motion Picture Classic 27:31+, Apr 1928
    Nation 124:562-4, May 18, 1927
           126:104-5, Jan 25, 1928
           124:562-4, May 18, 1927
           126:104-5, Jan 25, 1928
           198:249-50, Mar 9, 1964
    New Republic 53:272-3, Jan 25, 1928
    New York Theatre Critics' Reviews 1964:338
    New York Times VIII, p. 2, Jan 8, 1928
                    p. 28, Jan 10, 1928
                    VIII, p. 1, Jan 22, 1928
                    VIII, p. 2, Jan 22, 1928
                    IX, p. 2, Apr 29, 1928
                    p. 24, Mar 4, 1930
                    p. 36, Nov 24, 1938
                    IX, p. 3, Jan 15, 1939
                    II, p. 1, Feb 16, 1964
                    p. 33, Feb 21, 1964
                    II, p. 1, Mar 1, 1964
    New Yorker 40:106+, Feb 29, 1964
    Newsweek 63:56, Mar 2, 1965
    Saturday Review 4:590, Feb 11, 1928
                    47:23, Mar 7, 1964
    Theatre Arts 12:163-6, Mar 1928
                 23:175, Mar 1939
    Theatre Magazine 47:38, Mar 1928
                     47:45, Apr 1928
                     52:49, Aug 1930
                     53:42, Feb 1931
    Time 83:61, Feb 28, 1964
    Vanity Fair 30:52-3, Apr 1928

O'NEILL, EUGENE (cont.)
Marco Millions (cont.)
Vogue 71:82-3, Mar 1, 1928
143:40, Apr 1, 1964
Yale Review 17:173-4, Oct 1927

A Moon for the Misbegotten
Productions:
Opened May 2, 1957 for 68 performances.
(Off Broadway) Opened June 12, 1968 for 199 performances.
Reviews:
America 97:270, May 25, 1957
Catholic World 185:308-9, Jul 1957
Christian Century 74:657, May 22, 1957
Commonweal 66:541, Aug 30, 1957
88:504-5, Jul 26, 1968
Life 42:109-10+, Jun 24, 1957
Nation 178:409, May 8, 1954
184:446, May 18, 1957
New York Theatre Critics' Reviews 1957:277
New York Times p. 16, Feb 21, 1947
p. 29, Mar 12, 1947
II, p. 1, Aug 24, 1952
II, p. 1, Apr 28, 1957
p. 21, May 3, 1957
II, p. 1, May 12, 1957
p. 10, Jun 7, 1958
p. 14, Jan 22, 1960
p. 55, Jun 13, 1968
New Yorker 33:84+, May 11, 1957
Newsweek 49:70, May 13, 1957
Saturday Review 40:34, May 18, 1957
51:40, Jun 29, 1968
Theatre Arts 36:6-7+, Sep 1952
41:67-8+, May 1957
41:12-13, Jul 1957
Time 49:47, Mar 3, 1947
69:91, May 13, 1957
91:67, Jun 21, 1968
Vogue 152:70, Sep 15, 1968

Moon of the Caribees (See S.S. Glencairn for other productions)
Productions:
(Off Broadway) Opened December 20, 1918 (Province-town Players).

Reviews:
   Commonweal 9:349, Jan 23, 1929
                48:185, Jun 4, 1948
   New Republic 118:27-9, Jun 7, 1948
   New York Times p. 13, Dec 21, 1918
                  p. 31, Nov 4, 1924
                  VII, p. 1, Dec 28, 1924
                  p. 24, Jan 10, 1929
                  IX, p. 1, Jan 27, 1929
                  p. 23, Oct 30, 1937
                  p. 21, May 21, 1948
                  II, p. 1, May 30, 1948
   New Yorker 24:43, May 29, 1948
   School and Society 67:478, Jun 26, 1948
   Theatre Arts 13:172, Mar 1929
                27:400, Jul 1943
   Theatre Guild Magazine 9:12, Nov 1931
   Theatre Magazine 34:60, Jul 1921
                    40:22, Jan 1925
   Time 4:14, Nov 17, 1924

More Stately Mansions
   Productions:
   Opened October 31, 1967 for 142 performances.
   Reviews:
   America 117:622, Nov 18, 1967
   Commonweal 87:335-6, Dec 8, 1967
   Life 63:63-4, Oct 13, 1967
   Nation 205:538-40, Nov 20, 1967
   National Review 20:43-4, Jan 15, 1968
   New York Theatre Critics' Reviews 1967:230
                                     1967:234
   New York Times p. 1, Mar 18, 1957
                  p. 35, Mar 21, 1957
                  p. 16, Nov 10, 1962
                  p. 82, Nov 11, 1962
                  p. 41, Feb 23, 1967
                  p. 32, Feb 28, 1967
                  II, p. 1, Oct 29, 1967
                  p. 40, Nov 1, 1967
                  II, p. 1, Nov 12, 1967
   New Yorker 43:127, Nov 11, 1967
   Newsweek 70:125, Nov 13, 1967
   Reporter 37:34-5, Nov 30, 1967
   Saturday Review 45:26, Dec 1, 1962
                   47:46, May 30, 1964
                   50:26+, Nov 18, 1967

O'NEILL, EUGENE (cont.)
  More Stately Mansions (cont.)
          Time 90:76-7, Sep 22, 1967
          Vogue 151:62, Jan 1, 1968

  Mourning Becomes Electra
      Productions:
          Opened October 26, 1931 for 150 performances.
          Opened May 9, 1932 for 16 performances.
      Reviews:
          Arts and Decoration 36:52+, Jan 1932
          Bookman 73:440-5, Dec 1931
                  75:290-1, Jun 1932
          Catholic World 134:330-1, Dec 1931
          Commonweal 15:46-7, Nov 11, 1931
                  15:386, Feb 3, 1932
          Dramatist 23:1439-46, Jan 1932
          Life (NY) 98:19, Nov 13, 1931
          Literary Digest 111:18-19, Nov 21, 1931
          Living Age 342:276, May 1932
          Nation 133:551-2, Nov 18, 1931
                  134:210-11, Feb 17, 1932
          New Republic 68:352-5, Nov 11, 1931
          New York Times p. 25, Sep 9, 1931
                         p. 26, Oct 13, 1931
                         p. 22, Oct 27, 1931
                         p. 16, Oct 31, 1931
                         VIII, p. 1, Nov 1, 1931
                         p. 25, May 10, 1932
                         VIII, p. 1, May 22, 1932
                         p. 26, Jun 14, 1932
                         XI, p. 3, Dec 12, 1937
                         X, p. 1, Jan 30, 1938
                         II, p. 1, Sep 7, 1969
          Outlook 159:343, Nov 11, 1931
          Player's Magazine 8:11, Jan-Feb 1932
          Saturday Review 8:257-8, Nov 7, 1931
          Theatre Arts 16:13-16, Jan 1932
                  22:101-7, Feb 1938
          Theatre Guild Magazine 9:14-19, Dec 1931
                                 9:2, Jan 1932
                                 9:10, Mar 1932
          Town and Country 86:46, Dec 1, 1931
          Vanity Fair 37:24+, Jan 1932
                  37:46-7+, Jan 1932
          Vogue 79:56-7+, Jan 1, 1932

Movie Man (See The Lost Works of Eugene O'Neill)

The Rope
    Productions:
        (Off Broadway) Opened April 26, 1918 (Province-
        town Players).
    Reviews:
        Dramatic Mirror 78:730, May 25, 1918
        New York Times p. 11, May 14, 1918
        Theatre Magazine 27:358, Jun 1918

S. S. Glencairn ("Moon of the Caribees," "In the Zone,"
    "Bound East for Cardiff," "Long Voyage Home")
    Productions:
        Opened November 3, 1924 for 105 performances.
        Opened January 9, 1929 for 90 performances.
        Opened October 29, 1937 for 68 performances
        (WPA Federal Theatre Project).
        Opened May 20, 1948 for 14 performances.
    Reviews:
        Commonweal 9:349, Jan 23, 1929
                48:185, Jun 4, 1948
        New Republic 118:27-9, Jun 7, 1948
        New York Times p. 31, Nov 4, 1924
                VII, p. 1, Dec 28, 1924
                p. 24, Jan 10, 1929
                IX, p. 1, Jan 27, 1929
                p. 23, Oct 30, 1937
                p. 21, May 21, 1948
                II, p. 1, May 30, 1948
        New Yorker 24:43, May 29, 1948
        School and Society 67:478, Jun 26, 1948
        Theatre Arts 13:172, Mar 1929
                27:400, Jul 1943
        Theatre Guild Magazine 9:12, Nov 1931
        Theatre Magazine 40:22, Jan 1925
        Time 4:14, Nov 17, 1924

Sniper (See The Lost Works of Eugene O'Neill)

Strange Interlude
    Productions:
        Opened January 30, 1928 for 426 performances.
        Opened Mar 11, 1963 for 97 performances.
    Reviews:
        America 108:594, Apr 20, 1963
        American Mercury 11:499-506, Aug 1927

O'NEILL, EUGENE (cont.)
Strange Interlude (cont.)
<u>Arts and Decoration</u> 28:65, Apr 1928
Catholic World 127:77-80, Apr 1928
Commonweal 78:72-3, Apr 12, 1963
Dial 84:348-51, Apr 1928
Drama 18:170-71, Mar 1928
      19:174, Mar 1929
Dramatist 19:1356-8, Jan 1928
Life (NY) 91:21, Feb 16, 1928
Literary Digest 96:26-7, Feb 25, 1928
      103:19-20, Oct 19, 1929
Nation 126:192, Feb 15, 1928
     196:274-5, Mar 30, 1963
New Republic 53:349-50, Feb 15, 1928
     148:28-9, Mar 30, 1963
New York Theatre Critics' Reviews 1963:317
New York Times p. 28, Jan 31, 1928
     VIII, p. 1, Feb 5, 1928
     p. 24, Apr 30, 1928
     IX, p. 1, May 13, 1928
     IV, p. 4, May 20, 1928
     p. 29, Jun 27, 1928
     IX, p. 1, Jan 27, 1929
     p. 18, Jan 30, 1929
     p. 14, Apr 6, 1929
     IX, p. 2, Oct 13, 1929
     p. 1, Oct 18, 1929
     III, p. 2, Nov 3, 1929
     VIII, p. 1, Feb 22, 1931
     VIII, p. 4, Mar 29, 1931
     p. 19, Jan 5, 1937
     p. 5, Mar 13, 1963
     p. 34, Jun 18, 1963
New Yorker 39:73, Mar 23, 1963
Newsweek 61:97, Mar 25, 1963
Outlook 148:304-5, Feb 22, 1928
Overland ns 87:220, Jul 1929
Saturday Review 4:590, Feb 11, 1928
     4:641, Mar 3, 1928
     4:357-8, Sep 22, 1928
     46:36, Mar 30, 1963
Theatre Arts 12:237-40, Apr 1928
     15:286-9, Apr 1931
     47:12-13, May 1963
Theatre Magazine 47:39, Apr 1928
     53:25, Apr 1931

Time 81:74, Mar 22, 1963
Vanity Fair 30:52-3, Apr 1928
Virginia Quarterly Review 5:133-6, Jan 1929
Vogue 71:82-3+, Apr 1, 1928
    72:62, Jul 1, 1928

The Straw
  Productions:
    Opened November 10, 1921 for 20 performances.
  Reviews:
    Bookman 54:463-4, Jan 1922
    Drama 12:152, Feb 1922
    Dramatic Mirror 84:737, Nov 19, 1921
    Independent 107:236, Dec 3, 1921
    Life (NY) 78:18, Dec 8, 1921
    Nation 113:626, Nov 30, 1921
    New York Clipper 69:20, Nov 16, 1921
    New York Times VI, p. 1, May 8, 1921
                    p. 16, Nov 11, 1921
    Theatre Arts 6:6, Jan 1922
    Theatre Magazine 35:31, Jan 1922

A Touch of the Poet
  Productions:
    Opened October 2, 1958 for 284 performances.
    Opened May 2, 1967 for 5 performances (National
      Repertory Theatre).
  Reviews:
    America 100:118, Oct 25, 1958
    Catholic World 188:243-4, Dec 1958
    Christian Century 75:252-4, Feb 26, 1958
                      75:1401-2, Dec 3, 1958
    Commonweal 69:151-3, Nov 7, 1958
    Life 42:116, Jun 24, 1957
    Nation 187:298-9, Oct 25, 1958
    New Republic 136:21, Jun 3, 1957
                 139:23, Oct 20, 1958
    New York Theatre Critics' Reviews 1958:282
                                      1967:305
    New York Times p. 12, Mar 30, 1957
                   II, p. 3, Apr 7, 1957
                   II, p. 1, Sep 22, 1957
                   VII, p. 1, Sep 22, 1957
                   p. 23, Oct 3, 1958
                   II, p. 1, Oct 12, 1958
                   p. 85, Sep 30, 1962
                   p. 38, May 3, 1967

O'NEILL, EUGENE (cont.)
  A Touch of the Poet (cont.)
          New York Times Magazine p. 49, Apr 28, 1957
          New Yorker 34:87, Oct 11, 1958
          Newsweek 49:66, Apr 8, 1957
                  52:112, Oct 13, 1958
          Reporter 19:37-8, Nov 13, 1958
          Saturday Review 40:24, Apr 13, 1957
                      40:21+, Sep 21, 1957
                      41:56, Oct 18, 1958
          Theatre Arts 42:16-17+, Oct 1958
                      42:9-10, Dec 1958
          Time 69:77, Apr 8, 1957
                70:102+, Sep 30, 1957
                72:89, Oct 13, 1958
          Vogue 132:105, Nov 15, 1958

  Welded
      Productions:
        Opened Mar 17, 1924 for 24 performances.
      Reviews:
        American Mercury 2:115-16, May 1924
        Bookman 59:332, May 1924
        Dramatist 15:1208-10, Apr 1924
        Life (NY) 83:26, Apr 3, 1924
        Nation 118:376-7, Apr 2, 1924
        New York Times VIII, p. 2, Mar 9, 1924
                        p. 24, Mar 18, 1924
                        VIII, p. 1, Mar 23, 1924
                        VIII, p. 2, Mar 23, 1924
                        p. 17, Mar 13, 1965
        Outlook 137:238, Jun 11, 1924
        Theatre Arts 8:497-8, Jul 1924
        Theatre Magazine 39:16, May 1924

  Where the Cross Is Made
      Productions:
        (Off Broadway) Opened November 22, 1918 (Provinc
          town Players).
      Reviews:
        New York Times I, part 2, p. 5, Jun 3, 1923

OSBORN, PAUL

  A Bell for Adano (Based on John Hersey's novel)
      Productions:
        Opened Dec 6, 1944 for 304 performances.

Reviews:
Catholic World 160:356, Jan 1945
Commonweal 41:254, Dec 22, 1944
Hollywood Quarterly 1:38-9, Oct 1945
Life 17:76-80+, Dec 18, 1944
Nation 159:781, Dec 23, 1944
    161:67, Jul 21, 1945
New Republic 111:867, Dec 25, 1944
New York Theatre Critics' Reviews 1944:65
New York Times p. 24, Nov 10, 1944
    VI, p. 42, Nov 26, 1944
    II, p. 1, Dec 3, 1944
    p. 21, Dec 7, 1944
    p. 24, Dec 28, 1944
    p. 31, Sep 20, 1945
New Yorker 20:40+, Dec 16, 1944
Newsweek 24:78, Dec 18, 1944
    26:101, Jul 16, 1945
Photoplay 27:19, Aug 1945
Saturday Review 27:18-19, Dec 23, 1944
Theatre Arts 29:69-72+, Feb 1945
    29:583, Oct 1945
Time 44:75+, Dec 18, 1944
    46:86, Jul 2, 1945

Hotbed
Productions:
Opened November 8, 1928 for 19 performances.
Reviews:
New York Times p. 20, Nov 10, 1928
Theatre Magazine 49:46, Jan 1929

The Innocent Voyage (Adapted from a novel by Richard
    Hughes)
Productions:
Opened November 15, 1943 for 40 performances.
Reviews:
Catholic World 158:393-4, Jan 1944
Commonweal 39:172+, Dec 3, 1943
Nation 157:620, Nov 27, 1943
New Republic 109:746, Nov 29, 1943
New York Theatre Critics' Reviews 1943:224
New York Times p. 27, Nov 16, 1943
Player's Magazine 20:13, Jan 1944
    23:back cover, Nov-Dec 1946
    24:191, May 1948
Publishers' Weekly 144:2176, Dec 11, 1943

OSBORN, PAUL (cont.)
The Innocent Voyage (cont.)
        Theatre Arts 28:10+, Jan 1944
        Time 42:42, Dec 6, 1943
        Vogue 102:32-3, Dec 15, 1943

A Ledge (Suggested by Henry Holt's short story)
    Productions:
        Opened November 18, 1929 for 16 performances.
    Reviews:
        New York Times p. 26, Nov 19, 1929

*Maiden Voyage
    Reviews:
        New York Times p. 15, Mar 9, 1957
                       II, p. 1, Mar 10, 1957

Morning's At Seven
    Productions:
        Opened November 30, 1939 for 44 performances.
        (Off Broadway) Season of 1955-56.
    Reviews:
        Catholic World 150:468-9, Jan 1940
                       181:64, Oct 1955
        Commonweal 31:186, Dec 15, 1939
                   62:469, Aug 12, 1955
        Nation 149:686+, Dec 16, 1939
        New York Theatre Critics' Reviews 1940:445
        New York Times p. 30, Nov 7, 1939
                       IX, p. 1, Nov 12, 1939
                       p. 26, Dec 1, 1939
                       X, p. 5, Dec 10, 1939
                       IX, p. 3, Dec 17, 1939
                       p. 25, Jun 23, 1955
        Theatre Arts 24:88+, Feb 1940
                     39:80, Oct 1955
        Time 34:48, Dec 11, 1939

Oliver Oliver
    Productions:
        Opened January 5, 1934 for 11 performances.
    Reviews:
        New York Times p. 8, Jan 6, 1934
        Newsweek 3:35, Jan 13, 1934
        Stage 11:30, Feb 1934

On Borrowed Time (Based on the novel by Lawrence Edward Watkin)
Productions:
Opened February 3, 1938 for 321 performances.
Opened February 10, 1953 for 78 performances.
Reviews:
Catholic World 146:727-8, Mar 1938
                177:70, Apr 1953
Commonweal 27:468, Feb 18, 1938
              57:552, Mar 6, 1953
Life 4:39, Mar 28, 1938
Nation 146:225, Feb 19, 1938
        176:192, Feb 28, 1953
New Republic 94:74, Feb 28, 1953
New York Theatre Critics' Reviews 1953:365
New York Times p. 16, Feb 4, 1938
                X, p. 3, Feb 13, 1938
                p. 27, Oct 6, 1938
                IX, p. 1, Nov 6, 1938
                IX, p. 3, Nov 13, 1938
                p. 19, Jan 1, 1953
                p. 34, Feb 11, 1953
                p. 20, Feb 24, 1953
New Yorker 29:61, Feb 21, 1953
Newsweek 41:62, Feb 23, 1953
One Act Play Magazine 1:949, Feb 1938
Saturday Review 36:37, Feb 28, 1953
Stage 15:10, Jun 1938
Theatre Arts 22:180, Mar 1938
Time 31:36, Feb 14, 1938
      61:86, Feb 23, 1953
Vogue 91:108+, Mar 15, 1938

Point of No Return (Based on the novel by John P. Marquand)
Productions:
Opened December 13, 1951 for 364 performances.
(Off Broadway) Season of 1956-57.
Reviews:
Catholic World 174:391, Feb 1952
Commonweal 55:325, Jan 4, 1952
Life 32:59-60+, Jan 7, 1952
Nation 173:574, Dec 29, 1951
New Republic 126:22-3, Jan 7, 1952
New York Theatre Critics' Reviews 1951:140
New York Times p. 32, Oct 31, 1951
                p. 84, Dec 2, 1951

OSBORN, PAUL (cont.)
    Point of No Return (cont.)
                            VI, p. 24, Dec 9, 1951
                            p. 35, Dec 14, 1951
                            II, p. 3, Dec 23, 1951
                            p. 38, May 6, 1953
                            p. 17, Mar 23, 1957
        New Yorker 27:47, Dec 22, 1951
        Newsweek 38:43, Dec 24, 1951
        Saturday Review 35:24-5, Jan 5, 1952
                        35:22, Jan 26, 1952
        Theatre Arts 36:73, Feb 1952
                    37:31-3, Mar 1953
        Time 58:44, Dec 24, 1951

    *Tomorrow's Monday
        Reviews:
        New York Times p. 15, Jul 16, 1936

    The Vinegar Tree
        Productions:
        Opened November 19, 1930 for 229 performances.
        Reviews:
        Bookman 73:70, Mar 1931
        Catholic World 132:461, Jan 1931
        Drama Magazine 21:14, Feb 1931
        Life (NY) 96:18-19, Dec 12, 1930
        Nation 131:658, Dec 10, 1930
        National Magazine 59:172, Jan 1931
        New York Times p. 30, Nov 20, 1930
                        p. 9, May 30, 1931
                        VIII, p. 4, Nov 15, 1931
                        p. 16, Aug 14, 1935
        Theatre Arts 16:715, Sep 1932
        Theatre Magazine 53:25, Jan 1931
        Vogue 77:98, Jan 15, 1931

    The World of Suzie Wong (Based on Richard Mason's
        novel)
        Productions:
        Opened October 14, 1958 for 508 performances.
        Reviews:
        Catholic World 188:246, Dec 1958
        Commonweal 69:272, Dec 12, 1958
        Life 45:95-6, Oct 6, 1958
        Nation 188:76, Jan 24, 1959
        New Republic 139:22, Oct 27, 1958

New York Theatre Critics' Reviews 1958:266
New York Times II, p. 3, Oct 12, 1958
                 p. 47, Oct 15, 1958
                 p. 74, Oct 16, 1958
                 II, p. 1, Oct 19, 1958
                 p. 49, Nov 18, 1959
New Yorker 34:88+, Oct 25, 1958
Newsweek 52:64, Oct 27, 1958
Reporter 19:37-8, Nov 13, 1958
Saturday Review 41:28, Nov 1, 1958
Theatre Arts 42:10-11, Dec 1958
Time 72:84, Oct 27, 1958
Vogue 132:105, Nov 15, 1958

PARKER, DOROTHY

Close Harmony (with Elmer Rice)
    Productions:
    Opened December 1, 1924 for 24 performances.
    Reviews:
    Life (NY) 84:18, Dec 18, 1924
    Nation 119:686-7, Dec 17, 1924
    New York Times p. 23, Dec 2, 1924

The Ladies of the Corridor (with Arnaud d'Usseau)
    Productions:
    Opened October 21, 1953 for 45 performances.
    Reviews:
    America 90:157, Nov 7, 1953
    Catholic World 178:230-1, Dec 1953
    Commonweal 59:197-8, Nov 27, 1953
    Nation 177:378, Nov 7, 1953
    New Republic 129:21, Nov 9, 1953
    New York Theatre Critics' Reviews 1953:244
    New York Times II, p. 1, Oct 18, 1953
                     VI, p. 65, Oct 18, 1953
                     p. 33, Oct 22, 1953
                     II, p. 1, Nov 1, 1953
    New Yorker 29:58-60, Oct 31, 1953
    Newsweek 42:65, Nov 2, 1953
    Saturday Review 36:32, Nov 7, 1953
                     36:47, Dec 12, 1953
    Theatre Arts 38:20, Jan 1954
    Time 62:82, Nov 2, 1953

PATRICK, JOHN

The Curious Savage
   Productions:
      Opened October 24, 1950 for 31 performances.
   Reviews:
      Catholic World 172:227, Dec 1950
      Christian Science Monitor Magazine p. 8, Oct 28,
         1950
      Commonweal 53:121, Nov 10, 1950
      Nation 171:418, Nov 4, 1950
      New Republic 123:21, Nov 13, 1950
      New York Theatre Critics' Reviews 1950:230
      New York Times p. 44, Oct 25, 1950
                    p. 17, May 29, 1953
                    p. 12, Mar 17, 1956
      New Yorker 26:76+, Nov 4, 1950
      Newsweek 36:88, Nov 6, 1950
      Theatre Arts 34:17, Dec 1950
      Time 56:57, Nov 6, 1950

Everybody Loves Opal
   Productions:
      Opened October 11, 1961 for 21 performances.
   Reviews:
      America 106:132, Oct 28, 1961
      New York Theatre Critics' Reviews 1961:234
      New York Times p. 40, Oct 12, 1961
      New Yorker 37:131, Oct 21, 1961
      Theatre Arts 45:70, Dec 1961
      Time 78:64, Oct 20, 1961

Good As Gold (Based on Alfred Toombs' novel)
   Productions:
      Opened March 7, 1957 for 4 performances.
   Reviews:
      Nation 184:262, Mar 23, 1957
      New York Theatre Critics' Reviews 1957:321
      New York Times p. 22, Mar 8, 1957
      New Yorker 33:79, Mar 16, 1957
      Saturday Review 40:24, Mar 23, 1957
                      40:7-8, Apr 6, 1957
      Theatre Arts 41:19, May 1957

The Hasty Heart
   Productions:
      Opened January 3, 1945 for 207 performances.

(Off Broadway) Season of 1953-54.
(Off Broadway) Season of 1959-60.
Reviews:
Catholic World 160:452-3, Feb 1945
Commonweal 41:396, Feb 2, 1945
Life 18:103-4, Feb 5, 1945
Nation 160:81, Jan 20, 1945
New Republic 112:118, Jan 22, 1945
New York Theatre Critics' Reviews 1945:298
New York Times p. 14, Jan 4, 1945
            II, p. 1, Jan 14, 1945
            p. 10, Mar 13, 1954
            p. 45, Sep 15, 1959
New Yorker 20:38, Jan 13, 1945
Newsweek 25:78, Jan 15, 1945
Player's Magazine 22:10+, Nov-Dec 1945
            23:23, Sep-Oct 1946
Saturday Review 28:26-7, Mar 3, 1945
Theatre Arts 29:138+, Mar 1945
Time 45:55, Jan 15, 1945

Hell Freezes Over
Productions:
Opened December 28, 1935 for 25 performances.
Reviews:
Catholic World 142:602, Feb 1936
New York Times p. 14, Dec 30, 1935
Time 27:24, Jan 6, 1936

Lo and Behold
Productions:
Opened December 12, 1951 for 38 performances.
Reviews:
Catholic World 174:392-3, Feb 1952
Commonweal 55:300, Dec 28, 1951
Nation 173:574, Dec 29, 1951
New Republic 126:22, Jan 7, 1952
New York Theatre Critics' Reviews 1951:143
New York Times p. 45, Dec 13, 1951
New Yorker 27:48-9, Dec 22, 1951
Newsweek 38:43, Dec 24, 1951
Theatre Arts 36:73, Feb 1952
Time 58:44, Dec 24, 1951

The Story of Mary Surratt
Productions:
Opened February 8, 1947 for 11 performances.

379

PATRICK, JOHN (cont.)
The Story of Mary Surratt (cont.)
(Off Broadway) Opened December 9, 1961 for 9
performances (Equity Library Theatre).
Reviews:
Catholic World 164:551, Mar 1947
Commonweal 45:491, Feb 28, 1947
Nation 164:226-7, Feb 22, 1947
New Republic 116:40, Feb 24, 1947
New York Theatre Critics' Reviews 1947:461
New York Times II, p. 1, Feb 2, 1947
p. 25, Feb 10, 1947
New Yorker 22:50-1, Feb 15, 1947
Newsweek 29:88, Feb 17, 1947
Theatre Arts 31:20, Apr 1947
Time 49:53, Feb 17, 1947

The Teahouse of the August Moon (Based on Vern Sneid-
er's novel)
Productions:
Opened October 15, 1953 for 1,027 performances.
Opened November 8, 1956 for 14 performances.
Reviews:
America 90:186, Nov 14, 1953
Catholic World 178:228-9, Dec 1953
184:306, Jan 1956
Commonweal 59:163, Nov 20, 1953
Life 35:129-30+, Nov 2, 1953
36:101-2+, Jun 14, 1954
Nation 177:357-8, Oct 31, 1953
178:429-30, May 15, 1954
New Republic 129:21, Oct 26, 1953
130:28, May 17, 1954
New York Theatre Critics' Reviews 1953:254; 1956:214
New York Times II, p. 1, Oct 11, 1953
p. 32, Oct 16, 1953
II, p. 1, Oct 25, 1953
VI, p. 17, Nov 15, 1953
II, p. 3, Dec 20, 1953
p. 30, Mar 10, 1954
p. 23, Apr 23, 1954
II, p. 3, May 2, 1954
p. 37, May 20, 1954
II, p. 1, Sep 12, 1954
p. 13, Sep 18, 1954
p. 13, Dec 18, 1954
p. 22, Feb 17, 1955
p. 35, Mar 22, 1955

p. 24, May 10, 1955
p. 60, Aug 7, 1955
II, p. 1, Aug 14, 1955
p. 32, May 29, 1956
p. 25, Jun 4, 1956
p. 33, Nov 9, 1956
New Yorker 29:66+, Oct 24, 1953
Newsweek 42:60, Dec 21, 1953
42:92, Oct 26, 1953
Saturday Review 36:29, Oct 31, 1953
36:45, Dec 12, 1953
Theatre Arts 37:22-4, Dec 1953
39:32-3, Jun 1955
41:31-2, Jan 1957
Time 62:72, Oct 26, 1953

The Willow and I
  Productions:
    Opened December 10, 1942 for 28 performances.
  Reviews:
    Commonweal 37:256, Dec 25, 1942
    Nation 156:32, Jan 2, 1943
    New York Theatre Critics' Reviews 1942:144
    New York Times p. 32, Dec 11, 1942
    New Yorker 18:37, Dec 19, 1942
    Theatre Arts 27:76-7, Feb 1943

PAYNE, JOHN HOWARD

Love In Humble Life
  Productions:
    Opened March 9, 1937 in repertory (Federal
      Theatre Project).
  Reviews:
    New York Times p. 27, Mar 10, 1937

PETERSEN, LOUIS

Entertain A Ghost
  Productions:
    (Off Broadway) Opened April 9, 1962 for 8 per-
      formances.
  Reviews:
    New York Times p. 48, Apr 10, 1962

PETERSEN, LOUIS (cont.)
  Take a Giant Step
    Productions:
      Opened September 24, 1953 for 76 performances.
      (Off Broadway) Season of 1956-1957.
    Reviews:
      America 90:81, Oct 17, 1953
              96:56, Oct 13, 1956
      Catholic World 178:148, Nov 1953
      Commonweal 59:38, Oct 16, 1953
      Nation 177:298, Oct 10, 1953
      New York Theatre Critics' Reviews 1953:274
      New York Times II, p. 1, Sep 20, 1953
                       p. 16, Sep 25, 1953
                       II, p. 1, Oct 4, 1953
                       p. 30, Sep 26, 1956
                       VI, p. 31, Nov 11, 1956
      New Yorker 29:79, Oct 3, 1953
      Newsweek 42:54, Oct 5, 1953
      Saturday Review 36:33, Oct 10, 1953
                      36:47, Dec 12, 1953
      Theatre Arts 37:24, Nov 1953
      Time 62:78, Oct 5, 1953

POLLOCK, CHANNING

  The Crowded Hour (See entry under Selwyn, Edgar)

  The Enemy
    Productions:
      Opened October 20, 1925 for 203 performances.
    Reviews:
      Dramatist 17:1290-91, Jan 1926
      Nation 121:696, Dec 16, 1925
      New York Times p. 20, Oct 21, 1925
                     VII, p. 4, Oct 25, 1925
                     p. 27, Mar 3, 1926
                     VII, p. 1, Aug 19, 1928
      Theatre Magazine 42:18-19, Dec 1925
                       43:26+, Mar 1926
      Woman Citizen 10:20, Dec 1925

  The Fool
    Productions:
      Opened October 23, 1922 for 272+ performances.
    Reviews:
      Bookman 58:60-61, Sep 1923

Dramatist 14:1155-6, Apr 1923
Everybody's 48:120-26, Mar 1923
Hearst 43:93-5+, Mar 1923
Life (NY) 80:18, Nov 9, 1922
New York Clipper 70:20, Nov 1, 1922
New York Times p. 18, Oct 24, 1922
                 VII, p. 1, Oct 29, 1922
                 VII, p. 1, Nov 19, 1922
Theatre Magazine 37:28+, Mar 1923

The House Beautiful
    Productions:
        Opened March 12, 1931 for 108 performances.
    Reviews:
        Arts and Decoration 35:88, May 1931
        Catholic World 133:206, May 1931
        Commonweal 13:610, Apr 1, 1931
        Drama 21:10, May 1931
        Life (NY) 97:23, Apr 3, 1931
        Nation 132:360-1, Apr 1, 1931
        New York Times p. 20, Mar 13, 1931
                        VIII, p. 1, Mar 22, 1931
                        VIII, p. 2, Mar 22, 1931
        Theatre Arts 15:371-2, May 1931
        Vogue 77:76-7+, May 15, 1931

Mr. Moneypenny
    Productions:
        Opened October 17, 1928 for 61 performances.
    Reviews:
        Catholic World 128:336-7, Dec 1928
        New York Times p. 26, Oct 17, 1928
                        IX, p. 5, Oct 21, 1928
                        p. 1, Oct 28, 1928
        Theatre Magazine 48:45-6, Dec 1928
        Vogue 72:162, Dec 8, 1928

A Perfect Lady (with Rennold Wolf)
    Productions:
        Opened October 28, 1914 for 21 performances.
    Reviews:
        Dramatic Mirror 72:9, Nov 4, 1914
        Dramatist 6:534-5, Jan 1915
        Green Book 13:121, Jan 1915
        Munsey 54:94, Feb 1915
        Nation 99:561, Nov 4, 1915

383

POLLOCK, CHANNING (cont.)
A Perfect Lady (cont.)
New York Times p. 11, Oct 29, 1914
Theatre Magazine 20:266-7, Dec 1914

Roads of Destiny (Suggested by O. Henry's story)
Productions:
Opened November 27, 1918 for 101 performances.
Reviews:
Dramatic Mirror 79:865, Dec 14, 1918
Hearst 35:46-7+, Feb 1919
New York Times p. 15, Nov 28, 1918
VII, p. 8, Dec 1, 1918
Theatre Magazine 29:15+, Jan 1919

The Sign on the Door
Productions:
Opened December 19, 1919 for 187 performances.
Reviews:
Dramatic Mirror 81:2023, Jan 1, 1920
Dramatist 11:1007-8, Jul 1920
Forum 63:244-5, Feb 1920
New York Times p. 14, Dec 20, 1919
IX, p. 2, Jan 4, 1920
Theatre Magazine 31:99+, Feb 1920

Such a Little Queen
Productions:
Opened August 31, 1909 for 103 performances.
Reviews:
Collier's 44:23-4, Nov 6, 1909
Current Literature 47:543-50, Nov 1909
Dramatic Mirror 62:5, Sep 11, 1909
Forum 42:361-2, Oct 1909
Green Book 3:257-95, Feb 1910
Hampton 23:693+, Nov 1909
Harper's World 53:24, Oct 30. 1909
Leslies' Weekly 109:274, Sep 16, 1909
Life (NY) 54:379, Sep 16, 1909
Metropolitan Magazine 31:262-3, Nov 1909
Pearson 22:663-4, Nov 1909
Theatre Magazine 10:103-4+, Oct 1909
Vanity Fair 6:200, Nov 1909
World Today 17:1269-79, Dec 1909

RAPHAELSON, SAMUEL

Accent on Youth
  Productions:
    Opened December 25, 1934 for 229 performances.
    (Off Broadway) Opened May 16, 1969 for 9 per-
    formances (Equity Library Theatre).
  Reviews:
    Catholic World 140:600, Feb 1935
    Commonweal 21:318, Jan 11, 1935
    Literary Digest 119:19, Jan 12, 1935
    Nation 140:83-4, Jan 16, 1935
    New Republic 81:336, Jan 30, 1935
    New York Times p. 19, Dec 26, 1934
                    IX, p. 3, Jan 6, 1935
                    p. 24, Jul 2, 1935
                    p. 21, Jul 9, 1935
                    p. 24, Jul 11, 1935
                    p. 20, Aug 13, 1935
                    p. 18, Jun 29, 1937
    Theatre Arts 19:99, Feb 1935
    Time 25:40, Jan 7, 1935

Harlem (See White Man)

*The Heel
  Reviews:
    New York Times p. 33, May 27, 1954

Hilda Crane
  Productions:
    Opened November 1, 1950 for 70 performances.
  Reviews:
    American Mercury 72:351-3, Mar 1951
    Catholic World 172:225-6, Dec 1950
    Christian Science Monitor Magazine p. 8, Nov 11,
    1950
    Commonweal 53:171-2, Nov 24, 1950
    Nation 171:444, Nov 11, 1950
    New Republic 123:21-2, Nov 27, 1950
    New York Theatre Critics' Reviews 1950:221
    New York Times II, p. 1, Oct 29, 1950
                    p. 38, Nov 2, 1950
    New Yorker 26:79, Nov 11, 1950
    Newsweek 36:99, Nov 13, 1950
    Theatre Arts 35:11, Jan 1951
    Time 56:99, Nov 13, 1950

RAPHAELSON, SAMUEL (cont.)
Jason
Productions:
Opened January 21, 1942 for 125 performances.
Reviews:
Catholic World 154:727-8, Mar 1942
Commonweal 35:393, Feb 6, 1942
Nation 154:173, Feb 7, 1942
New York Theatre Critics' Reviews 1942:377
New York Times p. 12, Jan 22, 1942
New Yorker 17:28+, Jan 31, 1942
Player's Magazine 18:12, Mar 1942
Theatre Arts 26:221-2, Apr 1942

The Jazz Singer
Productions:
Opened September 14, 1925 for 303 performances.
Opened April 18, 1927 for 16 performances.
Reviews:
New York Times p. 29, Sep 15, 1925
                p. 25, Apr 19, 1927

The Perfect Marriage
Productions:
Opened October 26, 1944 for 92 performances.
Reviews:
Nation 159:624, Nov 18, 1944
New York Theatre Critics' Reviews 1944:104
New York Times p. 17, Oct 27, 1944
                II, p. 1, Nov 5, 1944
Newsweek 24:104, Nov 6, 1944
Theatre Arts 29:16, Jan 1945

Skylark
Productions:
Opened October 11, 1939 for 256 performances.
Reviews:
Catholic World 150:337, Dec 1939
Commonweal 31:14, Oct 27, 1939
Life 7:46-8, Nov 13, 1939
Nation 149:448-9, Oct 21, 1939
New Republic 100:368, Nov 1, 1939
New York Theatre Critics' Reviews 1940:475
New York Times XI, p. 2, Mar 19, 1939
                p. 32, Oct 12, 1939
                IX, p. 1, Oct 22, 1939

X, p. 3, Dec 10, 1939
p. 12, Jan 30, 1940
VIII, p. 1, Apr 12, 1942
North American Review 248 no. 2:404, Dec 1939
Stage 16:18-19, Apr 1, 1939
Theatre Arts 23:855, Dec 1939
Time 34:36, Oct 23, 1939

White Man
Productions:
Opened October 17, 1936 for 7 performances.
Reviews:
New York Times X, p. 3, Oct 11, 1936
p. 22, Oct 19, 1936
Theatre Arts 20:932+, Dec 1936

The Wooden Slipper
Productions:
Opened January 3, 1934 for 5 performances.
Reviews:
New York Times p. 16, Jan 4, 1934

Young Love
Productions:
Opened October 30, 1928 for 87 performances.
Reviews:
Life (NY) 92:17, Nov 23, 1928
Nation 127:556-7, Nov 21, 1928
128:397-8, Apr 3, 1928
New York Times VII, p. 1, Aug 12, 1928
IX, p. 1, Oct 21, 1928
p. 28, Oct 31, 1928
Vogue 72:82, Dec 22, 1928

RAYFIEL, DAVID

Nathan Weinstein, Mystic, Connecticut
Productions:
Opened February 25, 1966 for 3 performances
Reviews:
New York Theatre Critics' Reviews 1966:355
New York Times p. 15, Feb 26, 1966

P.S. 193
Productions:
(Off Broadway) Opened October 30, 1962 for 48

RAYFIEL, DAVID (cont.)
   P.S. 193 (cont.)
          performances.
      Reviews:
          Commonweal 77:254-5, Nov 30, 1962
          Nation 195:361-2, Nov 24, 1962
          New York Times p. 33, Oct 31, 1962
          New Yorker 38:146+, Nov 10, 1962
          Saturday Review 45:48, Nov 17, 1962

REED, MARK

   Mother's Day (See Yes, My Darling Daughter)

   The Partisans (See She Would and She Did)

   Petticoat Fever
      Productions:
          Opened March 4, 1935 for 137 performances.
      Reviews:
          Catholic World 141:90, Apr 1935
          Commonweal 21:600, Mar 22, 1935
          Literary Digest 119:16, Mar 16, 1935
          New York Times IX, p. 3, Jan 13, 1935
                         p. 22, Mar 5, 1935
                    VIII, p. 2, Mar 10, 1935
                         p. 14, Jun 25, 1935
                         p. 24, Jul 12, 1935
                         p. 21, Feb 21, 1936
                         p. 14, Jul 8, 1936
                      II, p. 7, Mar 21, 1937
                         p. 23, Jul 6, 1937
                         p. 19, Jul 20, 1937
          Newsweek 5:29, May 16, 1935
          Stage 12:22-3, Apr 1935
          Theatre Arts 19:325+, May 1935
          Time 25:25, Mar 18, 1935

   She Would and She Did
      Productions:
          Opened September 11, 1919 for 36 performances.
      Reviews:
          Dramatic Mirror 80:1504, Sep 25, 1919
          New Republic 20:234, Sep 24, 1919
          New York Times p. 18, Sep 12, 1919
                       IV, p. 2, Sep 21, 1919
          Review 1:457-8, Oct 4, 1919

Skyrocket
    Productions:
        Opened January 11, 1929 for 11 performances.
    Reviews:
        New York Times p. 14, Jan 12, 1929

Yes, My Darling Daughter
    Productions:
        Opened February 9, 1937 for 405 performances.
        (Off Broadway) Opened May 10, 1968 for 9 per-
            formances (Equity Library Theatre).
    Reviews:
        Catholic World 144:730-1, Mar 1937
        Nation 144:249, Feb 27, 1937
        New Republic 90:139, Mar 10, 1937
        New York Times p. 19, Feb 10, 1937
                       XI, p. 1, Feb 28, 1937
                       XI, p. 1, Mar 14, 1937
                       p. 26, Jun 4, 1937
                       X, p. 2, Jun 12, 1938
                       p. 17, Jun 14, 1938
                       p. 17, Jul 13, 1938
        Theatre Arts 21:262, Apr 1937
        Time 29:46, Feb 22, 1937

REGAN, SYLVIA

The Fifth Season
    Productions:
        Opened January 23, 1953 for 654 performances.
    Reviews:
        Catholic World 176:468, Mar 1953
        Look 17:4, Mar 10, 1953
        Nation 176:132, Feb 7, 1953
        New York Theatre Critics' Reviews 1953:380
        New York Times p. 13, Jan 24, 1953
                       II, p. 1, Jun 14, 1953
                       p. 24, Feb 25, 1954
                       II, p. 3, Sep 5, 1954
        New Yorker 28:48, Jan 31, 1953
        Saturday Review 36:25, Feb 7, 1953
        Time 61:49, Feb 2, 1953

Morning Star
    Productions:
        Opened April 16, 1940 for 63 performances.

REGAN, SYLVIA (cont.)
  Morning Star (cont.)
    Reviews:
        Catholic World 151:345-6, Jun 1940
        Commonweal 32:43, May 3, 1940
        New York Theatre Critics' Reviews 1940:328
        New York Times p. 26, Apr 17, 1940
                        p. 22, Apr 18, 1940
        Newsweek 15:34, May 6, 1940
        Theatre Arts 24:402, Jun 1940
        Time 35:64, Apr 29, 1940

  Zelda
    Productions:
        Opened March 5, 1969 for 5 performances.
    Reviews:
        New York Theatre Critics' Reviews 1969:336
        New York Times p. 38, Mar 6, 1969

REIZENSTEIN, ELMER (See Rice, Elmer)

RESNIK, MURIEL

  Any Wednesday
    Productions:
        Opened February 18, 1964 for 982 performances.
    Reviews:
        America 110:466, Mar 28, 1964
                110:552, Apr 18, 1964
        Look 28:100-4, Jun 16, 1964
        New York Theatre Critics' Reviews 1964:342
        New York Times p. 34, Feb 19, 1964
                        p. 24, Feb 20, 1964
                        II, p. 1, Aug 1, 1965
                        p. 45, Nov 11, 1965
                        p. 48, Jun 28, 1966
        New Yorker 40:106, Feb 29, 1964
        Newsweek 63:56, Mar 2, 1964
        Saturday Evening Post 237:83-7, Apr 25, 1964
        Saturday Review 47:23, Mar 7, 1964
        Time 83:61, Feb 28, 1964

RICE, ELMER

The Adding Machine
  Productions:
    Opened March 19, 1923 for 72 performances.
    (Off Broadway) Opened June 13, 1947 (Actor's
      Theatre).
    (Off Broadway) Season of 1948-49 (New York Reper-
      tory Group).
    (Off Broadway) Season of 1955-56.
  Reviews:
    Bookman 57:319-20, May 1923
           58:58, Sep 1923
    Dial 74:526-9, May 1923
    Drama 20:20, Oct 1929
    Freeman 7:184-5, May 2, 1923
          7:231-2, May 16, 1923
    Independent 110:270-2, Apr 14, 1923
    Life (NY) 81:20, Apr 12, 1923
    Nation 116:399, Apr 4, 1923
    New Republic 34:164-5, Apr 4, 1923
    New York Clipper 71:14, Mar 28, 1923
    New York Times p. 24, Mar 20, 1923
                VIII, p. 1, Mar 25, 1923
                VII, p. 1, Apr 1, 1923
                VII, p. 2, Apr 1, 1923
                X, p. 2, Dec 4, 1927
                VIII, p. 2, Jan 29, 1928
                p. 35, Nov 18, 1948
                p. 17, Feb 10, 1956
                VI, p. 28, Feb 12, 1956
    Theatre Magazine 37:19, May 1923
                37:30+, Jun 1923

American Landscape
  Productions:
    Opened December 3, 1938 for 43 performances.
  Reviews:
    Catholic World 148:472-3, Jan 1939
    Commonweal 29:273, Dec 30, 1938
    Nation 147:700, Dec 24, 1938
    New Republic 97:230, Dec 28, 1938
    New York Times p. 19, Dec 5, 1938
                X, p. 3, Dec 11, 1938
                IX, p. 3, Dec 25, 1938
    North American Review 247 no. 1:155, Mar 1939
    One Act Play Magazine 2:594-9, Dec 1938

RICE, ELMER (cont.)
American Landscape (cont.)
Theatre Arts 23:86-9, Feb 1939
Time 32:31, Dec 12, 1938

Between Two Worlds
Productions:
Opened October 25, 1934 for 32 performances.
Reviews:
Catholic World 140:342-3, Dec 1934
Nation 139:574, Nov 14, 1934
New York Times p. 24, Oct 26, 1934
Stage 12:28-9, Dec 1934
Theatre Arts 18:900-2, Dec 1934
Time 24:32, Nov 5, 1934
Vogue 84:51, Dec 15, 1934

Black Sheep
Productions:
Opened October 13, 1932 for 4 performances.
Reviews:
New York Times p. 22, Oct 14, 1932
Theatre Arts 16:961-2, Dec 1932

Close Harmony (See entry under Parker, Dorothy)

Cock Robin (See entry under Barry, Philip)

Counsellor-At-Law
Productions:
Opened November 6, 1931 for 292 performances.
Opened September 12, 1932 for 104 performances.
Opened May 15, 1933 for 16 performances.
Opened November 24, 1942 for 258 performances.
Reviews:
Arts and Decoration 36:68, Jan 1932
Catholic World 134:470-1, Jan 1932
156:601, Feb 1943
Commonweal 15:102, Nov 25, 1931
37:206, Dec 11, 1942
Current History ns 3:457, Jan 1943
Dramatist 23:1446-8, Jan 1932
Independent Woman 22:155, May 1943
Nation 133:621-2, Dec 2, 1931
New Republic 69:69, Dec 2, 1931
New York Theatre Critics' Reviews 1942:165
New York Times p. 17, Nov 7, 1931

VIII, p. 3, Mar 27, 1932
p. 13, Sep 17, 1932
IX, p. 3, Nov 6, 1932
p. 24, Apr 11, 1933
IX, p. 2, May 6, 1933
p. 17, Nov 25, 1942
p. 14, Mar 26, 1943
North American Review 233:75, Jan 1932
Outlook 159:407, Nov 25, 1931
Theatre Arts 16:21-2, Jan 1932
27:16, Jan 1943
Theatre Guild Magazine 9:6-7+, Dec 1931
Time 40:55, Dec 7, 1942
Vanity Fair 37:24+, Jan 1932

Cue for Passion
    Productions:
        Opened November 25, 1958 for 39 performances.
    Reviews:
        Catholic World 188:418, Feb 1959
        New York Theatre Critics' Reviews 1958:192
        New York Times p. 25, Nov 26, 1958
                        II, p. 5, Dec 7, 1958
        New Yorker 34:116-17, Dec 6, 1958
        Newsweek 52:66, Dec 8, 1958
        Theatre Arts 43:21-2, Feb 1959
        Time 72:77, Dec 8, 1958

Dream Girl
    Productions:
        Opened December 14, 1945 for 348 performances.
        Opened May 9, 1951 for 15 performances.
    Reviews:
        Catholic World 162:454-5, Feb 1946
                        173:306, Jul 1951
        Commonweal 43:456-7, Feb 15, 1946
                        54:165, May 25, 1951
        Forum 105:564, Feb 1946
        Harper's Bazaar 79:128, Dec 1945
        Life 19:36-8, Dec 31, 1945
        Nation 162:54, Jan 12, 1946
        New Republic 113:903, Dec 31, 1945
                        124:23, May 28, 1951
        New York Theatre Critics' Reviews 1945:66
                        1951:271
        New York Times p. 13, Dec 15, 1945
                        III, p. 3, Dec 23, 1945

393

RICE, ELMER (cont.)
Dream Girl (cont.)
II, p. 1, Mar 10, 1946
II, p. 1, Jun 9, 1946
p. 13, Sep 2, 1946
II, p. 1, Sep 8, 1946
p. 39, May 10, 1951
New Yorker 21:36, Dec 22, 1945
Newsweek 26:88, Dec 24, 1945
Theatre Arts 30:72, 78-9, Feb 1946
Time 46:77-8, Dec 24, 1945

Flight to the West
Productions:
Opened December 30, 1940 for 136 performances.
Reviews:
Catholic World 152:595, Feb 1941
Commonweal 33:328, Jan 17, 1941
Nation 152:53, Jan 11, 1941
New Republic 104:84, Jan 20, 1941
New York Theatre Critics' Reviews 1940:162
1941:434
New York Times p. 59, Dec 15, 1940
p. 19, Dec 31, 1940
IX, p. 1, Jan 19, 1941
New Yorker 16:33, Jan 11, 1941
Newsweek 17:52, Jan 13, 1941
Stage 1:10, Dec 1940
1:28-9, Feb 1941
Theatre Arts 25:112, Feb 1941
25:184-5, Mar 1941
Time 37:57, Jan 13, 1941

For the Defense
Productions:
Opened December 19, 1919 for 77 performances.
Reviews:
Dramatic Mirror 81:2023, Jan 1, 1920
Life (NY) 96:17, Aug 8, 1930
New York Times p. 14, Dec 20, 1919
Theatre Magazine 31:100+, Feb 1920

The Grand Tour
Productions:
Opened December 10, 1951 for 8 performances.
Reviews:
Commonweal 55:299, Dec 28, 1951

New York Theatre Critics' Reviews 1951:146
New York Times II, p. 5, Dec 9, 1951
                 p. 45, Dec 11, 1951
New Yorker 27:49, Dec 22, 1951
Newsweek 38:43, Dec 24, 1951
Theatre Arts 36:73, Feb 1952

The Home of the Free
    Productions:
        Opened October 31, 1917 in repertory (Washington
        Square Players).
    Reviews:
        Dramatic Mirror 78:620, May 4, 1918
        New York Times p. 7, Apr 23, 1917
                       p. 11, Apr 23, 1918
        Theatre Magazine 27:355, Jun 1918

The Iron Cross
    Productions:
        Opened February 13, 1917 in repertory.
    Reviews:
        New York Times p. 9, Feb 12, 1917
        Theatre Magazine 25:213-14, Apr 1917

It Is the Law (Adapted from the story by Hayden Talbot)
    Productions:
        Opened November 29, 1922 for 125 performances.
    Reviews:
        New York Clipper 70:20, Dec 6, 1922
        New York Times p. 28, Nov 30, 1922
        Theatre Magazine 37:19, Feb 1923

Judgment Day
    Productions:
        Opened September 12, 1934 for 93 performances.
    Reviews:
        Catholic World 140:89-90, Oct 1934
        Commonweal 20:509, Sep 28, 1934
        Golden Book Magazine 20:506, Nov 1934
        Literary Digest 118:20, Sep 29, 1934
        Nation 139:392, Oct 3, 1934
        New York Times p. 26, Sep 13, 1934
                       X, p. 1, Sep 23, 1934
                       p. 16, May 20, 1937
                       X, p. 1, Jun 20, 1937
                       p. 21, Aug 20, 1937
                       IX, p. 7, Dec 3, 1939

RICE, ELMER (cont.)
    Judgment Day (cont.)
        Newsweek 4:28, Sep 22, 1934
        Theatre Arts 18:814-15, Nov 1934
        Vogue 84:74, Oct 15, 1934

    The Left Bank
        Productions:
        Opened October 5, 1931 for 242 performances.
        Reviews:
        Arts and Decoration 36:68, Dec 1931
        Bookman 74:302, Nov 1931
        Catholic World 134:210, Nov 1931
        Nation 133:440-1, Oct 21, 1931
        New Republic 68:264+, Oct 21, 1931
        New York Times p. 35, Oct 6, 1931
                        VIII, p. 1, Oct 18, 1931
        Outlook 159:248, Oct 21, 1931
        Theatre Arts 15:983-4, Dec 1931
        Theatre Guild Magazine 9:4, Jan 1932
        Vogue 78:102, Dec 1, 1931

    *Love Among the Ruins
        Reviews:
        New York Times p. 85, May 5, 1963

    The Mongrel (Adapted from Herman Bahr's play)
        Productions:
        Opened December 15, 1924 for 32 performances.
        Reviews:
        Independent 114:51, Jan 10, 1925
        Living Age 324:70-76, Jan 3, 1925
        New York Times p. 28, Dec 16, 1924
        Theatre Magazine 40:62+, Feb 1925

    A New Life
        Productions:
        Opened September 15, 1943 for 70 performances.
        Reviews:
        Catholic World 158:187, Nov 1943
        Commonweal 38:585, Oct 1, 1943
        Nation 157:388, Oct 2, 1943
        New Republic 109:426, Sep 27, 1943
        New York Theatre Critics' Reviews 1943:279
        New York Times VI, p. 14, Sep 12, 1943
                        p. 26, Sep 16, 1943
        Newsweek 22:90, Sep 27, 1943
        Theatre Arts 27:640-4, Nov 1943

Not for Children
    Productions:
        Opened February 13, 1951 for 7 performances.
    Reviews:
        Commonweal 53:541, Mar 9, 1951
        New York Theatre Critics' Reviews 1951:348
        New York Times p. 23, Nov 25, 1935
                        IX, p. 3, Dec 22, 1935
                        IX, p. 2, Dec 29, 1935
                        IX, p. 2, Mar 1, 1936
                        II, p. 1, Feb 4, 1951
                        p. 35, Feb 14, 1951
        New Yorker 27:66, Feb 24, 1951
        Newsweek 37:49, Feb 26, 1951
        Theatre Arts 35:19, Apr 1951
        Time 57:50, Feb 26, 1951

On Trial
    Productions:
        Opened August 19, 1914 for 365 performances.
    Reviews:
        American Heritage 16:46-9+, Apr 1965
        American Magazine 79:42+, Jan 1915
        American Playwright 3:300-303, Sep 1914
        Book News 33:91-2, Oct 1914
        Bookman 40:181-3, Oct 1914
        Colliers 54:10, Jan 2, 1915
        Current Opinion 57:249, Oct 1914
                        59:24-7, Jul 1915
        Dramatic Mirror 72:8, Aug 19, 1914
                        72:8, Aug 26, 1914
        Dramatist 6:498-500, Oct 1914
        Everybody's 31:700-702, Nov 1914
        Green Book 12:772-84, Nov 1914
                    12:886-8, Nov 1914
                    12:901-3, Nov 1914
        Hearst 26:640-7, Nov 1914
        Life (NY) 64:395, Sep 3, 1914
        McClure's 44:18-21, Jan 1915
        Munsey 53:348-55, Nov 1914
        Nation 99:260-1, Aug 27, 1914
        New York Times p. 11, Aug 20, 1914
                        VIII, p. 6, Oct 18, 1914
                        p. 5, Apr 30, 1915
                        VII, p. 4, May 16, 1915
        Strand 48:685-8, Dec 1914
        Theatre Magazine 20:154+, Oct 1914
                        20:160+, Oct 1914

RICE, ELMER (cont.)
  See Naples and Die
    Productions:
      Opened September 24, 1929 for 62 performances.
    Reviews:
      Life (NY) 94:26, Oct 18, 1929
      Nation 129:409, Oct 16, 1929
      New Republic 60:243-4, Oct 16, 1929
      New York Times p. 30, Sep 27, 1929
      Theatre Magazine 50:70, Nov 1929

  Street Scene
    Productions:
      Opened January 10, 1929 for 601 performances.
    Reviews:
      Catholic World 128:720-2, Mar 1929
      Commonweal 9:348-9, Jan 23, 1929
      Dial 86:245-6, Mar 1929
      Drama Magazine 19:170, Mar 1929
      Life (NY) 93:23, Feb 1, 1929
      Nation 128:142, Jan 30, 1929
              128:680-1, Jun 5, 1929
      New Republic 57:296-8, Jan 30, 1929
      New York Times p. 20, Jan 11, 1929
                    VIII, p. 1, Jan 20, 1929
                    IX, p. 4, Jan 27, 1929
                    IX, p. 4, Feb 24, 1929
                    IX, p. 1, May 19, 1929
                    p. 24, Jan 10, 1930
                    IX, p. 4, Mar 16, 1930
                    p. 14, Sep 10, 1930
                    VIII, p. 2, Sep 28, 1930
      Outlook 151:140, Jan 23, 1929
      Saturday Review 30:24-6, Feb 1, 1947
      Theatre Arts 13:164-6, Mar 1929
              14:164-6, Feb 1930
              43:59-64+, Nov 1959
      Theatre Magazine 49:50, Mar 1929
              49:26-7+, Apr 1929
      Vogue 73:114, Mar 2, 1929

  The Subway
    Productions:
      Opened January 25, 1929 for 35 performances.
    Reviews:
      New York Times p. 15, Jan 26, 1929
                    p. 25, Jul 15, 1929
      Theatre Magazine 49:47, Apr 1929

Two On An Island
    Productions:
        Opened January 22, 1940 for 96 performances.
    Reviews:
        Catholic World 150:729-30, Mar 1940
        Commonweal 31:348, Feb 9, 1940
        Life 8:42-4, Feb 19, 1940
        Nation 150:136, Feb 3, 1940
        New York Theatre Critics' Reviews 1940:409
        New York Times p. 18, Jan 16, 1940
                      p. 17, Jan 23, 1940
                      IX, p. 1, Jan 28, 1940
                      IX, p. 1, Feb 4, 1940
        Newsweek 15:34, Feb 5, 1940
        Player's Magazine 25:192, May 1949
        Theatre Arts 24:167-8, Mar 1940
        Time 35:41, Feb 5, 1940

Wake Up, Jonathan! (See entry under Hughes, Hatcher)

We, The People
    Productions:
        Opened January 21, 1933 for 49 performances.
    Reviews:
        Arts and Decoration 38:58, Mar 1933
        Christian Century 50:231, Feb 15, 1933
        Commonweal 17:411, Feb 8, 1933
        Literary Digest 115:15, Feb 11, 1933
                       115:19, Mar 4, 1933
        Nation 136:158-60, Feb 8, 1933
               136:172, Feb 15, 1933
        New Outlook 161:10, Mar 1933
        New Republic 74:18-19, Feb 15, 1933
        New York Times p. 9, Jan 23, 1933
                      IX, p. 1, Feb 5, 1933
        Stage 10:20-21, Mar 1933
        Theatre Arts 17:258-60, Apr 1933
        Time 21:22, Jan 30, 1933
        Vogue 81:73, Mar 15, 1933
        World Tomorrow 16:176, Feb 22, 1933

The Winner
    Productions:
        Opened February 17, 1954 for 30 performances.
    Reviews:
        America 90:664, Mar 20, 1954
        New York Theatre Critics' Reviews 1954:365

RICE, ELMER (cont.)
The Winner (cont.)
New York Times II, p. 3, Feb 14, 1954
p. 34, Feb 18, 1954
New Yorker 30:78-80, Feb 27, 1954
Newsweek 43:71, Mar 1, 1954
Saturday Review 37:25, Mar 6, 1954
Theatre Arts 38:16, Apr 1954
Time 63:76+, Mar 1, 1954

RICHARDSON, JACK

Christmas in Las Vegas (See Xmas in Las Vegas)

Gallows Humor
Productions:
(Off Broadway) Opened April 18, 1961 for 40
performances.
(Off Broadway) Opened February 11, 1962 for 55
performances.
Reviews:
Nation 192:399, May 6, 1961
New York Times p. 35, Apr 19, 1961
New Yorker 37:93, Apr 29, 1961
Newsweek 57:62, May 1, 1961
Saturday Review 44:39, May 6, 1961
Theatre Arts (p. 30) 45:32, Jun 1961

Lorenzo
Productions:
Opened February 14, 1963 for 4 performances.
Reviews:
New Republic 148:29, Mar 9, 1963
New York Theatre Critics' Reviews 1963:174
New York Times p. 12, Jan 25, 1963
p. 5, Feb 16, 1963
New Yorker 39:112+, Feb 23, 1963
Newsweek 61:60, Feb 25, 1963
Saturday Review 46:24, Mar 9, 1963
Theatre Arts 47:13, Apr 1963
Time 81:75, Feb 22, 1963

The Prodigal
Productions:
(Off Broadway) Opened February 11, 1960 for 167
performances.

400

Reviews:
    Esquire 55:47-8, Apr 1961
    Nation 190:214, Mar 5, 1960
    New York Times p. 23, Feb 12, 1960
                    II, p. 1, Feb 21, 1960
    New Yorker 36:104+, Feb 20, 1960
    Time 75:54, Apr 18, 1960

Xmas in Las Vegas
    Productions:
    Opened November 4, 1965 for 4 performances.
    Reviews:
    Commonweal 83:243, Nov 26, 1965
    New York Theatre Critics' Reviews 1965:284
    New York Times p. 31, Nov 5, 1965
    New Yorker 41:154, Nov 13, 1965

RICHMAN, ARTHUR

All Dressed Up
    Productions:
    Opened September 9, 1925 for 13 performances.
    Reviews:
    Life (NY) 86:18, Oct 1, 1925
    New York Times p. 28, Sep 10, 1925

Ambush
    Productions:
    Opened October 10, 1921 for 98 performances.
    Reviews:
    Bookman 54:374-5, Dec 1921
    Dramatic Mirror 84:557, Oct 15, 1921
    Everybody's 46:137-44, Apr 1922
    Independent 107:110, Oct 29, 1921
    Life (NY) 78:18, Nov 3, 1921
    Nation 113:484, Oct 26, 1921
            113:599, Nov 23, 1921
    New Republic 28:301, Nov 2, 1921
    New York Clipper Vol. 69, Oct 19, 1921
    New York Times p. 22, Oct 11, 1921
                    VI, p. 1, Oct 16, 1921
    Outlook 129:507, Nov 30, 1921
    Theatre Magazine 34:426+, Dec 1921
                    35:292+, May 1922

RICHMAN, ARTHUR (cont.)
Antonia (Adapted from the play by Melchior Lengyel)
Productions:
Opened October 20, 1925 for 55 performances.
Reviews:
Dramatist 16:1280-81, Oct 1925
New York Times p. 20, Oct 21, 1925

*Arelene Adair
Reviews:
New York Times p. 15, Jun 12, 1926

The Awful Truth
Productions:
Opened September 18, 1922 for 144 performances.
Reviews:
Life (NY) 80:18, Oct 5, 1922
New York Clipper 70:20, May 1922
                70:20, Nov 8, 1922
New York Times p. 14, Sep 19, 1922
             VI, p. 1, Sep 24, 1922
Theatre Magazine 36:299, Nov 1922

The Far Cry
Productions:
Opened September 30, 1924 for 31 performances.
Reviews:
American Mercury 3:377, Nov 1924
Life (NY) 84:18, Oct 23, 1924
Nation 119:451, Oct 22, 1924
New York Times p. 24, Oct 1, 1924
Theatre Magazine 39:15-16, Dec 1924

Heavy Traffic
Productions:
Opened September 5, 1928 for 61 performances.
Reviews:
American Mercury 15:373-5, Nov 1928
Life (NY) 92:17, Sep 28, 1928
Nation 127:276-7, Sep 19, 1928
New York Times p. 23, Sep 6, 1928
Theatre Magazine 48:78, Nov 1928
Vogue 72:108, Oct 27, 1928

Isabel (Adapted from a play by Curt Goetz)
Productions:
Opened January 13, 1925 for 31 performances.

Reviews:
   Bookman 61:75, Mar 1925
   Life (NY) 85:18, Feb 12, 1925
   New York Times p. 19, Jan 14, 1925
   Theatre Magazine 40:64, Mar 1925

Not So Long Ago
   Productions:
   Opened May 4, 1920 for 31 performances.
   Reviews:
   Current Opinion 69:54-60, Jul 1920
   New York Times p. 14, May 5, 1920

A Proud Woman
   Productions:
   Opened November 15, 1926 for 7 performances.
   Reviews:
   New York Times p. 24, Nov 16, 1926

The Season Changes
   Productions:
   Opened December 23, 1935 for 8 performances.
   Reviews:
   New York Times p. 10, Dec 24, 1935

A Serpent's Tooth
   Productions:
   Opened August 24, 1922 for 36 performances.
   Reviews:
   Dial 73:463, Oct 1922
   Life (NY) 80:20, Sep 14, 1922
   New Republic 32:149-50, Oct 4, 1922
   New York Clipper 70:20, Aug 30, 1922
   New York Times p. 8, Aug 25, 1922
   Theatre Magazine 36:301, Nov 1922
                     36:310+, Nov 1922

RIGGS, LYNN

   Big Lake
   Productions:
   Opened April 11, 1927 for 11 performances.
   Reviews:
   New York Times p. 17, Apr 9, 1927

403

RIGGS, LYNN (cont.)
   Borned in Texas
      Productions:
         Opened August 21, 1950 for 8 performances.
      Reviews:
         Nation 171:213, Sep 2, 1950
         New Republic 123:23, Sep 4, 1950
         New York Times p. 23, Jun 4, 1945
                        p. 30, Aug 22, 1950

   *Cherokee Night
      Reviews:
         New York Times p. 19, Jun 21, 1932
                        IX, p. 1, Jun 26, 1932

   The Cream in the Well
      Productions:
         Opened January 20, 1941 for 24 performances.
      Reviews:
         Commonweal 33:375, Jan 31, 1941
         Nation 152:136, Feb 1, 1941
         New Republic 104:179, Feb 10, 1941
         New York Theatre Critics' Reviews 1941:404
         New York Times p. 19, Jan 21, 1941
         New Yorker 16:27, Feb 1, 1941
         Theatre Arts 25:190, Mar 1941

   Green Grow the Lilacs
      Productions:
         Opened January 26, 1931 for 64 performances.
      Reviews:
         Arts and Decoration 34:84, Apr 1931
         Bookman 73:293-4, May 1931
         Catholic World 132:179, Mar 1931
         Commonweal 13:414, Feb 11, 1931
         Drama 21:11-12, Mar 1931
         Life (NY) 97:18, Feb 20, 1931
         Nation 132:164-5, Feb 11, 1931
         New Republic 66:19, Feb 18, 1931
         New York Times IX, p. 3, Dec 14, 1930
                        p. 21, Jan 27, 1931
                        VIII, p. 1, Feb 8, 1931
                        VIII, p. 3, Mar 1, 1931
                        p. 20, Jul 23, 1952
         Outlook 157:234, Feb 11, 1931
         Theatre Arts 15:272-3, Apr 1931
         Theatre Magazine 53:26, Apr 1931
         Vogue 77:108, Mar 15, 1931

*Lonesome West
  Reviews:
    New York Times p. 15, Jun 30, 1936

Roadside
  Productions:
    Opened September 26, 1930 for 11 performances.
    (Off Broadway) Opened June 3, 1947 in repertory
      (Actors Theatre).
  Reviews:
    Drama 21:17, Nov 1930
    Life (NY) 96:19, Oct 17, 1930
    New York Times p. 21, Sep 27, 1930

Russet Mantle
  Productions:
    Opened January 16, 1936 for 117 performances.
  Reviews:
    Catholic World 142:725-6, Mar 1936
    Commonweal 23:386, Jan 31, 1936
    Nation 142:168, Feb 5, 1936
    New Republic 86:169, Mar 18, 1936
    New York Times p. 15, Jan 17, 1936
                IX, p. 1, Jan 26, 1936
                p. 15, Aug 18, 1936
    Newsweek 7:30, Jan 25, 1936
    Stage 13:36-7, Mar 1936
    Theatre Arts 20:176-8, Mar 1936
    Time 27:43, Jan 27, 1936

*Year of Pilar
  Reviews:
    New York Times p. 14, Jan 7, 1952

RILEY, LAWRENCE

Personal Appearance
  Productions:
    Opened October 17, 1934 for 501 performances.
    (Off Broadway) Opened January 5, 1941 (Lighthouse
      Players).
  Reviews:
    Catholic World 140:341, Dec 1934
    Commonweal 21:122, Nov 23, 1934
    Literary Digest 118:20, Nov 10, 1934
    Nation 139:517, Oct 31, 1934

RILEY, LAWRENCE (cont.)
Personal Appearance (cont.)
New York Times p. 26, Oct 18, 1934
IX, p. 1, Oct 28, 1934
IX, p. 3, Nov 17, 1935
p. 23, Jun 16, 1936
p. 27, Jun 23, 1936
p. 17, Jul 9, 1936
Theatre Arts 18:896+, Dec 1934
Time 24:44-5, Oct 29, 1934

Return Engagement
Productions:
Opened November 1, 1940 for 8 performances.
Reviews:
New York Theatre Critics' Reviews 1940:230
New York Times p. 19, Nov 2, 1940
Time 36:44, Nov 11, 1960

RINEHART, MARY ROBERTS

The Bat (with Avery Hopwood)
Productions:
Opened August 23, 1920 for 867 performances.
Opened May 31, 1937 for 18 performances.
Opened January 20, 1953 for 23 performances.
Reviews:
Catholic World 176:467, Mar 1953
Commonweal 57:473, Feb 13, 1953
Dramatic Mirror p. 371, Aug 28, 1920
Dramatist 12:1053, Apr 1921
Independent 103:261, Sep 4, 1920
Life (NY) 76:456, Sep 9, 1920
Literary Digest 68:27-8, Feb 12, 1921
New York Clipper 68:19, Sep 1, 1920
New York Theatre Critics Reviews 1953:390
New York Times p. 6, Aug 24, 1920
VI, p. 1, Nov 14, 1920
p. 11, Jan 24, 1922
VII, p. 1, Apr 30, 1922
p. 5, Sep 3, 1922
p. 27, Jun 1, 1937
II, p. 3, Jan 18, 1953
p. 28, Jan 21, 1953
New Yorker 28:49, Jan 31, 1953
Newsweek 41:68, Feb 2, 1953

Saturday Review 36:25, Feb 7, 1953
Theatre Magazine 32:240-2, Oct 1920
Time 61:49, Feb 2, 1953

The Breaking Point
Productions:
Opened August 16, 1923 for 68 performances.
Reviews:
New York Times p. 8, Aug 17, 1923
VI, p. 1, Aug 26, 1923
Theatre Magazine 38:16, Oct 1923

Cheer Up
Productions:
Opened December 30, 1912 for 24 performances.
Reviews:
Blue Book 16:1150-2, Apr 1913
Dramatic Mirror 69:7, Jan 8, 1913
New York Dramatic News 57:23, Jan 4, 1913

Seven Days (with Avery Hopwood)
Productions:
Opened November 10, 1909 for 397 performances.
Reviews:
American Mercury 71:271, Dec 1910
Burr McIntosh Monthly 22:126, Feb 1910
Cosmopolitan 48:484, Mar 1910
Dramatist 1:15, Jan 1910
Forum 43:183-4, Feb 1910
Green Book 3:77-9, Jan 1910
Hampton 24:135-6, Jan 1910
Harper's Weekly 53:25, Nov 27, 1909
Leslies' Weekly 109:535, Dec 2, 1909
110:107, Feb 3, 1910
Life (NY) 54:473, Nov 25, 1909
Lippincott 82:641-712, Dec 1908
Metropolitan Magazine 31:822-3, Mar 1910
Pearson 23:230, Feb 1910
Theatre Magazine 10:xv+, Dec 1909

ROTTER, FRITZ

Letters to Lucerne (with Allen Vincent)
Productions:
Opened December 23, 1941 for 23 performances.
Reviews:

ROTTER, FRITZ (cont.)
Letters to Lucerne (cont.)
Commonweal 35:294, Jan 9, 1942
New York Theatre Critics' Reviews 1941:168
New York Times p. 47, Dec 9, 1941
p. 14, Dec 24, 1941
New Yorker 17:28, Jan 3, 1942
Newsweek 19:55, Jan 5, 1942
Player's Magazine 18:14, Feb 1942
Theatre Arts 26:155-6, Mar 1942

ROYLE, EDWIN MILTON

Her Way Out
Productions:
Opened June 23, 1924 for 24 performances.
Reviews:
New York Times p. 18, Jun 24, 1924
VII, p. 1, Jul 13, 1924

Launcelot and Elaine (Dramatized from Tennyson's
"Idylls of the King. ")
Productions:
Opened September 12, 1921 for 32 performances.
Opened March 8, 1930 for 25 performances.
Reviews:
Dramatic Mirror 84:413, Sep 17, 1921
Independent 106:137, Sep 24, 1921
107:36, Oct 8, 1921
New York Times p. 12, Sep 13, 1921
p. 24, Mar 10, 1930
Theatre Magazine 34:340, Nov 1921

*Peace and Quiet
Reviews:
New York Times p. 9, Jun 20, 1916

The Silent Call
Productions:
Opened January 2, 1911 for 8 performances.
No Reviews.

The Squaw Man
Productions:
Opened January 9, 1911 for 8 performances.
Opened December 26, 1921 for 50 performances.

Reviews:
Dramatic Mirror 84:999, Dec 31, 1921
Dramatist 2:133, Jan 1911
New York Clipper 69:29, Jan 11, 1922
New York Times p. 10, Dec 27, 1921

The Unwritten Law
Productions:
Opened February 7, 1913 for 19 performances.
Reviews:
American Playwright 2:76-8, Mar 1913
Bookman 37:65, Mar 1913
Dramatic Mirror 69:6, Feb 12, 1913
Dramatist 3:265-6, Apr 1912
Life (NY) 61:374, Feb 20, 1913
New York Drama News 55:12, Apr 27, 1912
57:19, Feb 15, 1913
New York Times p. 13, Feb 8, 1913
Theatre Magazine 17:68+, Mar 1913

RYERSON, FLORENCE (Mrs. Colin Clements)

Glamour Preferred (with Colin Clements)
Productions:
Opened November 15, 1940 for 11 performances.
Reviews:
Commonweal 33:152, Nov 29, 1940
New York Theatre Critics' Reviews 1940:220
New York Times p. 13, Nov 16, 1940

Harriet (with Colin Clements)
Productions:
Opened March 3, 1943 for 377 performances.
Opened September 27, 1944 for 11 performances.
Reviews:
Catholic World 157:177-8, Apr 1943
Commonweal 37:568, Mar 26, 1943
Current Literature 4:156-8, Apr 1943
Independent Woman 22:65, Mar 1943
Life 14:37-8+, Apr 5, 1943
Nation 156:426, Mar 20, 1943
New Republic 108:381, Mar 22, 1943
New York Theatre Critics' Reviews 1943:364
New York Times p. 22, Jan 29, 1943
p. 24, Mar 4, 1943
II, p. 1, Mar 14, 1943

RYERSON, FLORENCE (cont.)
Harriet (cont.)
>p. 15, Jun 29, 1943
>II, p. 7, Dec 12, 1943
>p. 26, Sep 28, 1944
>VI, p. 16, Feb 14, 1943
New Yorker 19:43, Mar 13, 1943
Newsweek 21:82, Mar 15, 1943
Scholastic 44:13-16, Apr 24, 1944
Theatre Arts 27:265-7+, May 1943
Time 41:42, Mar 15, 1943

Morality Clause (See Glamour Preferred)

Strange Bedfellows (with Colin Clements)
Productions:
Opened January 14, 1948 for 229 performances.
Reviews:
Catholic World 166:552-3, Mar 1948
Commonweal 47:399, Jan 30, 1948
Life 24:71-2, Feb 16, 1948
New York Theatre Critics' Reviews 1948:386
New York Times p. 27, Jan 15, 1948
New Yorker 23:41, Jan 24, 1948
Newsweek 31:82, Jan 26, 1948
School and Society 67:243, Mar 27, 1948
Theatre Arts 32:22, Spring, 1948
Time 51:64, Jan 26, 1948

SACKLER, HOWARD

The Great White Hope
Productions:
Opened October 3, 1968 for 556 performances.
Reviews:
America 119:528-30, Nov 23, 1968
Commentary 47:22+, Feb 1969
Commonweal 89:283-4, Nov 22, 1968
Harper 238:108-9, Jan 1969
Nation 206:93-4, Jan 15, 1968
>207:446, Oct 28, 1968
National Review 20:1282-3, Dec 17, 1968
New Republic 159:36+, Oct 26, 1968
New York Theatre Critics' Reviews 1968:222
New York Times p. 58, Dec 14, 1967
>II, p. 3, Dec 24, 1967

                    X, p. 3, Dec 24, 1967
                    p. 40, Oct 4, 1968
                    p. 39, Oct 5, 1968
                    II, p. 1, Oct 13, 1968
                    p. 54, Oct 29, 1968
                    p. 26, Sep 27, 1969
                    II, p. 3, Oct 26, 1969
        New Yorker 44:103, Oct 12, 1968
        Newsweek 70:73, Dec 25, 1967
                    72:117, Oct 14, 1968
        Saturday Review 50:18, Dec 30, 1967
                    51:28, Oct 19, 1968
        Sports Illustrated 29:34-5, Oct 7, 1968
        Time 92:73, Oct 11, 1968
        Vogue 152:92, Nov 15, 1968

SAROYAN, WILLIAM

Across the Board on Tomorrow Morning (See Two By
    Saroyan)

The Beautiful People
    Productions:
        Opened April 21, 1941 for 120 performances.
        (Off Broadway) Season of 1955-56 (Theatre East).
    Reviews:
        Catholic World 153:342-3, Jun 1941
        Commonweal 34:38, May 2, 1941
        Life 10:128-31, May 19, 1941
        Nation 152:537, May 3, 1941
        New Republic 104:632, May 5, 1941
                    104:664, May 12, 1941
        New York Theatre Critics' Reviews 1941:328
        New York Times p. 27, Apr 22, 1941
                    p. 30, Apr 11, 1956
        New Yorker 17:30, May 3, 1941
        Newsweek 17:67, May 5, 1941
        Theatre Arts 25:411-13, Jun 1941
        Time 37:66+, May 5, 1941

The Cave Dwellers
    Productions:
        Opened October 19, 1957 for 97 performances.
        (Off Broadway) Opened October 16, 1961 for six
            performances.
    Reviews:

SAROYAN, WILLIAM (cont.)
  The Cave Dwellers (cont.)
          America 98:299, Nov 30, 1957
          Catholic World 186:305, Jan 1958
          Christian Century 74:1425, Nov 27, 1957
          Commonweal 67:287, Dec 13, 1957
          Nation 185:330-1, Nov 9, 1957
          New Republic 137:20, Nov 4, 1957
          New York Theatre Critics' Reviews 1957:211
          New York Times II, p. 1, Oct 13, 1957
                          p. 29, Oct 21, 1957
                          II, p. 1, Oct 27, 1957
                          p. 34, Oct 16, 1961
          New Yorker 33:85-7, Nov 2, 1957
                     37:138, Oct 28, 1961
          Saturday Review 40:22, Nov 2, 1957
          Theatre Arts 41:20-1, Dec 1957
          Time 70:92, Oct 28, 1957

  *Don't Go Away Mad
    Reviews:
          New York Times p. 28, May 10, 1949

  Fat Man in a Famine (See Jim Dandy)

  Floydada to Matador ("Hello Out There," "The Hunger-
        ers," "Opera Opera.")
    Productions:
          (Off Broadway) Season of 1955-56.
    Reviews:
          New York Times II, p. 5, Dec 18, 1955
                          p. 19, Dec 22, 1955

  Get Away Old Man
    Productions:
          Opened November 24, 1943 for 13 performances.
    Reviews:
          Commonweal 39:205, Dec 10, 1943
          New Republic 109:851, Dec 13, 1943
          New York Theatre Critics' Reviews 1943:312
          New York Times p. 40, Nov 25, 1943
          Player's Magazine 20:13, Jan 1944
          Theatre Arts 28:77-8, Feb 1944
          Time 42:42, Dec 6, 1943

  Hello, Out There
    Productions:

Opened September 29, 1942 for 47 performances.
(Off Broadway) Season of 1955-56 (See Floydada to
  Matador for reviews.)
Reviews:
    Catholic World 156:214, Nov 1942
    Commonweal 36:615, Oct 16, 1942
    Nation 155:357, Oct 10, 1942
    New Republic 107:466, Oct 12, 1942
    New York Theatre Critics' Reviews 1942:223
    New York Times p. 20, Sep 11, 1941
                 p. 28, Sep 30, 1942
    New Yorker 18:30, Oct 10, 1942
    Newsweek 20:82, Oct 12, 1942

*High Time Along the Wabash
    Reviews:
    New York Times p. 17, Dec 2, 1961
    Saturday Review 44:30, Dec 23, 1961

The Hungerers (See Floydada to Matador)

*Jim Dandy
    Reviews:
    Library Journal 67:229, Mar 1, 1941
    New York Times p. 26, Oct 8, 1941
                 p. 10, Nov 8, 1941
                 IX, p. 5, Dec 14, 1941
    Quarterly Journal of Speech 30:71-5, Feb 1944
    Time 38:68, Nov 17, 1941
    Vogue 110:129, Oct 15, 1947

*Life, Laughter and Tears (with Sean O'Casey)
    Reviews:
    New York Times p. 15, Feb 26, 1942

*A Lost Child's Fireflies
    Reviews:
    New York Times p. 11, Jul 16, 1954

*London Comedy: or, Sam the Highest Jumper of Them
    All
    Reviews:
    New York Times p. 24, Apr 8, 1960
                 p. 39, Apr 12, 1960
    Time 75:47, Mar 28, 1960

SAROYAN, WILLIAM (cont.)
  Love's Old Sweet Song
      Productions:
          Opened May 2, 1940 for 44 performances.
          (Off Broadway) Opened October 21, 1961 for 10
          performances (Equity Library Theatre).
      Reviews:
          Catholic World 151:344-5, Jun 1940
          Commonweal 32:82, May 17, 1940
          Nation 150:634-5, May 18, 1940
          New Republic 102:760, Jun 3, 1940
          New York Theatre Critics' Reviews 1940:319
          New York Times p. 44, Apr 7, 1940
                          IX, p. 3, Apr 4, 1940
                          p. 16, May 3, 1940
          New Yorker 16:28, May 11, 1940
          Newsweek 15:44-5, Apr 29, 1940
          Theatre Arts 24:832, Nov 1940
          Time 35:52, May 13, 1940

  My Heart's in the Highlands
      Productions:
          Opened April 13, 1939 for 44 performances.
          (Off Broadway) Season of 1938-39 (Group Theatre).
          (Off Broadway) Season of 1949-50 (Equity Library
          Theatre).
      Reviews:
          Catholic World 149:343-4, Jun 1939
          Commonweal 30:22, Apr 28, 1939
          Nation 148:538, May 6, 1939
          New Republic 98:379, May 3, 1939
          New York Times p. 29, Apr 14, 1939
                          X, p. 1, May 7, 1939
                          p. 36, Nov 22, 1949
                          p. 8, Feb 18, 1950
          Newsweek 13:45, May 1, 1939
          North American Review 247 no. 2:365, Jun 1939
          Theatre Arts 23:396+, Jun 1939
                       24:832, Nov 1940

  Once Around the Block
      Productions:
          (Off Broadway) Season of 1956-57.
      Reviews:
          New York Times p. 36, May 25, 1950
                          p. 34, Oct 29, 1956
                          VI, p. 31, Nov 11, 1956

Opera Opera (See Floydada to Matador)

*Sam Ego's House
  Reviews:
      New York Times p. 43, Nov 11, 1954

*Sam Ego's House of Angels Aghast
  Reviews:
      New York Times p. 11, Nov 1, 1947

Sam the Highest Jumper of Them All (See London
      Comedy)

*Settled Out of Court (with H. Cecil)
  Reviews:
      New York Times p. 44, Oct 20, 1960

*The Son
  Reviews:
      Christian Science Monitor Magazine p. 7, Aug 19,
        1950
      New York Times p. 12, Apr 1, 1950
                   p. 24, Aug 16, 1950

*Sunset Sonata
  Reviews:
      Newsweek 13:35, Jun 12, 1939

Talking to You (See Two By Saroyan)

The Time of Your Life
  Productions:
      Opened October 25, 1939 for 185 performances.
      Opened September 23, 1940 for 32 performances.
      (Off Broadway) Season of 1946-47.
      Opened January 19, 1955 for 15 performances.
  Reviews:
      America 92:518, Feb 12, 1955
      Catholic World 150:335, Dec 1939
                     180:467, Mar 1955
      Commonweal 31:78, Nov 10, 1939
                 32:512, Oct 11, 1940
      Life 7:46-9, Dec 4, 1939
      Nation 149:505-6, Nov 4, 1939
             180:124-5, Feb 5, 1955
      New Republic 101:169, Nov 29, 1939
      New York Theatre Critics' Reviews 1940:463
                                        1955:390

SAROYAN, WILLIAM (cont.)
   The Time of Your Life (cont.)
         New York Times p. 26, Oct 26, 1939
                         IX, p. 1, Nov 5, 1939
                         IX, p. 1, Nov 12, 1939
                         IX, p. 1, Nov 26, 1939
                         p. 27, Sep 24, 1940
                         II, p. 1, Jan 16, 1955
                         p. 35, Jan 20, 1955
                         II, p. 1, Jan 30, 1955
         New Yorker 30:44+, Jan 29, 1955
         Newsweek 14:30, Oct 23, 1939
                   14:35, Nov 6, 1939
                   45:80-1, Jan 31, 1955
         North American Review 248 no. 2:403-4, Dec 1939
         One Act Play Magazine 3:175-9, Feb 1940
         Theatre Arts 23:842+, Dec 1939
                       24:11-13, Jan 1940
                       24:832, Nov 1940
                       30:351, Jun 1946
                       39:22-4+, Jan 1955
                       39:22, 25, Apr 1955
         Time 34:32, Nov 6, 1939
              65:71, Jan 31, 1955
         Yale Review 30:422, Winter 1941

   Two By Saroyan ("Talking to You" and "Across the
         Board on Tomorrow Morning")
      Productions:
         Opened August 17, 1942 for 8 performances.
         (Off Broadway) Opened October 22, 1961 for 98
            performances.
      Reviews:
         Nation 193:460, Dec 2, 1961
         New Republic 107:257, Aug 31, 1942
         New York Theatre Critics' Reviews 1942:252
         New York Times p. 13, Mar 21, 1942
                        p. 17, Aug 18, 1942
                        p. 22, Oct 23, 1961
         New Yorker 37:129-30, Nov 4, 1961
         Player's Magazine 17:8, Apr 1941
         Theatre Arts 25:526-9, Jul 1941
         Vogue 100:82-3, Sep 15, 1942

416

The Devil's Advocate (Based on Morris L. West's novel)
Productions:
Opened March 9, 1961 for 116 performances.
Reviews:
America 105:161-3, Apr 15, 1961
Catholic World 193:8-12, Apr 1961
Christian Century 78:458, Apr 12, 1961
Commonweal 74:279, Jun 9, 1961
Nation 192:312, Apr 8, 1961
New York Theatre Critics' Reviews 1961:332
New York Times II, p. 3, Mar 5, 1961
            p. 20, Mar 10, 1961
            II, p. 1, Mar 19, 1961
New Yorker 37:126, Mar 18, 1961
Newsweek 57:88, Mar 20, 1961
Reporter 24:44, Apr 13, 1961
Saturday Review 44:35, Mar 25, 1961
Theatre Arts 45:54-5, May 1961
Time 77:42, Mar 17, 1961

The Highest Tree
Productions:
Opened November 4, 1959 for 21 performances.
Reviews:
America 102:253, Nov 21, 1959
New York Theatre Critics' Reviews 1959:235
New York Times II, p. 1, Nov 1, 1959
            p. 41, Nov 5, 1959
New Yorker 35:117-18, Nov 14, 1959
Reporter 21:39, Dec 10, 1959
Saturday Review 42:34, Nov 21, 1959
Time 74:57, Nov 16, 1959

One by One
Productions:
Opened December 1, 1964 for 7 performances.
Reviews:
New York Theatre Critics' Reviews 1964:123
New York Times p. 60, Dec 2, 1964

Sunrise at Campobello
Productions:
Opened January 30, 1958 for 556 performances.
Reviews:
America 98:735, Mar 22, 1958

SCHARY, DORE (cont.)
  Sunrise at Campobello (cont.)
            Catholic World 187:67, Apr 1958
            Christian Century 75:622-3, May 21, 1958
            Commonweal 67:592, Mar 7, 1958
            Life 44:91-4, Feb 10, 1958
            Look 22:98-101+, Apr 1, 1958
            Nation 186:146, Feb 15, 1958
            New Republic 138:20, Feb 10, 1958
            New York Theatre Critics' Reviews 1958:378
            New York Times VI, p. 42, Jan 19, 1958
                          II, p. 1, Jan 26, 1958
                          p. 16, Jan 29, 1958
                          p. 25, Jan 31, 1958
                          II, p. 1, Feb 9, 1958
                          II, p. 3, Apr 20, 1958
                          II, p. 4, Jan 25, 1959
                          p. 17, Mar 26, 1959
                          p. 15, Jun 8, 1959
            New York Times Magazine Jan 19, 1958
            New Yorker 33:93-6, Feb 8, 1958
            Newsweek 51:69, Feb 10, 1958
            Reporter 18:35, Mar 6, 1958
            Saturday Review 41:28, Feb 15, 1958
            Theatre Arts 42:15-16, Apr 1958
            Time 71:57, Feb 10, 1958

  Too Many Heroes
    Productions:
      Opened November 15, 1937 for 16 performances.
    Reviews:
      New York Times p. 26, Nov 16, 1937
      Theatre Arts 22:22, Jan 1938
      Time 30:36, Nov 29, 1937

SCHISGAL, MURRAY

  The Basement
    Productions:
      (Off Broadway) Opened October 2, 1967 for 24
        performances.
    Reviews:
      America 117:487-8, Oct 28, 1967
      Christian Century 85:26+, Jan 3, 1968
      New York Times p. 56, Oct 3, 1967
                     II, p. 3, Oct 15, 1967

New Yorker 43:151-2, Oct 14, 1967
Newsweek 70:106+, Oct 16, 1967

*Ducks and Lovers
Reviews:
New York Times p. 39, Oct 20, 1961

Fragments
Productions:
(Off Broadway) Opened October 2, 1967 for 24
performances.
Reviews:
America 117:487-8, Oct 28, 1967
Christian Century 85:26+, Jan 3, 1968
New York Times p. 56, Oct 3, 1967
II, p. 3, Oct 15, 1967
New Yorker 43:151-2, Oct 14, 1967
Newsweek 70:106+, Oct 16, 1967

Jimmy Shine
Productions:
Opened December 5, 1968 for 153 performances.
Reviews:
America 120:147-8, Feb 1, 1969
New Republic 160:32-4, Jan 25, 1969
New York Theatre Critics' Reviews 1968:152
1968:154
New York Times p. 52, Dec 6, 1968
II, p. 3, Dec 22, 1968
New Yorker 44:180-1, Dec 14, 1968
Newsweek 72:115, Dec 16, 1968
Saturday Review 51:13, Dec 21, 1968
Time 92:81, Dec 13, 1968

Luv
Productions:
Opened November 11, 1964 for 901 performances.
Reviews:
America 112:232-2, Feb 13, 1965
Catholic World 200:383, Mar 1965
Commonweal 81:389, Dec 11, 1964
Life 58:79-81+, Jan 8, 1965
Nation 199:415, Nov 30, 1964
New Republic 151:20, Dec 12, 1964
New York Theatre Critics' Reviews 1964:152
New York Times p. 43, Nov 12, 1964
p. 26, Nov 13, 1964

SCHISGAL, MURRAY (cont.)
    Luv (cont.)
                                II, p. 1, Nov 22, 1964
                                    p. 56, Nov 16, 1965
                                    p. 20, Feb 3, 1966
                                    p. 36, Dec 22, 1966
                    New Yorker 40:143, Nov 21, 1964
                    Newsweek 64:102, Nov 23, 1964
                    Saturday Review 47:29, Nov 28, 1964
                    Time 84:81, Nov 20, 1964
                    Vogue 145:68, Jan 1, 1965

    The Tiger
        Productions:
            (Off Broadway) Opened February 4, 1963 for 200
                performances.
        Reviews:
            Commonweal 77:665, Mar 22, 1963
            Nation 196:166-7, Feb 23, 1963
            New York Times p. 5, Feb 6, 1963
            New Yorker 38:116, Feb 16, 1963
            Newsweek 61:56, Feb 18, 1963
            Time 81:63, Feb 15, 1963

    The Typists
        Productions:
            (Off Broadway) Opened February 4, 1963 for 200
                performances.
        Reviews:
            Commonweal 77:665, Mar 22, 1963
            Nation 196:166-7, Feb 23, 1963
            New York Times p. 5, Feb 6, 1963
            New Yorker 38:114+, Feb 16, 1963
            Newsweek 61:56, Feb 18, 1963
            Time 81:63, Feb 15, 1963

SCHULBERG, BUDD

    The Disenchanted (with Harvey Breit) (Based on Schul-
            berg's novel)
        Productions:
            Opened December 3, 1958 for 189 performances.
            (Off Broadway) Opened January 6, 1962 for 9 per-
                formances (Equity Library Theatre).
        Reviews:
            America 100:557, Feb 7, 1959

Catholic World 188:419, Feb 1959
Christian Century 75:1488, Dec 24, 1958
Commonweal 69:386, Jan 9, 1959
Nation 187:501, Dec 27, 1958
New Republic 139:23, Dec 22, 1958
New York Theatre Critics' Reviews 1958:180
New York Times II, p. 4, Nov 4, 1958
            p. 53, Dec 4, 1958
            II, p. 1, Jan 11, 1959
New Yorker 34:107-9, Dec 13, 1958
Newsweek 52:63, Dec 15, 1958
Reporter 20:36-7, Jan 8, 1959
Saturday Review 41:31, Dec 20, 1958
Theatre Arts 43:11+, Feb 1959
          44:22-47, Aug 1960
Time 72:44, Dec 15, 1958

SELWYN, EDGAR

Anything Might Happen
  Productions:
    Opened February 20, 1923 for 63 performances.
  Reviews:
    Life (NY) 81:18, May 5, 1923
    New York Clipper 71:14, Mar 7, 1923
    New York Times p. 22, Feb 21, 1923
              VII, p. 1, Feb 25, 1923
    Theatre Magazine 37:16+, Apr 1923

The Arab
  Productions:
    Opened September 20, 1911 for 53 performances.
  Reviews:
    Dramatic Mirror 66:10, Sep 27, 1911
              66:5, Oct 4, 1911
    Everybody's 25:818, Dec 1911
    Green Book 6:966, Nov 1911
    Leslies' Weekly 113:493, Nov 2, 1911
    Life (NY) 58:618, Oct 12, 1911
    Munsey 46:282, Nov 1911
          55:695, Sep 1915
    New York Drama News 61:20, Jun 26, 1915
    Red Book 18:379+, Dec 1911
    Theatre Magazine 14:163, Nov 1911

SELWYN, EDGAR (cont.)
  The Country Boy
    Productions:
      Opened August 30, 1910 for 143 performances.
    Reviews:
      Canadian Magazine 36:287-8, Jan 1911
      Dramatic Mirror 64:7, Sep 10, 1910
      Dramatist 2:99-101, Oct 1910
      Everybody's 23:702-3+, Nov 1910
      Good Housekeeping 51:707, Dec 1910
      Green Book 5:536-9, Mar 1911
                5:1153-78, Jun 1911
      Hampton 25:674-6, Nov 1910
      Metropolitan Magazine 33:262-3, Nov 1910
      Munsey 44:270-6, Nov 1910
      Pearson 24:645, Nov 1910
      Theatre Magazine 12:100-1+, Oct 1910
      World Today 19:1224-35, Nov 1910

  The Crowded Hour (with Channing Pollock)
    Productions:
      Opened November 22, 1918 for 139 performances
    Reviews:
      Dramatic Mirror 79:831, Dec 7, 1918
      Forum 61:114-15, Jan 1919
      Hearst 35:42-3+, May 1919
      New York Drama News 65:10, Nov 16-23, 1918
      New York Times p. 13, Nov 26, 1918
                    VII, p. 6, Dec 8, 1918
                    VII, p. 8, Dec 8, 1918
      Theatre Magazine 29:20+, Jan 1919

  Dancing Mothers (with Edmund Goulding)
    Productions:
      Opened August 11, 1924 for 312 performances.
    Reviews:
      Bookman 60:211, Oct 1924
      Canadian Magazine 64:104-5+, May 1925
      Life (NY) 84:18, Aug 28, 1924
      Theatre Magazine 39:15+, Oct 1924
                       39:28-9+, Nov 1924

  I'll Be Hanged if I Do (with William Collier)
    Productions:
      Opened November 28, 1910 for 80 performances.
    Reviews:
      Blue Book 12:882-5, Mar 1911

Bookman 23:602, Feb 1911
Dramatic Mirror 64:7, Nov 30, 1910
64:9, Dec 14, 1910
Green Book 5:242-3+, Feb 1911
Munsey 44:710, Feb 1911
Pearson 25:260, Feb 1911
Red Book 16:764-8, Feb 1911

The Mirage
Productions:
Opened September 30, 1920 for 192 performances.
Reviews:
Dramatic Mirror p. 635, Oct 9, 1920
Independent 104:113, Oct 23, 1920
New York Clipper 68:29, Oct 6, 1920
New York Times p. 14, Oct 1, 1920
Theatre Magazine 32:349+, Dec 1920

Nearly Married
Productions:
Opened September 5, 1913 for 123 performances.
Reviews:
Blue Book 18:215-17, Dec 1913
Bookman 38:263, Nov 1913
Dramatic Mirror 70:6-7, Sep 10, 1913
Dramatist 5:440-1, Jan 1914
Green Book 10:870-1, Nov 1913
10:964-5, Dec 1913
Munsey 50:294-5, Nov 1913
New York Drama News 58:9, Sep 13, 1913
New York Times p. 7, Sep 6, 1913
Theatre Magazine 18:112-13+, Oct 1913

Possession
Productions:
Opened October 2, 1928 for 47 performances.
Reviews:
Life (NY) 92:19, Oct 19, 1928
New York Times VII, p. 1, Jul 22, 1928
IX, p. 2, Sep 23, 1928
p. 35, Oct 3, 1928

Rolling Stones
Productions:
Opened August 17, 1915 for 115 performances.
Reviews:
Bookman 42:159+, Oct 1915

SELWYN, EDGAR (cont.)
    Rolling Stones (cont.)
            Dramatic Mirror 74:8, Aug 25, 1915
            Green Book 14:620-1, Oct 1915
            Nation 101:269, Aug 26, 1915
            New York Times p. 11, Aug 18, 1915
            Theatre Magazine 22:169+, Oct 1915

    Something to Brag About (with William LeBaron)
        Productions:
            Opened August 13, 1925 for 4 performances.
        Reviews:
            New York Times VII, p. 1, Jul 12, 1925
                            p. 14, Aug 14, 1925

SHAW, IRWIN

    The Assassin
        Productions:
            Opened October 17, 1945 for 13 performances.
        Reviews:
            Commonweal 43:69, Nov 2, 1945
            New Republic 113:573, Oct 29, 1945
                        114:479-80, Apr 8, 1946
            New York Theatre Critics' Reviews 1945:138
            New York Times p. 13, Mar 23, 1945
                        II, p. 2, Apr 1, 1945
                        p. 20, Oct 18, 1945
            New Yorker 21:42, Oct 27, 1945
            Newsweek 26:90, Oct 29, 1945
            Theatre Arts 29:679+, Dec 1945
            Time 47:67, Mar 25, 1946

    Bury the Dead
        Productions:
            Opened April 18, 1936 for 97 performances.
        Reviews:
            Catholic World 143:338-40, Jan 1936
            Commonweal 24:48, May 8, 1936
            Literary Digest 121:11, May 2, 1936
            Nation 142:592-3, May 6, 1936
            New Republic 87:21, May 13, 1936
            New York Times p. 21, Mar 16, 1936
                        p. 17, Apr 20, 1936
                        IX, p. 1, Apr 26, 1936
                        X, p. 1, May 3, 1936

XI, p. 3, Nov 15, 1936
II, p. 1, Aug 20, 1950
Newsweek 7:29, Apr 25, 1936
Theatre Arts 20:417-19, Jun 1936
Time 27:56, Apr 27, 1936

Children from Their Games
Productions:
Opened April 11, 1963 for 4 performances.
Reviews:
New York Theatre Critics' Reviews 1963:352
New York Times II, p. 7, Apr 7, 1963
p. 33, Apr 12, 1963
New Yorker 39:96, Apr 20, 1963
Newsweek 61:90, Apr 22, 1963
Saturday Review 46:27, Apr 27, 1963
Theatre Arts 47:65, Jun 1963

The Gentle People
Productions:
Opened January 5, 1939 for 141 performances.
(Off Broadway) Opened July 5, 1947 (Actors' Theatre).
Reviews:
Catholic World 148:598, Feb 1939
Commonweal 29:358, Jan 20, 1939
Life 6:31, Feb 6, 1939
New Republic 97:343, Jan 25, 1939
New York Times p. 25, Jan 6, 1939
p. 12, Jul 7, 1939
IX, p. 1, Jul 30, 1939
p. 10, Apr 15, 1950
North American Review 247 no. 2:368-9, Jun 1939
Newsweek 13:26, Jan 16, 1939
One Act Play Magazine 2:675-7, Jan 1939
Stage 16:10-11, Feb 1939
Theatre Arts 23:170, Mar 1939
Time 33:41, Jan 16, 1939

Quiet City
Productions:
(Off Broadway) Opened April 16 and 23, 1939 (Group Theatre).
No Reviews.

Patate (Adapted from the play by Marcel Achard)
Productions:

SHAW, IRWIN (cont.)
  Patate (cont.)
      Opened October 28, 1958 for 7 performances.
    Reviews:
      Nation 184:554, Jun 22, 1957
      New York Theatre Critics' Reviews 1958:234
      New York Times p. 31, Oct 29, 1958
      New Yorker 34:91, Nov 8, 1958
      Saturday Review 41:27, Nov 15, 1958
      Theatre Arts 43:23-4, Jan 1959

Retreat to Pleasure
  Productions:
      Opened December 17, 1940 for 23 performances.
    Reviews:
      New York Theatre Critics' Reviews 1940:188
      New York Times p. 32, Dec 18, 1940
                  p. 24, Dec 19, 1940
      New Yorker 16:29, Dec 28, 1940
      Newsweek 16:38, Dec 30, 1940
      Stage 1:54, Feb 1941
      Theatre Arts 25:96, Feb 1941

Siege
  Productions:
      Opened December 8, 1937 for 6 performances.
    Reviews:
      New York Times p. 31, Dec 9, 1937

Sons and Soldiers
  Productions:
      Opened May 4, 1943 for 22 performances.
    Reviews:
      Catholic World 157:300, Jun 1943
      Commonweal 38:123, May 21, 1943
      Nation 156:715, May 15, 1943
      New Republic 108:669, May 17, 1943
      New York Theatre Critics' Reviews 1943:325
      New York Times p. 22, May 5, 1943
      New Yorker 19:36, May 15, 1943
      Time 41:73, May 17, 1943

The Survivors (with Peter Viertel)
  Productions:
      Opened January 19, 1948 for 8 performances.
    Reviews:
      Catholic World 166:552, Mar 1948

Commonweal 47:424, Feb 6, 1948
Forum 109:156-8, Mar 1948
New Republic 118:33, Feb 2, 1948
New York Theatre Critics' Reviews 1948:374
New York Times p. 27, Jan 20, 1948
                II, p. 1, Jan 25, 1948
New Yorker 23:38+, Jan 31, 1948
Newsweek 31:73, Feb 2, 1948

SHELDON, EDWARD

Bewitched (with Sidney Howard)
    Productions:
    Opened October 1, 1924 for 29 performances.
    Reviews:
        New York Times p. 26, Oct 2, 1924
                        VIII, p. 1, Oct 5, 1924
        Theatre Magazine 39:14+, Dec 1924

The Boss
    Productions:
    Opened January 30, 1911 for 88 performances.
    Reviews:
        Blue Book 13:22-4, May 1911
        Bookman 23:32, Mar 1911
        Colliers 46:16+, Feb 25, 1911
        Dramatic Mirror 65:7, Feb 1, 1911
        Dramatist 2:143-5, Apr 1911
        Everybody's 24:670-3, May 1911
        Leslies' Weekly 112:181, Feb 16, 1911
        Life (NY) 57:308-9, Feb 9, 1911
        Metropolitan Magazine 34:126, Apr 1911
        Munsey 45:133-4, Apr 1911
        Pearson 25:502, Apr 1911
        Theatre Magazine 13:72, Mar 1911
        World Today 20:282, Mar 1911

The Czarina (Adapted from the Hungarian of Melchoir
        Lengyel and Lajos Biro)
    Productions:
    Opened January 31, 1922 for 136 performances.
    Reviews:
        Hearst 41:45-7+, May 1922
        New Republic 29:340-41, Feb 15, 1922
        New York Clipper 70:20, Feb 8, 1922
        New York Times p. 22, Feb 1, 1922
        Theatre Magazine 35:211+, Apr 1922

SHELDON, EDWARD (cont.)
    Dishonored Lady (with Margaret Ayer Barnes)
        Productions:
        Opened February 4, 1930 for 127 performances.
        Reviews:
            Commonweal 11:453, Feb 19, 1930
            Life (NY) 95:18, Feb 28, 1930
            New Republic 62:20-1, Feb 19, 1930
            New York Times VIII, p. 2, Jan 26, 1930
                            p. 27, Feb 6, 1930
                            IX, p. 2, May 25, 1930
            Outlook 154:312, Feb 19, 1930
            Theatre Arts 14:283-4, Apr 1930
            Theatre Magazine 51:43, Apr 1930
            Vogue 75:54+, Mar 29, 1930

    The Garden of Paradise (Based on Hans Christian Ander-
        son's "The Little Mermaid.")
        Productions:
        Opened November 28, 1914 for 17 performances.
        Reviews:
            American Playwright 4:6-7, Jan 1915
            American Mercury 79:42-6, Apr 1915
            Book News 33:229, Jan 1915
            Bookman 40:548-9, Jan 1915
            Colliers 54:28, Jan 2, 1915
            Dial 60:75, Jan 20, 1916
            Dramatic Mirror 72:8, Dec 9, 1914
            Green Book 13:267-78, Feb 1915
            Life (NY) 64:1082, Dec 10, 1914
            Munsey 54:85-9+, Feb 1915
            Nation 9:669, Dec 3, 1914
            New Republic 1:23, Dec 5, 1914
            New York Times VII, p. 8, Jul 19, 1914
                            p. 9, Nov 30, 1914
                            IX, p. 2, Dec 6, 1914
            Smart Set 45:147-8, Feb 1915

    The High Road
        Productions:
        Opened November 9, 1912 for 71 performances.
        Reviews:
            American Playwright 1:391-4, Dec 1912
            American Magazine 75:61, May 1913
            Book News 31:653-4, Apr 1913
            Bookman 36:536-8, Jan 1913
            Colliers 50:19, Dec 28, 1912

Dramatic Mirror 68:6, Nov 27, 1912
Dramatist 4:319-20, Jan 1913
Everybody's 28:258, Feb 1913
Green Book 9:200-201+, Feb 1913
        9:367-8, Feb 1913
Literary Digest 46:183, Jan 25, 1913
McClure's 40:66-9, Mar 1913
Munsey 48:684-5, Jan 1913
New York Drama News 67:11, Nov 30, 1912
Red Book 20:689-96, Feb 1913
Theatre Magazine 17:2+, Jan 1913

Jenny (with Margaret Ayer Barnes)
    Productions:
        Opened October 8, 1929 for 111 performances.
    Reviews:
        Catholic World 130:332-3, Dec 1929
        Life (NY) 94:22, Nov 1, 1929
        Nation 129:504, Oct 30, 1929
        New York Times VIII, p. 1, Jun 2, 1929
                   p. 34, Oct 9, 1929
        Outlook 153:314, Oct 23, 1929
        Theatre Magazine 50:15+, Dec 1929
        Vogue 74:164, Dec 7, 1929

Lulu Belle (with Charles MacArthur)
    Productions:
        Opened February 9, 1926 for 461 performances.
    Reviews:
        Bookman 63:215-16, Apr 1926
        Life (NY) 87:21, Mar 4, 1926
        New York Times p. 17, Jan 27, 1926
                  p. 20, Feb 10, 1926
                  VIII, p. 1, Feb 14, 1926
        Theatre Magazine 43:15, Apr 1926
        Vogue 67:116-17, Apr 1926

The Nigger
    Productions:
        Opened December 4, 1909 in repertory.
    Reviews:
        Burr McIntosh Monthly 22:220-1, Mar 1910
        Dramatic Mirror 62:5, Dec 11, 1909
        Dramatist 2:161-3, Apr 1911
        Forum 43:186-7, Feb 1910
        Green Book 3:392-4, Feb 1910
                5:705-36, Apr 1911

SHELDON, EDWARD (cont.)
The Nigger (cont.)
Hampton 24:272-3, Feb 1910
Harper's Weekly 54:24, Jan 1, 1910
Life (NY) 54:886, Dec 16, 1909
Metropolitan Magazine 32:118-19, Apr 1910
Theatre Magazine 10:3-5, Jan 1910

*Proud Princess (with Dorothy Donnelly)
Reviews:
New York Times VII, p. 2, Feb 17, 1924

Romance
Productions:
Opened February 10, 1913 for 160 performances.
Opened February 28, 1921 for 106 performances.
Reviews:
Blue Book 17:242-4, Jun 1913
Bookman 37:308, May 1913
Current Opinion 54:379-83, May 1913
Dramatic Mirror 69:6, Feb 19, 1913
                83:408, Mar 5, 1921
Dramatist 5:468-9, Apr 1914
Editor 37:357-8, Jun 25, 1913
Everybody's 28:681-3, May 1913
Green Book 9:632-4, Apr 1913
            9:735-6, Apr 1913
            10:489-503, Sep 1913
Hearst 24:299-308, Aug 1913
Life (NY) 61:416, Feb 27, 1913
Munsey 49:148, Apr 1913
New York Clipper 69:23, May 9, 1921
New York Times VIII, p. 5, Feb 9, 1913
                p. 13, Feb 11, 1913
                p. 20, Jul 1, 1916
                p. 9, Oct 7, 1916
                p. 18, Mar 1, 1921
                VI, p. 1, Mar 6, 1921
                VIII, p. 2, Mar 11, 1928
                p. 23, Aug 27, 1935
                p. 23, Aug 17, 1937
Red Book pp. 113-16, May 1913
Theatre Magazine 17:65-6, Mar 1913

The Song of Songs (Based on Hermann Sudermann's novel)
Productions:
Opened December 22, 1914 for 191 performances.

Reviews:
Bookman 40:637-8, Feb 1915
Current Opinion 58:97-8, Feb 1915
Dramatic Mirror 72:8, Dec 30, 1914
Green Book 13:478-9, Mar 1915
13:570-1, Mar 1915
Hearst 27:299-301+, Mar 1915
Nation 100:87, Jan 21, 1915
New Republic 1:25, Jan 2, 1915
New York Times p. 13, Dec 23, 1914
VIII, p. 2, Dec 27, 1914
Smart Set 45:453-4, Jan 1915
Theatre Magazine 21:58+, Feb 1915

SHELLEY, ELSA

Foxhole in the Parlor
Productions:
Opened May 23, 1945 for 45 performances.
Reviews:
Commonweal 42:191, Jun 8, 1945
New Republic 112:815, Jun 11, 1945
New York Theatre Critics' Reviews 1945:210
New York Times p. 15, May 24, 1945
New Yorker 21:38, Jun 2, 1945
Theatre Arts 29:389, Jul 1945

Pick-Up Girl
Productions:
Opened May 3, 1944 for 198 performances.
Reviews:
Catholic World 159:264-6, Jun 1944
Commonweal 40:110-111, May 19, 1944
Life 16:68-70, Jun 12, 1944
New York Theatre Critics' Reviews 1944:196
New York Times p. 25, May 4, 1944
New Yorker 20:44, May 13, 1944
Theatre Arts 28:572, Oct 1944

With A Silk Thread
Productions:
Opened April 12, 1950 for 13 performances.
Reviews:
New York Theatre Critics' Reviews 1950:314
New Yorker 26:60+, Apr 22, 1950
Newsweek 35:95, Apr 24, 1950
Theatre Arts 34:17, Jun 1950

Chicago
    Productions:
        (Off Broadway) Opened April 12, 1966 for 16 per-
            formances.
    Reviews:
        Nation 202:403, Apr 4, 1966
        New York Times II, p. 15, Apr 10, 1966
                          p. 36, Apr 13, 1966

Forensic and the Navigators
    Productions:
        (Off Broadway) Season of 1967-68 in repertory,
            (Theatre Genesis).
    No Reviews.

La Turista
    Productions:
        (Off Broadway) Opened March 4, 1967 for 29 per-
            formances (American Place Theatre).
    Reviews:
        New York Times II, p. 5, Mar 5, 1967
                          II, p. 3, Apr 13, 1969

Red Cross
    Productions:
        (Off Broadway) Opened April 28, 1968 for 65 per-
            formances.
    Reviews:
        Commonweal 88:384, Jun 14, 1968
        Nation 202:224, Feb 21, 1966
        New York Times p. 47, Apr 29, 1968
        New Yorker 44:91, May 11, 1968

Up To Thursday
    Productions:
        (Off Broadway) Opened February 10, 1965 for 23
            performances (Theatre 1965 New Playwrights
            Series).
    Reviews:
        New York Times II, p. 1, Feb 7, 1965
                          p. 45, Feb 11, 1965
        Newsweek 65:93, Feb 22, 1965

SHERWOOD, ROBERT E.

*Acropolis
   Reviews:
      New York Times p. 25, Nov 24, 1933

Abe Lincoln in Illinois
   Productions:
      Opened October 15, 1938 for 472 performances.
      (Off Broadway) Opened January 21, 1963 for 40 per-
         formances.
   Reviews:
      Canadian Forum 19:355-6, Feb 1940
      Catholic World 148:340-1, Dec 1938
      Commonweal 29:20, Oct 28, 1938
                  77:543, Feb 15, 1963
      Forum 101:72, Feb 1939
      Independent Woman 17:348, Nov 1938
      Life 5:42+, Oct 31, 1938
      Nation 147:487-8, Nov 5, 1938
             196:125-6, Feb 9, 1963
      New Republic 97:18, Nov 9, 1938
                   98:134, Mar 8, 1939
      New York Times p. 20, Oct 4, 1938
                     p. 12, Oct 17, 1938
                     IX, p. 1, Oct 23, 1938
                     X, p. 3, Apr 23, 1939
                     IX, p. 1, Jul 30, 1939
                     IX, p. 1, Oct 22, 1939
                     p. 5, Jan 23, 1963
      New Yorker 38:69-70, Feb 2, 1963
      Newsweek 12:29, Oct 31, 1938
      North American Review 246 no. 2:373-4, Dec 1938
      Saturday Review 19:6, Feb 18, 1939
                      46:20, Feb 9, 1963
      Stage 16:7-9, Nov 1938
            16:48-9, Apr 1, 1939
      Theatre Arts 22:853-5, Dec 1938
                   47:58-9+, Mar 1963
      Time 32:53, Oct 24, 1938
      Vogue 92:45+, Nov 15, 1938

*Hannibal Ante Portas
   Reviews:
      New York Times VIII, p. 2, Jul 7, 1929

SHERWOOD, ROBERT E. (cont.)
Idiot's Delight
Productions:
Opened March 24, 1936 for 300 performances.
Opened August 31, 1936 for 179 performances.
Opened May 23, 1951 for 15 performances.
(Off Broadway) Season of 1956-57.
Reviews:
Catholic World 143:212, May 1936
173:306-7, Jul 1951
Commonweal 23:664, Apr 10, 1936
24:104, May 22, 1936
54:213, Jun 8, 1951
Drama 16:117, May 1938
Forum 95:348-9, Jun 1936
Literary Digest 121:20, Mar 28, 1936
Nation 142:490-2, Apr 15, 1936
New Republic 86:253, Apr 8, 1936
New York Theatre Critics' Reviews 1951:260
New York Times p. 26, Mar 10, 1936
p. 25, Mar 25, 1936
IX, p. 1, Apr 12, 1936
IX, p. 3, Oct 4, 1936
p. 26, May 19, 1937
p. 22, Aug 10, 1937
p. 19, Mar 23, 1938
X, p. 2, Apr 10, 1938
IV, p. 8, Oct 23, 1938
p. 46, May 24, 1951
p. 14, Feb 23, 1957
Newsweek 7:32, Apr 4, 1936
9:24, May 29, 1937
Pictorial Review 37:65, Jul 1936
Player's Magazine 12:11+, May-Jun 1936
Saturday Review 14:6-7, May 9, 1936
14:18, May 9, 1936
Stage 13:26-8, Apr 1936
Theatre Arts 20:340-1, May 1936
20:466-7, Jun 1936
22:410-11, Jun 1938
Time 27:38, Apr 6, 1936

The Love Nest (Based on Ring Lardner's story)
Productions:
Opened December 22, 1927 for 23 performances.
Reviews:
New York Times p. 17, Dec 23, 1927
Saturday Review 4:499-500, Jan 7, 1928

The Petrified Forest
    Productions:
        Opened January 7, 1935 for 197 performances.
        Opened November 1, 1943 for 8 performances.
    Reviews:
        Canadian Forum 15:194, Feb 1935
        Catholic World 140:601-2, Feb 1935
        Commonweal 21:375, Jan 25, 1935
        Literary Digest 119:19+, Jan 19, 1935
        Nation 140:111, Jan 23, 1935
        New Republic 82:21, Feb 13, 1935
        New York Theatre Critics' Reviews 1943:242
        New York Times p. 31, Dec 21, 1934
                      IX, p. 1, Dec 30, 1934
                      p. 26, Jan 8, 1935
                      IX, p. 1, Jan 13, 1935
                      X, p. 1, Jan 20, 1935
                      X, p. 1, May 12, 1935
                      II, p. 9, Nov 24, 1935
                      II, p. 12, Mar 1, 1936
                      VIII, p. 1, Jan 10, 1943
                      p. 30, Nov 2, 1943
                      p. 6, Mar 19, 1955
        Saturday Review 11:572, Mar 23, 1935
        Stage 12:4, Feb 1935
        Theatre Arts 19:169-70, Mar 1935
        Time 25:30, Jan 14, 1935
        Vanity Fair 44:48, Mar 1935
        Vogue 85:52-3, Feb 15, 1935

The Queen's Husband
    Productions:
        Opened January 25, 1928 for 125 performances.
    Reviews:
        Dial 84:351, Apr 1928
        Life (NY) 91:19, Feb 9, 1928
        New York Times p. 17, Jan 26, 1928
                      VIII, p. 4, Jan 29, 1928
                      VIII, p. 1, Feb 12, 1928
                      IX, p. 4, Apr 15, 1928
                      p. 23, Sep 6, 1928
                      VIII, p. 2, Nov 15, 1931
                      p. 23, Jun 2, 1936
        Outlook 148:225, Feb 8, 1928
        Theatre Magazine 47:28-30+, May 1928
        Vogue 71:146+, Mar 15, 1928

SHERWOOD, ROBERT E. (cont.)
  Reunion in Vienna
    Productions:
      Opened November 16, 1931 for 264 performances.
    Reviews:
      Arts and Decoration 36:68, Jan 1932
      Bookman 74:564, Jan 1932
      Catholic World 134:467-8, Jan 1932
      Commonweal 15:160, Dec 9, 1931
      Dramatist 23:1448-9, Jan 1932
      Nation 133:650, Dec 9, 1931
             134:608, May 25, 1932
      New Republic 69:70, Dec 2, 1931
      New York Times p. 29, May 12, 1931
                    VIII, p. 4, Oct 18, 1931
                      p. 31, Nov 17, 1931
                      p. 17, Jan 4, 1934
                    IX, p. 3, Jan 28, 1934
      North American Review 234:174, Aug 1932
      Outlook 159:438, Dec 2, 1931
      Sketch Book 8:19, Dec 1931
      Theatre Arts 16:96-7, Feb 1932
      Theatre Guild Magazine 9:3, Jan 1932
                             9:18-21, Mar 1932
      Vanity Fair 37:74, Jan 1932
      Vogue 79:68+, Jan 15, 1932

  The Road to Rome
    Productions:
      Opened January 31, 1927 for 392 performances.
      Opened May 21, 1928 for 440 performances.
    Reviews:
      Bookman 65:205-6, Apr 1927
      Dramatist 18:1335-6, Apr 1927
      Life (NY) 89:19, Feb 17, 1927
      New Republic 50:70-1, Mar 9, 1927
      New York Times p. 24, Feb 1, 1927
                    VII, p. 1, Feb 6, 1927
                    VIII, p. 4, Feb 5, 1928
                      p. 19, May 22, 1928
                      p. 23, May 17, 1928
                    VIII, p. 3, Jun 3, 1928
                    VIII, p. 1, Jun 10, 1928
                      p. 22, Apr 15, 1929
                    X, p. 4, Nov 10, 1929
      Outlook 146:546-7, Aug 24, 1927
      Theatre Magazine 45:20, May 1927

Theatre Magazine 45:28+, Jun 1927
Vogue 69:84+, Apr 1, 1927

The Rugged Path
    Productions:
        Opened November 10, 1945 for 81 performances.
    Reviews:
        Catholic World 162:264, Dec 1945
        Commonweal 43:168, Nov 30, 1945
        Forum 105:468, Jan 1946
        Life 19:88-90, Dec 3, 1945
        Nation 161:562, Nov 24, 1945
        New Republic 113:711, Nov 26, 1945
        New York Theatre Critics' Reviews 1945:109
        New York Times p. 17, Oct 13, 1945
                      p. 17, Nov 12, 1945
                      II, p. 1, Nov 18, 1945
        New Yorker 21:47, Nov 17, 1945
        Newsweek 26:84, Nov 19, 1945
        Saturday Review 28:18-20, Nov 24, 1945
        Theatre Arts 30:6, 8-10, Jan 1946
        Time 46:63, Nov 19, 1945
        Vogue 106:61, Dec 15, 1945

Second Threshold (See entry under Barry, Philip)

Small War on Murray Hill
    Productions:
        Opened January 3, 1957 for 12 performances.
    Reviews:
        Catholic World 184:470-1, Mar 1957
        Christian Century 74:201, Feb 13, 1957
        Commonweal 65:436+, Jan 25, 1957
        New York Theatre Critics' Reviews 1957:397
        New York Times II, p. 1, Dec 30, 1956
                      p. 19, Jan 4, 1957
                      II, p. 1, Jan 13, 1957
        New Yorker 32:58+, Jan 12, 1957
        Newsweek 49:58, Jan 14, 1957
        Saturday Review 40:48, Jan 19, 1957
        Theatre Arts 41:19, Mar 1957
        Time 69:68, Jan 14, 1957

There Shall Be No Night
    Productions:
        Opened April 29, 1940 for 115 performances.
        Reopened September 9, 1940 for 66 performances.

SHERWOOD, ROBERT E. (cont.)
There Shall Be No Night (cont.)
Reviews:
Catholic World 151:343-4, Jun 1940
Commonweal 32:62, May 10, 1940
Life 8:48+, May 13, 1940
Nation 150: 605-6, May 11, 1940
New Republic 102:641, May 13, 1940
New York Theatre Critics' Reviews 1940:322
New York Times p. 11, Mar 30, 1940
            p. 25, Apr 30, 1940
            X, p. 1, May 5, 1940
            IX, p. 1, May 12, 1940
            IX, p. 1, Sep 22, 1940
            IX, p. 1, Oct 13, 1940
            IX, p. 3, Mar 30, 1941
            p. 20, May 6, 1941
            XI, p. 1, May 11, 1941
            p. 34, Dec 16, 1943
            II, p. 1, Jan 2, 1944
New Yorker 16:28, May 11, 1940
Newsweek 15:34, May 13, 1940
            22:80, Dec 27, 1943
Survey Graphic 29:408, Jul 1940
Theatre Arts 24:398-401+, Jul 1940
            24:548, Aug 1940
            25:788+, Nov 1941
            28:209-10+, Apr 1944
Time 35:52, May 13, 1940
Yale Review 30:423, Winter, 1941

This Is New York
Productions:
Opened November 28, 1930 for 59 performances.
Reviews:
Bookman 72:516, Jan 1931
Catholic World 132:464, Jan 1931
Drama Magazine 21:13, Jan 1931
Harper's Bazaar Vol. 162, Mar 1931
Life (NY) 96:18, Dec 19, 1930
New York Times p. 21, Nov 29, 1930
Outlook 156:629, Dec 17, 1930
Theatre Magazine 53:25, Feb 1931
Vogue 77:118, Feb 15, 1931

Tovarich (Adapted from the play by Jacques Deval)
Productions:

Opened October 15, 1936 for 356 performances.
Opened May 14, 1952 for 15 performances.
Reviews:
Catholic World 144:335-6, Dec 1936
               175:309, Jul 1952
Commonweal 25:20, Oct 30, 1936
            56:224, Jun 6, 1952
Life 2:38-9, Jan 11, 1937
    3:22-3, Dec 20, 1937
Literary Digest 122:22, Oct 31, 1936
Nation 143:530, Oct 31, 1936
New Republic 89:21, Nov 4, 1936
New York Theatre Critics' Reviews 1952:281
New York Times p. 19, Apr 25, 1935
           IX, p. 1, May 19, 1935
           p. 35, Sep 29, 1936
           IX, p. 2, Oct 4, 1936
           IX, p. 1, Oct 15, 1936
           p. 31, Oct 16, 1936
           X, p. 1, Oct 25, 1936
           X, p. 1, Jan 24, 1937
           X, p. 2, Apr 25, 1937
           p. 39, May 15, 1952
Newsweek 8:40, Oct 24, 1936
       10:30, Dec 20, 1937
Saturday Review 35:26, May 31, 1952
Stage 14:48-9, Nov 1936
    15:95, Oct 1937
Theatre Arts 19:481, Jul 1935
         20:919-23, Dec 1936
         21:833, Nov 1937
         36:82, Jul 1952
Time 28:47, Oct 26, 1936
    31:29, Jan 3, 1938

Waterloo Bridge
Productions:
Opened January 6, 1930 for 64 performances.
Reviews:
Life (NY) 95:20, Jan 24, 1930
Nation 130:106, Jan 22, 1930
New Republic 61:251, Jan 22, 1930
New York Times X, p. 4, Dec 1, 1929
              p. 29, Jan 7, 1930
              VIII, p. 4, Nov 29, 1931
Outlook 154:152, Jan 22, 1930
Theatre Magazine 51:70+, Feb 1930
Vogue 75:108, Mar 1, 1930

Alley Cat (with Alan Dinehart) (Based on an original
   script by Lawrence Pohle)
   Productions:
   Opened September 17, 1934 for 8 performances.
   Reviews:
   New York Times p. 18, Sep 18, 1934

Behind Red Lights (with Beth Brown) (Adapted from
   Beth Brown's novel For Men Only)
   Productions:
   Opened January 13, 1937 for 177 performances.
   Reviews:
   New York Times p. 17, Jan 14, 1937
   Stage 14:64, Feb 1937

Cheaper to Marry
   Productions:
   Opened April 15, 1924 for 71+ performances.
   Reviews:
   Life (NY) 83:20, May 1, 1924
   New York Times p. 26, Apr 16, 1924
                  VIII, p. 1, Apr 20, 1924
   Theatre Magazine 39:19, Jun 1924

Children of Today (with Clara Lipman)
   Productions:
   Opened December 1, 1913 for 24 performances.
   Reviews:
   Dramatic Mirror 70:6-7, Dec 3, 1913
   Theatre Magazine 19:46, Jan 1914

Creoles (with Kenneth Perkins)
   Productions:
   Opened September 22, 1927 for 28 performances.
   Reviews:
   New York Times p. 33, Sep 23, 1927

Crime (with John B. Hymer)
   Productions:
   Opened February 22, 1927 for 133 performances.
   Reviews:
   Bookman 65:331-2, May 1927
   Life (NY) 89:21, Mar 24, 1927
   New York Times p. 27, Feb 23, 1927
   Theatre Magazine 46:26+, Sep 1927
   Vogue 69:87+, Apr 15, 1927

Crime Wave (See Crime)

Crooked Gamblers (with Percival Wilde)
    Productions:
        Opened July 31, 1920 for 82 performances.
    Reviews:
        Dramatic Mirror p. 229, Aug 7, 1920
        New York Clipper 68:23, Aug 4, 1920
        New York Times p. 12, Aug 2, 1920
        Theatre Magazine 32:187-8, Oct 1920

The Crooked Square (with Alfred C. Kennedy)
    Productions:
        Opened September 10, 1923 for 88 performances.
    Reviews:
        New York Times p. 10, Sep 11, 1923
                        VII, p. 1, Sep 16, 1923
        Theatre Magazine 38:19, Nov 1923

East Is West (with John B. Hymer)
    Productions:
        Opened December 25, 1918 for 680 performances.
    Reviews:
        Dramatic Mirror 80:47, Jan 11, 1919
        Dramatist 11:1016, Jul 1920
        Forum 61:244-6, Feb 1919
        Hearst 35:46-7+, Jun 16, 1919
        Nation 108:104, Jan 18, 1919
        New York Times p. 9, Dec 26, 1918
        Theatre Magazine 29:78+, Feb 1919

Elevating a Husband (with Clara Lipman)
    Productions:
        Opened January 22, 1912 for 120 performances.
    Reviews:
        American Playwright 1:41-2, Feb 1912
        Blue Book 14:244-7, Dec 1911
        Dramatic Mirror 67:7, Jan 24, 1912
        Dramatist 3:237-8, Apr 1912
        Green Book 7:700-1+, Apr 1912
                    8:901-20, Nov 1912
        Hampton 28:202+, Apr 1912
        Munsey 46:902, Mar 1912
        Theatre Magazine 15:75-6+, Mar 1912

Fast Life (with John B. Hymer)
    Productions:

SHIPMAN, SAMUEL (cont.)
    Fast Life (cont.)
        Opened September 26, 1928 for 21 performances.
    Reviews:
        Life (NY) 92:17, Oct 12, 1928
        New York Times p. 35, Sep 27, 1928

    First Is Last (with Percival Wilde)
        Productions:
        Opened September 17, 1919 for 62 performances.
    Reviews:
        Dramatic Mirror 80:1538, Oct 2, 1919
        New York Times p. 14, Sep 18, 1919

    Friendly Enemies (with Aaron Hoffman)
        Productions:
        Opened July 22, 1918 for 440 performances.
    Reviews:
        Dramatic Mirror 79:157, Aug 3, 1918
                        79:225, Aug 17, 1918
        Dramatist 9:899-900, Apr 1918
        Forum 60:361-2, Sep 1918
        Green Book 20:584-8, Oct 1918
        Hearst 34:286-7+, Oct 1918
        Leslies' Weekly 128:483, Apr 5, 1919
        National Magazine 47:509-10, Oct-Nov 1918
        New York Times p. 11, Jul 23, 1918
                        III, p. 6, Aug 11, 1918
                        III, p. 4, Aug 25, 1918
        Theatre Magazine 28:87, Aug 1918
                        28:143, Sep 1918

    A Lady Detained (with John B. Hymer)
        Productions:
        Opened January 9, 1935 for 13 performances.
    Reviews:
        New York Times p. 23, Jan 10, 1935
        Time 25:25, Jan 21, 1935

    Lawful Larceny
        Productions:
        Opened January 2, 1922 for 190+ performances.
    Reviews:
        Current Opinion 73:354-62, Sep 1922
        Dramatic Mirror 95:17, Jan 7, 1922
        Life (NY) 79:18, Jan 26, 1922
        New York Clipper 69:20, Jan 11, 1922

New York Times p. 20, Jan 3, 1922
VI, p. 1, Jan 8, 1922
Theatre Magazine 35:167, Mar 1922

Nature's Nobleman (with Clara Lipman)
Productions:
Opened November 14, 1921 for 74 performances.
Reviews:
Dramatic Mirror 84:736, Nov 19, 1921
New York Times p. 23, Nov 15, 1921

No More Women (with Neil Twomey)
Productions:
Opened August 3, 1926 for 6 performances.
Reviews:
New York Times p. 17, Aug 4, 1926
Theatre Magazine 44:16, Oct 1926

Scarlet Pages (with John B. Hymer)
Productions:
Opened September 9, 1929 for 72 performances.
Reviews:
Life (NY) 94:22, Oct 4, 1929
New York Times VIII, p. 1, Sep 1, 1929
p. 26, Sep 10, 1929
IX, p. 1, Sep 22, 1929
Outlook 153:155, Sep 25, 1929
Theatre Magazine 50:46, Nov 1929
Vogue 74:128, Oct 26, 1929

She Means Business
Productions:
Opened January 26, 1931 for 8 performances.
Reviews:
New York Times p. 21, Jan 27, 1931

That French Lady (with Neil Twomey)
Productions:
Opened March 15, 1927 for 47 performances.
Reviews:
New York Times p. 29, Mar 16, 1927

Trapped (with Max Marcin)
Productions:
Opened September 11, 1928 for 15 performances.
Reviews:
New York Times p. 25, Sep 12, 1928

SHIPMAN, SAMUEL (cont.)
    The Unwritten Chapter (with Victor Victor)
        Productions:
            Opened October 11, 1920 for 24 performances.
        Reviews:
            Dramatic Mirror p. 683, Oct 16, 1920
            Life (NY) 76:768, Oct 28, 1920
            New York Clipper 68:373+, Dec 1920
            New York Times p. 18, Oct 12, 1920

    The Woman in Room 13 (with Max Marcin)
        Productions:
            Opened January 14, 1919 for 175 performances.
        Reviews:
            Dramatic Mirror 80:125, Jan 25, 1919
            Forum 61:375, Mar 1919
            Independent 97:137, Feb 1, 1919
            Life (NY) 73:172, Jan 30, 1919
            New York Dramatic News 65:8, Jan 25, 1919
            New York Times p. 9, Jan 15, 1919
            Theatre Magazine 29:141+, Mar 1919

SHULMAN, MAX

    The Tender Trap (with Robert Paul Smith)
        Productions:
            Opened October 13, 1954 for 102 performances.
            (Off Broadway) Season of 1961-62.
        Reviews:
            America 92:257, Nov 27, 1954
            Catholic World 180:227-8, Dec 1954
            Commonweal 61:166, Nov 12, 1954
            Nation 179:390, Oct 30, 1954
            New Republic 131:23, Nov 1, 1954
            New York Theatre Critics' Reviews 1954:282
            New York Times p. 37, Oct 14, 1954
                        p. 15, Aug 26, 1961
            New Yorker 30:83, Oct 23, 1954
            Newsweek 44:94, Oct 25, 1954
            Saturday Review 37:27, Oct 30, 1954
            Theatre Arts 38:25+, Dec 1954
            Time 64:41, Oct 25, 1954

SIMON, NEIL

Barefoot in the Park
    Productions:
        Opened October 23, 1963 for 1,530 performances.
    Reviews:
        America 109:753, Dec 7, 1963
        Commonweal 79:226, Nov 15, 1963
        New York Theatre Critics' Reviews 1963:221
        New York Times p. 36, Oct 24, 1963
                       p. 35, Oct 25, 1963
                       II, p. 3, Nov 3, 1963
                       p. 28, Mar 10, 1966
                       p. 39, Jun 19, 1967
        New Yorker 39:93, Nov 2, 1963
        Newsweek 62:62, Nov 4, 1963
        Saturday Review 46:32, Nov 9, 1963
        Theatre Arts 48:68, Jan 1964
        Time 82:74, Nov 1, 1963

Come Blow Your Horn
    Productions:
        Opened February 22, 1961 for 677 performances.
    Reviews:
        America 105:355, May 20, 1961
        Nation 192:222, Mar 11, 1961
        New York Theatre Critics' Reviews 1961:356
        New York Times p. 31, Feb 23, 1961
                       II, p. 1, Mar 5, 1961
        New Yorker 37:93 Mar 4, 1961
        Saturday Review 44:38, Mar 11, 1961
        Time 77:60, Mar 3, 1961

The Odd Couple
    Productions:
        Opened March 10, 1965 for 964 performances.
    Reviews:
        America 112:810-11, May 29, 1965
        Commonweal 82:51-2, Apr 2, 1965
        Life 58:35-6, Apr 9, 1965
        Nation 200:373-4, Apr 5, 1965
        New York Theatre Critics' Reviews 1965:362
        New York Times VI, p. 42, Mar 7, 1965
                       p. 36, Mar 11, 1965
                       p. 25, Mar 12, 1965
                       II, p. 1, Mar 21, 1965
                       p. 28, Mar 10, 1966

SIMON, NEIL (cont.)
  The Odd Couple (cont.)
                      p. 34, Jun 29, 1967
          New Yorker 41:83, Mar 20, 1965
          Newsweek 65:90-1, Mar 22, 1965
          Saturday Review 48:44, Mar 27, 1965
          Time 85:66, Mar 19, 1965
          Vogue 145:142, May 1965

  Plaza Suite (Visitor From Mamaroneck, Visitor From
        Hollywood, Visitor From Forest Hills)
      Productions:
      Opened February 14, 1968 for 1,097 performances.
      Reviews:
          America 118:552, Apr 20, 1968
          Commonweal 88:597, Sep 6, 1968
          Nation 206:317, Mar 4, 1968
          New York Theatre Critics' Reviews 1968:346
          New York Times p. 49, Feb 15, 1968
                        p. 31, Feb 16, 1968
                        II, p. 1, Feb 25, 1968
                        p. 61, Dec 14, 1968
                        p. 90, Mar 22, 1970
          New Yorker 44:75-6, Feb 24, 1968
          Newsweek 71:56, Feb 26, 1968
          Saturday Review 51:39, Mar 2, 1968
          Time 91:54, Feb 23, 1968
          Vogue 151:132, Apr 1, 1968

  The Star-Spangled Girl
      Productions:
      Opened December 21, 1966 for 261 performances.
      Reviews:
          America 116:264, Feb 18, 1967
          New York Theatre Critics' Reviews 1966:194
          New York Times p. 38, Dec 22, 1966
                        II, p. 8, Jan 8, 1967
          New Yorker 42:59, Dec 31, 1966
          Newsweek 69:66, Jan 2, 1967
          Saturday Review 50:98, Jan 14, 1967
          Time 88:45, Dec 30, 1966
          Vogue 149:60, Feb 15, 1967

Visitor from Forest Hills (See Plaza Suite)

Visitor from Hollywood (See Plaza Suite)

Visitor from Mamaroneck (See Plaza Suite)

SINCLAIR, UPTON

Cicero
　　Productions:
　　　　(Off Broadway) Season of 1960-61.
　　Reviews:
　　　　New York Times p. 37, Feb 9, 1961
　　　　New Yorker 37:94-5, Feb 18, 1961

*Giant's Strength
　　Reviews:
　　　　New York Times p. 8, Jun 19, 1948

Singing Jailbirds
　　Productions:
　　　　Opened December 6, 1928 for 79 performances.
　　　　(Off Broadway) Opened November 24, 1934 in
　　　　　　repertory.
　　Reviews:
　　　　New York Times VIII, p. 2, May 20, 1928
　　　　　　　　　　　　　p. 34, Dec 5, 1928
　　　　　　　　　　　　VIII, p. 4, Dec 23, 1928
　　　　　　　　　　　　p. 20, Feb 10, 1929
　　　　Theatre Magazine 49:50+, Feb 1929
　　　　World Tomorrow 12:112, Mar 1929

SKINNER, CORNELIA OTIS

Edna His Wife (Adapted from the book by Margaret Ayer
　　Barnes)
　　Productions:
　　　　Opened December 7, 1937 for 32 performances.
　　Reviews:
　　　　New York Times p. 30, Dec 8, 1937
　　　　Time 30:33-4, Dec 20, 1937

The Loves of Charles II
　　Productions:
　　　　Opened December 27, 1933 for 23 performances.
　　No Reviews.

Mansion on the Hudson
　　Productions:
　　　　Opened April 2, 1935 for 16 performances.
　　Reviews:
　　　　New York Times p. 20, Apr 3, 1935

SKINNER, CORNELIA OTIS (cont.)
  The Pleasure of His Company (See entry under Taylor,
    Samuel)

  Paris '90
    Productions:
      Opened March 4, 1952 for 87 performances.
    Reviews:
      New York Theatre Critics' Reviews 1952:348
      New York Times p. 10, Feb 9, 1952
                     VI, pp. 10-11, Feb 24, 1952
                     VI, pp. 10-11, Mar 2, 1952
                     p. 33, Mar 5, 1952
                     II, p. 1, Mar 16, 1952

  The Wives of Henry VIII
    Productions:
      Opened November 15, 1931 for 69 performances.
    Reviews:
      New York Times p. 22, Nov 16, 1931
                     p. 33, Jun 29, 1949
      Theatre Guild Magazine 9:11, Dec 1931

SKLAR, GEORGE

  *And People All Around (with B. T. Bradshaw, Jr.)
    Reviews:
      New York Times II, p. 1, Aug 7, 1966
                     p. 46, Feb 12, 1968

  Laura (with Vera Caspary) (Based on the novel by Vera
    Caspary)
    Productions:
      Opened June 26, 1947 for 44 performances.
    Reviews:
      Catholic World 165:458, Aug 1947
      New York Theatre Critics' Reviews 1947:353
      New York Times II, p. 1, Jun 22, 1947
                     p. 16, Jun 27, 1947
      Newsweek 30:82, Jul 7, 1947
      Time 50:56, Jul 7, 1947

  Life and Death of an American
    Productions:
      Opened May 19, 1939 for 29 performances (WPA
        Federal Theatre Project).

Reviews:
Catholic World 149:471-2, Jul 1939
Commonweal 30:188, Jun 9, 1939
New York Times p. 11, May 20, 1939

Merry-Go-Round (See entry under Maltz Albert)

Peace On Earth (with Albert Maltz)
Productions:
Opened November 29, 1933 for 126 performances.
Opened March 31, 1934 for 18 performances.
Reviews:
Catholic World 138:478, Jan 1934
New Outlook 163:43, Jan 1934
New Republic 77:169, Dec 20, 1933
New York Times p. 39, Nov 30, 1933
                p. 22, Mar 9, 1934
Survey 23:240, May 1934
Theatre Arts 18:88-91, Feb 1934
Vanity Fair 41:41, Feb 1934
World Tomorrow 17:19, Jan 4, 1934

Stevedore (with Paul Peters)
Productions:
Opened April 18, 1934 for 111 performances.
Opened October 1, 1934 for 64 performances.
(Off Broadway) Season of 1948-49.
Reviews:
Catholic World 139:342-3, June 1934
Golden Book 20:246, Sep 1934
Literary Digest 117:23+, May 5, 1934
Nation 138:515-16, May 2, 1934
New Outlook 163:44, Jun 1934
New Republic 78:367, May 9, 1934
New York Times p. 33, Apr 19, 1934
                IX, p. 1, Apr 29, 1934
                p. 18, Oct 2, 1934
                IX, p. 3, Jan 13, 1935
                p. 26, May 7, 1935
                p. 20, Sep 23, 1935
                p. 30, Feb 23, 1949
Newsweek 3:38, Apr 28, 1934
Review of Reviews 89:48, Jun 1934
Saturday Review 10:797, Jul 7, 1934
Stage 11:8, Jun 1934
Theatre Arts 18:408-9+, Jun 1934
Time 23:26, Apr 30, 1934

SMITH, HARRY JAMES

Blackbirds
    Productions:
        Opened January 6, 1913 for 16 performances.
    Reviews:
        American Playwright 2:40-2, Feb 1913
        Bookman 36:644-5, Feb 1913
        Dramatic Mirror 69:6, Jan 8, 1913
        Green Book 9:376+, Mar 1913
                9:498-9, Mar 1913
        Munsey 48:1005-6, Mar 1913
        New York Drama News 57:24, Jan 11, 1913
        New York Times p. 11, Jan 7, 1913

Mrs. Bumpstead-Leigh
    Productions:
        Opened April 3, 1911 for 64 performances.
        Opened April 1, 1929 for 72 performances.
    Reviews:
        Blue Book 13:462-3, Jul 1911
        Bookman 33:358-9, Jun 1911
        Commonweal 9:722-3, Apr 24, 1929
        Dial 86:531-2, Jun 1929
        Dramatic Mirror 65:7, Apr 5, 1911
        Dramatist 2:169-70, Jul 1911
        Leslies' Weekly 112:451, Apr 10, 1911
        Life (NY) 57:788, Apr 20, 1911
                93:20, Apr 26, 1929
        Metropolitan Magazine 34:353, Jun 1911
        Munsey 45:419-20, Jun 1911
        New Republic 58:252-3, Apr 17, 1929
        New York Times p. 28, Apr 2, 1929
                IX, p. 2, May 12, 1929
        Red Book 17:376-7+, Jun 1911
        Theatre Magazine 12:176, Dec 1910
                13:142-3+, May 1911
        Vogue 73:104, Jun 8, 1929

The Little Teacher
    Productions:
        Opened February 4, 1918 for 128 performances.
    Reviews:
        Dramatic Mirror 78:7, Feb 16, 1918
        Forum 59:362, Mar 1918
        Green Book 19:580+, Apr 1918
        Life (NY) 71:262, Feb 14, 1918
        New York Times p. 11, Feb 5, 1918

A Tailor Made Man
    Productions:
        Opened August 27, 1917 for 398 performances.
        Opened October 21, 1929 for 8 performances.
    Reviews:
        Current Opinion 63:311-14, Nov 1917
        Dramatic Mirror 77:8, Sep 8, 1917
        Dramatist 10:930, Jan 1919
        Forum 59:360-1, Mar 1918
        Green Book 18:778-82, Nov 1917
        Hearst 32:378-80+, Nov 1917
        Life (NY) 70:424, Sep 13, 1917
        New York Drama News 64:3, Sep 1, 1917
        New York Times p. 5, Aug 28, 1917
                        IV, p. 5, Sep 2, 1917
                        p. 26, Oct 22, 1929
        Theatre Magazine 26:209+, Oct 1917

SMITH, WINCHELL

Bobby Burnit (Based on the novel by George R. Chester)
    Productions:
        Opened August 22, 1910 for 32 performances.
    Reviews:
        Dramatist 2:101-2, Oct 1910
        Hampton 25:524, Oct 1910
        Leslies' Weekly 111:271+, Sep 15, 1910
        Metropolitan Magazine 33:120-1, Oct 1910
        New York Dramatic News 64:5, Sep 3, 1910

The Boomerang (with Victor Mapes)
    Productions:
        Opened August 10, 1915 for 522 performances.
    Reviews:
        American Mercury 81:33+, Jan 1916
        Book News 34:73-4, Oct 1915
        Bookman 42:155+, Oct 1915
        Current Opinion 59:240-3, Oct 1915
        Dramatic Mirror 74:8, Aug 18, 1915
                        75:2, Jan 1, 1916
                        76:9, Oct 21, 1916
        Dramatist 7:612-13, Oct 1915
        Green Book 14:618-19, Oct 1915
                    14:796, Nov 1915
        Harper's Weekly 61:206-7, Aug 28, 1915
        Hearst 28:266-9+, Oct 1915

451

SMITH, WINCHELL (cont.)
The Boomerang (cont.)
                Munsey 57:333, Mar 1916
                        58:307, Jul 1916
                Nation 101:240, Aug 19, 1915
                New Republic 4:76, Aug 21, 1915
                New York Dramatic News 61:16, Aug 21, 1915
                New York Times p. 9, Aug 11, 1915
                                VI, p. 2, Aug 15, 1915
                                II, p. 5, May 28, 1916
                Smart Set 47:146-8, Oct 1915
                Theatre Magazine 22:107+, Sep 1915

The Fortune Hunter
        Productions:
                Opened September 4, 1909 for 345 performances.
        Reviews:
                Collier's 44:24, Oct 30, 1909
                Columbian 3:638-64+, Jan 1911
                Cosmopolitan 48:485, Mar 1910
                Current Literature 49:421-9, Oct 1910
                Dramatic Mirror 62:5, Sep 18, 1909
                Dramatist 1:20-21, Jan 1910
                Forum 42:437, Nov 1909
                Green Book 2:1015, Nov 1909
                        3:421-5, Feb 1910
                        4:257-85, Aug 1910
                Hampton 23:692-3+, Nov 1909
                Metropolitan Magazine 31:258-9, Nov 1909
                New York Dramatic News 55:10, May 18, 1912
                Pearson 22:664-6, Nov 1909
                Theatre Magazine 10:xiii, Oct 1909
                Woman's Home Companion 38:43, Feb 1911
                World Today 18:286-97, Mar 1910

A Holy Terror (with George Abbott)
        Productions:
                Opened September 28, 1925 for 32 performances.
        Reviews:
                New York Times p. 31, Sep 29, 1925

Lightnin' (with Frank Bacon)
        Productions:
                Opened August 26, 1918 for 1, 291 performances.
                Opened September 15, 1938 for 54 performances.
        Reviews:
                Catholic World 148:212, Nov 1938

Commonweal 28:589, Sep 30, 1938
Current Opinion 65:227-30, Oct 1918
Dramatic Mirror 78:33, Feb 2, 1918
                79:361, Sep 7, 1918
Dramatist 12:1040-41, Jan 1921
Everybody's 40:43, Jan 1919
Green Book 20:786-7+, Nov 1918
Hearst 34:454-5+, Dec 1918
Illus World 38:502-4, Dec 1922
Life (NY) 72:416, Sep 19, 1918
           78:18, Jul 21, 1921
Literary Digest 84:31, Mar 14, 1925
Nation 113:253, Sep 7, 1921
New York Times p. 7, Aug 27, 1918
                IV, p. 2, Sep 8, 1918
                p. 10, Aug 24, 1921
                p. 13, Aug 19, 1938
                X, p. 2, Sep 11, 1938
                p. 17, Sep 16, 1938
Outlook 126:182, Sep 29, 1920
Theatre Arts 22:774+, Nov 1938
Theatre Magazine 28:203+, Oct 1918
                32:272+, Nov 1920
Time 32:39, Sep 26, 1938

Love Among the Lions (Based on a novel by F. Anstey)
  Productions:
    Opened August 8, 1910 for 48 performances.
  Reviews:
    Dramatic Mirror 64:6, Aug 20, 1910
    Hampton 25:522+, Oct 1910
    Leslies' Weekly 111:213, Sep 1, 1910
    Life (NY) 56:399, Sep 8, 1910
    Metropolitan Magazine 33:126-7, Oct 1910
    Munsey 44:133-4, Oct 1910
    Pearson 24:530, Oct 1910
    Theatre Magazine 12:66-7+, Sep 1910

The New Henrietta (with Victor Mapes) (Based on Bron-
    son Howard's play)
  Productions:
    Opened December 22, 1913 for 48 performances.
  Reviews:
    Blue Book 18:1044-5, Apr 1914
    Bookman 38:611-12, Feb 1914
    Dramatic Mirror 70:10, Dec 24, 1913
                  70:2, Dec 31, 1913

SMITH, WINCHELL (cont.)
The New Henrietta (cont.)
71:2, Jan 21, 1914
Green Book 11:696-7, Apr 1914
Leslies' Weekly 118:59, Jan 15, 1913
Theatre Magazine 19:61-2+, Feb 1914
Woman's Home Companion 42:19, Nov 1915

The Only Son
Productions:
Opened October 16, 1911 for 32 performances.
Reviews:
American Playwright 1:21-3, Jan 1912
Blue Book 14:1140-3, Apr 1912
Bookman 34:367-8, Dec 1911
Dramatic Mirror 66:10, Oct 18, 1911
66:2, Nov 1, 1911
Dramatist 3:218, Jan 1912
Everybody's 26:88-90, Jan 1912
Green Book 6:1200+, Dec 1911
Leslies' Weekly 113:493, Nov 2, 1911
113:560, Nov 16, 1911
Life (NY) 58:762-3, Nov 2, 1911
Munsey 46:428-9, Dec 1911
Pearson 26:769-70, Dec 1911
Theatre Magazine 14:197+, Dec 1911

Thank You (with Tom Cushing)
Productions:
Opened October 3, 1921 for 257 performances.
Reviews:
Dramatic Mirror 84:556, Oct 15, 1921
Independent 107:63, Oct 15, 1921
New York Clipper 69:28, Oct 12, 1921
New York Times p. 10, Oct 4, 1921
VI, p. 1, Oct 16, 1921
Theatre Magazine 34:438, Dec 1921
35:103, Feb 1922

Turn to the Right (with John E. Hazard)
Productions:
Opened August 18, 1916 for 435 performances.
Reviews:
Collier's 58:8, Jan 27, 1917
Current Opinion 61:240-4, Oct 1916
Dramatic Mirror 76:8, Aug 26, 1916
76:4, Oct 21, 1916

                              76:9, Nov 11, 1916
                              77:8, Jan 6, 1917
                              77:4, Apr 7, 1917
        Dramatist 8:733-5, Oct 1916
        Everybody's 36:57-8, Jan 1917
        Green Book 16:790-3, Nov 1916
        Hearst 32:198-200+, Sep 1917
        Leslies' Weekly 123:629+, Dec 7, 1916
        McClure's 48:10, Jan 1917
        Munsey 59:286, Nov 1916
        Nation 103:183, Aug 24, 1916
        New York Times p. 7, Aug 18, 1916
        Theatre Magazine 24:140, Sep 1916
                              24:205, Oct 1916
        Woman's Home Companion 44:24, Jan 1917

The Wheel
    Productions:
        Opened August 29, 1921 for 49 performances.
    Reviews:
        Dramatic Mirror 83:893, May 21, 1921
                           84:341, Sep 3, 1921
        Independent 106:113, Sep 17, 1921
        New York Clipper 69:20, Sep 7, 1921
        New York Times p. 10, Aug 30, 1921
        Weekly Review 5:234, Sep 10, 1921

SPEWACK, SAMUEL

Boy Meets Girl (with Bella Spewack)
    Productions:
        Opened November 27, 1935 for 669 performances.
        Opened June 22, 1943 for 15 performances.
    Reviews:
        Catholic World 142:471, Jan 1936
        Commonweal 23:188, Dec 13, 1935
        Life 5:36-8, Aug 29, 1938
        Literary Digest 120:19, Dec 14, 1935
        New Republic 85:175, Dec 18, 1935
        New York Theatre Critics' Reviews 1943:316
        New York Times p. 27, Nov 19, 1935
                        p. 38, Nov 28, 1935
                        XI, p. 3, Dec 15, 1935
                        p. 18, May 28, 1936
                        IX, p. 1, Jun 28, 1936
                        X, p. 3, Nov 22, 1936

                              455

SPEWACK, SAMUEL (cont.)
Boy Meets Girl (cont.)
p. 23, Jul 6, 1937
p. 15, Jun 23, 1943
Newsweek 6:42, Dec 7, 1935
12:22-3, Sep 5, 1938
Stage 13:2+, Jan 1936
Theatre Arts 20:19, Jan 1936
Time 26:53, Dec 9, 1935
Vogue 87:57, Jan 15, 1936

Clear All Wires (with Bella Spewack)
Productions:
Opened September 14, 1932 for 93 performances.
Reviews:
Arts and Decorations 38:44-5, Nov 1932
Catholic World 136:209-10, Nov 1932
Commonweal 16:512, Sep 28, 1932
Literary Digest 114:21, Oct 15, 1932
Nation 135:290-1, Sep 28, 1932
New Outlook 161:38, Oct 1932
New York Times p. 19, Sep 15, 1932
IX, p. 1, Sep 25, 1932
IX, p. 3, Oct 2, 1932
Stage 10:9-10, Oct 1932
Theatre Arts 16:865-6, Nov 1932
Town and Country 87:26, Oct 15, 1932
Vogue 80:32, Nov 1, 1932

Festival (with Bella Spewack)
Productions:
Opened January 18, 1955 for 23 performances.
Reviews:
America 92:545, Feb 19, 1955
New Republic 132:22, Feb 7, 1955
New York Theatre Critics' Reviews 1955:393
New York Times p. 22, Jan 19, 1955
p. 35, Jan 20, 1955
New Yorker 30:46-7, Jan 29, 1955
Saturday Review 38:24, Feb 12, 1955
Time 65:71, Jan 31, 1955

The Golden State
Productions:
Opened November 25, 1950 for 25 performances.
Reviews:
Commonweal 53:253, Dec 15, 1950

456

New York Theatre Critics' Reviews 1950:183
New York Times p. 29, Nov 27, 1950
New Yorker 26:82, Dec 2, 1950
Newsweek 36:74, Dec 4, 1950
Theatre Arts 35:14, Feb 1951
Time 56:65, Dec 4, 1950

Miss Swan Expects (with Bella Spewack)
    Productions:
        Opened February 20, 1939 for 8 performances.
    Reviews:
        New York Times p. 15, Feb 21, 1939
        Newsweek 13:28, Mar 6, 1939

My 3 Angels (with Bella Spewack) (Based on Albert
        Husson's La Cuisine des Agnes)
    Productions:
        Opened March 11, 1953 for 344 performances.
        (Off Broadway) Season of 1955-56.
    Reviews:
        America 88:716-17, Nov 28, 1953
        Catholic World 177:149, May 1953
        Life 34:101-2+, May 11, 1953
        Nation 176:273, Mar 28, 1953
        New York Theatre Critics' Reviews 1953:334
        New York Times p. 23, Mar 12, 1953
                      p. 24, Feb 4, 1956
                      VI, p. 72, Feb 5, 1956
        New Yorker 29:64+, Mar 21, 1953
        Newsweek 41:98, Mar 23, 1953
        Saturday Review 36:27, Mar 28, 1953
        Theatre Arts 38:32-3, Jun 1954
        Time 61:80, Mar 23, 1953

Once There Was A Russian
    Productions:
        Opened February 18, 1961 for 1 performance.
    Reviews:
        New York Theatre Critics' Reviews 1961:363
        New York Times II, p. 1, Feb 12, 1961
                       p. 32, Feb 20, 1961

Poppa (with Bella Spewack)
    Productions:
        Opened December 24, 1928 for 96 performances.
    Reviews:
        New York Times p. 31, Dec 25, 1928

SPEWACK, SAMUEL (cont.)
Poppa (cont.)
VIII, p. 1, Dec 30, 1928
Theatre Magazine 49:46, Apr 1929

Spring Song (with Bella Spewack)
Productions:
Opened October 1, 1934 for 40 performances.
Reviews:
Catholic World 140:214, Nov 1934
New York Times p. 18, Oct 2, 1934
Theatre Arts 18:817, Nov 1934

Two Blind Mice
Productions:
Opened March 2, 1949 for 157 performances.
Reviews:
Catholic World 169:64, Apr 1949
Commonweal 49:592, Mar 25, 1949
Life 26:141-2+, Apr 4, 1949
New York Theatre Critics' Reviews 1949:342
New York Times p. 32, Mar 3, 1949
New Yorker 25:48+, Mar 12, 1949
Newsweek 33:81, Mar 14, 1949
School and Society 69:338, May 7, 1949
Theatre Arts 33:23, 26, May 1949
Time 53:58, Mar 14, 1949
Vogue 113:138, Apr 1, 1949

Under the Sycamore Tree
Productions:
(Off Broadway) Opened March 7, 1960 for 41 per-
formances.
Reviews:
Life 33:169, Oct 13, 1952
New York Times p. 38, Apr 24, 1952
p. 37, Mar 8, 1960
New Yorker 36:121-2, Mar 19, 1960

The War Song (with Bella Spewack and George Jessel)
Productions:
Opened September 24, 1928 for 80 performances.
Reviews:
Nation 127:406, Oct 17, 1928
New York Times p. 39, Sep 25, 1928
Vogue 72:150, Nov 10, 1928

Woman Bites Dog (with Bella Spewack)
    Productions:
        Opened April 17, 1946 for 5 performances.
    Reviews:
        Commonweal 44:72, May 3, 1946
        Forum 105:940-1, Jun 1946
        New York Theatre Critics' Reviews 1946:407
        New York Times II, p. 1, Apr 14, 1946
                        p. 21, Apr 18, 1946
        New Yorker 22:44, Apr 27, 1946

SPIGELGASS, LEONARD

Dear Me, the Sky Is Falling (Based on a story by Ger-
        trude Berg and James Yaffe)
    Productions:
        Opened March 2, 1963 for 145 performances.
    Reviews:
        Commonweal 78:47, Apr 5, 1963
        Nation 196:254, Mar 23, 1963
        New York Theatre Critics' Reviews 1963:366
        New York Times p. 9, Mar 4, 1963
                      p. 20, Jul 23, 1963
        New Yorker 39:132, Mar 9, 1963
        Newsweek 61:69, Mar 18, 1963
        Saturday Review 46:28, Mar 23, 1963
        Theatre Arts 47:10-12, Apr 1963
        Time 81:70, Mar 15, 1963

A Majority of One
    Productions:
        Opened February 16, 1959 for 556 performances.
    Reviews:
        America 100:671, Mar 7, 1959
        Catholic World 189:158, May 1959
        Commonweal 69:625, Mar 13, 1959
        Life 46:50+, Mar 9, 1959
        Nation 188:215, Mar 7, 1959
        New York Theatre Critics' Reviews 1959:370
        New York Times II, p. 1, Feb 15, 1959
                        p. 28, Feb 17, 1959
                        II, p. 1, Feb 22, 1959
                        p. 37, Mar 10, 1960
                        p. 39, May 16, 1960
        New Yorker 35:66+, Feb 28, 1959
        Newsweek 53:82, Mar 2, 1959

SPIGELGASS, LEONARD (cont.)
A Majority of One (cont.)
Reporter 20:40, Mar 19, 1959
Saturday Review 42:29, Mar 7, 1959
Theatre Arts 43:11+, Apr 1959
Time 73:49, Mar 2, 1959

The Wrong Way Lightbulb
Productions:
Opened March 4, 1969 for 7 performances.
Reviews:
New York Theatre Critics' Reviews 1969:344
New York Times p. 40, Mar 5, 1969

STALLINGS, LAURENCE

The Buccaneer (See entry under Anderson, Maxwell)

*Eldorado (with George S. Kaufman)
Reviews:
New York Times VIII, p. 2, Oct 25, 1931

A Farewell to Arms (Adapted from Ernest Hemingway's
novel)
Productions:
Opened September 22, 1930 for 24 performances.
Reviews:
Bookman 72:296, Nov 1930
Life (NY) 96:18, Oct 10, 1930
National Magazine 59:137, Dec 1930
New Republic 64:208-9, Nov 8, 1930
New York Times p. 30, Sep 17, 1930
                p. 30, Sep 23, 1930
Outlook 156:233, Oct 8, 1930
Vanity Fair 35:46, Dec 1930
Vogue 76:72+, Nov 10, 1930

First Flight (See entry under Anderson, Maxwell)

The Streets Are Guarded
Productions:
Opened November 20, 1944 for 24 performances.
Reviews:
Commonweal 41:205, Dec 8, 1944
Nation 159:725, Dec 9, 1944
New Republic 111:746-7, Dec 4, 1944

460

New York Theatre Critics' Reviews 1944:79
New York Times p. 19, Nov 21, 1944
                    II, p. 1, Nov 26, 1944
New Yorker 20:44, Dec 2, 1944
Newsweek 24:111, Dec 4, 1944
Theatre Arts 29:11-13, Jan 1945
Time 44:48, Dec 4, 1944

What Price Glory? (See entry under Anderson, Maxwell)

STEIN, GERTRUDE

Dr. Faustus Lights the Lights
    Productions:
        (Off Broadway) Season of 1951-52 (Living Theatre).
    Reviews:
        New York Times p. 19, May 26, 1952

In Circles
    Productions:
        (Off Broadway) Opened November, 1967 for 222
            performances.
        (Off Broadway) Opened June 25, 1968 for 56 per-
            formances (Judson Poets Theater).
    Reviews:
        New York Times p. 12, Oct 14, 1967
                        II, p. 1, Nov 5, 1967
                        p. 49, Jun 21, 1968
                        p. 36, Jun 28, 1968

What Happened
    Productions:
        (Off Broadway) Opened September 26, 1963 for 12
            performances (Judson Poets' Theater).
    Reviews:
        Commonweal 79:227, Nov 15, 1963

Yes Is for a Very Young Man
    Productions:
        (Off Broadway) June 1949
        (Off Broadway) Opened March 4, 1963 for 1 per-
            formance.
    Reviews:
        New York Times p. 27, Jun 7, 1949
                        p. 7, Mar 6, 1963
        Time 47:67, Mar 25, 1946

STEINBECK, JOHN

Burning Bright
    Productions:
        Opened October 18, 1950 for 13 performances.
        (Off Broadway) Season of 1959-60.
    Reviews:
        Catholic World 172:228, Dec 1950
        Commonweal 53:120, Nov 10, 1950
        Nation 171:396, Oct 28, 1950
        New York Theatre Critics' Reviews 1950:238
        New York Times II, p. 1, Oct 15, 1950
                        p. 40, Oct 19, 1950
                        II, p. 1, Oct 29, 1950
                        p. 27, Oct 17, 1959
        New Yorker 26:52+, Oct 28, 1950
        Newsweek 36:78, Oct 30, 1950
        Saturday Review 33:20-1, Nov 11, 1950
        Theatre Arts 34:16, Dec 1950
        Time 56:58, Oct 30, 1950

The Moon Is Down
    Productions:
        Opened April 7, 1942 for 71 performances.
    Reviews:
        Catholic World 155:213-14, May 1942
        Commonweal 36:14, Apr 24, 1942
        Current History ns 2:228-31, May 1942
        Harper's Bazaar 76:74, Apr 1942
        Life 12:32-4, Apr 6, 1942
        Nation 154:468, Apr 18, 1942
        New Republic 106:638-9, May 11, 1942
        New York Theatre Critics' Reviews 1942:318
        New York Times VII, pp. 6-7, Mar 29, 1942
                        p. 22, Apr 8, 1942
                        VIII, p. 1, Apr 12, 1942
                        VIII, p. 1, Apr 19, 1942
                        VIII, p. 1, May 10, 1942
                        II, p. 1, Jul 11, 1943
                        p. 5, Nov 15, 1963
        New Yorker 18:34+, Apr 18, 1942
        Newsweek 19:72, Apr 20, 1942
        Scholastic 40:19, Apr 27, 1942
        Theatre Arts 26:287-9, May 1942
        Time 39:36, Apr 20, 1942

Of Mice and Men
    Productions:
        Opened November 23, 1937 for 207 performances.
        (Off Broadway) Opened April 4, 1964 for 8 perform-
            ances (Equity Library Theatre).
    Reviews:
        Catholic World 146:468, Jan 1938
        Commonweal 27:191, Dec 10, 1937
                    28:161, Jun 3, 1938
        Life 3:44-6, Dec 13, 1937
        Literary Digest 124:34, Dec 18, 1937
        Nation 145:663-4, Dec 11, 1937
        New Republic 93:170, Dec 15, 1937
                     94:396, May 4, 1938
        New York Times p. 20, Nov 24, 1937
                        XII, p. 7, Dec 5, 1937
                        XI, p. 3, Dec 12, 1937
                        X, p. 1, Apr 24, 1938
                        XI, p. 3, Apr 30, 1939
                        p. 14, Jun 10, 1939
        Newsweek 10:32, Dec 6, 1937
        One Act Play Magazine 1:858-9, Jan 1938
        Scribner's Magazine 103:70, Feb 1938
        Stage 15:50-51, Jan 1938
              15:54-5, Jan 1938
        Theatre Arts 21:774-81, Oct 1937
                     22:13-16, Jan 1938
        Time 30:41, Dec 6, 1937

Tortilla Flat (See entry under Kirkland, Jack).

STEWART, DONALD OGDEN

How I Wonder
    Productions:
        Opened September 30, 1947 for 63 performances.
    Reviews:
        Catholic World 166:170-1, Nov 1947
        Commonweal 47:16, Oct 17, 1947
        Forum 108:372, Dec 1947
        New Republic 117:37, Oct 13, 1947
        New York Theatre Critics' Reviews 1947:332
        New York Times p. 34, Oct 1, 1947
        New Yorker 23:53, Oct 11, 1947
        Newsweek 30:80, Oct 13, 1947
        Science Illustrated 2:22-5, Dec 1947

STEWART, DONALD OGDEN (cont.)
How I Wonder (cont.)
School and Society 66:421, Nov 29, 1947
Theatre Arts 31:20, Nov 1947
31:14, Dec 1947
Vogue 110:132, Oct 15, 1947
110:190, Nov 15, 1947

*The Kidders
Reviews:
New York Times p. 40, Nov 13, 1957

Los Angeles (with Max Marcin)
Productions:
Opened December 19, 1927 for 16 performances.
Reviews:
New York Times p. 32, Dec 20, 1927

Rebound
Productions:
Opened February 3, 1930 for 114 performances.
Reviews:
Catholic World 131:80-1, Apr 1930
Commonweal 11:453, Feb 19, 1930
Life (NY) 95:16, Feb 21, 1930
Nation 130:254, Feb 26, 1930
New Republic 62:47-8, Feb 26, 1930
New York Times p. 29, Feb 4, 1930
p. 21, Feb 6, 1930
IX, p. 1, Feb 16, 1930
VIII, p. 4, Nov 1, 1931
Outlook 154:312, Feb 19, 1930
Theatre Magazine 51:42-3, Apr 1930
Vogue 75:90, Mar 29, 1930

STONE, JOHN AUGUSTUS
No Productions.

STRONG, AUSTIN

Bunny
Productions:
Opened January 4, 1916 for 16 performances.
Reviews:
Book News 34:322-3, Mar 1916

Dramatic Mirror 75:7, Jan 15, 1916
Green Book 15:440-2, Mar 1916
Harper's Weekly 62:84, Jan 22, 1916
Nation 102:56, Jan 13, 1916
New York Dramatic News 62:17, Jan 8, 1916
New York Times p. 13, Jan 5, 1916
Theatre Magazine 23:64+, Feb 1916

The Dragon's Claw
   Productions:
      Opened September 14, 1914 for 8 performances.
   Reviews:
      Dramatic Mirror 72:8, Sep 23, 1914
      Munsey 53:357, Nov 1914

A Good Little Devil (Based on Un Bon Petit Diable by
      Rosemonde Gerard and Maurice Rostand)
   Productions:
      Opened January 8, 1913 for 133 performances.
   Reviews:
      American Playwright 2:75-6, Mar 1913
      Blue Book 17:30-2, May 1913
      Bookman 37:61-3, Mar 1913
      Collier's 50:20, Feb 8, 1913
      Dramatic Mirror 69:4, Jan 15, 1913
                      69:2, Jan 22, 1913
                      69:2, Apr 2, 1913
      Everybody's 28:518-20, Apr 1913
      Green Book 9:372-5+, Mar 1913
                 10:44-6+, Jul 1913
      Harper's Weekly 57:19, Feb 8, 1913
      Hearst 23:973-84, Jun 1913
      Independent 74:303-4, Feb 6, 1913
      Life (NY) 61:200-1, Jan 23, 1913
      Munsey 48:1012-13, Mar 1913
      New York Dramatic News 57:3, Jan 11, 1913
                             57:17, Jan 18, 1913
      Red Book 20:1078-81, Apr 1913
      Theatre Magazine 17:35+, Feb 1913

The Little Father of the Wilderness (with Lloyd Osborne)
   Productions:
      Opened June 2, 1930 for 8 performances.
   Reviews:
      New York Times p. 27, Jun 3, 1930

465

STRONG, AUSTIN (cont.)
A Play Without A Name
Productions:
Opened November 26, 1928 for 48 performances.
Reviews:
Life (NY) 92:9, Dec 28, 1928
New York Times p. 30, Nov 26, 1928
IX, p. 4, Dec 16, 1928
Outlook 150:1355, Dec 19, 1928
Theatre Magazine 49:26+, Feb 1929
49:51, Feb 1929

Seventh Heaven
Productions:
Opened October 30, 1922 for 704 performances.
Reviews:
Current Opinion 74:441-7, Apr 1923
Dramatist 14:1160-61, Apr 1923
Hearst 43:93-5+, May 1923
Life (NY) 81:20, Feb 1, 1923
New Republic 33:97-8, Dec 20, 1922
New York Clipper 70:20, Nov 8, 1922
New York Times p. 11, Oct 31, 1922
VIII, p. 1, Nov 5, 1922
VIII, p. 1, Nov 12, 1922
Theatre Magazine 37:23, Jan 1923

Three Wise Fools
Productions:
Opened October 31, 1918 for 316 performances.
Opened March 1, 1936 for 9 performances.
Reviews:
Dramatic Mirror 79:723, Nov 16, 1918
79:827, Dec 7, 1918
Dramatist 11:1031, Oct 1920
Hearst 36:46-7+, Sep 1919
Life (NY) 72:712-13, Nov 14, 1918
New York Times p. 13, Nov 1, 1918
IV, p. 2, Nov 10, 1918
p. 25, Jan 14, 1936
p. 14, Feb 29, 1936
IX, p. 1, Mar 1, 1936
p. 12, Mar 2, 1936
Newsweek 7:30, Jan 25, 1936
Theatre Magazine 28:345, Dec 1918
29:8, Jan 1919

STURGES, PRESTON

Child of Manhattan
  Productions:
    Opened March 1, 1932 for 87 performances.
  Reviews:
    Arts and Decoration 37:56, May 1932
    Nation 134:351-2, Mar 23, 1932
    New Republic 70:127, Mar 16, 1932
    New York Times p. 15, Mar 2, 1932
    Theatre Arts 16:362, May 1932

The Guinea Pig
  Productions:
    Opened January 7, 1929 for 64 performances.
  Reviews:
    New York Times p. 35, Jan 8, 1929

Recapture
  Productions:
    Opened January 29, 1930 for 24 performances.
  Reviews:
    Life (NY) 95:16, Feb 21, 1930
    New York Times VIII, p. 2, Jan 19, 1930
                   p. 16, Jan 30, 1930
    Theatre Magazine 51:70, Mar 1930

Strictly Dishonorable
  Productions:
    Opened September 18, 1929 for 557 performances.
  Reviews:
    Commonweal 10:592, Oct 9, 1929
    Drama 20:40, Nov 1929
    Life (NY) 94:24, Oct 11, 1929
             95:18, Jun 6, 1930
    Nation 129:392-3, Oct 9, 1929
           130:659-60, Jun 4, 1930
    New Republic 60:270, Oct 23, 1929
    New York Times p. 37, Sep 19, 1929
                   IX, p. 1, Sep 29, 1929
                   p. 23, Mar 11, 1931
                   VIII, p. 2, Mar 29, 1931
                   IX, p. 1, Apr 12, 1931
    Outlook 153:232, Oct 9, 1929
    Theatre Magazine 50:20+, Nov 1929
                     50:45, Nov 1929
    Vogue 74:150, Nov 9, 1929

*Alice Adams
Reviews:
New York Times p. 9, Mar 9, 1946
p. 26, Aug 5, 1947

Beauty and Jacobin
Productions:
Opened November 29, 1912 for one matinee.
Reviews:
Dramatic Mirror 68:6-7, Dec 4, 1912
Harper's Weekly 125:390-9, 539-53, Aug 1912
125:539-53, Sep 1912

Cameo Kirby (with Harry Leon Wilson)
Productions:
Opened December 20, 1909 for 24 performances.
Reviews:
Dramatist 2:106-7, Oct 1910

Clarence
Productions:
Opened September 20, 1919 for 300 performances.
Reviews:
Current Opinion 67:296-300, Dec 1919
Dramatic Mirror 80:1539, Oct 2, 1919
Forum 62:502-3, Oct-Nov 1919
Life (NY) 74:592, Oct 2, 1919
New York Times p. 8, Sep 22, 1919
IV, p. 3, Sep 28, 1919

Colonel Satan
Productions:
Opened January 10, 1931 for 17 performances.
Reviews:
Nation 132:134, Feb 4, 1931
New York Times p. 24, Jan 12, 1931
p. 25, Jan 19, 1931
Vogue 77:88, Mar 1, 1931

The Country Cousin (with Julian Street)
Productions:
Opened September 3, 1917 for 128 performances.
Reviews:
Dramatic Mirror 77:5, Sep 15, 1917
Green Book 18:780-3, Nov 1917

Hearst 32:470-2+, Dec 1917
Life (NY) 70:506-7, Sep 27, 1917
New York Times p. 9, Sep 4, 1917
IV, p. 2, Sep 9, 1917
p. 12, Sep 11, 1917
Theatre Magazine 26:203+, Oct 1917

Getting a Polish (with Harry Leon Wilson)
Productions:
Opened November 7, 1910 for 32 performances.
Reviews:
Blue Book 12:858-60, Feb 1911
12:894-6, Mar 1911
Dramatic Mirror 64:9, Dec 7, 1910
Green Book 5:233+, Feb 1911
Metropolitan Magazine 33:797, Mar 1911
Munsey 44:560-1, Jan 1911
Theatre Magazine 12:xvii+, Dec 1910

How's Your Health (with Harry Leon Wilson)
Productions:
Opened November 26, 1929 for 47 performances.
Reviews:
Catholic World 130:469-70, Jan 1930
New York Times p. 30, Nov 27, 1929

The Intimate Strangers
Productions:
Opened November 7, 1921 for 91 performances.
Reviews:
Bookman 54:464-5, Jan 1922
Dramatic Mirror 84:700, Nov 12, 1921
Life (NY) 78:18, Dec 8, 1921
New York Clipper 69:20, Nov 16, 1921
New York Times p. 28, Nov 8, 1921
Theatre Magazine 35:30, Jan 1922

*Karabash
Reviews:
New York Times IX, p. 3, Aug 27, 1939

Magnolia
Productions:
Opened August 27, 1923 for 40 performances.
Reviews:
Hearst 44:85-7+, Dec 1923
Life (NY) 82:18, Sep 13, 1923

TARKINGTON, BOOTH (cont.)
Magnolia (cont.)
  Nation 117:273, Sep 12, 1923
  New York Times VII, p. 1, Jun 24, 1923
       p. 12, Aug 28, 1923
       VI, p. 1, Sep 2, 1923
       p. 10, Jul 29, 1940

Mister Antonio
 Productions:
  Opened September 18, 1916 for 48 performances.
 Reviews:
  Dramatic Mirror 76:7, Sep 23, 1916
  Harper's Weekly 134:187-203, Jan 1917
        134:374-87, Feb 1917
  Life (NY) 68:580, Oct 5, 1916
  Nation 103:330, Oct 5, 1916
  New York Times p. 9, Sep 19, 1916
       II, p. 4, Sep 24, 1916
  Theatre Magazine 24:281+, Nov 1916

Monsieur Beaucaire (with E. G. Sutherland)
 Productions:
  Opened March 11, 1912 for 64 performances.
 Reviews:
  Blue Book 15:233-5, Jun 1912
  Dramatic Mirror 67:7, Mar 13, 1912
  Green Book 7:1098-9+, Jun 1912
  Life (NY) 59:631, Mar 28, 1912
  New York Drama News 55:24, Mar 16, 1912
  New York Times IV, p. 2, May 25, 1919

Poldekin
 Productions:
  Opened September 9, 1920 for 44 performances.
 Reviews:
  Current Opinion 69:481-8, Oct 1920
  Dramatic Mirror 82:415, Mar 6, 1920
       82:503, Sep 18, 1920
  Dramatist 11:1025-6, Oct 1920
  Independent 104:1, Oct 2, 1920
  Life (NY) 76:582, Sep 30, 1920
  McClure's 52:8-11+, Mar 1920
      52:91, Apr 1920
  New York Clipper 68:27, Sep 15, 1920
  New York Times p. 12, Sep 10, 1920
       VI, p. 1, Sep 12, 1920

VI, p. 1, Sep 19, 1920
Theatre Magazine 32:371+, Dec 1920
Weekly Review 3:275-6, Sep 29, 1920

Rose Briar
    Productions:
        Opened December 25, 1922 for 88 performances.
    Reviews:
        Nation 116:128, Jan 31, 1923
        New York Clipper 70:20, Jan 3, 1923
        New York Times p. 11, Dec 26, 1922
        Theatre Magazine 37:5+, Mar 1923

Springtime (with Harry Leon Wilson)
    Productions:
        Opened October 19, 1909 for 79 performances.
    Reviews:
        Collier's 44:23, Nov 6, 1909
        Dramatic Mirror 62:5, Oct 30, 1909
        Everybody's 22:273, Feb 1910
        Green Book 3:83-4, Jan 1910
                  3:481-507, Mar 1910
        Hampton 24:133, Jan 1910
        Harper's Weekly 53:24, Nov 20, 1909
        Leslies' Weekly 109:439, Nov 4, 1909
        Metropolitan Magazine 31:532-3, Jan 1910
        Theatre Magazine 10:170+, Dec 1909

Tweedles (with Harry Leon Wilson)
    Productions:
        Opened August 13, 1923 for 96 performances.
    Reviews:
        Bookman 58:181, Oct 1923
        Current Opinion 75:445-50+, Oct 1923
        Life (NY) 82:18, Aug 30, 1923
        Nation 117:273, Sep 12, 1923
        New York Times p. 10, Aug 14, 1923
                      VI, p. 1, Aug 19, 1923
                      VI, p. 2, Aug 19, 1923
        Theatre Magazine 38:19, Oct 1923

Up From Nowhere (with Harry Leon Wilson)
    Productions:
        Opened September 8, 1919 for 40 performances.
    Reviews:
        Dramatic Mirror 80:1465, Sep 18, 1919
        Forum 62:501, Oct-Nov 1919

TARKINGTON, BOOTH (cont.)
Up From Nowhere (cont.)
New York Times p. 17, Sep 9, 1919
IV, p. 2, Sep 14, 1919
Theatre Magazine 30:280, Oct 1919

The Wren
Productions:
Opened October 10, 1921 for 24 performances.
Reviews:
Bookman 54:375-6, Dec 1921
Life (NY) 78:18, Oct 27, 1921
New York Clipper 69:20, Oct 19, 1921
New York Times p. 22, Oct 11, 1921
VI, p. 1, Oct 16, 1921

Your Humble Servant (with Harry Leon Wilson)
Productions:
Opened January 3, 1910 for 72 performances.
Reviews:
Dramatic Mirror 63:5, Jan 15, 1910
Dramatist 1:17-20, Jan 1910
Green Book 3:522, Mar 1910
Hampton 24:409-10, Mar 1910
Life (NY) 55:129, Jan 20, 1910
Metropolitan Magazine 32:122-3, Apr 1910
Munsey 42:891-2, Mar 1910
Theatre Magazine 11:37, Feb 1910

TAYLOR, SAMUEL

Avanti!
Productions:
Opened January 31, 1968 for 21 performances.
Reviews:
New York Theatre Critics' Reviews 1968:365
New York Times p. 29, Feb 1, 1968
New Yorker 43:86+, Feb 10, 1968

Beekman Place
Productions:
Opened October 7, 1964 for 29 performances.
Reviews:
New York Theatre Critics' Reviews 1964:198
New York Times p. 50, Oct 8, 1964
New Yorker 40:108, Oct 17, 1964

Saturday Review 47:30, Oct 24, 1964
Time 84:77, Oct 16, 1964

First Love (Based on Romain Gary's Promise At Dawn)
Productions:
Opened December 25, 1961 for 24 performances.
Reviews:
America 106:540, Jan 20, 1962
New York Theatre Critics' Reviews 1961:143
New York Times II, p. 5, Dec 17, 1961
                p. 20, Dec 26, 1961
New Yorker 37:56-7, Jan 6, 1962
Newsweek 59:45, Jan 8, 1962
Reporter 26:45, Feb 1, 1962

The Happy Time (Based on the book by Robert Fontaine)
Productions:
Opened January 24, 1950 for 614 performances.
Reviews:
Catholic World 170:470, Mar 1950
Commonweal 51:510, Feb 17, 1950
Life 28:107-8+, Feb 6, 1950
New Republic 122:20, Feb 27, 1950
New York Theatre Critics' Reviews 1950:370
New York Times p. 24, Jan 25, 1950
                II, p. 2, Feb 10, 1952
                p. 39, May 12, 1959
New Yorker 25:50-1, Feb 4, 1950
Newsweek 35:76, Feb 6, 1950
Saturday Review 33:26-8, Feb 18, 1950
Theatre Arts 34:12, Apr 1950
Time 55:66, Feb 6, 1950

Nina (Adapted from the play by Andre Roussin)
Productions:
Opened December 5, 1951 for 45 performances.
Reviews:
Commonweal 55:277, Dec 21, 1951
New York Theatre Critics' Reviews 1951:152
New York Times p. 44, Dec 5, 1951
                p. 36, Jun 24, 1952
New Yorker 27:71, Dec 15, 1951
Newsweek 38:69, Dec 17, 1951
Theatre Arts 36:31+, Feb 1952
Time 58:76, Dec 17, 1951

473

TAYLOR, SAMUEL (cont.)
The Pleasure of His Company (with Cornelia Otis Skinner)
    Productions:
        Opened October 22, 1958 for 474 performances.
    Reviews:
        America 100:255, Nov 22, 1958
        Catholic World 188:331, Jan 1959
        New York Theatre Critics' Reviews 1958:245
        New York Times p. 36, Oct 23, 1958
                       II, p. 1, Nov 2, 1958
                          p. 22, Apr 24, 1959
        New Yorker 34:97-8, Nov 1, 1958
        Newsweek 52:62-3, Nov 3, 1958
        Reporter 19:36, Nov 27, 1958
        Saturday Review 41:25, Nov 8, 1958
        Theatre Arts 43:9, Jan 1959
        Time 72:48+, Nov 3, 1958

Sabrina Fair
    Productions:
        Opened November 11, 1953 for 318 performances.
    Reviews:
        America 90:325+, Dec 19, 1953
        Catholic World 178:306, Jan 1954
        Commonweal 59:281, Dec 18, 1953
        Nation 177:454, Nov 28, 1953
        New Republic 129:20-1, Nov 23, 1953
        New York Theatre Critics' Reviews 1953:217
        New York Times p. 37, Nov 12, 1953
                       II, p. 1, Nov 22, 1953
                          p. 18, Aug 5, 1954
        New Yorker 29:85, Nov 21, 1953
        Newsweek 42:60, Dec 21, 1953
                 42:64, Nov 23, 1953
        Saturday Review 36:46, Dec 12, 1953
                        36:29-30, Nov 28, 1953
        Theatre Arts 38:24, Jan 1954
                     38:26-9, Feb 1954
        Time 62:78, Nov 23, 1953

Stop-Over (with Matt Taylor)
    Productions:
        Opened January 11, 1938 for 23 performances.
    Reviews:
        New York Times p. 16, Jan 12, 1938
        Theatre Arts 22:177-8, Mar 1938
        Time 31:46, Jan 24, 1938

THOMAS, A. E.

The Big Idea (with Clayton Hamilton)
Productions:
Opened November 16, 1914 for 24 performances.
Reviews:
American Playwright 3:398-9, Dec 1914
Book News 33:229-30, Jan 1915
Bookman 40:551-2, Jan 1915
Collier's 54:9-10, Jan 2, 1915
Current Opinion 58:29, Jan 1915
Dramatic Mirror 72:8, Nov 25, 1914
Green Book 13:379-80, Feb 1915
Munsey 53:812, Jan 1915
New Republic 1:24, Nov 21, 1914
New York Drama News 60:11, Nov 21, 1914
New York Times p. 13, Nov 17, 1914
            VIII, p. 6, Nov 22, 1914
Theatre Magazine 21:7-8+, Jan 1915

The Big Pond (See entry under Middleton, George)

The Champion (with Thomas Louden)
Productions:
Opened January 3, 1921 for 175 performances.
Reviews:
Collier's 67:15, Feb 5, 1921
Dramatic Mirror 83:59, Jan 8, 1921
Life (NY) 77:136, Jan 27, 1921
New York Clipper 68:19, Jan 4, 1921
New York Times p. 11, Jan 4, 1921
            VI, p. 1, Jan 9, 1921
            VI, p. 1, Jan 16, 1921
Theatre Magazine 33:181+, Mar 1921

Come Out of the Kitchen (Based on Alice Duer Miller's
    story)
Productions:
Opened October 23, 1916 for 224 performances.
Reviews:
Collier's 58:37-8, Jan 27, 1917
Dramatic Mirror 76:7, Oct 28, 1916
Dramatist 8:761-2, Jan 1917
Green Book 17:8-9+, Jan 1917
Nation 103:427, Nov 2, 1916
New York Drama News 63:10, Oct 28, 1916
New York Times p. 14, Oct 24, 1916
Theatre Magazine 24:356+, Dec 1916

THOMAS, A. E. (cont.)
   Embers (Adapted from the French of Pierre Wolff and
      Henri Duvernois)
      Productions:
         Opened February 1, 1926 for 25 performances.
      Reviews:
         New York Times p. 20, Feb 2, 1926

   Fool's Bells (Based on a story by Leona Dalrymple).
      Productions:
         Opened December 22, 1925 for 5 performances.
      Reviews:
         New York Times p. 8, Dec 24, 1925

   The French Doll (Adapted from the French of MM. Ar-
      mont and Gerbidon)
      Productions:
         Opened February 20, 1922 for 120 performances.
      Reviews:
         New York Clipper 70:22, Mar 8, 1922
         New York Times p. 20, Feb 21, 1922
         Theatre Magazine 35:308, May 1922

   Her Friend the King (with Harrison Rhodes)
      Productions:
         Opened October 7, 1929 for 24 performances.
      Reviews:
         New York Times p. 34, Oct 8, 1929
         Theatre Magazine 50:68, Dec 1929

   Her Husband's Wife
      Productions:
         Opened May 9, 1910 for 48 performances.
         Opened January 8, 1917 for 32 performances.
         (Off Broadway) Opened February 1946 (Playhouse
            des Artistes).
      Reviews:
         Bookman 33:359, Jun 1911
         Current Literature 49:192-7, Aug 1910
         Dramatic Mirror 63:10, May 21, 1910
                        77:7, Jan 20, 1917
         Dramatist 6:516-17, Oct 1914
         Everybody's 23:696+, Nov 1910
         Green Book 4:99-100, Jul 1910
         Life (NY) 55:922, May 19, 1910
                   69:102, Jan 18, 1917
         Metropolitan Magazine 32:542-3, Jul 1910

Nation 104:85, Jan 18, 1917
New York Drama News 63:2, Jan 13, 1917
New York Times p. 3, Jan 9, 1917
    II, p. 4, Jan 21, 1917
Pearson 24:92-4, Jul 1910
Theatre Magazine 11:175-7, Jun 1910
    25:88, Feb 1917

The Jolly Roger
 Productions:
  Opened August 30, 1923 for 52 performances.
 Reviews:
  Nation 117:304, Sep 19, 1923
  New York Times p. 10, Aug 31, 1923
     VII, p. 1, Sep 9, 1923

Just Suppose
 Productions:
  Opened November 1, 1920 for 88+ performances.
 Reviews:
  Dramatic Mirror p. 880, November 6, 1920
  Life (NY) 76:960, Nov 25, 1920
  New York Clipper 68:32, Nov 17, 1920
  New York Times p. 15, Nov 2, 1920
     VII, p. 1, Nov 7, 1920
     p. 24, Jul 2, 1935
  Theatre Magazine 33:7+, Jan 1921
  Weekly Review 3:509-10, Nov 24, 1920

Lost (with George Agnew Chamberlain)
 Productions:
  Opened March 28, 1927 for 8 performances.
 Reviews:
  New York Times p. 22, Mar 29, 1927

Merely Murder (Based on Georgette Heyer's novel)
 Productions:
  Opened December 3, 1937 for 3 performances.
 Reviews:
  New York Times p. 26, Nov 16, 1937
     p. 21, Dec 4, 1937

No More Ladies
 Productions:
  Opened January 23, 1934 for 162 performances.
  Opened September 3, 1934 for 16 performances.
 Reviews:

THOMAS, A. E. (cont.)
No More Ladies (cont.)
Catholic World 138:732-3, Mar 1934
Nation 138:167-8, Feb 7, 1934
New Outlook 163:32, Mar 1934
New York Times p. 20, Jan 24, 1934
p. 23, Sep 4, 1934
p. 14, Sep 19, 1934
p. 15, Aug 9, 1939
Newsweek 3:36, Feb 3, 1934
Review of Reviews 89:48, Apr 1934
Stage 11:7-8, Mar 1934
Theatre Arts 18:248, Apr 1934
Time 23:35, Feb 5, 1934

Only 38
Productions:
Opened September 13, 1921 for 88 performances.
Reviews:
Dramatic Mirror 84:413, Sep 17, 1921
Independent 107:36, Oct 8, 1921
New York Times p. 22, Sep 14, 1921
Theatre Magazine 34:422, Dec 1921

The Rainbow
Productions:
Opened March 11, 1912 for 104 performances.
Reviews:
American Playwright 1:110-12, Apr 1912
Blue Book 15:246-8, Jun 1912
Bookman 35:247-8, Jun 1912
Collier's 49:24, Apr 13, 1912
Current Literature 52:687-93, Jun 1912
Dramatic Mirror 67:7, Mar 13, 1912
Dramatist 3:245-7, Apr 1912
Green Book 7:1072, May 1912
7:1088-90+, Jun 1912
Hampton 28:294+, May 1912
Hearst 21:2473-88, Jun 1912
Munsey 47:281-2, May 1912
National Magazine 37:780-5, Jan 1913
New York Drama News 55:14, Mar 16, 1912
Red Book 19:380-4, Jun 1912
Theatre Magazine 15:108, Apr 1912

*Spin-Drift
Reviews:
New York Times p. 16, Feb 14, 1925

Vermont
    Productions:
        Opened January 7, 1929 for 15 performances.
    Reviews:
        New York Times p. 28, Jan 9, 1929
        Theatre Magazine 49:51, Mar 1929

What the Doctor Ordered
    Productions:
        Opened September 20, 1911 for 21 performances.
    Reviews:
        American Playwright 1:23-4, Jan 1912
        Bookman 33:359-60, Jun 1911
        Dramatic Mirror 66:10, Sep 27, 1911
        Life (NY) 58:567, Oct 5, 1911
                  90:19, Sep 8, 1927

THOMAS, AUGUSTUS

Arizona
    Productions:
        Opened April 28, 1913 for 40 performances.
    Reviews:
        Blue Book 17:659-61, Aug 1913
        Bookman 37:430-1, Jun 1913
        Dramatic Mirror 69:6, Apr 30, 1913
        Dramatist 3:252-3, Jul 1913
        Green Book 10:19-21+, Jul 1913
        Life (NY) 61:980, May 15, 1913
        New York Times p. 11, Apr 30, 1913
        Theatre Magazine 17:171, Jun 1913

As a Man Thinks
    Productions:
        Opened March 13, 1911 for 128 performances.
    Reviews:
        Blue Book 13:250-2, Jun 1911
        Book News 31:289, Dec 1912
        Bookman 33:354, Jun 7, 1911
        Current Literature 50:529-36, May 1911
        Dramatic Mirror 65:7, Mar 15, 1911
        Dramatist 2:142-3, Apr 1911
        Everybody's 25:688-89, Nov 1911
        Harper's Weekly 55:18, Apr 15, 1911
        Independent 70:664-5, Mar 30, 1911
        Leslies' Weekly 112:347, Mar 30, 1911

479

THOMAS, AUGUSTUS (cont.)
As a Man Thinks (cont.)
Life (NY) 57:580, Mar 23, 1911
Metropolitan Magazine 34:220, May 1911
Munsey 45:282-3, May 1911
Nation 93:197-8, Aug 31, 1911
Outlook 97:714, Apr 1, 1911
Pearson 25:663-72, May 1911
Red Book 17:369-74, Jun 1911
World Today 20:530, May 1911
21:1247-54, Oct 1911

The Copperhead (Based on a story by Frederick Landis)
Productions:
Opened February 18, 1918 for 120 performances.
Reviews:
Art World 3:460, Mar 1918
Bookman 47:291, May 1918
Current Opinion 65:23-6, Jul 1918
Dramatic Mirror 78:5, Mar 2, 1918
Dramatist 9:896-7, Apr 1918
Green Book 19:776-9, May 1918
Hearst 34:42-4+, Jul 1918
Life (NY) 71:382, Mar 7, 1918
New Republic 14:267, Mar 30, 1918
New York Times p. 11, Feb 19, 1918
V, p. 4, Feb 24, 1918
IV, p. 10, Mar 31, 1918
Theatre Magazine 27:21+, Apr 1918

The Harvest Moon
Productions:
Opened October 15, 1909 for 91 performances.
Reviews:
American Magazine 69:417, Jan 1910
Current Literature 47:661-8, Dec 1909
Dramatic Mirror 62:5, Oct 30, 1909
Dramatist 1:21-2, Jan 1910
Everybody's 22:130, Jan 1910
Forum 42:575-6, Dec 1909
Green Book 3:81-2, Jan 1910
3:705-49, Apr 1910
Hampton 24:128+, Jan 1910
Harper's Weekly 53:24, Nov 6, 1909
Independent 67:1123-4, Nov 18, 1909
Life (NY) 54:628, Nov 4, 1909

Metropolitan Magazine 31:536-7, Jan 1910
Nation 89:387, Oct 21, 1909
Outlook 93:571, Nov 13, 1909
Pearson 23:97-8, Jan 1910
Theatre Magazine 10:167-9+, Dec 1909
World Today 18:651-8, Jun 1910

Indian Summer
    Productions:
        Opened October 27, 1913 for 24 performances.
    Reviews:
        American Playwright 2:351-5, Nov 1913
        Bookman 38:364-5, Dec 1913
        Dramatic Mirror 70:6, Oct 29, 1913
        Dramatist 5:420-1, Jan 1914
        Harper's Weekly 58:24-5, Nov 22, 1913
        Life (NY) 62:838-9, Nov 13, 1913
        New York Times p. 11, Oct 28, 1913
        Theatre Magazine 18:177-9, Dec 1913

Mere Man
    Productions:
        Opened November 25, 1912 for 8 performances.
    Reviews:
        American Playwright 1:399-400, Dec 1912
        Dramatic Mirror 68:7, Nov 27, 1912
        New York Drama News 56:26, Nov 30, 1912
        Theatre Magazine 17:4, Jan 1913

The Model
    Productions:
        Opened August 31, 1912 for 17 performances.
    Reviews:
        American Playwright 1:288-90, Sep 1913
        Blue Book 15:701-4, Aug 1912
        Bookman 36:170-1, Oct 1912
        Dramatic Mirror 68:6, Sep 4, 1912
        Dramatist 3:252, Jul 1912
        Everybody's 27:673, Nov 1912
        Green Book 8:802-3, Nov 1912
                   8:898-9, Nov 1912
        Life (NY) 60:1767, Sep 12, 1912
        New York Drama News 55:18-19, Apr 13, 1912
                             56:12, Sep 14, 1912
        Theatre Magazine 16:102+, Oct 1912

481

THOMAS, AUGUSTUS (cont.)
    Nemesis
        Productions:
        Opened April 4, 1921 for 56 performances.
        Reviews:
            Dramatic Mirror 83:620, Apr 9, 1921
            Dramatist 12:1051-2, Apr 1921
            Everybody's 45:106-12, Jul 1921
            Life (NY) 77:572, Apr 21, 1921
            Nation 112:598, Apr 20, 1921
            New York Clipper 69:19, Apr 6, 1921
            New York Times p. 24, Apr 5, 1921
                            VI, p. 1, Apr 10, 1921
            Theatre Magazine 33:395+, Jun 1921
            Weekly Review 4:377-8, Apr 20, 1921

    Palmy Days
        Productions:
        Opened October 27, 1919 for 50 performances.
        Reviews:
            Nation 109:640, Nov 15, 1919
            New York Times p. 14, Oct 28, 1919
                            VIII, p. 2, Nov 2, 1919
            Theatre Magazine 30:367+, Dec 1919

    Rio Grande
        Productions:
        Opened April 4, 1916 for 55 performances.
        Reviews:
            Book News 34:401, May 1916
            Bookman 43:343, May 1916
            Dramatic Mirror 75:9, Mar 11, 1916
                            75:8, Apr 15, 1916
                            7:663-6, Apr 1916
            Green Book 15:972-3+, Jun 1916
            Hearst 30:97-9+, Aug 1916
            Life (NY) 67:759, Apr 20, 1916
            Nation 102:420, Apr 13, 1916
            New Republic 6:353-4, Apr 29, 1916
            New York Drama News 62:18, Apr 8, 1916
            New York Times p. 11, Apr 5, 1916
            Theatre Magazine 23:273-4+, May 1916

    Still Waters
        Productions:
        Opened March 1, 1926 for 16 performances.
        Reviews:

Catholic World 123:92-3, Apr 1926
New York Times p. 21, Sep 8, 1925
p. 29, Sep 10, 1925
p. 23, Sep 11, 1925
p. 24, Sep 15, 1925
p. 24, Feb 26, 1926
p. 23, Mar 2, 1926
VIII, p. 1, Mar 7, 1926
Theatre Magazine 43:16, May 1926

*When It Comes Home
Reviews:
New York Times VIII, p. 1, Jan 22, 1928

THURBER, JAMES

The Male Animal (with Elliott Nugent)
Productions:
Opened January 9, 1940 for 243 performances.
Opened April 30, 1952 for 317 performances.
Reviews:
Catholic World 150:597, Feb 1940
175:228, Jun 1952
Commonweal 31:307, Jan 26, 1940
56:173, May 23, 1952
Life 8:27-8+, Jan 29, 1940
Nation 150:81, Jan 20, 1940
175:58, Jul 19, 1952
New Republic 102:116, Jan 22, 1940
New York Theatre Critics' Reviews 1940:424
1952:297
New York Times IX, p. 1, Jan 7, 1940
p. 17, Jan 10, 1940
IX, p. 1, Jan 21, 1940
p. 27, Jul 1, 1941
p. 24, Jul 9, 1941
II, p. 2, Apr 27, 1952
p. 35, May 1, 1952
II, p. 1, May 18, 1952
New Yorker 28:58, May 10, 1952
Newsweek 14:34, Nov 6, 1939
15:32-3, Jan 22, 1940
39:84, May 26, 1952
Saturday Review 35:28, May 17, 1952
Theatre Arts 24:158-9+, Mar 1940
24:396+, Jun 1940

483

THURBER, JAMES (cont.)
The Male Animal (cont.)
                    36:17, 32-5, Jul 1952
        Time 35:49, Jan 22, 1940
              59:58, May 12, 1952

A Thurber Carnival
    Productions:
        Opened February 26, 1960 for 127 performances.
        Opened September 5, 1960 for 96 performances.
        (Off Broadway) Opened October 1, 1965 for 9 per-
            formances (Equity Theatre).
    Reviews:
        America 103:322-3, May 28, 1960
        Christian Century 77:489-90, Apr 20, 1960
        Nation 190:236, Mar 12, 1960
        New York Theatre Critics' Reviews 1960:342
        New York Times II, p. 1, Feb 21, 1960
                      p. 13, Feb 27, 1960
                      II, p. 1, Mar 6, 1960
                      VI, p. 18, Mar 6, 1960
                      II, p. 3, Sep 4, 1960
                      p. 41, Sep 13, 1960
                      VI, p. 28, Oct 16, 1960
                      p. 42, Apr 12, 1962
        New Yorker 36:125-6, Mar 5, 1960
        Newsweek 55:89, Mar 7, 1960
        Saturday Review 43:26, Mar 19, 1960
        Time 75:50, Mar 7, 1960

TOTHEROH, DAN

    Distant Drums
        Productions:
            Opened January 18, 1932 for 40 performances.
        Reviews:
            Catholic World 134:712-13, Mar 1932
            Commonweal 15:385, Feb 3, 1932
            Literary Digest 112:17, Feb 6, 1932
            Nation 134:177-8, Feb 10, 1932
            New Republic 69:320-1, Feb 3, 1932
            New York Times p. 24, Jan 19, 1932
                          VIII, p. 1, Jan 31, 1932
                          VIII, p. 2, Jan 24, 1932
            Outlook 160:151, Feb 3, 1932
            Player's Magazine 8:13, Mar-Apr 1932
            Theatre Arts 16:190-1, Mar 1932

Theatre Guild Magazine 9:11, Mar 1932
Vogue 79:73+, Mar 15, 1932

Live Life Again
    Productions:
    Opened September 29, 1945 for 2 performances.
    Reviews:
        Catholic World 162:164, Nov 1945
        New Republic 113:499, Oct 15, 1945
        New York Theatre Critics' Reviews 1945:154
        New York Times p. 14, Oct 1, 1945
        New Yorker 21:50-1, Oct 6, 1945
        Theatre Arts 29:621-2, 632-3, Nov 1945

Moor Born
    Productions:
    Opened April 3, 1934 for 63 performances.
    Reviews:
        Catholic World 134:213-4, May 1934
        Commonweal 19:692, Apr 20, 1934
        Literary Digest 117:24, Apr 21, 1934
        Nation 138:453-4, Apr 18, 1934
        New Outlook 163:43, May 1934
        New Republic 78:275, Apr 18, 1934
        New York Times p. 26, Apr 4, 1934
        New Yorker 3:37-8, Apr 14, 1934
        Review of Reviews 89:49, May 1934
        Stage 11:6-7, May 1934
        Theatre Arts 18:409, Jun 1934
        Time 23:55-6, Apr 16, 1934

Mother Lode (with George O'Neil)
    Productions:
    Opened December 22, 1934 for 9 performances.
    Reviews:
        New York Times p. 16, Dec 24, 1934
        Theatre Arts 19:103, Feb 1935

*Rough an' Ready
    Reviews:
        New York Times II, p. 3, May 22, 1949

Searching for the Sun
    Productions:
    Opened February 19, 1936 for 5 performances.
    Reviews:
        New York Times IX, p. 2, Feb 16, 1936
                      p. 22, Feb 20, 1936

TOTHEROH, DAN (cont.)
Wild Birds
    Productions:
        Opened April 9, 1925 for 44 performances.
    Reviews:
        American Mercury 5:247-8, Jun 1925
        Dramatist 16:1266-7, Apr 1925
        Independent 114:644, Jun 6, 1925
        New York Times p. 16, Apr 10, 1925
                        VIII, p. 1, Apr 26, 1925

*Wind in the Sails
    Reviews:
        New York Times p. 24, Aug 1, 1940

TREADWELL, SOPHIE

Gringo
    Productions:
        Opened December 12, 1922 for 35 performances.
    Reviews:
        Bookman 56:749-50, Feb 1923
        New York Times p. 26, Dec 15, 1922
                        VII, p. 1, Dec 24, 1922
        Theatre Magazine 37:19, Feb 1923

Hope for a Harvest
    Productions:
        Opened November 26, 1941 for 38 performances.
    Reviews:
        Catholic World 154:472-3, Jan 1942
        Nation 153:621, Dec 13, 1941
        New Republic 105:762, Dec 8, 1941
        New York Theatre Critics' Reviews 1941:198
        New York Times p. 18, Apr 5, 1941
                        p. 28, Nov 27, 1941
                        X, p. 5, Dec 7, 1941
        Theatre Arts 26:12, Jan 1942
        Time 38:39, Dec 8, 1941

Ladies Leave
    Productions:
        Opened October 1, 1929 for 15 performances.
    Reviews:
        New York Times p. 28, Oct 2, 1929
        Outlook 153:272, Oct 16, 1929
        Theatre Magazine 50:68, Dec 1929

Lone Valley
    Productions:
        Opened March 10, 1933 for 3 performances.
    Reviews:
        New York Times p. 18, Mar 11, 1933

*Lonely Lee
    Reviews:
        New York Times VIII, p. 2, Nov 11, 1923

Machinal
    Productions:
        Opened September 7, 1928 for 91 performances.
        (Off Broadway) Season of 1959-60.
    Reviews:
        America 103:203, Apr 30, 1960
        American Mercury 15:376-7, Nov 28, 1928
        Commonweal 72:306, Jun 17, 1960
        Dial 85:445, Nov 1928
        Life (NY) 92:17, Sep 28, 1928
        Nation 127:302, Sep 26, 1928
        New Republic 56:299-300, Oct 31, 1928
                    142:21-2, Apr 25, 1960
        New York Times p. 10, Sep 8, 1928
                        III, p. 4, Sep 16, 1928
                        IX, p. 1, Sep 16, 1928
                        X, p. 1, Nov 25, 1928
                        p. 27, Apr 8, 1960
                        II, p. 1, Apr 17, 1960
        New Yorker 36:134-6, Apr 16, 1960
        Theatre Arts 12:774-80, Nov 1928
        Theatre Magazine 48:46, Nov 1928
                         49:20, Jan 1929
        Vogue 72:74+, Oct 27, 1928

O, Nightingale
    Productions:
        Opened April 15, 1925 for 29 performances.
    Reviews:
        New York Times p. 25, Apr 16, 1925

Plumes in the Dust
    Productions:
        Opened November 6, 1936 for 11 performances.
    Reviews:
        Catholic World 144:336-7, Dec 1936
        Commonweal 25:104, Nov 20, 1936

487

TREADWELL, SOPHIE (cont.)
  Plumes in the Dust (cont.)
        New Republic 89:116, Nov 25, 1936
        New York Times p. 21, Oct 26, 1936
                     p. 14, Nov 7, 1936
                     XI, p. 1, Nov 15, 1936
        Newsweek 8:58+, Nov 14, 1936
        Time 28:89, Nov 16, 1936

TURNEY, ROBERT

  Daughters of Atreus
    Productions:
    Opened October 14, 1936 for 13 performances.
    Reviews:
      Commonweal 25:20, Oct 30, 1936
      Nation 143:529-30, Oct 31, 1936
      New York Times p. 33, Oct 15, 1936
      Player's Magazine 13:8, Nov-Dec 1936
      Saturday Review 14:18, Oct 17, 1936
      Scribner's Magazine 100:78, Dec 1936
      Stage 14:68-9, Oct 1936
            14:72, Nov 1936
      Theatre Arts 20:924-5, Dec 1936
      Time 28:48, Oct 26, 1936
      Vogue 88:66, Nov 15, 1936

  The Secret Room
    Productions:
    Opened November 7, 1945 for 21 performances.
    Reviews:
      Catholic World 162:263, Dec 1945
      Commonweal 43:140, Nov 23, 1945
      Life 19:51-2+, Nov 19, 1945
      New York Theatre Critics' Reviews 1945:124
      New York Times p. 16, Nov 8, 1945
      New Yorker 21:50+, Nov 17, 1945
      Newsweek 26:85, Nov 19, 1945
      Theatre Arts 30:13, Jan 1946
      Time 46:64, Nov 19, 1945

TYLER, ROYALL

  *The Contrast
    Reviews:

New York Times p. 27, Jul 20, 1948
             p. 45, Jul 20, 1966

VALE, MARTIN (MRS. BAYARD VEILLER)

The Two Mrs. Carrolls
Productions:
    Opened August 3, 1943 for 585 performances.
Reviews:
    Catholic World 157:635-7, Sep 1943
    Life 15:115-16+, Aug 23, 1943
    Nation 157:388, Oct 2, 1943
    New York Theatre Critics' Reviews 1943:304
    New York Times p. 14, Aug 14, 1943
    Newsweek 22:78, Aug 16, 1943
    Theatre Arts 27:575-6, Oct 1943
    Time 42:50, Aug 16, 1943

VAN DRUTEN, JOHN

After All
Productions:
    Opened December 3, 1931 for 20 performances.
Reviews:
    Arts and Decorations 36:56, Feb 1932
    Catholic World 134:468-9, Jan 1932
    Commonweal 15:187, Dec 16, 1931
    Nation 133:706, Dec 23, 1931
    New York Times IX, p. 1, May 26, 1929
               p. 28, Dec 4, 1931
    Outlook 159:502, Dec 16, 1931
    Theatre Arts 16:101, Feb 1932
    Town and Country 86:22, Jan 1, 1932

*Behold We Live
Reviews:
    New York Times p. 13, Aug 17, 1932
              IX, p. 1, Sep 11, 1932

Bell, Book and Candle
Productions:
    Opened November 14, 1950 for 233 performances.
Reviews:
    Catholic World 172:307, Jan 1951
    Christian Science Monitor Magazine p. 10, Nov 25,
      1950

VAN DRUTEN, JOHN (cont.)
Bell, Book and Candle (cont.)
Commonweal 53:197, Dec 1, 1950
Hobbies 57:38, Oct 1952
Life 29:111-12+, Dec 11, 1950
Nation 171:493, Nov 25, 1950
New Republic 123:22, Dec 25, 1950
New York Theatre Critics' Reviews 1950:206
New York Times II, p. 3, Nov 12, 1950
p. 37, Nov 15, 1950
II, p. 3, Dec 17, 1950
p. 86, Oct 11, 1953
p. 30, Oct 6, 1954
New Yorker 26:62+, Nov 25, 1950
Newsweek 36:76, Nov 27, 1950
Saturday Review 33:24, Dec 16, 1950
School and Society 73:104, Feb 17, 1951
Theatre Arts 35:15, Jan 1951
Theatre Arts 36:50-75, Jun 1952
Time 56:76+, Nov 27, 1950

The Damask Cheek (with Lloyd Morris)
Productions:
Opened October 22, 1942 for 93 performances.
Reviews:
Catholic World 156:335-6, Dec 1942
Commonweal 37:71-2, Nov 6, 1942
Independent Woman 21:368+, Dec 1942
Life 13:68+, Nov 23, 1942
Nation 155:599, Nov 28, 1942
New Republic 107:609-10, Nov 9, 1942
New York Theatre Critics' Reviews 1942:195
New York Times p. 24, Oct 23, 1942
VIII, p. 1, Nov 8, 1942
VIII, p. 1, Dec 6, 1942
New Yorker 18:30, Oct 31, 1942
Newsweek 20:86, Nov 2, 1942
Theatre Arts 26:740-1, Dec 1942
Time 40:57, Nov 2, 1942

The Distaff Side
Productions:
Opened September 25, 1934 for 153 performances.
Reopened for 24 performances.
Reviews:
Catholic World 140:212, Nov 1934
Commonweal 20:563, Oct 12, 1934

Golden Book Magazine 20:510, Nov 1934
Nation 139:418-9, Oct 10, 1934
New Republic 80:273, Oct 17, 1934
New York Times p. 24, Sep 6, 1933
              X, p. 1, Sep 24, 1933
              p. 17, Sep 26, 1934
              p. 22, Jul 7, 1936
Newsweek 4:22-3, Oct 6, 1934
Stage 12:15, Nov 1934
      12:12-13, Dec 1934
Theatre Arts 18:818, Nov 1934
Vanity Fair 43:45-6, Dec 1934

Diversion
    Productions:
        Opened January 11, 1928 for 62 performances.
    Reviews:
        Life (NY) 91:21, Feb 2, 1928
        New York Times VII, p. 2, Aug 14, 1927
                       p. 26, Jan 6, 1928
                       p. 25, Jan 12, 1928
        Vogue 71:114, Mar 1, 1928

The Druid Circle
    Productions:
        Opened October 22, 1947 for 70 performances.
    Reviews:
        Catholic World 166:265, Dec 1947
        Commonweal 47:95, Nov 7, 1947
        New Republic 117:36, Nov 3, 1947
        New York Theatre Critics' Reviews 1947:288
        New York Times II, p. 1, Oct 19, 1947
                       p. 29, Oct 23, 1947
                       II, p. 1, Nov 16, 1947
        New Yorker 23:44+, Nov 1, 1947
        Newsweek 30:76, Nov 3, 1947
        Player's Magazine 25:191, May 1949
        School and Society 66:507-8, Dec 27, 1947
        Theatre Arts 31:14, Oct 1947
                     32:11, Jan 1948
        Time 50:68+, Nov 3, 1947
        Vogue 110:133, Oct 15, 1947

Flowers of the Forest
    Productions:
        Opened April 8, 1935 for 40 performances.
    Reviews:

491

VAN DRUTEN, JOHN (cont.)
Flowers of the Forest (cont.)
Catholic World 141:216-18, May 1935
Commonweal 21:740, Apr 26, 1935
Nation 140:490-1, Apr 24, 1935
New Republic 82:316, Apr 24, 1935
New York Times p. 24, Oct 3, 1934
p. 23, Nov 21, 1934
X, p. 3, Dec 9, 1934
p. 21, Apr 5, 1935
p. 25, Apr 9, 1935
IX, p. 1, Apr 14, 1935
Newsweek 5:17, Apr 20, 1935
Theatre Arts 19:3, Jan 1935
19:400-1+, Jun 1935
Time 25:26, Apr 22, 1935

*Gertie Maude
Reviews:
New York Times p. 14, Aug 18, 1937
X, p. 2, Sep 5, 1937
Theatre Arts 21:847, Nov 1937

I Am A Camera (Based on the stories of Christopher
Isherwood)
Productions:
Opened November 28, 1951 for 214 performances.
(Off Broadway) Season of 1956-57.
Reviews:
Catholic World 174:309, Jan 1952
Commonweal 55:277, Dec 21, 1951
Nation 173:554, Dec 22, 1951
New Republic 125:22, Dec 24, 1951
New York Theatre Critics' Reviews 1951:156
New York Times p. 39, Nov 29, 1951
II, p. 5, Dec 9, 1951
p. 11, Mar 13, 1954
II, p. 2, Apr 11, 1954
p. 47, Oct 10, 1956
New Yorker 27:62+, Dec 8, 1951
Newsweek 38:50, Dec 10, 1951
Saturday Review 34:26+, Dec 22, 1951
35:27, Jul 5, 1952
School and Society 75:41, Jan 19, 1952
Theatre Arts 36:20-2, 30, Feb 1952
Time 58:63, Dec 10, 1951

I Remember Mama (Adapted from Kathryn Forbes' Ma-
    ma's Bank Account).
    Productions:
    Opened October 19, 1944 for 714 performances.
    Reviews:
    Catholic World 160:259, Dec 1944
    Commonweal 41:72, Nov 3, 1944
    Life 17:104-6+, Nov 20, 1944
        18:79, Apr 9, 1945
    Nation 159:568, Nov 4, 1944
    New Republic 111:836, Dec 18, 1944
    New York Theatre Critics' Reviews 1944:111
    New York Times p. 16, Oct 20, 1944
                    II, p. 1, Oct 29, 1944
                    VI, p. 16, Dec 3, 1944
                    VI, p. 24, Oct 14, 1945
                    p. 79, Dec 15, 1946
                    VI, p. 18, Mar 2, 1947
                    p. 51, Jan 4, 1948
                    II, p. 3, Apr 11, 1948
    New Yorker 20:39, Oct 28, 1944
    Newsweek 24:86, Oct 30, 1944
    Player's Magazine 22:10, Nov-Dec 1945
    Saturday Review 27:18+, Dec 16, 1944
    Theatre Arts 28:692+, Dec 1944
                    29:81-2, 87, Feb 1945
                    29:215-17+, Apr 1945
    Time 44:68, Oct 30, 1944

I've Got Sixpence
    Productions:
    Opened December 2, 1952 for 23 performances.
    Reviews:
    Commonweal 57:306, Dec 26, 1952
    New York Theatre Critics' Reviews 1952:167
    New York Times II, p. 1, Nov 30, 1952
                    p. 44, Dec 3, 1952
                    II, p. 5, Dec 7, 1952
    New Yorker 28:86, Dec 13, 1952
    Newsweek 40;62, Dec 15, 1952
    Saturday Review 35:25, Dec 20, 1952
    Theatre Arts 36:15, Dec 1952
                    37:26, Feb 1953
    Time 60:73, Dec 15, 1952

Leave Her to Heaven
    Productions:

493

VAN DRUTEN, JOHN (cont.)
Leave Her to Heaven (cont.)
Opened February 27, 1940 for 15 performances.
Reviews:
Commonweal 31:455, Mar 15, 1940
New York Theatre Critics' Reviews 1940:379
New York Times p. 16, Feb 28, 1940
Newsweek 15:35, Mar 11, 1940
Theatre Arts 24:317, May 1940
Time 35:32, Mar 11, 1940

*London Wall
Reviews:
New York Times p. 23, May 2, 1931
VIII, p. 1, May 24, 1931

Make Way for Lucia (Based on the novels of E. F. Ben-
son)
Productions:
Opened December 22, 1948 for 29 performances.
Reviews:
Commonweal 49:352, Jan 14, 1949
Nation 168:81, Jan 15, 1949
New Republic 120:19, Jan 10, 1949
New York Theatre Critics' Reviews 1948:115
New York Times p. 23, Dec 23, 1948
New Yorker 24:34, Jan 1, 1949
Newsweek 33:54, Jan 3, 1949
Time 53:49, Jan 3, 1949
Vogue 113:115, Jan 1949

The Mermaids Singing
Productions:
Opened November 28, 1945 for 53 performances.
Reviews:
Catholic World 162:358, Jan 1946
Commonweal 43:263, Dec 21, 1945
Harper's Bazaar 79:128, Dec 1945
New Republic 113:839, Dec 17, 1945
New York Theatre Critics' Reviews 1945:86
New York Times p. 26, Nov 29, 1945
II, p. 5, Dec 9, 1945
New Yorker 21:56-8, Dec 8, 1945
Newsweek 26:93, Dec 10, 1945
Saturday Review 28:14-16, Dec 15, 1945
Theatre Arts 30:7, Jan 1946
30:78, Feb 1946
Time 46:76, Dec 10, 1945

Most of the Game
    Productions:
        Opened October 1, 1935 for 23 performances.
    Reviews:
        Nation 141:448, Oct 16, 1935
        New York Times p. 27, Oct 2, 1935
        Theatre Arts 19:823, Nov 1935
        Vanity Fair 45:40, Dec 1935

Old Acquaintance
    Productions:
        Opened December 23, 1940 for 170 performances.
    Reviews:
        Catholic World 152:597, Feb 1941
        Commonweal 33:303, Jan 10, 1941
        Nation 152:137, Feb 1, 1941
        New York Theatre Critics' Reviews 1940:178
                                         1941:448
        New York Times p. 33, Dec 10, 1940
                       p. 18, Dec 24, 1940
                       IX, p. 2, Dec 28, 1941
        Newsweek 17:52, Jan 6, 1941
        Theatre Arts 25:93-4, Feb 1941
        Time 37:41, Jan 6, 1941
        Vogue 97:77, Mar 1, 1941

*Return of the Soldier
    Reviews:
        New York Times VIII, p. 1, Jul 8, 1928

Solitaire (Based on a novel by Edwin Corle)
    Productions:
        Opened January 27, 1942 for 23 performances.
    Reviews:
        Catholic World 154:730, Nov 1942
        Commonweal 35:418, Feb 13, 1942
        Nation 154:201-2, Feb 14, 1942
        New Republic 106:204, Feb 9, 1942
        New York Theatre Critics' Reviews 1942:362
        New York Times p. 22, Jan 28, 1942
                       IX, p. 1, Feb 8, 1942
        Newsweek 19:63+, Feb 9, 1942
        Player's Magazine 18:12, Mar 1942
        Theatre Arts 26:224-5, Apr 1942
        Time 39:47, Feb 9, 1942

495

VAN DRUTEN, JOHN (cont.)
*Somebody Knows
    Reviews:
        New York Times VIII, p. 1, May 29, 1932

There's Always Juliet
    Productions:
        Opened February 15, 1932 for 108 performances.
        Opened October 27, 1932 for 20 performances.
    Reviews:
        Bookman 74:667, Mar 1932
        Catholic World 135:73, Apr 1932
        Commonweal 15:495, Mar 2, 1932
        Nation 134:266, Mar 2, 1932
        New Republic 70:97, Mar 9, 1932
        New York Times p. 26, Oct 13, 1931
                      VIII, p. 4, Nov 8, 1931
                      p. 24, Feb 16, 1932
                      VIII, p. 1, Feb 28, 1932
                      p. 23, Oct 28, 1932
        North American Review 234:174-5, Aug 1932
        Theatre Arts 16:270-1, Apr 1932
        Theatre Guild Magazine 9:29-31, Apr 1932
        Vogue 79:96B, Apr 15, 1932

The Voice of the Turtle
    Productions:
        Opened December 8, 1943 for 1,557 performances.
        (Off Broadway) Season of 1961-62.
    Reviews:
        American Mercury 58:464-8, Apr 1944
        Catholic World 158:487-8, Feb 1944
        Collier's 113:16-17+, Apr 29, 1944
        Commonweal 39:253, Dec 24, 1943
        Life 15:45-6, Dec 27, 1943
        Nation 157:767, Dec 25, 1943
        New Republic 109:915, Dec 27, 1943
        New York Theatre Critics' Reviews 1943:199
        New York Times II, p. 5, Dec 5, 1943
                      p. 30, Dec 9, 1943
                      II, p. 3, Dec 19, 1943
                      II, p. 6, Dec 10, 1944
                      p. 27, Dec 19, 1944
                      p. 19, Feb 5, 1945
                      p. 16, Feb 6, 1945
                      II, p. 1, Jun 30, 1945
                      p. 16, Sep 3, 1946

II, p. 1, Sep 8, 1946
p. 35, Feb 26, 1947
II, p. 3, Jun 8, 1947
p. 12, Aug 22, 1947
II, p. 2, Aug 22, 1947
p. 41, Jun 28, 1961
New Yorker 19:44, Dec 18, 1943
Newsweek 22:86, Dec 20, 1943
Theatre Arts 28:73-5, Feb 1944
Time 42:36, Dec 20, 1943

Young Woodley
    Productions:
        Opened November 2, 1925 for 260 performances.
    Reviews:
        Bookman 62:595, Jan 1926
        Dramatist 17:1292-3, Jan 1926
        Independent 115:713, Dec 19, 1925
        Nation 121:582+, Nov 18, 1925
                126:130, Feb 1, 1928
        New Republic 45:133-4, Dec 23, 1925
        New York Times p. 34, Nov 3, 1925
                        VIII, p. 1, Nov 8, 1925
                        VIII, p. 2, Nov 29, 1925
        Outlook 141:508, Dec 2, 1925
        Theatre Arts 10:10-11, Jan 1926
        Theatre Magazine 43:15, Jan 1926
                        43:19, Jan 1926
                        43:26+, Feb 1926
        Vogue 67:63, Jan 1, 1926

VAN ITALLIE, JEAN-CLAUDE

    America Hurrah ("Interview," "T.V.," and "Motel")
    Productions:
        (Off Broadway) Opened November 6, 1966 for 634
            performances.
    Reviews:
        America 116:25, Jan 7, 1967
        Christian Century 84:596-7, May 3, 1967
        Commentary 43:87-8, Mar 1967
        Nation 203:587-8, Nov 28, 1966
        New Republic 155:31-3, Dec 3, 1966
        New York Times p. 66, Nov 7, 1966
                        II, p. 1, Nov 27, 1966
                        p. 59, Dec 20, 1966

497

VAN ITALLIE, JEAN-CLAUDE (cont.)
America Hurrah (cont.)
                         p. 13, Aug 4, 1967
                         II, p. 3, Aug 13, 1967
                         p. 25, Sep 4, 1967
                         p. 55, Oct 10, 1967
        New Yorker 42:69-70, Jan 21, 1967
        Newsweek 68:114, Nov 21, 1966
        Reporter 36:49-50, Mar 9, 1967
        Time 88:79-80, Nov 18, 1966

Interview (See America Hurrah)

Motel (See America Hurrah)

*The Serpent: A Ceremony
    Reviews:
        New York Times p. 92, Mar 10, 1968
                       p. 56, May 6, 1968

T.V. (See America Hurrah)

Thoughts on the Instant of Greeting a Friend on the Street
    Productions:
        (Off Broadway) Opened May 8, 1968 for 80 per-
            formances.
    Reviews:
        Harper's Bazaar 237:113-15, Oct 1968
        Nation 206:772+, Jun 10, 1968
        New York Times p. 55, May 9, 1968
                       II, p. 1, May 19, 1968
        New Yorker 44:74, May 18, 1968

War
    Productions:
        (Off Broadway) Opened December 22, 1963 for 2 per-
            formances (Theatre 1964 Playwrights Unit).
        (Off Broadway) Opened April 12, 1966 for 16 per-
            formances.
    Reviews:
        Nation 202:404-5, Apr 4, 1966
        New York Times II, p. 15, Apr 10, 1966
                       p. 36, Apr 13, 1966

VARESI, GILDA

Enter Madame (with Dolly Byrne)
    Productions:
        Opened August 16, 1920 for 350 performances.
    Reviews:
        Bookman 53:412-13, Jul 1921
        Current Opinion 70:199-207, Feb 1921
        Drama 11:130, Jan 1921
        Dramatic Mirror p. 327, Jan 1921
        Dramatist 12:1037-8, Jan 1921
        Everybody's 44:38-9, Jan 1921
        Hearst 38:41-3+, Nov 1920
        New Republic 24:300, Nov 17, 1920
        New York Clipper 68:19, Aug 25, 1920
        New York Times p. 11, Aug 17, 1920
                        VI, p. 1, Aug 22, 1920
                        VI, p. 1, Oct 17, 1920
        Outlook 126:221, Oct 6, 1920
        Review 4:40, Jan 12, 1921
        Theatre Magazine 32:240, Oct 1920
        Weekly Review 5:40, Jan 12, 1921

VEILLER, BAYARD

Back Home (Based on Irvin S. Cobb's "Back Home"
    stories)
    Productions:
        Opened November 15, 1915 for 16 performances.
    Reviews:
        Dramatic Mirror 73:9, Jun 30, 1915
                        74:8-9, Nov 20, 1915
        Munsey 56:622, Jan 1916
        New York Drama News 61:17, Nov 20, 1915
        New York Times p. 13, Nov 16, 1915

Damn Your Honor (with Becky Gardiner)
    Productions:
        Opened December 30, 1929 for 8 performances.
    Reviews:
        New York Times p. 14, Dec 31, 1929
        Theatre Magazine 51:66-7, Feb 1930

The Fight
    Productions:
        Opened October 31, 1912 for 4 performances.
        Opened September 2, 1913 for 80 performances.

VEILLER, BAYARD (cont.)
    The Fight (cont.)
        Reviews:
            Bookman 38:133-4, Oct 1913
            Dramatic Mirror 70:6, Sep 10, 1913
            Everybody's 29:679-82, Nov 1913
            Green Book 10:764-6, Nov 1913
            Life (NY) 62:476, Sep 18, 1913
            Munsey 50:297, Nov 1913
            New York Drama News 58:18, Sep 13, 1913
            Theatre Magazine 18:116, Oct 1913

    That's the Woman
        Productions:
        Opened September 3, 1930 for 29 performances.
        Reviews:
            Arts and Decoration 34:110, Nov 1930
            Life (NY) 96:18, Sep 26, 1930
            New York Times p. 27, Sep 4, 1930

    The Thirteenth Chair
        Productions:
        Opened November 20, 1916 for 328 performances.
        Reviews:
            Book News 35:206, Jan 1917
                      36:64, Oct 1917
            Collier's 58:38, Jan 27, 1917
            Dramatic Mirror 76:4+, Dec 2, 1916
                            77:4, Apr 7, 1917
            Dramatist 8:791-2, Apr 1917
            Green Book 17:205+, Feb 1917
            Life (NY) 68:949, Nov 30, 1916
            McClure's 48:11, Mar 1917
            New York Dramatic News vol. 63, Nov 25, 1916
            New York Times p. 9, Nov 21, 1916
            Theatre Magazine 25:20+, Jan 1917

    The Trial of Mary Dugan
        Productions:
        Opened September 19, 1927 for 437 performances.
        Reviews:
            Dial 83:530-31, Dec 1927
            Dramatist 18:1351-2, Oct 1927
            Independent 119:482, Nov 12, 1927
            Life (NY) 90:21, Oct 6, 1927
            Nation 125:406-7, Oct 12, 1927
            New York Times p. 33, Sep 20, 1927

```
                    VIII, p. 4, Oct 9, 1927
                    p. 28, Mar 7, 1928
                    IX, p. 1, Apr 1, 1928
                    p. 31, May 4, 1928
                    VIII, p. 1, Jun 24, 1928
                    p. 17, Jun 28, 1928
                    VII, p. 2, Sep 2, 1928
                    IX, p. 4, Sep 30, 1928
          Theatre Magazine 46:22+, Nov 1927
                    46:28-30+, Dec 1927
          Vogue 70:87, Nov 15, 1927
```

Within the Law
     Productions:
          Opened September 11, 1912 for 541 performances.
          Opened Mar 5, 1928 for 16 performances.
     Reviews:
          American Playwright 1:315-16, Oct 1912
                    2:205-7, Jun 1913
          Blue Book 15:682-5, Aug 1912
          Book News 32:255-6, Jan 1914
          Bookman 36:282, Nov 1912
          Collier's 50:24+, Oct 5, 1912
          Current Literature 53:682-9, Dec 1912
          Dramatic Mirror 68:6, Sep 18, 1912
                    68:2, Oct 9, 1912
                    69:2, Jun 11, 1913
          Dramatist 4:318-19, Jan 1913
          Everybody's 27:675, Nov 1912
                    28:394, Mar 1913
          Green Book 8:200-2, Aug 1912
                    8:984-7, Dec 1912
                    8:1005-6, Dec 1912
          Harper's Weekly 56:20, Oct 12, 1912
          Hearst 23:484-94, Mar 1913
          Independent 76:250, Nov 6, 1913
          Leslies' Weekly 115:411, Oct 24, 1912
                    115:613, Dec 12, 1912
          Life (NY) 60:1858, Sep 26, 1912
          Metropolitan Magazine 38:41-2, Jun 1913
          Munsey 48:350-1, Nov 1912
                    49:819-20, Aug 1913
          National Magazine 38:53, Apr 1913
          New York Dramatic News 55:18, April 13, 1912
                    56:10-11, Sep 21, 1912
          New York Times p. 20, Mar 6, 1928
          Red Book 20:186-8+, Nov 1912

VEILLER, BAYARD (cont.)
Within the Law (cont.)
Stage 14:77, Aug 1937
Theatre Magazine 16:36, Aug 1912
16:97+, Aug 1912
Woman's Home Companion 40:24, Mar 1913

VEILLER, MRS. BAYARD (See Vale, Martin)

VIDAL, GORE

The Best Man
Productions:
Opened March 31, 1960 for 520 performances.
Reviews:
America 103:422, Jul 2, 1960
Commonweal 72:128-9, Apr 29, 1960
Life 48:55+, Apr 25, 1960
Nation 190:343, Apr 16, 1960
New Republic 142:21-2, Apr 18, 1960
New York Theatre Critics' Reviews 1960:308
New York Times p. 39, Apr 1, 1960
II, p. 1, Apr 10, 1960
VI, p. 27, May 22, 1960
p. 44, Oct 5, 1960
p. 1, Dec 7, 1960
New Yorker 36:88+, Apr 9, 1960
Newsweek 55:86, Apr 11, 1960
Reporter 22:38-9, Apr 28, 1960
Saturday Review 43:33, Apr 16, 1960
Time 75:85, Apr 11, 1960

*Fire to the Sea
Reviews:
New York Times p. 20, Nov 15, 1961

Romulus (Adapted from the play by Friedrich Duerren-
matt)
Productions:
Opened January 10, 1962 for 69 performances.
Reviews:
America 106:772-3, Mar 10, 1962
Christian Century 79:233, Feb 21, 1962
Nation 194:106-7, Feb 3, 1962
National Review 12:173-4, Mar 13, 1962

New Republic 146:20+, Jan 29, 1962
New York Theatre Critics' Reviews 1962:380
New York Times p. 27, Jan 11, 1962
                p. 25, Mar 2, 1962
New Yorker 37:63, Jan 20, 1962
Newsweek 59:50, Jan 22, 1962
Saturday Review 45:29, Jan 27, 1962
Theatre Arts 46:62-3, Mar 1962
Time 79:68+, Jan 19, 1962

Visit to a Small Planet
    Productions:
    Opened February 7, 1957 for 388 performances.
    Reviews:
    America 96:629, Mar 2, 1957
    Catholic World 185:68, Apr 1957
    Christian Century 74:918, Jul 31, 1957
    Commonweal 65:662-3, Mar 29, 1957
    Life 42:87-8, Mar 4, 1957
    Nation 184:174, Feb 23, 1957
    New York Theatre Critics' Reviews 1957:356
    New York Times p. 18, Feb 8, 1957
                    II, p. 1, Feb 24, 1957
    New Yorker 32:78+, Feb 16, 1957
    Newsweek 49:95, Feb 18, 1957
    Reporter 16:40, Mar 7, 1957
            17:35-6, Jul 11, 1957
    Saturday Review 40:29, Feb 23, 1957
    Theatre Arts 41:17, Apr 1957
    Time 69:60, Feb 18, 1957

Weekend
    Productions:
    Opened March 13, 1968 for 21 performances.
    Reviews:
    Commonweal 88:74-5, Apr 5, 1968
    Nation 206:454, Apr 1, 1968
    New York Theatre Critics' Reviews 1968:326
    New York Times p. 50, Mar 14, 1968
                    II, p. 1, Mar 31, 1968
    New Yorker 44:101, Mar 23, 1968
    Newsweek 71:100, Mar 25, 1968
    Saturday Review 51:20, Mar 30, 1968
    Time 91:64, Mar 22, 1968

VINCENT, ALLEN

Letters to Lucerne (See entry under Rotter, Fritz).

VOLLMER, LULA

The Dunce Boy
Productions:
Opened April 1, 1925 for 43 performances.
Reviews:
American Mercury 5:247, Jun 1925
New York Times p. 20, Apr 4, 1925

The Hill Between
Productions:
Opened March 11, 1938 for 11 performances.
Reviews:
New York Times p. 12, Mar 12, 1938
One Act Play Magazine 1:1120-21, Apr 1938
Time 31:30, Mar 21, 1938

*Moonshine and Honeysuckle
Reviews:
New York Times p. 17, Jul 25, 1933

Sentinels
Productions:
Opened December 25, 1931 for 11 performances.
Reviews:
Commonweal 15:301, Jan 13, 1932
New York Times p. 15, Dec 26, 1931
Outlook 160:22, Jan 6, 1932

The Shame Woman
Productions:
Opened October 16, 1923 for 278 performances.
Reviews:
Nation 117:587-8, Nov 21, 1923
New York Times p. 14, Oct 17, 1923
VIII, p. 1, Oct 21, 1923
Theatre Magazine 38:68, Dec 1923

Sun Up
Productions:
Opened May 25, 1923 for 28+ performances.
Opened October 22, 1928 for 101 performances.

Reviews:
  Current Opinion 75:701-6+, Dec 1923
  Drama 17:116, Jan 1927
  New York Clipper 71:14, May 30, 1923
  New York Times p. 28, May 25, 1923
              p. 18, Dec 21, 1923
              VIII, p. 4, Dec 30, 1923
              VII, p. 2, Jan 13, 1924
              VII, p. 2, Feb 24, 1924
              VIII, p. 2, Mar 30, 1924
              p. 25, May 5, 1925
              p. 13, Aug 14, 1925
              p. 34, Sep 18, 1928
              p. 33, Oct 23, 1928
              IX, p. 4, Nov 4, 1928
              p. 34, Jan 8, 1929
              p. 22, Feb 19, 1929
              p. 47, Mar 4, 1929
  Theatre Magazine 38:16, Jul 1923
                38:26+, Oct 1923

Trigger
  Productions:
  Opened December 6, 1927 for 47 performances.
  Reviews:
  Life (NY) 90:19, Dec 22, 1927
  New York Times p. 32, Dec 7, 1927
  Theatre Magazine 47:39-40, Feb 1928

Troyka (Adapted from the Hungarian of Imre Fazekas)
  Productions:
  Opened April 1, 1930 for 15 performances.
  Reviews:
  Life (NY) 95:18, Apr 18, 1930
  New York Times p. 32, Apr 2, 1930
  Outlook 154:631, Apr 16, 1930
  Theatre Magazine 51:70+, May 1930

WALTER, EUGENE

The Challenge
  Productions:
  Opened August 5, 1919 for 72 performances.
  Reviews:
  Hearst 36:48+, Nov 1919
  New York Times p. 7, Aug 6, 1919

505

WALTER, EUGENE (cont.)
   The Challenge (cont.)
                        IV, p. 2, Aug 10, 1919
         Review 1:458, Oct 4, 1919
         Theatre Magazine 30:223-5, Oct 1919

The Easiest Way
   Productions:
      Opened January 19, 1909 for 157 performances.
      Opened September 6, 1921 for 63 performances.
   Reviews:
      Bookman 54:230-31, Nov 1921
      Craftsman 15:739-41, Mar 1909
      Current Literature 51:73-81, Jul 1911
      Dramatic Mirror 61:3, Jan 30, 1909
                        84:377, Sep 10, 1921
      Dramatist 4:379-80, Jul 1913
      Forum 41:215-7, Mar 1909
      Independent 66:191, Jan 28, 1909
      Life (NY) 53:166, Feb 4, 1909
                 57:682, Apr 6, 1911
      Literary Digest 42:679-80, Apr 8, 1911
      Munsey 41:578-9, Jul 1909
      Nation 88:72, Jan 21, 1909
             113:381, Oct 5, 1921
      New Republic 28:138-9, Sep 28, 1921
      New York Clipper 69:23, Sep 14, 1921
      New York Times p. 14, Sep 7, 1921
                        VI, p. 1, Sep 11, 1921
      Stage 14:80, Aug 1937
      Theatre Magazine 9:81-4, Mar 1909
      Weekly Review 5:255, Sep 17, 1921

Fine Feathers
   Productions:
      Opened January 7, 1913 for 79 performances.
   Reviews:
      American Playwright 2:37-40, Feb 1913
      Blue Book 16:8-11, Nov 1912
      Bookman 36:643-4, Feb 1913
      Collier's 50:15+, Oct 26, 1912
      Current Literature 53:443-50, Oct 1912
      Dramatic Mirror 69:4, Jan 15, 1913
      Dramatist 4:321-2, Jan 1913
      Everybody's 28:520-1, Apr 1913
      Green Book 9:142-67, Jan 1913
                 9:432-4, Mar 1913

Hearst 23:811-22, May 1913
Life (NY) 61:200, Jan 23, 1913
Munsey 48:1009-12, Mar 1913
New York Drama News 57:19, Jan 18, 1913
New York Times p. 11, Jan 8, 1913
Smart Set 39:147-9, Mar 1913
Theatre Magazine 16:194, Dec 1912
17:34+, Feb 1913
Woman's Home Companion 40:24, Mar 1913

The Heritage
Productions:
Opened January 14, 1918 for 16 performances.
Reviews:
Dramatic Mirror 78:7, Jan 26, 1918
Life (NY) 71:142, Jan 24, 1918
New York Drama News 64:23, Jan 19, 1918
New York Times p. 11, Jan 15, 1918
IV, p. 4, Jan 20, 1918

Jealousy (Based on the French of Louis Verneuil)
Productions:
Opened October 22, 1928 for 136 performances.
Reviews:
Life (NY) 92:17, Nov 9, 1928
Nation 127:502, Nov 7, 1928
New York Times p. 32, Oct 23, 1928
IX, p. 4, Nov 4, 1928
Theatre Magazine 49:45-6, Jan 1929
49:30-31+, Feb 1929
Vogue 72:146, Dec 8, 1928

Just a Wife
Productions:
Opened February 1, 1910 for 79 performances.
Reviews:
Bookman 31:142-4, Apr 1910
Dramatic Mirror 63:6, Feb 12, 1910
Dramatist 1:37-8, Apr 1910
Green Book 3:765-6, Apr 1910
Hampton 24:702-3, May 1910
Life (NY) 55:284, Feb 17, 1910
Theatre Magazine 11:vi, Mar 1910

Just A Woman
Productions:
Opened January 17, 1916 for 136 performances.

WALTER, EUGENE (cont.)
   Just A Woman (cont.)
      Reviews:
         Bookman 43:164+, Apr 1916
         Dramatic Mirror 75:8, Jan 22, 1916
         Dramatist 7:678-9, Apr 1916
         Green Book 15:655+, Apr 1916
         Harper's Weekly 62:134, Feb 5, 1916
         Hearst 29:281-3+, Apr 1916
         Life (NY) 67:160-1, Jan 27, 1916
         Nation 102:115, Jan 27, 1916
         New Republic 5:336, Jan 29, 1916
         New York Drama News 62:17-18, Jan 22, 1916
         New York Times p. 12, Jan 8, 1916
         Theatre Magazine 23:124, Mar 1916

   The Knife
      Productions:
         Opened April 12, 1917 for 84 performances.
      Reviews:
         Dramatic Mirror 77:4+, Apr 21, 1917
         Dramatist 8:821-2, Jul 1917
         Green Book 18:13-15, Jul 1917
         Life (NY) 69:728, Apr 26, 1917
         Nation 104:470, Apr 19, 1917
         New York Times p. 11, Apr 13, 1917
         Theatre Magazine 25:342+, Jun 1917

   The Man's Name (with Marjorie Chase)
      Productions:
         Opened November 14, 1921 for 24 performances.
      Reviews:
         New York Times p. 22, Nov 16, 1921
                        p. 16, Nov 28, 1921

   Nancy Lee (with H. Crowin Wilson)
      Productions:
         Opened April 9, 1918 for 63 performances.
      Reviews:
         Book News 36:377-8, Jun 1918
         Dramatic Mirror 78:548, Apr 20, 1918
         Green Book 19:977-8, Jun 1918
         Life (NY) 71:682, Apr 25, 1918
         Theatre Magazine 27:286, May 1918

   Trail of the Lonesome Pine (Based on the novel by John
      Fox, Jr.)

Productions:
Opened January 29, 1912 for 32 performances.
Reviews:
American Playwright 1:35-8, Feb 1912
Blue Book 14:478-80, Jan 1912
Dramatic Mirror 67:6, Feb 7, 1912
Dramatist 3:240-1, Apr 1912
Everybody's 26:542, Apr 1912
Green Book 7:26-7+, Jan 1912
7:798-9, Apr 1912
Leslies' Weekly 114:205, Feb 22, 1912
Munsey 47:130, Apr 1912
Theatre Magazine 15:76, Mar 1912

WARREN, ROBERT PENN

All the King's Men
Productions:
(Off Broadway) Season of 1959-60.
(Off Broadway) Season of 1966-67 for 9 performances
(Equity Library Theatre).
Reviews:
New York Times p. 19, Jan 19, 1948
p. 25, Jul 19, 1950
p. 27, Oct 17, 1959
II, p. 1, Oct 25, 1959
p. 12, Jul 12, 1963

*Brothers to Dragons
Reviews:
New York Times p. 86, Dec 8, 1968

WATKINS, MAURINE

Chicago
Productions:
Opened December 30, 1926 for 172 performances.
Reviews:
American Mercury 375-6, Mar 1927
Collier's 79:10, Jan 22, 1927
Dramatist 18:1329-30, Jan 1927
Life (NY) 89:19, Jan 20, 1927
New York Times p. 7, Jun 7, 1926
p. 21, Dec 28, 1926
p. 10, Dec 29, 1926

WATKINS, MAURINE (cont.)
  Chicago (cont.)
                        p. 11, Dec 31, 1926
                        IX, p. 1, Dec 18, 1927
                        p. 19, Mar 14, 1935
        Overland 85:243, Aug 1927
        Vogue 69:80-81+, Mar 1, 1927

  Revelry (Based on the novel by Samuel Hopkins Adams)
    Productions:
      Opened September 12, 1927 for 48 performances.
    Reviews:
      American Mercury 12:376-8, Nov 1927
      Life (NY) 90:19, Sep 29, 1927
      New Republic 52:148, Sep 28, 1927
      New York Times VII, p. 2, Sep 4, 1927
                        p. 37, Sep 13, 1927
                        VIII, p. 1, Sep 25, 1927

WATTERS, GEORGE MANKER

  Burlesque (with Arthur Hopkins)
    Productions:
      Opened September 1, 1927 for 372 performances.
      Opened December 25, 1946 for 439 performances.
    Reviews:
      American Mercury 12:375-6, Nov 1927
      Catholic World 164:455, Feb 1947
      Independent 119:362, Oct 8, 1927
      Life (NY) 90:21, Sep 22, 1927
      Nation 125:295, Sep 21, 1927
      New Republic 52:123, Sep 21, 1927
      New York Theatre Critics' Reviews 1946:208
      New York Times p. 15, Sep 2, 1927
                        VIII, p. 1, Sep 11, 1927
                        IX, p. 4, Nov 20, 1927
                        p. 17, Jun 10, 1928
                        II, p. 3, Dec 22, 1946
                        p. 30, Dec 26, 1946
                        II, p. 1, Jan 5, 1947
      New Yorker 22:44+, Jan 4, 1947
      Newsweek 29:64, Jan 6, 1947
      Saturday Review 30:22, Jan 4, 1947
      Theatre Arts 31:17, Mar 1947
      Theatre Magazine 46:22-4, Nov 1927
      Time 49:56, Jan 6, 1947
      Vogue 70:84-5+, Nov 1, 1927

WEITZENKORN, LOUIS

First Mortgage
    Productions:
      Opened October 10, 1929 for 4 performances.
    Reviews:
      New York Times p. 36, Oct 11, 1929

Five Star Final
    Productions:
      Opened December 30, 1930 for 175 performances.
    Reviews:
      Arts and Decoration 34:84, Mar 1931
      Catholic World 133:81-2, Apr 1931
      Commonweal 13:329, Jan 21, 1931
      Drama 21:9, Mar 1931
      Life (NY) 97:18, Jan 23, 1931
      Nation 132:53, Jan 14, 1931
      New York Times p. 11, Dec 31, 1930
                      VIII, p. 1, Jan 11, 1931
                      p. 32, Jun 9, 1931
      Outlook 157:112, Jan 21, 1931
      Theatre Arts 15:186, Mar 1931
      Vogue 77:88, Mar 1, 1931

*Name Your Poison
    Reviews:
      New York Times p. 27, Jan 21, 1936

WEXLEY, JOHN

All the World Wondered (See The Last Mile)

The Last Mile
    Productions:
      Opened February 13, 1930 for 289 performances.
    Reviews:
      Catholic World 131:214, May 1930
      Collier's 85:25, May 3, 1930
      Commonweal 11:658-9, Apr 9, 1930
      Life (NY) 95:18, Mar 7, 1930
              95:18, Jun 6, 1930
      Literary Digest 105:18-19, Apr 5, 1930
      Nation 130:278, Mar 5, 1930
      New Republic 62:152-3, Mar 26, 1930
      New York Times p. 21, Feb 14, 1930

WEXLEY, JOHN (cont.)
The Last Mile (cont.)
                        VIII, p. 1, Feb 23, 1930
                        VIII, p. 4, Mar 30, 1930
                        VIII, p. 3, Dec 21, 1930
                        VIII, p. 3, Feb 8, 1931
        Outlook 154:470, Mar 19, 1930
        Sketch Book 7:29, Jun 1930
        Theatre Arts 14:278-80, Apr 1930
        Theatre Magazine 51:43, Apr 1930
                        51:30, May 1930
                        51:14, Jun 1930
                        52:25, Aug 1930
        Vogue 75:92-3, Apr 12, 1930

Steel
    Productions:
        Opened November 17, 1931 for 14 performances.
        (Off Broadway) Fall, 1936 in repertory (Labor Stage,
            Inc.).
    Reviews:
        Commonweal 15:160-1, Dec 9, 1931
        New York Times p. 26, Nov 19, 1931

They Shall Not Die
    Productions:
        Opened February 21, 1934 for 62 performances.
    Reviews:
        Catholic World 139:90-1, Apr 1934
        Commonweal 19:554, Mar 16, 1934
        Literary Digest 117:22, Mar 17, 1934
        Nation 138:284-5, Mar 7, 1934
        New Outlook 163:44, Apr 1934
        New Republic 78:134, Mar 14, 1934
        New York Times IX, p. 2, Feb 18, 1934
                        p. 24, Feb 22, 1934
                        IX, p. 1, Mar 4, 1934
                        p. 19, Mar 5, 1934
                        X, p. 1, Mar 11, 1934
        Newsweek 3:34, Mar 3, 1934
        Review of Reviews 89:48, Apr 1934
        Stage 11:15, Apr 1934
        Survey Graphic 23:240, May 1934
        Theatre Arts 18:323-5, May 1934
        Time 23:40, May 5, 1934

WILDER, THORNTON

Childhood (See Plays for Bleecker Street)

The Happy Journey to Trenton and Camden
    Productions:
        (Off Broadway) Opened April 1939
        (Off Broadway) Opened February 9, 1948 (New
          Stages).
        Opened March 16, 1948 for 348 performances (Pre-
          sented with Satre's The Respectful Prostitute).
        (Off Broadway) Opened September 6, 1966 for 72 per-
          formances.
    Reviews:
        America 115:432, Oct 8, 1966
        Nation 203:334, Oct 3, 1966
        New York Times II, p. 1, Mar 21, 1948
                     p. 37, Apr 28, 1954
                     p. 53, Sep 7, 1966
        New Yorker 42:126, Sep 17, 1966
        Saturday Review 49:54, Sep 24, 1966

Infancy (See Plays for Bleecker Street)

*Life in the Sun
    Reviews:
        New York Times p. 34, Mar 18, 1955
                    p. 24, Aug 24, 1955
                  II, p. 1, Aug 28, 1955
        Saturday Review 38:42+, Sep 10, 1955

The Long Christmas Dinner
    Productions:
        (Off Broadway) Opened September 6, 1966 for 72
          performances.
    Reviews:
        America 115:431, Oct 8, 1966
        Nation 203:334, Oct 3, 1966
        New York Times p. 53, Sep 7, 1966
        New Yorker 42:126, Sep 17, 1966
        Saturday Review 49:54, Sep 24, 1966

The Matchmaker
    Productions:
        Opened December 5, 1955 for 486 performances.
    Reviews:
        America 94:363, Dec 24, 1955

WILDER, THORNTON (cont.)
  The Matchmaker (cont.)
          Catholic World 182:386, Feb 1956
          Collier's 137:6, Mar 2, 1956
          Commonweal 63:379-80, Jan 13, 1956
          Holiday 19:85+, May 1956
          Life 40:131-2+, Jan 23, 1956
          Nation 181:562-3, Dec 24, 1955
          New Republic 134:21, Jan 2, 1956
          New York Theatre Critics' Reviews 1955:194
          New York Times p. 18, Aug 24, 1954
                          II, p. 3, Sep 5, 1954
                          p. 16, Nov 5, 1954
                          II, p. 3, Nov 14, 1954
                          II, p. 1, May 8, 1955
                          VI, p. 66, Nov 27, 1955
                          p. 45, Dec 6, 1955
                          II, p. 3, Dec 18, 1955
                          p. 14, Aug 20, 1959
          New Yorker 31:78-80, Dec 17, 1955
          Saturday Review 38:26, Dec 24, 1955
          Theatre Arts 40:14-15, Feb 1956
          Time 66:80+, Dec 19, 1955

  The Merchant of Yonkers (Based on a play by Johann
          Nestroy)
      Productions:
      Opened December 28, 1938 for 39 performances.
      Reviews:
          Catholic World 148:599-600, Feb 1939
          Commonweal 29:330, Jan 13, 1939
          Nation 148:74, Jan 14, 1939
          New York Times p. 30, Dec 13, 1938
                          IX, p. 3, Dec 18, 1938
                          p. 14, Dec 29, 1938
                          IX, p. 1, Jan 8, 1939
          Newsweek 13:32, Jan 9, 1939
          Theatre Arts 23:173-4, Mar 1939
          Time 33:25, Jan 9, 1939

  Our Town
      Productions:
      Opened February 4, 1938 for 336 performances.
      Opened January 10, 1944 for 24 performances.
      (Off Broadway) Season of 1958-59.
      Reviews:
          America 101:231, Apr 18, 1959

Atlantic 197:38-9, Apr 1956
Canadian Forum 19:355-6, Feb 1940
Catholic World 146:729, Mar 1938
           189:242-3, Jun 1959
Christian Century 55:943-4, Aug 3, 1938
Commonweal 27:496, Feb 25, 1938
           28:161, Jun 3, 1938
           39:373, Jan 28, 1944
           70:128-30, May 1, 1959
Independent Woman 17:147, May 1938
Nation 146:244-5, Feb 19, 1938
           188:324, Apr 11, 1959
New Republic 94:74, Feb 23, 1938
New York Times II, p. 10, Jan 23, 1938
           p. 27, Jan 26, 1938
           X, p. 3, Jan 30, 1938
           p. 18, Feb 5, 1938
           X, p. 1, Feb 13, 1938
           p. 17, Sep 16, 1938
           p. 35, Jun 30, 1940
           p. 16, Jan 24, 1941
           p. 24, Jan 11, 1944
           II, p. 1, Jan 16, 1944
           p. 11, Feb 13, 1946
           p. 27, May 2, 1946
           p. 32, Mar 18, 1955
           VI, p. 26, Nov 27, 1955
           p. 46, Mar 24, 1959
           p. 40, Mar 25, 1959
           II, p. 1, Apr 5, 1959
           II, p. 1, Aug 23, 1959
           II, p. 3, Aug 21, 1960
           p. 20, Aug 28, 1961
           p. 14, Nov 4, 1961
           p. 77, Sep 29, 1968
           p. 62, Dec 14, 1968
New Yorker 35:80+, Apr 11, 1959
           44:98, Oct 5, 1968
One Act Play Magazine 1:948, Feb 1938
Saturday Review 18:11, May 7, 1938
           32:33-4, Aug 6, 1949
           42:35, Apr 11, 1959
Scribner's Magazine 103:65, May 1938
Stage 15:34-6, Apr 1938
Theatre Arts 22:172-3, Mar 1938
           24:815-24, Nov 1940
           28:137, Mar 1944

WILDER, THORNTON (cont.)
Our Town (cont.)
                              29:234-9, Apr 1945
            Time 31:36-7, Feb 14, 1938
            Vogue 91:108-9, Mar 15, 1938
            Yale Review 27:836-8, Summer 1938

Plays for Bleecker Street ("Infancy," "Childhood," and
      "Someone from Assisi")
      Productions:
          (Off Broadway) Opened January 11, 1962 for 349 per-
              formances.
      Reviews:
          Commonweal 75:516-17, Feb 9, 1962
          Nation 194:86-7, Jan 27, 1962
          New Republic 146:30, Feb 5, 1962
          New York Times p. 28, Jan 12, 1962
                              II, p. 1, Jan 21, 1962
          New Yorker 37:64+, Jan 20, 1962
          Newsweek 59:50, Jan 22, 1962
          Reporter 26:48, Mar 1, 1962
          Saturday Review 45:26, Feb 3, 1962
          Theatre Arts 46:63, Mar 1962
          Time 79:68, Jan 19, 1962

Pullman Car Hiawatha
      Productions:
          (Off Broadway) Opened December 3, 1962 for 33
              performances.
      Reviews:
          New York Times p. 46, Dec 4, 1962
          New Yorker 38:130+, Dec 15, 1962

Queen of France
      Productions:
          (Off Broadway) Opened September 6, 1966 for 72 per-
              formances.
      Reviews:
          America 115:431, Oct 8, 1966
          Nation 203:334, Oct 3, 1966
          New York Times p. 53, Sep 7, 1966
          New Yorker 42:126, Sep 17, 1966
          Saturday Review 49:54, Sep 24, 1966

Skin of Our Teeth
      Productions:
          Opened November 18, 1942 for 359 performances.

Opened August 17, 1955 for 22 performances.
(Off Broadway) Season of 1960-61 (Equity Library
  Theatre).
Reviews:
  America 93:574, Sep 10, 1955
  Atlantic 171:121+, Mar 1943
  Catholic World 156:473-4, Jan 1943
                 166:73-4, Oct 1947
                 181:62-3, Oct 1955
  Commonweal 37:175-6, Dec 4, 1942
             37:229, Dec 18, 1942
             63:13, Oct 7, 1955
  Cosmopolitan 114:19, Apr 1943
  Current History ns 3:458-9, Jan 1943
  Independent Woman 21:368, Dec 1942
  Life 13:93-4+, Nov 30, 1942
       39:71-2, Aug 29, 1955
  Nation 155:629, Dec 5, 1942
         181:210, Sep 3, 1955
  New Republic 107:714, Nov 30, 1942
  New York Theatre Critics' Reviews 1942:173
                                    1955:293
  New York Times VII, p. 20, Nov 1, 1942
                      p. 29, Nov 19, 1942
                 VIII, p. 1, Nov 22, 1942
                 VIII, p. 1, Dec 13, 1942
                 VIII, p. 1, Jan 3, 1943
                      p. 22, Mar 20, 1945
                 II, p. 1, May 27, 1945
                 II, p. 2, Nov 18, 1945
                      p. 32, Nov 5, 1946
                 VI, p. 26, Aug 7, 1955
                      p. 16, Aug 18, 1955
                 II, p. 1, Aug 28, 1955
                 VI, p. 64, Nov 27, 1955
                      p. 24, Oct 14, 1960
                 II, p. 1, Mar 5, 1962
                      p. 30, Mar 6, 1961
                      p. 43, Mar 15, 1961
                      p. 32, Mar 20, 1961
                      p. 40, Mar 28, 1961
                      p. 24, Mar 30, 1961
                      p. 11, Apr 1, 1961
                      p. 29, Apr 21, 1961
                      p. 35, May 1, 1961
                      p. 22, May 19, 1961
                      p. 28, May 31, 1961

WILDER, THORNTON (cont.)
The Skin of Our Teeth (cont.)

                             p. 27, Jun 16, 1961
                             p. 29, Aug 9, 1961
                             p. 20, Aug 21, 1961
                             p. 27, Aug 29, 1961
                             p. 37, Sep 18, 1961
                             p. 85, Oct 8, 1961
                             p. 13, Oct 14, 1961
                             p. 22, Oct 23, 1961
                             p. 51, Jun 2, 1966
                             p. 55, Sep 12, 1968
New York Times Magazine pp. 20-1, Nov 1, 1942
                           pp. 26-7, Aug 7, 1955
New Yorker 18:35, Nov 28, 1942
                19:32, May 8, 1943
                19:34, Jun 12, 1943
                31:72+, Aug 27, 1955
Newsweek 20:86-7, Nov 30, 1942
             46:67, Aug 29, 1955
Player's Magazine 22:12-13, Sep-Oct 1945
Poet Lore 49:187, Summer 1943
Saturday Review 25:3-4, Dec 19, 1942
                   38:22, Aug 27, 1955
Theatre Arts 27:9-11, Jan 1943
              27:334+, Jun 1943
              30:704-5, Dec 1946
              39:66-9, Sep 1955
Time 40:57, Nov 30, 1942
        40:62, Dec 28, 1942
        66:32, Aug 29, 1955

Someone from Assisi (See Plays for Bleecker Street).

The Trumpet Shall Sound
   Productions:
   Opened December 10, 1926 for 30 performances.
   Reviews:
      Life (NY) 89:21, Jan 13, 1927
      New York Times p. 15, Dec 11, 1926

The Victors (Adapted from the play by Jean Paul Sartre)
   Productions:
   (Off Broadway) Opened December 1948 (New Stages).
   Reviews:
      Commonweal 49:352, Jan 14, 1949
      Forum 111:162-3, Mar 1949

New Republic 120:19, Jan 10, 1949
New York Times p. 17, Dec 27, 1948
                II, p. 1, Jan 2, 1949
                II, p. 2, Jan 9, 1949
School and Society 69:85, Jan 29, 1949
Theatre Arts 31:44, Feb 1947
                33:17, Mar 1949
Time 53:49, Jan 3, 1949

WILLIAMS, JESSE LYNCH

And So They Were Married (See Why Marry?)

Lovely Lady
    Productions:
    Opened October 14, 1925 for 21 performances.
    Reviews:
    New York Times p. 27, Oct 15, 1925

Why Marry?
    Productions:
    Opened December 25, 1917 for 120 performances.
    Reviews:
    Book News 36:218, Feb 1918
    Bookman 47:75, Mar 1918
    Current Opinion 64:99-102, Feb 1918
    Dramatic Mirror 77:31, Nov 17, 1917
                    78:7, Jan 5, 1918
    Dramatist 9:917-18, Jul 1918
    Green Book 19:389-94, Mar 1918
    Hearst 33:362-4+, May 1918
    Life (NY) 71:64, Jan 10, 1918
    Nation 107:132, Aug 3, 1918
    New York Times p. 7, Dec 26, 1917
                    IV, p. 7, Jan 27, 1918
                    V, p. 3, Feb 8, 1918
                    V, p. 8, Feb 10, 1918
                    V, p. 10, Mar 3, 1918
    North American Review 207:278-81, Feb 1918
    Theatre Magazine 27:85+, Feb 1918

Why Not?
    Productions:
    Opened December 25, 1922 for 120 performances.
    Reviews:
    Dramatist 14:1159-60, Apr 1923

WILLIAMS, JESSE LYNCH (cont.)
  Why Not? (cont.)
           Nation 116:128, Jan 31, 1923
           New York Clipper 70:20, Dec 27, 1922
           New York Times p. 20, Dec 25, 1922
                           p. 13, Dec 30, 1922
                           VII, p. 1, Dec 31, 1922
                           VII, p. 1, Jan 7, 1923
                           p. 6, Jan 29, 1923
                           VIII, p. 1, Mar 11, 1923

WILLIAMS, TENNESSEE

  *Battle of Angels
    Reviews:
    New York Times p. 18, Dec 31, 1940
                   IX, p. 1, Jan 5, 1941

  Camino Real
    Productions:
    Opened March 19, 1953 for 60 performances.
    (Off Broadway) Season of 1959-60.
    Reviews:
    America 89:25, Apr 4, 1953
            89:59, Apr 11, 1953
            103:422-4, Jul 2, 1960
    Catholic World 177:148, May 1953
    Commonweal 58:51-2, Apr 17, 1953
    Look 17:17, May 5, 1953
    Nation 176:293-4, Apr 4, 1953
    New Republic 128:30-1, Mar 30, 1953
    New York Theatre Critics' Reviews 1953:330
    New York Times II, p. 1, Mar 15, 1953
                    p. 26, Mar 20, 1953
                    II, p. 1, Mar 29, 1953
                    p. 21, Mar 21, 1955
                    p. 41, Apr 9, 1957
                    II, p. 1, May 15, 1960
                    p. 42, May 17, 1960
                    II, p. 1, May 29, 1960
    New Yorker 29:69, Mar 28, 1953
               36:92+, May 28, 1960
    Newsweek 41:63, Mar 30, 1953
    Saturday Review 36:28-30, Apr 18, 1953
    Theatre Arts 37:88, Jun 1953
    Time 61:46, Mar 30, 1953

Cat On A Hot Tin Roof
    Productions:
        Opened March 24, 1955 for 694 performances.
    Reviews:
        Catholic World 181:147-8, May 1955
        Collier's 137:6, Mar 2, 1956
        Commonweal 62:230-1, Jun 3, 1955
        Life 38:137-8+, Apr 18, 1955
        Nation 180:314, Apr 9, 1955
        New Republic 132:28, Apr 11, 1955
                     132:22, Apr 18, 1955
                     132:23, Apr 25, 1955
        New York Theatre Critics' Reviews 1955:342
        New York Times p. 18, Mar 25, 1955
                       II, p. 1, Apr 3, 1955
                       II, p. 3, Apr 17, 1955
                       p. 37, Dec 20, 1956
                       p. 24, Jan 31, 1958
                       p. 23, Oct 23, 1959
        New Yorker 31:68+, Apr 2, 1955
        Newsweek 45:54, Apr 4, 1955
        Saturday Review 38:32-3, Apr 9, 1955
                        38:26, Apr 30, 1955
        Theatre Arts 39:18-19, 22-3+, Jun 1955
                     39:74-7, Jul 1955
        Time 65:98, Apr 4, 1955

Garden District (See Something Unspoken and Suddenly
    Last Summer)

The Glass Menagerie
    Productions:
        Opened March 31, 1945 for 561 performances.
        Opened November 21, 1956 for 15 performances.
        Opened May 4, 1965 for 175 performances.
    Reviews:
        America 112:888, Jun 19, 1965
        Catholic World 161:166-7, May 1945
                       161:263-4, Jun 1945
                       184:307, Jan 1957
        Christian Science Monitor Magazine p. 8, Apr 15,
            1950
        Commonweal 42:16-17, Apr 20, 1945
                   82:356-7, Jun 4, 1965
        Life 18:81-3, Apr 30, 1945
             18:12-14, Jun 11, 1945
             58:16, May 28, 1965

WILLIAMS, TENNESSEE (cont.)
The Glass Menagerie (cont.)
 Nation 160:424, Apr 14, 1945
 199:60, Aug 10, 1964
 New Republic 112:505, Apr 16, 1945
 New York Theatre Critics' Reviews 1945:234
 1956:190
 1965:332
 New York Times II, p. 2, Jan 14, 1945
 p. 15, Apr 2, 1945
 II, p. 1, Apr 8, 1945
 II, p. 1, Apr 15, 1945
 II, p. 1, Sep 9, 1945
 II, p. 1, Jan 27, 1946
 II, p. 1, Mar 31, 1946
 II, p. 2, Jun 2, 1946
 VI, p. 18, Mar 2, 1947
 p. 17, Jul 29, 1948
 p. 50, Nov 22, 1956
 II, p. 1, Dec 2, 1956
 p. 30, Mar 6, 1960
 II, p. 1, Mar 5, 1961
 p. 30, Mar 6, 1961
 p. 32, Mar 20, 1961
 p. 32, Mar 28, 1961
 p. 11, Apr 1, 1961
 p. 43, Apr 11, 1961
 p. 29, Apr 21, 1961
 p. 35, May 1, 1961
 p. 22, May 19, 1961
 p. 28, May 31, 1961
 p. 27, Jun 16, 1961
 p. 20, Aug 21, 1961
 II, p. 1, Mar 28, 1965
 p. 53, May 5, 1965
 II, p. 1, May 16, 1965
 New York Times Magazine pp. 28-9, Mar 4, 1945
 New Yorker 21:40, Apr 7, 1945
 41:158, May 15, 1965
 Newsweek 25:86, Apr 9, 1945
 65:92, May 17, 1965
 Player's Magazine 22:5+, Sep-Oct 1945
 Saturday Review 28:34-6, Apr 14, 1945
 39:29, Dec 8, 1956
 50:71, Nov 25, 1967
 Theatre Arts 29:263, May 1945
 29:325-7+, Jun 1945

29:554, Oct 1945
31:38-9, Aug 1947
41:24, Feb 1957
Time 45:86, Apr 9, 1945
85:64, May 14, 1965

The Gnadiges Freulein (See Slapstick Tragedy)

I Rise in Flame, Cried the Phoenix
    Productions:
        (Off Broadway) Season of 1958-59.
    Reviews:
        New York Times p. 30, Apr 15, 1959
        Saturday Review 42:23, Apr 25, 1959

In the Bar of a Tokyo Hotel
    Productions:
        (Off Broadway) Opened May 11, 1969 for 25 per-
        formances.
    Reviews:
        Life 66:10, Jun 13, 1969
        Nation 208:709-10, Jun 2, 1969
        New York Times p. 54, May 12, 1969
                     II, p. 5, May 25, 1969
        Newsweek 73:133, May 26, 1969
        Saturday Review 52:18, May 31, 1968
        Time 93:75, May 23, 1969

The Milk Train Doesn't Stop Here Anymore
    Productions:
        Opened January 16, 1963 for 69 performances.
        Opened January 1, 1964 for 5 performances.
    Reviews:
        America 108:449, Mar 30, 1963
        Commonweal 77:515-17, Feb 8, 1963
        Nation 196:106, Feb 2, 1963
        National Review 14:291+, Apr 9, 1963
        New Republic 148:27, Feb 2, 1963
        New York Theatre Critics' Reviews 1963:391
                                          1964:397
        New York Times p. 19, Jul 12, 1962
                       p. 7, Jan 18, 1963
                       p. 32, Sep 18, 1963
                       p. 33, Jan 2, 1964
                       p. 25, Jul 27, 1965
        New Yorker 38:72, Jan 26, 1963
        Newsweek 61:79, Jan 28, 1963

WILLIAMS, TENNESSEE (cont.)
  The Milk Train Doesn't Stop Here Anymore (cont.)
                63:70, Jan 13, 1964
          Reporter 28:48, Apr 25, 1963
          Saturday Review 46:20-1, Feb 2, 1963
                47:22, Jan 18, 1964
          Theatre Arts 47:66, Feb 1963
          Time 80:40, Jul 20, 1962
                81:53, Jan 25, 1963
                83:52, Jan 10, 1964

  The Mutilated (See Slapstick Tragedy)

  The Night of the Iguana
    Productions:
        Opened December 28, 1961 for 316 performances.
        (Off Broadway) Season of 1966-67 for 9 performances
          (Equity Library Theatre).
    Reviews:
        America 106:604, Feb 3, 1962
        Catholic World 194:380-1, Mar 1962
        Christian Century 79:169, Feb 7, 1962
        Commonweal 75:460, Jan 26, 1962
        Life 52:67+, Apr 13, 1962
        Nation 194:86, Jan 27, 1962
        New Republic 146:20+, Jan 22, 1962
        New York Theatre Critics' Reviews 1961:131
        New York Times VI, pp. 34-5, Oct 29, 1961
                II, p. 5, Dec 24, 1961
                  p. 10, Dec 29, 1961
                II, p. 1, Jan 7, 1962
        New Yorker 37:61, Jan 13, 1962
        Newsweek 59:44, Jan 8, 1962
        Reporter 26:45, Feb 1, 1962
        Saturday Review 42:23, Apr 25, 1959
                45:36, Jan 20, 1962
        Theatre Arts 46:57, Mar 1962
        Time 79:53, Jan 5, 1962

  Orpheus Descending
    Productions:
        Opened March 21, 1957 for 68 performances.
        (Off Broadway) Season of 1958-59.
        (Off Broadway) Season of 1959-60.
    Reviews:
        America 97:148-50, Apr 27, 1957
        Catholic World 185:226-7, Jun 1957

Catholic World 189:192-3, Jun 1959
Christian Century 74:455, Apr 10, 1957
Commonweal 66:94-7, Apr 26, 1957
Harper's 214:76-7, May 1957
Nation 184:301-2, Apr 6, 1957
New Republic 136:21, Apr 8, 1957
New York Theatre Critics' Reviews 1957:310
New York Times II, p. 1, Mar 17, 1957
      p. 28, Mar 22, 1957
      II, p. 1, Mar 31, 1957
      p. 44, Mar 18, 1959
      p. 23, May 15, 1959
      p. 45, Oct 6, 1959
      p. 21, Aug 28, 1961
New Yorker 33:84+, Mar 30, 1957
Newsweek 49:81, Apr 1, 1957
Reporter 16:43, Apr 18, 1957
Saturday Review 40:26, Mar 30, 1957
Theatre Arts 41:20, May 1957
      42:25-6, Sep 1958
Time 69:61, Apr 1, 1957

Period of Adjustment
  Productions:
  Opened November 10, 1960 for 132 performances.
  Reviews:
  America 104:410-11, Dec 17, 1960
  Catholic World 192:255-6, Jan 1961
  Christian Century 77:1536, Dec 28, 1960
  Commonweal 74:255, Jun 2, 1961
  Horizon 3:102-3, Mar 1961
  Nation 191:443-4, Dec 3, 1960
      195:59, Aug 11, 1962
  New Republic 143:38-9, Nov 28, 1960
  New York Theatre Critics' Reviews 1960:176
  New York Times p. 34, Nov 11, 1960
      II, p. 1, Nov 20, 1960
      p. 25, Jan 3, 1962
      p. 24, Jun 14, 1962
  New Yorker 36:93, Nov 19, 1960
  Newsweek 56:79, Nov 21, 1960
  Reporter 23:35, Dec 22, 1960
  Saturday Review 43:28, Nov 26, 1960
  Theatre Arts 45:57-8, Jan 1961
  Time 73:54+, Jan 12, 1959
      76:75, Nov 21, 1960

WILLIAMS, TENNESSEE (cont.)
  Portrait of A Madonna
    Productions:
      Opened April 15, 1959 for 37 performances.
    Reviews:
      New York Theatre Critics' Reviews 1959:320
      New York Times p. 21, Apr 1, 1957
                     p. 28, Apr 16, 1959
                     II, p. 1, Apr 26, 1959
      Theatre Arts 43:9, Jun 1959

  The Purification
    Productions:
      (Off Broadway) Season of 1959-60.
    Reviews:
      New York Times p. 12, May 29, 1954
                     II, p. 1, Jun 6, 1954
                     p. 57, Dec 9, 1959

  The Rose Tattoo
    Productions:
      Opened February 3, 1951 for 306 performances.
      Opened October 20, 1966 for 76 performances (City
        Center Drama Co.).
    Reviews:
      America 115:786, Dec 10, 1966
      Catholic World 172:467-8, Mar 1951
      Commonweal 53:492-4, Feb 23, 1951
      Life 30:80+, Feb 26, 1951
      Nation 172:161, Feb 17, 1951
             203:493, Nov 7, 1966
      National Review 19:99, Jan 24, 1967
      New Republic 124:22, Feb 19, 1951
      New York Theatre Critics' Reviews 1951:363
      New York Times II, p. 1, Jan 28, 1951
                     p. 19, Feb 5, 1951
                     II, p. 1, Feb 11, 1951
                     II, p. 3, Mar 25, 1951
                     II, p. 1, Jun 3, 1951
                     p. 23, Feb 21, 1952
                     p. 36, Oct 21, 1966
                     II, p. 1, Nov 20, 1966
      New Yorker 26:58+, Feb 10, 1951
      Newsweek 37:72, Feb 12, 1951
      Saturday Review 34:22-4, Mar 10, 1951
                      49:60, Nov 26, 1966
      School and Society 73:181-3, Mar 24, 1951

Theatre Arts 35:16, Apr 1951
Time 57:53-4, Feb 12, 1951
88:80, Nov 18, 1966

The Seven Descents of Myrtle
Productions:
Opened March 27, 1968 for 29 performances.
Reviews:
Commonweal 88:208-9, May 3, 1968
Nation 206:516-17, Apr 15, 1968
New York Theatre Critics' Reviews 1968:313
New York Times p. 54, Mar 28, 1968
II, p. 1, Apr 7, 1968
New Yorker 44:109, Apr 6, 1968
Newsweek 71:131, Apr 8, 1968
Saturday Review 51:30, Apr 13, 1968
Time 91:72, Apr 5, 1968

Slapstick Tragedy ("The Mutilated" and "The Gnadiges
Freulein")
Productions:
Opened February 22, 1966 for 7 performances.
Reviews:
Commonweal 84:82, Apr 8, 1966
Nation 202:309, Mar 14, 1966
New Republic 154:34, Mar 26, 1966
New York Theatre Critics' Reviews 1966:359
New York Times p. 42, Feb 23, 1966
p. 15, Feb 26, 1966
II, p. 1, Mar 6, 1966
New Yorker 42:83, Mar 5, 1966
Newsweek 67:90, Mar 7, 1966
Reporter 34:49-50, Mar 24, 1966
Saturday Review 49:28, Mar 12, 1966
Time 87:88, Mar 4, 1966
Vogue 147:109, Apr 1, 1966

Something Unspoken
Productions:
(Off Broadway) Season of 1957-58. (Billed as
Garden District)
Reviews:
Catholic World 186:469-70, Mar 1958
Christian Century 75:136, Jan 29, 1958
Commonweal 68:232-3, May 30, 1958
Nation 186:86-7, Jan 25, 1958
New Republic 138:20, Jan 27, 1958

527

WILLIAMS, TENNESSEE (cont.)
    Something Unspoken (cont.)
            New York Times p. 23, Jan 8, 1958
                            II, p. 1, Jan 19, 1958
                            p. 44, Sep 17, 1958
            New Yorker 33:66+, Jan 18, 1958
            Newsweek 51:84, Jan 20, 1958
            Reporter 18:42-3, Feb 6, 1958
            Saturday Review 41:26, Jan 25, 1958
            Theatre Arts 42:13, Mar 1958
            Time 71:42, Jan 20, 1958

*Stairs to the Roof
    Reviews:
            New York Times p. 35, Feb 26, 1947
            Theatre Arts 31:12, Jul 1947

A Streetcar Named Desire
    Productions:
            Opened December 3, 1947 for 855 performances.
            Opened May 23, 1950 for 16 performances.
            (Off Broadway) Season of 1954-55.
            Opened February 15, 1956 for 15 performances.
    Reviews:
            Atlantic 186:94-5, Jul 1950
            Catholic World 166:358, Jan 1948
                            183:67, Apr 1956
            Commonweal 47:254, Dec 19, 1947
            Forum 109:86-8, Feb 1948
            Life 23:101-2+, Dec 15, 1947
                27:66, Dec 19, 1949
            Nation 165:686, Dec 20, 1947
            New Republic 117:34-5, Dec 22, 1947
            New York Theatre Critics' Reviews 1947:249
                                            1956:362
            New York Times VI, p. 14, Nov 23, 1947
                            p. 42, Dec 4, 1947
                            II, p. 3, Dec 14, 1947
                            II, p. 1, Jun 6, 1948
                            II, p. 1, Jun 12, 1949
                            p. 38, Sep 29, 1949
                            p. 33, Oct 13, 1949
                            p. 36, May 24, 1950
                            p. 18, Mar 4, 1955
                            p. 24, Feb 16, 1956
                            p. 27, Feb 19, 1965
            New York Times Magazine p. 14, Nov 23, 1947

New Yorker 23:50+, Dec 13, 1947
            32:90+, Feb 25, 1956
Newsweek 30:82-3, Dec 15, 1947
Saturday Review 30:22-4, Dec 27, 1947
            39:22, Mar 3, 1956
School and Society 67:241-3, Mar 27, 1948
Theatre Arts 31:18, Dec 1947
            32:10-11, 13, Jan 1948
            32:35, Feb 1948
            32:30, Apr 1948
            32:21, Oct 1948
            33:44, Jun 1949
            33:14, Nov 1949
            40:24, Apr 1956
Time 50:85, Dec 15, 1947
     54:54, Oct 31, 1949
     67:61, Feb 27, 1956

Suddenly Last Summer
    Productions:
        (Off Broadway) Season of 1957-58.   (Billed as
            Garden District).
        (Off Broadway) Opened October 30, 1964 for 9 per-
            formances (Equity Library Theatre).
    Reviews:
        Catholic World 186:469-70, Mar 1958
        Christian Century 75:136, Jan 29, 1958
        Commonweal 68:232-3, May 30, 1958
        Nation 186:86-7, Jan 25, 1958
        New York Times p. 23, Jan 8, 1958
                       II, p. 1, Jan 19, 1958
                       p. 44, Sep 17, 1958
        New Yorker 33:66+, Jan 18, 1958
        Newsweek 51:84, Jan 20, 1958
        Reporter 18:42-3, Feb 6, 1958
        Saturday Review 41:26, Jan 25, 1958
        Theatre Arts 42:13, Mar 1958
        Time 71:42, Jan 20, 1958

Summer and Smoke
    Productions:
        Opened October 6, 1948 for 100 performances.
        (Off Broadway) Season of 1951-52.
    Reviews:
        Catholic World 168:161, Nov 1948
                       176:148-9, Nov 1952
        Commonweal 49:68-9, Oct 29, 1948

WILLIAMS, TENNESSEE (cont.)
  Summer and Smoke (cont.)
        Forum 110:352-3, Dec 1948
        Life 25:102-3, Oct 25, 1948
        Nation 167:473-4, Oct 23, 1948
        New Republic 119:25-6, Oct 25, 1948
                        119:27-8, Nov 15, 1948
        New York Theatre Critics' Reviews 1948:205
        New York Times p. 18, Jul 9, 1947
                        p. 21, Aug 1, 1947
                        II, p. 1, Aug 10, 1947
                        II, p. 1, Oct 3, 1948
                        p. 33, Oct 7, 1948
                        II, p. 1, Oct 17, 1948
                        II, p. 7, Dec 5, 1948
                        p. 21, Aug 9, 1949
                        II, p. 3, Oct 29, 1950
                        p. 32, Nov 23, 1951
                        p. 13, Jan 25, 1952
                        p. 19, Apr 25, 1952
                        II, p. 1, May 4, 1952
        New York Times Magazine pp. 66-7, Sep 26, 1948
        New Yorker 24:51, Oct 16, 1948
        Newsweek 32:88, Oct 18, 1948
        Saturday Review 31:31-3, Oct 30, 1948
                        35:28, May 10, 1952
        School and Society 68:303-4, Oct 30, 1948
        Theatre Arts 31:11, Sep 1947
                        33:10-11+, Jan 1949
        Time 52:82-3, Oct 18, 1948

  Sweet Bird of Youth
    Productions:
        Opened March 10, 1959 for 375 performances.
    Reviews:
        America 101:55-6, Apr 4, 1959
        Catholic World 189:158-9, May 1959
                        189:191-4, Jun 1959
        Christian Century 76:726, Jun 17, 1959
                        76:854, Jul 22, 1959
        Life 46:71-3, Apr 20, 1959
        Nation 188:281-3, Mar 28, 1959
        New Republic 140:21-2, Apr 20, 1959
        New York Theatre Critics' Reviews 1959:347
        New York Times p. 27, Apr 17, 1956
                        p. 39, Mar 11, 1959
                        p. 26, Mar 12, 1959

                    II, p. 1, Mar 22, 1959
                        p. 27, Oct 27, 1961
        New Yorker 35:98-100, Mar 21, 1959
        Newsweek 53:75, Mar 23, 1959
        Reporter 20:34, Apr 16, 1959
        Saturday Review 42:26, Mar 28, 1959
        Theatre Arts 40:66-7, Aug 1956
                      43:21-2, May 1959
        Time 73:58, Mar 23, 1959

This Property Is Condemned
    Productions:
        (Off Broadway) Season of 1956-57.
    Reviews:
        New York Times p. 34, Oct 29, 1956
                      VI, p. 31, Nov 11, 1956

Twenty-Seven Wagons Full of Cotton
    Productions:
        Opened April 19, 1955 for 47 performances.
    Reviews:
        America 93:193, May 14, 1955
        Catholic World 181:227, Jun 1955
        Commonweal 62:255, Jun 10, 1955
        New Republic 132:22, May 2, 1955
        New York Theatre Critics' Reviews 1955:325
        New York Times p. 23, Jan 19, 1955
                      p. 40, Apr 20, 1955
                      II, p. 1, Apr 24, 1955
        New Yorker 31:69-71, Apr 30, 1955
        Saturday Review 38:26, May 14, 1955
        Theatre Arts 39:17, 23+, Jul 1955
        Time 65:78, May 2, 1955

*Two Character Play
    Reviews:
        New York Times p. 54, Dec 13, 1967
        Time 90:63, Dec 22, 1967

You Touched Me (with Donald Windham) (Suggested by a
        short story by D. H. Lawrence)
    Productions:
        Opened September 25, 1945 for 109 performances.
    Reviews:
        Catholic World 162:166, Nov 1945
        Commonweal 42:623, Oct 12, 1945
        Nation 161:349, Oct 6, 1945

WILLIAMS, TENNESSEE (cont.)
  You Touched Me (cont.)
          New Republic 113:469, Oct 8, 1945
          New York Theatre Critics' Reviews 1945:164
          New York Times II, p. 2, Oct 17, 1943
                          VI, p. 28, Sep 23, 1945
                          p. 27, Sep 26, 1945
                          II, p. 1, Sep 30, 1945
          New York Times Magazine p. 28-9, Sep 23, 1945
          New Yorker 21:48, Oct 6, 1945
          Theatre Arts 29:618-21, Nov 1945
                        29:680, Dec 1945
          Time 46:77, Oct 8, 1945

WILLIAMS, WILLIAM CARLOS

  Many Loves
      Productions:
          (Off Broadway) Season of 1958-59 (Living Theatre).
          (Off Broadway) Opened October 13, 1961 for 19 per-
            formances.
      Reviews:
          Nation 188:125, Feb 7, 1959
          New York Times p. 28, Jan 14, 1959
                         p. 29, Jun 16, 1961

WILSON, LANFORD

  The Gingham Dog
      Productions:
          Opened April 23, 1969 for 5 performances.
      Reviews:
          New York Theatre Critics' Reviews 1969:304
                                            1969:306
          New York Times II, p. 18, Oct 13, 1968
                           p. 41, Apr 24, 1969
                           II, p. 22, May 4, 1969
          New Yorker 45:107, May 3, 1969
          Saturday Review 51:32+, Oct 26, 1968

  Home Free
      Productions:
          (Off Broadway) Opened February 10, 1965 for 23
            performances (Theatre 1965 New Playwrights
            Series).

Reviews:
New York Times II, p. 1, Feb 7, 1965
              p. 45, Feb 11, 1965
Newsweek 65:93, Feb 22, 1965

Ludlow Fair
Productions:
(Off Broadway) Opened March 22, 1966 for 15 per-
formances.
Reviews:
Commonweal 84:178, Apr 29, 1966
New York Times p. 42, Mar 23, 1966
New Yorker 42:124, Apr 2, 1966

The Madness of Lady Bright
Productions:
(Off Broadway) Opened March 22, 1966 for 15 per-
formances.
Reviews:
Commonweal 84:178, Apr 29, 1966
New York Times p. 42, Mar 23, 1966
New Yorker 42:124, Apr 2, 1966

The Rimers of Eldritch
Productions:
(Off Broadway) Opened February 20, 1967 for 32 per-
formances.
Reviews:
America 116:354-5, Mar 11, 1967
New York Times p. 53, Feb 21, 1967
New Yorker 43:132+, Mar 4, 1967
Saturday Review 50:30, Mar 11, 1967
Time 89:52, Mar 3, 1967

This Is The Rill Speaking
Productions:
(Off Broadway) Opened April 11, 1966 for 16 per-
formances.
Reviews:
Nation 202:403-4, Apr 4, 1966
New York Times II, p. 15, Apr 10, 1966
              p. 43, Apr 12, 1966

Untitled Play
Productions:
(Off Broadway) Season of 1967-68 (In repertory),
(Judson Poet's Theatre).
No Reviews.

WILSON, LANFORD (cont.)
Wandering
Productions:
(Off Broadway) Opened May 8, 1968 for 80 performances.
Reviews:
Harper's Bazaar 237:113-15, Oct 1968
Nation 206:772+, Jun 10, 1968
New York Times p. 55, May 9, 1968
II, p. 1, May 19, 1968
New Yorker 44:74, May 18, 1968

WINCELBERG, SHIMON

Kataki
Productions:
Opened April 9, 1959 for 20 performances.
(Off Broadway) Season of 1959-1960.
Reviews:
New York Theatre Critics' Reviews 1959:326
New York Times p. 24, Apr 10, 1959
p. 55, Dec 16, 1959
New Yorker 35:79, Apr 18, 1959
Newsweek 53:75, Apr 20, 1959
Saturday Review 42:23, Apr 25, 1959
Theatre Arts 43:10-11, Jun 1959
Time 73:71, Apr 20, 1959

WISHENGRAD, MORTON

The Rope Dancers
Productions:
Opened November 20, 1957 for 189 performances.
(Off Broadway) Season of 1958-59.
Reviews:
America 98:437, Jan 11, 1958
Catholic World 186:384, Feb 1958
Christian Century 74:1514, Dec 18, 1957
Commonweal 67:616, Mar 14, 1958
67:640, Mar 21, 1958
Nation 185:442, Dec 7, 1957
New York Theatre Critics' Reviews 1957:174
New York Times II, p. 1, Nov 17, 1957
p. 39, Nov 21, 1957
II, p. 1, Dec 1, 1957

p. 26, Mar 14, 1959
p. 26, Jul 15, 1959
New Yorker 33:94+, Nov 30, 1957
Newsweek 50:70-1, Dec 2, 1957
Reporter 17:34, Dec 26, 1957
Saturday Review 40:51, Dec 7, 1957
Theatre Arts 42:21-2, Feb 1958
Time 70:77, Dec 2, 1957

WOLFSON, VICTOR

American Gothic (Based on Wolfson's The Lonely Steeple)
    Productions:
    (Off Broadway) Season of 1953-54.
    Reviews:
        America 90:251, Nov 28, 1953
        Catholic World 178:309, Jan 1954
        New Republic 129:21, Nov 30, 1953
        New York Times p. 35, Nov 11, 1953
        New Yorker 29:85-6+, Nov 21, 1953
        Saturday Review 36:30, Nov 28, 1953

Bitter Steam (Based on Ignazio Silone's Fontamara).
    Productions:
    Opened March 30, 1936 for 61 performances.
    Reviews:
        Catholic World 23:696, Jan 17, 1936
        Commonweal 23:696, Apr 17, 1936
        Literary Digest 121:18, Apr 11, 1936
        New York Times p. 16, Mar 31, 1936
        Newsweek 7:43, Apr 11, 1936
        Theatre Arts 20:339, Apr 11, 1936

Excursion
    Productions:
    Opened April 9, 1937 for 116 performances.
    Reviews:
        Catholic World 145:214-15, May 1937
        Commonweal 26:20, Apr 20, 1937
        Literary Digest 123:22, Apr 24, 1937
        New Republic 91:74-5, May 26, 1937
        New York Times p. 11, Apr 10, 1937
                    XI, p. 1, Apr 18, 1937
                    p. 24, Jul 27, 1937
        Newsweek 9:32, Apr 17, 1937
        Stage 14:49, May 1937

WOLFSON, VICTOR (cont.)
    Excursion (cont.)
        Theatre Arts 21:422-4, Jun 1937
        Time 29:62, Apr 19, 1937

    The Family (Based on Nina Fedorova's novel)
        Productions:
        Opened March 30, 1943 for 7 performances.
        Reviews:
            New York Theatre Critics' Reviews 1943:344
            New York Times p. 22, Mar 31, 1943
            Theatre Arts 27:333-4, Jan 1943

    Pastoral
        Productions:
        Opened November 1, 1939 for 14 performances.
        Reviews:
            New York Times p. 26, Nov 2, 1939
            Newsweek 14:32, Nov 13, 1939

    Prides' Crossing
        Productions:
        Opened November 20, 1950 for 8 performances.
        Reviews:
            Christian Science Monitor Magazine p. 10, Nov. 25,
                1950
            Commonweal 53:231, Dec 8, 1950
            New York Theatre Critics' Reviews 1950:198
            New York Times p. 37, Nov 21, 1950
            New Yorker 26:83, Dec 2, 1950
            Theatre Arts 35:17, Jan 1951
            Time 56:65, Dec 4, 1950

WOUK, HERMAN

    The Caine Mutiny Court-Martial (Adapted from Wouk's
        novel)
        Productions:
        Opened January 20, 1954 for 415 performances.
        Reviews:
            America 90:516+, Feb 13, 1954
            Catholic World 178:466, Mar 1954
            Collier's 132:50-3, Nov 13, 1953
            Commonweal 59:523, Feb 26, 1954
            Life 35:75-6+, Dec 14, 1953
            Nation 178:138, Feb 13, 1954

536

178:260-1, Mar 27, 1954
New Republic 130:21, Feb 15, 1954
New York Theatre Critics' Reviews 1954:382
New York Times p. 35, Oct 14, 1953
           p. 52, Dec 15, 1953
           II, p. 1, Jan 17, 1954
           p. 27, Jan 21, 1954
           II, p. 1, Jan 31, 1954
           VI, p. 12, Mar 21, 1954
           pp. 12-13+, Mar 21, 1954
           p. 6, Apr 4, 1954
           p. 13, Dec 8, 1954
           p. 40, Jun 14, 1956
New Yorker 29:66+, Jan 30, 1954
Newsweek 43:73, Feb 1, 1954
Saturday Review 37:24+, Feb 6, 1954
Theatre Arts 39:58-61, Jan 1955
            38:18-19, Apr 1954
Time 63:36, Feb 1, 1954

Nature's Way
   Productions:
   Opened October 16, 1957 for 61 performances.
   Reviews:
   Christian Century 74:1384, Nov 20, 1957
   Nation 185:310, Nov 2, 1957
   New York Theatre Critics' Reviews 1957:219
   New York Times VI, p. 29, Aug 25, 1957
              p. 42, Oct 17, 1957
   New Yorker 33:96-8, Oct 26, 1957
   Theatre Arts 41:25-6, Dec 1957
   Time 70:92, Oct 28, 1957

The Traitor
   Productions:
   Opened April 4, 1949 for 67 performances.
   Reviews:
   Catholic World 169:145, May 1949
   Commonweal 50:45-6, Apr 22, 1949
   New Republic 120:30, Apr 18, 1949
   New York Theatre Critics' Reviews 1949:322
   New York Times p. 30, Apr 1, 1949
              II, p. 1, Apr 10, 1949
   New Yorker 25:55, Apr 9, 1949
   Newsweek 33:79+, Apr 11, 1949
   Saturday Review 32:34-6, May 21, 1949
   School and Society 69:339, May 7, 1949

WOUK, HERMAN (cont.)
  The Traitor (cont.)
        Theatre Arts 33:13, Jun 1949
        Time 53:87, Apr 11, 1949

WRIGHT, RICHARD

  Daddy Goodness
    Productions:
        (Off Broadway) Opened June 4, 1968 for 64 per-
          formances (Negro Ensemble).
    Reviews:
        New York Times p. 37, Jun 5, 1968

  The Long Dream (See entry under Frings, Ketti)

  Native Son (See entry under Green, Paul)

WYCHERLY, MARGARET (See Vale, Martin)

YORDAN, PHILIP

  Anna Lucasta
    Productions:
        (Off Broadway) Opened June 16, 1944 in repertory
          (American Negro Theatre).
        Opened August 30, 1944 for 957 performances.
        Opened September 22, 1947 for 32 performances.
        (Off Broadway) Season of 1955-56.
    Reviews:
        Catholic World 160:71-2, Oct 1944
        Commonweal 40:517, Sep 15, 1944
        Life 17:69-72, Oct 4, 1944
            18:79, Apr 9, 1945
        New Republic 111:334-40, Sep 18, 1944
        New York Theatre Critics' Reviews 1944:143
        New York Times p. 10, Jun 17, 1944
                      p. 15, Aug 31, 1944
                      II, p. 1, Sep 10, 1944
                      II, p. 1, Sep 24, 1944
                      II, p. 1, Mar 3, 1946
                      II, p. 1, Aug 25, 1946
                      II, p. 3, Sep 21, 1947
                      p. 31, Oct 7, 1947

                    p. 31, Oct 30, 1947
                    p. 21, Apr 13, 1956
New Yorker 20:40, Sep 4, 1944
Newsweek 24:107-9, Sep 11, 1944
                  30:74, Nov 10, 1947
Theatre Arts 28:632-4, Nov 1944
Time 43:56, Jun 26, 1944

Any Day Now
    Productions:
    (Off Broadway) Opened June 3, 1941.
    Reviews:
    New York Times p. 28, Jun 10, 1941

ABOUT THE DRAMATISTS

Name	Birthplace	Dates
Abbott, George	Hamburg, N. Y.	born 1887
Ade, George	Kentland, Ind.	1866-1944
Akins, Zoe	Humansville, Mo.	1886-1958
Albee, Edward	Washington, D. C.	born 1928
Alfred, William	New York	born 1922
Allen, Woody	New York	born 1935
Anderson, Maxwell	Atlantic, Pa.	1888-1959
Anderson, Robert	New York	born 1917
Anspacher, Louis K.	Cincinnati	1878-1947
Archibald, William	Trinidad, West Indies	born 1919
Ardrey, Robert	Chicago	born 1908
Atlas, Leopold	New York	born 1907
Aurthur, Robert Alan	Freeport, N. Y.	
Axelrod, George	New York	born 1922
Balderston, John	Philadelphia	1889-1954
Baldwin, James	New York	born 1924
Barry, Philip	Rochester, N. Y.	1896-1949
Beach, Lewis	Saginaw, Mich.	born 1891
Behrman, S. N.	Worcester, Mass.	born 1893
Belasco, David	San Francisco	1859-1931
Bellow, Saul	Lachine, Quebec, Canada	born 1915
Benet, Steven Vincent	Bethlehem, Pa.	1898-1943
Berg, Gertrude	New York	born 1899
Bolton, Guy	England	born 1881
Boothe, Clare	New York	born 1903
Bouicicault, Dion	Dublin, Ireland	1820-1890
Bowles, Jane	New York	born 1917
Breit, Harvey	New York	1910-1968
Browne, Porter Emerson	Beverly, Mass.	1879-1934
Buck, Pearl S.	Hillsboro, West Va.	born 1892
Burrows, Abe	New York	born 1910
Caldwell, Erskine	White Oak, Ga.	born 1903
Capote, Truman	New Orleans	born 1924
Chase, Mary Coyle	Denver	born 1907
Chayefsky, Paddy	New York	born 1923
Chodorov, Edward	New York	born 1904
Chodorov, Jerome	New York	born 1911
Cohan, George M.	Providence, R. I.	1878-1942
Conkle, E. P.	Peru, Neb.	born 1899
Connelly, Marc	McKeesport, Pa.	born 1890

Coxe, Louis O.	Manchester, N. H.	born 1918
Craven, Frank	Boston	1880-1945
Crothers, Rachel	Bloomington, Ill.	1878-1958
Crouse, Russel	Findlay, Ohio	1893-1966
Crowley, Mart	Vicksburg, Miss.	born 1935
Cummings, E. E.	Cambridge, Mass.	1894-1962
Daly, Augustin	Plymouth, N. C.	1838-1899
Davis, Ossie	Cogdell, Ga.	born 1921
Davis, Owen	Portland, Maine	1874-1956
Dell, Floyd	Barry, Ill.	1887-1969
Dodd, Lee Wilson	Franklin, Pa.	1879-1933
DosPassos, John	Chicago	born 1896
Dreiser, Theodore	Indiana	1871-1945
Duberman, Martin	New York	born 1930
Dunlap, William	Perth Amboy, N. J.	1766-1839
Dunning, Philip	Meriden, Conn.	1890-1968
d'Usseau, Arnaud	Los Angeles	born 1916
Eliot, T. S.	St. Louis	1888-1965
Emery, Gilbert	Naples, N. Y.	1875-1945
Faulkner, William	New Albany, Miss.	1897-1962
Ferber, Edna	Kalamazoo, Mich.	1885-1968
Ferris, Walter	Green Bay, Wis.	born 1882
Fields, Joseph	New York	1895-1966
Fitch, Clyde	Elmira, N. Y.	1865-1909
Fitzgerald, F. Scott	St. Paul, Minn.	1896-1940
Flavin, Martin	San Francisco	1883-1967
Forbes, James	Salem, Ontario, Canada	1871-1938
Foster, Paul	Salem, N. J.	born 1931
Franken, Rose	Dallas	born 1895
Friedman, Bruce Jay	New York	born 1930
Frings, Ketti	Columbus, Ohio	born 1916
Frost, Robert	San Francisco	1874-1963
Gale, Zona	Portage, Wis.	1874-1938
Gardner, Herb	Brooklyn	born 1934
Gelber, Jack	Chicago	born 1932
Gibbs, Wolcott	New York	1902-1958
Gibson, William	New York	born 1914
Gillette, William	Hartford, Conn.	1855-1937
Gilroy, Frank D.	New York	born 1925
Glaspell, Susan	Davenport, Iowa	1882-1948
Gleason, James	Alameda, Calif.	1886-1959
Goetz, Augustus	Buffalo, New York	1901-1957
Goetz, Ruth	Philadelphia	born 1912
Goldman, James	Chicago	born 1927
Goldsmith, Clifford	East Aurora, N. Y.	born 1900
Goodrich, Frances	Belleville, N. Y.	born 1933
Gordon, Ruth	Wollaston, Mass.	born 1896
Gordone, Charles	Elkhart, Ind.	born 1925
Gow, James	Iowa	1907-1952

Name	Birthplace	Dates
Green, Paul	Lillington, N. C.	born 1894
Hackett, Albert	New York	born 1900
Haines, William Wister	Des Moines, Iowa	born 1908
Hanley, William	Lorain, Ohio	born 1931
Hansberry, Lorraine	Chicago	1930-1965
Hart, Moss	New York	1904-1961
Hayden, John	Hartford, Conn.	born 1889
Hayes, Alfred	London	born 1911
Hayes, Joseph	Indianapolis	born 1918
Hecht, Ben	New York	1893-1964
Heggen, Thomas	Fort Dodge, Iowa	1918-1949
Heller, Joseph	Brooklyn	born 1923
Hellman, Lillian	New York	born 1905
Hemingway, Ernest	Oak Park, Ill.	1899-1961
Herbert, F. Hugh	Vienna	1897-1958
Herne, James A.	Cohoes, N. Y.	1839-1901
Heyward, Dorothy	Wooster, Ohio	1890-1961
Heyward, Dubose	Charleston, S. C.	1885-1940
Hopkins, Arthur	Cleveland	1878-1950
Howard, Bronson	Detroit	1842-1908
Howard, Sidney	San Francisco	1891-1939
Howells, William Dean	Martin's Ferry, Ohio	1837-1920
Hoyt, Charles Hale	Concord, N. H.	1860-1900
Hughes, Hatcher	North Carolina	1886-1945
Hughes, Langston	Joplin, Mo.	1902-1967
Hurlbut, William	Belvedere, Ill.	born 1883
Huston, John	Nevada, Mo.	born 1906
Inge, William	Independence, Kan.	born 1913
James, Daniel Lewis	Kansas City, Mo.	born 1911
James, Henry	New York	1843-1916
Jeffers, Robinson	Pittsburgh	1887-1962
Jones, Leroi	Newark	born 1934
Kanin, Fay	New York	born 1917
Kanin, Garson	Rochester, N. Y.	born 1912
Kaufman, George S.	Pittsburgh	1889-1961
Kelly, George	Philadelphia	born 1887
Kennedy, Charles Rann	England	1871-1950
Kerr, Jean	Scranton, Pa.	born 1923
Kesselring, Joseph O.	New York	1902-1967
Kingsley, Sidney	New York	born 1906
Kirkland, Jack	St. Louis	1902-1969
Kober, Arthur	Brody, Austria-Hungary	born 1900
Koch, Howard	New York	born 1902
Kopit, Arthur L.	New York	born 1937
Kramm, Joseph	South Philadelphia, Pa.	born 1928
Krasna, Norman	Long Island	born 1909
Kummer, Clare		1873-1958

Lardner, Ring	Niles, Mich.	1885-1933
Laurents, Arthur	New York	born 1918
Lavery, Emmet	Poughkeepsie, N. Y.	born 1902
Lawrence, Jerome	Cleveland	born 1915
Lawson, John Howard	New York	born 1895
Lee, Robert E.	Elyria, Ohio	born 1918
Levin, Ira M.	New York	born 1919
Lewis, Sinclair	Sauk Center, Minn.	1885-1951
Lindsay, Howard	Waterford, N. Y.	1892-1968
Logan, Joshua	Texarkana, Texas	born 1908
Long, John Luther	Pennsylvania	1861-1927
Loos, Anita	Sisson, Calif.	born 1893
Lowell, Robert	Boston, Mass.	born 1917
MacArthur, Charles	Scranton, Pa.	1895-1956
McCullers, Carson	Columbus, Ga.	1917-1967
McEnroe, Robert E.	New Britain, Conn.	born 1916
McGuire, William Anthony	Chicago	1887-1940
MacKaye, Percy	New York	1875-1956
MacLeish, Archibald	Glencoe, Ill.	born 1892
McLellan, C. M. S.	Maine	1865-1916
McNally, Terrence	Corpus Christi, Texas	born 1939
Mailer, Norman	Long Branch, N. J.	born 1923
Maltz, Albert	Brooklyn	born 1908
Marquand, John P.	Wilmington, Del.	born 1893
Marquis, Don	Walnut, Ill.	1878-1937
May, Elaine	Philadelphia	born 1932
Mayer, Edwin Justus	New York	1897-1960
Michaels, Sidney	New York	born 1927
Middleton, George	Patterson, N. J.	1880-1967
Millay, Edna St. Vincent	Maine	1892-1950
Miller, Arthur	New York	born 1915
Mitchell, Langdon	Philadelphia	1862-1935
Mitchell, Thomas	Elizabeth, N. J.	born 1895
Moody, William Vaughn	Spencer, Ind.	1869-1910
Mosel, Tad	Steubenville, Ohio	
Mowatt, Anna Cora	Bordeaux, France	1819-1870
Nichols, Anne	Dales Mills, Ga.	1899-1966
Nicholson, Kenyon	Crawfordsville, Ind.	born 1894
Nugent, Elliott	Dover, Ohio	born 1900
Odets, Clifford	Philadelphia	1906-1963
O'Neill, Eugene	New York	1888-1953
Osborn, Paul	Evansville, Ind.	born 1901
Parker, Dorothy	West End, N. J.	1893-1967
Patrick, John	Louisville, Ky.	born 1910
Peterson, Louis	Hartford, Conn.	born 1922
Pollock, Channing	Washington, D. C.	1880-1946
Raphaelson, Samuel	New York	born 1896
Rayfield, David	Brooklyn	born 1923

Name	Birthplace	Dates
Reed, Mark	Chelmsford, Mass.	born 1893
Rice, Elmer	New York	1892-1967
Richardson, Jack	New York	born 1935
Richman, Arthur	New York	1886-1944
Riggs, Lynn	Claremore, Ok.	1899-1954
Rinehart, Mary Roberts	Pittsburgh	1876-1958
Royle, Edwin Milton	Lexington, Mo.	1862-1942
Ryerson, Florence	Glendale, Calif.	1895-1965
Sackler, Howard	New York	born 1930
Saroyan, William	Fresno, Calif.	born 1908
Schary, Dore	Newark, N.J.	born 1905
Schisgal, Murray	New York	born 1926
Schulberg, Budd	New York	born 1914
Selwyn, Edgar	Canada	1875-1944
Shaw, Irwin	New York	born 1912
Sheldon, Edward	Chicago	1886-1946
Sherwood, Robert E.	New Rochelle, N.Y.	1896-1955
Shipman, Samuel	New York	1888-1937
Shulman, Max	St. Paul, Minn.	born 1919
Simon, Neil	New York	born 1927
Sinclair, Upton	Baltimore	born 1878
Skinner, Cornelia Otis	Chicago	born 1901
Sklar, George	Meriden, Conn.	born 1910
Smith, Harry James	New Britain, Conn.	1880-1918
Smith, Winchell	Hartford, Conn.	1871-1933
Spewack, Bella	Hungary	born 1899
Spewack, Samuel	Russia	born 1899
Stallings, Laurence	Macon, Ga.	1894-1968
Stein, Gertrude	San Francisco	1874-1946
Steinbeck, John	Salinas Valley, Calif.	1902-1968
Stewart, Donald Ogden	Columbus, Ohio	born 1894
Strong, Austin	San Francisco	1881-1952
Sturges, Preston	Chicago	1898-1959
Tarkington, Booth	Indianapolis, Ind.	1869-1946
Taylor, Samuel	Chicago	born 1912
Thomas, A. E.	Chester, Mass.	1872-1947
Thomas, Augustus	St. Louis, Mo.	1857-1934
Thurber, James	Columbus, Ohio	1894-1961
Totheroh, Dan	California	born 1894
Treadwell, Sophie	California	1890-1970
Turney, Robert	Nashville, Tenn.	born 1900
Van Druten, John	London, England	1902-1957
van Itallie, Jean-Claude	Brussels	born 1936
Varesi, Gilda	Milan, Italy	born 1887
Veiller, Bayard	Brooklyn	1869-1943
Vidal, Gore	West Point, N.Y.	born 1925
Vollmer, Lula	North Carolina	1898-1955

Walter, Eugene	Cleveland	1874-1941
Warren, Robert Penn	Guthrie, Ky.	born 1905
Watkins, Maurine	Kentucky	1901-1969
Watters, George Manker	Rochester, N. Y.	1891-1943
Weitzenkorn, Louis	Wilkes-Barre, Pa.	1893-1943
Wexley, John	New York	born 1902
Wilder, Thornton	Madison, Wis.	born 1897
Williams, Jesse Lynch	Sterling, Ill.	1871-1929
Williams, Tennessee	Columbus, Miss.	born 1914
Williams, William Carlos	New Jersey	born 1883
Wilson, Lanford	Lebanon, Mo.	born 1938
Wincelberg, Shimon	Germany	born 1915
Wishengrad, Morton	New York	1913-1963
Wolfson, Victor	New York	born 1910
Wouk, Herman	New York	born 1915
Wright, Richard	Natchez, Miss.	born 1909
Yordan, Philip	Chicago	born 1914

PROLIFIC AMERICAN PLAYWRIGHTS

Playwright	Plays Reviewed
Owen Davis	52
Eugene O'Neill	41
Maxwell Anderson	30
George S. Kaufman	29
Elmer Rice	29
Rachel Crothers	25
Tennessee Williams	25
John VanDruten	24
Paul Green	23
Samuel Shipman	23
Zoe Akins	22
George M. Cohan	22
Philip Barry	21
William Saroyan	21
S. N. Behrman	21
Guy Bolton	20
Booth Tarkington	20
Sidney Howard	19
William Hurlbut	18
A. E. Thomas	18
Robert E. Sherwood	16
Clare Kummer	14
George Abbott	13
Edward Albee	13
Marc Connelly	13
Ben Hecht	13
Howard Lindsay	13
Elliott Nugent	13
J. C. Nugent	13
Clifford Odets	13
Samuel Spewack	13
Augustus Thomas	13
Kenyon Nicholson	12
Paul Osborn	12
Arthur Richman	12
Edward Sheldon	12
Thornton Wilder	12
Susan Glaspell	11
Moss Hart	11
Lillian Hellman	11
Percy MacKaye	11
George Middleton	11

Edgar Selwyn	11
Winchell Smith	11
Eugene Walter	11
David Belasco	11
George Kelly	10
Norman Krasna	10
Arthur Miller	10
Samuel Raphaelson	10
Irwin Shaw	10

FREQUENTLY PRODUCED AMERICAN PLAYWRIGHTS

Playwright	Productions
Eugene O'Neill	73
Owen Davis	54
George S. Kaufman	40
Tennessee Williams	38
Elmer Rice	36
Maxwell Anderson	34
William Saroyan	31
Paul Green	29
Rachel Crothers	28
John VanDruten	28
Edward Albee	26
George M. Cohan	26
Sidney Howard	24
Philip Barry	23
Clifford Odets	23
Robert E. Sherwood	23
Samuel Shipman	23
Zoe Akins	22
S. N. Behrman	21
A. E. Thomas	21
Guy Bolton	20
Booth Tarkington	20
Thornton Wilder	19
William Hurlbut	18
Arthur Miller	17
Marc Connelly	16
George Kelly	16
Clare Kummer	16
Howard Lindsay	16
Elliott Nugent	16
Moss Hart	15
Ben Hecht	15
Lillian Hellman	15
J. C. Nugent	15
Paul Osborn	15
Samuel Spewack	15
George Abbott	14
William Gillette	13
Kenyon Nicholson	13
John Patrick	13
Edward Sheldon	13
Augustus Thomas	13

Susan Glaspell	12
Sidney Kingsley	12
Percy MacKaye	12
Samuel Raphaelson	12
Arthur Richman	12
Winchell Smith	12
Eugene Walter	12
David Belasco	11
George Middleton	11
Edgar Selwyn	11
Irwin Shaw	11
Joseph Fields	10
Charles Rann Kennedy	10
Norman Krasna	10
Arthur Laurents	10
Lynn Riggs	10

POPULAR AMERICAN PLAYWRIGHTS

Playwright	Productions over 100 performances
George S. Kaufman	21
Eugene O'Neill	17
Owen Davis	15
Maxwell Anderson	14
S. N. Behrman	13
Philip Barry	11
Rachel Crothers	11
Howard Lindsay	11
Elmer Rice	11
Edward Albee	10
Moss Hart	10
Tennessee Williams	10
George M. Cohan	9
Lillian Hellman	9
Robert E. Sherwood	9
Guy Bolton	8
Russel Crouse	8
Arthur Miller	8
Clifford Odets	8
John VanDruten	8
Marc Connelly	7
George Kelly	7
Channing Pollock	7
Edward Sheldon	7
David Belasco	6
Joseph Fields	6
Sidney Howard	6
Sidney Kingsley	6
Norman Krasna	6
Edgar Selwyn	6
Samuel Shipman	6
George Abbott	5
Frank Craven	5
Ben Hecht	5
Clare Kummer	5
Charles MacArthur	5
Paul Osborn	5
Neil Simon	5
Winchell Smith	5
Thornton Wilder	5

LONG RUNNING AMERICAN PLAYS

(*Off Broadway Productions)

Performances	Play and Year of Production	Author
3, 224	Life With Father (1939)	Lindsay
3, 182	Tobacco Road (1933)	Kirkland
2, 327	Abie's Irish Rose (1922)	Nichols
1, 775	Harvey (1944)	Chase
1, 642	Born Yesterday (1946)	Kanin
1, 572	Mary, Mary (1961)	Kerr
1, 557	Voice of the Turtle (1943)	Van Druten
1, 530	Barefoot in the Park (1963)	Simon
1, 444	Arsenic and Old Lace (1941)	Kesselring
1, 291	Lightnin' (1918)	W. Smith
1, 234	Cactus Flower (1965)	Burrows
1, 157	Mister Roberts (1948)	Logan
1, 141	Seven Year Itch (1952)	Axelrod
1, 097	Plaza Suite (1968)	Simon
1, 027	Teahouse of the August Moon (1953)	Patrick
1, 007	Never Too Late (1962)	Long
*1, 002	Boys in the Band (1968)	Crowley
982	Any Wednesday (1964)	Resnik
964	Odd Couple (1965)	Simon
957	Anna Lucasta (1944)	Yordan
956	Kiss and Tell (1943)	Herbert
924	Moon Is Blue (1951)	Herbert
901	Luv (1964)	Schisgal
867	Bat (1920)	Rinehart
865	My Sister Eileen (1940)	Fields
855	Streetcar Named Desire (1947)	T. Williams
837 (see 255)	You Can't Take It With You (1936)	Hart
835	Three Men on a Horse (1935)	Abbott
832	Subject Was Roses (1964)	Gilroy
806	Inherit the Wind (1955)	Lawrence
796	No Time for Sergeants (1955)	Levin
789	Ladder (1926)	J. E. Davis
780	Forty Carats (1968)	J. Allen
*780	View from the Bridge (1965)	Miller
765	State of the Union (1945)	Lindsay

760	First Year (1920)	Craven
755	You Know I Can't Hear You When the Water's Running (1967)	R. Anderson
750	Two for the Seesaw (1958)	Gibson
742	Death of A Salesman (1949)	Miller
739	Man Who Came To Dinner (1939)	Hart
*722	Connection (1959)	Gelber
722	Claudia (1941)	Franken
717	Diary of Anne Frank (1955)	Goodrich
714	I Remember Mama (1944)	Van Druten
712	Tea and Sympathy (1953)	R. Anderson
710	Junior Miss (1941)	J. Chodorov
704	Seventh Heaven (1922)	Strong
700	Miracle Worker (1959)	Gibson
694	Cat On A Hot Tin Roof (1955)	T. Williams
*692	Scuba Duba (1967)	Friedman
691	Children's Hour (1934)	Hellman
687	Dead End (1935)	Kingsley
683	Dear Ruth (1944)	Krasna
680	East Is West (1918)	Shipman
677	Come Blow Your Horn (1961)	Simon
671	Doughgirls (1942)	Fields
670	Impossible Years (1965)	Fisher
669	Boy Meets Girl (1935)	Spewack
664	Who's Afraid of Virginia Woolf? (1962)	Albee
657	Women (1936)	Boothe
654	Fifth Season (1953)	Regan
642	Janie (1942)	Betham
640	Green Pastures (1930)	Connelly
639	Auntie Mame (1956)	Lawrence
*634	America Hurrah (1966)	Van Itallie
623	Tenth Man (1959)	Chayefsky
618	Is Zat So? (1925)	Gleason
615	Anniversary Waltz (1954)	J. Chodorov
614	Happy Time (1950)	Taylor
613	Separate Rooms (1940)	Carole
*607	Hogan's Goat (1965)	Alfred
603	Broadway (1926)	Dunning
601	Street Scene (1929)	Rice
600	Kiki (1921)	Belasco
598	Don't Drink the Water (1966)	W. Allen
585	Two Mrs. Carrolls (1943)	Vale
*582	Zoo Story (1960)	Albee
581	Detective Story (1949)	Kingsley
577	Brother Rat (1936)	Monks
*571	Crucible (1957)	Miller
571	Show Off (1924)	Kelly
564	Happy Birthday (1946)	Loos
564	Look Homeward, Angel (1957)	Frings
561	Glass Menagerie (1945)	T. Williams

552

557	Strictly Dishonorable (1929)	Sturges
556	Majority of One (1959)	Spiegelgass
556	Sunrise at Campobello (1958)	Schary
556	Great White Hope (1968)	Sackler
556	Toys in the Attic (1960)	Hellman
*546	Adaptation (1969)	May
*546	Next (1969)	McNally
541	Within the Law (1912)	Veiller
538	What A Life (1938)	Goldsmith
530	Raisin in the Sun (1959)	Hansberry
526	Solid Gold Cadillac (1953)	Kaufman
522	Boomerang (1915)	W. Smith
520	Best Man (1960)	Vidal
508	World of Suzie Wong (1958)	Osborn
501	Member of the Wedding (1950)	McCullers
501	Personal Appearance (1934)	Riley
500	Room Service (1937)	Murray
500	Sailor, Beware! (1933)	Nicholson
500	Tomorrow the World (1943)	Gow
*493	In White America (1963)	Duberman
486	Matchmaker (1955)	Wilder
478	Bus Stop (1955)	Inge
477	Deep Are The Roots (1945)	d'Usseau
477	Middle of the Night (1956)	Chayefsky
477	Picnic (1953)	Inge
474	Pleasure of His Company (1958)	Taylor
472	Abe Lincoln in Illinois (1938)	Sherwood
468	Dark at the Top of the Stairs (1957)	Inge
461	Lulu Belle (1926)	Sheldon
453	Play It Again, Sam (1969)	W. Allen
446	Goodbye, My Fancy (1948)	Kanin
444	Will Success Spoil Rock Hunter? (1955)	Axelrod
440	Friendly Enemies (1918)	Shipman
440 (see 392)	Road to Rome (1928)	Sherwood
439 (see 372)	Burlesque (1946)	Watters
437	Trial of Mary Dugan (1927)	Veiller
435	Turn to the Right (1916)	W. Smith
429	Price (1968)	Miller
428	Thousand Clowns (1962)	Gardner
426	Strange Interlude (1928)	O'Neill
424	Get-Rich-Quick Wallingford (1910)	Cohan
423	John Loves Mary (1947)	Krasna
423	Old Soak (1922)	Marquis
417	Jacobowsky and the Colonel (1944)	Behrman
417	Philadelphia Story (1939)	Barker
417	Tunnel of Love (1957)	J. Fields
415	Caine Mutiny Court-Martial (1954)	Wouk
411	Twin Beds (1914)	Field
410	Heiress (1947)	Goetz
410	Little Foxes (1939)	Hellman
409	Cocktail Party (1950)	Eliot

408	Command Decision (1947)	Haines
406	Once in a Lifetime (1930)	Kaufman
405	Yes, My Darling Daughter (1937)	Reed
398	Hatful of Rain (1955)	Gazzo
398	Tailor Made Man (1917)	H. J. Smith
397	Seven Days (1909)	Rinehart
392 (see 440)	Road to Rome (1927)	Sherwood
390	Long Day's Journey Into Night (1956)	O'Neill
388	Visit to a Small Planet (1957)	Vidal
385	Late George Apley (1944)	Marquand
382	Oh, Men! Oh, Women! (1953)	E. Chodorov
*380 (see 208)	Desire Under the Elms (1963)	O'Neill
*380	To Be Young, Gifted and Black (1969)	Hansberry
378	Prime of Miss Jean Brodie (1968)	J. Allen
378	Watch on the Rhine (1941)	Hellman
377	Harriet (1943)	Ryerson
375	Sweet Bird of Youth (1959)	T. Williams
373	Mulatto (1935)	L. Hughes
372 (see 439)	Burlesque (1927)	Watters
372	Having Wonderful Time (1937)	Kober
*370	American Dream (1961)	Albee
367	Porgy (1927)	Heyward
367	Season in the Sun (1950)	Gibbs
366	Coquette (1927)	Abbott
365	On Trial (1914)	Rice
364	J. B. (1958)	MacLeish
364	Point of No Return (1951)	Osborn
360	Craig's Wife (1925)	Kelly
360	She Loves Me Not (1933)	Lindsay
359	Skin of Our Teeth (1942)	Wilder
356	Tovarich (1936)	Sherwood
351	Men In White (1933)	Kingsley
350	Enter Madame (1920)	Varesi
350	Mrs. McThing (1952)	Chase
*349	Plays for Bleecker Street (1962)	Wilder
348	Dream Girl (1945)	Rice
348	Happy Journey to Trenton and Camden (1948)	Wilder
345	Fortune Hunter (1909)	W. Smith
345	Royal Family (1927)	Kaufman
344+	Six-Cylinder Love (1921)	McGuire
344	Another Language (1932)	Franken
344	My 3 Angels (1953)	Spewack
342	Bad Man (1920)	Browne
336	Hit-the-Trail-Holiday (1915)	Cohan
336	Lunatics and Lovers (1954)	Kingsley
336	Our Town (1938)	Wilder
333	All the Way Home (1960)	Mosel
332	Bad Seed (1954)	M. Anderson
328	All My Sons (1947)	Miller

*328	Death of Bessie Smith (1961)	Albee
328	Thirteenth Chair (1916)	Veiller
322	One Sunday Afternoon (1933)	Hagan
321	On Borrowed Time (1938)	Osborn
320	Seven Keys to Baldpate (1913)	Cohan
318	Sabrina Fair (1953)	Taylor
318	Searching Wind (1944)	Hellman
317 (see 243)	Male Animal (1952)	Thurber
316	Night of the Iguana (1961)	T. Williams
315	Polly With a Past (1917)	Bolton
312	Adam and Eva (1919)	Bolton
312	Dancing Mothers (1924)	Selwyn
312	Forever After (1918)	Owen Davis
310	Saturday's Children (1927)	M. Anderson
307	Eve of St. Mark (1942)	M. Anderson
306	Rose Tattoo (1951)	T. Williams
305	Old Maid (1935)	Akins
304	Bell for Adano (1944)	Osborn
303	Jazz Singer (1925)	Raphaelson
303	Little Accident (1928)	Dell
300	Clarence (1919)	Tarkington
300	Idiot's Delight (1936)	Sherwood
299	Generation (1965)	Goodhart
299	What Price Glory? (1924)	M. Anderson
*295	Tom Paine (1968)	Foster
292 (see 258)	Counsellor-At-Law (1931)	Rice
289	Ah, Wilderness (1933)	O'Neill
289	Last Mile (1930)	Wexley
288	Shannons of Broadway (1927)	Gleason
288	Susan and God (1937)	Crothers
286	Anne of the Thousand Days (1948)	M. Anderson
286	Kiss the Boys Good-Bye (1938)	Boothe
284	Touch of the Poet (1958)	O'Neill
283 (see 267)	Biography (1934)	Behrman
279	King of Hearts (1954)	Kerr
279	Nervous Wreck (1923)	Owen Davis
278	Shame Woman (1923)	Vollmer
273	Dylan (1964)	Michaels
273	June Moon (1929)	Lardner
272+	Fool (1922)	Pollock
272	Anastasia (1954)	Bolton
271	Far Country (1961)	Denker
271	Great God Brown (1926)	O'Neill
267 (see 283)	Biography (1932)	Behrman
265	For Love or Money (1947)	Herbert
265	Life with Mother (1948)	Lindsay
264	Margin for Error (1939)	Boothe
264	Reunion in Vienna (1931)	Sherwood
263	Time of the Cuckoo (1952)	Laurents
261	Dracula (1927)	Baldwin
261	Firebrand (1924)	Mayer
261	Purlie Victorious (1961)	Ossie Davis

261		Star-Spangled Girl (1966)	Simon
260		Young Woodley (1925)	Van Druten
258	(see 292)	Counsellor-At-Law (1942)	Rice
257		Declassee (1919)	Akins
257		Thank You (1921)	W. Smith
256		Skylark (1939)	Raphaelson
*256		U. S. A. (1959)	Dos Passos
255		Pre-Honeymoon (1936)	Nichols
255	(see 837)	You Can't Take It With You (1965)	Hart
253		Greeks Had a World For It (1930)	Akins
253		Soldier's Wife (1944)	Franken
252		Little Journey (1918)	Crothers
250		Golden Boy (1937)	Odets
*250		No Place To Be Somebody (1969)	Gordone
248		Mary of Scotland (1933)	M. Anderson
248+		Merton of the Movies (1922)	Kaufman
248		Tarnish (1923)	Emery
246		Dulcy (1921)	Kaufman
246		First Lady (1935)	Dayton
246		I Know My Love (1949)	Behrman
243		Butter and Egg Man (1925)	Kaufman
243	(see 317)	Male Animal (1940)	Thurber
242		Case of Libel (1963)	Denker
242		Left Bank (1931)	Rice
236		Gideon (1961)	Chayefsky
235		Country Girl (1950)	Odets
234		Paris Bound (1927)	Barker
233		Bell, Book and Candle (1950)	Van Druten
232		Dinner at Eight (1932)	Kaufman
232		Tommy (1927)	Lindsay
231		Return of Peter Grimm (1911)	Belasco
229		Accent on Youth (1934)	Raphaelson
229		Berkeley Square (1929)	Balderston
229		Holiday (1928)	Barker
229		Lark (1955)	Hellman
229		Strange Bedfellows (1948)	Ryerson
229		Vinegar Tree (1930)	Osborn
228		Rollo's Wild Oat (1920)	Kummer
224		Come Out of the Kitchen (1916)	A. E. Thomas
224		Her Master's Voice (1933)	Kummer
224		Late Christopher Bean (1932)	S. Howard
223		Son-Daughter (1919)	Belasco
223		Star Wagon (1937)	M. Anderson
223		Too Many Cooks (1914)	Craven
*222		In Circles (1967)	Stein
222		Tchin-Tchin (1962)	Michaels
221		Calculated Risk (1962)	J. Hayes
221		Over 21 (1944)	Gordon
220		Sinners (1915)	Owen Davis
219		Gigi (1951)	Loos
219		Silver Whistle (1948)	McEnroe
216		Light Up the Sky (1948)	Hart

ANTOINETTE PERRY (TONY) AWARDS
FOR BEST PLAY

1946-47   All My Sons, by Arthur Miller

1947-48   A Streetcar Named Desire, by Tennessee Williams (Best New American Play)

             Mister Roberts, by Joshua Logan and Thomas Heggen (the Outstanding Play)

1948-49   Death of A Salesman, by Arthur Miller

1949-50   The Cocktail Party, by T. S. Eliot

1950-51   Darkness At Noon, by Sidney Kingsley

1951-52   No American winners.

1952-53   The Crucible, by Arthur Miller

1953-54   Teahouse of the August Moon, by John Patrick

1954-55   The Desperate Hours, by Joseph Hayes

1955-56   The Diary of Anne Frank, by Frances Goodrich and Albert Hackett

1956-57   Long Day's Journey Into Night, by Eugene O'Neill

1957-58   Sunrise at Campobello, by Dore Schary

1958-59   J. B., by Archibald MacLeish

1959-60   The Miracle Worker, by William Gibson

1960-61   No American winners.

1961-62   No American winners.

1962-63   Who's Afraid of Virginia Woolf?, by Edward Albee

1963-64   No American winners.

1964-65   The Subject Was Roses, by Frank D. Gilroy

1965-66   No American winners.

1966-67   A Delicate Balance, by Edward Albee

1967-68   No American winners.

1968-69   The Great White Hope, by Howard Sackler

NEW YORK DRAMA CRITICS' CIRCLE AWARDS

(Best American Play)

1935-36 Winterset, by Maxwell Anderson

1936-37 High Tor, by Maxwell Anderson

1937-38 Of Mice and Men, by John Steinbeck

1938-39 No Award.

1939-40 The Time of Your Life, by William Saroyan

1940-41 Watch On the Rhine, by Lillian Hellman

1941-42 No Award.

1942-43 The Patriots, by Sidney Kingsley

1943-44 Jacobowsky and the Colonel, Adapted by S. N. Behrman
      (considered as Best Foreign Play)

1944-45 The Glass Menagerie, by Tennessee Williams

1945-46 No Award.

1946-47 All My Sons, by Arthur Miller

1947-48 A Streetcar Named Desire, by Tennessee Williams

1948-49 Death of A Salesman, by Arthur Miller

1949-50 The Member of the Wedding, by Carson McCullers
      The Cocktail Party, by T. S. Eliot (considered as Best
       Foreign Play)

1950-51 Darkness At Noon, by Sidney Kingsley

1951-52 I Am A Camera, by John Van Druten

1952-53 Picnic, by William Inge

1953-54 Teahouse of the August Moon, by John Patrick

1954-55 Cat On a Hot Tin Roof, by Tennessee Williams

1955-56	The Diary of Anne Frank, by Frances Goodrich and Albert Hackett
1956-57	Long Day's Journey Into Night, by Eugene O'Neill
1957-58	Look Homeward, Angel, by Ketti Frings
1958-59	A Raisin in the Sun, by Lorraine Hansberry
1959-60	Toys in the Attic, by Lillian Hellman
1960-61	All the Way Home, by Tad Mosel
1961-62	*The Night of the Iguana, by Tennessee Williams
1962-63	Who's Afraid of Virginia Woolf?, by Edward Albee
1963-64	No Award.
1964-65	The Subject Was Roses, by Frank D. Gilroy
1965-66	No Award.
1966-67	No Award.
1967-68	No Award.
1968-69	*The Great White Hope, by Howard Sackler

*Best Play, regardless of category.

PULITZER PRIZE WINNERS

(AMERICAN DRAMA)

1917-18   Why Marry?, by Jesse Lynch Williams

1918-19   No Award.

1919-20   Beyond the Horizon, by Eugene O'Neill

1920-21   Miss Lulu Bett, by Zona Gale

1921-22   Anna Christie, by Eugene O'Neill

1922-23   Icebound, by Owen Davis

1923-24   Hell-bent fer Heaven, by Hatcher Hughes

1924-25   They Knew What They Wanted, by Sidney Howard

1925-26   Craig's Wife, by George Kelly

1926-27   In Abraham's Bosom, by Paul Green

1927-28   Strange Interlude, by Eugene O'Neill

1928-29   Street Scene, by Elmer Rice

1929-30   The Green Pastures, by Marc Connelly

1930-31   Alison's House, by Susan Glaspell

1931-32   musical

1932-33   Both Your Houses, by Maxwell Anderson

1933-34   Men in White, by Sidney Kingsley

1934-35   The Old Maid, by Zoe Akins

1935-36   Idiot's Delight, by Robert E. Sherwood

1936-37   You Can't Take It with You, by Moss Hart and George S.
Kaufman

1937-38   Our Town, by Thornton Wilder

1938-39	Abe Lincoln in Illinois, by Robert E. Sherwood
1939-40	The Time of Your Life, by William Saroyan
1940-41	There Shall Be No Night, by Robert E. Sherwood
1941-42	No Award.
1942-43	The Skin of Our Teeth, by Thornton Wilder
1943-44	No Award.
1944-45	Harvey, by Mary Chase
1945-46	State of the Union, by Howard Lindsay and Russel Crouse
1946-47	No Award.
1947-48	A Streetcar Named Desire, by Tennessee Williams
1948-49	Death of a Salesman, by Arthur Miller
1949-50	musical
1950-51	No Award.
1951-52	The Shrike, by Joseph Kramm
1952-53	Picnic, by William Inge
1953-54	The Teahouse of the August Moon, by John Patrick
1954-55	Cat on a Hot Tin Roof, by Tennessee Williams
1955-56	The Diary of Anne Frank, by Frances Goodrich and Albert Hackett
1956-57	Long Day's Journey into Night, by Eugene O'Neill
1957-58	Look Homeward, Angel, by Ketti Frings
1958-59	J.B., by Archibald MacLeish
1959-60	musical
1960-61	All the Way Home, by Tad Mosel
1961-62	musical
1962-63	No Award.
1963-64	No Award.

1964-65	The Subject Was Roses, by Frank D. Gilroy
1965-66	No Award.
1966-67	A Delicate Balance, by Edward Albee
1967-68	No Award.
1968-69	The Great White Hope, by Howard Sackler
1969-70	No Place To Be Somebody, by Charles Gordone

MAJOR AWARDS IN AMERICAN DRAMA:
A COMPILATION

Triple Award-Winning Plays

Season	Play	Dramatist
1947-48	A Streetcar Named Desire	Tennessee Williams
1948-49	Death of A Salesman	Arthur Miller
1953-54	Teahouse of the August Moon	John Patrick
1955-56	The Diary of Anne Frank	Frances Goodrich and Albert Hackett
1956-57	Long Day's Journey Into Night	Eugene O'Neill
1964-65	The Subject Was Roses	Frank D. Gilroy
1968-69	The Great White Hope	Howard Sackler

Multiple Award Winning Playwrights

Playwright	Total Awards	Drama Critics'	Tony	Pulitzer
Tennessee Williams	7	4	1	2
Arthur Miller	6	2	3	1
Eugene O'Neill	6	1	1	4
Edward Albee	4	1	2	1
Maxwell Anderson	3	2	-	1
Frank D. Gilroy	3	1	1	1
Frances Goodrich and Albert Hackett	3	1	1	1
Sidney Kingsley	3	2	1	-
John Patrick	3	1	1	1
Howard Sackler	3	1	1	1
Robert E. Sherwood	3	-	-	3
T. S. Eliot	2	1	-	1
Ketti Frings	2	1	-	1
Lillian Hellman	2	2	-	-
William Inge	2	1	-	1
Archibald MacLeish	2	-	1	1
Tad Mosel	2	1	-	1
William Saroyan	2	1	-	1
Thornton Wilder	2	-	-	2

INDEX OF CO-AUTHORS, ADAPTORS,
AND ORIGINAL AUTHORS

INDEX OF TITLES

571

591

WITHDRAWAL